IN
BYRON'S
WAKE

The Turbulent Lives of
Lord Byron's Wife and Daughter:
Annabella Milbanke and Ada Lovelace

MIRANDA SEYMOUR

**SIMON &
SCHUSTER**

London · New York · Sydney · Toronto · New Delhi

A CBS COMPANY

First published in Great Britain by Simon & Schuster UK Ltd, 2018
This edition published in Great Britain by Simon & Schuster UK Ltd, 2018
A CBS COMPANY

1 3 5 7 9 10 8 6 4 2

Simon & Schuster UK Ltd
1st Floor
222 Gray's Inn Road
London WC1X 8HB

www.simonandschuster.co.uk
www.simonandschuster.com.au
www.simonandschuster.co.in

Simon & Schuster Australia, Sydney
Simon & Schuster India, New Delhi

A CIP catalogue record for this book
is available from the British Library

Paperback ISBN: 978-1-4711-3858-4
eBook ISBN: 978-1-4711-3859-1

Typeset in Sabon by M Rules
Printed and bound by CPI Group (UK) Ltd, Croydon, CR0 4YY

In memory of Peter Cochran, who was so kind to all those of us who benefited from his work in the world of Byronic studies. And to the future of Talia and Shira, two of Ada Lovelace's youngest and most loyal admirers.

CONTENTS

PART TWO:
Ada

PART THREE:
Visions

PART FOUR:
The Making and Breaking of a Reputation

The Noels, Milbankes, Byrons & Kings

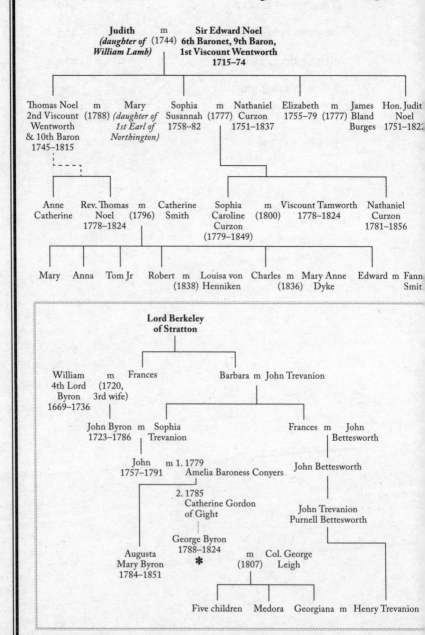

Judith m (1744) Sir Edward Noel
(daughter of William Lamb) 6th Baronet, 9th Baron, 1st Viscount Wentworth 1715–74

Thomas Noel m (1788) Mary (daughter of 1st Earl of Northington)
2nd Viscount Wentworth & 10th Baron 1745–1815

Sophia Susannah 1758–82 m (1777) Nathaniel Curzon 1751–1837

Elizabeth 1755–79 m (1777) James Bland Burges

Hon. Judith Noel 1751–1822

Anne Catherine

Rev. Thomas Noel 1778–1824 m (1796) Catherine Smith

Sophia Caroline Curzon (1779–1849) m (1800) Viscount Tamworth 1778–1824

Nathaniel Curzon 1781–1856

Mary   Anna   Tom Jr   Robert m (1838) Louisa von Henniken   Charles m (1836) Mary Anne Dyke   Edward m Fann Smit

Lord Berkeley of Stratton

William 4th Lord Byron 1669–1736 m (1720, 3rd wife) Frances

Barbara m John Trevanion

John Byron 1723–1786 m Sophia Trevanion

Frances m John Bettesworth

John 1757–1791 m 1. 1779 Amelia Baroness Conyers

2. 1785 Catherine Gordon of Gight

John Bettesworth

John Trevanion Purnell Bettesworth

Augusta Mary Byron 1784–1851

George Byron 1788–1824
✱

m (1807) Col. George Leigh

Five children   Medora   Georgiana m Henry Trevanion

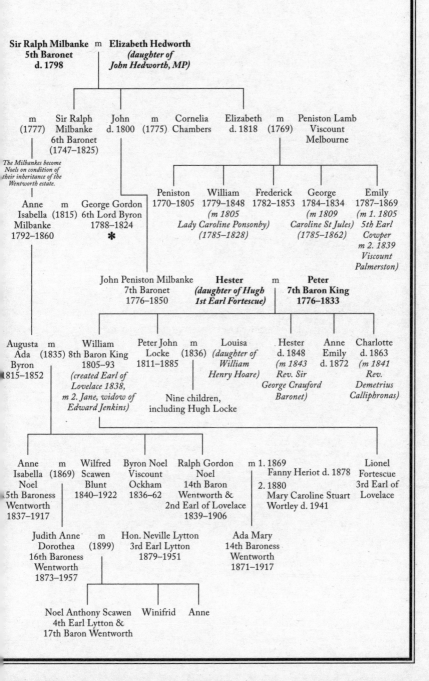

Sir Ralph Milbanke m **Elizabeth Hedworth**
5th Baronet   *(daughter of*
d. 1798   *John Hedworth, MP)*

m   Sir Ralph   John   m   Cornelia   Elizabeth   m   Peniston Lamb
(1777)   Milbanke   d. 1800   (1775)   Chambers   d. 1818   (1769)   Viscount
         6th Baronet   Melbourne
         (1747–1825)

The Milbankes become
Noels on condition of
their inheritance of the
Wentworth estate.

                                              Peniston   William   Frederick   George   Emily
                                              1770–1805   1779–1848   1782–1853   1784–1834   1787–1869
Anne   m   George Gordon   *(m 1805*   *(m 1809*   *(m 1. 1805*
Isabella   (1815)   6th Lord Byron   *Lady Caroline Ponsonby)*   *Caroline St Jules)*   *5th Earl*
Milbanke   1788–1824   *(1785–1828)*   *(1785–1862)*   *Cowper*
1792–1860   ✳   *m 2. 1839*
                                                                                                   Viscount
                                                                                                   Palmerston)

                    John Peniston Milbanke   **Hester**   m   **Peter**
                    7th Baronet   *(daughter of Hugh*   **7th Baron King**
                    1776–1850   *1st Earl Fortescue)*   **1776–1833**

Augusta   m   William   Peter John   m   Louisa   Hester   Anne   Charlotte
Ada   (1835)   8th Baron King   Locke   (1836)   *(daughter of*   d. 1848   Emily   d. 1863
Byron   1805–93   1811–1885   *William*   *(m 1843*   d. 1872   *(m 1841*
1815–1852   *(created Earl of*   *Henry Hoare)*   *Rev. Sir*   *Rev.*
                 Lovelace 1838,   *George Crauford*   *Demetrius*
                 m 2. Jane, widow of   Nine children,   *Baronet)*   *Calliphronas)*
                 Edward Jenkins)   including Hugh Locke

Anne   m   Wilfred   Byron Noel   Ralph Gordon   m 1. 1869   Lionel
Isabella   (1869)   Scawen   Viscount   Noel   Fanny Heriot d. 1878   Fortescue
Noel   Blunt   Ockham   14th Baron   2. 1880   3rd Earl of
5th Baroness   1840–1922   1836–62   Wentworth &   Mary Caroline Stuart   Lovelace
Wentworth   2nd Earl of Lovelace   Wortley d. 1941
1837–1917   1839–1906

         Judith Anne   m   Hon. Neville Lytton   Ada Mary
         Dorothea   (1899)   3rd Earl Lytton   14th Baroness
         16th Baroness   1879–1951   Wentworth
         Wentworth   1871–1917
         1873–1957

              Noel Anthony Scawen   Winifrid   Anne
              4th Earl Lytton &
              17th Baron Wentworth

PART ONE

Annabella

CHAPTER ONE

ANTICIPATION
(1761–92)

The year is 1799, almost the dawn of a new century, but this is presently of less interest than the fact that she, Miss Annabella Milbanke, is posing for her portrait to John Hoppner, one of England's most celebrated artists.

It was her own decision to wear the white dancing dress, bound high above the waist with a blue satin sash, short-sleeved to show how elegantly she holds her arms. Annabella dances extremely well. Her mother declares that her minuet steps are perfection and Mr Watts, the dancing master, declares that he has never seen such strength in a child's ankles. He is quite right; that is why Annabella finds it so easy to hold her pose on the dais, stepping forward as if to greet the world.

It was also her own idea that Mr Hoppner should paint rocks behind her, and the sea, as if she were skipping along the beach below their country home in the faraway north of England. But mostly, when she is alone on the beach at Seaham, it is not dancing that preoccupies Annabella. She likes to make up stories: it is so interesting to picture herself as a brave soldier in the pass at Thermopylae, or comforting a prisoner in his lonely dungeon ...

'Head up, my angel,' her mother instructs from the stiff gilt chair where she sits in watchful attendance. 'Think of your *pas grave* in the minuet. Hold your body straight as a little queen.'

She feels like a little queen, the centre of attention as Mr Hoppner bobs out from behind his easel to praise her for her patience. He has a long pale face with no hint of a smile. She can't decide whether he is interesting enough to become a chosen friend.

'Shall we visit Great Aunt Mary later?' asks Annabella. 'I want to read her one of my new poems.'

Her mother darts a look at Mr Hoppner. 'She's such a clever little creature.'

'Indeed!' says Mr Hoppner. 'A most remarkable infant.'

'I'm not an infant! I'm seven years of age!' The smile undoes the pompous phrasing, bringing such dimples into the round and rosy cheeks that the adoring old lady (she must be nearing fifty) jumps up and runs forward to embrace her proud-backed, blue-eyed daughter. It's a charming scene, reflects Hoppner. Perhaps mother and child would have formed a better subject. But time is pressing on and the artist is growing weary of Lady Milbanke's chatter.

Discreetly, Mr Hoppner rattles the oily brushes in his jar. Sighing, Judith Milbanke resumes her seat.

'She is so very coaxing,' she murmurs by way of apology.

'Indeed.' He hesitates. 'And you have others like her, madam?'

'We did!' the child interrupts. 'But Sophy's leaving to get married. And now I must remember to write to her as Lady Tamworth. I shall write to her every week!'

But Lady Milbanke has folded her hands across her stomach, almost as if to ward off a blow.

'Sophy Curzon is her cousin. My poor late sister's daughter has always lived with us. But Annabella – Anne Isabella, I should say, since she bears the names both of a royal lady and our dear friend, Mrs Baker of Elemore Hall – is our only child. And born on Ascension Day! Her father and I are much blessed.'

'And so,' the child sweetly adds, 'am I.'

Completed and framed, Hoppner's portrait of Miss Milbanke was despatched to Seaham Hall, perched high on the cliffs of County Durham, above the German Ocean. Here, the new painting was hung alongside the 1778 portrait by Joshua Reynolds (one of his best) of Annabella's newly married father, Sir Ralph Milbanke, dark-browed and kind-eyed, all ready to burst out with one of those silly jokes for which a loving daughter could never find the heart to tease him. Flanking it was the sharp-nosed profile of Annabella's mother, Judith Noel, posed in the fiercely fashionable convention of the time (the portrait was painted in 1784, six years after Judith's marriage), hair powdered and plucked up into a pyramid of ruffles and bows, a black waist ribbon stressing the anguish of her childless frame.

Looking at the three family members together, an entire generation might seem to have been skipped. And so it has been. Awaited for fifteen long years, it is no wonder that Annabella, born at last on 17 May 1792, can do as she pleases with her adoring parents. The result is already peeping through in Hoppner's portrait. Everything about this child – her steadfast stare; the poised way she stands; the tilt of a determined chin – speaks of a formidable and, so far, well-founded confidence. The world, little Miss Milbanke seems to assume, lies at her feet.

CHAPTER TWO

A VERY FINE CHILD
(1792–1810)

From 1792 on, Judith Milbanke's letters to her family and friends dwelt upon a single theme: the wonder that was her daughter, Annabella. Never in the history of mankind had a mother been blessed with such a flawless little creature! Happy someday would be the winner of such a bride! Visiting grand neighbours with Sophy and Annabella (when Miss Milbanke was still only fifteen months old), Judith took less interest in a park newly landscaped by Humphry Repton than in the fact that the Earl and Countess Fitzwilliam's son 'quite doated [*sic*] on Annabella'. Lord Milton, aged just seven, seemed a most eligible candidate for her hand. Having seen 'Miss *naked*,' Judith raunchily joked to her broadminded aunt, Mary Noel, 'therefore he can tell whether he will like her or no.'

Travelling on to stay with other old friends from earlier, Yorkshire days, before the Milbankes moved east to Seaham, Judith complacently reported how the county folk flocked in to see their Annabella 'as if she had been something miraculous'. On 20 April 1794, as little Miss neared her second birthday, the proud mother was happy to credit her offspring as '*Governess in Chief*' of Papa, Mama & the whole Family'.

The word was out. Pleasing Judith Milbanke depended upon how many bouquets a friend was willing to throw in the direction of her daughter. Judith, while priding herself on her forgiving nature, was better known for her hot temper. Annabella, therefore, was warmly praised: 'one of the finest girls of her age I ever beheld,' Mrs Baker of Elemore gushed in a tactful postscript to one of Judith's letters from Seaham to Mary Noel.

Admirers were rewarded with more information than they might have wished to receive. Aged two, Annabella could already identify twenty flowers (and weeds) by name. Annabella always performed her 'Do Do' as soon as she got up. Annabella had bathed in the sea and, rising from the waves, looked 'like a little Venus'. The princesses (George III's daughters) had personally requested news of Annabella, having heard report – the words were seldom off the lips of a besotted mother – that 'she was a *very fine Child*'.

Few dared suggest the likely result of all this adulation. In 1794, Sophy Curzon masked her own anxiety behind a neighbour's comment. Apparently, Lady Liddell of Ravensworth Castle thought Judith far too indulgent: 'she does not *ever deny* that if it is possible to spoil a very fine Girl, *Annabella's Mama is determined to do it*.' The words were Lady Liddell's; the emphatic underlining was Sophy's own.

Warnings – rarely offered – were a waste of breath. Events conspired to strengthen Judith's belief that Miss Milbanke was destined for great things. Her brother, Viscount Wentworth of Kirkby Mallory, had always made it clear that the handsome estate over which he presided in the Midlands would not be passed down to his own illegitimate son. Thomas Noel, following his marriage to Kitty Smith in 1796, was understandably disgruntled about receiving only a modest sum of money and the living of the church at Kirkby Mallory (to which he became a notoriously absentee rector, employing a curate as his substitute). The following year, Lord Wentworth made arrangements to leave his considerable property, together with his title, to his sister Judith, and after her, to his niece. A conscientious brother, he now began the task of setting his affairs in order by paying off a substantial number of gambling debts. (Both Wentworth and Mary Ligonier, the wealthy little wife he married after the death of his live-in mistress, Catherine Vanloo, were addicted to the tables; Judith and Ralph preferred betting on horses.)

In January 1798, Ralph Milbanke's father died. It was years since either Judith or her husband had visited Halnaby Hall, the north country mansion at which the long-widowed baronet had consoled himself with various lady-friends. Now, Halnaby and the annual rents from a second grand house (Moulton Hall) passed into the new baronet's hands, together with an agreement that the 5-year-old Annabella, when she married, would receive a dowry of £16,000 (worth approximately £800,000 nowadays). In due course, the whole of this estate would pass down to her as well.

The new Lady Milbanke had no difficulty in adjusting to her improved circumstances. In London, a splendid new house on Lower Berkeley Street, near Manchester Square, was rented at £300 per year. Plans were swiftly made to entertain the Wentworths at Halnaby; Annabella, now grown too grand for a mere nurse, was allotted a personal maid of her own.

Mary Anne Clermont had arrived nine years earlier to help care for the orphaned Sophy Curzon. Self-taught and possessed of modest independent means, this timid, plain but capable young woman had already established her worth as a housekeeper and tactful smoother of Judith's volatile temper when she was promoted to the role of Annabella's admiring attendant.

Judith felt a twinge of apprehension about her brother's first visit to Halnaby. The house, elegantly furnished in the French style, was sure to impress, but what opinion would Thomas and his fashionable wife form of their nieces? Sophy, at nineteen, was going through a plain phase ('very journalière') and Annabella, while an undeniably appealing child with her deep blue eyes, flushed cheeks and high pale forehead, was a law unto herself. 'She is excessively talkative and entertaining if *she likes* people & very *coaxing* to her *favourites*' Judith confided to Aunt Mary Noel, 'but she will judge for *herself* & cannot be *made* to *like* any body.'

Annabella's thoughts about her uncle are unknown, but she did not take long to reach an opinion of Halnaby. Certainly, the big red-brick house (supposedly designed by Inigo Jones) was very splendid, symmetrical and ornate; certainly, it was pleasant to march along stone terraces as broad as a small town square, or to dash through high, quiet rooms that unfolded each into the next as neatly as a set of perfect equations. She liked the panelled library. She enjoyed being taken on carriage rides through the deer park, or to try her skill at fishing in Halnaby's ornamental lake. But Halnaby was not Seaham and, as Sophy Curzon reported to Aunt Mary during the family's first winter visit to this landlocked palace, 'the *Angel* . . . regrets the Sea and the Sands'.

All through her life, Annabella would be drawn back to the sea, and Seaham Hall, completed in the year of her birth, was the home that she never ceased to love. The hall's long windows and terraced gardens faced the sea. Sealight glinted off the windowpanes. The smell of salt sharpened the northern air. From the house, a sandy descent led down beyond the garden to the beach, where a wilful Annabella liked to pull off her big cotton bonnet and scamper into the waves. 'She . . . is sadly tanned, which I know would annoy you,' Judith told Aunt Mary, '. . . I believe it is the bathing makes the sun & air catch her skin so much.'

Ancient tunnels wound down from the hamlet above into the deep caves once used by smugglers; off in the hazy distance, the deceptively named Featherbed Rocks obscured the long line of coast curving south, down to distant Whitby and Scarborough.

The village, although largely rebuilt during the transformation of old Seaham Manor into the smart new hall, remained a feudal community. Eliza Grant, visiting Seaham as a child in 1808, remembered seeing only a dozen or so cottages, all occupied by Milbanke employees. Staying at the village inn with her mother and sisters, Eliza noticed the graceful manners and wistful face of the innkeeper's daughter. Young Bessy, she learned, had been summoned up to the hall as that summer's chosen companion for Lady Milbanke's daughter. Restored to the inn, Bessy hankered after the privileged world into which she had briefly stepped.

Quick-tempered and bossy though Judith Milbanke was, she

shared with her husband a warm sense of social duty that was imparted to her daughter. In politics (Sir Ralph was a Whig MP), Judith inclined to the left. A fierce opponent of the hangings that took place after the Gordon Riots, she had expressed outrage in 1797 at the English government's persecution of 'the poor oppressed Irish'. Rebuilding Seaham village along with the hall, the Milbankes had replaced a row of 'miserable Cottages' with sturdy, habitable homes. It was customary, whenever one of the community fell ill, for Sir Ralph to send in the family's own Dr Fenwick, while adding the comfort of a bottle or two of his own best claret. Annabella, nostalgically recording these details some forty years later, stressed the fact that – while her father gave the orders concerning his workers' welfare – it was Judith who enforced them. 'She did not leave it to Servants. She saw that the execution was as good as the Intention.'

Sentimentality was at play in a middle-aged lady's recollections of her long-dead parents. Nevertheless, it was these early experiences that helped to make a committed philanthropist of Annabella. Equally enduring was the influence of her parents' own Unitarian faith in a forgiving God, one who preferred active benevolence to the slavish following of Christian doctrine that Annabella later mocked as 'Pye-house'. Relations between the owners of Seaham Hall and their rector, Richard Wallis, were cordial, but never so close as with their tenant workforce in the village.

Annabella's education, like that of most girls of her time, was a haphazard affair. A governess, passed on by the Bakers of Elemore Hall, was dismissed for neglectful behaviour before her charge had reached the age of five. Miss Walker had no successor. Mary Anne Clermont taught Annabella the clear handwriting that caused Lord Wentworth jovially to request his niece to take over the role of family correspondent. (Nobody except his own wife could decipher Sir Ralph's crabbed penmanship.) A skilled sketcher, Annabella learned her attractive technique when William Mulready was touring great houses of the north as a drawing-master. She left a strong impression upon the young man; many years later, Mulready recalled that Miss Milbanke, while not quite so handsome as her parents thought her, was an exceptionally kind and friendly child: 'very gentle and good'.

Drawing, together with dancing (for which Annabella evinced both aptitude and relish), formed an essential part of a young Georgian lady's education. Music, despite the fact that her parents enjoyed duetting on the violin and harpsichord, interested her less than learning to make her own petticoats. Greek was a struggle – demonstrated by the awkwardly shaped letters in the Greek list of friends' names that Annabella drew up during her teens. (William Mulready was among them.) Reading tastes were dictated by Sir Ralph's affection for the plays of Dryden, Otway and Shakespeare and by her early and surprised delight in poetry. By the age of fourteen, Annabella was swooning over Edward Young's fashionably gloomy *Night Thoughts*. Young, as she started to try her hand at scanning verses, became her model.

Poetry became the private vehicle through which Annabella voiced the passions – a reaction against her mother's noisy impulsiveness – that she concealed from public view. Letters were her downfall. Aged eleven, anxious to praise her mother for giving (it was most unusual at that time) a political speech in public, Annabella could not manage it without condescension:

> You never forgot one word of your speech nor was any fear discernable in your speech, addressing a very numerous &
> in part a very respectable audience you never once forgot the proper action (for action is a very essential part in a good speaker . . .)
>   Have I praised or have I flatter'd? let those who heard them judge – as it is I remain an impartial Tory.
>
> *AI*

Letter-writing was a medium in which Annabella was never at ease. Whether offering advice, making jokes or presenting a criticism, the tone invariably went wrong. It was a failing of which she was painfully aware and for which – from time to time – she offered touchingly gauche apologies. The didactic tone of Annabella's written voice led – it still does today – to misinterpretation of her personality. Often, to her mortification, it resulted in a broken friendship.

Versifying provided a welcome outlet for the feelings that she imperfectly expressed in prose. Mathematics, taught to Annabella by William Frend from Euclid, the standard children's textbook at that time, provided a reliable refuge from emotion; here was a world of numbers over which, with diligent application, she could exert control.

It was Frend's politics rather than his mathematics (or his avid interest in astronomy) that first captured the interest and sympathy of the Milbankes. A hard-working priest with a living just outside Cambridge, Frend had to relinquish his position when he became a Unitarian (and thus unable to accept the Church of England's Thirty-nine Articles). Six years later, in 1793 – the year that England declared war on France – Frend caused a stir among his colleagues at Cambridge by publishing a pamphlet that favoured peace. A trial was held, with fervent support for Frend from his students, including the young Samuel Coleridge. Formally banished from his post at Jesus College (while retaining all the perks, excepting residence, of a bachelor don), this unlikely rebel became part of the hotbed of London radicals that surrounded the philosopher William Godwin, author of the inflammatory *An Enquiry Concerning Political Justice*.

The Milbankes liked what they heard about Frend's views. Peace remained the favoured option in their own northerly part of England: the letters that Judith wrote during Annabella's childhood dwelt on the local consequences of economic hardship almost as insistently as the latest achievements of her little daughter. 'I wish any thing to put an End to the War for my part,' she told Mary Noel in 1794. One year later, she sadly described 'a state of almost general Bankruptcy, no Trade, no Credit, no Money – People breaking every day ... A peace would set all afloat again.'

Annabella first met William Frend while visiting London with her mother in 1806. Aged fourteen and hungry for knowledge, she began a mathematical correspondence. By the end of the year, Frend was complimenting his pupil's progress with Euclid and explaining how she should use his new arithmetical toy, a sophisticated abacus which enabled numbers to be computed up to 16,665. References to algebra, verse-scanning, Latin, and Roman history ('I think it may be time for you to begin Livy') show that Frend became Annabella's personal teacher, a role he would also perform for her daughter, Ada. (Frend was the father-in-law of Ada's more famous tutor, Augustus De Morgan.)

A middle-aged academic was no substitute for a confidante and ally of her own age. Annabella had felt bereft when Sophy Curzon, whom she would always look upon as a beloved older sister, left Seaham in 1800. Judith, too, described herself as wandering around like a lost soul during the months after Sophy's wedding to Lord Tamworth. Sir Ralph had done his best, when not preoccupied by the considerable costs of maintaining his political career, to keep his daughter diverted with play-reading and backgammon. But a real consolation was finally in sight, one that would help provide an enduring substitute for Sophy's absence.

Judith's closest friend, Millicent Gosford, became a widow in 1807, the year in which Millicent's son married Mary Sparrow, an heiress from Worlingham in Suffolk. Deprived of their main home in Ireland after Gosford burned down in 1805, the younger Gosfords moved to England, bringing with them two orphaned Irish cousins, Hugh and Mary Millicent Montgomery.

The junior Lady Gosford was just thirteen years older than Annabella. It was exactly the gap that had separated her from Sophy. Mary Montgomery was herself already twenty-two when she met the fifteen-year-old Miss Milbanke for the first time. Frequently represented in family letters simply as 'MG' and 'MM', these two agreeable women became the closest of all Annabella's friends.

Annabella was not short of female company up in her northern eyrie. The Bakers of Elemore had a daughter, a second Isabella;

Louisa and Elizabeth Chaloner lived close by; Emily Milner's beautiful sister Diana had married Francis (Frank) Doyle, the older brother
of another Irish friend, Selina Doyle. All of these young northerners
were and remained devoted to Annabella; nevertheless, during those
early days, they had lives and preoccupations of their own. Mary
Montgomery proved different. Clever, musical and highly social,
but hindered by a cruelly persistent spinal complaint, she welcomed
the affectionate care that Annabella was eager to lavish. Seaham,
offering comfort, healthful sea air and the company of an admiring younger friend, provided a pleasant escape from the brooding
atmosphere in Mary Gosford's London house. (Lord Gosford, when
present, which was rare, was a notoriously unkind husband.)

Poetry loomed large among the interests shared by Annabella and
her new friend. Walter Scott was the most celebrated poet of the
moment and Mary Montgomery could boast of having almost met
him through a mutual friendship with the renowned Scottish-born
dramatist Joanna Baillie. But Annabella had a little trump card of
her own. Visiting Seaham in 1808, 'MM' was introduced to Joseph
Blacket, Miss Milbanke's very own poet-in-residence.

A handsome young consumptive with a motherless child, Blacket
was a professional cobbler whose historical plays and romantic
poems ('Now awful night, array'd in sable gloom, / Draws her
dark curtain round one half the globe') had caught the interest of
a few northern patrons, including the Duchess of Leeds and Judith
Milbanke. Learning that Blacket was temporarily homeless, Judith
urged her husband to provide a Seaham cottage, together with fuel,
food and – in those hard times, it was a generous gift – the sum of
twenty pounds.

Perhaps Joseph Blacket fell in love with Annabella; perhaps, he
simply knew on which side his bread was buttered. When Miss
Milbanke and her friend set up a competition to see who could
best inspire their pet poet, he found himself quite unable to set the
musical Miss Montgomery's airs to verse. But Annabella's awkward
notion – she requested an ode to the tree which had provided a muse
to one of her Whig heroes, Charles Fox – bore instant fruit. Writing

to thank Lady Milbanke for all her kindnesses on 23 November 1809, Blacket lavished praises on her daughter's own gift for verse. ('In Miss Milbanke's lines I find sublimity ... Her Ideas are wove in the finest Loom of Imagination ...')

Blacket, who died at the age of twenty-three in August 1810, was not alone in admiring Annabella's first poems. Sarah Siddons, the great Shakespearean actress, was a close friend of Judith Milbanke. Shown one of Annabella's verses during a visit to Halnaby, Mrs Siddons declared it to be 'the most extraordinary production, in any point of view, that ever came under my observation'.

Mrs Siddons was besotted by Miss Milbanke, declaring that she perceived something 'nearly resembling the heavenly, in the divine illumination of that countenance of hers'. The villagers of Seaham, while less garrulous in the expression of their feelings, tended to agree. Annabella, in her mid-teens, struck them as both sweet and kind, a friendly visitor to their homes whose 'natural simplicity and modest retirement' was accompanied by 'a... charming manner'.

Aged seventeen, Annabella had become a pretty, slightly built young woman with an unusually high forehead, blue eyes, fair curling hair and an open, friendly face that lit up (the 'divine illumination' that Mrs Siddons raved about) whenever her interest was caught. Gentle, clever, good-hearted and eager to be of service in the world (the word 'benevolence' appears with uncommon frequency in her early correspondence), the flaws for which this paragon would later be viciously condemned were also beginning to appear. Among them was a disturbing zeal for passing judgement upon people she scarcely knew.

Escorted to London by Judith in February 1810 for her first taste of a London season, Miss Milbanke was eager to demonstrate how skilfully she, like Mrs Siddons, could interpret character from a person's appearance. Dining out on 3 March at the home of Lord Ellenborough, the lord chief justice, she studied one of the guests across the table – Lord Grey – and discovered him to be self-important. Back at home again, Annabella opened the journal in which she proudly recorded her impressions: '*His* seems to me the politeness of a gentleman, not the politeness resulting from a principle of benevolence.' Another new acquaintance was condemned, despite a brilliant naval record, for lacking the manners of a true gentleman. The Persian ambassador might think himself lucky for having escaped with a briskly noted commendation for his fine black beard and splendid teeth.

Whisked from the noisy gatherings of celebrity guests who were always on show at Lady Cork's home in New Burlington Street to the primmer parties held by the formerly rather wicked Lady Elizabeth Foster (newly recast as the decorous widow of her long-term lover, the Duke of Devonshire), Annabella's favourite evenings were those that she spent with the kindly old Ellenboroughs. Ample space was made for a rapturous note in her journal of the latest such occasion (10 July), and not only because Mrs Bates (a former factory-worker) had sung Handel arias in a way 'that made me forget all but Heaven . . .'

The real point of the 'happifying' summer evening of songs from Mrs Bates was that Annabella had discovered her ideal in Anne Ellenborough. Not only did the great judge's wife appear incapable of unkindness, but she was motivated by the wish to do nothing but good. 'She appears constantly actuated by a principle of disinterested universal benevolence. She says ill of none . . .'

What Annabella did not care to admit to the self-conscious little journal that she kept during her first season in London was that she had immensely enjoyed her transformation from the virtuous 'Northern Light' (a nickname that acknowledged Miss Milbanke's growing reputation for doing good works) into becoming, largely thanks to the great fortune that she was in line to inherit from her uncle, one of the most courted young women of the year.

CHAPTER THREE

THE SIEGE OF ANNABELLA
(1810–12)

'How disgusting he is!' Annabella noted after being ogled at a London party by a portly bride-hunting Duke of Clarence (the future William IV). Her private comment upon one happily oblivious London hostess, naughty old Lady Cork, was even harsher: 'she is to be shunned by all who do not honour iniquity'.

Annabella's outrage (prudently restricted to the pages of her journal) was understandable in a high-minded young woman of provincial background. The London she entered early in 1810 offered a startling contrast to life in remote northern England. Living at Seaham through the closing years of the Napoleonic Wars, she had witnessed and admired her parents' generous response to the evident hardships of their employees and tenants. In London, by contrast, the occupants of the various grand houses into which she was invited seemed (with the exception of kindly Lady Ellenborough) indifferent to everything but politics, gossip and the scent of the money for which, beneath the sheen of compliments and smiles, everybody was on the hunt. Up in County Durham, an evening's entertainment occasionally rose to a cheerful 'hop' at the Bakers' or the Milners', with a carpet rolled back for the twirl, thump and rush of a dance in which young and old, servants and masters, jogged merrily together. In London, chaperoned into the candlelit, red-walled opulence of such popular assembly halls as the Argyll Rooms, the sense of being thrust into the marriage market, exposed to a cool appraisal of precisely which unmarried maiden carried the largest cargo of disposable wealth, was inescapable.

Stern though Annabella's private opinions often were, her journal also provides clear evidence that Miss Milbanke relished her introduction to high society, displaying a newfound pleasure in having fun that came as a relief to her anxious parents.

The Milbankes were determined that their clever daughter – rosily open-faced and (for a young lady who devoured her beloved mutton chops as eagerly as a soldier on the march) remarkably slender – should make a good impression in the world. A handsome house had been rented for just that purpose in Portland Place, a favourite street among the country-loving northern gentry, who appreciated its proximity to the good air and fine walking on the broad open pastures (already earmarked for urbanisation as part of the Regent's Park) to be found just north of the Euston Road.

A house was merely the starting point in the campaign required to launch the Milbankes' cherished child. Judith, while not over-fond of her husband's formidably well-connected sister, Elizabeth, had hastened to announce Annabella's arrival in London to Lady Melbourne, and to express a candid hope that this most artful of hostesses might smooth the social progress of her niece. (It was while dining at her aunt's palatial home in Whitehall that Annabella formed her first – and poor – opinion of Lady Melbourne's giddy little daughter-in-law, Lady Caroline Lamb, as 'clever in everything that is not within the province of commonsense'.)

Judith Milbanke was growing too old for the role of chaperone through evenings that often extended into the dawn, but Mary Gosford was delighted to help out with the task. Staying in the Gosfords' fine house in Great Cumberland Place, or at Mary Montgomery's snug abode in nearby Seymour Street, Annabella deepened her already settled friendship with the two Marys into an abiding love. Meanwhile, Miss Montgomery discreetly encouraged her beloved older brother, Hugh, to believe that Annabella might be prepared to consider a match. It was a notion which Annabella's teasingly friendly manner towards tall, cheerful Hugh did nothing to discourage.

Confined to her bed for lengthy periods, Mary Montgomery read all that was current and received all who amused her (many failed the test), while fixing an attentive eye on the world beyond her window. For Mary Gosford, as for Annabella, leading as adventurous a cultured life as possible was an act of positive kindness to their abidingly inquisitive invalid friend. Chaperoned by Lady Gosford and often joined by Mrs George Lamb (Lady Melbourne's clever and level-headed second daughter-in-law), Annabella performed her duty with a vengeance. Musical evenings; gazing upon painted panoramas that were cranked past the viewers (just as backdrops would later be on early cinema screens); attending high-minded lectures upon poetry and plays; visiting exhibitions of curious objects (Annabella was fascinated to see a meteorite that fell on Yorkshire earth in 1795 and was now on display in the London home of James Sowerby, the great fossil-collector of the day): being benevolent to a sick friend had never been more enjoyable.

But marriage, not culture, was the true purpose of Annabella's three seasons in London. Candid, pretty, virtuous and clever, her prospects as an heiress made her – as she was calmly aware – the object of considerable interest. One catch existed. It was widely reported that Miss Milbanke's wealthy uncle, Lord Wentworth, planned to make her his eventual beneficiary, in lieu of his own illegitimate son. (Nobody was informed that the fortune was to pass to Annabella only after her mother's death.) But Viscount Wentworth remained in robust health, while the Milbankes were becoming steadily impoverished both by Sir Ralph's political expenses and by the rapidly shrinking revenue from his north-country mines. The bailiffs were not yet knocking on the door, but Halnaby, by 1810, was proving impossibly expensive to maintain. The future of Seaham itself had grown uncertain. It was for this reason that Annabella's three years on the London marriage market were frequently interrupted by the Milbankes' retreat to a cheaply rented house in Richmond-upon-Thames, while Portland Place discreetly closed its doors. Without the hospitality of Lady Gosford and the precious connection to her Aunt Melbourne – lodged at the very heart of London society in her great house on Whitehall – it is not entirely clear how Miss Milbanke would have survived.

Money was needed. It was up to Annabella – there was no other way, bar the selling of land or interminably waiting for Uncle Wentworth to die – to secure her parents' future comfort. A match must be made, and a good one.

Courtships

The first prospective alliance was to a man to whom Annabella's friends believed she was ideally suited.

George Eden (his father had been elevated to the peerage as Lord Auckland), was the nephew of Sir John Eden, a former MP and close neighbour to the Milbankes in the north. In January 1810, the Edens had been devastated by a suicide: the body of George's older brother, William, had been found floating in the Thames. Comfort lay in the knowledge that George himself was built of sterner stuff. Admired by his family, respected by his peers, George had always seemed more capable than poor, conflicted William of running the family's handsome estate at Eden Farm, lying a few miles east of London.

Grave and high-principled, George Eden was so eager and assiduous a suitor that the Milbankes must have been ready to tear their hair out with frustration at Annabella's steady refusal (it was the first of many such displays of obstinacy) to commit herself to anything deeper than a fond friendship. Her respect and affection for Mr Eden was beyond doubt. The most regular of her dancing partners, George was praised in Annabella's journal as both just and wise. Lady Auckland, desperate to see George married to such a suitable young woman, assured Miss Milbanke (this was during Annabella's second London season) that Mr Eden's sisters thrived upon her 'cheerful & improving society', while expressing her heartfelt admiration for 'a character so far beyond what any of your years possess'.

All was in vain.

George Eden's misfortune was to be too perfect. Where, with such a paragon of virtue, lay the chance to exercise that redemptive benevolence which 18-year-old Annabella longed to bestow? How could Miss Milbanke foresee what an excellent wife she might one day make to the future governor-general of India? At the time of George's proposal, back in the late summer of 1811, Annabella knew only that this particular alliance was not to her taste.

Friendship was a different matter. Rejecting Mr Eden's offer, Miss Milbanke promised her absolute discretion. Nobody should know that he had been turned down; her affection for him would continue undiminished. A kindly consolation, instantly accepted ('Be a friend still to my Mother and to my sisters,' poor George humbly entreated), Annabella's readily bestowed friendship did nothing to speed her progress to the altar. Seeing them continually in each other's company; noting the regularity of the Milbanke family's visits to Eden Farm; remarking the closeness that had grown up between Annabella and one of George's eight sisters, Mary Dulcibella: how could society be blamed for assuming that the future of this evidently well-suited couple was a foregone conclusion?

Lady Melbourne may have been at work behind the scenes to promote an alternative match for her uppish little niece. In this new instance, however, the courtship was kept well out of view. The first public reference to Sir Augustus Foster's wistful pursuit of Annabella Milbanke was not made until almost eighty years later, when Foster's third son, Vere, published a family correspondence that included many of his father's personal letters.

Tall, florid and – to judge from the official portrait of him painted in diplomatic attire – justly proud of his shapely legs, Sir Augustus was still holding down his post at the British embassy in Sweden when Annabella first arrived in London. Banished from Stockholm by Napoleon, Foster reached London in May 1810 and rapidly – he was notoriously susceptible – fell in love with the latest novelty on the marriage market: a girl possessed of rare intelligence and fiercely independent mind.

The Milbankes, eager for what sounded a most suitable match, expressed cautious enthusiasm. Annabella kept her distance. Foster's mother, Lady Elizabeth, newly married to the Duke of Devonshire after twenty-four years of living with him and his wife in London's most notorious *ménage à trois*, did not disguise her impatience with an obsession that she regarded as a waste of time. The duchess was on excellent terms with the Prince of Wales; discreet arrangements were made to scupper Augustus's plans. When a lovesick Augustus actually declined to exchange Stockholm for a royal appointment to Washington, on the other side of the Atlantic, his mother lost her temper. Was he mad? Would he refuse the opportunity of a lifetime in order to engage upon – the angry duchess could not even bring herself to identify Miss Milbanke by name – 'an unfounded pursuit of other objects?'

Augustus gave in, but he did not give up. In the spring of 1812, the now widowed duchess was still being entreated to soften her view. 'I see you don't like Annabella much,' the disconsolate diplomat wrote from Washington on 26 May. Wistfully, Foster defended his chosen one ('she has good eyes, is fair, has right ideas, and sense, and mildness') while bewailing his misfortune in being so far away: 'No Minister ever had such temptation to break up a negotiation and come home. I would give the world to go back for six months ...'

Either the spectacle of such devotion softened his steely mother's heart or a shrewd woman had realised that Annabella would never be won. Throughout the summer of Annabella's third season in London, the dowager duchess made a dutiful effort to promote her son's cause. Augustus was informed that his mother now liked Annabella's countenance and manners and that she was getting to know her much better. On 4 July, shortly before dining at Portland Place with Lady Milbanke and 'Old twaddle Ralph', the duchess passed on a further crumb of comfort to her son. Judith ('*la madre*') had enquired after Augustus 'most kindly'. Perhaps Annabella's strange indifference was a mask. 'I shall live in hope for you,' the duchess wrote with a conspicuous effort at goodwill.

It was always the sisters who benefited most from their brother's courtship of Annabella; close female confidantes were of intense importance to this only child of an ageing couple. By the springtime of 1812, a strong mutual friendship had already sprung up between Miss Milbanke and Augustus Foster's clever sister, Caroline. (Mrs George Lamb, like Mary Gosford, belonged to the same age group as Annabella's adored cousin, Sophy Tamworth.)

In April 1812, following a brief visit to George Eden's agreeable home near Beckenham in Kent, Annabella spent three days with the Lambs at Brocket Hall, Lord and Lady Melbourne's house in Hertfordshire. On 9 April, she finally told a disappointed Sir Ralph that Caro George (as Mrs George Lamb was often named to distinguish her from that other, wilder Caroline Lamb, her sister-in-law) had promised to transmit her refusal to Sir Augustus. But nothing was said. Possibly, Caro George feared, as she confided to Annabella, that a despairing Augustus would plunge into marriage with – unimaginable horror! – an American. Possibly, she hoped that Miss Milbanke (for whom she was developing a great affection) might yet change her mind. Exiled to Washington, out of sight of Annabella during the most flirtatious summer of her young life, Augustus continued to take hope from his mother's softening view and words of reassurance.

On 31 August, Caro George finally delivered her report to Augustus of the discussion she had held with Annabella at Brocket in April. Asked directly about her intentions, Miss Milbanke had fidgeted, reddened and done all she could to change the subject. Clearly, it was one that was not to her taste: 'she was much embarrassed', Mrs Lamb wrote; worse, she 'has never mentioned you since'.

And that was that. Back in Sweden by 1816 and married to a congenial Danish bride, Augustus would read about the sensational break-up of Miss Milbanke's short-lived marriage and feel smugly consoled. The problem had been that he, like the admirable George Eden, was just too good for a young lady whose heart – from the moment she placed one pretty foot in a London drawing room – had been obstinately set upon the reformation of a rake. Now, the 'icicle' – as she was privately referred to by Augustus's mother – had got what she deserved.

Foster was being wise with hindsight. In part, Annabella did sincerely believe in her duty to marry a good and wealthy man, one who could both secure the future of Seaham and Halnaby and ensure her parents' peace of mind. A virtuous intention did not preclude enjoyment along the way. While it would be improper to suggest that she put herself about during her three seasons in London, Miss Milbanke certainly showed a smiling face to an impressive number of gentlemen.

That number, by the summer of 1812, had burgeoned to six or seven. Up in Durham, Annabella won the heart of a bewitched young clergyman named William Darnell; in London, she turned down Lord Longford's brother, General Edward Pakenham, and reduced William Bankes, the wealthy heir to Kingston Lacy, to disappointed tears. The Irish Earl of Roden's attractively ugly son, Lord Jocelyn, seems never to have become more than a dancing partner, but Lord Seaforth's heir, Frederick Mackenzie, liked Annabella enough to pay a visit of his own to Seaham (where an absent daughter requested her father to be sure to bestow 'paternal tenderness'). It sounds as though the young man intended to offer his hand, and Sir Ralph would have been delighted by the union. No proposal was made, however – and no tears were shed. 'I do not believe that Mac[kenzie] has any thoughts of me though I am sure Lady Seaforth has,' Annabella wrote cheerfully home in April 1812.

Annabella's parents could – and did – worry about the future of a clever and increasingly independent daughter who seemed to have outgrown an elderly couple of provincials. Often out dancing until sunrise and merrily conscious that she had become one of the most courted girls in London, Annabella set thoughts of Frederick Mackenzie aside as she began planning to hold a splendid dinner party at Portland Place. The guest list would prove demanding, she informed her dazed parents on 9 April, for she intended only to ask men who could not possibly be in love with her. Such gentlemen had become difficult to find. 'I am much the fashion this year. Mankind bow before me, and womankind think me somebody.'

Life was full of interest and the fact would seem to be that Annabella, in the summer of 1812, and having reached the ripe old age of twenty, had no great wish to get married. One reason for this lack of impatience was that she relished the freedom to do as she pleased and see whom she wished, liberties that she had never experienced during her years at Seaham. Another reason was the example offered by her friends.

It is striking how many of Annabella's older women friends had chosen not to marry. Mary Montgomery had the excuse of invalidship. For Selina Doyle, as for the much older Joanna Baillie and her sister Agnes, there was no reason other than the strong wish of these three intelligent women to remain independent. Looking around her in London, Annabella could understand why. Lady Gosford made no secret of the relief she felt whenever her grouchy husband left home. William Lamb put as good a face as he could on what appeared to be a wretched home life with the giddiest of wives. The examples of such unblushingly scandalous spouses as Augustus Foster's mother and her own Aunt Melbourne were hardly appealing. Why, seeing the misery that a supposedly good marriage could make of a woman's life, should a strong-willed young female relinquish her newly gained independence?

A BARLEY-SUGAR DAUGHTER

No tears had been shed in the summer of 1811 when an exhausted Lady Milbanke retreated to take the waters at Tunbridge Wells, leaving her daughter in the gentle care of Lady Gosford. Annabella had not enjoyed being escorted through her first season in London by a mother whose rouged cheeks were always a touch too bright, whose wigs seemed always to slide askew, and who talked with too noisy an insistence about the marvellous achievements of her brilliant daughter. It was not pleasant to detect how mischievously Lady Melbourne patronised her sister-in-law, nor to observe how Judith, rising to the bait, innocently resumed her hymns of praise, never noticing the fan-masked yawns and stifled sniggers of her captive audience. The ladies who ruled London society were easily bored. They found garrulous Lady Milbanke only a shade more diverting than her beloved 'Ralpho', an equally loquacious husband who regularly drank a bottle a night.

But now Judith had gone to Tunbridge, and her daughter rejoiced.

Farewell old Woman – make yourself merry with thinking how merry I am. I shall write to you tomorrow on a subject which I have not now time to discuss. This I declare now because I like to excite your curiosity, and to delay gratifying it. I am a sweet chicken!!! You ought to think me the most barley-sugar daughter in the creation. I am tired of paying myself compliments but you may pay me as many as you like.

Seaham, for the moment, had lost its lonely charm. A long, dank autumn of estrangement from friends in London was briefly enlivened by the agreeable company of Mary Montgomery; alone again, Annabella contemplated the prospect of a glum family Christmas with a nagging mother and no kind father on hand to defend her. (Sir Ralph had developed an illness which would keep him in bed for most of the winter.) When an invitation to join the Tower family at nearby Elemore Hall arrived, Annabella jumped at the chance to escape.

Still at Elemore in January 1812 and only mildly diverted by the compliments of her new local admirer, William Darnell, Annabella began plotting for a speedy return to London. Grave concerns were expressed as to the health of that invaluable invalid, Mary Montgomery. When Judith proved unresponsive, Annabella took herself off to see old Dr Fenwick at Durham. Fenwick had personally examined poor, ailing Mary during his summer visit to London; surely, he would agree that a conscientious Annabella should rush back to London and care for her sick friend?

Dr Fenwick, to his young visitor's dismay, thought nothing of the kind. Instead, writing *in loco parentis* ('except your parents, there is not a friend of yours who loves you more sincerely than myself'), he advised Annabella to stay quietly up at Seaham and stop picking quarrels with a mother who, for all her faults, loved nothing in the world so much as her cherished child.

> If she sometimes is mistaken as to the best method of securing
> your comfort, she is so truly affectionate, her confidence in
> you is so liberal, so entire & honourable to both; in short her
> feelings as a Mother occupy so large a portion of her existence,
> that you cannot be too studious to make a suitable return.

Fenwick, writing to Annabella in early February 1812, a day or two after her visit to his home, flattered himself that he understood her personality. In fact, he was oblivious to one of Miss Milbanke's greatest flaws. Intensely critical of others, Annabella could never bear to be at fault herself. To be advised to mend her ways was as painful as the realisation that Dr Fenwick had no intention of championing her proposed return to London. There was no help here. Another strategy must be devised.

On 9 or 10 February, shortly after her visit to Fenwick's house, Annabella retired to her own room at Seaham in order to justify her intentions to her parents. (Since they all lived under the same roof, her painstaking, elaborate letter was presumably slipped under their bedroom door.) Beginning with Dr Fenwick's homily ringing in her ears, she apologised for the 'irritable humours' by which she had recently caused hurt to her dear 'Mam' when Sir Ralph was seriously ill. Perhaps, she conceded, it was possible that Miss Montgomery's weakening health might be the product of her own anxious wonderings? Nevertheless – this was a difficult leap in the argument, but a determined Annabella bridged it without a blink – did she have the right to distress beloved parents with the spectacle of an anguish that no truthful daughter would wish to conceal? (Truth was a weapon that Annabella was learning to wield with inventive skill.) Or should she – by going to London – where it was conceivable that Mary would prove to be less ill than her loving friend imagined – allow them to rejoice at her own restored peace of mind?

This amazingly tortuous letter ended with a concessionary flourish. She would, after all, leave Seaham only when her father's health showed signs of being on the mend. 'I therefore propose not to be in London till this day fortnight ...'

Annabella proved resolute. By 24 February 1812, she was snugly ensconced at Lady Gosford's London home and – so the Milbankes learned – bestowing happiness upon all who saw her, including the poor invalid, so lit up with joy that 'for a time [it] gave her the appearance of blooming health.'

As often with Annabella, truth and wishful thinking were inextricably entwined. Miss Montgomery was indeed less blooming than when she visited Seaham the previous autumn. Death, however, was a long way off. By mid-March, Mary was able to chaperone Annabella to the London studio at which, for a price of twenty guineas, Judith's barley-sugar daughter was having her portrait painted by George Hayter. Within two years, Mary was travelling to Granada, followed by the first of many long sojourns in Italy. Nearly forty years later, when Annabella herself lay close to death, her old – and still beloved – friend Miss Montgomery was presiding over supper parties at her home in Hampstead.

Annabella can easily be condemned (several of her parents' friends voiced their disapproval at the time) for behaving like a heartless humbug, but six lonely and often fogbound months at Seaham might have rendered any lively young woman desperate for escape. Plainly, the jubilant tone of her first letter from London had far more to do with her sense of regained freedom than with the discovery that Mary Montgomery was not yet upon her deathbed.

On 23 March 1812, George Hayter put the finishing touches to his portrait of a smilingly confident Annabella, her head tossed back, her hair unpinned and loosely curled.

Two days later, she met Lord Byron.

CHAPTER FOUR

ENTERING THE LISTS
(1812–13)

'Childe Harold ... is on every table, and himself courted,
visited, flattered and praised whenever he appears. He has
a pale, sickly, but handsome countenance, a bad figure,
animated and amusing conversation and in short, he is
really the only topic of almost every conversation – the men
jealous of him, the women of each other ...'

ELIZABETH, DUCHESS OF DEVONSHIRE TO HER SON,
SIR AUGUSTUS FOSTER, IN WASHINGTON, 1812

Annabella's first encounter with Byron took place at Lady Caroline Lamb's morning waltzing party, held in the glorious entrance hall of Melbourne House. Byron – as he later recalled – was intrigued by Miss Milbanke's reserved manner and air of 'quiet contempt'. The curiosity was mutual. Writing up her journal that evening at Lady Gosford's home, Annabella noted that Lord Byron's disdainful expression – she drew near enough to notice his restless eyes and the frequency with which he masked the impatient twitch of full lips with his hand – suggested a proper degree of scorn for the frivolity that surrounded him. Lord Byron, lame since birth and always conscious of the halt in his step – he wore loose pantaloons to conceal the defect – declared his preference for boxing to waltzing; Annabella, an enthusiastic dancer, now decided that she, too, despised such trivial amusements.

Writing to her mother the following day with a careful account of Lord Byron's appearance and manner, Annabella reported that his opinions were both eloquent and sincere. Byron, meanwhile, baffled a captivated Caroline Lamb by the keen interest he displayed in her husband William's young cousin from the north: 'the first words you ever spoke to me in confidence were concerning Annabella,' Caroline later reminded him, before adding with more frankness than tact: 'I was astonished – overpowered – I could not believe it.'

How much did Annabella already know about the young man whose small, proud head and aloof manner she studied with such eager interest on 25 March?

Reading the *Edinburgh Review*'s advance puff of *Childe Harold* and its author in February 1812, Annabella had learned from Francis Jeffrey's unsigned and influential review that the poem's author could stand comparison with Dryden and (he was one of Annabella's particular favourites) George Crabbe. Thrillingly, she learned that there was an evident and powerful connection between the young poet and his poem's eponymous Childe, a 'sated epicure . . . his heart burdened by a long course of sensual indulgence', who wanders through Europe's loveliest scenery with the restless displeasure of Milton's Lucifer, 'hating and despising himself most of all for beholding it with so little emotion'.

Since everybody in London society was talking about *Childe Harold*'s author by the time that Annabella met him, it's probable that she also knew that he, like herself, was an only child. (His half-sister Augusta was the daughter of Captain Byron's first marriage to Lady Conyers, the once wealthy and – so shockingly – divorced wife of the Marquis of Camarthen.) She may not have known that young Byron and his own once wealthy Scottish mother, Catherine Gordon of Gight, had been subsequently abandoned by his philandering, financially reckless, and finally debt-ridden father. She would certainly have learned that he had returned from his two-year tour of Europe in the summer of 1811, just before the sudden death of his mother at Newstead Abbey, an appealingly derelict family mansion of precisely the kind that a romantic young poet ought to own. (Byron spent little time at Newstead, leaving it under the sporadic supervision of a cheerful young sailor cousin, his namesake and – at the present time – his heir.)

This was mere background detail. Annabella was more interested to discover that Lord Byron's scornful expression concealed a generous heart and a strong social conscience, clear evidence of which had already emerged in his first – and widely discussed – public speech.

Byron was paying one of his occasional visits to Newstead in December 1811, when the tranquil surface of country life in Nottinghamshire was ruffled by an outbreak of rioting. The introduction of new mechanical looms threatened the livelihood of stocking-makers at a time when weaving provided the sole source of income for many poor families. A few bold rebels smashed the new frames that were intended to put them out of work. The punishment, at a time of vicious repression, was transportation and fourteen years of exile to a penal colony in Australia. In February 1812, a bill was introduced to change that penalty from deportation to death.

The government's brutal response to Nottinghamshire's angry frame-breakers was the subject that Byron picked for his maiden speech in the House of Lords.* Parliamentary speeches during that period tended to be stupefyingly dull. Byron's, delivered on 27 February, was inflammatory: 'Will you erect a gibbet in every field, and hang up men like scarecrows?' he demanded of a largely admiring House. A week later, his angry poem on 'Framers of the Frame Bill' ('Who, when asked for a remedy, sent down a *rope*') was printed in the *Morning Chronicle*. The poem appeared anonymously, but Byron's distinctive voice was easily identified.

Scores of the young ladies who panted after Byron in 1812 were

---

* Byron's second speech, given on 21 April 1812, objected to Britain's ongoing discrimination against Catholics.

attracted by the mad, bad and dangerous aspect of his volatile personality. Annabella saw a man who – like herself – sought to be of service to the world. Had he not proved it, during their very first conversations, by the concern he evinced for the orphan of her former protégé, Joseph Blacket? (Annabella was unaware that Byron's *English Bards and Scotch Reviewers*, written before his departure for the Continent, had poked fun at the former cobbler for his high-flown poetry.)

Besieged by admirers during that happy spring of 1812 as she had never been before, Annabella's letters home dwelt increasingly upon one subject. Lord Byron was 'without exception of young or old more agreeable in conversation than any person I know ... a very bad, very good man,' she informed her mother on 16 April. Byron, so Sir Ralph learned on the following day, was 'deeply repentant' for his youthful sins; by 26 April, Annabella was ready to proclaim it as her 'Christian duty' to offer him spiritual guidance. Was this really a mission to redeem Lord Byron's soul, her nervous mother wondered, or had Annabella fallen in love with a hardened reprobate? Writing to Lady Melbourne, never her favourite member of the Milbanke family, Judith confessed her fears and solicited – for the first time in her life – that worldly lady's personal intervention.

Judith's appeal fell into outstretched hands. 'My cousins cannot live without me,' Annabella had innocently boasted to her parents on 15 April, during a month in which she spent almost as much time at Melbourne House as under Mary Gosford's roof. Flattered by the smooth courtesies of Lady Melbourne and her daughter, Emily (Lady Cowper), Annabella remained blissfully unconscious of her value as a pawn in their scheme to sabotage Byron's increasingly public relationship with Lady Melbourne's daughter-in-law, the lovesick, married and scandal-prone Caroline Lamb.

Judith's information was swiftly put to use. Hints of Byron's growing interest in William Lamb's starchy little cousin were intended to discourage Lady Caroline; instead, they spurred a jealous mistress into action. Towards the end of April, Annabella was persuaded – without much difficulty – to hand over a selection of her own poems, in order – so Caroline sweetly declared – that she might obtain Lord Byron's sincere opinion of their merit.

Lord Byron did not, as Caroline must have hoped, jeer at Annabella's high-minded verses: if anything, he rated them too highly. A poem about a cave at Seaham was singled out for its pleasing turn of thought – albeit of a somewhat different turn from his own – while favourable comparisons were made to the works of Joseph Blacket, Annabella's verses being 'better much better'.

> But these are all, has she no others? She certainly is a very extraordinary girl, who would imagine so much strength & variety of thought under that placid countenance? ... You will say as much of this to Miss M. as you think proper. I say all this very sincerely. I have no desire to be better acquainted with Miss Milbank [*sic*]; she is too good for a fallen spirit to know, and I should like her more if she were less perfect.

Although hardly the missive that Caroline had hoped for, Byron's response offered enough fuel to serve her purpose. On 2 May, Annabella received a morning summons to visit her cousin's wife in the suite of upper rooms at Melbourne House which Caroline shared with her husband and their lovable, mentally handicapped young son, Augustus.

Caroline kept no record of the encounter; Annabella, with uncharacteristic terseness, noted that she had received Lord Byron's written opinion of her verses, answered Cousin Caroline's questions with 'a painful acknowledgement' and that she had then – this was most unlike her – returned home to dine alone.

Annabella's handwritten copy of the letter with which Lady Caroline presented her visitor (it survives within the Lovelace Byron Papers) omitted that final sentence about her own discouraging perfection. There can be little doubt, however, that the letter in its entirety was read aloud to the guest – and taken to heart. Over the next two years, the single fear consistently expressed by Annabella was that Byron would be disillusioned when he discovered her flaws.

And the 'painful acknowledgement'? An admission that Annabella had already refused George Eden – he remained her most regular escort – is ruled out by Caroline's insistent assertions, from May on, that Mr Eden was Miss Milbanke's preferred suitor and that Byron himself stood no chance. More probably, Caroline extracted and then mocked her young cousin's wistful dream of reforming Byron. Either way, Annabella left Melbourne House in low spirits.

Caroline's own obsession with Byron found its way into one of Annabella's rare attempts at comic verse. In 'Byromania', an undated satirical poem that seemingly emerged from that spring, she poked fun at her cousin's wife for 'smiling, sighing o'er his face'. Fortunately for her own peace of mind, Annabella remained unaware of the extremes to which Caroline was prepared to go in pursuit of the desired object (snippets of her pubic hair were hand-delivered to Byron's rooms towards the end of the summer) or of the easy duplicity with which Byron himself – while assuring Lady Melbourne that he was doing everything to escape from Caroline's clutches – continued to dally with a woman he fondly addressed as 'the cleverest most agreeable, absurd, amiable, perplexing dangerous fascinating little being that lives'.

While Byron never presumed to call Annabella 'a fascinating little being', observers noted his interest and evident respect. Byron liked the idea of Miss Milbanke, Augustus Foster's mother shrewdly informed her absent son during the summer of 1812, not as a mistress, but as a wife. Caroline, meanwhile, despatched a warning to Annabella to forget all about the salvation of 'Falling Angels'. Filing this letter of 22 May away for future reference, Annabella pencilled a terse underlined comment on the envelope: '*Very remarkable*'.

By 22 May, Annabella's parents had been in town for three weeks. It was the mother, so Byron convinced himself, who was responsible for an unwelcome alteration in Miss Milbanke's manner. Friends with a vested interest hastened to produce other reasons for her coolness: 'C[aroline] told me she was engaged to Eden, so did several others. Mrs [George] L[amb] her great friend, was of opinion (& upon my honour I believed her) that she neither did could nor ought to like me ... was I to hazard my heart with a woman I was very much inclined to like, but at the same time sure could be nothing to me ...?'

It is not necessary to suppose that Byron was being devious in this letter, addressed to Lady Melbourne on 28 September. (She had asked about his intentions towards her niece.) While passion was the keynote of his affair with the married Lady Caroline, an entirely different quality emerged in his search for a perfect wife. The Byron whom Annabella was getting to know was thoughtful, kind, friendly and courteous. 'I have met with much evidence of his goodness,' she had informed her mother on 13 April, after only two meetings with Byron. If only – as she continued to wish without results – her new friend would not show quite such respect, and even awe. A pedestal offered a lonely perch for a young lady with a romantic heart.

Outwardly calm, Annabella betrayed her growing feelings for Byron to her journal. On 20 June, she sat near enough to him at a lecture to see that what discomforted him was not Thomas Campbell's allusion to religion, but the way the audience turned to watch Lord Byron's reaction. (He was, she was beginning to perceive, intensely shy.) On 14 July, a week after enjoying a friendly chat with Byron at an evening hosted by Sarah Siddons, Annabella met him again at a party given by vivacious old Lady Cork. At this encounter, however, Byron wanted only to know whether she shared his high opinion of Miss Bessy Rawdon, the likeable and well-travelled niece of Lord Moira (later Lord Hastings).

Annabella's discomfort was increased by her rigorous sense of fair play. Much though she wished it, she could not find a single bad word to say about the admirable Miss Rawdon. Going on from Lady Cork's soirée to a party given that same night by Lady Melbourne's married daughter, she felt puzzled by her own unhappiness. Cousin Emily's evenings were always lively, and yet, alone with her journal, Annabella confessed that she had returned home 'wearied with want of tranquillity and found no pleasure!' More revealingly still, Annabella actually confided her jealous fears of the engaging Miss Rawdon to a mother whom she knew for an inveterate chatterbox.

Judith, as Annabella had guessed would be the case, took the information directly to her sister-in-law. Who better than Lady Melbourne, so closely involved in all Byron's affairs, would know where his affections truly lay?

Judith herself, or so she would proudly declare to Lady Melbourne at a later date, had known from the start that Annabella was interested only in one man. Chaperoning her niece around London during late August (the Milbankes had decamped from the sultry city to savour Richmond's fresher air), Lady Melbourne swiftly reached the same opinion. Plainly, Annabella adored Byron. Far more surprising was the news from Lord Holland's home at Cheltenham that Byron not only liked her niece, but that he actually wanted to marry her.

Byron's declarative letter was written in the early autumn, when Caroline Lamb had been whisked away to Ireland and her lover had settled into Lord Holland's Gloucestershire retreat to work on *The Giaour*, the first in a series of immensely successful romantic poems featuring an eastern setting. Lady Melbourne had asked what he meant to do about Caroline. Uneasy in the face of such directness, Byron mumbled that writing friendly letters helped to keep her under control. He then, writing on 13 September, sprang his surprise.

> Now my dear Ly M. You are all out as to my real sentiments. I was, am & shall be I fear attached to another ... one whom I wished to marry ... had not some occurrances rather discouraged me ... As I have said so much I may as well say all – the woman I mean is Miss Milbank [*sic*]. I know nothing of her fortune, & am told that her father is ruin'd ... I never saw a woman whom I *esteemed* so much. But that chance is gone and there's an end.
>
> Now – my dear Ly M. I am completely in your power ... If through your means, or any means, I can be free, or at least change my fetters, my regard & admiration could not be increased, but my gratitude would.

Lady Melbourne had become Byron's cherished confidante during the course of his hectic six-month affair with Lady Caroline Lamb. No friend had a better understanding than she of the emotional volatility that was deployed with such lethal effect upon the women Byron loved – or thought he loved. But Lady Melbourne had also become quite attached to her strong-willed little niece during a summer in which Annabella had confided some of her own feelings about Byron. Noting that the suitor appeared both to believe that his cause was hopeless and yet to invite her help, Lady Melbourne answered with care. Love had not been mentioned in Byron's letter; might she learn what he proposed to offer in its stead?

Directness produced as candid an answer as could have been expected from a man who was notoriously capable of changing his affections within the space of a few lines. Was Byron sure of himself? Frankly: 'no'. Nevertheless, praising Annabella as 'a clever woman, an amiable woman & of high blood', Lord Byron believed that she would make him an excellent wife, one who would always find out the best in him.

> As to Love, that is done in a week (provided the Lady has a reasonable share) besides marriage goes on better with esteem & confidence than romance, and she is quite pretty enough to be loved by her husband, without being so glaringly beautiful as to attract too many rivals.

Intent on gathering documentary evidence of the sincerity of his feelings for her niece, Lady Melbourne persisted in her quest. Wriggling on the hook that remained firmly in place, Byron displayed a bewildering variety of impulses (sudden enthusiasm for a black-eyed married lady; a dislike of Lady Milbanke; impatience with the time involved in courtship of such a virtuous girl; an ardent wish to address Lady Melbourne as his aunt). On 28 September, in what seems to have been his final letter on the subject, he began by denying his queried interest in Bessy Rawdon, before enquiring whether Annabella intended to marry George Eden. He was halfway through writing it when a frantic letter from the tenacious Lady Caroline galvanised her hounded lover into flight.

> I see nothing but a marriage and a speedy one can save me; if
> your Niece is attainable I should prefer her ... I wish somebody
> would say at once that I wish to propose to her – but I have
> great doubts of her; it rests with her entirely.

The letter was hardly reassuring: Byron had preceded the above announcement by frivolously announcing that everything depended upon whether Annabella waltzed or not. Nevertheless, Lady Melbourne had already decided upon her course of action. On 29 September, in a letter which crossed with Byron's own to her, she offered hardheaded advice that tallied with the suitor's own current line of thought: 'the result of all this seems to me that ye best thing you can do, is to marry & that in fact you can get out of this Scrape by no other means'. At the beginning of October, she sent news to her niece of Byron's offer to make her his wife.

Curiously, Byron's proposal by proxy arrived on Annabella's breakfast table almost simultaneously with a declaration from one of his friends. William Bankes had been courting Annabella since the spring. Having wished Bankes a brisk farewell on his imminent journey to Granada, Annabella (in her journal entry for 6 October 1812) reveals how coolly she dismissed unwelcome suitors. Bankes had already been deemed 'odious' for preventing her from talking with Byron at a dinner party; now, he was dismissed as a pathetic waverer, incapable of defending himself. 'In short he is a *feeble* character – a good heart without Judgment, Wit & Ingenuity without common sense.'

So much for poor Bankes. Byron, upon whose more thoughtful 'Character Sketch' Annabella embarked two days later, was assessed with a shrewder understanding and more forbearance. On the minus side (for which she blamed an indulgent mother), she identified pride, inability to control his passions and a disturbing volatility of temperament: 'his mind is constantly making the most sudden transitions, from good to evil, from evil to good ...' On the plus side (far outweighing the faults listed in her careful appraisal of his personality), she saw chivalrous generosity and kindness: 'In secret he is the zealous friend of all the human feelings.' Evidently recalling the tenor of their earliest conversations, she remarked upon his uncommon candour: 'He is inclined to open his heart unreservedly to those whom he believes good, even without the preparation of much acquaintance. He is extremely humble towards persons whose characters he respects & to them he would penitently confess his errors.'

The choice of words is revealing. Clearly, Annabella relished the prospect of becoming the confessor and saviour of a celebrated rake. Marriage was quite another matter.

On 13 October, Lady Melbourne summoned her niece for an overnight stay at Melbourne House. Together, they attended a performance of *Much Ado About Nothing*, and heard an actor deliver Byron's speech in honour of the reopening of Drury Lane (a theatrical project with which Byron had become closely involved). The following morning, Annabella addressed herself to Lady Gosford, while using the letter to clarify her own thoughts.

Annabella, by any reading of the elaborate screed she wrote to Mary Gosford, was flattered both by Byron's proposal and by the careful selection of his letters through which her Machiavellian aunt had chosen to transmit it. Clearly, it was not his fault that friends had misled him about her relationship with George Eden. Equally apparent was the inherent goodness which would always triumph over his passions. He loved her. Proudly, she quoted Byron's words about having always wished to marry her, no matter what the future might hold. Complacently, she cited his account of her superiority to all other women.

And yet.

It was the issue of her declared perfection that remained the sticking point. Painfully conscious of her faults, and in particular, of the hot temper which she was still struggling to subdue, Annabella could not bear (or so she wrote to Lady Gosford) the prospect of witnessing his disillusion.

He speaks of my character as the only female one which could
have secured his devoted affection and respect. Were there no
other objection, his theoretical idea of my perfection which
could not be fulfilled by the trial would suffice to make me
decline a connection that must end in his disappointment.

A decision had been reached. Having loaned her aunt the character sketch of Byron (of which she was evidently proud), Annabella
retreated to her parents' house at Richmond, before despatching a
letter informing Aunt Melbourne that she did not love the noble gentleman enough to marry him. That blunt piece of news was sent on to
Byron at Cheltenham, together with a copy of the character sketch.
Also transmitted by her aunt was Annabella's habitual sweetener:
the offer of a dignified continuation of friendship, with no reference
to the past.

Annabella's aunt was displeased. Byron's own chagrin was so
well hidden as to pass for relief. Writing back to Lady Melbourne on
17 October, he asked her to reassure Miss Milbanke that discretion
would be maintained. A second letter (it was written the following
day) began by praising the character sketch of himself as 'very exact'
in parts, although 'much too indulgent, overall'. A graceful allusion
to Annabella as the 'Princess of Parallelograms' (a tribute to her
mathematical skill) signalled his own comfortable retreat: 'we are
two parallel lines prolonged to infinity side by side but never to meet'.
By 20 October, he had drawn a line under the proceedings. Miss
Milbanke was to be informed (second-hand, as always), that 'I am
more proud of her rejection than I can ever be of another's acceptance.'

Two weeks later, Byron hinted at new interests; by 14 November,
he was off again, making love to the lusciously available and safely
married Lady Oxford. Weary of behaving like the hero of a sentimental novel, he now adopted a tone of brutal honesty. Annabella's
delicacy was all very nice, Lady Melbourne heard from her self-
adopted nephew, but 'I prefer hot suppers.'

Neither Lord Byron nor Annabella had reckoned with the determination of their jointly appointed go-between: the intelligent and blushlessly treacherous Lady Melbourne. Annabella's rejection – a decided setback in the ongoing battle to extricate Byron from the tenacious grasp of Caroline Lamb – might yet be overcome. And so, having complimented Miss Milbanke on 21 October for the dignity with which she had conducted herself, and having offered assurance that Byron was 'much touch'd' by her confidence in his future good conduct, Lady Melbourne summoned her niece back from Richmond for a second interview.

Very sweetly, Lady Melbourne now asked to be told just what dear Annabella did want from a man in order to marry him; very demurely, Annabella presented her written shopping list. Calm, equable, pleasant-looking and of good birth (a title was not required), the ideal husband would consult, but not rely upon, his wife, displaying an attachment that was balanced, never excessive. No emotional displays or ill humour would be permitted at any time, lest they should affect her. 'I am never sulky,' she added in an explanatory aside, 'but my spirits are easily depressed, particularly by seeing anybody unhappy.'

If Annabella was slyly poking fun at her aunt's blatant determination to marry her off, Lady Melbourne, a woman whose wit was sharper than her sense of humour, failed to see the joke. The wish list was, by and large, granted to her niece; the absurd request for a husband who would always control his feelings in order not to irritate those of his wife was angrily dismissed. Overall, Miss Milbanke was recommended to climb down from her 'stilts' and expect a great deal less from any man who was willing to marry her. On the subject of ill temper, she was advised to study self-control: 'till you can attain this power over Yourself never boast of your command over yr passions, – and till you can practise it – you have no right to require it in others.'

Annabella's answer was engagingly frank. She had not meant to suggest that she hungered after a righteous prig: 'I am always repelled by people of that description.' As to her aunt's advice against seeking an impossible ideal, surely a young lady might be allowed to hope? And now, 'After so full an explanation you will perhaps take off my *stilts*, and allow that I am only *on tiptoe*.'

Lady Melbourne had been beaten back, but the topic of Byron could never be long avoided. In Richmond, where Mary Montgomery arrived to spend two autumn months, his name was warmly praised by a friend who persisted in seeing the unlikely couple as a perfect match. Reunited with her faithful journal, Annabella approvingly noted that Lord Byron never allowed religion to be mocked at his table and that he had generously given away John Murray's payment for *Childe Harold* to Robert Dallas, an impoverished friend. (Dallas had helped to secure the poem's publication.) Warned against becoming too friendly with Lady Melbourne by Dr Fenwick up in Durham (the canny old practitioner was full of stories about that estimable lady's deceiving ways), Annabella declined to admit that her aunt's chief value was as the last remaining line of communication to Lord Byron. Within the privacy of an increasingly wistful Miss Milbanke's mind her rejected suitor remained firmly to the fore.

In February 1813, newly arrived in London from visiting the Wentworths and then Cousin Sophy, Annabella made the only kind of overture that was now open to her. Lady Melbourne was requested to ask Lord Byron if they could now meet without awkwardness. His response was prompt, but disappointingly casual. Miss Milbanke might be informed that 'if she does not misunderstand me nor my views – we shall be very good friends – & "live happy ever after" – in that state of life to which "it may please God to call us".'

Poor Annabella. What was she to make of a man grown heartless enough to add that he had actually smiled at her rejection? Even aloof Mr Darcy (whose character she greatly admired when reading *Pride and Prejudice* during a second winter visit to Cousin Sophy's home) would have shown more feeling.

Annabella's journal reveals little about her thoughts during her final summer on the London marriage market. Arriving in London on 7 May 1813 (following her third stay of the year with Sophy

Tamworth), Annabella attended a ball. It was the first occasion of the year at which she set eyes on Byron – but only from a distance. He was present at another party three days later, but there was no chance to speak with him. Nine days later, her private journal expressed disgust at the envy Samuel Rogers – a poet whom Byron rated only just below Walter Scott – betrayed of his literary confrère. The warmth of Annabella's own feelings is clear in her indignant private comment: 'I always thought Rogers mean, but I did not think him capable of such petty artifices as he used on this occasion to blast a rival's name.'

No further mention of Byron's name appears in the journal. In her private 'Auto-Description' of 1831, however, Annabella recalled Byron's exceptional pallor when she gave him her hand at their first May meeting, and how that betrayal of feeling had given her hope. ('Perhaps, unconscious as I was, the engagement was then formed on my part.') Several further such encounters had apparently taken place, 'but every time I felt more pain, & at last I shunned the occasions'.

Lord Byron, who had been toying with the idea of travelling abroad with his new mistress, the lovely Lady Oxford, overstepped a line when he flirtatiously presented her 11-year-old daughter with some trinkets he had recently retrieved from Caroline Lamb. The Oxfords indicated their displeasure by leaving Byron behind when they went abroad at the end of June 1813. It was at a party given around this time that Annabella observed her former suitor seated on a sofa beside a woman whose pleasant face, framed in corkscrews of brown ringlets, was new to her. Enquiries revealed that the brown-haired lady was Byron's older and married half-sister, the Honourable Augusta Leigh.

ରେ

Augusta Leigh was always short of money. She was especially so when she arrived in London at the end of June 1813 (just as the Oxfords set off for the Continent). Colonel Leigh was away, as was his habit, at the races. Their three small children – the eldest, Georgiana, was Byron's god-daughter – had been left in the care of a nurse at The Paddocks in Six Mile Bottom. (The Leighs' home suited the sporting Colonel's wish to live close to the thoroughbred mecca of Newmarket.) Augusta's choice of city lodgings was a giveaway of her hard-up state. Beginning at the noisily inelegant abode of Byron's grasping lawyer, John Hanson, she moved on to lodge with Theresa Villiers, a loyal friend whose excellent connections to the royal circle might be worked upon to advantage.

Augusta arrived in town at the very moment when Byron was unattached. Comic, easygoing, delightfully unreproachful and unfailingly affectionate, Augusta's unhesitating readiness to become Byron's favourite companion may have been related to the fact that her half-brother – of whose own financial woes she was at best dimly aware – appeared to be a source of wealth.

Few, in the late summer of 1813, saw anything unusual in Byron's loving reunion with an older sister to whom he had become almost a stranger. Caroline Lamb was merely signalling a frenzied wish to recapture her lost lover's interest when, on 5 July, she used the occasion of a waltzing party to cut herself with a broken glass before slashing her wrists (not deeply enough, according to an exasperated Lady Melbourne) with a pair of pocket scissors. Hostesses were quick to spread the tale of Lady Caroline's theatrical stunt, but no eyebrows were raised when Byron requested to bring Augusta to their houses. His own half-sister: what could be more innocently respectable?

Annabella Milbanke was thinking only of how to renew a friend-ship that she valued and feared she had forever lost – Byron was reported to be departing for the Continent, perhaps never to return – when she wrote once again to Lady Melbourne from Seaham on 18 July. A newspaper had reported that day on Lord Byron's purported use of legal trickery to enforce the sale of Newstead. Annabella begged her aunt to pass along the fact that she herself knew Lord Byron to be incapable of such base behaviour. Her more ardent message followed.

As I shall not have an opportunity of seeing him again I should be glad if you would tell him that however long his absence may be, I shall always have pleasure in hearing that he is happy, and if my esteem can afford him any satisfaction, he may rely on my not adopting the opinions of those who wrong him.

The newspaper had got its facts wrong. Byron had indeed agreed to sell his crumbling family estate in Nottinghamshire for £140,000 (close to £5 million in today's terms), back in 1812. Over a year later, he had still received only £5,000. The prospective buyer, a lawyer called Thomas Claughton, was now belatedly questioning the originally agreed price. Responding on 18 July to Lady Melbourne's letter with an explanation (Byron himself had already seen the article and angrily ordered John Hanson to take corrective action), Byron saved Annabella for his postscript. Miss Milbanke could be told – whatever it pleased her aunt to say: 'I have not the skill – you are an adept – you may defend me if it amuses you.' (Lady Melbourne's envoy to her niece, if she ever wrote one, has not survived.)

The Milbankes had little personal knowledge of Lord Byron – Sir Ralph had met him only once – but they were growing anxious about Annabella.

Evidence of parental concern, rather than of any cunning strategy for their daughter's future, showed up in their prompt support for Annabella's decision, on 22 August, to write directly, for the first time in her life, to Lord Byron. Informing him of her parents' approval, she imposed only one condition upon the epistolary friendship that she wished to initiate: 'In particular I would not have it known to Ly Melbourne ... she is perhaps too much accustomed to look for design, to understand the plainness of my intentions ...'

CHAPTER FIVE

AN EPISTOLARY COURTSHIP

(1813–14)

Not tell Lady Melbourne! How little Annabella knew Byron, or indeed, her aunt. How could she have guessed that – within a fortnight of her own resolutely secret suit to Byron – Lady Melbourne would be sending him (although for what mischievous purpose, it is hard to conjecture) the private list of husbandly requirements that she herself had persuaded Annabella to draw up a year earlier?

Returning that curious document to his favourite correspondent on 5 September 1813, Byron expressed concern that Miss Milbanke's faith in her own infallibility 'may lead her into some egregious blunder'. The blunder that he evidently had in mind lay in soliciting the friendship of himself, a rejected suitor. So far, however, Lady Melbourne knew only that he had embarked upon a sentimental correspondence with somebody referred to as 'X.Y.Z.'. By 7 September, however, Annabella's aunt had been enlightened. Doubtless, she hoped that this high-minded friendship with her niece might steer a young man she adored away from a far more dangerous relationship: his newly discovered passion for Augusta Leigh.

Byron had entered the month of August 1813 with the intention of running away to Europe accompanied by the latest object of his desire. (Mrs Leigh, he told a horrified Lady Melbourne on 5 August, was even keener than himself on the elopement plan.) By the end of the month, he was having second thoughts. Augusta, for her part, had returned to the ramshackle, debt-ridden house at Six Mile Bottom that she shared with her husband and their three young children. Byron, while dropping enticing hints to his friend Tom Moore on 22 August about having landed himself in a 'far more serious – and entirely new – scrape', was by now pondering how best to dig himself out.

On that same day (22 August), Annabella had posted off from Seaham her laboriously prolix request to become Lord Byron's special penfriend. Love formed no part of her suit: fearful of raising false expectations or – which seems more likely – anxious to save her face, she alluded to another secret and unrequited passion. 'I signified the existence of an attachment in my mind,' she would admit to Mary Gosford on 3 December, mournfully adding that she had been betrayed into this uncharacteristic act of deception by her own imprudent enthusiasm.

Annabella's intentions were sincere; her indication of unavailability acted like catnip upon a man accustomed to reducing ladies to a state of prostrate compliance. But here, incredibly, was one – the only one who had dared to refuse him – calmly announcing that she preferred another man. When Byron wrote back (25 August) to say that he himself 'still' preferred her to all others and that friendship was impossible ('I doubt whether I could help loving you'), Annabella scored another point by retreating. If friendship was not on offer, she announced, 'I will trouble you no more ... God bless you.'

Unavailable still? Such coolness was irresistible! On 31 August, an increasingly intrigued Byron wrote back to announce that – despite having once aspired to be her husband – he accepted Miss Milbanke's newly imposed conditions. Friendship it should be, and he was ready to obey commands: 'if you will mark out the limits of our future correspondence & intercourse they shall not be infringed. – Believe me with the most profound respect – ever gratefully yrs. Byron.'

And so it all began.

Byron's letters to Annabella during that autumn, when read alongside the opinions that he was simultaneously expressing to her aunt, might cause an impartial reader to gasp at such insouciant betrayal of a friendship. But Byron's left hand was seldom aware of what his right was doing. Inconsistency was as instinctive to him as wit. 'If I am sincere with myself (but I fear one lies more to one's self than to anyone else),' he would admit to his journal on 6 November, 'every page should confute, refute, and utterly abjure its predecessor.'

Writing to his self-appointed friend (so conveniently remote in her northern fastness), Byron became earnest, sincere and grati-fyingly deferential. He told her (when asked) about his childhood introduction by a Scottish nurse to the grim doctrine of Calvinism and a vengeful God, a deity far removed from Annabella's own forgiving Maker. He chastised her view of his solemnity. ('Nobody laughs more ...') He acquainted her with his notion of the purpose of life ('The great object of life is Sensation – to feel that we exist even though in pain – it is this "craving void" which drives us to Gaming – to Battle – to Travel ...'), but expressed warm approval when Miss Milbanke disagreed. He teased her about rumours of a newly rejected lover (Stratford Canning, a cousin of the Whig pol-itician)* and asked her to be kind to his little cousin Eliza Byron, about to go away to school up in the remote north of England. He informed Miss Milbanke that she herself wrote 'remarkably well', sulked when Annabella did not respond at once to his own letters, wondered when she next would be in town, and (on 26 September, a month after their correspondence began) humbly sought permission to address her as 'My dear friend'.

So far, so promising. Writing to Annabella in that same late September letter, Byron asked her (in a tone that sounded agreeably filial) to convey his 'invariable' respects to Miss Milbanke's parents. Of Augusta Leigh, of the always-returning Caroline Lamb and of his new love interest, a certain Lady Frances (the flirtatious wife of his friend, Sir Godfrey Wedderburn Webster), Lord Byron mentioned

---

* Stratford Canning is best known as Britain's ambassador to the Ottoman Empire during the Crimean War.

not one word.* Annabella was to be his mentor, not his confidante. The most that he would allow her to know – driven by a pride that matched her own – was that he did not languish uncomforted.

Writing simultaneously to Lady Melbourne throughout that same autumn of 1813, Byron used an entirely different tone. On 28 September, just two days after requesting the honour of addressing Annabella as his own dear friend, he groaned to her aunt about the persevering epistles of 'your mathematician' and mocked the earnestness of such a prim little virgin – 'the strictest of St Ursula's 11000 what do you call 'ems' – who, nevertheless, chose to write letters to a rake. Annabella was unchivalrously categorised behind her back as the kind of young woman who

> enters into a clandestine correspondence with a personage generally presumed a great Roué – & drags her aged parents into this secret treaty – it is I believe not usual for single ladies to risk such brilliant adventures – but this comes of *infallibility* ...

Ominously, Byron added his opinion that Annabella was doing 'a foolish thing' by corresponding with him at all.

Byron's bravado may have been more of a pose than he himself knew. Ten days later, he failed to disguise his discomfiture when Lady Melbourne revealed that Annabella, while writing to him with all the considerable gravity that she could muster, was meanwhile displaying the gayest of spirits in the letters she despatched to Melbourne House. Was she indeed? – 'the little demure Nonjuror!' Byron burst out on 8 October.

He had revealed too much, and it seems that he knew it. Before the end of the month, Lady Melbourne was being untruthfully informed (by Byron himself) that his correspondence with her niece was at an end.

---

* Lady Frances's charms were heightened by the fact that the Wedderburn Websters had recently moved to Aston Hall in Yorkshire. Aston was, as Byron had learned from Augusta, the very house in which she herself had been conceived.

By the close of 1813, so far as her aunt knew, Annabella Milbanke had passed out of her former suitor's thoughts. On 6 February 1814, Byron mischievously reminded Lady Melbourne of the doomed proposal ('that brilliant negociation with the Princess of Parallellograms') he had once persuaded her to make on his behalf. Now, back in London from a long and secluded Christmas at Newstead with the pregnant Augusta and her children, Byron asked his favourite mentor to find him some docile, trouble-free consort: 'What I want is a companion – a friend rather than a sentimentalist.'

Lady Melbourne knew better than to trust Byron's shimmering impulses. Annabella was more easily deceived. Bewitched by her correspondence with the most dangerously seductive letter-writer of the age, it took just three months for austere vows of friendship to change into ardent hopes of a requited love. On 26 November 1813, she confessed to Mary Gosford her secret dream of becoming Byron's wife: 'a thought too dear to be indulged'. The following day, Annabella set out to charm Byron with a letter in which, shyly angling for a romantic response, she asked whether their closer acquaintanceship might have caused him to like her – less?

The tactic almost worked. Responding on 29 November, Byron sounded both serious and tender. Annabella wronged herself, he told her, both in fearing that 'the charm' had been broken by correspondence and in imagining that she had overstepped a mark through her question. 'No one can *ass*ume or *pre*sume less than you do,' he reassured her. As for love, none could supplant her. It was simply the case – she had told him so herself – that 'the only woman to whom I ever seriously pretended as a wife – had disposed of her heart already . . .'

November 1813 was the month in which Byron first began to keep a journal. On the last day of the month, just after writing that affectionate response to Annabella's 'very pretty' letter, he sat down at his desk in Bennet Street to assess their relationship.

What an odd situation and friendship is ours! – without one spark
of love on either side, and produced by circumstances which in

general end in coldness on one side, and aversion on the other. She is a very superior woman, and very little spoiled, which is strange in an heiress – a girl of twenty – a peeress that is to be, in her own right – an only child, and a *savante*, who has always had her own way. She is a poetess – a mathematician – a metaphysician, and yet, withal, very kind, generous, and gentle, with very little pretension. Any other head would be turned with half her acquisitions, and a tenth of her advantages.

Byron had done his homework. Always in debt himself, he was evidently attracted by (it was a charge he would later vigorously deny) Annabella's position as an only child – and future peeress – who was due to inherit her uncle's fortune. Overall, nevertheless, the most striking aspect of Byron's private journal entry was that his exalted respect for Annabella – for all his initial denial of any such implication – came curiously close to love.

Close, but he was not yet ready to be caught. Annabella, by late November 1813, found herself in torment over her own folly. Three times now, she wailed to Lady Gosford, Byron had mentioned her unidentified lover as his sole reason not to propose. How could she now signal her availability without admitting that she had lied – and risk losing his respect? 'He has never yet suspected me,' she sighed. Mary Gosford, while sympathetic, could offer no solution.

A deeper question, one that Annabella had perhaps not paused to examine, was whether Byron actually wished to know that his dear friend's heart was free? In February 1814, Miss Milbanke launched herself upon the impossible mission of acknowledging the deception she had practised without compromising her own lofty integrity. So baffling was her explanation that Byron quoted one sentence back to her with a request for its elucidation. 'I cannot by total silence acquiese [*sic*] in that which if supported when its delusion is known to myself would become deception.' What exactly did she mean by those elaborate words, he asked, before torturing her with the reminder (he had just returned from a private holiday with Augusta at Newstead) of the circumscribed role to which she herself had so strictly confined him: 'the moment I sunk into your friend ... you never did – never for an instant – trifle with me nor amuse me with what is called encouragement ...'

Extracted from its context, this reminder that they were friends – and nothing more – offered scant cause for hope. However, Byron's long letter (his often matched Annabella's own voluminous epistles in length) also included expressions of regret that ill-health would keep her from London (Annabella had been ailing for some weeks), flattering comments about some verses that she had thoughtfully sent him, pleasure at her generous tribute to *The Corsair* (Byron's most recent eastern romance was enjoying a massive success) and a tender farewell: 'God bless you.' Enough emotion was on show here for Annabella to try once more. On 17 February, she again signalled her availability. Byron promptly thanked her for indicating the exact opposite and thereby saving them both a deal of trouble: '& so adieu to the subject,' he wrote with airy dismissiveness, before inquiring her age and revealing that he, at twenty-six, felt 'six hundred in heart and in head & pursuits about six.'

Annabella's best chance, as she was too innocent to realise, was in keeping her distance. In March, a month when Byron presided over a cynical alliance – the hastily arranged marriage of Mary Anne Hanson, the toughly sexy daughter of his own unscrupulous lawyer, to the mentally deficient and extremely rich Earl of Portsmouth, whom Hanson also represented – Byron confided to Annabella that religion, advocated by her as a source of comfort, offered no solace to his all too sensitive spirit.* Writing back with complete sincerity that she nevertheless hoped the best for him, as she had always done, Miss Milbanke won his heart. 'I shall be in love with her again, if I don't take care,' Byron warned himself on 15 March. Addressing

---

* Hanson promised Byron a substantial amount of money (£30,000) from Lord Portsmouth's estate in exchange for acting as best man and for later confirming the bridegroom's sanity at the time of the marriage. Anecdotal report adds that Byron himself had already slept with the bride. So Byron himself later boasted to his own wife – but Byron did love to shock (Elizabeth Foyster, *The Trials of the King of Hampshire* (Oneworld Publications: 2016)).

Annabella directly on the same day, he spoke of his desire for her company.

It was the enticing sentence 'You do not know how much I wish to see you' that inspired Annabella to venture one further cautious step. On 13 April, she asked if she had correctly understood that Lord Byron might be willing to visit her at Seaham? This was bold. Byron had expressed no such wish. For a bachelor to invite himself to stay at the house of a young unmarried woman with whom he had been in regular correspondence was tantamount to asking for her hand. How, then, would he answer? The response, written a week later from Byron's new London lodging at Albany (a bachelor's set of rooms off Piccadilly that he had inherited from the recently married Lord Althorp), was encouraging. He would visit Seaham Hall with pleasure, requesting only not to intrude upon her studies: 'you will do as you please – only let it be *as you* please ...' Distance, he added airily of a five-day journey by stagecoach from London, was of no consequence in the matter.

Annabella's complete ignorance of what was taking place in Byron's life during the period of her negotiations for a visit helps to explain the extreme distress with which – two years later – she would belatedly unravel the intrigue that had formed the background to Byron's capricious courtship of herself: a woman whose intelligence and virtuous high-mindedness he had respected almost too much to exploit. Almost, however, was not quite enough.

Byron, at the time he answered Annabella's timid request, had just learned of the birth (on 15 April) of Augusta Leigh's fourth child, christened Elizabeth Medora and always known to her family as Elizabeth or Libby. Conception had taken place in July 1813, the month during which Augusta and Byron had first consummated their love. Never supposing that his half-sister might also still be sleeping with her husband (as was the case), the guilty lover assumed from the start that the child was his.

Incapable of keeping a secret, Byron allowed his pen to betray what his lips were forbidden to utter. *The Bride of Abydos* (November 1813) approached a public confession of his passion, close enough for Byron to hesitate about sending an early copy of his poem to Annabella, while almost begging Lady Melbourne to connect its narrative to his earlier hints of an incestuous love. (The poem's original version presented the besotted and garrulous Selim as Zuleika's brother, rather than as her cousin.)

Lady Melbourne remained, as Annabella had become aware, her suitor's closest confidante. While Annabella herself was writing wistful letters to her aunt throughout the spring of 1814 about a life of studious isolation, Byron was confessing to the unshockable Lady M that he was embarked upon the most enjoyable love affair of his life. 'However I will positively reform,' he told her on 25 April:

> – you must however allow – that it is utterly impossible I can
> ever be half as well liked elsewhere – and I have been all my life
> trying to make someone love me – & never got the sort that I
> preferred before. – But positively she & I will grow good – & all
> that – & so we are *now* and shall be these three weeks & more
> too ...*

Byron did not reserve his shocking tales for Lady Melbourne alone. 'Frightful suspicions', noted his friend John Cam Hobhouse after visiting the Drury Lane Theatre with Byron on 19 May. Horrors 'not to be conceived' were revealed on 24 June to a suddenly prudish Caroline Lamb. Lady Melbourne, however, was not only his confidante but his mentor. In between swaggering about his dreadful wickedness, Byron sought her views about the wisdom of his going to Seaham. By 24 April, the date on which Annabella disclosed that she had herself informed Aunt Melbourne of his proposed visit (of which 'I think she will be very glad to learn'), Lady Melbourne had thrown icy water upon the project. 'Credo di *No*!' Byron scrawled to the side of Annabella's words, before underlining his negation. Miss Milbanke's letter went unanswered.

---

* In other words, until Elizabeth Medora was weaned. Making love to a nursing mother was evidently not to Byron's taste.

Hopeful and oblivious, Annabella sailed on towards her destiny. On 29 April, she reminded Byron that her parents still awaited confirmation of his visit. No confirmation arrived.

On 30 April, however, while pleading for Augusta ('not aware of her own peril – till it was too late') to Lady Melbourne, Byron began to wonder if marriage to a quietly respectable woman like Annabella might encourage him 'to sever all other pursuits'. Lady Melbourne, advising him on that same day, had independently reached the same conclusion, but from a more cynical motive. Such a respectable young woman could provide the perfect camouflage for the adulterous siblings, and dear Annabella was far too naive to be suspicious of what was going on: 'she will understandably make a friend (a female one) of any person you may point out – & *all friends* is very much to be wished . . .'

Up at Seaham, time crawled. Temporarily deprived of her favourite confidante – Mary Montgomery had gone abroad for her health – Annabella had nobody with whom to share the anxiety she felt about her dismayingly reticent correspondent. She wrote to praise Byron's 'Ode to Napoleon Buonaparte'. (In Seaham village, a bonfire had been lit to celebrate the emperor's abdication.) Its author did not respond. Lady Melbourne, writing to Miss Milbanke on 25 May as if Byron was a perfect stranger to her niece, airily declared that Annabella was certain to enjoy the poet's company when he visited her parents' northern home. Byron himself said nothing at all.

On 19 June, while Judith Milbanke went to Kirkby Mallory to visit her heartbroken brother – comforting him through Lady Wentworth's final days – Annabella plucked up the courage to make one final appeal. 'Pray write to me,' she pleaded, pathetically adding that she knew Lord Byron would never mean to hurt her. 'Prim and pretty as usual' comprised Byron's tart comment to her aunt. Three days later, writing to Annabella on 24 June, he explained that he was still trying to fix a date for his visit. His sign-off was a little warmer than before: 'ever yrs most sincerely' had progressed into 'very affectly & truly yrs'. From this, Annabella could take her crumb of comfort.

Byron wrote nothing more to Annabella until 1 August. Between times, he had been asking Augusta to scout out his chances for marrying her pretty young friend, Lady Charlotte Leveson-Gower. By August, he, Augusta, her children, Byron's college friend Francis Hodgson and his naval cousin George Byron were all off enjoying a beachside summer holiday at Hastings. Colonel Leigh, as usual, was absent from the party.

Later, after they became close friends, Captain Byron would tell Annabella that Augusta made use of the Hastings summer vacation to urge her brother to press for a marriage to Miss Milbanke. If she did so, it was without success. Annabella had written to Byron at the end of July to hint once more at her availability, while entreating a fixed date for his long-promised visit to Seaham. Responding from Hastings, Byron wilfully misunderstood her. Of course, he knew that she remained committed to another man, he wrote. No need, then, for her to worry that he – blessed with an excellent memory of that unfortunate fact – would intrude upon their happy trysts. Trapped, Annabella could only repeat that his rival had been dispatched ('nothing could now induce me to marry him') and ask, wrapping the most transparent of hopes in the most obscurely elaborate language at her disposal, where Byron now stood?

> My doubt then is – and I ask a solution – whether you are in
> any danger of that attachment to me which might interfere
> with your peace of mind ... Next, on the supposition of a reply
> unfavourable to my wishes, I would ask you to consider by what
> course the danger may be avoided ...

On 10 August, briefly back at his Albany rooms, Byron replied with something that came thrillingly close to a declaration. 'I will answer your question as openly as I can,' he wrote. 'I did, do, and always shall love you –' From here, however, he perversely proceeded to remind her that she had already turned him down once and – given the chance – would doubtless do so again. Since she had tendered no offer of affection, he did not intend to sue for pity.

At this point, Annabella lost her temper. Enraged by Byron's obdurate failure to understand her, she now announced (on 13 August) that her own feelings about him were and always had been limited by the knowledge that she and he were thoroughly incompatible. 'Not, believe me, that I depreciate your capacity for the domestic virtues ... Nevertheless you do not appear to be the person whom I ought to select as my guide, my support, my example upon earth ...'

The: *So there!* was almost audible. Two formidable personalities had clashed with as much spirit as Petruchio and his shrew; unexpectedly, Byron took his hit on the chin. 'Very well – now we can talk of something else,' he responded nonchalantly on the 16th. A short and extremely proper exchange of letters about literature followed on, with Byron's cancellation of his promised visit softened by his sending (at Annabella's meek request) his list of recommendations for her reading course. He suggested Sismondi, Hume and Gibbon with the promised loan of his own dual-language Tacitus. Climbing down from her stilts, the scholarly Annabella graciously agreed to give Gibbon a second chance.

At the end of August, Byron and Augusta travelled to Newstead, following the final withdrawal of the Abbey's dilatory purchaser, Thomas Claughton. There, having learned that the beguiling Lady Charlotte Leveson-Gower had rejected the proposal made by Augusta on her brother's behalf, the couple fell back on their original plan. Terrified by the prospect of a scandal which would jeopardise her social position (Mrs Villiers was helping to smooth the way to a place at court and free lodgings for life), Augusta was desperate to see her brother respectably married. Wealthy, affectionate and seemingly unaware of the scandalous tales that were beginning to be whispered in London, Miss Milbanke eminently fitted the bill.

On 9 September, in a letter which he hesitated a full day before finally despatching, Annabella's laggardly suitor referred to the petulant August epistle in which Annabella announced that she would never be his because their characters were 'ill adapted to each other'. Now, Byron humbly asked if that meant all was lost. 'Are the "objections" – to which you alluded – insuperable?' And if so, 'is there any line or change of conduct which could possibly remove them?' In short, he was finally ready to propose marriage.

On 18 September, Byron was dining alone at Newstead with Augusta and the local apothecary (liver problems had plagued the young poet since his return to England in 1811) when a gardener brought in the late Mrs Byron's wedding ring. Mysteriously disinterred from a Newstead flower bed just before Miss Milbanke's prompt consent (she wrote back on the very day that his proposal arrived), ring and letter together were laid upon the breakfast table. It may have been the odd coincidence that caused the intensely superstitious Byron to turn ashen white. Later, and with extraordinary spite, Augusta would add another detail for Annabella's benefit. Byron's only response to the news of her acceptance, so she said, had been to comment: 'It never rains but it pours.'

Lady Melbourne was the first to hear the news, in a letter which once again announced her protégé's intention of reforming 'most thoroughly' (by which, he meant her to understand, his ceasing to sleep with Augusta) in preparation for an altered way of life for which he requested her aunty blessing. Answering Annabella on that same day (18 September), Byron declared that her response, while 'unexpected', had given him 'a new existence': he was truly moved by her earnest wish to make him happy. 'It *is* in your power to render me happy – you have made me so already.'

On the following day, Byron and Augusta walked together into a part of the estate grimly known as Devil's Wood and carved their names – like the lovers they doubtless still were – into the bark of an old tree. Back in the abbey, Byron wrote to appoint Annabella as his guide, philosopher and friend: 'my whole heart is yours'. To Thomas Moore, a favourite confidant about financial matters, he announced on that same day that his bride-to-be was both virtuous (a later letter to Moore admiringly described Annabella as 'a *pattern* of the north') and rich.

Annabella's great expectations formed a regular feature of Byron's letters to Moore. Confirmation of her status as an heiress had come to him via Lady Melbourne. Apparently, there would be a house, together with a fine second residence and a 'very considerable' inheritance. Judith Milbanke had herself informed an attentive sister-in-law of these valuable particulars on 25 September before collapsing into bed, exhausted by the emotional travails of Annabella's snail-paced journey to the altar with a man – her mother now proudly declared – whom she herself had always known to be The One: 'and I was right . . .'

Not everybody was so ecstatic. As she opened her letters – from Emily Milner, Selina Doyle and Joanna Baillie – Annabella found her female friends, both old and young, united in one chorus of commiseration. William Darnell, her northern suitor, teased her for yielding her fair person 'without a sigh' and 'to the unspeakable regret of her friends', to 'that insatiable Lord' who now chose 'talent and beauty as his rightful prey'. Delighted by his own eloquence, Darnell sought approval: 'Very good – Don't you think?' And she did, enough to copy it out, while preserving the undated original into her old age.*

Mary Montgomery, who had always encouraged the match, was still abroad when news of the engagement was given out. Her brother Hugh (yet another of Annabella's suitors) seems not to have responded to a jaunty proclamation (delivered on 22 September and softened by a sympathetic note from Lady Milbanke) that 'The Thane is found.' Mary Gosford, treated on 6–8 October to an artlessly pompous explanation of the care that Annabella had taken to single out Byron as 'the man most calculated to support me on my journey to Immortality', was tactfully acquiescent.

Elation swept Annabella along for a couple of joyous weeks. Caroline Lamb managed, despite Byron's fears of an outburst, to produce a friendly note of congratulation, together with an engagingly

---

* Darnell, who later became the prebendary of Durham Cathedral and had his sermons published in the *Edinburgh Review*, was devoted to Annabella. In another undated autumn letter, from the Lovelace Byron Papers, he told her that 'there is no young person to whom I have been so much in the habit of looking up to as yourself' and sweetly ended by saying he would be proud to call Lady Byron his friend only 'because she was Miss Milbanke'.

naive drawing of the happy couple. Augusta, writing what would be perceived three years later as 'ingenious compositions', smoothly apologised for the delays which still kept her brother lingering in the south. Mrs Leigh, so Byron tactlessly boasted to Annabella on 7 October, was 'more attached to me than anyone in existence can be'. Writing to Lady Melbourne on the same day, he revealed that Augusta, increasingly terrified that scandalous reports might prevent her coveted court appointment, was 'especially anxious' for this marriage to take place.

Four weeks after her acceptance, and still separated from an absentee fiancé by almost three hundred miles, Annabella started to fret. Everything seemed like a dream, she confessed to Byron on 10 October, and yet doubts were creeping in. 'God bless you ... my own ... my only dearest.' Promising her three days later that his lawyer was at last setting off for Durham with the necessary papers (hard legal questions about the validity of Hanson's daughter's swift and strangely discreet marriage to Lord Portsmouth would pre-occupy the wily lawyer until April the following year*), Byron tried to soothe his fiancée's nerves. Indeed, he did not deserve either such happiness or her anxiously honourable explanation of the phantom lover with whom she had kept him at bay. But 'I never doubted *you* –' Byron wrote on 13 October: 'I know you to be Truth herself.' Augusta was urged to reassure the nervous bride-to-be. 'I can most fully appreciate the motives for your doubts & fears of being able to make my dear Brother happy,' she wrote to Seaham on 15 October. 'He writes me word that he hopes very soon to see you ...'

Four days later, Byron's mood had darkened. Writing to Lady Melbourne on 19 October, he blamed Annabella for failing to accept him, back in 1812. Had she done so then ('if she had even given me a *distinct* though distant hope'), he now believed that he would have

---

* On 22 November 1814, Portsmouth's brother (and heir) formally requested that the earl should be certified as a lunatic and thus retrospectively unfit to have married Miss Hanson. Byron's marriage preparations came further down John Hanson's list of concerns than protecting the lucrative aggrandisement of his daughter (see E. Foyster, *op. cit.* pp. 192–3).

acted upon it and pressed his suit. Augusta (always free of blame in Byron's eyes) would thus have been spared the unhappiness and guilt for which her brother was now ready to throw all the blame upon a reluctant bride.

A cruelly unjust view had been formulated. It was one from which Byron would never again deviate.

Isolated, apprehensive and perfectly unaware of any sexual flavour in Byron's relationship to his sister, Annabella wrote on 22 October to thank Augusta for all her kindness and to assure her that such generous warmth would not be forgotten. To Byron (his letters now dwelt with ominous repetitiveness upon his need for a wife who would control his wayward passions), she expressed her wistful hope for news of his visit. Her Uncle Wentworth, travelling up to Seaham from Leicestershire especially to meet her fiancé, was forced to return home unsatisfied. The villagers, while complimenting 'our Miss' on her glowing appearance, seemed puzzled by her continuing solitude.

On 29 October, pausing only for an overnight stay at Augusta's house (it was, so he explained to Annabella, at his sister's explicit request) and to hurl a final angry instruction at his malingering lawyer to hasten to Durham with the crucial documents, Byron finally set off for Seaham.

It was Lady Melbourne who, writing to a friend about the engagement back in September, had remarked upon the oddity of a courtship carried on entirely by correspondence. When Annabella entered the drawing room in which Byron awaited her, the couple had not even glimpsed each other for fifteen months. He, so she later remembered, fiddled with a large fob watch that dangled from his fingers. Pale and gaunt after one of his ferocious stints of dieting, he made no effort to move towards her. When she held out her hand, he bent his lips to her fingertips.

I stood on the opposite side of the fireplace. There was a silence. He broke it. 'It is a long time since we have met', – in an under-tone. My reply was hardly articulate. I felt overpowered by the situation . . .

Joined by her parents (at their daughter's request), Byron grew more conversational, talking about his new hero, Edmund Kean, with an unnatural excitement that Annabella ascribed to nerves. Informed – as the little party picked up their candlesticks at last and climbed Seaham's airily graceful staircase to their bedrooms – that the family normally rose around ten, Byron kept to his room until midday. Annabella spent a disconsolate two hours in the library before setting off for a solitary stroll. Returning, she found that their guest had also walked out alone.

It was an unpromising beginning. Two days into his fortnight-long visit, on 4 November, Byron despatched the first of three bulletins to Lady Melbourne. Sir Ralph seemed entirely agreeable; Lady Milbanke was tiresomely businesslike, not at all to his taste. More worryingly, Annabella showed no signs of being able to control him ('& if she don't it won't do at all'). Her silence was unnerving: ('the most *silent* woman I ever encountered'). Her degree of affection – unfortunately for a man who wrote that 'I never could love but that which *loves*' – remained impossible to judge.

Two days on, Byron wrote again. Annabella and he were getting along famously. She had become more talkative. Her parents were kind. He hoped (once again) she would be happy: 'I am sure she can make & keep me so if she likes.'

A week later, Byron was at his most mercurial. Perhaps there would be no marriage. Annabella talked interminably about fine feelings, analysed everything he said and retired to bed with an unexplained ailment every third day. Once, to his alarm, she had actually made a scene almost worthy of Caroline Lamb.* Nevertheless, concluding

---

* In 1856, Annabella presented an entirely different portrait of the scene to Harriet Beecher Stowe. In this version, she offered to break the engagement if Byron had some private reason to regret his offer. Collapsing on a sofa, Byron had 'murmured indistinct words of anger & reproach – "you don't know what you have done".' The subject was never renewed except by hints at 'fearful mysteries' in the past. This is less convincing than the rage described by Byron. Only in her late twenties did Annabella learn to suppress her own violent temper. (Harriet Beecher Stowe, *Lady Byron Vindicated* (Sampson Low & Son, 1870), p. 289.)

a complaint-filled letter to Lady M with the ungallant recollection of how swiftly a kiss or two could soothe her niece ('entre nous, it is really amusing'), and how pleasantly '*caressable*' into good humour she was, Byron decided that Annabella's temper was not bad, only 'very *self*-tormenting – and anxious – and romantic'. Having threatened a rupture, he concluded by declaring after all that 'if there is a break – it shall be *her* doing not mine'.

Lady Melbourne offered worldly advice. She herself had seen Annabella display a furious tantrum that ended in a two-day headache, but – since she always hurried to atone and he was so skilful a seducer – 'everything is in your power – for though you are dextrous in most things, that is your forte'.

The advice proved superfluous. By the time Lady Melbourne's letter reached Seaham, Byron had already made demonstration of his desire, frightened Annabella, angered her mother and stormed out of the house. His spirits, sullen at the northern staging post of Boroughbridge (from where Annabella learned that he felt 'cold as Charity – Chastity or any other Virtue'), improved at the pliant Augusta's home (from which his sister gushed forth 'her hundred loves'). Safely back in London, he hoped that those 'hot luncheons of salubrious memory' had helped to brighten Annabella's own mood.* Signing his saucy letter off in high good humour, Byron wished a tender good morning – as if across the pillow – to 'Ma Mignonne'.

The sense of games – dangerously silly games – being played by the amorous siblings is inescapable. 'Mignonne' was the pet name Augusta and Byron used for little Elizabeth Medora Leigh. On 15 December 1814 (this letter was one which Annabella would later regard as clear evidence of her husband's crime), Augusta blithely informed Byron that a visitor 'has found out a likeness to your picture in Mignonne' – that is, Medora – 'who is of course very good-humoured in consequence'. On 30 November, Augusta even dared to

---

* Byron had previously told Lady Melbourne that he preferred his suppers 'hot': the sexual meaning was plain. Here, he is clearly inviting Annabella to recall more than the 'hot luncheons' he had enjoyed under her roof.

tell Annabella that she shared all of her feelings about Byron, causing Annabella to respond – with pitiable innocence – that she expected them to form 'a very amiable trio'.

Annabella's obliviousness to what would later be illuminated by the glare of hindsight invites sympathy. But what is to be made of Augusta, blandly reporting to her brother on one day that racecourse bets were being laid against his marriage to Miss Milbanke, and on another that Annabella's scholarly habits were said to be ruining her health (meaning, her looks)? Was Mrs Leigh really the goose that her young brother affectionately nicknamed her, or was she a jealous sister deliberately throwing spokes in the wheels of a marriage that, if it proved a happy one, might threaten her own secret supremacy?

Certainly, that first and long-awaited visit to Seaham by Byron had not been an unqualified success. The letters that flew after his retreating form were imploring. On 16 November (the day of his departure), Annabella entreated Byron to have faith in her love. On 17 November, she recalled the terrible quarrel that had evidently taken place when she begged him not to 'turn me out of doors in revenge as you threatened'. Two days later, she urged him not to believe in 'the grave didactic, deplorable person that I have appeared to you'. Hearing by the same post from an anxious Judith Milbanke that his fiancée had recovered her former good spirits, being 'delighted and happy with her future prospects', the bridegroom softened. On 20 November, he signed himself 'most entirely and unalterably your attached B'. Six days later, Annabella wrote with candid passion of her desire for his embraces: 'I wish for you, want you, Byron mine, every hour ... Come, come, come – to my heart.'

∽

'Remember – I have done with doubts,' Annabella wrote to Byron on 24 November. But had he? Unexpectedly sympathetic when she told him on the previous day of having to sack a newish maid ('a hardened sinner') and take back her old one, Jane Minns, Byron was incensed to hear that the bells of Sunderland Minster had been rung to proclaim his approaching nuptials. 'Dearest A,' he snapped on 12 December, 'I must needs say – that your Bells are in a pestilent hurry ... I am very glad however that I was out of their hearing – deuce take them ...'

For Annabella, busying herself with wedding arrangements, arranging for a winter honeymoon at Halnaby and overseeing the sale of Milbanke properties (to boost her dowry and save Seaham Hall, the clifftop home that she adored), all the other problems raised by Byron (the challenges faced by his lawyer over Lord Portsmouth's mental status; the acquiring of a marriage licence; continuing worries about Newstead's future) appeared surmountable. All was ready, she pleaded. Her own papers were in perfect order.* Nobody objected to Byron's request for a simple drawing-room ceremony, least of all a Unitarian bride who would take pride throughout her life in never having attended a church service.

And yet still the bridegroom delayed.

On 16 December, Annabella spoke out plainly, telling Byron that his absence had become 'as unwelcome as possible to everybody'. (Her northern friends had already been advised of a deferral, from December to January 1815.) Four days later, she told him not to come at all if he had cause for dissatisfaction. Addressing him more directly still in a postscript, she wrote: 'Are you less confident than you were in the happiness of our marriage?'

Byron's answer was freezing.

I do not see any good purpose to which questions of this kind are to lead – nor can they be answered otherwise than by time and events. You can still decide upon your own wishes and conduct before we meet – and apprize me of the result at our interview – only make sure of your own sentiments – mine are yours ever, *B*.

---

* Annabella, now aged twenty-two, had unofficially taken on the role of family lawyer. It was one that equipped her well to face the challenges of an unknowable future.

Next day, 23 December, while sullenly preparing to set out for Seaham (via Augusta's home in Cambridgeshire), Byron fired off a final salvo in which he reminded his bride-to-be of the unhappy way in which they had last parted.

Dearest A – if we meet let it be to marry – had I remained at S[eaham] it had probably been over by this time – with regard to our being under the same roof and *not* married – I think past experience has shown us the awkwardness of that situation – I can conceive nothing above purgatory more uncomfortable ... I shall however set out tomorrow ... Hobhouse I believe accompanies me – which I rejoice at – for if we don't marry I should not like a 2nd journey back quite alone – and remaining at S[eaham] might only revive a scene like the former and to that I confess myself unequal –

Arriving at Six Mile Bottom armed with a marriage licence and the drafts of his latest work (a ravishing reworking of various psalms, to be set to the music of Isaac Nathan), Byron tactlessly informed Annabella that his beloved sister was looking as perfect as ever ('better can't be in my estimation'), before wishing his bride-to-be as pleasant a time as he was having himself at the Leighs' home: 'much merriment and minced pye – it is Christmas Day'.

CHAPTER SIX

A Sojourn in Hell
(January to March 1815)

The role of elder sister had been vacant in Miss Milbanke's home circle ever since Sophy Curzon left Seaham Hall to marry Lord Tamworth in 1800. Annabella was fondly imagining she had found a Sophy substitute (Augusta was nine years older than herself) when she invited Mrs Leigh to join the wedding party and to accompany the couple, as was a regular convention in those days, on their January honeymoon.

Augusta's explanation for refusing this invitation – Byron enclosed it with his own Christmas letter to Annabella from the Leighs' Cambridgeshire house – was strikingly lame. The four young children (whom Augusta produced as her sole reason for staying at home) had never yet prevented their mother from going wherever she wished. When the fact that Byron did not once write to his increasingly plaintive sister during the entire first two months of his marriage is added to his almost hysterical opposition to the two women's initial encounter in March, it becomes clear that it was he, not Augusta, who feared the consequences of such a meeting. Guilt, a quality upon which Byron's work flourished (while his spirit suffered), was – and would remain – entirely foreign to Augusta's cheerful and less complex personality. Years later, an enlightened Annabella would ascribe Mrs Leigh's sins to the state of 'moral idiotcy' [sic] in which she seemed to thrive.

Augusta Leigh had a vested interest in supporting a marriage that would help to divert growing public attention from Byron's illicit affection for herself. John Hobhouse, accompanying Byron on the bachelor's last and far from hasty stage of his carriage journey towards matrimony, held a different view. Byron had alarmed Hobhouse in the summer of 1814 by hinting about lurid secrets in his private life. Six months later, those unnamed secrets had been forgotten and Hobhouse was conscious only of the fact that he was about to lose his cherished friend and fellow rake to a dowdy little North Country bride. Hobhouse's *Diary*, our main guide to the wedding visit, is richly peppered with qualifications and barbs. In tone and content, it denigrated pretty much everything except his own friendship with Byron.

The Milbanke family's continuing fears of a last-minute matrimonial cancellation were apparent from the moment that Byron's carriage drew up at Seaham. It was eight in the evening. Supper had been eaten, the shutters long since closed. A distraught Lady Milbanke had retired to her room. Annabella, intercepting Byron as he limped upstairs to his former bedroom, flung her arms around his neck and burst into tears. ('She did this *not before us*,' Hobhouse noted with queasy relief.) Subsequently, meeting the bride-to-be by candlelight in the Seaham library, the rakish young man noted a frank manner, expressive eyes and good ankles. Miss Milbanke's dresses, as Byron had previously warned him, were unfashionably long and high-necked, affording little chance for an intimate assessment of the young lady's assets. To her credit (in the diarist's opinion), their hostess showed no affectation either in the way she greeted her guest or in the way she behaved with Byron, 'gazing with delight on his bold and animated face – this regulated however with the most entire decorum. Byron loves her personally when present,' Hobhouse noted, before adding a snide qualification of his own: 'as it is easy for those used to such indications to observe.'

A night's rest helped to thaw Hobhouse's reservations. Marriage settlement documents were signed first thing next morning in the presence of William Hoar, the Milbankes' lawyer, who had come up weeks earlier from London for that specific purpose, and who departed the following day. Celebratory entertainments provided by the Seaham villagers included a colliers' sword dance that culminated in a sinister little ritual, the beheading of the fool. At the hall, a mock wedding ceremony was rehearsed, with Hobhouse playing an improbable bride to Mr Hoar's stately groom. Annabella, having gained Hobhouse's respect during the morning's discussions with Hoar about Byron's financial position, was now declared to be 'most attractive', while her father's stories (since Hobhouse was hearing them for the first time) seemed pleasantly entertaining. Only Byron, after a muted family supper, appeared wistful. ('Well H, this is our last night – tomorrow I shall be Annabella's – *absit omen*!!') That Byron might have been joking about his desire for a last-minute reprieve was beyond the imagining of his fond but humourless companion.

Mr Hobhouse's temper had been improved by the acquisition of an unexpected admirer. Thomas Noel, Lord Wentworth's illegitimate son and the absentee Rector of Kirkby Mallory, was invited to preside at his cousin Annabella's wedding as a special honour; alluring promises had been made (Noel was always short of money) of a handsome gift from the groom. Having already cooled his heels among the anxious family for three long weeks while the wedding plans went on hold, Thomas Noel was hungry for entertainment; Hobhouse and Byron offered all that a lively and most unclerically minded rector could have wished for.

The groom, so Noel informed Kitty and their family of six on his return home,* was not in the least surly and aloof. Far from it. The melodious-voiced Lord Byron (as young Mary Noel was happy to pass along to her favourite female correspondent of the time, 'is very engaging in his manners, exceedingly good-humoured, and has great spirits'. Mr Hobhouse, who spoke of Lord Byron's goodness, nobility and generosity in the highest of terms, had proved equally delightful, telling stories of his travels 'in such pleasing language that Papa says he could never be tired of listening to him'.

---

* Thomas and Catherine Noel were the parents of two girls (Mary and Anna) and four boys (Tom Jr, Robert, Charles and Edward).

What Thomas Noel did not tell his children was that Mr Hobhouse had privately urged him to do everything in his power to stop the marriage going ahead, advice that Noel decided to ignore.

On 2 January 1815, the long-awaited ceremony took place with the couple kneeling upon on two hard little cushions (Byron later remarked that he thought they were stuffed with peach stones) in Seaham's airy first-floor drawing room. Hobhouse, while omitting to record his friend's oddly informal wedding attire (a black coat instead of the customary blue, and loose trousers instead of the wedding breeches that would draw attention to the thinner calf above his deformed foot), noted that Annabella was simply dressed in white muslin ('very plain indeed'), and that she spoke her responses clearly ('firm as a rock'). Following the bride's quick change into a warmer dress and fur-trimmed grey travelling pelisse, the couple had both sat quietly in the room. Tellingly, Hobhouse observed that he felt 'as if I had buried a friend'.

Byron's devoted comrade provided a final glimpse of his own feelings as the honeymooners set off on their thirty-mile carriage journey inland to Halnaby, near Darlington. Annabella, to whom Hobhouse had condescendingly presented a yellow morocco-bound set of her husband's works (as if she did not already have copies of her own!), confided that any future absence of happiness would be entirely her own fault. Innocently stated, the remark would be stored up by the resentful Hobhouse as a declaration of Annabella's personal responsibility for the fate of the marriage. Byron, meanwhile, had seemed to cling to Hobhouse's hand as the two friends bade a last farewell. Or was it the other way round? 'I had hold of his out of the window when the carriage drove off,' Hobhouse reported.

The Reverend Thomas Noel's feelings were less tender. Something 'substantial' had been promised for his time and efforts. His recompense consisted of a mere ring pulled by the poet off his own white finger (rings, frequently conferred, were an item of which Byron always possessed a superabundance) and a request to wear it in remembrance of the donor.

Mr Wallis, the Seaham vicar who was also in attendance, got nothing at all.

⨳

Until now, Annabella had spent little time alone with her spouse. If her frequently revised later accounts are to be trusted, solitude brought a sharp awakening. Journeying to Halnaby with his new bride in a closed private carriage, Byron began by singing, fell into silence and then informed Bell (the pet name he bestowed upon his bride from this point on) that she should have married George Eden. When this produced no results, he announced, firstly, that she would learn to regret not having accepted his own first proposal; secondly, that she should not have married him at all; and finally, that he shared the dislike which Lady Melbourne had told him she felt for Annabella's mother.

Byron was as capricious in his moods as the wind. He was also suffering from a filthy cold, one that lasted throughout the entire first week of the honeymoon. Ill health did not improve his spirits. It is entirely possible that he did indeed say all these attributed unpleasantries, and mean them. It is also well within the bounds of belief that Byron announced, shortly after their first dinner as a married couple, a strong preference for sleeping alone, and that he greeted Annabella's arrival in the Halnaby library the following morning with the announcement that she had married into a family rich only in insanity. Apparently, he added that he had damned himself by marrying her.

So Lady Byron recorded later and – prone though Annabella became to dressing her marital recollections in the plumage of a bad gothic novel – there is no reason to doubt that their essential basis was factual. Byron, referring to his estranged wife as 'Truth herself', meant to convey that Annabella did not lie. What she may have done instead was to focus an obliging memory upon those truths that would most help to make her legal case for separation. Those truths – and no others – were what Lady Byron presented in her formal depositions. That purposeful testimony tells part of the story, but not the whole.

Annabella was not alone in creating the myths in which the three-week January honeymoon at Halnaby has been enshrouded as thoroughly as by the snow which marooned the handsome, bleak old house, blanketing its long stone terraces and holding the world outside at bay. Jane Minns, reporting that her young mistress had been all smiles on her arrival at Halnaby (Mrs Minns had travelled ahead to prepare the household), was herself looking back over a gap of fifty-four years. Tom Moore's frequently repeated tale of Byron ravishing his wife on a Halnaby sofa within minutes of their arrival is not verified elsewhere. Moore claimed to have come across the scene in Byron's unpublished memoirs, but no other reader – and there were many – alluded to any such memorable occasion. A rape scene is hard to square with Byron's only extant mention of a sofa encounter at Halnaby, when he informed Lady Melbourne that he and his Bell were snugly sharing a couch even as he wrote (she being curled up fast asleep in its far corner). 'You would think,' he complacently reported on this first day of wedlock, 'that we had been married these fifty years.'

It was perhaps inevitable that the honeymoon of such a notorious literary figure would invite embellishment. Samuel Rogers also cited the conveniently unverifiable Byron 'Memoirs' (they were burned in John Murray's Albemarle Street drawing room in 1824) as his source for a story of the poet waking his wife from slumber during their first night at Halnaby with a shriek of terror. Firelight, flickering behind the closed red damask curtains of the couple's four-poster bed, had caused a guilty spirit to picture himself in Hell.

Again, this was a case of fanciful thinking. The anecdote was first published in 1856 by Rogers' personal Boswell, Alexander Dyce, as an example of his hero's lively table talk. Rogers was evidently conflating the Byrons' imagined wedding night with a subsequent event at Seaham Hall, when Annabella rescued her sleeping spouse from being suffocated by the noxious fumes of sea coal. (An intoxicated Byron had imprudently doused the smoking fire in his dressing room with a bucket of water.) That incident was widely reported, especially since Byron took great pride in his wife's resourcefulness. 'This has been a trial of Bell's presence of Mind, & adroitness which I am delighted to hear she possesses,' Lady Melbourne complimented her protégé on 11 February, six days after his account of the event.

What do we know for certain about the week during which Byron laid aside his charming surface (Annabella later wistfully referred to it as his 'company kindness'), allowing her to see the personality which Walter Scott privately described as 'irritable to the point of mental disease' (and which Byron himself would later plead made him 'violent', but 'not malignant')?

We know that, early on the first morning of their marriage, a misadventure occurred. Finding her fingers too slender for the wedding ring that had belonged to Byron's chubbier mother, the new Lady Byron hung it around her neck on a black ribbon. For Byron, that innocent act was bad enough; a black ribbon signified misfortune to his superstitious mind. Worse followed when the ring fell into the fireplace; here was sure evidence that trouble lay in store for their marriage.

A letter was delivered to Byron while the honeymooners consumed their first post-nuptial breakfast. Augusta, never diplomatic, had seized the occasion to hail her younger brother as the 'Dearest, best & first of human beings' before informing him that she herself had trembled like the sea in an earthquake during his wedding ceremony. Byron read the letter aloud to Bell and asked for her thoughts. She told him (Annabella's calmness in the face of provocation always infuriated her husband) that the letter was very agreeable. 'My answers on all such occasions appeared to convince him of my unsuspecting goodwill towards her [Augusta],' she would tell her lawyer the following year.

It is unlikely that the newly married Annabella felt anything other than 'unsuspecting goodwill' towards the unknown sister-in-law with whom she swiftly began to share her concerns about Byron's odd behaviour. While Byron cheerfully informed Lady Melbourne that Halnaby was 'just the spot' for a honeymoon and that he now entertained 'great hopes this match will turn out well' (7 January 1815), Augusta tried to reassure his anxious wife. 'At Halnaby he did several times declare that he was guilty of some heinous crime,' Annabella later recalled. But Augusta asserted that such tales were all a sham. 'It is so like him *to try and persuade* people that *he is disagreeable and all that* Oh dear!', she lamented to Annabella on 9 January 1815. Nine days later, she countered news of Byron's 'fit of *grumps*' and 'malicious insinuations' with praises for the way that Annabella had taken control:

> I think and with joy that you are the most sagacious person and
> have in one fortnight made yourself as completely Mistress of
> the 'art of making B happy' as some others would in 20 years.

Strangely, given Annabella's lawyerly habit of making copies of everything she wrote, no trace remains of her own side of the copious correspondence with Augusta during those first months of 1815. But Augusta's eulogy suggests that the stay at Halnaby was less resolutely black than Annabella's memory later painted it. Expeditions were rendered impossible by heavy snow. Music offered no diversion for a couple who neither played instruments nor – apart from Byron's occasional wild Albanian chantings – sang. In certain other respects, they were well matched. Insistently though Annabella would later dwell upon Byron's belief in a vengeful God, he was intrigued by her own more forgiving creed. At Halnaby, she read a discussion of miracles, at his request, and argued the case against atheism. Byron was listening to his hardheaded wife when he briskly instructed John Hanson, on 19 January 1815, to start raising money from his encumbered estates in Nottinghamshire and Lancashire.

Money worries would haunt Byron throughout his marriage, leading to times (so he later told Hobhouse) when he was '*bereaved of reason* during his paroxysms with his wife'.* Money was preying

---

* The words 'bereaved of reason' were underlined later by John Hobhouse, not by Byron himself.

on his mind following the couple's return to Seaham Hall for the second part of their honeymoon. On 26 January, five days after their arrival back at the Milbankes' home, Byron glumly told Hobhouse that his debts were in excess of £30,000 (just under £2.5 million in today's money). Unmentioned was the £30,000 he was due to receive in three annual payments, a reward for supporting John Hanson's underhand marriage of his daughter to the wealthy – and mad – Earl of Portsmouth.

Privately, Byron was uneasy. Publicly, the handsome young husband was all smiles. Lady Milbanke complacently reported to her remarried brother-in-law, Sir James Bland Burges, that the newlyweds were 'well, and as happy as youth and love can make them ... neither of them seems in any haste to visit London'. In 1846, Mrs Clermont would declare that Annabella had left Seaham for Halnaby looking like 'a flower' and returned looking 'as if she cared for nothing', but that ardent supporter's memory may have been corrupted by subsequent events and the passage of over thirty years.

In 1818, Annabella would return to Seaham for the express purpose of reliving her joyful memories of this visit to her family home as a honeymooning bride. Down in Cambridgeshire, Augusta heard about jolly games of charades, in which a frisky Byron had pulled off Lady Milbanke's wig while Annabella donned his greatcoat and yachting cap, together with false whiskers and a moustache. What a pity that 'certain people whom I know & many others whom I don't know could not peep through the door', Augusta giggled on 28 January. And how splendid that Byron was in such spirits! 'I rather suspect he rejoices at the discovery of your "ruling passion" for making mischief in private,' she added, leaving her sexual innuendo almost as naked as the guilelessness of an artless Annabella's confidence.*

---

* What was the 'mischief' involving Annabella's self-acknowledged 'ruling passion'? Flagellation? Or is it possible that Byron had introduced his wife to oral and/or anal sex, and that Annabella found that she enjoyed it? At least one later defendant of Lady Byron (John Fox, writing in 1869–71 and seeming to cite Annabella's lawyer as his authority) hinted that sodomy, rather than incest, was the embarrassing charge of which no proof could be offered to a court.

Less reassuring were the *Bouts-Rimés* that were forwarded to
Augusta from Seaham the following day. The game had been to
write alternate lines of rhymed verse; the result was a tease with a
troublingly barbed edge. Annabella (or so she later recalled) had
annoyed her husband by innocently suggesting that each line-maker
should mark their contribution with an 'X', not knowing that this
was the code symbol for sex used by Byron in his relationship with
Augusta. Two lines run as follows:

> BELL: *The lord defend us from a honeymoon.*
> BYRON: *Our cares commence – our comforts end so soon.*

The sour tone of the jangling rhymes (of which there were many
more) was echoed in the letters which Byron fired off from Seaham
during the following days. So, 'the treaclemoon is over, and I
am awake, and find myself married,' he wrote to Tom Moore on
2 February, adding that he missed their friend Douglas Kinnaird's
brandy and was bored of dancing to the jangle of the Milbankes'
tea bell ('damn tea'). Lady Melbourne, busily urging her protégé to
put himself under his wife's affectionate direction, received a similar
signal ('the *Moon* is over'), together with a reminder of Byron's persisting passion for Augusta, although 'I have quite enough at home
to prevent me from loving any one essentially for some time to come'.

Diligently searching – the request had come from her niece – for a
rentable London property large enough to suit Byron's extravagant
taste (but cheap enough to satisfy his prudent wife), Lady Melbourne
took comfort from Byron's announcement in this same letter of
2 February 1815 that – moon apart – 'Bell & I are as lunatic as
heretofore – she does as she likes – and don't bore me ...' Familiar
with Lord Byron's capricious moods, Elizabeth Melbourne remained
cautiously optimistic. Governing him, and doing so with kindness
and affection: this delicate skill, as she never ceased to remind her
niece, was the key to a successful marriage.

Augusta, meanwhile, grew alarmed at hearing that Byron
frequently proclaimed his preference for his sister over his wife,

introducing mentions of his 'Gus' in a way that she unhappily agreed with Annabella was 'very *mal-a-propos*'. She took hope, nevertheless, from Lady Byron's hints at sexual pleasure and – as the chilly days at Seaham lengthened into weeks – signs of a growing companiability.

Returning alone to Seaham three years later, Annabella would walk down the cliff path to the shore. Here, and out on the moors where she and Byron had once set off on a day-long 'ramble-scramble-tumble-cum-jumble' that ended with them floundering, laughing, into a bog, she had merrily followed Byron's lead. In company, and even in private (as she noticed by his discomfort when they encountered country folk out on the lonely roads around Seaham), her halt-footed husband was always conscious of the painful deformity that a ruthless God had personally condemned him to endure. Alone with her, Byron grew unselfconscious and boyish, 'jumping & squeaking on the sands' or scrambling ahead of his wife up to the crag of the Featherbed Rocks where, side by side, the two of them gazed tranquilly out across the white crests of a grey and wintry sea. These small and modest recollections evoked happy memories. When preparing her legal depositions of a wretched marriage, Lady Byron resolved to omit such scenes.

Annabella's maid, Jane Minns, concerned by her mistress's evident sadness during the lonely weeks at Halnaby, had urged her to confide in her father, kind Sir Ralph. Pride forbade it. Augusta, that warmly reassuring unknown sister, was clearly the person who knew Byron best and who was thus most able to advise a wife on how to handle him. True, Byron had dropped mysterious hints of a forbidden relationship with his sister, but there was no serious reason to believe him. Two months of marriage had taught Annabella that Lord Byron was at any moment capable of saying whatever popped into his head, especially after a generous swig from the brandy bottle that was always on hand at hospitable Seaham Hall. (Augusta, knowing him better, futilely entreated Annabella to hide the brandy away.)

That Byron loved Augusta was beyond doubt; that he might love her more than he should cast only a faint shadow across the unsuspecting mind of his wife. It is likely that Annabella's firm refusal to stay alone at Seaham while her husband travelled to London – via another visit to The Paddocks* at Six Mile Bottom – was based simply upon an eager desire to meet for herself the charmingly demonstrative Mrs Leigh. Augusta, justifiably fearful of her brother's intentions, began by opposing any visit by either party, proceeded to the suggestion that the couple should take over some nearby house and ended, joylessly, by acquiescing to Lady Byron's request to stay under her roof. (Colonel Leigh was not in residence.)

Byron's anger at his wife's wilful insistence upon accompanying him to the Leighs' Cambridgeshire home evaporated in the face of unexpected good news. The elusive Thomas Claughton was once again considering the purchase of Newstead Abbey and the Duchess of Devonshire's grand London house in Piccadilly was available for the Byrons to rent. Household arrangements were to be settled between Annabella and Lady Melbourne, who instantly despatched floor maps, inventories and screeds of helpful recommendations. Byron, meanwhile, now informed Tom Moore that he had 'vastly' enjoyed his stay at Seaham Hall, where his wife was in 'unvaried good-humour and behavior [*sic*].' A reference to Annabella as being 'in health' hinted at a better reason for good cheer than either news about houses or of Milbankian hospitality. Lady Byron believed that she was pregnant. Byron never doubted that their child would be a boy.

∞

'What I suffered at Six Mile Bottom was indescribable,' Annabella later recalled. As always, the darkest elements came to the fore in quasi-legal statements that required a tale of unmitigated horror. For once, however, she included a moment of unexpected joy. Shortly after leaving Seaham on 9 March, Byron turned to his wife in the carriage and told her that she had succeeded in making him a happy

* Recently reborn as Swynford Manor, a wedding venue.

man. Kissed and caressed in front of her own maid, Annabella grew embarrassed; nevertheless, the declaration was truly tender. It made up for the coldness and the 'sort of unrelenting pity' she had been subjected to at Halnaby.

That moment of affection stood out in Annabella's mind because it contrasted so painfully with what followed. The newly-weds spent three long March weeks under Augusta's roof. Byron, throughout that period, behaved as if he wished that he had never met his wife. Thwarted by Augusta's unexpected resistance to his sexual overtures, he reacted with all the considerable malice of which, when denied his wishes, Byron was always capable. His target became Annabella.

The portrait of life at the Leighs' isolated house that Lady Byron later painted to her lawyer was unyieldingly grim. Sent early to bed ('We can amuse ourselves without you my dear'), and greeted by a shriek of 'Don't touch me!' when once she reached towards her husband for comfort in the night, Annabella was meanwhile informed – however absurd she then believed the announcement to be – that little Elizabeth Medora Leigh was Byron's own child. Instructed to listen while a reluctant Augusta unwillingly read out the letters in which her brother had pondered which wealthy bride to pursue, Annabella was commanded to sit with Mrs Leigh upon a sofa while Byron – lounging between them – decided which of the two women could kiss him more ardently. Constantly exposed to what one of her subsequent accounts simply but eloquently described as 'deep horrors', it's small wonder that Lady Byron's private record of her feelings at the time included the pitiful line: 'My heart is withered away, so that I forget to eat my bread.'

The unexpected result of Byron's perverse behaviour was to drive the two women (literally, some would suggest) into each other's arms. Confidences had already been exchanged about Byron's boasts of an incestuous relationship. Watching Augusta closely throughout the visit, an anxious Annabella noted that Mrs Leigh 'submitted to his [Byron's] affection, but never appeared gratified by it'. True, Augusta made a point of wearing her monogrammed brooch containing a lock of hair (Byron had ordered one for his sister and one for himself back at Seaham, when he anticipated staying alone under her roof), but she did so under his instruction. True, Augusta read out painful passages from letters, but it was always at Byron's insistence. Also true, and less forgivably, Mrs Leigh never protested when her guest was sent off early to bed. (One of Annabella's most wretched memories of her stay in Cambridgeshire was the sound of Byron and his beloved, merry 'Gus' laughing together behind closed doors.)

Superficially, the new sisters-in-law had little in common. Annabella was cautious, rational, intellectual; Augusta was impulsive, illogical and happy to accept Byron's affectionate description of herself as 'a ninny'. What drew the two women together was the callousness with which Byron sought to manipulate their feelings. His success was qualified. Gus – chestnut-haired, hazel-eyed, softly rounded as a damaged peach and nervous as a hunted hare – was awed by the calm dignity with which the younger woman endured her husband's manic goading. 'I think I never saw nor heard of a more perfect being in mortal mould than she appears to be,' Augusta wrote of Annabella in a letter to Francis Hodgson, on 18 March. On 1 April, she wrote to Hodgson again, to announce that her poor brother's debts had plunged him into despair.

And throughout all of this, what did Annabella think? 'She [Augusta] was always devotedly kind to me and consulted my wishes on every occasion,' Lady Byron firmly stated a year later, and added: 'I cannot think how feelingly [Augusta acted] without emotions of gratitude.' Nevertheless, leaving the Leighs' cluttered and claustrophobic home for London on 28 March, Annabella experienced profound relief. Augusta had seemed equally thankful for the visit's end. Recalling their departure in her legal statement the following year, Annabella simply noted that she 'did not wish to detain us'.

CHAPTER SEVEN

UNLUCKY FOR SOME:
13 PICCADILLY TERRACE
(1815–16)

The house which Lady Melbourne had picked out for her niece's future abode was the London home of Augustus Foster's mother. (The widowed Duchess of Devonshire – Georgiana's successor – was solacing herself in Rome.) Built in the 1760s in the neoclassical style, 13 Piccadilly Terrace* looked across the fields of Green Park from the western and airier end of a palatial row of Georgian mansions, beneath the tall windows of which – much to the delight of the late 4th Duke of Queensberry, one of the terrace's most famously lecherous inhabitants – available ladies marketed their wares. 'Old Q' had become quite a feature of the street himself, ogling the passing traffic from a balcony, and then, from an armchair drawn up within a specially designed bay window. The Byrons, to the relief of their neighbours, would prove more reticent.

An assortment of pets, a long-suffering valet (William Fletcher was helped out by an occasional understudy, James Brown), an eccentric old cleaning lady called Mrs Mule and a formidable wardrobe: these were Lord Byron's contributions to setting up the household, plus the rent he had agreed to pay of £700 per annum

---

* Still standing, 13 Piccadilly Terrace has been renumbered as 139.

(around £28,000 today). A semi-tame squirrel was installed, together with a bad-tempered parrot – it once bit Annabella's finger, whereupon Byron hurled it, cage and all, out of the window, only to rush downstairs to save the bird from death – and a mastiff. The dog guarded its master's door, not from a wife who regularly shared his bed, but from the menace of a swelling band of creditors.

Annabella's miserable experiences at Augusta's Cambridgeshire home were briefly forgotten in the task of setting up a sixteen-bedroom house which, while adequately furnished by the duchess, possessed not one scrap of linen, glass or cutlery. By 5 April, all was orderly enough for John Murray, Byron's publisher, to be invited in to show off a new bookplate print of the poet (Annabella agreed with her husband that its unflattering predecessor was unusable), a portrait of Byron as he had appeared to visitors at the Royal Academy in the summer of 1814: a glorious figure in Albanian costume, represented to the sitter's own entire satisfaction by the well-known artist Thomas Phillips. (The painting so enchanted Byron's proud mother-in-law that she purchased it for herself.)

Byron was not alone in being able to assume a charming public manner. Mr Murray went away from Piccadilly Terrace with an excellent impression of the poet's young bride. It was not yet apparent how rare the honour of paying a social visit to these reclusive newly-weds was to be. As a girl, Annabella had enjoyed hosting London dinner parties. There were to be no such occasions at her new home. Among her closest friends – the Milners, the Gosfords, the Doyles, the Montgomerys, the Eden family, Mrs George Lamb – not one seems ever to have crossed the threshold of her marital abode. Lady Melbourne, paying an official call, was turned away. Even Hobhouse, returning from a European trip in the summer of 1815, found it difficult to gain access to his oldest friend.

Signs of domestic unrest behind the house's austere façade showed up almost immediately. News had come while the Byrons were still visiting Augusta that Mrs Leigh had secured a £300 per annum appointment as a Woman of the Bedchamber to the Regent's mother, old Queen Charlotte. Free and spacious lodging in St James's Palace (a welcome bonus for a couple who had no London home) was not, however, to be provided until 1818. On 31 March, a mere three days after the Byrons' traumatic stay at The Paddocks, the queen's new court lady was invited to lodge herself – and to stay for as long as she wished – under her brother's roof. The offer came not from Byron, but his wife.

Why did Lady Byron turn so readily to the very woman for whom her husband had recently displayed a woundingly amorous affection? Possibly, Annabella thought it would create an impression of estrangement if Augusta stayed – as she could easily have done – with Mrs Villiers, the worldly older friend who had helped secure her new royal post. (Mr Villiers was a Groom of the Bedchamber to George III.) More likely, having formed a bond of sisterly kinship under stressful conditions, Annabella felt that cheerful, sympathetic Gus was the only person with whom she could safely share her private worries and that she would – Augusta made no secret of her longing for a livelier existence than she could obtain in a Cambridgeshire village – gladly take up the proposal.

Accepting with speed, Augusta nevertheless displayed unease about the chances for success of the *ménage à trois* that Annabella had once blithely envisaged as 'an amiable trio'. 'You will perhaps be a better judge by & bye [*sic*] whether I shall not be a plague,' Mrs Leigh presciently advised her 'dearest Sis' on 31 March '– & you must tell me truly if I am likely to prove so . . .'

Augusta arrived at Piccadilly Terrace on 15 April. Accompanying her were a maid and her eldest daughter, Georgiana ('Gee'), Byron's quiet, slow-witted godchild. The newcomers had scarcely settled in as guests before – from the debt-ridden Lord Byron's point of view – good news arrived. Wealthy old Lord Wentworth, grief-stricken since the loss of his lively little wife in the summer of 1814, had been taken ill at his London house. Death was imminent. While Judith hurried to make her way down from Seaham, Annabella set out from Piccadilly Terrace to act as her dying uncle's companion and comforter. Hints that the early stages of pregnancy were taxing her health appear in the anxious letter Byron sent to Lord Wentworth's house on 13 or 14 April:

> Dearest –
> Now your mother is come I won't have you worried any longer – more particularly in your present situation which is rendered very precarious by what you have already gone through. Pray – come home
> Ever thine *B*

Lord Wentworth died on 17 April. The anger with which Byron greeted his wife upon her return home – she later recalled that he did not speak to her for four days, preferring to use Augusta as his envoy – was fuelled by a disappointment that he was ashamed to put into words. Lord Wentworth had been expected to leave his fortune to his niece, Annabella. Instead, it was to pass to her only upon the death of his one surviving sister, and with conditions. The Milbankes, in return for adopting Judith's maiden name (Noel), became the new owners of Wentworth's London home and of Kirkby Mallory, the Leicestershire estate at which Judith had spent her early years. Lord Wentworth's money, of which they all stood in urgent need, remained entailed. Sir Ralph was still struggling to raise the last portion of his daughter's £20,000 settlement (a sum on which Byron, a year after his marriage, was still receiving only the interest). For the present, however, Wentworth's large legacy was untouchable.

Chattels offered meagre comfort to a man hounded by creditors. The sole evidence that some of these personal objects did reach Piccadilly Terrace survives in a French violin on which Lord Wentworth had enjoyed duetting with his equally musical wife. Byron's feelings about the promised legacy can be guessed from the sour little verse scratched on to its back:

> Hey diddle! diddle,
> I am now Byron's fiddle,

Pray what do you think of my shape?
You may touch me and feel me
But beware if you steal me
I may get you into a 'Scrape!'
[Signed]: *mme Muse* 1815

Annabella later claimed that nursing a dying uncle had been light duty compared to the misery she was enduring at Piccadilly Terrace. Confined to her bedroom for days and sometimes weeks on end by an unexpectedly difficult pregnancy, she found herself torn between gratitude for Augusta's efforts to act as the buffer between an increasingly estranged couple and growing discomfort about the nature of Byron's relationship with his sister. Once again, Annabella puzzled over the significance of distant gigglings and laughter. What was taking place elsewhere in the house? How, fed with Byron's hints about a terrible crime, one for which her original delay in agreeing to marry him was held to be mysteriously responsible, could she not wonder?

On one humiliating evening, or so Annabella recalled, a smiling Augusta brought a request from her brother that his wife should stop pacing the creaky floorboards of the upstairs library and return quietly to her bed. Just for a moment, young Lady Byron had felt a black desire to plunge a dagger into her gentle rival's heart. 'It was an instant of revenge,' she wrote over a year later:

and her voice of kindness extinguished it – yet if I ever should go mad perhaps those remembrances would be prevailing ideas, & to a principle of Forgiveness I feel indebted for the possession of my intellects under circumstances that made my brain burn.

By the autumn of 1816, when Annabella recorded this memory, she had no doubt that there had been a pre-marital relationship between brother and sister, and that Byron had always been eager to resume it. Back in the summer of 1815, uncertainty was overruled by a grateful consciousness that Augusta, during the two summer months

that Mrs Leigh resided at Piccadilly Terrace, was doing everything
to help that lay within her power.

It is tempting to dismiss Annabella's elaborate retrospective statements about her marriage as jealous fantasies, but Lady Byron was
not a fanciful woman. The upstairs room in which she paced was
clearly identified by her as having 'then' been the library, thus indicating a subsequent change of use. The dagger that she had longed
to plunge into Augusta's heart was identified as having always been
kept in Byron's adjacent bedroom. These are concrete details, and
convincing ones. Likewise, when Annabella recalled how Byron had
tried to frighten her with Harriet Lee's *The German's Tale* (1801)
by associating himself with its protagonist (a son who murders to
obtain a legacy), the accuracy of the memory is confirmed by Lady
Byron's recollection that her husband began writing a play based
upon Lee's tale. Passages were read out to her, but 'I believe he burnt
it afterwards.'

Annabella was correct. Byron did write an early draft of *Werner*
(1822), a play based on Lee's tale and also, perhaps, upon a dramatic
version written by Elizabeth Devonshire's friend and predecessor,
Georgiana.* But was Annabella right to see personal menace in
her husband's presentation of himself as another such murderer?
Byron's hints at having committed a homicide haunted her. It
seems more likely that a sometimes unkind husband stored up
trouble for himself by his spoofing of a credulous and increasingly
terrified bride.

'My Night Mare is my own personalty [*sic*],' Byron confessed
to his close friend Douglas Kinnaird in 1817. Throughout their
courtship, Annabella had presented herself as eager to play what we
would today see as the therapist's role to a troubled man of whose
essential goodness she remained convinced. Byron encouraged her
to assume the part, urging her to act as his friend and guide. 'I

---

* Since 13 Piccadilly Terrace was the home of Elizabeth, Duchess of Devonshire,
it is reasonable to imagine that a copy of her close friend Georgiana's play would
have been in its library.

meant to marry a woman who would be *my friend* – I want you to be *my friend*,' Annabella remembered him insisting. So, were Byron's declarations and hints intended to wound and alarm, or was he simply treating his wife as the understanding mentor and mother confessor that she had promised to become? Who was failing whom?

Some light on Byron's increasingly erratic behaviour is cast by his frustrated knowledge that Annabella's well-meant endeavours could do nothing to alter the circumstances in which he found himself trapped.

The year 1815 was when Byron's personal crises reached a head. His financial problems seemed insoluble. Laudanum and calomel (a powerful mercury-based medication) were failing to ease the continual irritation caused by a diseased liver. His feelings about Augusta remained both strong and ambivalent (he was damned by having slept with her; it was intolerable that she should be under the same roof and yet resist him). Gentle reason – Annabella's mild panacea for all his troubles – drove him mad.

Back in November 1813, while attempting to identify the source of his own quicksilver emotional transitions in the journal that he had just begun to write, Byron believed that he had brought an ungovernable temper almost under control. One unfailing goad to fury remained: 'unless there is a woman (and not any or every woman) in the way, I have sunk into tolerable apathy'. Annabella was precisely that stubborn woman who, by standing in the way, brought out the worst in her husband. Faced by his wife's implacable, maddening tranquillity, Byron set out to shatter it. He did so with all the considerable verbal and imaginative power at his disposal. Later, Annabella would recall every last wild word, claim and threat that had been used to provoke a reaction from her heroically imperturbable self. Unfortunately for Lord Byron, she took his taunts and violent dramatics very seriously indeed.

ᘓᕲ

Five months into the Byrons' marriage, Annabella had good reason to feel both unhappy and isolated. Apart from Augusta, she had nowhere to turn for help. Mrs Clermont, who had stayed elsewhere in London throughout the summer, was apparently in receipt of daily confidential letters, as – to a lesser degree – was Selina Doyle. Neither woman could offer more than sympathy. The Noels (the Milbankes legally changed their name in May, a month after Lord Wentworth's death) were kept at arms' length by a husband who had no wish to dance attendance either on a woman he disliked or her garrulous old husband. The fact that Sir Ralph, an ardent Whig, shared both Byron's elation at Napoleon's escape from Elba and the poet's disgust at the outcome of Waterloo, provided a route through which Annabella struggled to promote a friendship between the two men in her life. 'B has just found out an Etymology for Blücher's name which is quite in your way,' she wrote to her father, before carefully spelling out his pun upon the name of Wellington's ally on the battlefield: '"There goes the *Blue Cur*".' On another occasion, Byron had noticed the word 'Dad' scrawled on a Piccadilly wall: 'B said it was a memento left us by our honoured parent.'

Such well-meant efforts proved useless. Byron rejected all invitations to the Noels' new London and country homes (formerly Lord Wentworth's properties), leaving Annabella to travel alone to the family celebration of her birthday on 17 May 1815. The most her husband would do was to extend an occasional family invitation to a play. (Douglas Kinnaird had just persuaded Byron to join the committee of the Drury Lane Theatre.) Byron did, however, consent to accept the occasional gift of food. 'Yours confectionately,' Annabella signed off her filial thanks for a homebaked goose pie, 'gratefully acknowledged by B's voracious stomach.' Her figure-conscious husband had apparently polished off at the same meal an entire turbot.

Hard though it is today to interpret the Byrons' secretive marriage, it presented an equally inscrutable façade to their contemporaries. George Ticknor's record of his week in London offers a good example.

George Ticknor was a New Englander whose father had set up Boston's first free primary schools, a parent enlightened enough to allow his son to exchange a legal career for the study of languages and literature. Arriving in London in the summer of 1815, en route to the University of Göttingen, young Ticknor requested an interview with Byron, one of his literary heroes.

The American visitor proved personable, well-read and in complete agreement with his host in his dislike of the boarding-school system that Lord Byron had experienced at Harrow. Paying his first visit to Piccadilly Terrace on 20 June (just after Augusta and little 'Georgy' Leigh had returned to Cambridgeshire), Ticknor caught no more than a glimpse of Annabella as she set off for a drive. Seeing her again three days later, he was impressed by Lady Byron's eloquent face and intelligent conversation.

> She is diffident – she is very young, not more, I think, than nineteen – but is obviously possessed of talent, and did not talk at all for display. For the quarter of an hour during which I was with her, she talked upon a considerable variety of subjects – America, of which she seemed to know considerable; of France, and Greece, with something of her husband's visit there – and spoke of all with a justness and light good humour.

Byron, with whom the young American subsequently spent a full hour discussing contemporary literature, was much taken by his visitor. Bidden to return on 26 June, Ticknor noticed on that occasion how affectionately his host saw Lady Byron to her carriage, walking her to the door and shaking her hand as warmly 'as if he were not to see her for a month'. On 27 June, Ticknor went to watch a historical drama, *Charles the Bold*, from Byron's Drury Lane box. The only other guests that night were Annabella's parents, of whom Ticknor greatly preferred Sir Ralph to his 'fashionable' wife. Lady Byron, in comparison, was 'more interesting than I have yet seen her', while Byron himself was praised for his kindness, gentle manners and unaffected ways. The poet, Ticknor noted with faint regret, was not in the least like the gloomy heroes of his romances.

⧼⧽

Ticknor was a rare witness to the fact that the Byrons' marriage could have a happy side. Annabella was, so her husband declared when he was feeling sentimental, 'a good kind thing'; 'the best little wife in the world'. Writing several months later to Tom Moore (in March 1816), Byron rhetorically demanded to be told whether 'there ever was a better or even brighter, a kinder or a more amiable & agreeable being than Lady B'. Sleeping together regularly and seemingly with pleasure, the young couple employed tender nicknames: 'Duck' for him, 'Pippin' (from her round and rosy cheeks) for her.

Their affectionate diminutives were already in regular use by 7 July when, shortly after George Ticknor's week of visits, Annabella's father offered to loan the couple his own recently vacated Durham home, ordering Seaham to be cleaned and whitewashed in preparation for their visit. Lady Noel, hearing that the Byrons planned to retreat there only for the December lying-in, grew anxious. 'Annabella I am sure requires country air,' she urged her son-in-law in August, a month when most Londoners who could afford it left town; 'her looks shew it, and it will do you both good'. Byron did not take kindly to instructions. Unusually for their social class, the couple remained in residence at their London home throughout the parched height of summer and on into the autumn.

Annabella, writing to Augusta early in August to express her approval of Byron's drawing up a new will (one that provided support for the improvident Leighs), admitted that this protracted London sojourn was not ideal. Confiding her longing to be out of 'this horrid town' to her 'Dearest Lei', she dwelt upon the dwindling prospect of Seaham where, she was sure, her spirits and her looks '(if I was ever blest with any)' would soon be restored. Was it to console her, she wondered, that Byron had unexpectedly invited Lady Noel to visit Seaham for the lying-in, or was it a thoughtful Augusta who had proved quietly persuasive? 'I always feel,' Annabella wrote with interesting ambivalence, 'as if I had more *reasons* to love you than I can exactly know'.

Annabella's gratitude to a loving sister-in-law was put to the test in early September. Byron had been in unusually savage spirits at the end of August, due in part to the increasing pressure of his debts. The Leighs, during this same period, were seeking to preserve Colonel Leigh's right to a relative's bequest, defending it from an unexpected challenge. Augusta, afraid that her husband's habitual inertia would cause them to lose out, summoned her brother to their aid.

Byron left for Cambridgeshire on 31 August, accompanied by his valet, the faithful William Fletcher. Requesting 'Dearest Pip' to send his forgotten medical drops, Byron tactlessly announced an instant and marvellous improvement in his temper. (A coded 'Not *frac*.' signified 'not fractious'.) Writing back to her 'Darling Duck' later the same day, Annabella adopted a characteristically optimistic tone.

I feel as if B— loved *himself*, which does me more good than anything else, and makes young Pip jump.

You would laugh to see and still more hear the effects of your absence in the house – Tearing up carpets, deluging staircases, knocking, rubbing, brushing!– By all these I was early awakened, for Ms Mew [*sic*] seems convinced that my ears and other senses have departed with you. She no longer flies like a sylph on tip-toe, but like a troop of dragoons at full gallop. The old proverb –

'When the Cat's away, the Mice will play –'

They shall have their holiday, but I can't fancy it mine. Indeed indeed *nau* [naughty] B– is a thousand times better than no B.

I dare not write any more for fear you should be frightened at the length, and not read at all. So I shall give the rest to Goose [Augusta].

I hope you call out 'Pip, pip, pip' – now & then. I think I hear you – but I won't grow lemoncholy –A—da!

The allusion to 'nau B' glossed the aggression to which Annabella had been exposed during the days leading up to his departure from Piccadilly Terrace for Six Mile Bottom. 'I was very ill,' she later recalled: '– he had kept me awake almost all the previous night to exercise his cruelty upon my feelings, & notwithstanding the self-command I could generally maintain, my convulsive sobs at last forced me to get up & leave the room.' From a safe distance, however, Byron was now ready to become a devoted husband. A second letter to 'Dearest Pip' was filled with jokes about Fletcher's courtship by letter of Annabella's maid, Ann Rood, while 'Goose' took 'a quill from her wing to scribble to you'. Byron's own was signed, as Annabella's had been, with the mysterious '–A—da', raising the intriguing possibility that little Augusta Ada Byron's second name contained some secret meaning for her parents.

ᙢᙣᙢ

Whatever grief Annabella may have been experiencing in private, she maintained before others a tranquil face. Judith, on 4 September, heard only that her daughter was 'marvellous happy' at the prospect of Byron's return and that Augusta reported his having been 'very disconsolate' without his wife. When Judith insisted that the Byrons should relocate to Kirkby Mallory, Annabella responded with a firm refusal: 'I wish I could see the practicality of our going to Kirkby,' she wrote to her mother on 8 September, 'but I do not.' Byron was apparently willing for her to travel alone, but 'I *will not*. As long as I am with him I am comparatively comfortable.' 'Comparatively' was a word that tempted further questioning, but Lady Noel, yielding to a will as firm as her own, backed down. It was agreed that Annabella's confinement would take place in town. Her choice of a reputable but unfashionable accoucheur, Dr Francis Le Mann of Soho Square, was also approved.

Money remained a subject for intense concern. Up in the north, Annabella's parents had been hit hard by the failure of the Durham Bank. While Judith painted a shrewdly optimistic picture of the future value of country estates like Kirkby Mallory, the shortage of available cash made it difficult for the Noels to help a needy son-in-law. Annabella, during her husband's absence in Cambridgeshire, paid hasty visits to Mr Hanson and her uncle, Sir James Bland Burges, executor of Lord Wentworth's will. Sir Francis Doyle, reported by his sister Selina to have 'a good deal of intercourse with people of business', was consulted about the possibility of taking out a mortgage on Kirkby Mallory. Sadly, as Annabella wrote to her mother on 30 August, Sir Frank had dashed any hopes of raising money by that route. Or any other. Even Sir Ralph's effort to realise some of the marriage settlement money – it had been due to Byron since May – by the sale of farms near Seaham was blocked by the ludicrous raising of a legal possibility that the 64-year-old Lady Noel might bear a second child. It was at this point that an exasperated Sir Ralph left William Hoar for a sharper firm of lawyers. Wharton & Ford would still be satisfactorily representing his descendants in 1900.

At Newstead, meanwhile, where young Captain Byron was acting as his cousin's unpaid agent and gamekeeper, Mr Claughton continued to dither over his prospective purchase with no imminent sign of reaching a decision.

Wherever the Byrons looked, the route to financial security was barred. The poet's creditors were reaching the end of their patience. On 8 September, in the letter explaining her decision to remain at Piccadilly Terrace, Annabella dropped the first hint of her husband's darkest fears. If Lord Byron were presently to leave town now for more than a few days, she warned her mother, 'some measures that are now suspended would immediately ensue'. Three days later, Annabella mentioned the possibility that Byron's beloved library of books would be seized for sale. A month on, she observed that only the prospect of becoming a father was giving her husband a little comfort amidst 'the very distressing circumstance to which we must look forward ... It seems a labyrinth of difficulties.'

Writing to his friends and literary confrères during the autumn of 1815, Byron sounded his normal self. Samuel Coleridge, from whom Byron entreated a play to put on at Drury Lane, was charmed by the thoughtfulness of a younger man who took the trouble to apologise about having unconsciously lifted a couple of lines from his own unpublished 'Christabel' for the almost completed *The Siege of Corinth*, the last and possibly the best of Byron's wildly successful Turkish tales.* Leigh Hunt was also moved by Lord Byron's generous enthusiasm and suggestions for the poem that Hunt rightly believed would be his masterpiece: *The Story of Rimini*. (Annabella shared her husband's admiration and copied out a long extract of Hunt's poem.) At the theatre, where Byron was playing an increasingly active role in commissioning new works, his indiscreet relationship with Susan Boyce, a young actress with a fondness for expensive jewellery, seemed par-for-the-course behaviour from a randy Regency rake whose wife was in the last stages of pregnancy.

Tom Moore, seeking advice from Byron – of all people! – on the stockmarket, received a letter on 31 October which indicated that his friend was still anxiously awaiting the promised marriage payment from Sir Ralph. Annabella was rather coolly described as 'in full progress' towards the production of a son. (Always referred to as 'Pip' by his mother and as 'Byron' by the rest of the family, the baby's sex remained a foregone conclusion.) The main substance of Byron's letter to Moore, a drinking crony, concerned the first of a series of dinners that Annabella would learn to dread.

As described by one of the world's most enchanting correspondents, the occasion sounded hilarious. The theatre crowd (it included the ageing and always convivial playwright Richard Brinsley Sheridan, and Byron's close friend, Douglas Kinnaird) had foregathered for an evening of hard drinking in an upstairs dining room. Here, the party rapidly progressed from being 'silent' to 'talky, then argumentative, then disputatious, then unintelligible,

---

* Byron had half-remembered a cluster of lines from Coleridge's 'Christabel' that an admiring Walter Scott had recited to him earlier that summer.

then altogethery, then inarticulate, and then drunk'. Kinnaird and Byron, between them, had managed to guide an intoxicated Sheridan down 'a damned corkscrew staircase, which had certainly been constructed before the discovery of fermented liquors'. All had ended in 'hiccup and happiness'.

What sounded so delightful in Byron's chatty account marked the beginning of the end for his marriage. That largely liquid supper was one of several gatherings at which Byron and Kinnaird settled their disputes about how to run the Drury Lane Theatre over copious amounts of brandy. Kinnaird was a hardened drinker; Byron had the will, but not the constitution. The effect – as Augusta had previously warned Annabella – was terrifying. Byron, when in his cups – especially when the cups were filled with gin or brandy – was mad, bad and a danger to anybody who happened to cross his path. Sober again, he would recollect none of it.

The Noels, as usual, were kept in the dark. Judith, suffering from a serious ailment that autumn, confined herself to her bed at Mivart's Hotel in Brook Street (now Claridge's) just behind Piccadilly. Sir Ralph's anxiety was lulled by his daughter's playful account of a visit to Piccadilly Terrace by the woman everybody wished the late Lord Wentworth had married in the first place instead of taking a mistress into his house. Lady Anne (Lindsay) Barnard, a well-travelled Scotswoman of exceptional brilliance and charm, came as chaperone to a group of young ladies who sought to impress Byron with tasteful accounts of the beauty of a Scottish autumn. Byron responded by expressing his personal admiration for the lovelier tint of a good malt whisky. 'In short,' wrote Annabella, 'they *yelped* and he *snapped*.'

On 1 November, the day after the drinking banquet described by Byron to Moore, Annabella still felt hopeful enough to draw up one of her earnest projects for Byron's reform: 'Wicked people have, for a time, induced him to act on wrong motives, by discrediting his right ones ... on the contrary, by insisting on the right ones, we may rouse *him* to do them justice ...' She concluded with a scolding for Byron's 'indulgence of foibles beyond the Christian temper of forbearance & forgiveness'.

Paper resolutions were all very fine, but the moment for marital reforming had passed. The arrival of a live-in bailiff on the premises meant no more to Annabella than the welcome addition of a much-needed male protective presence in the house. To a man who had been as poor – and who had grown as proud – as Byron, a resident debt-collector became the ultimate humiliation. 'God knows what I suffered yesterday & am suffering from B's distraction,' Annabella confided to Augusta on 9 November, specifying this new 'distraction' as 'of the *very worst* kind'. The combination of a bailiff and brandy, together with the rising terror – if he did not flee the country first – of bankruptcy and thus of a debtors' prison, had tipped her husband's behaviour from the unreasonable into the irrational. 'I have thought that since last Saturday [the night of Byron's first drinking dinner with Kinnaird] his *head* has never been right,' Annabella wrote, predicting in this same letter that she feared he would add 'more and more to the cause'. It was the first hint that Annabella had found a new explanation for her husband's strange behaviour. Byron was not consciously malevolent. He was going insane.

On 11 November, Annabella wrote once again to Mrs Leigh. This time, she issued a direct and urgent appeal. Augusta must come back to London, and soon.

Don't be afraid for my Carcase – it will do very well. Of the rest I scarcely know what to think – I have many fears.

Let me see you the middle of next week – at latest ... You will do good I think – if any can be done.

∞

By the time that Annabella despatched her letter to Cambridgeshire, Byron had already informed his wife, with much circumstantial detail (his boast of toying with two naked women at once was a detail that would stay in the mind of Annabella's straitlaced lawyer for the rest of his days), of his relationship with Susan Boyce. On 15 November, the day that an apprehensive Augusta arrived at

Piccadilly Terrace, a grim-faced Byron greeted her with the same information, while adding that he was tired of indulging his expensive young mistress's whims. A search was currently afoot for a new brooch that Susan had managed to drop in the Byron carriage. For the time, at least, Byron himself dropped Miss Boyce.

A break-up with Susan Boyce was small beer compared to the dismaying change that Augusta instantly perceived in her brother's behaviour. Both Byron's valet and Annabella's maid told Mrs Leigh that they were worried about the safety of Lady Byron and her unborn child. Summoning Mrs Clermont to join the household (with Annabella's approval), Augusta issued a dramatic warning: 'God knows what he may do.' Mrs Clermont, already fearful for her young mistress, came at speed.

It was Annabella who decided to import Byron's jolly young cousin into the house as a supportive male presence. George, whose future bride had been brought to London by her Derbyshire family, was delighted by the chance to continue his courtship of Elizabeth Chandos-Pole, and from such a fine address. Lady Melbourne, in a letter that has not survived, meanwhile received a troubling hint from her niece that she was ready to 'break loose' and leave. Addressing her aunt again early in the New Year, Annabella credited Augusta's reassuring company with having prevented her from doing so.

Was Annabella preparing the legal ground for a future case for divorce when she gathered these valuable witnesses around her in the house? Or was an intimidated young woman simply surrounding herself with supportive figures during a period of fear and extreme isolation? One of Lady Byron's earliest retrospective statements about the marriage suggests that the second reason was uppermost. She was not only afraid, but also lonely.

> ... for a considerable time before my confinement he [Byron] would not see me himself for above an hour – or two – if so much throughout the day & left me therefore alone all the evening till Mrs L[eigh] came, for he had always objected to my having *any* society at home.

> When he did stay at home himself, it was to drink Brandy –
> & he would then dismiss me to my room in the most unkind
> manner. He told me he must have either *his Brandy or his*
> *Mistress*.

The comfort of Augusta's presence at Piccadilly Terrace during the month before Ada's birth was a subject upon which Annabella never deviated. Mrs Leigh's former relationship with her brother was difficult to dismiss or deny. Those days were seemingly now in the past. Augusta had become unflinching in her efforts to defend a sister-in-law whom she loved, and for whom she feared.

The benefit of a sisterly presence at Piccadilly Terrace was instantly apparent. Byron, after his chilling initial reaction to Augusta's arrival at his home, swiftly resumed his familiar and enchanting manner. Towards his sister, he was once again affectionate, teasing and amorous. Towards his wife, his behaviour remained ferocious enough for Mrs Clermont to believe him capable of murder.

> The impression ... made upon my mind was that he was likely to
> put her to Death at any moment if he could do it privately. I told
> Mrs Leigh such was my opinion. She replied I will never leave him
> alone until she is brought to bed, and then you must stay always
> with her.

Dramatic though Mrs Clermont's statement sounds, it is supported by her assertion in 1816 that she never saw Lord Byron in a rational state at Piccadilly Terrace except during the first days after his daughter's birth. Alarm was now rife in the household. Fletcher kept close watch on his master's pistols. Augusta sat up late in order to ensure that a drunken Byron did not try to break past the nightly guard they had established to protect his wife from harm. Even the usually unobservant John Hobhouse, visiting the house on 25 November, noted that things were going badly there and that Byron had spoken out to him against marriage: 'talking of going abroad – &c.'

Going abroad was a good deal better than going to a debtors' prison. Hobhouse saw nothing extraordinary in the notion that Byron might abandon his wife. The London house (for which six months' rent was still unpaid) had only been leased for a year. A wife could always take shelter beneath her parents' roof. What neither Hobhouse nor anybody else could have predicted in late November was the particular way in which this anticipated result would actually come to pass.

∽∾

On 9 December, shortly before the beginning of her labour pains, Annabella managed to summon the strength to leave Piccadilly Terrace for long enough to consult Samuel Heywood, a respected attorney and close friend of the Milbanke family, about the possibility of her making an escape. Augusta's approval of the project suggests that the contemplated departure was intended to be of a temporary nature. (It was always in the scandal-prone Mrs Leigh's interests that her brother's marriage should survive.)

Heywood's response is unknown, but Byron got wind of the conversation. When Annabella returned and asked for the nurse – labour had already begun – Byron asked her when she meant to leave. Back from the theatre later that night, he sat up in the drawing room, knocking the tops off soda bottles with a poker. (Soda, as Byron would later recall in his *Ravenna Journal* of 1821, was as necessary to him as brandy during that traumatic autumn of 1815.) The nervous tenor of the household can be gauged from the fact that the racket of flying bottle tops, when heard upstairs, was mistaken for gunshots.

The baby – a healthy girl – was born at one o'clock the following afternoon, 10 December 1815, a Sunday. Annabella's nurse and her delivering physician, Francis Le Mann, were the sole others in attendance. Strange tales would later emerge. Lord Byron had enquired if the child had been born dead. Inspecting the newborn infant, he had hailed the arrival of a perfect instrument of torture to employ, presumably, against his wife. Annabella was informed by Byron, during labour, that her mother had just died.*

Such obviously anecdotal records, like many of the allegations that later became part of a copiously documented case for legal separation, must be taken with a judicious measure of salt. Mrs Clermont remembered that Byron's first concern had been to know whether the baby was physically perfect (a reasonable worry for a man born with a deformed foot). Lady Noel, visiting Piccadilly Terrace during the week after her grandchild's birth (Judith herself was still frail enough to require an invalid couch for her journey up the grand marble staircase to Annabella's bedroom) noticed nothing that disturbed her. Later, justifying her lack of concern, Lady Noel explained that she had been 'studiously deceived', due to her daughter's wish not to alarm an ailing parent.

Augusta Leigh's continuing fears for the physical safety of her sister-in-law would form one of the sturdiest pillars in Annabella's legal case for a marital separation. Two days after the birth of Augusta Ada (named in honour of her chosen godmother), Mrs Leigh confided in Francis Hodgson, the only male friend of Byron's with whom she had established a close personal friendship. She wanted to meet him urgently, and in private. No direct mention of this request must be made in Hodgson's response, since Byron was sure to recognise his friend's handwriting and enquire what was going on. As a future clergyman – and as a man who had observed the siblings' intimacy during their 1814 summer holiday at Hastings – Hodgson feared the nature of Augusta's confidences

---

* The stories in circulation about what might have been said and done by Byron during his marriage have gained much in colour from their retelling. It is not necessary to assume that his question about the baby's being dead or alive was put (to Augusta) in a vindictive spirit: Byron displayed a keen interest in the production of an heir. Annabella herself stated to a sympathetic Lady Anne Barnard only that Byron looked *ready* to use the baby as a perfect instrument of torture. The more credible version of his remark about Lady Noel (who was indeed seriously ill, worn out by money worries and taking over the running of a new estate) was that her condition had become critical.

and declined to comply. Instead, acting with Annabella's approval, Augusta turned to her own aunt.

Miss Sophia Byron was an imperturbable old lady of forthright views. (She often scolded a dieting Byron about his bouts of starvation.) The advice received from this familial quarter was unequivocal. Her nephew's symptoms suggested insanity, a trait with which Miss Byron had gained first-hand experience from observing the mental instability of her brother, aptly nicknamed 'Mad Jack'. The best thing Annabella could do, according to this authoritative source, was to have her husband closely observed and then take medical counsel upon the wisest course of action.

Aunt Sophia's brisk advice stiffened Annabella's resolve. Derangement required treatment: who better to assist in Lord Byron's restoration to sanity than a devoted wife? It was at this point that Annabella first formulated a plan by which the patient might be temporarily confined within her parents' secluded country home and nursed back to health by herself.

Christmas passed unmarked at Piccadilly Terrace. At some stage before the end of December, Annabella wrote a cautious letter to her parents, preparing them for the possibility of a family visit of an unspecified duration. Judith, having consulted Augusta in advance, sent a friendly invitation to her son-in-law, assuring Byron of all the space, peace and freedom that he could possibly wish for either at Seaham, or at Kirkby Mallory. All she asked in return was that 'a poor Grand-mama' might be granted the pleasure of wee Augusta's company. (The Noel family's use of the name 'Ada' emerged only after the Byrons' separation.) Tactful for once, Judith forbore to mention that the imminent difficulty of renewing an unpaid annual lease on 13 Piccadilly Terrace might make such an offer particularly welcome.

On 3 January 1816, Byron paid one of his rare daytime visits to the room in which Annabella was breastfeeding their daughter. It was a spectacle that gave him no pleasure. (One of Byron's rare early allusions to Ada, in a letter sent two days later to Tom Moore, noted that the infant 'squalls and sucks incessantly'.) Still, the visit began agreeably. In March 1816, Annabella stated that Mrs Grimes, the attending nurse, 'would probably say that she has seen Lord B appear personally fond of me during the few minutes she has seen us together'.

Swiftly, the visitor's mood changed. It was during this same visit that Byron apparently intimated that he meant 'to *do every thing wicked*' [Annabella's emphasis] and to begin by resuming his affair with Miss Boyce. He spoke of bringing his mistress to live in the house. And he said more, as if he dreaded what she herself might reveal.

> Amongst other unkind things said to me on Jan 3rd was this declaration 'A woman has no right to complain if her husband does not beat or confine her – and you will *remember* I have neither *beaten* nor *confined* you. I have never done an Act that would bring me under the Law – at least on this side of the Water.'

Byron's reported declaration was one which would prompt widespread and prurient speculation – it still does – about just what that mysterious act might have been been. Did Byron mean that he had never committed sodomy (a criminal offence in England) in his own country? Or did he mean that he had committed incest (which was a criminal offence only abroad)? How well did Byron himself know the law? And what did Annabella, the woman her husband paid sincere tribute to as 'Truth herself', understand by the words that she so carefully set down? These words were not idly recalled. Strikingly, they were added to Annabella's original statement only after she had decided that for her there could be no going back.

The gravity of Byron's outburst is underlined by the fact that he avoided his wife for the following three days. On 6 January, however, Augusta was sent upstairs by her brother with a curt note requesting Lady Byron to prepare herself for a visit to her parents' home at the earliest possible date. The reasons Byron gave were rational enough: bailiffs were closing in on him; the lease was almost up; the time had come to begin dismissing the household.

Byron's note mentioned that the child and her nurse would 'of course' accompany his wife on her journey. He proposed that they should all travel in his personal (and at that time, his only) carriage. There is no indication that Byron was contemplating a permanent break when he dashed off his brusque note. This, however, was the interpretation that Annabella placed upon his letter – or so Mrs Clermont recalled: 'She [Annabella] cryed & said although I expected it I cannot help feeling *this – to think* that I have lived to be hated by my husband.' On the following day, 7 January, Annabella confirmed that she was prepared to leave, as instructed, on the earliest day 'that circumstances will admit'.

'Circumstances' might suggest that Annabella desired time to recover from the shock of childbirth. She meant no such thing. A week before her final departure, the young mother threw herself into establishing by every means in her power that her husband was not responsible for his own behaviour.

Annabella's mission began with a visit to Matthew Baillie, an eminent London doctor (Baillie's uncle was the great Scottish surgeon John Hunter) and brother to Annabella's revered older friends, Joanna and Agnes. Dr Baillie may have imagined that his visitor had come to seek his advice; his role, as he rapidly discovered, was to act as audience and professional guarantor of a theory that had already been formed.

Annabella wrote up her account of the interview on that same day, 8 January 1816. The impression deliberately conveyed was that Baillie – not she – had presented the case for Byron as a madman. 'The principal insane ideas are – that he must be wicked – is foredoomed to evil – and compelled by some irresistible power to follow this destiny, doing violence all the time to his feelings.'

In fact, after listening carefully, Baillie had refused to become involved, suggesting that Lady Byron would do better to obtain written evidence from Francis Le Mann, who had treated the 'patient' with calomel for his chronic irritability (ascribed to a 'torpid' liver). But here, Annabella's quest once again had fallen short of her hopes. Le Mann would not commit his thoughts on insanity to paper,

preferring to fob Lady Byron off with an article about hydroceph-
alus, a condition in which excess fluid puts pressure on the brain.
Passages that seemed relevant to Byron's case were highlighted. Le
Mann did, however, promise to remain watchful and to send a report
of his more fully considered view.

On 12 January, Annabella took a step too far. Armed with Le
Mann's marked-up paper, she went to the office of John Hanson,
Byron's lawyer, to present her case. That hasty action betrayed
poor judgement. Although it had not yet been proved that Lord
Portsmouth was insane at the time of his marriage to Miss Hanson,
the last thing Byron's lawyer needed was to have his chief witness
declared a lunatic. Hanson declared that he saw nothing mad at all
in Lord Byron's behaviour. Shortly after Annabella left his house,
the alarmed lawyer reported her visit to her husband.

The following day, an enraged Byron spoke to Annabella in a
manner that caused her real terror. According to her later statements, this was the only occasion upon which Lady Byron feared
for her life.

The final step was probably taken on 14 January. Entering her
husband's dressing room, Annabella searched it for evidence to support her theory of Byron's madness. (Later, she fiercely denied having
picked the locks of her husband's letter trunks in order to carry off
a marked-up copy of de Sade's notorious *Justine*. If she did so, she
chose not to preserve such a controversial book.)

Armed with Dr Le Mann's instructions upon how best to proceed
with the salvation of a husband whom she still adored, Annabella left
13 Piccadilly Terrace in the cold dawn of 15 January 1816. Some kind
of parting ceremony took place on the previous evening. Annabella
had – or so her romantic memory later recalled – entered the drawing room in which Byron stood talking to Augusta by the fireplace.
Asked by him (with a mocking nod to Macbeth's three witches) when
she thought the three of them might next meet, Annabella responded
with the pious wish that it might be in heaven, before fleeing the
room – this motif was a regular feature of her recollections – in order
to conceal her tears.

Leaving at last, Annabella paused – or so she remembered the scene – outside her sleeping husband's door. Looking down at his mastiff's empty mat, she felt an urge to curl up on it and stay. Instead, Lady Byron hurried downstairs and out to the carriage where Nurse Grimes and baby Ada awaited her, together with her maid, the newly married Susan Fletcher, and a young footman. Nobody wished her farewell. Nobody knew of her departure.

Halting for a night at Woburn along the road to her parents' new Leicestershire home, Annabella wrote two letters. The first, despatched to Mrs Clermont, explained that she intended to comply with the advice given by Augusta Leigh (whom Mrs Clermont then held in high regard) and Dr Le Mann. She would immediately write to Byron with affection and without reproach. Her plan was to lull any suspicion, preparing the way for a country reunion with the troubled and violent man whom she hoped to nurse back to his senses.

Annabella's letter from Woburn was the first of two by her that would later contribute more than anything else to the view that Byron's young wife was either a liar or a hypocrite. Both letters are given here in full, just as Byron himself first saw them.

Woburn, January 15 1816

Dearest B –

The Child is quite well, and the best of Travellers, and quite well. I hope you are *good*, and remember my medical prayers & injunctions. Don't give yourself up to the abominable trade of versifying – nor to brandy – nor to anything nor any body that is not *lawful & right*.

Though I disobey in writing to you, let me hear of your obedience to Kirkby.

Ada's love with mine – *Pip*

The second letter was seemingly written on the following day, shortly after Annabella had settled into her parents' home.

Kirkby Mallory, January 16 1816

Dearest Duck

We got here quite well last night, and were ushered into the kitchen instead of drawing-room, by a mistake that might have been agreeable enough to hungry people. Of this and other incidents Dad wants to write you a jocose account, & both he & Mam long to have the family party completed. Such a W.C. and such a *sitting*-room or *sulking*-room all to yourself. If I were not always looking about for B. I should be a great deal better already for country air. *Miss* finds her provisions increased, & fattens thereon. It is a good thing she can't understand all the flattery bestowed upon her, 'Little Angel'. Love to the good goose, & everybody's love to you both from hence.

Ever thy most loving
Pippin ... Pip—ip

Certainly, these letters succeeded in their immediate purpose. Whatever Byron's own intentions may have been during January 1816 with regard to going abroad or staying with his wife (and Byron during this period changed his mind from hour to hour), even he probably never imagined, while reading these cheery bulletins from an unshakably rational spouse, that he would never again set eyes either upon his wife or his child.

CHAPTER EIGHT

THE SEPARATION

(1816)

'*Where there is blame, it belongs to myself, and if I cannot redeem, I must bear it.*'

BYRON TO THOMAS MOORE, MARCH 1816

Forty-three years later, in 1869, the letters which Annabella Byron wrote to her husband on 15 and 17 January 1816 were published as evidence of her duplicity. How could a woman who was intending either to leave her husband or else presently to put him under private restraint have written to him in such an apparently loving way? What might also have been asked, however, was why Byron himself saw nothing unusual in the playfulness of her tone, perplexed only by her teasing suggestion that he should give up his 'abominable habit of versifying'*? Evidently, although Annabella preserved scant

---

* Teasing, because Annabella was a lifelong admirer of Byron's poetry, large tracts of which she committed to memory. One of her last marital duties had been to copy out *Parisina* and *The Siege of Corinth*, published on 7 February 1816. When a nervous Murray expressed concern about the incest references in *Parisina*, Byron reassured him (this was the day before Annabella's departure in January 1816) that 'my copyist would write out anything I desired in all the ignorance of innocence'. (*BL&J*, 5)

evidence of any such trait in her archives, she was capable of being as light-hearted in her relationship with her husband as she was with her father. (Annabella's letters to Sir Ralph were full of saucy puns and jokes.) Sensing nothing odd about his wife's two letters, and evidently untroubled by her recent departure, Byron did not even feel the need to answer them. It was almost three weeks before he did, and he did so then for a very particular reason.

Annabella was conscious of Dr Le Mann's advice to adopt a reassuring tone, but her letters offer no evidence of hypocrisy. At the time that she despatched them, Lady Byron was confidently anticipating medical confirmation that her husband had become temporarily insane (and thus, crucially, not responsible for his many recent acts of cruelty towards her). If such proved to be the case, she planned to begin by nursing Byron back to health. Such was her strategy.

The Noels were expecting Byron to join them when Annabella left London. On 13 January 1816, two days before her departure, Sir Ralph had innocently asked his daughter when his hopes of 'seeing you all here in a moment' were to be gratified. On the 16th, the day of Annabella's own arrival at Kirkby Mallory, she confirmed to Augusta that the expectation of Byron's imminent arrival remained firmly in place.

By 17 January, Annabella had shared with her parents the news of Byron's volatile state and secured their support for her plan. Lady Noel despatched a friendly assurance to Piccadilly Terrace that her son-in-law would be granted as much rest and privacy as he could wish for at their new home in the Midlands. Annabella followed up with a letter to Captain Byron, urging him to press her husband (referred to as 'the Patient') to join her at her parents' house. 'I deem the change of scene of greatest consequence – and this place particularly eligible,' Annabella wrote on 18 January. Mention had previously been made that the Noels' family house contained a magnificent library. Probably, Lady Byron remembered how much her husband had been delighted by the library at Halnaby.

But Byron remained oddly silent. On 16 January, Augusta had

reported that she saw good signs of 'ye possibility of his following you'. Next day, John Hobhouse (regarded as a thoroughly bad influence on his friend by everybody but Byron himself) appeared at Piccadilly Terrace. The effect of Hobhouse's visit was disastrous. Writing the occasion up in his diary, Hobhouse cheerfully recorded that Byron and he had stayed up drinking brandy on 17 January till two in the morning and that his friend had grown decisive: 'Lady Byron into the country – Byron won't go!'

The following day, while Captain Byron crossed London to propose marriage to the soberly pretty Elizabeth Chandos-Pole (she accepted), Augusta tried to persuade Annabella that Byron's new decision was in fact an act of prudence. He looked ill and swollen-faced after his drinking exploits; Hanson, Mrs Clermont and Le Mann all agreed that it would be dangerous at the moment to put pressure on him to leave.*

It's unlikely that Augusta was being devious. Life in Piccadilly Terrace during this period was exceptionally difficult. Every day, and sometimes every hour, Byron changed his mind. At one moment, he was calling for Le Mann and calomel pills for his liver; at the next, he demanded brandy, the theatre and diversion. (Miss Boyce had been traded in for one of her colleagues, a Miss Cooke.) On the night of 17 January, Hobhouse helped convince Byron not to go to Kirkby. Two days later, Byron decided (but without communicating the change of heart to his wife) that country air was just what his constitution required.

On 19 January, seemingly unaware of how serious the situation had become, Augusta despatched two letters to Kirkby. Writing to Lady Noel, she supported Dr Le Mann's proposal to keep her brother under close medical supervision in London. Writing less formally to Annabella, Augusta passed along a bizarre piece of information. Byron had arranged for a fashionable artist, John Holmes, to paint

---

* Hobhouse ascribed the peculiarity of Byron's appearance at this time to liver trouble; he remarked that one eye had shrunk up, giving his poor friend a squint (Hobhouse's *Diary*, 12 February 1816).

a miniature of his sister. Augusta's likeness was to be twinned with a portrait of himself, and the pair of paintings sent ahead to Kirkby. Only think what wicked tales would be told about such a shocking coupling by Caroline Lamb, tittered Augusta, not to mention all the gossips at Melbourne House, 'a fine affair in their imagination your absence – & my story!'

Granted, Augusta was not an especially intelligent or intuitive woman. Nevertheless, this was a strange way to write to a wife who was supposedly oblivious to the rumours of incest. While Augusta's letter shows that Annabella was already acquainted with the gossip, it also explains why Mrs Leigh was simultaneously begging her husband to join her in London, thereby adding a tenuous veneer of respectability to Lord Byron's depleted household. (Cousin George had now left, and Byron was living there alone with Augusta and a handful of servants.)

Augusta plainly believed that Annabella would dismiss this new cause for gossip as just that: fodder for the spiteful anecdotes that seemed to be forever swirling around the doors of Melbourne House. Augusta was right. Annabella had already considered what she would later describe as 'intimations' of an unnatural relationship between Byron and Augusta. Lacking any tangible proof, she had firmly dismissed the rumours from her mind. Augusta could gossip and giggle. Annabella herself intended to protect a goose-like but beloved sister by keeping quiet. She was, as her younger friend the actress Fanny Kemble would later remark, always good at holding her tongue.

Public silence, however, went hand in hand with a less heroic trait in Annabella's character, one for which Sir Francis Doyle would scold her in a year when she found herself constantly torn between the need both for public discretion and for private declarations. Lady Byron, as Frank Doyle memorably observed, had a 'too confiding disposition'. It was this impulse that had led Annabella, throughout the last and most agonising months of her marriage, to share all her most secret fears and apprehensions with Doyle's sister, Selina. Writing to Annabella on 18 January 1816, Selina stated that 'I have gone over the same ground so often with you that you will be able to fill up the chasms.'*

Selina, who herself would never marry, had been profoundly shocked by Annabella's tales of Byron's cruelty. Personally, she favoured the pursuit of a permanent separation. Sir Frank shared that opinion. Shortly before Annabella left Piccadilly Terrace, the Doyles had urged their friend to abandon her romantic dream of restoring a possibly mad husband to his senses, and to leave him forever.

Writing to Selina from Woburn, twelve hours or so after quitting Piccadilly Terrace, Annabella reviewed the possible consequences of taking what the Doyle siblings darkly referred to as 'the final step'. She did not wholly oppose their counsel, she told Selina. What she requested now was a reasoned letter that stated precisely why Frank believed that she should undertake 'that Measure, which Duty, not Timidity, now determines me to postpone for a short time'.

Annabella must have known what she was doing when she solicited that written response and asked for it to be sent to Kirkby Mallory. Her parents knew the Doyles well. Selina's neat hand would be instantly familiar to them; letters, back in 1816, were commonly regarded as shared property within a family group. (Caroline Lamb had felt no compunction about reading and copying juicy extracts from the letters about the birth of Elizabeth Medora Leigh that passed between Byron and Lady Melbourne in 1814.) The Noels would be eager to know what dear Selina had to say – and Annabella knew that fact just as well as she knew in advance what Selina's letter would disclose.

Selina's prompt response reached Kirkby Mallory – a compactly handsome greystone house that commanded broad views across a Leicestershire landscape of sloping fields and scattered hamlets – on 19 January 1816. The letter was not circumspect. Reading of 'the

---

* On 6 April 1816, Byron sent on to Selina Doyle a packet of letters that Annabella had copied after writing to her friend. Annabella had – deliberately? – left this clear proof of her unhappiness at Piccadilly Terrace lying in an unlocked drawer. The letters have not survived.

outrages committed one after another' and of 'ill treatment & every thing calculated to inspire hatred', Lady Noel saw confirmation of all her darkest fears about her beloved daughter's marriage. ('I had many suspicions but ... dreaded agitating Lady B by questions,' she explained later that same week to a lawyer.) Sir Ralph was equally dismayed. Selina wrote that her brother believed the time had come for action. For the shocked Noels, Frank Doyle's view was decisive.

No clear account survives of what happened during the rest of that traumatic day of revelations. Annabella wrote to Mrs Clermont in London that she had suffered 'one wild fit' which rendered her 'frantic'; apparently, her mother 'had agonised me about the child'. Ann Rood Fletcher later recalled that her mistress had been continuously low and depressed since her departure from London, and that she broke down, on certain occasions, in hysterical fits of sobbing.

Annabella was evidently conflicted. (She begged Lady Noel not to record anything she might rashly disclose in conversation.) Nevertheless, the written statement of her trials that she submitted to her mother on the evening of 19 January (she misdated it as the 18th and continued to misdate her letters throughout a long and anxious week) was both articulate and detailed. This testimony was, so Annabella informed Mrs Clermont that evening, 'the strongest statement that I can swear to'. What she meant – although she did not say so in her letter to Mrs Clermont – was that she had made no allusion to the pernicious gossip about Augusta.

The omission was prudent. Armed with her daughter's statement, a furious, red-faced and wigless Lady Noel (Judith was still suffering from erysipelas, the vicious skin ailment that had plagued her throughout the previous autumn) hurried off for a week of fierce activity in London. Lawyers were visited, while Mrs Clermont was briefed to act as a recording scribe. Both Augusta and George Byron proved willing to declare that Annabella's life would be in danger if she returned to Piccadilly Terrace. Byron, still (astonishingly) oblivious to what was going on, assumed – or so Augusta reported to Annabella – that Lady Noel was enraged because her son-in-law had not yet gone to Kirkby.

Augusta wrote this on 23 January. It was on the same day that Lady Noel reported to Sir Ralph and Annabella that both Sir Samuel Romilly and their legal friend Sergeant Heywood agreed with Frank Doyle: Byron must from now on be kept away from his wife. Dr Le Mann, Judith added almost as an afterthought, had been unable to find any conclusive proof of insanity. Lord Byron was judged to be – and, more significantly, to have been throughout his abusive marriage – in full possession of the rational forces of his mind. He knew what he was doing.

Lady Noel was clearly relishing her moment of power. Annabella, always afraid of her mother's terrible loquacity, entreated her to be discreet. 'I hope you will keep my Mother sober,' she wrote to Mrs Clermont, one of the few people capable of subduing Lady Noel's temper. 'She will break my heart if she takes up the thing in bitterness against him. The more I think of the whole conduct on his part, the more unaccountable it all is. I cannot believe him *all bad*.'

Judith Noel, amidst her bustling and rushing and rage, had been compelled to confront a disquieting possibility. Sir Samuel Romilly, one of England's most eminent legal figures (and a personal friend of the Noels), did not think Lord Byron would wish to end the marriage voluntarily. To leave his wife – as Byron had upon occasion told both Hobhouse and Cousin George that he intended to do – was one thing. For Byron himself to be left by his young spouse – with all the humiliation that such an act implied – was quite another. A nuanced approach was required. Romilly knew just the man to undertake it.

In 1816, Stephen Lushington, the first man later to be offered (and twice to refuse) a life peerage for his services to the law, was thirty-four years old. Handsome, reserved and coolly intelligent, Lushington was a Fellow of All Souls, a passionate opponent to the Slave Trade and a rising star in the world of civil law. On 23 January 1816, Lady Noel showed Lushington her daughter's statement about the marriage (and doubtless added a great many comments of her own). 'I would not but have seen Lushington for the World,' Judith wrote to Annabella with unguarded satisfaction: 'he seems the most gentlemanlike, clear headed and clever Man I ever met with – and agrees with all others that a proposal should be sent by Your Father for a *quiet adjustment*.'

Lushington had told Lady Noel only what he sensed that she wished to hear. Writing to Annabella fourteen years later, he confirmed that her mother's voluble account of a husband's threats, his keeping of a mistress and of Byron's cruel aversion to his wife's company rendered separation 'justifiable', but not 'indispensable'. While prepared to supervise and edit the declaration of intent that Sir Ralph (so all the lawyers agreed) must now despatch to Lord Byron, Lushington felt uneasy about the process. Based upon what he had so far heard, the lawyer had privately 'deemed a reconciliation with Lord Byron practicable, and felt most sincerely a wish towards effecting it'.

Annabella herself, when not seeking release from unhappiness in reckless rides across the frost-bound fields surrounding Kirkby Mallory, remained divided. She feared the scandalmongers would blame poor Augusta for her own departure ('a cruel injustice', so Lady Byron told her mother on 26 January). She wept at the thought of all the love she had expended upon her husband, seemingly to no avail. 'It is worth the sadness if it brings anything good to him,' Annabella wrote in an earnest little memorandum which set out her determination to maintain loyalty and goodwill. For the present, she struggled to remain calm. The visible and daily failure of that daily attempt was daily witnessed by Mrs Fletcher, her observant maid.

On 28 January, following the arrival at Kirkby of Lady Noel, Mrs Clermont and Selina Doyle, Sir Ralph drew up and took to town for Dr Lushington's approval a letter in which he told Byron the reasons for his daughter's decision to leave. Augusta, recognising the untidy handwriting and guessing what Sir Ralph would have to say, sent his letter back unopened. On 30 January, the newly married Captain Byron, who was househunting in Leicestershire for a future marital home, visited Kirkby Mallory to comfort Annabella. He sent a report to London. Judith, writing to her husband at Mivart's Hotel in London, passed along to him George's belief that their daughter's actions had merely pre-empted Byron's own. Had Annabella not left him, George Byron declared, her husband would certainly have left her. In fact, he could now disclose that Byron had talked about going abroad alone ever since the birth of the couple's daughter.

It cannot have been a coincidence that Byron chose Friday, 2 February – the very day that he received Sir Ralph's re-sent letter – to make hasty preparations for a visit to Leicestershire. Annabella had heard nothing from him since she left. On 3 and again on 5 February, her husband belatedly attempted to fill up the gap. Striving for non-chalance, Byron sounded apprehensive. At first, he suggested that Sir Ralph must have written without Bell's approval. Two days later, he announced that his wife had only to speak the word and – it was a bad moment to cast Annabella as Shakespeare's stroppy Shrew to his own fancy-free Petruchio – 'Kate! I will buckler thee against a million!'

Annabella understood her husband better than he did her. On 7 February, she coolly reminded Byron of 'the misery that I have experienced almost without an interval from the day of marriage'. So now he missed her? How predictable! 'It is unhappily your disposi-tion to consider what you have as worthless – what you have lost as invaluable. But remember that you believed yourself most miserable when I was yours.'

These were brave words and ones which commanded Byron's grudging respect. A third and far more passionate epistle from her husband ('did I deem *you* so – did I ever so express to you – or of you – to others?') almost undid her: almost, but not quite. Collecting her thoughts for the benefit of Dr Lushington, Annabella acknow-ledged that her own 'softness' was making resistance difficult: 'one tender remembrance sweeps away accumulated injuries. I have a good Memory – but it is sad to employ it in recollecting wrongs'. In an afterthought addressed to Mrs Clermont, the carrier of her letter to Lushington's home in Great George Street, Lady Byron added that the baby girl had now been 'necessarily' weaned. The necessity was due to the fact that Annabella, usually blessed with a fine appetite, had nearly ceased to eat.

In London, news of the separation was beginning to spread. On 12 February, Lady Melbourne asked her brother Ralph why he had instructed friends 'to give the event every possible publicity'. Had he not considered the consequences for his daughter, who had now become 'the subject of conversation for every gossiping Man & Woman in town without knowing what to contradict or assert'?

Visiting Kirkby in February, the ageing Sarah Siddons grieved over Annabella's sufferings, while marvelling at 'the unexampled gentleness, goodness, and wise forbearances of the perfectest of human beings imaginable.' Mrs Siddons had caught the mood of the times. It was Byron, not his wife, of whom nothing quite bad enough could now be proclaimed. As young Thomas Macaulay would remark in 1831, when reviewing Moore's *Life and Letters of Lord Byron*, the handsome poet who had been society's darling had grown ripe for his comeuppance: 'he had been guilty of the offence which, of all offences, is punished most severely; he had been over-praised'.

The source of some of the most vicious anti-Byron gossip was Lady Caroline Lamb. Annabella's marriage had compelled an unforgiving Caroline to hold her tongue about the lover who had once rejected her so publicly. Now, having ransacked Lady Melbourne's papers and revisited her own copious records of a tumultuous affair, Caroline was ready to let rip. Hobhouse, on 9 February 1816, noted that Lady Caroline had accused Byron of '[-----]', by which he almost certainly meant sodomy. On 13 February, Mrs Clermont informed Annabella that 'very scandalous tales' had reached Dr Lushington from Brocket, the Lamb family's Hertfordshire home. On 17 February, an agonised Augusta (she was now doing everything in her power to persuade Lady Byron to return to her husband and forgive him) told Annabella that the latest stories were 'of a nature too horrible to repeat . . . Every other sinks into nothing before this most horrid one.' Byron himself had apparently declared that for a man to have such a thing said of him 'is utter destruction & ruin to a man from which he can never recover'. When Annabella coolly answered (19 February) that she would certainly speak out against anything she personally knew to be untrue, Augusta panicked. How much exactly did Annabella know? What might she not dare to declare in public?

On 20 January, Augusta wrote once more to Annabella, this time in a tone that combined shameless cajoling ('I do think in my heart dearest A, that *your return* might be the *saving & reclaiming* of him') with threats ('Most likely you are aware you will have to depose against him *yrself*, & that without witnesses yr depositions will go for nothing').

Augusta's letter was ill-timed. It reached Kirkby Mallory on the day that Annabella, accompanied by her father, returned to London, where they stayed at Mivart's Hotel. On the evening of 22 January, Annabella paid her first visit to Dr Lushington's home in Great George Street.

Slight, pale, calm and exceptionally articulate, Annabella created a very different impression from that made upon Lushington by the intemperate Judith Noel. It is not certain that Annabella mentioned incest, but it is striking that Lushington instantly requested (Annabella would disobey) a severance of all communication with Augusta. The following day, 23 January, Annabella asked her mother to follow Dr Lushington's wishes by maintaining only a cautiously friendly tone to Mrs Leigh, 'as being essential to my justification, *whatever she may turn out*'. (The emphasis was Annabella's own.) The lawyer's third request was that Lady Byron's maid should immediately be released from duty to rejoin her husband (Byron's valet) in London, even if this event should later lead to an unhelpful deposition – as indeed it did.

Fifty-five years later, Sir John Fox, a Master of Chancery who was friendly with Stephen Lushington, published part of a private letter in which the great lawyer, following Lady Byron's death, had revealed some of the details that had so shocked him back in 1816. Fox himself was too prim to include Lushington's report of Byron's boasts to Annabella 'of his adulteries and indecencies with loose women, toying with more than one at the same time naked'.

Incest; sodomy; unseemly revelations; acts of violence: whatever it was that Annabella revealed on that chilly March evening at Lushington's home, it shook the lawyer to the core. Writing to Lady Byron (she would become his family's lifelong friend) in

1830, Lushington confirmed that 'when I was informed by you of facts utterly unknown, as I have no doubt, to Sir Ralph and Lady Noel ... my opinion was entirely changed: I considered a reconciliation impossible'. Lushington went further than that. From then on, he refused to assist in the pursuit of any course but separation.

'I am in boundless respect of her,' Lushington would write years later of his favourite client: '... of her heart, intellect and governed mind.' Back in 1816, however, Lushington chafed against the way in which, while determined to achieve a dignified separation from her husband while retaining custody of her daughter, Annabella continued to defend her adversaries. She had no wish to slander Byron. She actively sought to protect Augusta Leigh from being engulfed by a scandal that was reaching uncontainable proportions.

Shortly after visiting Lushington, Annabella sent a confidential letter to Mrs Leigh's aunt, Sophia Byron. On 29 February, that spirited sexagenarian confirmed that she herself had attempted to persuade Augusta to leave Byron's house: '*Le Sposo* [Colonel Leigh] and her friends have been equally anxious for it,' Sophia wrote. There was no need to spell out the reason why. On 26 February, Annabella reassured Augusta's friend, Mrs Villiers, that she had never personally sanctioned the ugly tales that were beginning to taint the name of Mrs Leigh. On 5 March, Annabella held a private interview with Augusta. It was the first time the two women had met since Lady Byron's departure on 15 January from Piccadilly Terrace.

The meeting had been requested by Lord Byron and it is unclear what Annabella expected to achieve by it. Possibly, she hoped to plead against Byron's reported plan to abduct her baby daughter and place the little girl under Aunt Augusta's guardianship. (Frank Doyle warned Lady Noel on 4 March to defend the child 'with every possible vigilance' against 'a *coup de main*'.) Possibly, Annabella hoped Augusta might persuade Byron to sign the preliminary deed of separation which had been delivered to Piccadilly Terrace on 2 March. But Augusta, while horrified by Annabella's gaunt appearance ('positively reduced to a skeleton – pale as *ashes*', she lamented to Francis Hodgson on the day of the meeting), was pursuing her own agenda. Once more, while delivering a letter in which her brother begged Annabella to accept his regret for 'unknown faults' and to respect her high position as his wife ('Oh – Bell – to see you thus stifling and destroying all feeling, all affections – all duties'), Augusta entreated Annabella to come back. Byron, she averred, remained bewildered by his wife's protracted absence. What unforgivable injuries had he committed? What were these awful charges that Bell refused to name? Why would she not return home and grant her remorseful husband a second chance?

A return was not on the cards. Following the meeting with Augusta, Annabella instantly wrote to tell Byron that she had no intention of rejoining him. Contrary to his fixed belief that her parents, abetted by Mrs Clermont, were controlling her actions, the decision to leave him was hers and hers alone: 'for the consequences I alone am responsible'. Byron was unconvinced. 'Her nearest relatives are a ***** [*sic*],' he angrily informed an inquisitive Thomas Moore on 8 March. Nevertheless, while eager to remove his child 'from the contagion of its grandmother's society', Byron had nothing but good to say to Moore about his wife. None could be more agreeable. Never once in their time together had Annabella given him the least cause for reproach.

It is possible that Byron's affectionate words were fuelled by a sincere relief. On the evening of 9 March, a rejoicing Augusta told Francis Hodgson that 'L[ad]y Byron has given a *written contradiction* of the 2 principal and most horrible reports into Mr Wilmot's hands.' Robert Wilmot – a country cousin of Byron's who sympathised with Annabella's decision to leave him – had delivered this document to her husband. Byron promptly agreed to the separation.

Drawn up by Lushington and revised by Annabella, the document of retraction had not said quite what Augusta supposed. The 'horrible reports' (incest and sodomy) had neither been contradicted nor denied. A promise had, however, been made that these particular accusations would not be included in Lady Byron's formal charges if matters should ever come to court.*

On 11 March, primed by John Hanson with warnings about the need to protect his claim upon Annabella's expected fortune, Byron reneged on the deal. Wilmot was so angry that he considered challenging his cousin to a duel. As the alarming possibility of a public court case began to loom, Annabella once again took steps to protect the reputation of Augusta Leigh.

Lushington's respect for Annabella was constantly tested by her loyalty to Augusta, a woman whom the lawyer himself regarded as not only unprincipled but immoral. On 10 March, Annabella suggested that a personal commitment from Augusta to stay away from the baby girl would prevent 'the cruel necessity of stigmatising [her] either directly or indirectly'. When Lushington disagreed, Annabella composed a statement by which she intended to protect from further harm Augusta's already damaged reputation.

Annabella's handwritten defence of her sister-in-law was both warm and generous. Reshaped by the super-cautious Stephen Lushington, it became a nebulous web of conditionals and hypotheses. Tribute was still paid to Mrs Leigh's attempts to protect Lady Byron from her husband's 'violence & cruelty'. (These claims of abuse were crucial to Lushington's case.) Regarding the 'suspicion' of incest, Annabella was allowed only to say, amidst a web of 'mays' and 'mights', that the offence might – just possibly – not have taken place during her own marriage to Lord Byron.

Annabella's fears for Augusta were heightened by the growing likelihood of a public trial. On 14 March, she told her mother that Byron's sudden backtracking upon their agreement had been 'a dirty job', and one for which she blamed his advisors (meaning Hanson and Hobhouse).

---

* Lushington wanted to avoid any hint that his client had condoned either incest or sodomy by remaining in the marriage. Adultery, menaces and insulting behaviour offered more substantial cause for a legal separation.

It was at this point that a new and yet more explosive report was first mentioned.

The precise nature of this mysterious accusation has never been established, but the charge seems to have frightened Byron almost out of his wits. The most likely possibility is that Annabella had passed on to Lushington her earnest conviction that Byron, during a past paroxysm of madness, had committed murder. Mention was made of this belief during one of Lady Byron's many statements about their marriage. Certainly, Byron had alluded to some unnameable crime in his past. He had also intimidated Annabella by reminding her of *Caleb Williams*, William Godwin's gothic tale – much admired by both the Byrons – of a man who will stop at nothing to conceal the murders he has committed. Shocking a woman as innocent as Annabella amused Byron a great deal. It never occurred to him that his colourful romancing might one day be recalled as gospel truth.

Was there any truth in the suspicion? It is striking that Augusta instantly guessed the content of this new rumour. Reporting on it to Hodgson on 14 March, Mrs Leigh referred to a notorious case in which Lord Ferrers had been hanged for murdering a servant. Was it possible, she wondered, that her brother, while deranged, could once have committed 'some act which he would not avow even to his dearest friend – scarcely to his own soul'? Byron's present state of terror certainly pointed to some such horror. Ironically – remembering Annabella's theory of her husband's insanity – Byron himself now told Augusta that (if accused) he would plead madness as his defence.

This frightening moment was the one at which Byron reconciled himself to legal surrender and exile. On Sunday 17 March, a relieved Annabella told her mother that her husband had finally signed his name to the beginning of procedures. It was time for Judith to relax – 'for I really think it all finished in the best possible manner'.

∞

As often before, Lady Byron's faith in the word of her unpredictable husband proved premature. On 20 March 1816, a poem arrived in

Annabella's post. It carried the harrowing title: 'Fare Thee Well.' Filled with wrenching images (the broken-hearted husband – the remorseless wife – the fatherless child), the poem was swiftly published in a limited edition of fifty copies. Reading of the poet's blighted future, Byron's royal admirer, young Princess Charlotte, declared that she had wept 'like a fool'. Annabella herself was sufficiently affected to share her softened feelings with her mother.

From saccharine sentiment, Byron swung back to savage fury.

Mrs Fletcher's March deposition to John Hanson had convinced Byron that the true enemy of his marriage – worse even than the Noels – was Mrs Clermont. On 25 March, while accusing Annabella of helping to blacken his name ('as if it were branded on my forehead'), he circulated fifty copies of 'A Sketch from Private Life', a vicious skit which spared nothing but her name to the woman he called 'this hag of hatred'. Passing along Mrs Clermont's indignant request to her accuser for any proofs of his slanderous allegations, Annabella received in response a rant even more violent than the poem.

> The curse of my Soul light upon her & hers forever! – may my
> Spirit be deep upon her in her life – & in her death – may her
> thirst be unquenchable – & her wretchedness irrevocable – may
> she see *herself* only & eternally – may she dwell in the darkness
> of her own heart & shudder – now & for existence. Her last
> food will be the bread of her enemies – I have said it. –To you
> dearest Bell – I am as ever, very truly *BYRON*

Annabella declined to comment upon this remarkable document. She returned it to her husband only after having copied it in her own clear hand.

လ၅၅

Annabella's feelings towards both her husband and his sister had begun to harden. On 25 March, Mrs Leigh offended Lady Byron by publicly refusing, at a supper given by the Wilmots, to shake Selina Doyle by the hand. Two days later, meeting Caroline Lamb by arrangement at the house of Caroline's sister-in-law and namesake, Annabella's suspicions of Byron's incest were finally converted – as she wrote to Lushington that night – into *'absolute certainty'*. Lady Caroline had arrived armed to the teeth with proofs. Among her bulky sheaf of documents were extracts from Lady Melbourne's exchanges with Byron about the birth of Augusta's fourth child, Elizabeth Medora Leigh.

Medora's paternity was never mentioned by Lady Byron to Dr Lushington, but the little girl was pointedly singled out in a later journal entry of Annabella's in which, having just seen the Leigh children, she described her own 'most tender affection for — . What is the reason?' That coy query, together with the omitted name, leaves scant room to doubt that Annabella, by 1820, believed little Miss Leigh, then aged six, to be her husband's child.

∞

Heaping his fury upon the hapless head of Mrs Clermont offered little solace to Byron for the experience of becoming a social outcast. On 8 April 1816 (following the distressing and long-deferred sale by legal order of personal chattels that included his beloved books), the poet attended an evening hosted by Lady Jersey, one of London's most respected hostesses. His companion was the heavily pregnant Augusta Leigh. Byron expected to be cold-shouldered. What hurt him more was to see Augusta being ignored and snubbed by everybody other than their hostess and Miss Mercer Elphinstone, a sweet-natured heiress to whom Byron had once considered proposing. 'Stanzas to Augusta', written the following day, was Byron's tender tribute to his sister's unfaltering devotion.

The three-month separation battle had reached its end. On 14 April, Henry Brougham, an ardent supporter of Annabella, mischievously arranged for Byron's sentimental 'Farewell' to be published alongside his excoriation of Mrs Clermont in *The Champion* newspaper. (Annabella sent the 'Farewell' to her mother the following day, together with a gratefully punning tribute to Brougham as 'my warmest champion throughout'.)

On the day that *The Champion* poems appeared, Byron addressed his wife once more. From Augusta – with whom he had just parted for the last time – he had asked only that she should keep him informed about herself, her dog, his god-daughter Georgiana, and Medora (or little 'D'), the dark-haired child whose pet name was so like the one he had bestowed upon wee Augusta Ada ('little Da'). Writing to Annabella, Byron reminded her that he had already changed his will in order to leave all that he owned to his sister and her children (their own daughter being well provided for 'by other & better means'). All he asked now was that his wife should recall Mrs Leigh's kindness to herself and repay it. Implicit in that request was the hope that Annabella would help to combat the continuing rumours of incestuous behaviour on Augusta's part.

Byron enclosed with his letter a gift for his daughter: a ring beneath the sealed lid of which, so Byron believed, a strand of Charles I's hair lay coiled. On Annabella herself, he bestowed only his old coach, the one that had carried her to Kirkby.

On 23 April, Byron left Piccadilly Terrace for the last time. A thoughtfully alerted crowd had gathered to observe his departure for Dover and to admire the poet's flamboyant new carriage. (Unpaid for, it was modelled on the one used by another fallen hero, Napoleon Bonaparte, when travelling across Europe.) Minutes later, the bailiffs swooped on Piccadilly Terrace to reclaim the unpaid half-year's rent in chattels. Among the household goods that they confiscated from the abandoned house were Byron's pet squirrel and caged parrot.

CHAPTER NINE

IN THE PUBLIC EYE

(1816–24)

Viewed as part of the public relations exercise by a departing husband portraying himself as a martyred hero, Byron's 'Fare Thee Well' was not a complete success. In America (if Harriet Beecher Stowe's memory of her impressions as a 5-year-old were to be trusted), the poem was set to music and sung, with appropriate sobs, by heartbroken schoolgirls. In England, it invited public mockery. Isaac Cruickshank's *The Separation, or A Sketch from the private Life of Lord Iron*, pictured a balding Byron setting off for Europe with his arm wrapped around a buxom actress. George Cruickshank (Isaac's more famous son) depicted the poet waving a gallant handkerchief to a shorebound mother and child, while reciting 'Fare Thee Well' to a boatload of adoring strumpets.

Up in Scotland, a month after Byron's departure, one of his warmest admirers poked gentle fun at the poet's double standards. 'In the meanwhile,' Walter Scott wrote to his friend J. B. S. Morritt on 16 May 1816:

> I think my noble friend is something like my old peacock
> who chooses to bivouac apart from his lady, and sit below
> my bedroom window to keep me awake with his screeching
> lamentations. Only I own he is not equal in melody to Lord
> Byron, for *Fare-thee-Well* ... is a very sweet dirge indeed.

Looking back in the summer of 1831 at the 15-year-old scandal of Lord Byron's separation, Thomas Macaulay employed his review of Moore's recent two-volume *Life and Letters of Lord Byron* to point up the dangers that had arisen from confusing the poet with his heroic persona. How was it possible, Macaulay asked, to equate the lone and brooding Childe, celebrated for the scorn with which he abjured public sympathy, with a man who wanted the entire world to weep over the supposedly private farewell that he had flamboyantly offered to his wife and daughter?

Macaulay cast no aspersions upon Lady Byron for leaving a husband whom he designated a spoiled child ('not merely the spoiled child of his parents, but the spoiled child of nature, the spoiled child of fortune, the spoiled child of fame, the spoiled child of society').* The target of his witty but fair-minded essay in the *Edinburgh Review* was the great British public which, having begun by idolising a libertine genius, had gleefully sacrificed their hero in one of its 'periodical fits of morality'. Byron, so Macaulay argued, had probably done nothing more dreadful than a great many other English husbands. His misfortune had been the celebrity which allowed him to be transformed overnight from an unsatisfactory spouse into a universal scapegoat.

> True Jedwood justice was dealt out to him. First came the execution, then the investigation, and last of all, or rather not at all, the accusation. The public, without knowing anything whatever about the transactions in his family, flew into a violent passion with him, and proceeded to invent stories which might justify its anger. Ten or twenty different accounts of the separation, inconsistent with each other, with themselves, and with common sense, circulated at the same time. What evidence there might be for any one of these, the virtuous people who repeated them neither knew nor

---

* The phrase 'spoilt child' [*sic*] was frequently applied to Lady Byron, but never to her late husband, during the posthumous attacks upon her reputation that were to be published in 1869–70.

cared. For in fact these stories were not the causes, but the effects of the public indignation.

Focussing on the poet and on the ephemeral nature of mortal fame ('a few more years will destroy whatever remains of that magical potency which once belonged to the name of Byron', Macaulay predicted with unfounded confidence), the young critic found almost nothing to say about Lord Byron's wife. Not a word was spared to consider the impact upon Annabella's life of such an immense and public scandal as the separation from her husband had proved to be. Neither – perhaps Macaulay was among the very few who had failed to read them – did the future historian comment upon the privately printed and widely distributed 'Remarks' of 1830 in which Annabella defended her dead parents from Moore's proposal that they, not she, had led the way in separating an innocent young wife from a troubled but hardly diabolical husband.*

ᘓᘔᘓ

Annabella, in the month when Byron left England, was still living with her parents. She remained extremely apprehensive about her personal reputation. For the present, discretion seemed to be working in her favour. Satirised by the cartoonists, excoriated in the papers, cut in public and denounced from the stage, Lord Byron – as Macaulay would note – had been transformed from the nation's melancholy hero into a monster capable of any heinous act that could conceivably be attributed to his name. That such a change had been achieved without any visible act of vindictiveness on her own part was remarkable.

The public's mood could alter in a flash, and Annabella had lived alongside celebrity long enough to know it, better than Stephen

---

* It is especially strange that they went unmentioned by Macaulay, given that the 'Remarks' were subsequently bound in with Moore's 1831 edition, at Annabella's request.

Lushington, who advised her to stop worrying about her image; better than pugnacious Lady Noel, who was still itching for a court case and the satisfaction of yet further public revenge. 'How can you be so inconsiderate for me as to wish that the Cause had come into court?' Annabella asked her mother on 21 April 1816:

> For I should have died of it certainly – and now every object is attained without an exposure which revenge only could have desired, and which would have reflected some of its disgraceful consequences upon myself?

Preserving herself and her child from calumny now became Annabella's chief objective. It was a goal for which she was prepared to undertake considerable sacrifices. For her estranged husband, lovers would never be in short supply. Shortly before leaving England, he had enjoyed a covert affair with Claire Clairmont, the clever but egregiously pushy step-sister of Mary Shelley. (Mary, Claire and Shelley would soon join Byron beside Lake Geneva for that now legendary summer of 1816 during which *Frankenstein* would be conceived.) For Annabella, a 24-year-old mother and wife – the Byrons were never to divorce – there could be no such recklessness, no romance, no unconsidered steps. Her only chance of escaping scandal was to behave impeccably, and to choose her friends with scrupulous care. Among the first was Anna Jones, step-daughter of the vicar who altruistically took services at Kirkby Mallory. (The living and its proceeds still belonged to Annabella's absentee cousin, Thomas Noel.) Anna Jones, safely remote from London society, received many of Annabella's confidences about her marriage – and seemingly kept them to herself.

The first threat to Lady Byron's privacy came with the publication on 9 May 1816 of Caroline Lamb's sensationally revealing novel, *Glenarvon*. Byron was thinly disguised as the licentious and glamorously heartless Lord Ruthven. Annabella's fate was merely to seem insipid. Robert Wilmot, writing on 17 May, told her that she appeared in the book as Miss Monmouth, 'a most delightful person';

Lady Caroline's sister-in-law, Mrs George Lamb, opined that the portrait was 'very indulgent'. Miss Monmouth, as Annabella herself eventually discovered, was in fact dull as a dry ditch.

Byron had only been out of the country for a fortnight when *Glenarvon* returned him to centre stage. In London, so Mrs Lamb said, the book was the talk of the town. Retreating from gossipy Leicestershire to Lowestoft, a quiet seaside town on the remote coast of East Anglia, Annabella stopped to rest along the way at Ely and Peterborough. Writing the first of many imaginary baby letters to 'Dear GrandMama' at Kirkby, Annabella recorded in little Ada's fictive voice that the 'people at Ely and Peterborough Stared at us very much, and Mama said we were Lionesses – pray what does that mean?' Lady Byron's adopted tone was jaunty; the humiliation of being pointed out and stared at by groups of strangers was one that Annabella in her old age could still recall with pain. A private tour of Ely's majestic cathedral as guest of the dean's wife offered scant consolation.

Safely arrived at Lowestoft, Annabella took a seafront house next to her old (and herself also now separated) friend, Lady Gosford, returning to her Suffolk roots as little Mary Sparrow, the heiress to Worlingham Hall. Annabella was welcomed as an intermediary and peacemaker, the go-between for Mary and a widowed Irish aunt, Lady Olivia Sparrow, who presided nearby over a sternly evangelical household.

The irony of her new situation was not lost upon Annabella. Invited by Lady Olivia to meet her close friends, the Vicar of Lowestoft and his wife, she found herself being patronised by the very people she had once mocked – and still did within the safety of letters to her parents – as 'pye-house' bores. Lady Olivia was condescendingly kind. The Reverend Francis Cunningham, however, proved unexpectedly agreeable. Following a happy September return to George Eden's family home in Kent, Annabella agreed to visit Mr Cunningham's brother, William, the Vicar of Harrow. Byron had gone to school at Harrow. Annabella, who would also pay a secret visit to Newstead Abbey in 1818, could not resist the chance to see a place so intimately connected with her husband's past. Once there, laying aside her Unitarian principles, she even attended the services over which Mr Cunningham (Trollope's model for the unctuous Obadiah Slope) mellifluously presided.

Times were rapidly changing in England. Six years later, when seeking to erect a burial plaque at Harrow's church for 'Little Illegitimate', his tragically short-lived daughter by Claire Clairmont, Lord Byron was informed that Dr Cunningham objected because Allegra's plaque would be within sight from the hallowed pew of his own valued friend, Lady Byron.* The notion that his wife would ever occupy a pew at Harrow's church – let alone keep company with Dr Cunningham, at whom he could clearly recall her having poked fun – struck her husband as hilarious. Initially, Byron refused to believe it.

The report was true and her behaviour was part of a conscious choice. Annabella Byron and her little daughter each now carried around her neck the millstone of a name that instantly connected them to a man who had become as notorious for his lifestyle as for the ferociously witty poetry in which, with increasing contempt for the cant of a newly prudish England, he exposed his country's hypocrisy. If Lady Byron wished to keep her name free from the scandal in which her husband appeared to revel, her only option was to undertake good works, live in quiet places and keep company solely with reformers who at their best were thoughtful, intelligent and kind, while others proved to be sanctimonious bores of the Obadian variety. It was circumstance, allied to a passionate desire to be of service to society, that led Annabella into her long, productive career as an enlightened educational reformer, a passionate opponent to slavery and earnest advocate of a kinder penal system. Her achievements would eventually earn her an honoured place on the Reformers' Memorial at Kensal Green. Sadly, she did not live to know it.

---

* Byron's former master at Harrow, Dr Drury, arranged for Allegra's burial close to the church door. A plaque was finally erected in 1980.

Concern for her own reputation caused Annabella to reassess some of her closest friendships. When Mary Montgomery returned to England in 1818, Annabella felt nervous. Miss Montgomery had lived in Venice. She had been on visiting terms with Byron at a time when the scandalous poet boasted of having at least two mistresses on the go, both equipped with husbands. An old and deep friendship was renewed and lovingly maintained, but only after Selina Doyle had been delegated to evaluate the moral status of a dangerously well-travelled lady.

Mrs Clermont was less gently dealt with. Although often at loggerheads with each other, Lady Noel and her daughter both agreed that Clermont's role in the separation, followed by the glare of public interest that Byron's satire had attracted, made any continued intimacy impossible. Revisiting Seaham at a time when the house was being rented by her old friends the Bakers of Elemore Hall, Annabella received a request from Mrs Clermont, who was by then living nearby, to pay a visit. The risk of gossip just when Annabella was arranging to set up a new school for Seaham was too great. She turned the appeal down.

Ill health would plague Annabella for the rest of her life. Sending a report to John Hobhouse (evidently at Byron's request) soon after seeing her niece in October 1816, Lady Melbourne remarked that Lady Byron's face was 'sad and strained'. Her nerves were plainly 'shatter'd', Annabella's aunt continued, adding that 'although she might have conducted herself better, yet she is much to be pitied as her sufferings must be great'. (The letter, evidently designed to be seen by Byron, ascribed much of the blame for those sufferings upon the young woman's interfering parents.) Percy Shelley, meanwhile, brought news to Lake Geneva that Lord Byron's estranged wife had undergone a miraculous recovery. Douglas Kinnaird had pronounced her to be 'in perfect health'. What was more, Kinnaird knew for a certainty 'that she was living with your sister'. And thus,

Shelley happily told Byron, an end could be put to all that nasty gossip about incest: 'the only important calumny that ever was advanced against you'.

Kinnaird's own gossip contained a kernel of truth. In the spring of 1816, Mrs Leigh had briefly experienced the pain of becoming a social outcast. When Annabella invited a resumption of friendship, following Byron's departure, Augusta accepted with alacrity. The two women met frequently and exchanged many affectionate letters during the late summer of 1816. They would remain – so long as a subdued Augusta addressed Lady Byron as her 'guardian angel' and obeyed her commands – upon careful but cordial terms for a further fourteen years.

Financially, socially and morally, Annabella held almost every card in the altered relationship with her once-beloved sister-in-law. To retain any contact with Byron, however, she remained unwillingly dependent upon Augusta's aid. Annabella, plainly, could not continue to write to her husband herself, nor seek to receive letters from him. The agreement initiated by her, and reluctantly accepted by Mrs Leigh, was that Augusta would – without ever allowing her brother to know it – share all of their own private correspondence with Byron's wife.

The most intriguing feature about this remarkable arrangement was the readiness with which Augusta complied. Perhaps, she embraced the sense of power that it placed in her hands. Lady Byron could force her to grovel. She could – and did – withdraw all access to little Ada. (Lady Noel replaced Augusta in the promised role of godmother at a private autumn christening to which neither Colonel Leigh nor his wife were invited.) But Augusta could still inflict pain. She could read Byron's letters and transmit as many of them (or as few) as she chose. She could relish the hurt that Annabella must surely have felt to see how lovingly her husband wrote to his half-sister and how savagely he wrote about his wife.

The cruellest of Byron's letters were withheld by Augusta until 1834, by which time the relationship between the two women was beyond repair. Enough had already been shown to inflict a pain that Annabella struggled hard to conceal.

Had Augusta swiftly revealed the letter-passing arrangement to her self-exiled brother? That possibility would help to explain the consistent malice with which Byron wrote to Augusta about his wife. On 9 September 1816, he compared Annabella to an elephant who had clumsily trodden on his heart, before going on to announce that a charmingly determined young lady (Claire Clairmont) 'had scrambled eight hundred miles to unphilosophise me'. Forwarding the letter to her 'Guardian Angel', Augusta twisted her own knife in the wound by confessing that she, not Byron, had been the chief mover in their incestuous affair: 'in fact I am the one *much* the more to blame ... *quite* inexcusable'. In a letter to Augusta (likewise in a poem to John Murray which Byron's publisher declined to print), Lady Byron was described as a 'moral Clytemnestra',* one who had been 'formed for my destruction' (28 October). On 11 November 1816, Annabella was damned as a heartless torturer and on 18 December as a 'virtuous monster', one whose memory her husband intended to eradicate. On 17 May 1819 (Annabella's birthday, as Byron assuredly knew), the poet described his wife to Augusta as 'that infamous fiend who drove me from my Country & conspired against my life'.

And yet, writing directly to Annabella, as he had promised not to do, Byron was all tenderness. One letter pleaded that he was miserable without her, pining only for her love. Another (1 November 1816) assured her that 'if there were a means of becoming reunited to you I would embrace it'. As always, Byron seems to have been guided by the impulse of the moment. Writing to Augusta, he cursed the implacable wretch who had separated him from the woman he loved best. Writing to Annabella, he rued the bitterness of banishment, and regretted the loss of his admired wife.

༄

---

* Byron used this startling epithet on several occasions: it appears in *BL&J* (5) on pp. 144, 186, 191, and in *BL&J* (10) on p. 142.

John Murray's decision not to print one of Byron's most direct attacks upon his wife was an act of caution, but also of affectionate respect. Following the separation, Lady Byron signalled (27 March 1816) her wish to maintain a friendly relationship with the publisher. Murray became a regular visitor to Branch Hill Lodge, an eighteenth-century mansion amply decorated with gloomy stained-glass windows by a previous owner, in which Annabella intermittently dwelt upon the airy heights of Hampstead from 1817 until 1825. He was meticulous in supplying her with early copies of all his publications. Naturally, these included Byron's works. In the autumn of 1816, when the ranting 'Lines, on Hearing Lady Byron was Ill' arrived from Italy, the separation scandal was still vivid in the public's mind. Murray's decision not to publish a poem that referred to Annabella as 'The Moral Clytemnestra of Thy Lord' was motivated by concern for Lady Byron as much as for the damage it might inflict upon the sales of a lucrative author. Byron's poem was filed away, to remain unpublished until 1832, when Moore's affectionate life of the poet had helped usher in a more forgiving attitude towards his misdeeds.

Externally, Lady Byron appeared relaxed about her husband's satiric use of her. Writing to Theresa Villiers on 15 July 1819 about her appearance as Donna Inez, the hero's prim mother, in *Don Juan*, Annabella remarked that Byron's satire was 'so good as to make me smile at myself – therefore others are heartily welcome to laugh'.

Given such a good-natured approach, Murray felt no qualms, in February 1817, about informing Lady Byron that her husband's latest work was selling well, although 'not quite up to the mark of former times'. The news disturbed Annabella less than Murray's gift of the very first copy of the Autumn 1816 *Quarterly Review*.* The journal, as its publisher proudly pointed out, carried 'an article on a great Poet . . . written in a tone calculated to do some good'.

It did none for Annabella. Walter Scott's long essay, ostensibly a review of Canto III of *Childe Harold*, was both lavish in its generosity and unintentionally comical in the earnest way that it dwelt upon

---

* Late publication was a regular occurrence with journals of that time.

Byron's noble antecedents. What angered Annabella was the great Scottish writer's determination to present her husband as a victim.

Annabella was staying with Scott's close friends, Agnes and Joanna Baillie, at their own Hampstead home when Murray's gift was delivered. Letters from her mother and from the Wilmots (Byron's cousins) declared Scott to be outrageously prejudiced: action must be taken! But Annabella recognised the danger of antagonising one of Britain's most admired authors. Instead, she adopted a course which would soon become familiar to those who had angered or distressed her. She did not write to Scott herself. Instead, the Baillie sisters were asked to convey their house guest's detection of a criticism of herself which – as even Annabella had to admit – Scott had 'not expressed, but I think directly implied'.

The technique worked. Scott, under pressure, apologised. Visiting one of her literary heroes at Abbotsford by her own request, late in the summer of 1817, Annabella's graceful acceptance of her sad situation, one 'which must have pressed on her thoughts', caused a penitent Scott to describe his guest to Joanna Baillie as one of the most interesting women he had yet encountered. They walked together along riverbanks. Annabella admired the landscape. No reference was made to Scott's article in the *Quarterly*.

It was by such circuitous routes – hiding behind the testimony of friends, citing trusted supporters, and quoting copiously from Byron's past correspondence (of which she made and preserved meticulous copies) – that Annabella increasingly chose to defend her reputation. Insistent, elaborate and always self-righteous, Lady Byron's tactics would unfortunately contribute to her posthumous reputation as a hypocritical tamperer with the truth.

And yet, initially, there was no need for such paranoia. Byron's name, not his wife's, had been severely damaged by the scandal surrounding the couple's separation. In 'Canto IV' of *Childe Harold*, he offered what appeared to be a profession of remorse, causing one of his more loyal supporters, Francis Jeffrey, in the December 1816 *Edinburgh Review*, to bestow upon the author the famous epithet of a 'ruined archangel'. But Childe Harold's remorse was not a confession of his creator's guilt. That admission never came. Byron's one passionate document of self-defence, written on 9 August 1817 at La Mira, a villa near Venice, was circulated to friends and journalists on the express understanding that it must not be published. Clearly, Byron feared the legal consequences of such a public step.

The British public had always preferred to follow the lead of its press. Encouraged by Francis Jeffrey and his literary colleagues, public disapproval of Byron began to wane after the appearance in the winter of 1816 of 'Canto IV' with its sorrowing Childe. Outrage would flare to new heights again in the summer of 1819, with the appearance of the first jaunty canto of *Don Juan*. *Blackwood's*, a magazine that was partly run by Walter Scott's future son-in-law and biographer, John Gibson Lockhart, was first to leap into the fray. How could the seemingly chastened author of *Childe Harold*'s final canto stoop to producing such impious filth? For Lord Byron to offend his wife was wrong – and to desert her was frankly ungentle-manly – 'but to injure, and then to desert, and then to turn back and wound her widow'd privacy with unhallow'd strains of cold-blooded mockery was brutally, fiendishly, inexpiably mean'. Only an insen-sate brute would dare 'to pour the pitiful chalice of his contumely on the surrendered devotion of a virgin's breast, and the holy hopes of the mother of his child'. And so on.*

This was harrowing stuff and Annabella won further support by expressing only quiet amusement at Byron's mocking portrait of herself as Juan's sedate mamma. It's unlikely that she knew of the far crueller skit in which, writing to Tom Moore on 10 December 1820, Byron lampooned his wife as 'The Witch'. The spur, on this occasion, was a newspaper cutting that announced Lady Byron's role as patroness of a town hall charity dance. To Byron, at his most irrational, a Leicestershire soirée glittered with all the brilliance of the humiliating Almack's Assembly at which he and Augusta had been so stonily received.

And yet, Byron's feelings about his wife still veered like a

---

* The author of the *Blackwood's* review was John Wilson.

weathercock in a storm. Despatching to Moore a snappy epigram upon marriage a month earlier, Byron had identified Annabella both as Medea and Penelope. Which was she: demon or angel? Until the end, her husband never could decide.

And neither, even thirty years after his death, could his widow make up her mind about her husband. Byron had something of the angel in him, the ageing Annabella would murmur to her confidantes, including an avidly attentive Harriet Beecher Stowe. None of these intimates dared to enquire why she had abandoned such a paragon.

Back during Byron's lifetime, a sensation-loving press faced no such quandaries. 'I was thought a devil, because Lady Byron was allowed to be an angel,' the poet sighed to a sympathetic Lady Blessington at Genoa in 1823.

One year later, Byron's unexpected death, aged thirty-six, while risking himself in the cause of rescuing Greece from her Turkish oppressors, triggered the beginning of the poet's slow redemption. Writing in *Blackwood's* (August 1825), John Gibson Lockhart invited his readers to admire the heroic spectacle 'of youth, and rank, and genius, meeting with calm resignation the approach of death, under circumstances of the most cheerless description . . .'

∽❀∾

'Let people think as they please – it matters little now,' Augusta Leigh had entreated Annabella back on 28 February 1822. But Lady Byron would never cease to care what people thought. Justifying the role that she had played in her husband's life, while blaming others – and blaming, above all, Augusta for contributing to the destruction of a marriage increasingly gilded by memory's broad and idealising brush – would become the occupation and obsession of a lifetime. It was an obsession that would shape the way that an earnest and well-meaning mother would seek to govern and protect the one precious gift left by her celebrated husband: their brilliant, wayward child.

PART TWO

Ada

'I really believe that you hatched me simply for the entertainment of your old age'

AUGUSTA ADA BYRON TO HER MOTHER,
10 OCTOBER 1844

CHAPTER TEN

In Search of a Father

'The little boy [Hugo, an orphaned nephew of Mary Montgomery] is a very nice child on the whole he speaks nothing but Italian and Spanish which I now perfectly understand.'

ADA BYRON AGED EIGHT, TO HER MOTHER,
7 DECEMBER 1824

Lord Byron was exceptionally angry to discover, early in 1817, that Annabella, advised by his own former legal counsel, Sir Samuel Romilly, had made their daughter a Ward of Chancery.* (Formally, Ada remained in Chancery until 1825, a year after her father's death.) Nevertheless, he never doubted that his estranged wife would make an excellent and conscientious parent to little Ada. 'A girl is in all cases better with the mother,' Byron informed Augusta Leigh (by then the mother of seven) on 21 December 1820, 'unless there is some moral objection.'

Claire Clairmont, having courageously decided to bring up Clara

---

* Annabella had agreed to Romilly's suggestion after Augusta Leigh, in February 1816, indicated that she might personally oppose her sister-in-law's right to keep the child. Annabella feared seeing Ada shuffled off into the Leigh household almost more than the prospect of losing her to Lord Byron.

Allegra, her illegitimate child by Byron, as part of Percy Shelley's bohemian household, was granted less respect. Byron liked Shelley and admired the poet's wife, Mary, but the couple's proclaimed aversion to monogamy presented the 'moral objection' of which he disapproved (in anyone other than himself). While Annabella was threatened with a lawsuit if she dared to expose young Ada to the dangers of continental travel, the Shelleys, in 1818, were commanded to arrange for little Allegra's transportation from England to Italy, where Claire was tearfully compelled to surrender her maternal rights.

Byron's caution about continental travel was well-founded. The Shelleys' own baby daughter (another Clara) died of dysentery at Venice in September 1818. Their son William died of malaria in Rome the following summer. Clara Allegra – a child whose extra-ordinary resemblance to (of all people) Annabella was immediately noticed both by Byron and his valet, Fletcher – died of malaria or typhus in an Italian convent in 1822.* She was five years old.

Byron, from afar, expressed an erratic but fatherly interest in his legitimate child. His parting gift to Ada had been one of his talis-manic rings. Further small gifts were despatched while off upon his alpine travels in the summer of 1816, followed in due course by a locket, inscribed, in Italian: 'Blood is thicker than water.' He asked for his daughter to be taught music (in which neither parent had any skill) and Italian (a language for which Annabella shared her husband's deep love).

A taste for poetry, however, was to be discouraged in the child of the greatest poet of the age. Arriving in Greece in the autumn of 1823, and about to embark upon what would prove to be his last adventure, Byron made his feelings clear in a letter that entreated his

---

* It says much for Byron's underlying affection for his wife that he observed this inexplicable similarity with the keenest of pleasure. To an outsider, the descrip-tion of Allegra's features raises the intriguing possibility that she may have not been Byron's child at all. Claire herself was dark-haired. Her daughter's fair hair, blue eyes and high forehead were all well-observed aspects of Shelley's delicate countenance. His paternity is not unthinkable; Claire and Shelley's intimacy has been widely noted.

wife (via Augusta) to provide him with a full report of their daughter, now almost seven years old.

> Is the Girl imaginative? … Is she social or solitary – taciturn or talkative – fond of reading or otherwise? and what is her *tic*? I mean her foible – is she passionate? I hope that the Gods have made her anything save *poetical* – it is enough to have one such fool in a family.

Annabella delayed her response, possibly because Ada at the time was experiencing her first serious illness and her mother did not want to raise alarm. On 1 December, six weeks after her husband's enquiry, Lady Byron sent him a miniature (the artist prided herself on having captured a perfect likeness of Ada's profile), together with the details he required.

> Her prevailing characteristic is cheerfulness and good-temper. Observation. Not devoid of imagination, but it is chiefly exercised in connection with her mechanical ingenuity – the manufacture of ships and boats etc. Prefers prose to verse … Not very persevering. Draws well. Tall and robust.

Annabella was never to receive Byron's grateful response for a letter he described as her first kind action since the seemingly tender address to 'dearest Duck' that she had written even as she left him, back in 1816. The letter in which he expressed his gratitude – while fondly noting the similarities to his own boyish self in his wife's account of little Ada – was still lying, unsent, on the poet's desk at Missolonghi at the time that he died.

Possibly, Lord Byron's very last thoughts were of his unseen daughter. William Fletcher, conveying the news of his master's death to John Murray on 21 April 1824, was anxious to stress that Byron's 'pertickeler wish' had been that his valet should carry a message to his wife and child. Lady Byron, so Fletcher later noted, had broken down in sobs during that harrowing visit, weeping until her whole body shook as she begged him – vainly – to recall what her husband's final message to her had been. By the end of her own life, Annabella had convinced herself that some 'unuttered' tender words had been thought, even if they had not been spoken.

❧

The cheerful docility mentioned by Annabella in 1823 marked the emergence of an endearing trait in Ada's nature. Squabbles lay ahead, especially with a mother whose authority she often opposed, but Ada, throughout her life, would win affection by her good humour, her kindness and – unlike either of her parents – her quickness to forgive.

Ada had not always been so equable. Back in November 1821, when Lord Byron was renting a palace in Pisa, he heard that his 6-year-old daughter was thought to be 'a fine child', but one who possessed 'a violent temper'. The news troubled him less than it did a mother who had witnessed her husband's own ungovernable rages. What Byron began to fret about in Pisa was Ada's isolation. Listing the members of her family who lacked siblings, he reached a disconcerting result. There were his own mother, Augusta's mother, Augusta, he himself, Annabella and now young Ada: 'Such a complication of only children ... looks like fatality almost', he brooded in his journal. Pride returned to comfort him. After all, 'the fiercest Animals have the rarest number in their litters – as Lions – tigers – and even Elephants,' Byron could not help adding, 'which are mild in comparison.'

❧

Initially, once Ada was weaned, she served only to remind her unhappy mother of the final weeks of a disastrous marriage. 'My Child! Forgive the seeming wrong / The heart with-held from thee', Annabella wrote in a private poem dated 16 December 1819 and guiltily entitled 'The Unnatural Mother'. A month earlier, Annabella confessed that the first real evidence of Ada's affection had come as a huge relief: 'I had a strange prepossession that she would never be fond of me.'

The commencement of Lady Byron's relationship with her daughter was not made easier by the first of many breakdowns in Annabella's health. Back in 1816, following the tremendous strain imposed by her marital separation, she became nervous, unhappy and ill. It was a relief, then, after taking Ada off to Lowestoft to meet up with Mary Gosford and her own little girls during that summer, to bequeath her daughter to the care of Nurse Grimes and Lady Noel at Kirkby. Meanwhile, Annabella went to London to seek an independent abode in Hampstead, close to the sympathetic Baillie sisters and the intelligent, motherless daughters of their neighbour, a prosperous and pious Mr Carr. In the summer of 1817, Annabella made just one brief halt at Kirkby Mallory before setting off on a tour of the Lake District with Miss Sarah Carr.*

In September, following another hasty visit from her daughter, Judith Noel decided it was time to tweak her maternal conscience. Ada was declared to be missing her mamma. 'She looked round the Bed and on the Bed, and then into the Closet – seemed disappointed and said "gone-gone"!'

The prod worked. Annabella returned home, to be rewarded with a scolding. Lady Noel possessed a notoriously sharp tongue, and it was one that Judith had not restrained on this occasion. Where would her daughter have been without Lady Noel's support in her time of need? Did she ever pause to consider the pain her separation had caused, or the social embarrassment which had compelled Judith to remove from public view Phillips's magnificently showy portrait of Lord Byron in order to nail it up in a box designated for the attic?†

---

* Sarah Carr later married Annabella's lawyer and devoted friend, Stephen Lushington. Her sister Frances (Fanny to her family) would one day become the most formidable of the three trustees of Lady Byron's papers.

† Lady Noel went further. In 1818, she wrote to ask the Prince Regent to permit a name change for her 'insulted and injured daughter'. Annabella was not informed and the Prince did not oblige. (JN to HRH the Prince Regent, 14 September 1818. A copy, or what may have been a draft, survives in the Lovelace Byron Papers.)

Her mother's reproaches struck home. Filled with remorse, Annabella vowed to change her ways. It had become, so she guiltily wrote to Sarah Siddons's widowed daughter-in-law, Harriet, her 'dearest wish to prove a better child than she [Lady Noel] has yet found me'.

Most biographers and historians have adopted a stern view of Annabella's behaviour during the first years after her separation from Byron. A fondness for mutton ('divine mutton!') has been cited by Doris Langley Moore as evidence, not only of her gluttony, but of her heartless greed. Her ever-increasing dependence on doctors – often while visiting agreeable spas – has been ascribed to self-indulgent hypochondria. More seriously, Lady Byron stands reproached, not simply of being an absent mother, but also of being a neglectful and ungrateful daughter.

The indictments are unjust. Through 1818 until Lady Noel's death in 1822, Annabella spent at least a third of every year living with her parents at the isolated Leicestershire estate where Ada, spoiled by adoring grandparents and an indulgent household of servants, enjoyed a cherished country childhood. For Annabella, however, imprisoned at Kirkby, the life of a dutiful daughter offered little solace beyond the admiring company of the vicar's daughter (rudely referred to by Lady Noel as 'the Anna').

Anna Jones offered a sympathetic audience to a frustrated young woman who was eager to be of use in the world beyond Kirkby's confining walls. Escaping briefly to Seaham in the summer of 1818, and enjoying the company of Harriet Siddons's young daughter, Lizzie, as her guest, Annabella rushed through her pet project for a much-needed local school, modelled after one that Harriet had successfully established in Edinburgh.* Back at Kirkby, and at her mother's mercy, she was powerless. Driving out in her carriage with

---

* Harriet's own pioneering school in Scotland seemingly inspired Annabella's lifelong interest in education, while Harriet's personable brothers-in-law, George and Andrew Combe, introduced Lady Byron to another enduring interest: phrenology. That would-be science sought to interpret personality from the shape of a skull. George Combe, the husband of Cecilia Siddons, was its leading authority. Annabella became an ardent convert.

Miss Jones, an ardent young social reformer, she noticed evidence everywhere of the need for enlightened philanthropy. Several of the villages on the Wentworth estate were entirely dependent upon weaving for a living. The weavers were the people for whom Byron had spoken out in his first political speech, and now they were starving, put out of work by the thriving new mills of Derbyshire and of the North. Here, surely, was a way to bury her sadness through offering help to others while – it was always important to Annabella – undertaking something of which Byron would approve. But the estate belonged to Judith, and Lady Noel had grown too old and self-absorbed to concern herself with good works. Lady Byron, like her father, was Lady Noel's dependent. Until her mother's death, Annabella's hands were tied.

Only an infrequent departure by Judith for an occasional health cure at Leamington Spa or Tunbridge Wells could open up a rare window of freedom. In January 1820, Annabella briefly joined the friendly Carrs and Baillies in Hampstead and, while there, found herself a future home: Branch Lodge. In May, she took Ada to Hastings, where the now intensely religious Mary Gosford was spending a quiet summer by the sea. 'Hastings will be good for me,' Annabella wrote to Harriet Siddons, before wistfully revealing her reason. 'The place will be retired.' Brighton, not Hastings, was where smart society spent its summer months. Four years after the separation, Lady Byron still shrank from placing herself anywhere that she might be noticed.

Towards the end of that year, Judith gradually declined into senility. Physically, however, she remained strong. By May 1821, Annabella had resigned herself to what threatened to become a lifetime of duty as a nurse-companion. But it was the news that her beloved Seaham was to be sold that seemed to break her heart. Writing to the always sympathetic Harriet Siddons, Annabella sounded near to tears. No more visits to help keep her little school in order; no more nostalgic strolls along that beloved beach; no more connection to the only place in which she and Byron had been, however briefly, alone and happy together. Contemplating the dreary years ahead of enacting 'a calm performance of duty' towards a decrepit parent, Annabella preserved just enough humour to smile at the doleful image she had conjured up of herself. While resolved to turn herself into a model of 'sober-minded' devotion, she feared it was too late for 'a probability of complete success'.

Diversion offered itself in the form of Ada's education. In the summer of 1821, Annabella's daughter was five years old. Up in the Kirkby nursery, she was now cared for by a kindly and outspoken nanny named Eliza Briggs, who took a pleasing interest in Ada's newest acquisition, a Persian kitten called Puff. Puff was a gift from her mother and – to judge from Ada's adoring tales of Mistress Puff's exploits and fairylike beauty – a much beloved one. Miss Lamont – fresh from Ireland and equipped with excellent references from an impressive young educationalist called Arabella Lawrence – was viewed with excitement by her pupil as a link to the larger world beyond her nursery's iron-barred windows. Perhaps – who could tell? – Miss Lamont might even become a friend.

Arriving at a large country house in May 1821 for what seems to have been her first proper job, the governess immediately found herself trapped between the conflicting desires of two formidable personalities. Lady Byron clearly held the upper hand, but Ada, endeavouring to blossom into an autonomous being, was fighting her corner with a combination of charm, determination and active intelligence that inspired her novice tutor with a secret desire to cheer. Instantly in love with the child but terrified of annoying Lady Byron, her employer, Miss Lamont found herself walking a tightrope that offered no safety net.

Annabella's own intentions for her daughter had already been made clear in the thank-you note 'Ada' addressed to her grandmother on New Year's Day 1821. Written in Annabella's own clear hand (Ada's sole contribution was a wobbly 'ADA'), the letter informed Lady Noel that the sky above Hastings was grey, while the sea below was yellow and white. Expressing gratitude for the useful Christmas gift of a knife and fork, Ada sounded as though she had sprung straight from a pedant's manual on childcare. Consciously or not, Lady Byron seemed intent upon moulding her daughter into an extremely dull little girl.

Miss Lamont's Kirkby journal, begun on 14 May of that same year, revealed a very different child. Ada had hailed her arrival with delight. She expressed a wish to start learning at once, and about everything possible. 'She is brim full of life, spirit and animation,' Miss Lamont remarked with pleased relief, 'and is most completely happy.'

Pleasure was put at a premium under the rigorous schedule upon which Ada's mother insisted. Each lesson must last precisely fifteen minutes. Good behaviour – demonstrated by obedience, application or simply sitting still – would be rewarded by a ticket. The emphasis upon sitting still was deliberate: Ada could no more stay still than a sudden streak of sunlight. (Miss Lamont was oddly reminded of a reindeer by the way her small charge dashed about; later, up in Hampstead, the old Baillie sisters would similarly fall under the spell of the lively, rosy-cheeked child they so loved to watch racing across the garden of Branch Lodge.)

It did not take long for the governess to realise how torn Ada was between bold defiance and the sincere desire to please a mother whom she evidently revered. Challenged by Annabella over her bold claim to sing far better than Mamma, the little girl refused to recant, but she wept when Lady Byron punished her impertinence with silence. Her sobs redoubled when Mamma further showed her disapproval by departing on a promised visit to Hinckley (Ada was enchanted by the local market town) with not a word of farewell.

Two weeks into Miss Lamont's stay at Kirkby, the young governess had failed to establish ascendancy over her pupil. Short spells of solitary confinement completely failed to bring Ada to heel. Annabella, writing to Miss Lawrence in Liverpool on 30 May, expressed frustration. What was the use of a governess, when she herself was so often obliged to take her employee's place – 'as if I were the teacher'? Miss

Lamont had failed to instil the desired attitude in her small charge: 'a sense of duty, combined with the hope of approbation from those she loves'. Her period of trial would not be extended.

It seems that Arabella Lawrence – for whom Lady Byron felt respect – defended her protégée. Miss Lamont was permitted to remain at Kirkby – although only until 7 July – as an increasingly uneasy witness to the ongoing battle between a forceful mother and an increasingly assertive child. Ada was stepping up her demands for independence. On 11 June, Annabella compelled her to express regret for saying that she did not want to learn about figures. ('I was not thinking quite what I was about. The sums can be done better, if I tried, than they are.') Four days later, the little rebel declared that she cared less about arithmetic than in being told '*every every* thing' about the cruel practice of beating donkeys. Out of Annabella's sight, Ada built cities of coloured bricks and turned geography lessons into flights of fantasy. (Could the waves in Norway really surge higher than her own tall house?) Ada, not her mother, had gained control when her governess was persuaded to skip dull lessons to play to her upon the piano, to come and admire how she could gallop like a horse, and to hear how heartily she could bray to entertain her old grandfather: ('*à merveille!*' exclaimed an admiring Miss Lamont).

Signs of Ada's rebelliousness appeared in the governess's journal as regularly as Lady Byron's instructions for their suppression. When a housemaid was summoned to imprison Ada's fidgety fingers within black cotton bags, the young woman was greeted with a fierce nip. Despatched to a distant corner in disgrace, Ada sank her teeth into the dado rail. Released after tea, she was allowed into the drawing room, where a forgiving Lady Byron calmed the stormy little girl with soothing poetry. (It was a few months after this scene that Byron first heard about his daughter's violent temper.)

Exhausting though Miss Lamont's experience of teaching Ada had been, the governess departed from Kirkby Mallory in a state of bewitchment. 'No person can be more rational, companiable [*sic*] and endearing than this rare child,' she rhapsodised, before adding that Ada would do almost anything in order to win her mother's praise.

∞

Lady Noel died in 1822. The following year, Ada, together with her ageing grandfather, Nurse Briggs and Mistress Puff (the Persian cat), exchanged the grandeur of Kirkby Mallory for Annabella's rented home in Hampstead. A portrait of Sir Ralph was left behind at Kirkby; instead, Annabella carried away the portrait of Lord Byron posing as an Albanian chief. Removed from its box, the famous painting was now hung, discreetly screened by a green velvet curtain behind which Ada – as it is frankly impossible not to suppose – occasionally granted herself a daring peep.

On 19 April 1824, Ada's father died in Greece of fever, exacerbated by bloodletting. Death – he was only thirty-six – in the romantic cause of restoring Greece to independence transformed Byron's reputation overnight. Later, Lord Tennyson remembered how, as a 16-year-old boy, he had solemnly chiselled the words 'Byron is dead' in a rock as a record of his own sombre emotions on hearing the news. At English country houses, Byron's death was announced to guests with the solemnity due to a fallen hero.

Brought back to London from Missolonghi on the *Florida*, the poet's body was laid out for a week in the room that a grief-stricken John Hobhouse had hired in order that final respects could be paid to his lost friend. The crowds who gathered in Westminster on the final two days, when public tickets were sold, were immense. They gathered again on 12 July, when the funeral cortège left Westminster, and they were present at every staging post along the poet's three-day journey to rejoin his ancestors in the family vault at Hucknall Torkard in Nottinghamshire. At Newstead, the artist Cornelius Varley added a note to his new sketch of the abbey's ruined arch that it had been executed during the year of Lord Byron's death.

Annabella, informed of her husband's death on 12 May by the new Lord Byron, reserved any visible signs of distress for the occasion of William Fletcher's later visit, bringing no final tender message from her late husband. Byron had apparently spoken of Ada, but it was evidently on Annabella's instructions that as little as possible was said about her father's death to the little girl. Taken to inspect the *Florida*, Ada wrote about 'Papa's ship' in a way that suggests she conceived him to have been the ship's brave captain. Confusion was understandable, especially in a year when her mother's good friend, who now held the Byron title, sailed for the Sandwich Islands in command of HMS *Blonde*.

At Hampstead, where she was taken into a church for the first time, Ada was more disturbed by the sense of imprisonment that she felt within a high-walled box pew than by regrets for a father she had never known. She yawned throughout the sermons and sighed for her lack of playmates. Other than the sedate Misses Carr and the ageing Baillie sisters, the most regular visitors to Branch Lodge were the briskly intelligent group of women who had been acquainted with Annabella since her youth. True, Ada had young Flora Davison (*'ma chère Flore'*) upon whom to practise her epistolary skills, but Flora lived outside London. True, Miss Montgomery brought along a nice little nephew, Hugo, who had a nurse of his own, and whose shiny brown hair matched the fur trim of his Russian-style tunic. But what Ada wanted was a proper brother of her own. She lit upon the perfect candidate in the new Lord Byron's son. Her own mysteriously absent father was now dead, while George Byron's was sailing across some faraway ocean. George, too, must need an ally, a sister to comfort him. Besides, didn't the two of them even share a name?

Young George had little chance to argue once his forceful cousin had determined upon him as her choice. On 9 September 1824, Ada offered her undying affection and sincere consolation to 'my sweet George' for his father's absence, while reaffirming her own loyal devotion: 'but no more about this at present for should your death take you from me though I do not feel it much now I should when it happened'. Undeterred by her cousin's resounding silence, she tried again. Perhaps George would like to know her thoughts about love? (George was six; Ada almost eight.) Ada was eager to share her ideas. 'I think the greatest happiness is in loving and being loved I dare say my love you will feel that.'

Ada was already displaying signs of having inherited her late father's mesmerising volatility. After broaching (9 September) the subject of her sturdy little cousin's possibly imminent death, she moved along without a blink on that same day to telling her mother about her recent enjoyment of a tasty meal of 'fryed fish', before again switching to the latest hunting exploits of the adventurous Mistress Puff. Ada had also invented a new word to describe her own passion for intensive reading: 'gobblebook'.

∽

'Gobblebook' signalled a marked change in Ada. She had become not only an eager reader, but a voracious learner. Although unequipped with a formal governess during her three years at Branch Lodge, it's likely that Ada was being informally tutored by the clever ladies whose visits filled her letters at the time. If so, they did well by her. Ada started to ask probing questions about arithmetic, while trying her hand at writing in French. A letter addressed to Cousin George's mother, now also known as Lady Byron, proudly announced her near perfect command of Spanish and Italian. Emotionally, too, Ada was making progress. She could understand her mother's enduring affection for gentle Sophy Tamworth ('Lady Tam') well enough to connect it to her own sisterly devotion to little George.

The Baillie sisters would later remember Ada as a cheerful, energetic little girl, full of life and affection. Neither they nor her mother were surprised when she announced her plan to raise money (by making plaster casts of gems) to finance the painting of a portrait of her grandfather. The project was still in progress in the summer of 1825, when Sir Ralph died. Having dozed his last months placidly away at Branch Lodge, he was buried beside Judith in the windswept churchyard of their lost, but beloved, Seaham estate.

∽

Sir Ralph's death marked the last stage in his daughter's transformation into Lady Noel Byron, a woman of thirty-three who was determined to make good use of the immense wealth and vast estates that she now possessed through Uncle Wentworth's legacy.

A great injustice had occurred, however. It was one that Annabella acted swiftly to redress. In 1825, Lord Wentworth's six grandchildren were left virtually destitute, thanks to the fact that he had refused to leave his fortune to their father, his own (fiercely resentful) illegitimate son. The children's mother, Kitty Smith, was a sweet but ineffectual woman, long since abandoned by the absentee rector of Kirkby Mallory. While Annabella delegated the two young Noel girls to care for their somewhat helpless mother, her primary concern was for their brothers.

The four Noel sons stood halfway in age between Annabella and Ada. Tom, the eldest, now aged twenty-six, was a pleasant but irresponsible young man who liked writing poems. It was Robert, a clever, Pickwickian youth of twenty-two, whom Annabella singled out to act as trustee for his younger siblings, Charles (aged twenty) and Edward (nineteen). From 1825 on, while always taking care to consult and respect their mother's wishes, the Noel boys would become virtual extensions of Lady Byron's own tiny family. Writing to Robert from Italy in 1827, she addressed him as '*Caro Fratello*', but the relationship was nearer to that of mother and son. The warmth of the relationship is apparent from the fact that Robert described Annabella in 1847 as his oldest and kindest friend. It was from conscience as much as for convenience that Annabella chose the third Noel, Charles, to act as her agent and overseer at Kirkby. It was, she reasoned, only right that a male Noel, a Wentworth grandson, should be placed in charge of a vast estate that had been under Noel ownership since the sixteenth century.

ॐ

Released at last from filial duty, Annabella herself fell ill. Branch Lodge was abandoned as Lady Byron travelled from one spa to the next in her fruitless search for a cure. Ada, together with Miss Briggs, Puff and an additional fine black cat (an inky kitten had been promised to Cousin George), also found herself once again on the move.

Bifrons (originally so named because of its two contrasting façades, although the old house had long since been replaced) stood just outside Canterbury, on the Dover road. All that remains today of the house that Annabella rented for the next few years is bare land and a dwindling avenue of ancient trees. It was here, while being looked after by Mary Montgomery, one of her favourites among Annabella's friends, that Ada decided that she, like the literary father of whose fame she was now becoming dimly aware, would become a writer. Evidence that Annabella knew of her daughter's plan and actively set out to thwart it emerges from a curious letter that has survived, tucked away within the archive of John Murray.

On 31 March 1826, Annabella, conscious that Byron's publisher was always anxious to placate the poet's widow, issued Murray with a clear directive. He was to publish absolutely nothing initialled 'AB' that might appear to have received her authority, 'tho from the accidental delay of a letter, my consent may have been inferred by the party in question'. And what on earth, a baffled John Murray must have wondered, did Lady Byron mean to convey to him by that strangely ambiguous defence? If an 'accidental delay' on her part had caused the problem, why not write again? Few letter-writers were more zealous, after all, than Byron's widow. And why did she write to him, and not to the mysterious AB? The most likely answer seems to be that Annabella shrank from explicit censorship and chose this elaborate course as the easier route to suppression. It doubtless explains why an enchanting twenty-five-page story by Ada, carefully worked over by another hand, still lies unpublished – and seemingly unknown – within the Murray papers, held at the National Library of Scotland.*

---

* 'The Neopolitan Brothers', completed in 1827, possibly during her time in Europe, suggests that Ada had been dipping into the ladies' annuals which were published (in lavish editions) for the Christmas market. A gothic romance, Ada's tale features a murder, a haunting, a vividly imagined Italian setting and unspeakable remorse. As the work of a child of eleven, it is impressive. The reviser was most likely to have been Ada's sympathetic governess, Charlotte Stamp. (John Murray Archive, MS 43363, NLS.)

Briefly lodged during the spring of 1826 with Miss Montgomery, at Library House in Hastings, Ada had begun to look upon Lady Byron's old friend almost as a second mother. (Among the many reasons for Mary Montgomery's popularity with Ada were that she played the guitar, that she had a pleasingly exotic little nephew, and that she allowed Ada to sit in her dressing room and chatter, while practising her Italian with a lady who spoke the language fluently.) It was not, then, with much gratitude for her real and absent mother's endeavours that Ada learned that a new governess was on her way. After glumly admitting that it had been 'quite shocking' of her to announce she did not believe in prayers, Ada resignedly accepted that this unknown educator was God's way of punishing her.

A pleasant surprise was due. Miss Charlotte Stamp transformed young Ada's life. Kind, thoughtful and entertaining, she was everything that a clever, inventive and ebullient little girl could have wished for. An 'apt scholar' at chess, a ready partner in the quadrille, a willing collaborator in Ada's story-writing endeavours, Miss Stamp was extolled by her pupil as 'an enchantress' and a treasure. Twenty years later, Ada would still regard this impeccable governess as her chosen model of perfection.

Annabella also approved. Planning the most adventurous step she had taken since leaving Byron, she included Ada and Miss Stamp in the carefully picked group who were to travel with her around Europe for fifteen months.

The Napoleonic Wars had deprived Annabella herself of any chance to visit the Continent as a child. Aged thirty-five, she had still voyaged no further than Edinburgh. Understandably – for a widow whose name remained tainted by the scandal surrounding her separation from Byron – Annabella wanted to travel within a protective circle of friends. Robert Noel, a fluent linguist, acted as her interpreter during the first months of the trip before travelling alone to Lyons, where the base was laid for Robert's future career as one of Europe's most eminent phrenologists. (Lady Byron had reluctantly abandoned her wish to settle him in England as a clergyman.) Along with Ada and Miss Stamp, Annabella was accompanied through various stages of the 1826–7 trip by Harriet Siddons, Mary Montgomery and Louisa Chaloner, a friend from her northern youth. Ada, who respected Harriet and loved Miss Montgomery, struggled to feel equal enthusiasm for Miss Chaloner, an outspoken Yorkshirewoman who had recently told Ada that she was a plain child. Intended as a corrective to vanity, the observation had stung. 'I do like to look well,' Ada wistfully confessed to her mother on the day of Miss Chaloner's comment (2 June 1826). The announcement which followed ('I think it is well for me I am not beautiful') fell short of true conviction. Physical appearance would become, from this time on, a regular feature of Ada's letters.

The European tour offers poignant evidence of Lady Byron's feelings for her late husband. In England, she had paid anonymous visits to Harrow, to the deserted house at Piccadilly Terrace and even to Newstead Abbey, where the emotional experience of standing for the first time in Byron's own private rooms, back in 1818, had almost overwhelmed her. Arriving in Switzerland, Lady Byron arranged a sailing trip on Lake Geneva, within eyesight of the shuttered villa where her husband had spent the summer of 1816. In Genoa, the city from which Byron had set out for Greece, his final adventure, Annabella rented an elegant palace. Here, Ada's tutor in singing and drawing was selected precisely because Signor Isola claimed to have known and felt affection for Lord Byron. When the party of travellers moved on to Turin, they took Isola along with them. Annabella declared that Ada needed to continue her drawing lessons, but Isola's primary role was to talk with his employer about Byron, and his life in Italy.

Such nostalgic indulgence was always camouflaged by Lady Byron's interest in a higher cause. A second sentimental visit to Switzerland during this same extensive pilgrimage was ostensibly undertaken solely in order to settle Tom Noel as a young teacher at Dr Emmanuel Fellenberg's celebrated school.

While Tom Noel failed to fit into Hofwyl's demanding regime, Annabella swiftly established a warm relationship with the school's creator. A voluminous correspondence commenced, in which Dr Fellenberg's French addresses to 'Milady' were matched by Annabella's stately responses in her own tongue. Plans were swiftly laid for Tom's younger brother, Edward, and little Hugo Montgomery to complete their schooling at Hofwyl.

It would be hard to overstate the influence of Emmanuel Fellenberg's enlightened and progressive school upon Annabella's future life as a reformer. Recommended to her by Harriet Siddons, herself an ardent educationalist, Hofwyl provided the model for the schools through which Annabella, in her mid-thirties, decided to provide practical knowledge and technical skills to the poor. As at Hofwyl, which she had also heard praised by Henry Brougham, she would raise her pupils up to become teachers and spreaders of learning for a class to whom it had hitherto been denied. Thrillingly ahead of the times when Annabella paid her first visit to Fellenberg's country academy in 1826, Hofwyl showed her how to start using her great fortune for the public good. It became the mainspring for her lifework.

Little record survives of Ada's feelings about her travels, other than some drawings, along with anxious reports to her mother's friends in England on the subject of Lady Byron's failing health. Hofwyl had proved inspiring, but the tour reawakened an unforeseen storm of emotion and grief in Annabella. The near loss of Harriet Siddons to a severe attack of 'brainfever' seemed to be the final blow from a remorseless fate. Returning to England in the autumn of 1827, Lady Byron managed a month of supervising Ada at Bifrons (Miss Stamp had gone on holiday) before she herself altogether collapsed. The gravity of her illness is apparent from the fact that Ada, composing in February one of many worried little notes, expressed relief that her mother could now manage to scrawl in her own hand the simple words 'much better'. Two months later, Ada admitted that there had been times when 'I really thought ... you could not live.'

While travel had brought Annabella to what seemed to be her deathbed, it fired her precocious 11-year-old daughter with further dreams of escape. On 3 February 1828, Ada excitedly revealed her newest project. She was teaching herself to fly.

I am going to begin my paper wings tomorrow and the more
I think about it, the more I feel almost convinced that with a
year or so's experience & practise I shall be able to bring the art
of flying to very great perfection. I think of writing a book of
Flyology illustrated with plates ...

The following day, having joyfully conveyed the news that Miss
Doyle's niece Fanny Smith was looking forward to flying alongside
her when she next visited Bifrons, Ada set out the next phase of her
plan. Once she had mastered the art of flight, she would become
a 'carrier pigeon', an airborne messenger who would transport
her mother's letters across the skies. As an extra incentive to the
recovery of her health, Lady Byron learned that her wish to become
godmother to Puff's new kitten was granted. Puff, so she learned,
had become especially bold of late, hiding up the chimney, when not
crunching bird bones beneath Ada's bed.

In part, Ada was making an endearing attempt to comfort an ailing
mother to whom she now frequently signed herself off as 'Carrier
Pigeon' or even 'Your affectionate Young Turkey'. Nevertheless, as
her flying schemes grew ever more elaborate, it became clear that
Ada wished her aerial aspiration to be treated seriously. Writing to
Annabella at the spa of Tunbridge Wells on 2 April, she requested a
scientific book about bird anatomy. A bird's wings, as Ada explained,
offered an ideal model for her own paper constructions. Five days
later, Ada's plans had taken a further leap. She was going to build
a flying machine.

I have got a scheme about a ... steamengine which, if ever I
effect it, will be more wonderful than either steam packets or
steam carriages, it is to make a thing in the form of a horse
with a steamengine in the inside so contrived as to move an
immense pair of wings, fixed on the outside of the horse, in such
a manner as to carry it up into the air while a person sits on its
back.

Ada's plans had begun with a wonderful fantasy of flying about in 'the great room' at Bifrons and astonishing her mother with her feats. Now, a disused tack room for horses at Bifrons was converted into a 'flying room' hung with ropes (presumably for swinging about in simulated flights). Miss Stamp's discovery of an old saddle stand languishing in a corner led on to another bright idea. Might Ada be allowed to take up riding? Mamma had doubtless forgotten that there was the dearest little pony who was kept in the park at Bifrons: 'very gentle . . . just a little pottering thing . . . I really think that when you come back, an arrangement might be made without any trouble or inconvenience to any one for me to ride little Shag, as I call him.'

Miss Stamp, who dryly remarked that she now featured so often in her pupil's letters that she had best just become 'Miss S', decided that it was wisest to indulge her excited young pupil's projects and boasts. ('When you come home you shall see me *ride*,' Ada swaggered to her mother. She had never yet even sat upon a horse.)

Miss Stamp was tolerant. Annabella, recovering her health, grew apprehensive. A brisk course in theorems might calm her daughter's overexcited state. Arabella Lawrence was consulted, while William Frend and his daughter Sophia were invited to see if they could not help to restrain Miss Byron's fancies by confining her energies to figures and logic. In vain: instead of furthering Lady Byron's plan, Frend found himself being recast as her daughter's pet astronomer. Lady Byron had asked for lessons in geometry. Ada requested a map of the stars. Frend surrendered. People always did, when Ada set her heart upon something. By February 1829, the elderly mathematician had become the bewitched recipient of the young girl's confidences about her newest project. Flying had been abandoned for the creation of 'my Planetarium'.

Overexcitement; illness; the onset of puberty; the departure of her beloved Charlotte Stamp to get married (never, sadly for Ada, to return). A combination of these things brought Ada's year of elated dreaming to a shocking close. William Frend, writing to Lady Byron on 27 May 1829 to enquire if her daughter would be observing the course of Jupiter that June, was informed that a severe attack of measles had left Ada paralysed, semi-blind and bedridden.* It remained impossible to predict how much time might be required for her recovery.

---

* It is unlikely that Ada's measles was related to the paralysis. Although this has happened (most recently, in 1964), such consequences are extremely rare. At the time, a connection did seem possible. (See the appendix on Ada's health on pp. 475–6.)

CHAPTER ELEVEN

A RAINBOW'S ARC
(1829–35)

Utterly mysterious in its origins – Annabella theorised about a latent weakness of the spine – Ada Byron's state of semi-paralysis lasted for three years. Short periods of improvement were followed by sharp relapses. By the summer of 1830, following one of these brief respites from invalidism, 13-year-old Ada – formerly an active girl, one who had been eager to take up riding at the time of her collapse – had become chronically bedbound. Letters to her new tutor were shakily written in pencil (to avoid spattering the bedlinen with ink). Brief expeditions, when not confined to a wheelchair, were taken on crutches, with the gold-braided and wasp-waisted black jacket of a hussar that she adopted for these excursions lending a frail but resolutely cheerful Ada the look – although nobody dared to comment on it – of the dashing boy-heir for whom her father had longed. (The birth of a son, as the often surprisingly conventional Lord Byron once remarked, would have made him think twice about parting with Newstead, the ancestral home that he had profitably sold off in 1818 to Thomas Wildman.)

 ✆

A dashingly Byronic young man had formally joined Ada's larger family circle in 1826, when Henry Trevanion married Byron's niece and god-daughter, Georgiana Leigh. Three years later, impoverished and homeless, Georgiana and Henry were generously installed at Bifrons, Annabella's rented country home near Canterbury. Ada, meanwhile, was brought away from Bifrons to live on the fringes of London, first at Notting Hill and then, during 1830, at The Limes, a large, pretty house standing above the Thames at Mortlake. Here, close to the best physicians that London could provide, no expense was spared in Lady Byron's attempt to cure her daughter's baffling condition.

ၐ

Annabella had first heard about Henry Trevanion, a Cornish-born youth with Byronic connections (the poet's grandfather, best known as Admiral Byron of the *Wager*, had married Sophia Trevanion of Caerhays), from Augusta Leigh. On 9 December 1825, Mrs Leigh had sent Lady Byron a gushing account of Sophia's personable 21-year-old descendant as 'the *Hero* of my present fate'. Penniless – his father had disinherited him – and on the make, Henry had recently presented himself as a suitor to Georgiana, the Leighs' eldest daughter. Augusta's widely reported role as her brother's heir added pound signs to the attraction of marrying a slow-witted but exceptionally docile 17-year-old.* Unfortunately for Augusta's wish to support the marriage, her husband detested Trevanion. Together with Henry's father, Colonel Leigh refused to grant consent.

Henry remained assiduous and Augusta had a weakness for a handsome face: Henry's reminded her of Byron's own. Frantic to do something that might bind this solicitous youth to herself (Henry's precise role in Augusta's life remains murky, but it involved a strong sexual frisson), Mrs Leigh enlisted the aid of Annabella. Glad to assist Byron's god-daughter along the road to happiness, Annabella

---

* Had Henry Trevanion known of the arrangements restricting Mrs Leigh's access to funds that were held in trust, he might have thought twice. Even so, Georgiana's marriage settlement proved substantial enough for him to raise £8,332 against it in 1836.

provided a discreet loan of £200 via Louisa Chaloner. It was enough to ensure that a strangely low-key wedding was able to take place in London on 4 February 1826. The ceremony's sole guests were Augusta, her friend Colonel Henry Wyndham (standing in for the absent and furious George Leigh) and 12-year-old Elizabeth (at this point known as 'Libby') Medora, the child whom both Byron and Augusta believed to be their own.

Mrs Leigh's valiant endeavours to stay out of debt had never been helped by a wastrel husband and her own weak grasp of finance. Annabella, trained from her youth to act as her family's lawyer and accountant, was an excellent businesswoman, one who always saw to it that she was well advised. Since her father's death, she had added an inheritance of substantial coal-mining interests in the north to a portfolio that she managed with exceptional competence. In judgement of character, however, Annabella was often just as fallible as her sister-in-law. Both women were to be deceived by Henry Trevanion and by Elizabeth Medora Leigh in a saga that finally snapped the frail chain of duty by which Lord Byron sought to ensure the future security and comfort of his sister, Augusta.

'Look after Augusta,' Byron had insisted to Annabella, both during and after the couple's separation. Annabella had kept her word, but the limited personal affection she retained for Mrs Leigh was already dwindling by 1828, when the first warning signs emerged of serious trouble ahead.

In 1828, Augusta casually announced that she had authorised her charming son-in-law to edit a selection of Byron's letters, through which young Trevanion had already been trawling. Murray had sensibly steered clear of the negotiations, but Henry Colburn, one of the sharpest publishers in London, had offered £300. Augusta, delighted for her protégé, sought Annabella's approval for a done deal.

A close perusal of Byron's letters may have introduced Henry Trevanion to the possibility that Georgiana's younger sister was the product of an incestuous relationship. It is not known whether any of Byron's rashly intimate correspondence with Lady Melbourne was intended to form part of the published selection; certainly, the inclusion of such explosive material would explain Henry Colburn's eagerness and Annabella's dismay. Laying their own past differences aside, John Cam Hobhouse and Lady Byron united forces to scotch a project that they both believed would worsen Byron's still badly damaged reputation. Augusta, whose only concern was to please the beguiling Henry, announced in April 1829 that she felt personally 'very hurt'.

Annabella followed her blocking of the Colburn publication by refusing to give Augusta the thousand-pound sweetener she required as balm for her disappointment. Nevertheless, Augusta was a skilful piercer of Lady Byron's tender conscience about the harm that had been caused both by the separation and by Annabella's own meditated silence. Reputations had been damaged and the fault lay with Lady Byron. ('My sin is ever before me' ran the sad opening line of one of Annabella's private poems.*) Now, however, while financial assistance was withheld, practical help might still be bestowed.

In April 1829, Annabella informed Augusta that she was willing to lend her own newly vacated house to Byron's homeless godchild and her husband, a man whom she herself had never yet met. (She never did.) Sending thanks, Augusta neglected to mention that the couple would be accompanied to Bifrons by Georgiana's sister. Tall, lively and high-spirited, the 15-year-old Libby would act as a companion to the pregnant Georgiana, while entertaining her charming Henry: this, so it seems, was the idea that Augusta had hatched. It remains unguessable whether Mrs Leigh fully recognised what a gift she was making to a bored and unprincipled young man. Perhaps, the answer is best summed up by Annabella, when she commented upon Mrs Leigh's curious lack of any form of moral principle. Augusta simply didn't register the rights and wrongs of such behaviour. Nevertheless,

---

* 'Those who, like myself, are animated by an ever-new succession of hopeful visions, have dangers of a different kind to contend with ...' Annabella wrote to Lizzie Siddons on 13 June 1834, adding revealingly that: 'my states of depression ... arise, not from apprehension of the future, but from regret for the past'. (HRC, bound vol.1, Byron Collection)

she guessed what Lady Byron's views would be shrewdly enough to hold her tongue.

ॐ

Eighteen-twenty-nine would prove to be an active and stressful year for Lady Byron. Concerned about Ada, and far from well herself, she was busily engaged in helping to set up a number of co-operative schools, and also farms where – a bold concession at that time – tenants could unite to buy their own plots of land. Sailing around the coast from Brighton to Bristol and from Devon to Newport in her search for pleasing locations in which to establish these new ventures, Lady Byron's wealth was revealed by the fact that she now travelled on her own yacht, the *Prince Leopold*.

At Hastings, taking advice from William Frend, Annabella set up a co-operative institute in George Street. In London, she conducted discussions with Robert Owen about methods of schooling for the underprivileged whose chances in life she was determined to improve. (A shocking 90 per cent of all children received neither formal education nor apprenticeship training in early nineteenth-century England.) At Liverpool, she talked with Arabella Lawrence about Miss Lawrence's own successful school for the city's poor. At Brighton, Annabella formed a new and enduring friendship with zealous Dr King, founder of that town's own first co-operative. Annabella's reaction of dislike to Robert Owen, whom she swiftly judged to be both complacent and autocratic, was soon forgotten in her wholehearted enthusiasm for the modest, religious – and most obligingly compliant – William King.

In the early autumn of 1829, Augusta Leigh took it upon herself to criticise Byron's executor, Douglas Kinnaird, causing him to resign. A new trustee was required. Augusta put forward a Leigh family supporter, Colonel George D'Aguilar. Annabella, who had been exchanging friendly notes with Augusta about the injustice of denying Lord Byron a monument in Westminster Abbey, now suggested that the more experienced Dr Lushington might offer better service. Lushington had acted as her own lawyer for the past twelve years. His wife Sarah Carr, handpicked by Annabella, was one of her closest friends. Nobody could be more suitable.

By the end of November, the discussion between the two ladies had turned quarrelsome. Annabella was insistent; Augusta refused to back down. Mrs Leigh's reason was transparent; the cultured and agreeable Colonel D'Aguilar was ready to do just as she pleased. Lushington, who held as low an opinion of Augusta's prudence as of her morals, would sanction nothing without careful consideration. (In fact, Lushington strove to help the Leighs, a family whose attitude to money remained alarmingly close to that of Mr Micawber's.) By 1 December, Annabella was feeling angry enough to identify Lushington to young Lizzie Siddons as 'my protector when injury (I speak the language of the world for I know no injuries) was designed by the very person I was seeking to serve!' By January 1830, the two ladies were quivering with mutual resentment and indignation.

The voices that speak out from ancient, tissue-thin letters still vibrate with animosity and distrust, but it was Augusta's offer of forgiveness that finally tipped the balance for a furious Lady Byron.

Augusta Leigh (undated, but probably 16 January 1830):
   I can forgive and do forgive freely, all and everything that has antagonised and I may say almost destroyed me. I can believe that you have been actuated throughout by a principle which you thought a right one, but my own self-respect will never allow me to acknowledge an obligation where none has been originally conferred ...

Writing her response from Ealing (where she was renting a second home close to a projected school) on 17 January 1830, Annabella was at her chilliest and most implacable:

From your representations and the conclusions you draw, it is evident to me that your mind is not in a state to admit the truth – I must therefore decline any further discussion of facts which are already as well known to you as to me.

> *Believe me, ever faithfully yours*
> *A I Noel Byron*

The deliberate use by Lady Byron of her formal name was indicative of her rage. The employment of that innocuous word 'faithfully' conveyed a stinging reminder of the promise she had been compelled to make to her late husband. The Leigh family might drive Annabella up the wall, but they would never be deprived of what Byron's wife recognised to be their rightful due.

Augusta's refusal to acknowledge any obligation to a patient and on the whole generous benefactor was absurd, but it was the use of that awful word 'forgiveness' that had caused such anger. 'I can never pass over her insolence,' Lady Byron informed Sarah Lushington on 27 February 1830. She meant it. Augusta's decorous gift of a prayer-book for Ada's fourteenth birthday in December 1830 produced no response. Silence was an insult that Mrs Leigh did not forget. Relations between the two women, for the entirety of a fierce decade, would become nearly non-existent.

Augusta was evidently unconscious of any particular reason why such characteristic behaviour on her own part (voluminous lamentations about Mrs Leigh's sufferings and her shortage of money habitually followed Lady Byron around the country like a Greek chorus) had provoked such unreasonable wrath. A reason existed, however, and it was not a pretty one.

∽

It was during the autumn of the ongoing dispute about trusteeship that Annabella had received disquieting news from George and Mary Byron. (That kind and cheerful couple's loyalty to Annabella since 1816 had been rewarded in 1824, when Lady Byron put them in receipt of an annual £2,000, having learned that her husband had disinherited his cousin: this was Byron's punishment for siding against himself during the separation.) George, now 7th Lord Byron, had recently been approached by William Eden, the vicar of a church not far from Bifrons. Eden's parishioners reported tales of dreadful goings-on at Lady Byron's home since the Trevanions and Miss Leigh had moved into it that spring. Young Miss Leigh was now visibly pregnant. The Bifrons workforce spread the news that Henry Trevanion was responsible.

Annabella's first shocked thought was that the past had repeated itself, under her own roof, seemingly with her own approbation. On 4 December 1829, Lady Byron wrote to Georgiana Trevanion. A carefully phrased letter indicated that, while offended by Augusta's quarrelsomeness about the new trustee, and appalled by these new revelations, she would stand by her promise to help her husband's family. In January 1830, she arranged and paid for the disgraced trio to sail together to Calais. There, in lodgings that were paid for by Annabella, the illicit child was born. (Farmed out for adoption, the little boy died later that summer.) Augusta, while dimly conscious of a move to France, presumably for financial reasons, remained unaware either of her doomed first grandchild's birth or that Lady Byron was discreetly paying all the Trevanions' household bills.

Given this bizarre background scenario, it is not surprising that Annabella rejected Augusta's offer of forgiveness. Quite possibly, Lady Byron relished a moment of justifiable scorn. What kind of mother could conceivably have placed her 15-year-old daughter in such a compromising situation? How different was her own devoted care for poor, fragile Ada!

∽

Annabella's indignation would have justifiably increased, had she been informed of what happened next. Slipping quietly back into England during the following summer (1830), the Trevanions lodged at a family house in Chelsea, from which Henry paid regular visits to his unabashed young mistress, demurely lodged at her mother's apartment in St James's Palace. In February 1831, Trevanion informed an appalled Mrs Leigh that he and her younger daughter were expecting a child. (No mention was made of the previous pregnancy, or of Lady Byron's assistance.)

Augusta's response was hysterical. To Henry, she despatched a plaintive squawk of command: 'You will comfort me! I need not point out the means! Your own heart will dictate them – and as you are dear! MOST dear! *Much*, MUCH is in your power!' Elizabeth Medora, meanwhile, was apprised by Mrs Leigh of the agonies she had inflicted upon a mother's tortured soul: 'I have suffered much – long (neither you or ANY human Being knows how much) but – I never knew sorrow like this … I was not prepared for this wretchedness – Spare! Oh spare me, Dearest!' The greatest of all Augusta's sorrows, so it appeared from an interminably theatrical lament, was that her cherished daughter would not now be able to complete her religious education. ('You know that I confidently hoped and intended you to be confirmed this Easter! I suppose it is *now* hopeless – consult your own heart and wishes!') As was aptly observed in 1929 by Ethel Mayne, first biographer of Lady Byron: 'The pitiful absurdity of these letters paralyses the judgement.'

Plainly, little help for Henry and his victim (this was the role that Miss Leigh adopted, and maintained) was to be expected at this juncture from an agonised mother; Annabella, who supposed the trio still to be safely lodged (at her own expense) in France, was equally unlikely to prove sympathetic. Retiring to a village near Bath, the Trevanions and Elizabeth Medora decided to lie low. This was the point at which – informed at last by Henry Wyndham of what had been hidden from view for two full years – a distraught Colonel Leigh intervened. Never the brightest of men, George Leigh's solution was to abduct his unmarried and once again pregnant child and lock naughty Libby up within a discreet abode in north London. Following suit with the support of an eagerly collaborative Georgiana and (it is conjectured) funded by the ever-gullible Augusta – Henry Trevanion now 'liberated' a most co-operative young mistress and carried Medora (as we will from now on, for convenience, name Elizabeth Medora Leigh) off to live with him in France.

Nothing improved. In England, a husbandless Georgiana struggled to bring up three small children on her own. In France, in 1836, a penniless Trevanion set about raising funds against his abandoned wife's marriage settlement in order to buy himself – but not Medora – a home. Back in England, John Hanson (Byron's unsavoury lawyer had by now been publicly disgraced for his exploitation of the lunatic Lord Portsmouth) piously opined that 'poor Mrs Leigh and all connected with her are mad'. In 1838, Medora, still in France, was striving to obtain the title deed to a £3,000 settlement extravagantly promised by Augusta to Marie, Medora's illegitimate 4-year-old child.* (Henry Trevanion was, once again, the father.)

Trevanion remained the nemesis to whom Medora always returned. It was he – or he and Georgiana – who had first informed her that she was Byron's daughter.† In 1840, that alleged parentage would be used to clinch Medora's hold over Lord Byron's always wistful and conscience-stricken wife.

രജ്

By the spring of 1830, while the Trevanions and Medora were still living at Calais, illness had muted Ada's vibrant, quirky voice for almost a year. In March, the kindly old Baillie sisters expressed a hope that their young friend might soon be well enough to venture outside the house. Three months later, at Mortlake, Ada admitted to her correspondence tutor, Arabella Lawrence, that she was often in too much pain even to sit upright. Chair rides (or an occasional stumbling walk) along the terrace above the Thames to watch the boats and river birds now represented her entire external life. Within the seclusion of The Limes and with her closest girlfriend, Flora

---

* Augusta's settlement was predicated upon the always sickly Lady Byron's early death. None of the money could be released until that eventuality.

† Georgiana, for reasons that remain obscure, was always a co-operative member of the trio. By telling Medora that she was not the daughter of Colonel Leigh, she seemingly intended the girl to feel less guilt about sleeping with Henry Trevanion, her own sister's husband.

Davison,* for an audience, Ada – on her good days – endeavoured
to practise the piano ('I especially love the waltz'), and – with characteristic gallantry – attempted little jokes. Selina Doyle and she
were struggling to read German together, she told Robert Noel, a
fluent speaker of the language who was himself now out in Dresden
studying phrenology: *'und wie der Lahme und der Blinde helfen
wir uns einander'* ('and are as much use to each other as the lame
and the blind').

One of Ada's greatest resources was an absolute refusal to
repress her feelings, in marked contrast to the self-control that
Annabella had determinedly acquired. Writing to Miss Lawrence
in Liverpool from her Mortlake sickroom, the pupil made no secret
of her despair: 'This has been a sad irregular week. Monday I
missed nothing but was [so] desponding & despairing that I could
have cried with very great pleasure.' On another day during that
same bleak July of 1830, Ada grew tearful about the difficulties of
German grammar: 'I began to read it [her grammar book] as usual,
not thinking right ... however, I found my head in a state of sad
confusion, and getting extremely discouraged began to cry.' Striving
to keep a full record of a life in which there was a pitiful dearth
of distraction from her pain and isolation, Ada acknowledged that
she remained 'very far' from any condition that could in any way
be described as happiness.

Arabella Lawrence had known about Ada ever since she despatched young Miss Lamont to Kirkby Mallory as a governess, back
in the summer of 1821. Now, visiting Mortlake during her holiday
breaks, Lawrence was quick to realise that her pupil disliked rules
and thrived upon imaginative stories. History was consequently
taught, not by rote, but according to whichever period Ada might
suddenly find appealing. Debate was never discouraged. Laughing
at her own 'disputation habits', Ada blamed her relish for a good

---

* Flora's father was one of Lady Byron's closest friends and advisors. He was
among the initial three trustees she later appointed to protect her personal papers
from scrutiny. On his death, Mr Davison was replaced in that role by Henry
Bathurst.

argument on 'the quiet & unvaried life I have necessarily led for the last year and a half'.

But Lady Byron worried about such capriciousness. Constantly peering over Ada's shoulder, while adding comments to the young invalid's pencil-written letters, she asked Miss Lawrence to help her to control this argumentative tendency in her daughter. It came (she felt) too close to disrespect. Ada continued to tease. How restful it would be over the holidays with Miss Lawrence to decide everything for her, she wrote: 'it will be so nice ... and I shall have no trouble in making up my mind about anything'.

It was while her daughter was still bedridden that Annabella decided to introduce Ada to her father's poems. A first copy of every new poem and play her husband produced had been provided to Lady Byron by John Murray (at her own request) every year since 1816. The works she chose to read aloud to the poet's own child upon this momentous occasion were strangely chosen. 'Fare Thee Well' was understandable, as were the romantic lines about Greece which Lady Byron selected from *The Giaour*. But why would Annabella have singled out 'The Satire', Byron's vicious demolition of their old family friend, Mrs Clermont, for the ears of his ailing and sensitive daughter?

Ada's response was disappointing. To Annabella (who loved to write verse herself), all the glory of her late husband lay within his work. To Ada, while she expressed polite enthusiasm for *The Giaour*, Byron's enchantment derived entirely from his legend. The father she already admired was the glowing hero of the 'hidden' portrait (that shrouded image behind its alluringly mysterious green curtain): an image of which only her mother seemed to imagine that an inquisitive and intelligent girl of fourteen might remain unaware.

Lord Byron was much in Annabella's thoughts in 1830. Thomas Moore's newly published *Letters and Journals of Lord Byron: with Notices of his Life* had done no favours to Byron's widow. But what distressed Annabella most was Moore's assumption (it was based upon his subject's own notoriously volatile letters) that the Byron couple's separation had been arranged and controlled by Annabella's parents. Lady Byron's dignified response was bound – with the consent of John Murray, Moore's publisher – into the second edition of Moore's book. Her 'Remarks' included a letter from Stephen Lushington, in which the now-eminent lawyer stated that it had been Lady Byron's own account, not that of her parents, which had led him to advise her against a marital reconciliation.

What hovered, unspoken, behind the careful phrases in a letter from Lushington which Annabella had solicited and personally revised, was the question of what it had been, precisely, that Lady Byron had divulged to him. Annabella would never publicly accuse her sister-in-law of incest. She must have been aware, nevertheless, that by including Lushington's letter within the 'Remarks', she was giving new life to a half-forgotten but deliciously scandalous tale.

Towards the memory of Byron himself, Annabella remained supportive and loyal. On 2 August 1831, she revealed to Robert Noel her plans to send his younger brother Edward out to Greece. The connection was never explicitly stated, but it is clear that, by purchasing from its Turkish owner a 15,000-acre estate on Euboea (modern Evia), where Edward and a German friend intended to set up a school on the Hofwyl model, Lady Byron was following what she believed would have been her late husband's wishes. Byron would have applauded the establishing of a family connection to Greece (one which survives until this day).*

෴

'The vagrant is located at last. I have bought Mr Duval's house,' Annabella announced to Harriet Siddons on 29 August 1831. Duval's home was Fordhook, a gentrified and bay-windowed farmhouse in which the novelist Henry Fielding had once lived. Situated amidst flat fields to the east of Ealing Common, Fordhook was conveniently close to Acton Lodge (where Mary Montgomery frequently visited her brother Hugh).

Dr Fellenberg's renowned school had not done quite so well by

---

* The Noel-Bakers are landowners in modern Evia.

the temperamental Edward Noel as Lady Byron had hoped, but Annabella still chose the Swiss establishment for her model as she moved on from making loans to the co-operative schools which focussed on technical education for the poor, to set up her own new school at Ealing. The difference that set Annabella's project apart from the co-operatives, from Hofwyl and even from the school (one she greatly admired) set up at Cheam in 1826 by Dr Charles Mayo and his sister, was the focus upon constant occupation, and upon character development rather than any religious doctrine. It was one of the most remarkable features of Lady Byron's educational system that it was open to all creeds, or even none.

Ealing Grove was a bold venture, one which would become Lady Byron's most influential educational monument. There were many teething problems, especially with finding the right headmaster and with administering a pioneering allotment scheme that enabled the poorest pupils to pay their modest fees by selling produce that they themselves had grown. By 1836, however, Joanna Baillie was impressed by the spectacle of sixty attentive and happy pupils. Other educationalists began paying visits to Ealing, to learn from Lady Byron's success.

Sixteen years later, writing to a new friend, Dr Elizabeth Blackwell, Annabella explained that her project had simply been to offer a basic education, sound morals and clear personal goals to children who would always have to earn their own keep in life.

Today, this sounds unremarkable. Back in the 1830s, however, Annabella's undidactic and humane approach was revolutionary. Everything about the programme of education that she described to Dr Blackwell proclaimed Lady Byron's enduring abhorrence of the English public-school system that she believed had caused such damage to her husband. The banning of any form of religious teaching headed her list of directives for a scheme in which benevolence was united with discipline.

No creed. No scripture books. No continual sedentary indoor employment. No *under*-demand on any of these faculties. No over-excitement of feelings by prizes or other

artificial stimulants. No definite boundary between work
and play, the former as much as possible a pleasure, the latter
not a contrast with lessons. No corporal punishment. No
over-legislation.

Annabella's school, despite the problem of finding male teachers
who would consent to be controlled and supervised by a formidably demanding woman, was a success. Turning to her own
daughter, however, Lady Byron sometimes forgot her policy of
making work pleasurable. Ada, it was always understood, would
not only learn, but excel. Aged fifteen, she spoke three languages.
In basic arithmetic, she was advanced for her age, but no prodigy. In her knowledge of history and current affairs, however,
coached by a mother whose knowledge of global politics had once
so impressed young George Ticknor, Ada was precociously well
informed. Granted the freedom to read as she wished during three
years of extreme ill health, her exceptional powers of imagination had also flowered, unrestrained. 'God knows I have enough
of it, and a great plague it often is,' Ada later told a mother who
possessed no imagination (and who feared its liberating powers).
A plague to its possessor, perhaps, but mathematics alone would
never have enabled Ada Lovelace to become a visionary prophet
of our own technological age.

∽∾

By the summer of 1832, while mother and daughter were still settling
into their new home at Ealing, 16-year-old Ada had recovered her
health enough to accompany Lady Byron on a first jaunt to Brighton,
favourite home of William IV, England's sea-loving king. There, at
long last, Ada was deemed well enough to indulge her cherished
childhood dream: to ride upon a horse. At the beginning of that
year, Joanna Baillie had praised Miss Byron's ability to amble upon
a docile mount across Fordhook's two outlying fields; by August, in
Brighton, Ada was able to boast to Selina Doyle's illegitimate niece,

Fanny Smith,* that both her riding-master and 'Mamma' were delighted by her equestrian progress. She could actually canter up the curving street to their hotel (Albion House in Preston Street)! What was more, she had been professionally advised that she now held her reins to perfection!

There was more. Not without triumph, Ada informed Fanny that she had just started taking guitar lessons from a Spanish count, a truly romantic exile who (so an admiring Ada thought) produced the sounds of an entire orchestra from his soulfully plucked strings.

'[T]ake care to keep strait Dear,' an anxious Lady Gosford counselled Ada on 13 September 1832. She was referring, not to Ada's riding, but to an exuberant young lady's need to be prudent.

Like many others in Lady Byron's watchful circle of female friends, Mary Gosford was reassured when she learned that Ada's new project – allegedly inspired by the allotment scheme that her mother was pioneering in Ealing – was to become a farmer. 'Mamma encourages me very much,' Ada reported to Fanny Smith. Mamma was considerably less delighted to learn from Selina Doyle, early in 1833, that her daughter's ardent interest in the Ealing allotments had become a cover for secret meetings in a Fordhook garden shed, where she exchanged passionate embraces – and something more – with a young man who had been recruited to teach Miss Byron shorthand (for taking lecture notes).† Ordered to behave herself, Ada ran away and promptly showed up at her lover's family home. His parents, fearful of angering so powerful a figure as Ada's mother, just as promptly escorted the young lady back to Fordhook.

Years later, and plainly relishing a chance to shock one of her most susceptible confidantes, Ada boasted to Mary Somerville's son

* Fanny Smith was the child of Selina Doyle's handsome second brother, Charles ('Carlo'), and an Indian begum whom he was not able to marry. Fanny had known Ada since 1828, when Miss Smith promised to practise flying with her at Bifrons. Fanny became like a second daughter to Annabella during the Fordhook years. Later, she married Edward Noel.

† The abrupt termination of William Turner's employment as a shorthand teacher suggests that he was Ada's first beau, although the culprit was never named.

that relations between the unnamed youth and herself went 'as far as they could without actual penetration [the word 'connexion' was later coyly substituted in Woronzow Greig's unpublished record] being actually completed.' Miss Byron's public disgrace had just been avoided, but enough people in Lady Byron's own social circle knew what had happened for her daughter commonly to be perceived as damaged goods.* It is noteworthy that one of the first letters Ada would one day write to her future husband thanked him for overlooking her blotted past, and for a consequent debt of gratitude 'of which I am so sure I shall never need to be reminded by you'.

'Make amends to your mother before it is too late!' Nanny Briggs scolded Ada on 6 March 1833. Two days later, Ada announced her reform to her mother by stating, with heavy underlinings, that '*I am an altered person.*'

Repentance proved shortlived. By 27 April, as a letter written a full year later reveals, Ada was already hatching plans to resume the affair.† When a scandalised and despairing Annabella announced that she herself had been appointed 'by God *forever*' to supervise and restrain her wayward daughter, Ada struck back. She was willing to be guided, but not even by divine appointment would she be governed by her mother. Writing from Brighton in May 1833, Ada set out the case for her right to be free.

I cannot consider that the parent has any right to direct the child or to expect obedience in such things as concern *the child only.* I will give a practical illustration of my meaning. [The example given was of a window to be closed in Annabella's own room by her own instructions – fair enough – or of a window in

---

* Evidence that gossip had spread appears in *The New York Mirror* of 1833, which told its readers that 'Ada Byron, the sole daughter of the "noble bard", is the most coarse and vulgar woman in England'. Small wonder that Annabella was dismayed.
† On 27 April 1834, Ada referred to her state of mind '*this very day last year –* believing myself most noble & virtuous, [while] I was made up of deceit & selfishness' (AAB to Mrs William King, 27 April 1834, Lovelace Byron Papers: the italics are my own).

Ada's chamber: unacceptable.] ... The one case concerns *you &
your comfort*, the other concerns *me only* and cannot affect or
signify to you. Do you see the line of distinction that I draw? I
have given the most familiar possible illustration, because I wish
to be as clear as possible. Till 21, the law gives you a power of
enforcing obedience on *all points*; but at that time I consider
your power and your claim to cease ...

Smart, fierce and articulate, Ada's letter marked the beginning of a
lifelong battle between two intransigent characters: an exceptionally strong-willed mother and her equally strong-willed daughter.
The letter also demonstrates that Miss Byron, now seventeen, had
developed an uncommon gift for expressing herself. This faculty, as
much as her still nascent mathematical ability, would prove crucial
to Ada's remarkable future.

∞

The stronger Ada grew (she could by now rejoice at her skill in 'leap-
ing' a horse over a gate), the more complex her relationship with
Annabella became. She had fired off her letter of teenage defiance
while consenting – as a sop to her mother – to make her first presentation curtsey in that summer of 1833 at the Brighton-based court
of William IV. Arrayed in white satin and tulle and still limping a
little as the 7th Lord Byron's wife gently shepherded her towards
the throne, Ada betrayed the same critical eye that her mother had
trained on London society when she herself first arrived there from
the north of England. Healthy enough by now to stand for fifteen
minutes – but no more – without fatigue, Miss Byron was introduced to the Duke of Orléans ('very pleasing'), to Wellington (who
passed muster) and to Talleyrand (whose face reminded her of an old
monkey). Visiting Brighton again in the autumn of 1833, a proud
Ada boasted to Fanny Smith about how warmly her mother had been
received by the royal couple. Lady Byron had actually been invited to
sit next to the queen and had conversed at length with the king, Ada

informed her friend. Dressed (so Ada bragged) in a dashingly low-cut dress of crimson brown and wearing a pale straw hat decorated with white feathers, 'my illustrious parent' had looked 'very pretty indeed'. Lady Byron herself was shyly surprised by the kindness of the welcome she had received. The king and queen had been really friendly to her, Annabella wrote with evident pleasure to Sophia Frend.

Ada's pride in her mother's warm reception did not mean that she herself had become suddenly submissive. Over a decade later, she would offer a heartfelt apology for the way she had behaved as a wilful teenager, deceiving Lady Byron about 'all my *real* feelings'. (Ruefully, she added: 'And a pretty mess I made of it.') Back in 1833, a less conscience-stricken Ada evinced every sign of becoming alarmingly uncontrollable. At the end of the year, running short of ways to rein her daughter in, an exhausted Annabella turned to religion for salvation. Perhaps contemplation of the heavens would serve to calm the rattled nerves, not only of a volatile daughter, but of a mother unsettled by the recent evidence of new and shocking misbehaviour by the erring Mrs Leigh.* By March 1834, Ada noted that her mother and she were reading together and enjoying Dr Whewell's Bridgewater Treatise. A religious interpretation of Laplace's theorising of a godless universe, Whewell's contribution to the series of treatises commissioned on his deathbed by the Earl of Bridgewater appealed greatly to Ada's growing interest in astronomy.

It was around this time that Annabella settled upon the earnest and flawlessly respectable Dr William King as that ideal tutor who might combine sober instruction in calming mathematics for her daughter with an uplifting course of religious education. Ada's response was suspiciously meek. Mrs King, who had previously been

---

* On 22 July 1833, Annabella confided to Harriet Siddons that 'Self-will has involved one to whose moral and religious welfare all my efforts have been directed, in evils of the greatest magnitude, such as must bring retribution ...' Reference to Mrs Leigh rather than to Ada's recent misdemeanours is clear from the fact that she turned calmly to Ada in the next paragraph: 'Ada is quite well. We shall move soon ...' It remains unclear what Augusta Leigh had done to incur Lady Byron's wrath on this particular occasion (HRC, bound vol. 1, Byron Collection).

shocked to hear about Miss Byron's Ealing romance, was demurely informed by her husband's new pupil that religion was having an excellent effect. Ada took such comfort from the 'pleasant walks' and interesting discussions she had been experiencing with kind Dr King. She was absorbing his wise advice about controlling her imagination. She was so truly grateful for his thoughtful care.

Evidence that Ada was receiving instruction from somebody with a far livelier mind than Dr King began to appear that spring. On 15 March 1834, while reading Whewell and being urged by Dr King to lift up her thoughts unto God, Ada wrote to consult her mother's old tutor, William Frend, about rainbows.

Dogmatic though Frend could be upon certain topics – he had controversial views on algebra and rejected the idea of negative numbers – he had never underrated Ada's capacity to look at life from original angles. Her new preoccupation concerned prismatic light. 'I cannot make out one thing at all,' Ada wrote to his London home in Gower Street, 'viz: why a rainbow always appears to the spectator to be an arc of a circle. Why is it a curve at all, and why a circle rather than any other curve?' Sadly, Frend's response to an intriguing but not unanswerable question is not preserved.*

It was precisely this enterprising, inquisitive aspect of Ada's mind that Dr King had been urged to harness. A careful examination of the lengthy and seemingly dutiful letter Ada wrote to him on 9 March that year should have warned the earnest cleric that he was on a hiding to nothing. Ada was perfectly aware that mathematics had been singled out by her mother as a means to shackle her unruly mind. Here, however, she gave a completely different reason for her interest in the subject. 'My wish is to make myself well acquainted with Astronomy, Optics & c,' Ada explained to her well-meaning instructor, 'but I find I cannot study these satisfactorily for want of a thorough acquaintance with the elementary parts of Mathematics.'

---

* The higher the sun, the more of a rainbow's circle do we perceive. At a certain height, where the horizon presents no cut-off, the whole circle (caused by varied wavelengths of light being refracted off raindrops) becomes visible.

Mathematics, in fact, was perceived by Ada as a crucial stepping stone on an adventurous journey not into the conventional world of Dr King's theology, but into the mysterious realm of physics.

Ada already possessed a skill with words that enabled her to encircle, bewilder and trounce poor Dr King. While sweetly assenting to the prudence of controlling that dangerous imagination of hers, Miss Byron invited him to consider the worrying vacancy that might be created by the sudden extinction of any source of excitement. How fortunate that science offered a better solution – as she was about to explain:

> [For] nothing but *very close & intense* application to subjects
> of a scientific nature now seems to keep my imagination from
> running wild, or to stop up the void which seems to be left in
> my mind from a want of excitement. I am most thankful that
> this strong source of interest does seem to be supplied to me
> now almost providentially, & think it a duty vigorously to use
> the resources thus as it were pointed out to me.

And on Ada smoothly passed, requesting Dr King to be so gracious as to counsel her as to the best '*plan*' of study: 'I may say that I have *time* at my command, & that I am willing to take *any* trouble.' Dr King, in short, was to advise, but not control. His pupil would herself make the final decision about what she wished to learn from him. As to the ultimate purpose of her researches, she would keep that secret to herself.

Ada's reference to her new and unexpected access to 'subjects of a scientific nature' held the clue – had Dr King been able to follow it – to what had happened. In February that year, she had found a new and sympathetic mentor in her mother's friend Mary Somerville, a slight, smiling, pink-cheeked Scotswoman who was recognised to be one of the most brilliant expositors of science in England. The following month, Ada – for once, without her mother – attended a party held at the London home of one of Mary Somerville's closest friends. His name was Charles Babbage.

CHAPTER TWELVE

MATHEMATICAL FRIENDSHIPS
(1834–5)

Twelve years older than Lady Byron, Mary Somerville was fifty-four when Ada first visited the damp little house beside Chelsea Hospital where the Somerville family had resided, on and off, for the past fifteen years. Here, having recently returned from a heady year of being fêted in Paris, Mrs Somerville offered her young friend a friendly home into which Ada happily settled almost as an adopted daughter. For Mary's own two girls, Martha and Mary, the arrival of an eager disciple of mathematics offered a blessed release. Time spent in explaining propositions to Ada meant liberty for these sprightly and resolutely unmathematical young ladies to go and polish up their dance steps for a quadrille.

Known in her teens as 'The Rose of Jedburgh', Mary Somerville's still-glowing cheeks and a fondness for brightly coloured clothes (she sometimes wore an orange kimono) caused the less discerning to underrate her extraordinary mind. Ada never doubted that she had been introduced to a genius, while others sometimes found it difficult to equate Mrs Somerville's formidable intelligence with her cheerful social manner. Encountering Mrs Somerville only at the dances which her daughters were attending, the Irish novelist Lady Morgan decided she resembled 'one of the respectable twaddling chaperones one meets with at every ball, dressed in a snug mulberry velvet gown and a little cap with a red flower'. Maria Edgeworth was predictably more discerning. Writing to her mother on 17 January 1832, at the height of Mrs Somerville's fame, Maria expressed admiration for her absolute lack of pretension: 'while her head is among the stars her feet are firm upon the ground'.

The journey to international celebrity had not been easy. Brought up in the Scottish Borders by parents who disapproved of educated women, Miss Somerville taught herself mathematics by reading Euclid under the bedclothes. Other than her brief attendance of a school, her grasp of the subject was facilitated by a sympathetic brother who gave her access both to his textbooks and his tutors. The long absences at sea of her first husband (Samuel Greig was a naval officer) enabled Mary to continue with her studies while bringing up two children.

Widowed at twenty-seven, Mary remarried in 1812, when she was thirty-two. She found in her cousin William Somerville a devoted husband who revered his wife's exceptional mind.* Tall, kindly and self-effacing, Dr Somerville shared in Mary's pride when, twenty years later, the great educationalist Lord Brougham finally provided Jedburgh's 'Rose' with the chance to flower into full bloom.

That opportunity was an invitation to translate into English the recently deceased Marquis de Laplace's five-volume *Mécanique céleste*, a detailed and complex analysis of the movements of the planets in the light of Newton's gravitational theory. It's possible that Brougham had been prompted by Laplace himself. Mary and her husband were fond of telling the story of how France's homegrown Newton, praising the only three women clever enough to under-stand his writings, had identified just two: Caroline Herschel, Mrs

---

* Expounding upon Italian painting to a septuagenarian Mrs Somerville in the 1850s, the art historian Anna Jameson was silenced with a scowl: 'Mrs Somerville,' Mary's husband informed their loquacious visitor, 'had rather talk about science than art.' Dr Somerville's irritation was understandable: his wife was attempting to conduct a conversation with another visitor. Maria Mitchell, America's first professional woman astronomer, had come to pay her respects (H. V. Morton, *A Traveller in Italy* (Methuen, 1964), pp. 482–4).

Somerville – and, a little comically, a certain 'Mrs Greig, of whom I know nothing'. Published by John Murray in 1831, Somerville's translation achieved the challenging task of simplifying Laplace's often almost impenetrable text, while adding to it in a way that arguably surpassed the original.

The Laplace translation won Mrs Somerville the admiration of the scientific world. In 1834, the year that Ada became her protégée, the 54-year-old mathematician was about to publish a work of her own. *On the Connexion of the Physical Sciences* confirmed Mary Somerville as one of the most brilliant minds of her time: a mathematician who could effortlessly explain the newest ideas about astronomy, electricity, time, motion, light and even music. Nobody, with the possible exception of Somerville's close friend Michael Faraday, had such a gift for putting difficult ideas into simple language. It was a technique that Ada would absorb and put to powerful use.

It was not Somerville's unabashed femininity, but the plain fact that she was not a man that caused her still to be undervalued in England. Back in 1829, she had been hailed by an admiring fellow Scot, Sir David Brewster, as 'the most extraordinary woman in Europe, a mathematician of the very first rank'. In 1835, the year after Ada began paying regular visits to her home, Mrs Somerville joined Caroline Herschel as one of the first two women to become honorary fellows of the Royal Astronomical Society. (Women – with the exception of Queen Victoria – were not permitted full fellowship until 1945.) It was Mrs Somerville's marble bust that greeted the gentlemen members of the Royal Society as they walked into the entrance hall of that illustrious building. The lady herself was forbidden entry.

∽∾

Mrs Somerville, when Mary Montgomery first brought Ada Byron to her home in February 1834, had been feeling wistful. Her Chelsea riverside home was damp and chilly enough to make her yearn to be settled back in the heart of London. (William Somerville had taken on a dull job at the Chelsea Hospital only after a cousin cheated the couple out of their hard-won savings.) For Mary, Ada was not only a beguilingly eager pupil, but a breath of fresh air. Woronzow Greig, the son of Mrs Somerville's first marriage, remembered Miss Byron as pale, plump and shy. Alone with Mrs Somerville, however, Ada became confident and demonstrative. 'Ada was much attached to me,' Mrs Somerville would later recall, adding with evident pride that 'it was by my advice that she studied mathematics'.

The claim was not precisely true. It was an anxious mother who had first steered Ada towards what was intended to be only a calming discipline; Mary Montgomery had taken the next step of finding her a superlative teacher. What nobody anticipated was that Ada would take to mathematics with such relish, displaying an eager determination to master and understand whatever she was shown. 'She always wrote to me for an explanation,' Mrs Somerville remembered; like Dr King, the kindly Scotswoman urged her impetuous pupil to proceed with care. By 24 March, Ada was boasting to Dr King that she had learned 'to imagine to myself a figure in the air, and go through the construction & demonstration without any book or assistance whatsoever'. It was a typically exuberant claim from a young woman who was still working her way through the second book of Euclid.

Ada's enthusiasm appeared to be boundless. Returning to his orderly home on Regency Square in Brighton from an exhausting April fortnight in the company of Miss Byron and her mother at the spa town of Tunbridge Wells, poor Dr King was thankful to escape his protégée's endless interrogations and demands. 'You must *trammel* your mind . . .' he warned, while urging her to calm herself with soothing readings from William Whewell. If Ada ignored the worthy Dr King's advice, her excitement was understandable. By the time of her visit to Tunbridge, she had met Charles Babbage twice and been introduced to his remarkable, albeit unfinished, machine.

꩜

The second and more significant introduction to Babbage had been brought about by Mary Montgomery. Miss Montgomery deserves more credit than she has received for the formative role she played in Ada Byron's life. An invalid herself, she understood better than most the hunger Ada felt for all the experiences of which three semi-bedridden years had deprived her. An alert, clever and empathetic woman, Mary was on friendly terms with many of the giants of London's leading intellectual circles. It was she who provided Ada with her entrée to the world that opened her eyes to an imaginable future.

The word 'scientist' was first coined by William Whewell for his anonymous and laudatory review of Mary Somerville's *On the Connexion of the Physical Sciences* in April 1834. The study of science was already in the air and Ada, guided by Mary Montgomery, was escorted to the lecture rooms of London at which the latest inventions and ideas were being displayed and discussed. At the Royal Institution, Ada attended the thrillingly eloquent and vivid lectures of Michael Faraday. Beneath the domed roof of the Surrey Institution at Blackfriars, she listened to talks about geology, chemistry and natural philosophy. Respectably chaperoned by the indefatigable Miss Montgomery (an 18-year-old with the notorious surname of Byron could never have gone alone), she entered the wonderful circus of scientific entertainments on the Strand that had recently been named in honour of William IV's royal spouse (despite the fact that Queen Adelaide never passed its doors).

Ada must have adored her visits to the Adelaide. Here, shortly after it first opened its doors in 1832, visitors could watch a Jacquard loom weaving intricate designs by the use of hole-punched cards, before admiring the acrobatic dances of Thalia, an infant prodigy, who performed beneath the floating bulk of a tethered gas balloon. Electrical displays involving Leyden jars and numerous magnets dazzled the gallery-goers with showers of fiery sparks. A central canal – broad enough for Thomas Telford to conduct experiments with his new steamboat paddles – bestowed an unexpected touch of serenity on this palace of educational delights.

But the ever-helpful Miss Montgomery had further tricks up her sleeve. Some of the most interesting scientific discussions in London at that time took place within the drawing rooms of private houses. In the same month as Ada's introduction to Mrs Somerville, Mary took her into the home of Roderick Murchison, where fireside debates about geology were raising questions about the divine versus the natural order of the world. (Lady Murchison's interest in fossils had led to her husband's identification – while walking in Wales – of an ancient and largely aquatic period of the earth's history that Sir Roderick named the Silurian Age.) But the introduction through which Mary Montgomery made her biggest contribution to Ada's life came a month later.

On 19 March 1834, Miss Montgomery took Ada to dine with the Murchisons before conducting her to a house on Dorset Street, just off Manchester Square. It was here, in his private London home, that Charles Babbage held his famous Saturday soirées. While excited and doubtless intrigued (Mr Babbage's parties were celebrated for the extraordinary range of guests that they attracted), Ada had no idea that she was about to encounter a mind that was every bit as enquiring, lively and playfully capricious as her own.

∽✧∾

Born into wealth, Charles Babbage was one year older than Ada's mother. Like Ada, he had suffered from a long period of illness during his youth. Like her again, he had early discovered himself to be both inventive and ambitious. Ada had wanted to use a steam-powered Pegasus for her proposed flights about the world. Babbage had attempted to walk on water (using home-made paddleboards to cross Devon's River Dart). Further signs that Babbage would follow no conventionally charted path emerged during university. At Cambridge, he was punished for defending a supposedly blasphemous thesis. Forbidden to sit a formal exam, the brilliant young mathematician graduated without honours.

Aged twenty-one when he married in 1812 and settled in Marylebone, Babbage suffered bitter disappointment when he was refused a mathematics chair at Edinburgh in 1819 (it went instead to a Scotsman, William Wallace). Instead, Babbage spent part of the following year in helping his friend John Herschel to found the Royal Astronomical Society. It was while working with Herschel on various mathematical tables that Babbage dreamed up the idea of a steam-powered computing machine. If his contraption worked, it would simplify the process – and reduce the chances of error – in a core aspect of what was needed for the nation's military and industrial success.

This was where Babbage's travails as an inventor had begun. By 1823, the British government had been persuaded to invest in the ingenious new calculating engine.* Ten years later, an official fireproof room had been expensively constructed within government-owned property to house a machine that remained incomplete. 'The logarithmetical Frankenstein' was one journalist's sneering put-down for the creator of a half-finished monster.

The construction of Babbage's ambitious device had offered the inventor welcome distraction during a bleak period in his life. In 1827, Babbage lost a son, a daughter, his father and his wife. Leaving his surviving children in the care of his mother, the widower set off for Europe, to discuss his project with such eminent figures as Laplace and von Humboldt. Interest on the Continent proved encouragingly strong. Back home, however, the British government was in no hurry to invest further sums in a machine that still remained incomplete. The chances of its being finished did not improve when Babbage's master craftsman, Joseph Clement, responded to criticisms for overspending by withdrawing the expensive precision tools which he, as a professional craftsman, owned and without which the miraculous Difference Engine could not be

---

* Both Pascal and Leibniz had produced forms of calculating machines over a hundred years earlier, but those mechanical devices were intended to perform specific arithmetical tasks, and were operated by hand. Babbage's machine, operating autonomously, was designed to produce a long series of numbers from the setting of a very limited number, functioning upon the repeated use of differences. Most importantly, it was designed to print out the result.

built. Babbage's pleas for more backing from the government were rejected. (It didn't help that Babbage was a witty but lethally tactless man: Thomas Carlyle did not forgive the inventor's pointed vote of thanks to him for treating his fellow dinner guests to an interminable lecture on the merits of silence.)

By 1833, matters had stalled in a deadly stalemate. A government representative pointed out that two British battleships could have been built for the £15,000 that had already been loaned to Mr Babbage. The embittered inventor retorted that he had invested more than twice that amount himself, subsidising an invention which – unlike James Watt's steam engine – had been developed without any prototype, as the production of a single brilliant mind: his own.

The plain fact was that by the beginning of 1834, Babbage's glorious machine remained unbuilt. Only a tiny portion of his projected invention was on display for potential investors to inspect on the night (19 March 1834) when Ada paid a second visit to the inventor's Dorset Street home.

∞

Beauty, rank or intellect were declared by the attractive second wife of one scientist (Andrew Crosse) to be the sole criteria for joining Mr Babbage's Saturday soirées. Wealth – enough to fund an unbuilt machine – was an asset that could buy anyone a ticket of entrance. Ada, bright, aristocratic and appealingly youthful, was the only child of a woman widely known to be immensely rich.

Eager to please, Babbage began by introducing one arresting young woman to another: the expressive-eyed and attitude-striking 'Silver Lady', who balanced an animated bird upon her outstretched fingers, was a gleaming automaton that he had rescued from destruction and painstakingly repaired for display as an amusing curiosity. Did Miss Byron wish to guess which turban the Lady would wear for the next soirée? (Babbage strove to amuse his favoured female guests by making small changes in the Lady's attire.) But Ada – to the inventor's astonishment – showed no interest in her host's pretty automaton. All she cared about was the neatly clicking combination of wheels and cogs tucked away within Mr Babbage's back-room sanctum.

Ada's evident preference for a piece of machinery to a pretty automaton seemed remarkable to those who witnessed her March visit to Babbage's home. Sophia Frend later described how, 'young as she was', Ada had immediately grasped the concept of its operation. More importantly, with an intuitive appreciation of what was to come, she instantly saw 'the great beauty of the invention'.

March 1834 marked the birth of Ada's deep interest in Charles Babbage and his work. In June, she attended a lecture in which Dr Dionysius Lardner stressed the urgent need for funds to complete Babbage's remarkable machine. Nevertheless, credit is also due to Lady Byron who – during the very difficult summer that followed upon her daughter's attempted elopement – had herself conducted Ada on a brief visit to Dorset Street. It may have been during this earlier visit, paid in June 1833, that an attentive Sophia Frend was struck by the young girl's interest in engineering. Mary Somerville had been more interested in hearing Lady Byron's views – and Annabella (expressing her opinion that June to both Mrs Somerville and Dr King) did not disappoint her.

> We both went to see the *thinking* machine (for so it seems) last Monday. It raised several Nos. to the 2nd and 3rd Powers, and extracted the root of a quadratic equation – I had but faint glimpses of the principles by which it worked. [Babbage had explained its ability to count regularly to 10,000.] There was a sublimity in the views thus opened of the ultimate results of intellectual power.

Clearly, Annabella had grasped the machine's capabilities. Nevertheless, the praises which Mrs Somerville lavished that summer upon the really exceptional elegance of dear Lady Byron's own wonderful understanding of the Difference Engine were suspiciously obsequious. Mrs Somerville was a good friend to Babbage and she knew the financial quandary in which he was trapped. Quite possibly, she was flattering someone whom she thought might be persuaded to invest in the unfinished machine. Mary Somerville was not lacking in guile.

∽✧∾

Ada had inherited two of her father's most dangerous qualities: changeability and the ability to manufacture a persona. The Ada who wrote to Dr King and Mary Somerville that summer of 1834 was entirely under the spell of Charles Babbage's machine. 'I am afraid that when a machine, or a lecture, or anything of the kind, come[s] in my way, I have no regard for time, space or any other ordinary obstacles,' Ada wrote to Mary Somerville on 8 July.

Lady Byron, knowing her daughter better, remained sceptical about the depth of Ada's new passion. On 26 May, for the second year running, Annabella had asked Harriet Siddons's brother-in-law, Andrew Combe, to provide her with a phrenological reading of Ada's skull. For the second time, Combe's reading confirmed Lady Byron's fears: her daughter's intelligence was considerable, but it was of an impetuous and wilful kind. Writing to her 'dearest kitten' (Harriet Siddons's daughter, Lizzie) that summer, Annabella sighed that Ada's mercurial mind had already darted off in a new direction. 'Ada does not think anything the world offers worth trouble, except Music.'

Lady Byron was right. The harp – much admired at that time for its romantic ability to reveal the player's soul through the rippled communion of fingertips and vibrating strings – was the latest object to have caught fickle Ada's fancy. Who knew what might come next?

Music had never interested Lady Byron. Towards the end of July, she decided to revive Ada's interest in figures by a statistics-seeking tour of England's factories. In 1832, Charles Babbage had written a hard-nosed study of industry and its time use. *On the Economy of Machinery and Manufactures* (a book which helped to inspire Dickens's creation of Mr Gradgrind) had won its author considerable respect in the world of commerce. It was Lady Byron's intention to introduce her impulsive daughter to a real-world context against which Ada might more accurately evaluate the worth of Mr Babbage's unbuilt Difference Engine.

Officially, the 1834 tour took mother and daughter to observe spar-cutting at Ashby, ribbon manufacture at Coventry and the operation of Jacquard looms at a Matlock mill. (Here, Annabella demonstrated her own keen interest in technology by making a careful drawing of one of the machine's innovative punch cards.) In Staffordshire, where they inspected the roaring furnaces and kilns of Stoke-on-Trent, the travellers stayed with Florence Nightingale's parents. A visit to Doncaster was entirely unconnected to the town's celebrated racecourse. Unlike her sporting parents, Lady Byron detested racing. 'The risk to man and beast – the desperate gambling among the spectators – the futility of the object – press upon my mind in a painful manner,' she wrote in an undated letter to Mrs Siddons.

Unofficially, the tour enabled Lady Byron to make a quiet evaluation of her daughter's state of mind. Writing to Harriet Siddons from Harrogate, Annabella sounded reassured. The worries of 1833 were at last beginning to recede, she remarked in an oblique reference to Ada's attempted elopement with William Turner. As Ada grew calmer, her mother's own health began to improve. 'I feel my intellect reviving . . .'

Ada's own skittishly active mind required livelier fodder than factory inspections. Yawning her way through a sleepy summer month at Buxton Spa in the company of Lady Gosford and her daughters, she decided to pass on some of her newfound mathematical knowledge to the countess's eldest child. While Olivia Acheson, Lady Gosford's younger daughter, was humoured with affectionate notes about ponies and cats ('Livy' had inherited the now venerable Puff), her older sister Lady Annabella ('my dear little Friend') was treated to a gruelling course in Euclid. Trying to encourage a reluctant pupil ('You are going on as well as possible'), Ada could not resist the temptation to lecture.

My dear Annabella. You must pardon my scolding! You know
as a master, I am bound to tell truth! After studying your
Prop[osition] for some time, I have come to this conclusion:
either that you do not understand what you have written about,
or that if you do understand, you certainly have not *expressed*
your meaning. So try again, and do not be at all discouraged,
for it requires much practice to explain with clearness, & I
assure you *I* was *not* '*born*' with the power ... attend to my
orders pray. Let me hear as soon as you can.

Poor little Annabella; it was patently a relief when her stern
teacher turned to the less taxing subject of music, begging the
Acheson girls to look out for a harp in the attics of Worlingham, the
charming Norfolk house where they now spent most of each year,
together with Lady Gosford. Lady Byron had not been exaggerating
her daughter's passion for music: 'I am now so excessively fond of
my harp & my hour's practice,' Ada informed her small pupil, 'that
it is a much greater merit in me not to practice for three hours a day,
than it is to practice steadily for one.'

Keen to mentor, Ada knew herself to be still essentially a beginner.
While delivering a course that she spoke of publishing as a mathematical correspondence (in the style of Jane Marcet's educational
conversation books), Ada paid acknowledgement to the patience
of her own tutors: 'indeed I think I *am* making great progress,'
she advised little Annabella from Fordhook on 26 November. 'Mr
Babbage and Mrs Somerville are very kind indeed to me. The latter
generally enquires with interest "how my pupil" is going on.'

It must have been an urgent need for medical attention (Lady
Byron had fallen into one of her recurrent declines in health) that
caused a temporary move from Fordhook to a house in Wimpole
Street in the autumn of 1834. It was during this time that Ada found
herself present at a couple of remarkable conversations between
Charles Babbage and Mary Somerville.

Hot competition from the harp had not lessened Ada's enthusiasm
for Babbage's invention. On 1 September, she rapturously described

it to Dr King as 'a gem of all mechanism'. By November, she was copying out some of Babbage's notes and even borrowing some of the plans for his Engine from his son, Herschel. (Herschel was his father's chief draughtsman.) On 28 November, Ada sat in on a discussion between Babbage and Mrs Somerville about the straitened inventor's lack of financial backing and Babbage's fears that Robert Peel, the new prime minister, would do even less for him than Peel's predecessor, the Duke of Wellington. (Babbage was correct.) The fact that this information went straight back to Wimpole Street, where Annabella carefully recorded it, suggests that the ever-prudent Lady Byron was still weighing up the merits of herself investing in Mr Babbage's ill-fated Engine.

On 15 December, Ada returned to Wimpole Street with far more exciting news. That night, her mother's diary recorded a thrilling discovery that Babbage had made. It was 'in the highest department of mathematics – I understand it to include the means of solving equations that hitherto had been considered insoluble'.

Frustratingly, we don't know precisely what the conversation had involved. Just possibly, Ada had witnessed Babbage's long-nourished plans for a contraption which would perform more complex tasks than Difference Engine 1 (which could most simply be described as a long line of gears designed to produce a calculated figure). That autumn, or so Babbage latterly recalled in his autobiography, plans had been drawn up from the inventor's own notoriously messy diagrams for machinery that would enable the final figure to be fed back into the Engine, ready for further calculations. Such a machine would – in Babbage's later and splendidly graphic term – be capable of 'eating its own tail'.* Lady Byron was herself a forward-looking

---

* The curious expression 'eating its own tail' can be applied both to the Analytical Engine, a model of which is currently being built in the UK, and to Difference Engine 2, of which a model is on display in the Mathematics Gallery at London's Science Museum. While plans were allegedly being drawn for the Analytical Engine during the autumn of 1834, mathematicians and computer scientists incline to believe that Babbage was discussing Difference Engine 2 with Mrs Somerville. My suggestion that it could have been the Analytical Engine is, perhaps, wishful thinking.

woman who took a keen interest in technology and who was surprisingly open to new ideas. (During her autumn at Wimpole Street, she wrote a poem in which God the Father was boldly replaced by a maternal deity.) But Annabella had her limits. While Ada waxed ecstatic about the possibilities that Babbage's conversation with Mrs Somerville had unfolded to her own imaginative mind, Lady Byron briskly rejected this first intimation of the machine that we know today as Babbage's Analytical Engine. His new idea, so she firmly noted, was 'unsound'.

✆

Annabella's ongoing fears about her excitable daughter's capacity for mental strain proved justified. In February 1835, Mrs Somerville wrote – mother to mother – to ask if it were better that the lessons should stop. During her last visit, Ada had passed from evident fatigue to extreme agitation. Her face had undergone a curious change.* Anxiously, Mrs Somerville hoped that she herself had not been pushing Miss Byron beyond her capabilities.

Mrs Somerville remembered all too well the tragic death of her own firstborn daughter, aged only twelve, under circumstances of excessive academic pressure. But Ada now intervened, imploring Mrs Somerville not to abandon her. She was not ill, she pleaded, only nervous and frightened, and more now at the prospect of losing such a treasured friend:

> In a few weeks I dare say I shall be quite strong (particularly
> if I see a good deal of you). When I am weak, I am always
> so exceedingly terrified, *at nobody knows what*, that I can
> hardly help having an agitated look & manner, & this was the
> case when I left you. – I do not know how I can ever repay or
> acknowledge all your kindness, unless by trying to be a very

---

* This reference to a startlingly altered face crops up again and again in Ada's later medical history. See the appendix on Ada's health on pp. 475–6.

good little girl & showing that I profit by your excellent advice.
I feel that you are indeed a very sincere friend, & this makes me
very happy I assure you.

Ada's plea was effective. Her dreaded banishment did not take
place; instead, a change of pace and scenery was briskly enforced.
In April 1835, Ada wrote to Mrs Somerville from Brighton, where
she was enjoying daily visits to a nearby riding school. Riding – and
especially soaring over a delicious little jump – was the best exercise imaginable, a newly ebullient Ada declared, 'even better than
waltzing'. As for mathematics, she was prepared to slow down: 'I
have made up my mind not to care at present about making much
progress, but to take it very quietly ...'

Ada kept her word. The subject of mathematics was not raised
again until the autumn of 1835.

By the autumn of 1835, however, a great change had taken place.
The worryingly unconventional Miss Ada Byron had become an
outwardly most respectable married woman.

CHAPTER THIRTEEN

ADA'S MARRIAGE
(1835–40)

By the spring of 1835, when Ada had just turned nineteen, Mrs Somerville regarded her almost as a daughter, a substitute for her first and long-departed child. Mary was well aware of Ada's intense but mercurial nature and her delicate physical health. (The two were, as she soon realised, closely entwined.) Mrs Somerville also knew how profoundly anxious Lady Byron was about her only child, and how fearful for her reputation.

If only a husband could be found for the young woman, some special man who would cherish and understand this rare, eccentric girl. But where was a mother to find such a paragon? Annabella had not taken to the smoothly eligible youths who swarmed around her daughter in the year of Ada's debut at court. Ada, to be fair, had not helped herself. An engaging lack of concern for how she dressed attracted censorious comment. The folly of her runaway affair had caused a scandal, whispers of which had even crossed the Atlantic. Her enthusiasms – whether for maths, for riding, or for music – were always too fervent and extreme. Clearly not cut out to become a bishop's wife or even a conventionally well-behaved lady of the manor, Miss Byron now stood in real danger of joining Mary Montgomery, relegated in her maturity to the position of a clever semi-invalid, one who was forever socially dependent upon the indulgent care of understanding friends.

Such a future was not the one that any loving mother would wish upon her child. It was then with real pride, if not relief, that Mary Somerville identified a man who seemed (at least, in the opinion of her own son) to be the ideal candidate for Ada's hand. His name was Lord King. He had for some time lived abroad, remote from spiteful gossip about Ada's misdemeanour. Better still, Lord King was utterly captivated by the legendary figure of Lord Byron.

Woronzow Greig, Mary's son, had become acquainted with the reclusive and intelligent William King in the mid-1820s, when both young men were being tutored by William Whewell at Trinity, the former college of Byron himself. Stories of the poet's wild exploits, his brilliance and his eccentricity still abounded at Trinity in 1824, the year of Byron's tragically premature death. It was not by chance that Lord King, after leaving Cambridge, took up an invitation to work as secretary to his cousin and fellow-Byronist, Lord Nugent, High Commissioner of the Ionian Islands that Byron had visited during his doomed journey to Greece. There, living on Corfu while he saturated himself in Byron's poetry, William commissioned a portrait of himself in full Byronic mode.

A brocaded Ionian costume and fez cap failed to bestow quite such an aura of panache upon William King as had the dashing Albanian turban donned by Byron for Thomas Phillips's famous portrait (the one that had officially been hidden from view behind its own green curtain throughout Ada's youth). But William King's intense sense of identification would never wane. One of his first actions after returning to England in 1833 had been to rename the fields of his newly inherited Surrey estate after his hero's poems. The map still exists on which the new names are carefully penned in: Lara's Field, Corsair's Field, Ali's Field, Harold's Meadow, Chillon. All that was missing from this exoticised landscape was the ultimate connection to Lord Byron himself: the intimate link that only Ada Byron herself could provide.

William King had grown up in the expectation of becoming a grand landowner. The King family possessed large estates in Surrey and North Somerset, to which his mother, Lady Hester Fortescue, had added her own West Country domains and considerable personal wealth. It's unlikely that William's father had meant to cause difficulties for his heir when he made his wife the interim beneficiary of his will. William certainly foresaw no trouble when he wrote home from Corfu on 29 June 1833 that – following the news of his father's untimely death, aged fifty-seven – he intended Lady Hester and his four siblings to lack for nothing in the future. William was aware that his mother preferred her second son, Locke. (Peter Locke King's middle name honoured John Locke, the most famous of the family's ancestors.) Nevertheless, so William assured Lady Hester, 'nothing shall be wanting on my part to you and for you ... to meet all your wishes will always be my first duty's pleasure'.

William was in for a shock. Reaching home two weeks later, he discovered that Lady Hester was making full use of her new powers. Locke had already been granted an extensive portion of the King estate in Surrey. In the West Country, while William was permitted to retain the steep and wooded hillside enclosing his father's hunting lodge above Porlock, Locke had been given the giant's share. William had scarcely set his foot within Ockham Park, the King family's principal home near Guildford, when Lady Hester had it gutted. The furniture, as she barely troubled to explain, would be divided between 38 Dover Street, the Kings' London residence (it was now to become her personal domain) and Woburn Park, the new Surrey mansion in which Locke King, together with two of his three young sisters, Hester and Charlotte, were to live as their mother's companions. (A third and mentally impaired daughter, Emily, was packed off to London to act as a companion to 'Aunt Lucy', an elderly relative who was eking out an existence in Charlotte Street and to whom, when Lady Hester deigned to remember, she would grudgingly send money for coals and rent.)

It's an awful story and there's little room for doubt that Lady Hester was an awful woman. Every year, with tenacious glee, she once more wrote out a new will in which she once again bestowed the generous sum of just ten pounds upon her eldest son. (Seeking to justify her abominable treatment of William, his mother once drafted a letter in which she said that he intimidated her by asking difficult questions and that she would fear being alone in the presence of her firstborn.) Locke salved his own conscience by offering his older brother £3,000 raised from personal investments.

Locke's position was in fact as unenviable as was William's. Chained to a tyrant mother, he dwelt with his sisters in what was effectively Lady Hester's private prison at Woburn Park. Designed by William Kent, Woburn stood ostentatiously close to Ockham, which it dwarfed. Nominally under Locke's control, it was ruled by the iron fist of his mother, who ran it as her own fiefdom. The son whose obligations included writing his mother an annual letter of obsequious homage (while apologising every time he went away for more than a day) was in effect a mere dependant.

Lady Hester's callous behaviour had not only robbed William King of the major portion of his inheritance, but it aimed to separate him from the young sisters who adored him. No communication was permitted between the two estates. When Hester and Charlotte King visited Ockham, they did so clandestinely, rather than risk the scourge of their mother's displeasure.

It is unclear how much Mrs Somerville herself knew of this ugly history, but it is likely that William King, who had few friends, shared most of it with Woronzow Greig, his lifelong confidant and loyal supporter.*

Encountering William in 1835, for the first time in several years, Greig saw a handsome and thoughtful man, almost eleven years older than Miss Byron, who worshipped Ada's late father, took a keen interest in the world of science and who plainly stood in need of a wife. Ockham Park had been robbed of its pretty old furniture, its charming paintings and its library (even the contents of the wine cellar and William's own amateur science laboratory – left over from his college days – had been carried off to Woburn). Nevertheless, the King

---

* Greig's name was given in honour of his Russian godmother, Countess Woronzow (pronounced Voronzoff), daughter of Russia's ambassador to Britain. She married Lord Pembroke.

family's principal home remained ready to enchant a new young mistress. Serene, light and spacious, Ockham stood at the end of an avenue lined by stately trees. Its windows looked out across rolling parkland. Close by, the family church housed a glorious Rysbrach monument to William's forbears. And how could Byron's daughter not fall in love with Ashley Combe, a remote and ravishingly beautiful West Country estate of twisting paths and forested cliffs, its shimmering, sealike views across the Bristol Channel rivalling those that Ada's father had enjoyed during his summer beside Lake Geneva? All that Ockham and Ashley lacked in 1835 was a mistress worthy of their master.

The connection seemed simply to rise up and stare the Somervilles in the face. Here, close to the heart of their own family, stood Miss Byron's ideal mate. While no correspondence survives through which to trace the trail of discussion, it is clear that Greig's notion was put to Lady Byron by his mother, and found pleasing. Towards the end of May 1835, Ada was despatched on a visit to Warwickshire. There, William King was due to attend a ball being held at Weston House, the newly Gothicised home of Sir George Philips, founder of the *Manchester Guardian*. A jovial textile magnate whose strong interest in science had brought him into contact with the Somervilles and Charles Babbage, Sir George had met Annabella and her daughter the previous year during their inspection tour of Midlands factories. A regular visitor that summer both to Fordhook and to the Somervilles' house at Chelsea, Sir George and his brightly social wife were eager to assist in the plot to further what all parties perceived to be an ideal alliance.

Introduced to each other by their hostess (elegant Lady Philips did not approve of Miss Byron's evidently home-made frock), the meeting of William and Ada proved an instant success. The couple danced several quadrilles together, during one of which William plucked up the courage to tell Ada that he would love to show her Ockham Park and its pretty little church. 'I thought to myself how few young men whom one meets at balls would talk with so much feeling about their country church,' Ada demurely wrote to him, '& I admired you very much.'

Admiration had burgeoned into love. A week after the Weston ball, William and Ada rode together along the banks of the Thames. By the time that they returned to the Somervilles' home at Chelsea, William's proposal had been accepted. Four days later, on 8 June, Ada was saucily reminding him about a certain ride 'of which it is possible you may have some recollection', before teasing him with the news that she was just off on a similar excursion, with jolly Sir George as her escort. Writing from Somerset, where he was busily hewing down trees around what he tenderly referred to as Ada's very own hermitage, William confessed that he felt as though he were living in a dream. 'How I envy your chaperon his ride with you.'

Fearful that Lord King might hear about Ada's past history from the wrong person, Annabella asked Woronzow Greig to deliver a discreet account of the elopement incident. Writing to her fiancé shortly after that difficult disclosure, Ada expressed her gratitude to him for overlooking her imprudence. She promised to reward William's trust by becoming a model wife, one who would never forget his generous behaviour. 'Now do not be angry with me, because I have only just spoken the truth – neither more nor less.' A week later, Ada's mood had shifted. *Did* she actually possess 'the requisite perseverance & self denial' to make a dutiful spouse? But if William grew apprehensive about his fiancée's changeability – and it seems likely that he did – he could always take comfort from the evident fact that Lady Byron, so calm, so kind, so splendidly rational, exerted a powerful influence over her skittish daughter.

Lady Byron herself was delighted by the match. Writing to Harriet Siddons, Annabella praised Lord King, not merely as 'a man of rare worth and superior abilities', but because 'he has returned good for evil towards those who have wronged him.' Her allusion was plainly to the Woburn branch of Lord King's family. The tale was deplorable, but it enabled an admiring Annabella to highlight William's magnanimous nature. 'Schooled in adversity and guided by Christian principles, he has reached the age of 30 without a stain upon his reputation.' His tastes, so Harriet learned, were reassuringly domestic. Best of all, from a loving mother's point of view, Ockham Park was only half a day's carriage drive away from Annabella's own house at Ealing.

Given Lady Hester's hostility to her eldest son, it was clear that she would forbid any member of the Woburn-based family to attend the wedding. It was probably in order to suppress public comment upon this scandalous absence that the wedding was celebrated quietly – as Annabella's own had been – at home. Samuel Gamlen, a kindly and broadminded vicar whom Ada often treated as a substitute father, travelled down to Ealing from his Yorkshire rectory. On 8 July 1835, Gamlen presided over the nuptials at Fordhook. Little Olivia Acheson (Lady Byron's own special favourite among Mary Gosford's three daughters, singled out by Ada from a yearning trio of candidates) was the only bridesmaid. The following day, while the newly-weds visited Ockham, en route to a two-month West Country honeymoon at Ashley Combe, Annabella threw a party for both servants and her friends at which – so she gaily reported to the absent Ada – Fordhook's roof almost caved in from all the cheers.

No tears were shed in Ealing that Lord Byron's last mistress, Teresa Guiccioli, attempting to gatecrash the wedding of the great man's daughter, had turned up instead at a smart London church where, thanks to her choice of a coyly revealing veil, the countess was recognised and publicly mocked for making a fool of herself. Writing her voluminous homage to Byron some thirty years later, Teresa repaid his widow for that painful hour of humiliation with an acid portrait, one of such peculiar venom that it would help to destroy Annabella's hard-won status as one of the secular saints of Victorian England.

ᪿᣇᣱ

Before the marriage came the settlements. The documents were intimidating and vast: the History Centre in Woking, Surrey still holds the bullhide on which – despite the gifting to Locke King, via Lady Hester, of at least an equal part of the family estates – over 200 King properties were recorded under William's name, bringing in an annual income of £8,000 (around £396,000 in modern terms).

What catches the eye, however, is not the handsome flourishes which adorn the names of Ada, of the 7th Lord Byron and – he was the well-meaning peacemaker in the conflicted King family – of Lady Hester's brother, Lord Ebrington. Two names dominate all the others: those of Lord King and his formidably wealthy future mother-in-law, Lady Byron.

Writing to Robert Noel in Dresden on 28 July (Robert happened also to be getting married, to the well-born and charming Louisa von Henniken), Lady Byron described Lord King's fortune as 'sufficient, though not ample'. An immediate gift of £30,000 from Lady Byron helped to remedy matters. Given his mother-in-law's notoriously fragile health, William naturally assumed that he might soon receive a good deal more. Ada, meanwhile – although her mother was keen to point out that the cost of her trousseau alone equalled the expense of educating eighty poor children – was to receive precisely the same figure that her mother had herself been granted as a wife back in 1815. The modest sum of £300 a year (around £13,500 in modern terms) was expected to cover the cost of all Lady King's personal expenses, including her books, travel, pets, a maid and even her best clothes.

The amount, for a bride of Ada's status, was startlingly meagre. (Tom, the oldest of the four Noel brothers, was given £500 a year by Annabella during that same period; Annabella presented Robert Noel with £100 at the same time, merely as Ada's personal wedding gift for Louisa and himself.) 'Dear little Canary Bird, may the new "cage" be gladdened by your notes,' Annabella wrote to her daughter on 9 July, the day after Ada's wedding. The allusion to a cage, however playful, suggests that Annabella still regarded Ada as in need of supervision.* Her recollection of Byron's own extravagance had not dimmed. Confining her daughter to a tiny budget was Lady Byron's way of protecting an impetuous and financially naive young woman from running amok.

---

* Ada's husband and mother were still describing – to each other – her marital home as a 'cage' in 1844.

CHAPTER FOURTEEN

AN UNCONVENTIONAL WIFE
(1836–40)

Ada's marriage marked the beginning of a halcyon five years both for the newly-weds and for the mother whom they now fondly called 'the Hen'. (William was quickly nicknamed 'the Crow' for his glossy dark hair and slender legs, while flighty, elusive Ada became 'the Bird'.) A disappointingly pompous George Ticknor, calling in at Fordhook to inspect Lady Byron's Ealing school just a few days after the wedding, carried away the impression of an earnest little widow, whose gravity was appropriate to her 'peculiar' position in the world. To nearer friends, Annabella seemed almost giddy with joy. Witnessing Ada's happiness had at last secured her own, she confided to Robert Noel, while thanking him for introducing her to a wonderful new friend, Mrs Anna Jameson, the art historian. Writing to Harriet Siddons on 22 July, Lady Byron admitted that 'for the first time in my life – I may say that I feel without a care on earth ...'

Settled into a modest seaside cottage at Southampton for the autumn, Annabella remained almost girlishly merry. Chugging along the Solent on one of the popular steam packets that marked the advent of public tourism, she gloried in a spectacular sunrise and wondered that her fellow passengers appeared to be so oblivious. Snug in her newly rented home, she stitched herself a working-woman's hemp frock (both Annabella and her daughter were deft needlewomen) and got the giggles when young William, her only manservant, dropped a plate of chicken fricassee – there was nothing else in the larder that night – on the floor. William was a sweet boy, but hopelessly clumsy, she wrote to Harriet Siddons's daughter, Lizzie: perhaps her giggles gave off the wrong message? 'These catastrophes are very frequent in my house, I think I will act being in a rage next time ...' Signing off her letter to this cherished correspondent, Lady Byron cheerfully referred to herself as 'The Old Pup' – she was forty-three – '[who] sometimes frets to think you will scarce know it again with its unwearied degree of tabbyism'.

Lizzie Siddons's mother, Harriet, came down to Southampton from Edinburgh that September, eager to discuss the philanthropic ambitions that the two women shared. Annabella had finally reached the day when she felt able to step back from the Ealing school, where a new headmaster had replaced an annoying Mr Craig who, despite being trained in the Fellenberg system, had proved both ineffectual and sullen. ('Did not this answer for his truthfulness and humility!' Annabella burst out to Mrs Siddons, after hearing the Heep-like Craig tell the pupils how fortunate he felt to be supervised by a patron who could teach him so much.) Together, the two ladies discussed prison design (Annabella favoured Jeremy Bentham's plan for a central watchtower, thus saving on the cost of numerous guards). Together, they went over an article that Lady Byron was writing about industrial schools and the innovative system pioneered by Fellenberg at Hofwyl. Possibly, the two women also discussed phrenology. Robert Noel was exploring the idea of using head casts taken from the skulls of felons, in order to examine criminal traits. Nobody was more influential in the phrenological world than Harriet's handsome brother-in-law, George Combe, author of the wide-ranging *The Constitution of Man* (1828), a book that had become more widely read and discussed than any other in England, bar the Bible.*

October brought a happy and newly pregnant Ada to her mother for a two-week stay. Writing to her husband, she playfully reported that the Hen would have to inform William about a '*bad bird*', so bad that she had failed to pay her tuppence for walking along Southampton's pier, and had gambled away four whole shillings at a charity auction 'in exchange for a most vile basket'. Meanwhile, Ada pined for livelier company than her mother's estimable circle of fellow reformers at the seaside. The absent William had turned from a crow into his wife's 'dear cock': 'I want my Cock at night to keep me warm.'

Ada's sexual message is hard to miss, both here and in a later request to William not to 'eat her up' at their next reunion. ('*Ou* won't hurt her I think, will *ou*?') Chatting to Mary Somerville's attentive son during the 1840s about her sexual life, Ada revealed to Woronzow Greig that she and her husband always slept together, and were always naked under the sheets between which their firstborn had often been allowed to romp with his parents, just so. It's fair to deduce that this good-looking, strong-willed and most unconventional couple were happy during their first years of matrimony.

☙❧

Annabella's pride in Ada's marriage showed itself in her decision, following the Southampton visit, to commission an official portrait of her daughter, one that could be embarked upon before her pregnancy began to show. Ada was enthused neither by the project nor the artist, an outspoken Scotswoman called Margaret Carpenter. Writing to Mrs Somerville, the reluctant sitter assured her mentor that such trivia would never distract her from mathematics, the

---

* Both of the Combe brothers, Andrew and George, were ardent phrenologists. George was by far the better known of the two, but Annabella preferred his gentler and more modest sibling.

study of which had recently been resumed. ('I ... am occupied with Trigonometry in the preliminaries of Cubic and Biquadratic equations'.) Grumbling to the Hen, she complained that Mrs Carpenter had worse manners than her harp teacher; Miss d'Espourrin would never dream of stretching out on the Ockham drawing-room floor for a refreshing nap. (Ada had inherited her father's paradoxically conventional streak; always wild herself, she wished others to behave with propriety.) Worse still, Mrs Carpenter had scraped her sitter's bright brown hair off her face to emphasise her jaw. The result, in the view of a displeased Ada, was that she looked like 'a crop-eared dog'.

Ada joked that the only use of owning an unusually broad jawbone was to write the word 'mathematics' across it. To Annabella, as to her Byron-worshipping son-in-law, the entire point of the Carpenter portrait was to maximise that feature in which Ada's genetic heritage was most apparent. Mrs Carpenter was simply following orders. The three-quarter profile view of Lady King's head that she produced for her full-length portrait was an exact replication of Byron's stance in the Albanian portrait that had been long ago acquired by Lady Noel. Annabella, inspecting the result on 26 November, was delighted. The likeness to Lord Byron was declared by her to be 'most striking'. As a mark of her approval, she sent her mother's magnificent purchase along, cleaned and reframed, to adorn Ada's new country home. Mrs Carpenter's Byronic Ada received disappointingly muted praise the following summer when displayed at the Royal Academy.

༄

The first winter of Ada's marriage was a time of great contentment. Ada, visiting Fordhook in early December, wrote fondly to William of plans hatched by 'the dear old Hen' to introduce her son-in-law to the poet's publisher, John Murray. The Somervilles and Charles Babbage spent Christmas together with Lady Byron and their hosts at Ockham Park. In February 1836, Ada invited the Somervilles' two daughters to rejoin their lawyer half-brother, Woronzow, for a further few days at her home in Surrey. Writing to their mother, Ada

teased that warnings would be sent if either Martha or Mary decided
to elope, although she intended to keep the musically minded sisters
occupied in accompanying, on the piano and in song, her newest
pieces for the harp.

Lady Byron, meanwhile, had finally renewed acquaintanceship
with her cleverest and most worldly cousin. Lady Caroline Lamb was
dead and her widower had since inherited his father's title. Meeting
Prime Minister Melbourne in January 1836, after a gap of over
twenty years, Annabella saw a sharp face that had softened into a
poignant echo of Lord Melbourne's Uncle Ralph, the jovial, loving
father whom she had buried eleven years earlier. Plucked suddenly
back into the past, she almost wept.

The two-hour meeting between the two middle-aged cousins at
Windsor Castle reaped a useful reward. Two years later, when Lady
Byron sought to distinguish her daughter (Lady King) from an odious
mother-in-law (Lady Hester King) by giving Ada a different name,
Lord Melbourne supported Annabella's request for an upgrade. Lord
and Lady King became the Earl and Countess of Lovelace.* Lady
Hester's furious protest at such a step, despatched to a baffled Lord
Holland, went unanswered. (Her excessive prejudice against Ada's
husband had become well-known and was widely deplored.)

CS69

Writing a character portrait of her daughter during the early years
of Ada's marriage, a doting Lady Byron described an angel: here was
a young woman who combined a singing voice 'like the bonnie bird
on the banks of Doone' with an exceptional talent for studies 'of a
deep and scientific nature'. It was a clear indication of Lady Byron's
approval that the Kings were swiftly lodged at a London house that
could stand comparison with Lady Hester's frigid palace on Dover

---

* The choice of title (although taken from a valid claim through ancestry) must
have caused Prime Minister Melbourne to smile a bit. It remains a mystery why
the well-read and discreet Lady Byron should have chosen to attach to her own
daughter and son-in-law the name of Samuel Richardson's notorious libertine.

Street. The Hen's reward was to be invited to name the baby boy who was born at his parents' elegant new home, 12 St James's Square, in May 1836. It surprised neither the Crow nor the Bird that Annabella chose to call the future Viscount Ockham after her late husband, or that she named Byron's baby sister, born in 1837, Anne Isabella, after herself. History was being deliberately replayed: Byron and Annabella (the name was instantly shortened, as Lady Byron's own had been) were reborn. Performing the same agreeable role for Ada's third child in 1839, Annabella chose to echo her husband's Scottish heritage in Ralph Gordon King's second name. ('Ralph' honoured Lady Byron's beloved father.)

Ada, who had been playfully writing to Mrs Somerville in the summer of 1836 about her hopes of producing 'a mathematical child', was relieved by the painlessness of little Byron's arrival into the world. The hard part came later. Hester King, William's sister, gladly obeyed a summons to come and act as a companion and nursemaid to the convalescing young mother. Visiting Lady Byron in Brighton three months after giving birth, Ada could still only walk with the help of a cane and her gentle sister-in-law's supportive arm. Every evening, the two young women visited Annabella in her own seaside lodgings, where they took turns to read aloud to Lady Byron from her favoured diet of scientific and educational papers. But when Ada accidentally locked herself into her bedroom and had to be rescued by means of a ladder, Hester grew as hysterical with mirth as the prisoner herself. 'Hester and I are very happy together,' Ada told William, 'and it is a real comfort to me to have such a sister.'

It was a comfort for young Hester, too. At Woburn Park, things had been going from bad to worse following Locke King's marriage to Louisa Hoare, a commanding heiress from Northamptonshire. Sidelined by the new arrangements and angered by Locke's request that his sisters should display deference to his wife, the girls were making increasingly determined efforts to achieve an independent life. The helping hands of Ada and her mother were evident in the appearance of the two young women that autumn at several of

Babbage's soirées. It was at one of these occasions that Hester fell disastrously in love.

By the summer of 1837, Hester's calamitous love affair was over and her mother was issuing dire warnings from Woburn of the punishments due to be meted out to neglectful daughters. On 11 June, a sick and pregnant Ada tried to transform an increasingly bitter dispute into an opportunity for peace. Could a truce be called, now that Hester's love affair was over? Would William's mother consider paying a visit to Ockham – it was a mere seven-mile drive from Woburn Park – for a few days? 'You will however I trust remember that *if either at present or at any future time*, you should feel inclined to prefer inviting us, it would be most welcome,' a wistful Ada pleaded.

Predictably, Ada's generous suggestion was rebuffed by silence.

In the early autumn of 1837, when Byron's baby sister was born, Ada's sister-in-law once again offered her services as a nurse and companion. The birth process was unexpectedly painful and protracted (which might help to explain Ada's early animosity to her daughter). She had scarcely begun to recover when a serious attack of cholera – a deadly illness at that time – struck her down. Illness and disappointment – she had made no secret of her hopes for a second boy – contributed to the debilitating combination of frailty and nervousness that Ada would struggle against throughout her adult life. Little Annabella's birth also marked the onset of Ada's enduring obsession with weight. She began to starve herself. Her husband – William harboured a curious horror of heavily built people of either sex – approved. Lady Byron's anxious protests (she told friends that Ada was starting to adopt her late father's odd eating habits) were ignored.

More troubling than dietary fads, to Hester's gentle eyes, was Ada's insouciant attitude to motherhood. And yet, Hester loved her sister-in-law's wild enthusiasms. She readily joined in with a 'shilling' experiment by which a suspended coin chimed out the hours on the side of a glass, while causing heated sensations to the brain. (A thrilled Ada asked Mrs Somerville to alert that wizard of the electrical world, Michael Faraday, to the results of their trial.) While it sometimes worried a conventional young woman that Ada seemed to care more about science than her children, it was to Ada that Hester would still turn for her own salvation.

By the end of the year 1837, matters at Woburn Park had reached such a pass for Charlotte and Hester that the sisters fled to Ockham, vowing never to return. A new and appalling row broke out. Terrible things were said by the mistress of Woburn until Ada, beloved by everyone for her exceptional good nature and her cheerful optimism, thought that she had glimpsed a haughtily extended olive branch. Perhaps, Ada wrote to her mother-in-law on 12 February 1838, Lady Hester did not appreciate the pain she was inflicting and how sad it made Ada herself feel. 'No matter ... The occurrence of last week will of course now be blotted out from the record of events.'*

No record survives of what the mysterious 'occurrence' was, but Ada's conciliatory words would be thrown back in her teeth by the venomous Lady Hester eight years later, as offering clear proof that the fault lay all on Ada's side. On this later occasion, Ada rebelled. The fault was theirs, she wrote fiercely back to Lady Hester's brother on 23 June 1846. (All direct contact with Lady Hester had already been severed, at her own wish.) It was his sister and her son Locke, with their 'repeated and unjust condemnations' of both Lady Lovelace and her husband, who had finally killed 'the almost *romantic* generosity & warmth of feeling with which *at just 22 years of age* I regarded everything relating to Lovelace's family'.

Poor Ada. She might as well have held her tongue. Nothing would ever have the power to shake William King's vindictive mother from her invincible pinnacle of self-righteousness.

---

* Locke King, drawing up a peevish retrospective record of injuries done to him, his wife and his mother, identified 1838 as the year in which 'my sisters were so ill natured to Louisa [his wife] that I could not go on & intended to speak to them but he [William] said oh no doubt but let me send for them & Ly King [Ada] will talk with them & they will make peace ... I was not allowed to see them unless I would promise to say nothing of the past ...' (Peter Locke King, undated note in the Locke King family archive at Brooklands Museum.)

Ada's closeness to Hester King the younger is apparent from her sister-in-law's inclusion in the grand plans being hatched in 1838 for Ada's two new schools at Ockham. Here, thanks to lavish injections of money from Annabella, the Ealing model was being replicated, but on an expanded scale. Carpentry shops and a printing press had been introduced; a gym and a specially designed music room were next on the agenda. 'Our school is doing so well, that I am very anxious it should do better,' an elated Ada proclaimed to the approving Hen. All that they lacked in 1838 were suitable teaching manuals, a deficiency which Ada intended to enlist her sister-in-law's assistance to remedy.

Naturally, Ada had it all planned out in a trice. Charles Knight, the biggest name in educational books, would be the publisher. William Frend's daughter, Sophia, recently married to Augustus De Morgan, one of the leading logicians of the time, would write on mathematics. Harriet Martineau, the mother of sociology (and respected translator of Auguste Comte), would add a book on rules for a modern education. Ada – besides writing 'a good and amusing book about geography' and a children's version of George Combe's *Constitution* – was going to collaborate with Hester on a practical guide to thrift. 'I think the history of boiling a pot or making a mess of oatmeal porridge might be just as entertaining as the history of anything else,' a hopeful Ada informed her mother.

Lady Byron approved. Composing a glowing tribute to her clever daughter in her notebooks, Annabella praised her enthusiasm and skill. 'Ada teaches so that one cannot help learning,' an admiring friend had exclaimed. Lady Byron herself was especially impressed by the gift for communicating difficult ideas in simple language that Ada had learned from Mary Somerville.

It was not for lack of encouragement that Ada's schoolbook project collapsed, but because a rescue plan for the King sisters had emerged from Lady Byron's organising mind, robbing Ada of her chief collaborator. Hester and Charlotte, subsidised by their sympathetic sponsor, were to spend a year in Europe.

In April 1838, Ada and William wistfully put Lord King's excited sisters on to a boat bound for Antwerp. Charlotte travelled on to Weimar, where she was looked after by Lady Byron's new friend, Anna Jameson. Hester settled at Dresden as the cherished guest of kindly Robert Noel (just beginning to make his name as one of Germany's leading phrenologists) and his wife, Louisa von Henniken. That crucial visit to Germany – young Hester's first journey out of England – would lay the foundations for an enduring friendship. By the following summer, Hester trusted Robert Noel well enough to let him take a 'living mask', a process that required her head to be covered by a sheet and smothered with wet plaster. The experience was one that Hester thought equivalent to Ada's greatest terror; the notion of being buried alive ...

Years later, Robert Noel took down Hester's cast from one of his laboratory shelves and wrote up his notes about the sitter. Fond personal recollections played a larger part than phrenological diagnosis when Robert described Miss King as a sweet and touchingly maternal young woman, always cheerful and kind, with a strong sense of the ridiculous (a quality that had always endeared Hester to Ada).

It was on Hester's dislike of ostentation that Robert Noel would lay particular emphasis in his affectionate word portrait. Returned from Germany in the summer of 1839 and newly established with Charlotte in modest lodgings near Charing Cross (safely out of reach of Woburn Park), Hester was disconcerted to find dolled-up portraits of Ada smiling at her out of all the fashionable printshop windows. The brand-new Lady Lovelace was enjoying a great success at 7s 6d a sale, Hester wrote to Louisa Noel in Germany. Her letter, although spiky, stopped just short of a sneer.

Hester was being unjust. Ada herself had never asked to be made a countess. It was largely to please her mother that she had granted Alfred Chalon's request to create a marketable image of the young peeress. Chalon was the new queen's favourite watercolourist and it would have seemed ungracious to refuse, but it's hard to imagine that Ada relished seeing herself represented as the ringletted heroine of a velvet-covered ladies' annual, any more than she enjoyed the mandatory court visit to receive Queen Victoria's formal approval of her elevation to the rank of a countess.

Hester's greater concern was about Ada's capriciousness as a mother. Little Byron, described by Hester to Robert Noel's wife as 'an exceedingly odd boy', had already become – and would always remain – his mother's darling, capable of doing no wrong. If sturdy Byron knocked his tiny sister down, Ada laughed. If he answered his mother back, she laughed again and passed along his commands as jokes ('Now Ma may go ... Now Ma can go downstairs') together with her response ('No, my dear, I'm *not* going, so you need not talk about it'). Wee Annabella, meanwhile, was declared to be 'doggedly naughty' and 'to scream like a pig'. When Lady Byron volunteered to take charge of her small granddaughter for a week, Ada wondered how her mother found the patience to suffer so much tiresome 'chatteration'; she even asked Lady Byron frankly how she 'could endure her [the child] so much alone with you?' With ease, it seems. Hester King described Lady Byron to the Noels as a besotted granny, and one who took a keen interest in observing the children's progress.

Maternity bored Ada and she made no secret of the fact. Five years into her marriage, Lady Lovelace finally admitted to her mother that she would never have chosen to bear a child. She did not quite dare to voice the thought that had perhaps passed through her exiled father's mind as he contemplated the sale of Newstead, that she had most especially never desired to have a girl.

The acquisition of a new title had no noticeable effect upon Ada. For William, however, his earldom was a righting of all those wrongs inflicted by his mother. Felt as an act of justice, the title conferred a new sense of self-importance upon an insecure man. Invited to become Lord Lieutenant of Surrey, he eyed the neighbours whose homes were being built in the new baronial mode; William's impulse to outdo both them and his usurper of a younger brother took root. Why should the Earl of Lovelace be outshone by mere bankers like William Currie of East Horsley and Henry Drummond of Albury?

As William became increasingly involved both in the redesigning of his homes and the duties and ritual appropriate to his new rank, Ada remained loyal to the mother who had taught her always to rate intellectual achievement above social position. Back in the autumn of 1835, it was to Lady Byron that Ada had first turned for scientific advice about the refraction of sunlight. Two years later, it was to her mother that she boasted of her victory over a visiting clergyman who queried her belief that Isaac Newton had been a Unitarian: 'to say the truth I do not think Mr H. Fellows knows much about the Trinity or the Unity either'.

Increasingly, Ada spoke to Lady Byron, not as a parent, but as a colleague and equal. Annabella, too, was growing more relaxed. Her easy communion with Ada was seldom more apparent than in the light-hearted reports she sent home from Germany in the summer of 1838.

Annabella had undertaken this journey abroad as honeymoon companion and purse-carrier to Edward Noel (by now running his Fellenberg-style school on her island estate in Greece) and his bride, the former Fanny Smith. The couple had met at Fordhook the previous year when Edward returned from Euboea to convalesce from a serious illness. Nursing him back to health, Selina Doyle's pretty niece fell in love. It was a match of which Annabella heartily approved. Her favourite of the Noel boys happily married to her own sweet 'Fan' (a young woman to whom Lady Byron sometimes fondly signed herself 'Your Bag o'Bones'!) What could be better?

It was in the same playful tone as in her letters to Fanny that Annabella wrote to Ada from Germany. Staying at a hotel in Wiesbaden, she merrily reported how – the culprit was seated, all unaware, at a neighbouring breakfast table – a former curate from Ealing had reported upon that village's best-known inhabitant. Lady

Byron was, he bellowed (as if for one and all to hear), a drab little woman, quite undistinguished: 'very short, of a swarthy complexion . . . looks as if she could never smile'. Edward and Fanny had been outraged. Annabella thought the incident hilarious. 'I shall get some rouge and a brown wig to make myself captivating,' she promised Ada. 'I ought to get stilts too, it seems.'

∾

For four happy years, Ada had enjoyed the rewarding experience of having two formidably intelligent female mentors. While Annabella would always urge her daughter towards science, Mary Somerville sympathised with the passion for music that often drew her away from it. Mrs Somerville's main role, nevertheless, was to assist Ada with her mathematics. Seeking to scale the abstract slopes of spherical trigonometry in the same year that her eldest son was born, Ada had asked Mary to help her to obtain a full set – 'all that are used' – of solid wooden models. That request was made on 2 December 1836. Cooing over her mother's Christmas present to her of a telescope a week later, Ada's delight was heightened by learning that it was kind Mrs Somerville who had personally selected the gift. Meekly, she asked Mary's advice on how best to use this essential instrument for exploring the heavens.

That humble request was symptomatic of Ada's unassuming attitude towards a woman she wholeheartedly revered. Just occasionally, she forgot herself. In June 1837, Ada fired off an opinionated letter to Mrs Somerville about Charles Babbage's new contribution to the Bridgewater Treatises (Babbage had attacked William Whewell's more orthodox view of the universe). Mr Babbage's work was so careless, so fragmentary and unconnected, Ada announced before going on to deplore the waste of his fine mind on producing such 'crude outlines . . . I fear the work will be underrated.' But then Ada remembered to whom she was writing. It would not be well for Mrs Somerville to discover the truth, that Ada was simply quoting her mother's opinion, not having bothered to read Babbage's Treatise for herself. A little more candour was in order. 'I think when *I have* read it ... I shall probably give my opinion to Mr Babbage himself,' Ada declared before another pause, and a further step down. What was Mrs Somerville's own honest opinion? Would such behaviour be a bit 'presumptuous, do you think?'

The greatest lesson Mrs Somerville provided was not in mathematics itself, but in how to approach its study. When Ada told Babbage in 1839 that she had acquired 'a peculiar way of learning', what she meant was that Mrs Somerville had approved of Dr King's emphasis upon the discipline of perfectly memorising each new step until it could instantly be recalled, and without conscious effort. That careful approach offered no dazzling leaps, only a slow, tenacious struggle towards what Ada wistfully described to Babbage (in this same 1839 letter) as 'a very bright light a good way farther on'. Anathema to a young woman of Ada's mercurial character, this lesson in patience was practised (sporadically) out of an intense respect for the woman who showed her its value. Valuable as a discipline for an impetuous student, it had not been fully absorbed (as Ada's next tutor would discover), but the foundations had been laid.

In the summer of 1838 – that same summer in which the King sisters and her mother were all out of the country – Ada lost this most cherished of all her connections. Mrs Somerville's health had been impaired by fifteen years of living in a damp house near a smog-shrouded river. A shortage of money contributed to Dr Somerville's decision, in 1838, to quit his medical post and exchange cold, expensive England for a warmer, more affordable life abroad. Martha and Mary accompanied their parents on the family's journey to Italy, a country where Mrs Somerville's gender offered less impediment than in Victorian England to her recognition as a woman of pre-eminent intellectual achievement. Mary made only a couple of brief returns to Britain, where her son Woronzow Greig, having married a charming and pious Scottish girl in 1837, continued to work as an attorney.

Mary had gone and Ada was bereft, not only of a woman who had become close to her as a second mother, but of a magnificent tutor,

without whom she was lost. In 1839, she began to put pressure on
Charles Babbage to come to her rescue.

In February 1840, at a time when Babbage was in especially low
spirits about the future of his unbuilt Analytical Engine, Ada showed
the first hint of her secret and immense ambitions. If Mr Babbage
would only hurry up and find her a new teacher, the world might
benefit from the results.

> I hope you are bearing me in mind. I mean my mathematical
> interests. You know this is the greatest favour any one can
> do me. Perhaps, none of us can estimate how great. Who can
> calculate to *what* it *might* lead ... Am I too imaginative for you?
> I think not ...?

Babbage took his time in looking, but he did not let Lady Lovelace
down. The wonder was only that it had occurred neither to Lady
Byron nor to her daughter that Augustus De Morgan, the brilliant
mathematical logician who had recently married Sophia Frend,
might be able to take Mrs Somerville's place.

By October 1840, the new arrangement had taken shape. De
Morgan had not only rejected the idea of payment, but he had
willingly taken this most unconventional student under his personal wing. The boost to Ada's confidence and energy proved to be
immense. Writing to her absent mother that month, she boasted that
she felt 'wonderfully altered as to courage'. Better than this: 'I am
absolutely afraid of nothing. I never was so bold & full of nerve at
any time in my life.'

There's no doubt that much of Ada's new-found elation stemmed
from her new connection to the witty, intelligent and empathetic
Augustus De Morgan, the very teacher whom she craved. ('Never
was a better hit than that,' she rejoiced to Lady Byron.)

It's possible that some of Ada's new-found confidence also derived
from the fact that Lady Byron – that 'merry old hen' who had been
clucking about nothing but educational reforms and Ada's need
to be more closely involved in the field of good works all summer

long – was once again safely out of the country. For the present, the Hen's relentless interest in reform, Ada and even her grandchildren had been unexpectedly cast in the shade by a new and enthralling link to Annabella's own Byron-haunted past.

CHAPTER FIFTEEN

AMBITIONS AND DELUSIONS
(1840–1)

Charles Babbage, by 1840, was a disappointed man. His uncompleted Difference Engine had passed into the control of a government that showed no faith either in it or in its infinitely more complex and dynamic successor, the Analytical Engine, upon which Babbage had expended all of his considerable inventive genius. On the Continent, he was justly regarded as a genius; in England, his career had utterly stalled.

In Italy, the far-sighted Charles Albert, King of Sardinia (father of the future King of Italy, Victor Emmanuel II), encouraged the setting-up in the autumn of 1840 of a scientific conference in Turin. Babbage, formally invited by his elderly admirer and fellow mathematician, Count Giovanni di Plana (Mary Somerville, now settled in Italy, had acted as intermediary), would explain the significance of his revolutionary invention.

Bringing with him as interpreter Fortunato Prandi (one of the Young Italy group focussed around the exiled Giuseppe Mazzini in London), Babbage was treated with gratifying respect at that September conference.* The contrast to the indifference shown

---

* Police suspicions about Fortunato Prandi's return to Italy increased when it was reported that Prandi himself had not attended the conference. Possibly, Babbage was providing cover. Several years later, in an undated note in the Lovelace Byron Papers, Ada summoned Prandi to a secret midnight tête-à-tête at her London home, but the reason for it remains unknown.

to the inventor in his own country was poignant. Charles Albert, a stickler for etiquette, permitted Babbage to remain seated in the royal presence. The king even – this was an unprecedented honour – allowed Mrs Somerville's brilliant friend to present the queen with a portrait of the famous M. Jacquard, woven upon one of the industrialist's own automated silk looms at Lyons. (Babbage had inspected the Lyons looms and had purchased the artefact en route to Italy, evidently intending to highlight the respects in which that successful invention resembled the projected activity of his own unbuilt machine.) Ill health marred the end of Babbage's visit and forced him to cancel his plans to visit the Somerville family at their new home in Florence. Nevertheless, Babbage's feathers, ruffled by English indifference, were smoothed by Italian courtesy. In 1842, King Charles Albert would present the British inventor with a commendatore's order. It was the only award that the prickly Charles Babbage ever consented to accept.

Babbage pinned very high hopes upon the Turin conference. Writing to an Italian colleague, he explained why.

> The discovery of the Analytical Engine is so much in advance
> of my own country, and I fear even of the age, that it is very
> important for its success that it should not rest upon my
> unsupported testimony. I therefore selected the meeting at Turin
> as the time of its publication, partly from the celebrity of its
> academy, and partly from my high estimate of Plana.

Babbage's reasonable supposition was that his official host, Count di Plana, would write up a full and positive report before submitting his personal appreciation of the Analytical Engine to Britain's Royal Society. Armed with this impartial endorsement, the inventor stood a far better chance of gaining the support from the British government that he required. Unfortunately, di Plana himself had grown too old and infirm for the demanding task of describing such a complex – and still unbuilt – machine. In 1841, encouraged by Mary Somerville and in the hope of further developments, Babbage again travelled out to Italy – this time for a conference at Florence. His reception was as enthusiastic as before but, apart from the pleasure of seeing the Somervilles, his hopes were once more crushed. Di Plana had done nothing.

By the summer of 1842, almost two years after the Turin conference, no report had yet been published upon Babbage's wondrous invention.

೦೯೨

In the autumn of 1840, as Babbage set off for Italy with such high hopes, his future interpreter embarked upon the most significant phase of her mathematical education. Following the recommendation of Babbage (and bowing to the unyielding persistence of Lady Lovelace herself), Augustus De Morgan had taken over the role of mathematics coach to a strong-willed young woman whose intelligence and determination still greatly outstripped her mathematical skills.

The challenge of tutoring Ada was considerable. Aged just under twenty-four, and still equipped with only a modest understanding of either algebra or trigonometry, Lady Lovelace wanted to launch straight into differential calculus. Mrs Somerville's counsel about cautious progress was forgotten in Ada's habitual impatience to rush ahead. '*Festina lente*,' De Morgan reproved her on 15 September 1840: ' . . . it is no use trying to catch the horizon.' A few days later, he was again obliged to rein back his ambitious pupil. Lady Lovelace might wish to bestride Parnassus, but the problems of calculus must wait until attention had been paid to the more basic skills which, as De Morgan bluntly stated, 'you have left behind'.

It was not immediately pleasing to an impetuous young woman to be compelled to follow the sage advice that she herself, aping Mrs Somerville, had once been keen to dish out to Mary Gosford's little daughter. 'I work on very slowly,' Ada sighed to her mother on 21 November 1840. 'This Mr De Morgan does not wish otherwise.' A month later, however, she was beginning to get the point. 'I have materially altered my mind on this subject,' she confessed to her tutor. 'I often gain more from the discovery of a mistake of this sort [a simple oversight caused by hasty reading] than from 10 acquisitions made at *once* without any kind of difficulty ...' Ada's impulse to swagger about her own cleverness remained strong, but how could De Morgan not be disarmed by the frankness with which his pupil expressed her gratitude? ('I can only end by repeating what I have often said before,' she wrote: 'that I am very troublesome, & only wish I could do you any such service as you are doing me.')

Ada was lucky. Thanks to Babbage and possibly to Mrs Somerville (still advising from afar), she had acquired her ideal teacher. Only ten years older than his pupil, De Morgan himself had been just fourteen when his gift for mathematics was first noticed. Educated at Trinity at the same time as Woronzow Greig and William King, he was soon moving at the same intellectual level as their brilliant tutors. One, William Whewell, became a lifelong friend. Another, George Peacock (who had helped his own fellow student, Charles Babbage, to found the Cambridge Analytical Society back in 1815), had written the study of differential and integral calculus from which Ada would first begin to learn about algebra. In 1828, De Morgan – still aged only twenty-two – became the new University of London's first professor of mathematics. He taught there – with one gap of five years (due to a personal dispute) – for the next thirty years. Unremittingly industrious, he filled his spare time (when not composing his own celebrated study of differential calculus) with writing over 700 articles on mathematics for the general reader.

De Morgan's readiness to help Ada was based in part upon a close family connection. His wife, Sophia Frend, was the daughter of Lady Byron's own first tutor. In 1838, while Annabella visited Germany with the newly-wed Noels, the De Morgans were allowed to honeymoon for free at Fordhook for ten happy weeks. Early in 1841, they moved into the book-crammed house where Sophia's late father had lived in Gower Street, near the British Museum. Here, more often than not, Ada went to a quick informal supper that was followed by a session of coaching by De Morgan. When his pupil was unwell – as was increasingly the case – De Morgan often accepted a ride in the Lovelace coach, in order to teach Ada at 12 St James's Square. Invited to Ockham and beguiling Ashley Combe, however, De Morgan always refused. A college library held more charm for this modest and unworldly man than the social demands of life at a country house.

Lady Lovelace had adored and revered Mary Somerville, but De Morgan's mischievous wit lent an unexpected bonus to her lessons. 'I don't quite hear you, but I beg to differ entirely with you,' was one of De Morgan's celebrated dry asides; another was that 'it is easier to square the circle than to get round a mathematician'.

He meant it. Sophia, writing a tribute to her brilliant husband in the 1880s, described how little sympathy De Morgan had for Ada's impulse to race towards any new goal, as soon as it was first glimpsed. 'Show me,' he would command wherever an error had occurred. Caution was De Morgan's creed: no progress was permitted until he was shown the exact progress of thought from which the fault had risen, in order that all confusion could be resolved.

The correspondence between pupil and tutor, at its most intense during the period 1840–1, offers evidence of Ada's potential to become a remarkable mathematician. What it also reveals is how – carefully coached towards this end by Mrs Somerville and held to that same course by De Morgan – Ada became willing to persist with a single point until her mastery of it was certain. What De Morgan evidently admired in her was the energy and perseverance with which, even during periods of the grave sickness that had periodically begun to afflict her, his sweet-natured pupil bound herself to the task of her own mathematical improvement. Anything that she did not understand was instantly acknowledged. Writing to Mrs Somerville about her new telescope back in 1836, Ada had shown no qualms about admitting her absolute ignorance of how to use the instrument. So it was now when, writing to De Morgan on 13 September 1840, she freely admitted that she had no idea what was meant by an equation to a curve. Cock-a-hoop two months later when she thought she had spotted errors in George Peacock's text-book on algebra, she readily accepted (10 November) that Peacock's mistakes were in fact those arising from her own beginner's mind, one 'which long experience & practices are requisite to do away with'. Always eager to plunge into the mysteries of differential cal-culus, Lady Lovelace was beginning, nevertheless, to grasp (writing in this same letter) 'the importance of *not* being in a hurry'.

Ada's lessons with De Morgan took place approximately every fortnight. Frustratingly, no account survives of what was said during these sessions. Did Ada ever actually hear her teacher pronounce his well-known maxim, 'The moving force of mathematical invention is not reasoning but imagination'? Or had Ada's own faith in the power of imagination inspired De Morgan's pronouncement? The connection is intriguing because, on 5 January 1841, during the time that Ada was closest to De Morgan, she wrote an essay about the potentially fruitful collaboration between the scientific faculties and the inventive aspects of the mind.

Imagination is the *Discovering* faculty, pre-eminently. It is that which penetrates into the unseen worlds around us, the world of Science. It is that which feels & discovers what *is*, the *real* which we see not ...

Mathematical Science shows what *is*. It is the language of unseen relations between things. But to use & apply that language we must be able fully to appreciate, to feel, to seize, the unseen, the unconscious. Imagination too shows what *is*, the *is* that is beyond the senses. Hence she is or should be especially cultivated by the truly Scientific, – those who wish to enter into the worlds around us.

Writing the essay in which this intriguing passage appears, Ada laid particular emphasis upon what she described as 'the Combining Faculty': an ability to seize upon points in common, 'between sub-jects having no very apparent connexion, & hence seldom or never brought into juxtaposition'. That analogical capacity was precisely the quick-witted, insightful approach that would glow out of the one piece of work for which Ada would later become famous.

It's apparent that De Morgan respected what he recognised, more than any of his contemporaries, to be an extraordinary mind. Writing a long letter to Lady Byron in 1844 about the way it might develop, the logician expressed no doubt about what Ada had the potential to achieve. The worry – one upon which Annabella now sought his opinion – was the danger presented to a delicate constitution by an excess of mental strain. Caution was required. Nevertheless:

I feel bound to tell you that the power that Lady L[ovelace]'s thinking has always shewn, from the beginning of my correspondence with her, has been so utterly out of the common way for any beginner, man, or woman, that this power must be duly considered by her friends, with reference to the question whether they should urge or check her obvious determination to try not only to reach, but to get beyond the present bounds of knowledge.

If you or Lord L[ovelace] think it is a fancy for that particular kind of knowledge which, though unusual in its object, may compare in intensity with the usual interests of a young lady, you do not know the whole ... Mrs Somerville's mind never led her into any other than the *details* of mathematical work. Lady Lovelace will take quite a different route.

De Morgan liked Lady Byron, regarding her (according to his wife's memoir), as 'impulsive and affectionate almost to a fault'. But his was not a letter that set out to flatter or please. He was simply stating what seemed to him to be the obvious fact. Ada Lovelace was a one-off, like no other, neither in her ambitions nor her abilities. She might go beyond them all. The question – one that troubled her mother as much as it did De Morgan himself – was whether it was safe to allow her to do so.

Back in the autumn of 1840, Ada Lovelace felt no such fears. Woronzow Greig heard only that she had never been so happy. Annabella, out in France, was told that Mr De Morgan was a wonderful teacher, the answer to her daughter's prayers. No two people could suit each other better, Ada announced, blithely oblivious to the fact that Mr De Morgan had been happily married for just two years to one of Lady Byron's most cherished friends. (Perhaps it is not surprising that Sophia De Morgan's memoirs would later portray her husband's protégée in a less than flattering light.)

It seemed, during that halcyon autumn of 1840, as though the nearly 25-year-old Ada had discovered a perfect balance. Down in Somerset, she broke away from her studies only to ride up the hills flanking Ashley Combe, in order to enjoy a long, wild gallop across the empty heathland of Exmoor. When at Ockham Park or St James's Square, she cheerfully relinquished the children to the care of Hester and Charlotte. It was really so much better for them as well as herself, she explained:

> ... the less I have *habitually* to do with children the better for them & me. When my sisters are with me, I see *far more* of the children & am of much greater use ... because then there is some one *exclusively devoted* to them, under my direction & superintendence.

Viewed from the comfortable distance of her study, Ada's son Byron Ockham, at the beginning of 1841, remained his mother's firm favourite: 'His affable, communicative, manly & I may say elegant manners, charm people much,' Ada wrote to Louisa Barwell, a childcare specialist in whom her mother placed great faith. Little Annabella, meanwhile, remained in the doghouse, a noisy little girl who was notable only for her 'vile' chubbiness. (Ada, slender as a reed herself by now and fiercely energetic, had come to share her whippet-thin husband's view of weight as a symptom of indolence.)

Writing to Babbage during this same January week – and reminding him to humour her new passion for ice-skating when he visited

Ockham – Ada reverted to a more engrossing topic. The results might occur '*many* years hence', but she wanted to talk 'most seriously' about her plans to offer him valuable assistance.

> You have always been a kind & real & most invaluable friend to *me*; & I would that I could in any way repay it, though I scarcely dare so exalt myself as to hope however humbly, that I can ever be intellectually worthy to attempt serving *you*.

In January 1841, Babbage was still aglow from his recent autumn visit to Turin. Unconscious of the disappointments to come, he felt no present need for help. He had not reckoned upon Ada's persistence. On 22 February, Lady Lovelace wrote again. From hinting at the 'great good' likely to emerge from what she saw as 'the possible (I believe I may say the *probable*) future connexion between us', she proceeded to issue commands. Mr Babbage was instructed to visit her London home to discuss plans: 'the sooner the better'.

Ada Lovelace was entering one of her mercurial phases. It's hard to guess how De Morgan felt on being informed that mathematical forms reminded Ada of the fairies she had read about in fiction. It's equally difficult to imagine how Ada's mother felt on receiving a letter (it had been written on 6 February 1841) that demanded serious consideration for 'one of the most logical, sober-minded, cool, pieces of composition (I believe) that I ever penned; the result of much accurate, matter-of-fact, reflection & study'.

Ada Lovelace's letter to her mother was not logical; neither was it sober, nor cool. Ada had often speculated upon what her goal in life might be; now, so it seemed, she knew. Thanks to her incredible powers of intuition, reasoning and concentration, she foresaw the time when this 'scientific Trinity [would] make me see *anything*, that a being not actually *dead*, can see & know . . .' A 'vast apparatus' had been put into her power. All that remained was for Lady Lovelace to direct it over the next twenty years (the time scale had increased to thirty before the end of the letter) 'to make the engine what I please. But haste; or a restless ambition, would quite ruin the whole.'

So far, so fairly peculiar. It was when Ada proceeded to the bold declaration that 'I can throw *rays* from every quarter of the universe into *one* vast focus' that her letter appeared to enter the realms of lunacy. Something had evidently tipped the always fragile balance of Lady Lovelace's dancing, quicksilver mind. What was it that had taken place?

The most likely cause for Ada's bizarre demand to be seen as superhuman was that she felt an imperative need to stake her claim to superior powers. Her role as Byron's only surviving child, the heir to his legendary genius, was under challenge from a usurper. By February 1841, Lady Byron was living in Paris, where an intrusive cuckoo – a rival daughter – had found snug lodgings in an agreeably well-feathered nest.

Elizabeth Medora Leigh was back in the picture and telling strange tales about her parentage. Was it possible that Ada herself was no longer unique?

༼ঔ༽

Medora had returned at a moment when Lady Byron found herself – for once in an exceptionally busy period of her life as a reformer – frustratingly underoccupied.

Reform is seldom a glamorous subject, but it was one in which Lady Byron, by 1841, possessed few peers. It was a role which, as she would ruefully observe in later years, was made more difficult by her social position. ('The services which I am so willing to render are not asked ... A Right Honourable wall surrounds me.')

Such difficulties were heightened by the fact that Annabella's formidable administrative skills went hand in hand with an implacable will and a capacity for autocratic behaviour that was not always admired by her fellow reformers. There is no doubt – to take one example from many – that the first Ealing headmaster, Mr Craig, had proven unworthy of the time and money that Lady Byron expended upon sending him out to Hofwyl, before housing his family and even having to supervise the truculent pupils over whom Craig himself failed to exert adequate control. It was the dispute with Mr Craig (he was brusquely dismissed from his post, with modest provision for his future) which led his employer to review the system that had let both her and the unfortunate schoolmaster down.

Teaching during the 1840s was a thankless and under-funded profession. The country's attitude to it was dismally reflected in the fact that, in the England of 1840, £30,000 was allocated for national education, while £70,000 was expended upon improving the kennels and stabling at Windsor Castle. Teachers, unlike the clergy, received no pensions; as a result, the church received a great many more worthy applicants than did the schools, which made no special provisions for anybody who did not belong to the gentry class.

The scheme which Lady Byron devised was simple. If teachers were known to receive a family allowance – Annabella had in mind one that would benefit both widows and orphans – their status would instantly improve. And thus, as she argued in a long and earnest letter to Harriet Siddons, the profession would come to be held in higher regard and 'persons of a higher cast of mind' would aspire to become teachers.

Lady Byron had chosen her correspondent with care. Harriet was asked to show Annabella's long letter – it bore the look of a meditated formal proposal – to her brother-in-law. George Combe, as Lady Byron was perfectly aware, had become one of the most admired and influential figures in the world of progressive education. The celebrated author of *The Constitution of Man* was a man who would be able to make things happen.

In London, throughout the 1840s, Annabella oversaw the gradual transformation of Ealing Grove into a model school (one that she helped to replicate on a larger scale at Ockham). At Battersea Training College, Lady Byron's fellow reformer, Dr James Kay, trained several of the former Ealing pupils to become future head-masters. Each was taught to follow the Fellenberg principle that Annabella had introduced: the basics of a formal education were to be combined with a training in technical skills that would enable graduates to earn themselves a living in an increasingly mechanised society.

As in London, so in Leicestershire. By 1840, at least five schools had been set up in the area of Kirkby Mallory. Each school was subsidised by Lady Byron. Each followed the admired Swiss model. In Leicester itself, Annabella helped to fund the city's first public hospital. At Kirkby, Charles Noel was urged by Lady Byron to improve the cottages and to arrange that each family should have its own vegetable allotment. More impressively, her loyal land agent was instructed to argue for the rights of those families as if he himself stood in their shoes. When a weaving community faced hardship in one of the poorest villages on the estate, Annabella stepped forward to offer funds. When Charles Noel deferred action, she scolded him ('The great thing is not to delay as the people are starving.'). Urged to reduce the wages of a retired stableman, Lady Byron refused. ('I do not like the idea of lessening Pegg's subsistence now that he is old and infirm.')

Lady Byron had rounded off the improvements to her family estate, in the summer of 1840, by paying a rare personal visit to Kirkby. Her specific purpose was to inspect a new village school for girls that had been created from a converted cottage. Habitually reticent, Lady Byron was overcome by the welcome she received: 'So many mothers came that it seemed each child had two Mothers!' Annabella reported to Harriet Siddons, adding that the warmth of her reception encouraged her so much that she had managed to deliver a little speech with absolute confidence: 'an odd thing in a shy person ... I acquitted myself well.' Her reticence returned in force a few weeks later, when she learned that Benjamin Haydon was working on a grand group portrait of the 500 British and American abolitionists who had recently been addressed in London by the elderly Thomas Clarkson, William Wilberforce's sturdiest ally in Britain's campaign against slavery. Haydon did not warm to Lady Byron. Nevertheless, impressed by the evidence of suffering that he saw etched into the wan face of one of the very few Englishwomen who had been permitted to attend, Haydon quietly overruled Annabella's request to be omitted from the portrait and placed her well to the fore.

Ada had been scolding her mother – as she frequently did – for putting a frail constitution at risk through overwork. (Ada, as her mother might have countered, was a fine one to talk.) In March, there had been a brief collapse; by July 1840, Annabella was exhausted. It was at this point that Lady Byron decided it would do her good to spend a few months out of the country. George Combe's brother, Andrew, was too busy to accompany her to Paris; instead Dr Fitton, an elderly geologist, was recruited to act as Lady Byron's escort.

It was that exact moment – and it would be interesting to know just how the news of Lady Byron's vacation plans had reached Pontivy, a remote and tiny village in Brittany – that Annabella's relatively carefree mind was diverted into a new and dangerous channel of concern. Word reached her from Pontivy, where Augusta Leigh's 26-year-old runaway daughter Elizabeth Medora was living with her third illicit child, Marie, that the young woman was destitute, dying and in despair. Omitted from this harrowing report was the fact that still on hand, living only four miles away, was a wife-free Henry Trevanion. (Georgiana, together with Henry's legitimate offspring, remained in England.)

Medora was not dying, but the doctor whom Lady Byron despatched to Brittany to assess her situation confirmed that the young woman was indeed in dire straits. Requests had been sent to her mother for the deed to a £3,000 gift that Augusta Leigh had – with unusual prudence – put in trust for her unseen little granddaughter, Marie.* But Augusta (possibly conscious that Henry Trevanion was hovering close enough to seize upon any unexpected windfall) had refused to part with the requisite papers. How could a mother possibly be more heartless to her own neglected and penniless child?

Such a story – as Medora was shrewd enough to intuit – rang like

---

* Medora was planning to draw out an advance against the deed. The £3,000 gifted by Augusta to her granddaughter was contingent upon the death of Lady Byron.

music in the ears of her Aunt Annabella. The always inexplicable affection between two incompatible sisters-in-law had long ago withered into mutual distrust. By 1840, even the levelheaded Mary Montgomery was willing to view Mrs Leigh as 'one of the wickedest woman ever born', a sister who had actually continued to sleep with her brother during his marriage. (Mary's source for this account was a woman whose inviolate truthfulness she would never question: Annabella herself.)

Here, then, was the dawning of a golden opportunity for Lady Byron to lay claim to the high ground. She herself would rescue Medora Leigh, the unhappy product of a relationship in which Augusta, by her own admission, had always led the way. Annabella had never doubted the paternity to which Byron had alluded in his letters to Lady Melbourne – and of which it seems clear that he boasted in private to his credulous wife. Annabella was simply doing her duty, as Byron himself would have wished her to do, for his own unfortunate daughter.

Strengthened by this virtuous self-image, and perhaps a little excited by the adventure upon which she had embarked, Lady Byron prepared for action. Summoning Medora to meet her clandestinely at Tours, an out-of-the-way medieval town set on the Loire (and a testing 300-mile journey from Pontivy), Annabella instructed her niece to protect her respectability (and that of her aunt) by posing as a widowed mother, a certain Madame St Aubin.

Welcomed at Tours, the prodigal completed her redemption at Fontainebleau where, nursing her exhausted aunt through one of Annabella's most serious collapses, the sinning Elizabeth became the sinned-against Medora. It was there – or that is how she later chose to tell the tale – that Medora first learned the incredible truth about her parentage. By the time the pair of women left Fontainebleau for Paris in the mid-autumn of 1840, Medora's role as a newly adopted daughter and beloved protégée was secure. Settled into her own handsome suite of rooms on Place Vendôme as Madame St Aubin – Lady Byron's honoured guest – Medora Leigh could congratulate herself on having brought off the most impressive coup of a hitherto erratic career. Henry Trevanion himself would have applauded.

୨୧

Slender, dark-eyed and outrageously charming (her similarity to Ada was often remarked upon), Medora was also a compulsive liar. Quick to appreciate how profoundly her patroness had come to dislike her mother, Medora was still nursing her patient at Fontainebleau when she began to create her poisonous posy of scandalous tales. Every one of them related to Augusta and each became more shocking than the last.

Publicly, Lady Byron was honoured during her lifetime for her almost superhuman discretion. Privately, Annabella leaked secrets like a bucket with a hole in it. By Christmas 1840, most visitors to her elegant new home on Place Vendôme (one of Paris's most fashionable addresses) were conscious of Medora's history. Back in England, Anna Jameson gasped at the horrors that were being unfolded by her respected friend. Had Mrs Leigh actually played a knowing part in the downfall of her daughter?

> I can believe – alas! that I should confess it – even to you – any
> excess of wickedness in my own sex – even that a mother should
> conspire against the virtue & chastity of her own child; that
> she should corrupt one & sell the other – *this* even I know to be
> possible ... or have I mistook – have I fearfully exaggerated the
> purport of what you tell me?

No, she was not mistaken, and it says much for Medora's skill in storytelling that her preposterous tales were believed by women as intelligent as Anna Jameson and Mary Montgomery, who heard most of them first-hand while visiting Paris.

Fuelled by the wine that Lady Byron herself never touched, Medora recalled how she had been drugged and pinned to the floor by her sister and her mother, while Trevanion raped her. An obsessed Augusta had tried to lure Henry Trevanion into her bed by offering him the use of Emily (Annabella's god-daughter and the youngest of the Leigh children). All this was merely the beginning.

Lady Byron was gullible (as Byron had discovered), but she was not a fool. On one level, in the early days, she knew that she was being manipulated by a skilful trickster. Writing to young Olivia Acheson on the brink of moving from Fontainebleau to Paris, Annabella offered a bittersweet account of how judiciously 'your personified Bon-bon' was being sweetened with hints and half-truths and outright lies.

> She [Medora] knows that the throat of my conscience is small, and she adapts the sweet sin to the size of it, with wonderful precision ... One more edifying instance – if you can't tell a downright falsehood, tell that half of it which will convey the other half inaudibly to the mind of the receiver.

Six weeks later, however, Medora's compelling tales had swept all Annabella's caution away, leaving only a sense of excited outrage. Answering a meek enquiry from Mrs Leigh about her daughter's health, an almost hysterical Annabella ordered the unfortunate woman to hold her tongue. 'I would save you, if it be not too late, from adding the guilt of her death to that of her birth. *Leave her in peace*!' Mrs Villiers, striving to intercede on Augusta's behalf, met with complete resistance. Certified statements of Augusta's goodwill towards her erring child were returned from Paris, unopened.

All – all – in the wild version of events that Medora depicted and in which Annabella was now eager to believe, was the work of wicked Mrs Leigh. Did Medora's presence in Paris not prove how things stood? It was to Byron's wife that his dying child had now turned in her hour of need. It was his forgiving widow who had reached out to save Augusta's abused and wantonly abandoned daughter from her deathbed.

Etc. No gothic novel could surpass the lurid version of Augusta Leigh's misdoings that was now being circulated by a woman who had once been praised by Lord Byron for her absolute inability to utter an untruth.

The only person to whom Annabella delayed in speaking out was her own daughter.

෴

Back at the beginning of the year 1841, Ada had been writing, with complete control of her wits, an essay about the connection between imagination and scientific thought. She was ready to describe the past six months as the happiest period of her life, a time when the twin deities of music and mathematics had held her in thrall. Of Medora, she knew only that the ever-charitable Lady Byron had taken a hapless daughter of Augusta Leigh's under her wing in Paris. How typical of the Hen! 'I quite revere & adore the Hen's whole conduct & feelings respecting this singular & apparently unfortunate being,' Ada wrote to her mother in early January, shortly after receiving the unknown Medora's Christmas gift of a handmade red-and-gold pincushion. 'It *well* paints your whole principle & character; – at least it does so to *me*.'

And then, the bombshell descended.

CHAPTER SIXTEEN

A CUCKOO IN THE NEST
(1841–3)

*But if you knew one half the harum-scarum extraordinary
things I do, you would certainly incline to the idea that I
have a Spell of some sort about me. I am positive that no
She-Creature of my years could possibly attempt many of
my everyday performances, with any impunity.*

ADA LOVELACE TO WORONZOW GREIG,
31 DECEMBER 1841

During the year of 1840, Ada Lovelace and her husband began to be drawn apart, not by any lack of affection, but by their consuming and divided interests. Ada, while pursuing the elusive quarry of finite differences that brought her ever closer to understanding the intricate workings of Charles Babbage's unbuilt Analytical Engine, remained deeply committed to music.

The year 1840 was when Ada decided, out of her own modestly lined pocket, to sponsor the education at the Royal Academy of Music of a 14-year-old Welsh harpist, John Thomas. (Thomas, who went on to become Queen Victoria's harpist, gratefully named his daughter after his first patron.) Harp-playing occupied as much as half of every day for the young countess herself. Every new musical event was a must-do in a busy London calendar during a period when Lady Lovelace was dabbling in mesmerism (Anton Mesmer believed in a mysterious bodily fluid enabling the hypnotism of one person by another) while also acting as her mother's scout for new areas in which to invest. On 11 March 1841, Ada was a thrilled observer of the brand-new atmospheric railway, in which Lady Byron had expressed an interest.*

William Lovelace, handsomely funded by the doting Hen's judicious sales from the vast Wentworth estates (of which she held sole ownership), was meanwhile embarking on a lavish programme of architectural development in Surrey, Somerset and London. In 1840, while still living at Ockham, William bought East Horsley Place, the Barry-designed house owned by his Surrey neighbour William Currie. (Currie moved down the road to occupy his preferred second home at West Horsley.) In London, the Lovelaces' elegant home in St James's Square underwent a facelift major enough for Ada to have to move out into nearby lodgings during the early summer of 1842. During this same period, Lord Lovelace oversaw the ongoing transformation of his father's simple woodland hunting box in north Somerset. Ashley Lodge was converted into Ashley Combe, a fairytale palace perched between two wooded flanks of cliffside that climb up to Exmoor's heathland from the sweeping inlet of Hurlstone Bay. Inspired, it seems, by one of Byron's favourite poems (Coleridge's dreamlike *Kubla Khan* was written while the poet was exploring this ravishing corner of north Somerset), Ada's favourite of all her husband's architectural fantasies featured hanging gardens, balustraded terraces, winding tunnels and concealed bridges. It was – and remains, despite ruined gardens and a vanished house – a ravishing setting.

---

* The atmospheric railway scheme drove carriages uphill at 25 mph by means of a series of magnificently designed pumping stations and traction piping. Speeds of as much as 45 mph were achieved on the stretch of line in West Croydon visited by Ada. Lady Byron was unimpressed. Her eventual rail portfolio of £67,000 in 1860 (worth about £3 million today) did not include shares in the atmospheric railway.

The news that arrived from Place Vendôme in the spring of 1841 shook a congenially independent marriage to its foundations, sparking what Ada described the following year as 'a frightful crisis in my existence ... Heaven knows what intense suffering & agony I have gone thro'; & how *mad* & how *reckless* & how *desperate* I have at times felt.'

The first bulletin, sent towards the end of the month, revealed what Ada now felt licensed to speak to her mother about as 'the *fact*' of her father's incest. 'I am not in the least *astonished*,' she informed the disconcerted Hen on 27 February. 'In fact you merely confirm what I have for *years & years* felt scarcely a doubt about, but should have considered it most improper in me to hint to you that I in any way suspected.' Asked for the source of her knowledge, Ada grew evasive. 'Perhaps I may some day [remember],' she teased on 3 March. Quite possibly, it was Lady Byron herself who had made the revelation; Annabella seldom recollected just what she had said in private, or to whom.

The bombshell for Ada Lovelace was the news that Medora Leigh was the product of that incestuous relationship, and thus Ada's own half-sister. 'I should tell you that I did not suspect the daughter as being the result of it [the incest],' Ada responded. Evidently discomfited by the idea, she challenged it. How could her mother have come to such a monstrous conclusion? 'The natural intimacy & familiarity of a Brother & Sister certainly could not suggest it, to any but a very depraved & vicious mind ...'

Ada's reaction was understandable in a young woman who suddenly saw her own position – that of the treasured and sole product of an exceptional marriage – under threat. When no answer came from Paris, she took counsel with William. The news from France was worrying and unwelcome. Nevertheless, both husband and wife knew how obstinate Lady Byron could be. Like it or not, Medora Leigh (or the widow Madame St Aubin, as she was being described in Paris to cover the awkward presence of little Marie) must be accepted, not as a cuckoo in the nest, but as part of the family.

Evidence of the furious anger that Ada was forcing herself to suppress would only emerge two years later. By March 1843, when time had brought about a considerable change both in Lady Byron's feelings, and those of her demanding protégée, Ada would be ready to speak out and unmask her true feelings. But back in the spring of 1841, as she prepared to join the Paris household, she remarked only upon the fact that her mother had grown nervously solicitous. Urging her habitually informal daughter to pack at least one good dress for a court presentation, an almost supplicant Lady Byron promised to clothe her sweet Bird in the finest of Parisian plumage, to purchase whatever type of harp Ada might wish to play, and to leave plenty of time for Ada's own amusements.

'You hold out great temptations,' Ada dryly responded on 12 March. Nevertheless, she stated that her visit would be brief, while ill health made it unlikely that her husband (he was being nursed by his sisters) would come at all. Irritated at being obliged to defer her mathematics lessons, Ada promised the De Morgans that nothing would cause her to abandon her studies.

> Indeed the last fortnight is rather a convincing proof that nothing can. I have been out either to the Opera, German Opera, or somewhere or other, every night. I have had music lessons every morning, & practised my Harp too, for an hour or two, & I have been on horseback nearly every day also. I might add many sundries & et-ceteras to this list.
>
> I must however maintain that Differential Calculus is king of the company – & may it ever be so!

❧

Ada's unfaltering interest in Babbage's unbuilt machine, as much as the seriousness of her friendship with the ageing and frustrated inventor, is well illustrated by the fact that one of Ada's first visits in Paris was to the home of the great mathematician Jean Arago. Head of the Paris Observatory, Arago had been Babbage's facilitator in obtaining the silk portrait of Jacquard for his 1840 visit to Turin and it was Babbage who now provided Ada with the introduction to a man of whom she stood in some awe. Back at Place Vendôme with her mother and their old friend, Mary Montgomery, Ada found herself reluctantly surrendering to the persuasive charm of her new-found sister.

Graceful in her manner and tall in stature (a doting Annabella nicknamed Elizabeth Medora 'Lanky Doodle', while permitting her niece – and no one else – to address her by Byron's old pet name of 'Pip'), 'Madame St Aubin' seemed content with an arrangement that kept her in a private suite of rooms, ones from which little Marie and her mother had no rights of access into Lady Byron's home without prior invitation. 'I therefore go there whenever I choose,' Ada wrote to her husband on 8 April, adding that her initial feelings about Medora were 'very favourable ... She impresses me with the idea of *principle* very strongly.'

Ada, like Miss Montgomery and Annabella, swallowed the stories that Medora told without a blink. 'How comes it my Mother is not dead, mad or depraved?' Ada asked William:

> A *new language* is requisite to furnish terms strong enough to express my horror & amazement at the appalling facts! – That *viper* Mrs L[eigh] – crowned all by suppressing letters of my mother's to my father when he was abroad after the separation, & *forging others* in their place. *She-monster!**

Adding to the bitterness of a lengthy letter that Ada would write to Medora two years later was the sense of how much she herself had fallen under the spell of a persuasive liar. Out in Paris, while

---

* Medora's revelation chimed with suspicious neatness with a letter that Miss Montgomery had written to Annabella in 1823 from Genoa, where she learned from the gossipy Lady Blessington that some vindictive correspondent was slandering the reputation of Byron's wife (*LP*). Miss Montgomery, Medora and Lady Byron were all living under the same roof in Paris; the echo of the conversation preceding Medora's wild claim is almost audible.

her mother arranged to exchange her expired ten-year leasehold
of Fordhook for a similar arrangement with two adjoining houses
near Esher (conveniently close to Ockham), it was Ada who gave the
hardest thought to how Medora could most decorously be housed
in the smaller of the two. Following her own formal presentation to
the French King, Louis Philippe, Lady Lovelace spoke to Madame
de Talleyrand about two former employees, Nathalie and Victor
Beaurepaire, who might suitably serve as Madame St Aubin's private
servants at Esher, enabling her to live like a lady of means. (And so,
until the money ran out and the Beaurepaires took to blackmail,
indeed they did.)

The Paris party returned to England in May 1841. The new houses
at Moore Place were in need of considerable refurbishment before
they could be inhabited. Ada, living between Ockham and St James's
Square during that part of the year, was reluctant to provide house-
room for a sister who, she probably surmised, might never leave.
Instead, Medora was temporarily lodged in London with relatives
of Sophia De Morgan. Meanwhile, Anna Jameson arranged for little
Marie to attend a school in the pleasant West London hamlet of
Notting Hill. By August, Mrs Jameson was among that small group
of Annabella's friends who were willing to declare of Medora that
'it is impossible to know her without loving her – or to look into her
mind without respecting all she has done.' Writing to her beloved
confidante, Harriet Siddons, up in Edinburgh, at the beginning
of that month, Annabella confessed that the presentation of her
protégée was nevertheless causing friction among her friends. Only
Harriet, she sighed, seemed willing to look at things 'in the unre-
fracted light of truth – and to know the truth it brings'. The truth,
as Lady Byron's closest friends were ruefully aware, meant accepting Annabella's own judgement to be infallible. Harriet Siddons
remained prudently quiet on the subject of a young woman she had
never met.

☙

The immediate effect of Medora's introduction as her rival and half-sister upon Ada was to make her take up the challenge to show herself, uniquely, as the heir to Byron. Writing to her mother after the first revelation of incest, Lady Lovelace had declared her intention of surpassing her father's achievements: 'I think he has bequeathed this task to me! ... I *have a duty* to perform towards him.' What that duty might be, she remained unsure. For a time, Ada considered becoming a poet. Writing to Mary Somerville's son, Woronzow Greig, on the final day of 1841, she represented herself as a swashbuckling breaker of convention.

> You know I am a d—d odd animal! And as my mother often
> says, she never has quite yet made up her mind whether it [be]
> *Devil* or *Angel* that watches *peculiarly* over me; only that it is
> one or the other, *without doubt*! – (And for *my* part, I am quite
> indifferent *which*) –

For a couple of high summer months, Lady Lovelace played the daredevil. William, busy supervising his grand building projects, raised no objections to behaviour that caused one admirer to describe his wife as an elusive 'will o'the whisp', forever eluding capture as she sped along her way. In America, however, the *New York Times* had harsh words to say of a woman who rode about in fashionable Hyde Park with married men. Ada's riding companions were Sir William Molesworth, owner of the respected *Westminster Review*, and Frederick Knight, a Somerset landowner who had newly returned from Italy. Today, such behaviour seems almost laughably tame; back in 1841, when a woman was still forbidden to watch parliamentary proceedings without a husband planted at her side, such a bold wife – and Byron's daughter, to boot – attracted censure.

Mathematics was never far from Ada's mind. In June 1841, she confessed to Augustus De Morgan that her studies had been neglected during her stay in Paris. She wished to resume work: 'I am quite in a fuss about my mathematics, for I am much in want of a lift at the moment' suggests that abstract thinking offered Ada a welcome refuge from her confused emotions.

The new link to William Molesworth (his wife would become one of Ada's closest friends) was connected both to this wealthy and scientifically minded gentleman's interest in Babbage's unbuilt machine and Ada's own persistent wish to help that mechanical monster into existence. She kept up a regular correspondence with Babbage throughout the summer, while making increasingly frequent reference to Charles Wheatstone, the rotund and quietly charming inventor of the first electric telegraph, with whom Ada regularly discussed her scientific projects. By August 1841, Ada was addressing both Babbage and Wheatstone by their surnames alone. In an age that frowned upon gender equality, this marked a rare level of egalitarian professionalism.

Ada had kept faith with Augustus De Morgan throughout her hectic summer. An almost daily correspondence between them was maintained from August to late November, during which Lady Lovelace strove to narrow the gap between her deficiencies and her aspirations. On the one hand, she now felt confident enough to recommend and send Gabriel Lamé's *Cours de Physique* to her tutor; on the other, she was still struggling to apply differential and integral calculus to the subject of accelerated velocity ('It has interested me beyond anything.').* On 15 August 1841, conscious that she would never lure De Morgan away from the metropolis, she arranged to come up to London from Ockham for a lesson at Gower Street, before her family beat their annual two-month retreat to remote Ashley Combe. By 14 November, while still at Ashley, Ada was so deeply immersed in mathematics that a pleased Hen, writing to William Lovelace, joked that he should send 'love to the Bird when you can insinuate it between two problems'.

---

* Probably by measuring the speed at which a ball rolled down a sloping tray, which is still a popular experiment with budding mathematicians.

Annabella's seemingly light-hearted message arrived at the end of a series of cryptic bulletins despatched from Ashley Combe to De Morgan, during which Ada informed her tutor of sudden and private plans to visit London.

My intended journey to Town is only on particular business.
And by the bye it is *not to be known that I am going.* My
mother even has no idea of it; and I do not wish that she should.

The first visit, announced on 27 October, was deferred; on 10 November, it was reset for the following day, 'in consequence of letters unexpectedly received'. Again, Ada enjoined discretion to De Morgan ('I do not wish my journey to be known'). Once again the trip was delayed.

On 14 November, a hasty visit to London was rescheduled for the third time. Writing to her mother from Somerset on the same day, Ada made no mention of her travel plans. Instead, she confined herself to talk of Byron Ockham ('a true scion of the Parent Stock') and her son's vivid wish (aged five) to become a workman rather than a lord of leisure. Such an ambition, at a time when the local workforce was helping to reconstruct Ashley Combe as a palatial residence, was unsurprising; the Porlock bricklayers and masons must have appeared like gods to a small and often neglected boy who welcomed their friendly company.

Ada adored her oldest son. Quite deliberately, she recounted to her mother in this same letter that William, celebrating 5 November at home with the family, had let a firecracker off 'intentionally, almost in B[yron's] face, by way of fun'. She added that Miss Boutell, the young governess who witnessed the scene, had been astonished by the child's pluck. (He 'never winced even'.) Still, it was a curious tale to pass on to a doting grandmother. Was Ada alerting her mother to a darker side of Lord Lovelace's nature? (There would be several later references to the Crow's black temper and even to a flight that the Bird had taken from home until her husband had calmed down.) Or was Ada merely trying to distract attention from a London visit, one about which she was peculiarly anxious that her mother should not know?

Lady Byron's careful pruning of the family archive makes speculation difficult. It's likely that Ada's secret visits had to do with Charlotte King's marriage that autumn to a divinity student called Demetrius Calliphronas. It is also possible that Ada's discreet visit to London was connected to Dr James Kay.

On 21 October, James Kay, doctor, educational reformer and general good egg, had sent Ada the equivalent to a love letter. Seemingly bewitched by the 'waywardness, beauty & intangibility' of Lord Byron's daughter, he compared Ada to a fairylike mirage, always flitting from view or plunging him 'into some bog, while I am gazing at you half in admiration, somewhat in apprehension and altogether in kindness'. It's rash, without knowing more detail, to read too much into this flowery tribute. Annabella, who was herself an admiring friend and work colleague of Dr Kay's, read the good doctor's letter years later and agreed with his description of her daughter's elusive charm; one of Ada's chosen alter egos was that of a benevolent, if capricious, fairy.

Certainly, Dr Kay grew close to Ada during the summer of 1841. Recruited in his medical capacity as a supplier of laudanum to 'a naughty sick Bird', Dr James Kay became a regular attendant of the mesmeric sessions which were hosted by the Lovelaces during the summer of 1841.

Mesmerism in England during the 1840s was uneasily poised between charlatanism (France's leading mesmerist, Charles Lafontaine, drew huge audiences when he mesmerised a lion at London Zoo) and medical science. (Mesmerism aimed to spare patients from the pain of surgery in the years before the introduction of ether and chloroform.) A serious purpose behind the simple experiments performed at the Lovelaces' home by the country's best-known mesmerist, John Elliotson, might be argued from the fact that meetings were attended not only by Hester and the newly engaged Charlotte King, but by Dr Kay, Charles Wheatstone and William Lovelace's good friend, Britain's first Egyptologist, Sir John Gardner

Wilkinson. The results, judging by Dr Kay's unpublished journal, were mildly silly. Charlotte King and an unnamed housemaid fell into a trance in which they responded only to the soothing voice of the mesmerist. Ada believed that the process had caused her head to heat up and tingle. Kay himself remained more intrigued by his hostess than by Elliotson's demonstrations of his hypnotic powers.

Four months after writing his love letter to Ada, Dr Kay married a Yorkshire heiress and changed his name to Kay-Shuttleworth. Might the news that her admirer was courting Janet Shuttleworth have given rise to Ada's boasts of wild behaviour, and have caused her subsequent collapse? (She suffered a breakdown at the end of the year 1841.) Probably not. Listing the candidates for a colony of her favourite people the following July, Ada teasingly informed her husband that she would include both Dr Kay and himself ('tho really what use an old Crow would be to me I know not'.) In February 1843, Dr Kay was one of a very select group invited to Ockham, in order to celebrate Hester King's marriage to Sir George Crauford. (It was a marriage which Ada had been most anxious to bring about.)

A far more likely cause than Dr Kay's marriage for the despair which Ada confessed to Woronzow Greig on 31 December 1841 (in the same letter that boasted of her 'harum-scarum' ways and indifference to convention) was the continuing sense that Medora Leigh had usurped her right to feel that she was Lord Byron's unique heir. Writing to a concerned Greig from her London home, Ada begged the newly married barrister not to worry about her: 'I am doing very well indeed: – as well as possible. And I have no notion whatever of either taking myself *out of the world*, or being a useless invalid *in it*. So be easy.' Nevertheless, and to the considerable dismay of the Crow, the Hen and the Greigs (Woronzow's wife, Agnes, had swiftly joined the inner circle of Ada's friends), Lady Lovelace suddenly announced her need for a change. Maths was dropped for six months in favour of plays, operas – and new plans for a singing career.

In the spring of 1842, Ada's letters sound as though she has suddenly vaulted into our times. Her energy appears to be boundless. She writes of taking her meals on the run at a 'nice respectable shop in Oxford Street' where breakfast, dinner and supper can be obtained, 'at a moment's notice'. She loans the elegant Lovelace carriage to carry 'that *nice old gentleman* the Hen' off to visit the 7th Lord Byron's home in Belgravia, before dashing off herself for a two-hour chat about science with Charles Wheatstone. Between times, she attends a lecture, inspects another railway, takes a singing lesson and then finds the energy to spend '4 or 5 hours at least' playing her harp. And this, in the spring and early summer of 1842, was just an average day.

Throughout this hectic period of her life, as indicated by frequent references to physical pain and consultations with a new father figure, the kindly eyed royal obstetrician, Charles Locock, Ada was also combating serious problems with her health.

Singing was the antidote to illness, or so Lady Lovelace chose to persuade herself. (She told Wheatstone in 1842 that she thought mathematics made her feel worse.) In singing, she had found her true vocation. The courteous words of teachers (one said she had 'a wonderful *facility*', while another artfully suggested that such genius 'must not be lost to my friends and Society') were all that Ada needed to convince herself of her rare talent. William, who like the Hen and the Greigs, longed for his wife to return to mathematics, heard instead about the ways Ada now planned to dazzle their guests at Ockham. She would sing arias from the newly fashionable *Norma* to an audience gathered in their library. How proud he would be of her! Everybody admired her innate sense of theatre:

> ... and the more scope I have in prospect for it, the more
> settled, calm & happy, does my mind become ... Think how
> merrily & joyously evenings would go: how delightful when
> we have company, to be able to *improve* them a little, as I
> know I could through song ... For there is a mysterious kind of
> Mesmerism in *such* expressions as I am likely to be able to give,
> which ennobles the hearts of those who *listen* ...

The quotation is taken from the torrent of exuberant letters in which Ada swamped a distant William – busy with his building projects at Ashley Combe – during her short-lived love affair with the stage. With each fresh epistle, Ada's horizon expanded. Singing was just the start: poetry might well be her true destiny. 'And if so, it will be poetry of a unique kind – far more philosophical & higher in its nature than aught the world has perhaps yet seen.'

One thing was clear. Ada Lovelace would not be stopped. Her 'undevelopped [sic] power' must find expression, she wrote in the same letter. It could do so only by the provision of 'very powerful, & continually-acting stimulants', and for these, money was required. Vague about the stimulants, she was clear about her urgent need of funds. 'Money,' Ada informed her husband, 'is the rub.' Threats followed: 'it will be the very Devils' own work, if the wants of this case cannot be supplied'. But then she became alarmed that William might ask her mother for the cash that he himself lacked. Not a word to the Hen, she instructed him: all plans would be discussed with her by 'myself only at present'.

Ada was always a little apprehensive of her mother's uncompromising personality. Fortunately for her, Lady Byron was far too distracted by her protégée's erratic behaviour in the summer of 1842 to focus on that of her daughter.

Nothing could have been more calculated to provoke Elizabeth Medora Leigh, now viewing herself as Ada's co-heir and social equal, than to see Byron's more brilliant child free, at liberty to enjoy a life of adventurous independence of the kind that she herself – now imprisoned within a sedate mansion situated on the fringes of the quiet English village of Esher – now craved. In April, a disillusioned Anna Jameson predicted troubles to come. In May, following Augusta's unexpected relinquishing of the coveted financial deed and Annabella's prudent decision to place it in the care of her own solicitors, Medora erupted. Annabella, the object of her fury, was forced to admit that she had never – not even from Lord Byron at his wildest – seen the like of Medora's rage. Fleeing from Moore Place and its screechingly aggressive inhabitant, Annabella took refuge with the sympathetic George Byrons in London, at their home on Eaton Place. There, having regained her composure, Annabella drew up a list of observations on her niece and sealed them up in an envelope she temptingly inscribed: '*Not to be opened without my leave.*'

It has naturally been opened long since. What the document reveals is that, even at this late stage, Annabella was trying to mitigate her protégée's behaviour. Medora's anger had been pure drama, not deeply felt. Her obsession with money had by now become unavoidably apparent, but it was not the poor young woman's fault. All could be blamed on the way Medora's character had been shaped by her dissolute and neglectful mother. Nevertheless, mindful of her past promise to Byron, Annabella added a memo to herself. While declining to name her reasons, she noted that she must try to protect 'the mother' by some future arrangement. Relations between the two sisters-in-law had seemingly reached their nadir when Lady Byron could not bring herself to identify by name Augusta Leigh.

ᏬᎬᎩ

Family issues of a happier nature had provided Ada with a welcome break from trying to soothe the tantrums of an importunate and increasingly temperamental half-sister. Visiting Cambridge in the high summer of 1842 (Ada wanted to be on hand for the birth of Charlotte King's first child, while her husband completed a Cambridge degree in divinity), Lady Lovelace discovered that a new and promising romance was budding. Ada, who looked upon Hester as the true sister of her heart, was determined to help.

Lord Lovelace doted on his younger sisters. He had been perturbed when Charlotte married a penniless seminarian. Sir George Crauford was a vastly more eligible candidate. An old friend of Demetrius Calliphronas, Sir George was a large, shy baronet with an enormous head and a heart to match it. Recently returned from years in India and possessed of a splendid new

Miss Annabella Milbanke: 'a fine child' in her adoring parents' view.

Annabella Milbanke as a much-courted heiress, and as Byron would have first seen her.

Comte d'Orsay seems to have painted little Ada Byron
before he met her father at Genoa in 1823. He captures
her lively charm.

Ada's beloved Persian cat, Puff, drawn by
her mother with an accompanying tribute
in verse.

Lady Byron commissioned this handsome
portrait of Ada in the year of her marriage.
Ada disliked both it and the artist.

Lord Byron. Annabella's mother was so delighted by Thomas Phillips's portrait of her future son-in-law that she purchased it for herself. It was how the 25-year-old author of *Childe Harold* wished to be seen.

George Anson Byron (8th Lord) was Ada's 'sweet cousin'. She looked upon George as a brother. He married a Nottinghamshire heiress.

Lady Melbourne, here in her splendid prime, was Byron's most worldly advisor. She was also the mother-in-law of Lady Caroline Lamb and the aunt of Annabella Milbanke.

Augusta Leigh, half-sister to Lord Byron.

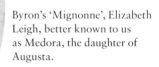

Byron's 'Mignonne', Elizabeth Leigh, better known to us as Medora, the daughter of Augusta.

(*Left*) As a young man, Ada Lovelace's future husband modelled his appearance upon Lord Byron. Like him, William King also travelled to Greece. (*Right*) Lady Hester King, the mother of William, was a cold and unhappy woman. Even Ada Lovelace failed to pierce her armour.

(*Left*) Ada was especially fond of her sweet-natured sister-in-law, Hester, Jr. (*Right*) Ada helped to facilitate Hester's marriage to the kind and devoted Reverend Sir George Crauford.

Lord Lovelace's exuberant creation helped to ruin him. Ada never inhabited her special Mathematical Room in the tower above the moat. The Lovelaces' daughter nicknamed Horsley Towers 'Glum Castle'.

Charles Babbage was of an age to have been a father figure to Ada. Their relationship was both fiery and playful.

The remarkable Mary Somerville furthered Ada's mathematical education and became a second mother to her. The close connection continued through Ada's daughter into the next generation.

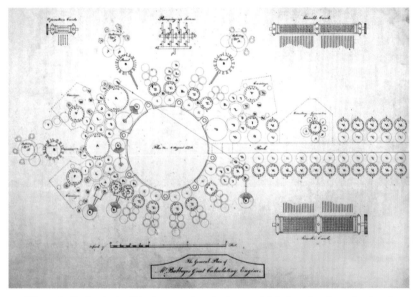

The unbuilt Analytical Engine stood at the heart of Ada Lovelace's professional friendship with Charles Babbage.

Antoine Claudet made a series of daguerreotypes of Ada and her children in the 1840s. Ada was fascinated by this technique of early photography.

Lady Byron drew this heartbreaking final image of Ada while helping to watch over her in London.

Byron Ockham, Ada and William's first son, wears his midshipman's uniform. This is by Claudet, *c.*1849.

Claudet's daguerreotype of Ada and William's second son, Ralph (later Lord Wentworth), *c.*1849.

Ada's clever and long-suffering daughter Annabella (later Anne) married William Scawen Blunt. She is in Eastern dress, beside one of her celebrated Arabian horses.

mansion (Burgh Hall in Lincolnshire), Sir George, having fallen deeply in love with Hester King, planned to install the impoverished Calliphronases in a wing at Burgh and to allow Hester, until such time as he could marry her, to live with them there. Sir George's one wish, so Ada reported to William from Cambridge in early July, was to make the King sisters happy and comfortable, '& indeed to give them every luxury almost'. There was just one problem: William Lovelace's morbid horror of obesity.* Sir George's girth was comparable, even in the devoted Hester's view, to that of a wine cask.

Ada's attempt to circumnavigate the problem of Sir George's massive proportions was endearing. Not having yet met the baronet, she described him to Lovelace as allegedly *very handsome and attractive*. As to size, Hester had said that her suitor was really 'not at all *too big*, or what exceeds the proportions of a fine well-made man'. Goodness evidently shone out of the dear man and – although bashful in company – Sir George was reported to have plenty to say, when aroused in 'particular' conversation. Really, Ada pleaded, no man could be better suited to their dear Hester, or more likely to produce the happiness that she so richly deserved.

Ada's commendations won through. Plans were made for a wedding to take place at Ockham in February 1843. (Locke King and his wife Louisa risked maternal wrath to attend the ceremony. William's mother, furious at what she perceived as Hester's selfish desertion, maintained her usual unforgiving distance.) Writing to Ada, whom he had still not met, back on 3 November 1842, Sir George thanked his unknown advocate for the 'so strangely so surprisingly kind' way in which she had represented and welcomed him into her branch of Hester's family. Her affectionate message of congratulation, so he told a gratified Ada, had given him more pleasure than any other letter he had received. It was a kindness which was never forgotten,

---

* Photographed in his late sixties, Lord Lovelace could still proudly squeeze into the tightly fitting cavalry officer's uniform that he had worn upon his wedding day.

as the grateful Crauford would demonstrate in his fond attentions in later years to all three of Ada's children.*

Lady Byron had been equally delighted by the news of Hester's suitor, signifying her approval by providing both a trousseau and a gift of £300 to a young woman whose tender affection for Ada's children had long since won their grandmother's own heart. Concern for Hester's welfare offered a welcome distraction from the unpleasant memory of how easily she had again exposed herself to Medora's manipulations.

Medora had lost favour with her aunt after her tantrums at Moore Place. Seeking to regain her old ascendancy, she took the only route that never failed. On 19 July 1842, having fuelled herself with alcohol, Medora concocted the most ignoble letter she ever addressed to 'Dearest Pip'. The subject, once again, was Augusta Leigh.

It was by chance that Medora, while lodging at the Lovelaces' home in St James's Square, had happened to catch a passing glimpse of her own mother. (Augusta had been visiting another resident in the square, her cousin the Duke of Leeds.) Mrs Leigh had not weathered well. Nevertheless, she is unlikely to have represented the nightmarish portrait conjured up for Lady Byron's delectation by an inebriated correspondent. 'I have drunk quantities of wine since,' Medora admitted before launching forth:

God forgive her. Oh how horrible she looked – so wicked – so hyena-like – that I could have loved her so ... Had death passed over me the chill – the horror – could not have been so great. Pity & forgive me if I involuntarily pain, I do not mean – but I do suffer ...

Reverting to more practical details and suddenly recalling that she was meant to be preparing to go back to France in less than a week,

* Ada's kindness is too often overlooked. In 1840, she turned down a personal invitation to the queen's birthday party, preferring to accompany a nervous former children's governess to the East London docks. (Miss Boutell was making her first visit to the Continent.)

Medora added as a (characteristically ungrammatical) afterthought that 'Ada and me will consult about road.'

By July 1842, Lady Byron was perfectly aware that Medora was an inveterate liar (one against whom she had already resolved to protect Augusta Leigh from future financial pressure). Nevertheless, Medora's awful account was nodded through as no more than the truth. 'I could not read of that meeting without great pain,' Annabella responded (forgetting that no actual encounter had been described), 'and yet I believe it best that you should see what it is.'

It was not one of Lady Byron's finest moments.

To Ada, the news that Medora, paid off with a small allowance from Lady Byron, was to be settled in a remote French village with her daughter and servants, came as an unqualified relief. Writing to her mother on 23 July, the day of Medora's departure, Ada thankfully noted the arrival of a warm west wind as 'the very thing' to speed their intrusive relative on her way.

Ada Lovelace's relief was understandable. At the end of her own patience after a series of difficult interviews with Medora (undertaken at Lady Byron's request), she made no effort to hide her scorn. Lady Byron heard how Medora had insulted both her kind patron and Anna Jameson before announcing her intention of getting the money (of which she had been so unjustly deprived) by 'throwing herself down the throat of the first man she could get hold of to marry'.

The language of Ada's paraphrasing of Medora's threat revealed her own contempt. Acting with just a touch of malice, Lady Lovelace had apparently offered to arrange a marriage to her own French dentist, adding that Medora could think herself lucky if the gentleman agreed to such a match. At this point, Miss Leigh completely lost her temper.* 'And then came all sorts of vituperations; some so really *ridiculous*, that one could scarcely feel otherwise than inclined to laugh.'

---

* Ada's suggestion was less insulting than it appears to have sounded to a furious Medora. In France, dentistry was regarded as an art that conferred upon its practitioners a high degree of social status. The dentist whom Ada named was French.

Writing to William at approximately the same time, Ada was more candid still. The whole Medora business had been both miserable and infuriating, she told her husband. But what saddened her most was to see the hurt that had been caused, both to her mother and to loquacious, well-meaning Anna Jameson. 'I cannot bear to think of it, & the *folly* of so many people.'

By the end of July 1842, Medora – modestly subsidised by her aunt and supposedly under the close supervision of the Beaurepaires – was gone. Annabella, although disillusioned, grieved at the loss of a niece who had become close as a daughter, one in whom she had seen a vivid glimpse of the irresistible, volatile husband she could never forget. Ada, freed from a disturbing and exhausting presence, reverted to her good-humoured self again. While sending teasing thanks two days later for her mother's generosity – Annabella had just funded the expensive purchase of an Ockham stud of horses – she offered sympathy for a loss that she knew her mother felt more deeply than she cared to admit. It was sad that 'a nice stingy Old Hen, (especially about *horses* . . .)' should be feeling bereft. 'I am afraid you are lonely this evening. I wish I were with you.' To William, Ada sent her promise to please him by a change of lifestyle. For the rest of the year, his wife planned to stay quietly at home in the country. 'I know you would prefer such a state of things . . . dear Mate.'

෨෧

Ada kept her word. Throughout the August of 1842 and on into the autumn, she retreated to the now partly habitable splendour of Ashley Combe. There, dwelling within her husband's Gothicised riff on a medieval castle, its lancet windows looking across Porlock's broad and silvery bay, Ada played her harp and resumed her mathematical studies. Writing to Augustus De Morgan at the end of August, she told him that she had been working hard, and with good results.

All that mattered was to find the right balance.

Writing to Woronzow Greig on 16 December 1842, in answer to

one of his annual and always searching letters about her projects, Ada chided Mrs Somerville's sober son for treating her ambitions as mere whims. Slyly, Greig had compared her to Madame de Staël's Corinne, a woman possessed of exceptional imagination, sensibility and – like her creator – an immense ego. And how many worlds did their very own Corinne plan to conquer, he had enquired?

Greig's reference touched a raw nerve. Tartly, Ada responded that she did not care for de Staël's loquacious heroine and her Werther-like dramas of the heart. For herself, she aspired only to reconcile her desire to excel in music (she thought now both of singing and of composing) with what might still prove to be 'my ultimate vocation: namely, Science and Mathematics'.

Brave words. And yet, Mr Greig and his wife must have shuddered when they read what followed:

> Time must show. To say the truth, I have less ambition than I had. And what I *really* care most about is now perhaps to establish in my mind those *principles & habits* that will fit me best for the next state. There is in my nervous system such utter want of *all* ballast & steadiness, that I cannot regard my life or powers other than precarious ... there are the seeds of destruction, within me. This I know.

Ada Lovelace's egocentricity – the words 'I', 'me', 'my' and 'myself' appeared twenty-seven times in a not especially lengthy letter – bore out Greig's reference to Corinne. Here was the ego written on a de Staël-like scale. And with cause. Aged just twenty-eight, Ada was a young woman who lived under the constant threat of a total breakdown in her health. The projects she described were always overshadowed by the intimations of her own frailty. How could Byron's brilliant, ambitious daughter not obsess about her own mortality as she remembered the cruel shortness of her father's own life span. Ada was twenty-eight. Byron had died at thirty-six. Time was running out.

Ada had chosen to be a little reticent with Woronzow Greig.

Writing an undated letter to Lord Lovelace from St James's Square sometime during the final weeks of 1842, she began with generalities. She was taking the affianced Hester off to the theatre to hear Adelaide Kemble sing. Her interest was now confined entirely to matters that were either musical or scientific. And then, as if to tease her husband, for 'I have nothing *very* particular to tell you', Ada released the information that an admiring Crow and a devoted Hen had been patiently hoping to hear:

> Wheatstone has been with me a long while today, & has taken
> my translation away with him, after reading it over with me.
> I hope to receive the proofs of it for corrections, by & bye as I
> trust [Richard] Taylor will not reject it. I am now translating a
> beautiful Italian scientific paper.

It is not known what the 'beautiful' Italian paper was, but the translation that Charles Wheatstone had carried off to submit for future publication – considerable revisions still lay ahead – was the first account to be published in English – from French – of Charles Babbage's magnificent, and still unbuilt, Analytical Engine. And it was Ada – wild, unpredictable, brilliant Ada – who was the translator.

CHAPTER SEVENTEEN

MY FAIR INTERPRETRESS
(1843–4)

Charles Babbage was a busy man and, despite his truculent manner, he was a popular one. In February 1843, he received, according to his own calculations, thirteen invitations for every day of the month. Among them, one of the most charmingly insistent came from Ada Lovelace. Hester King ('so happy that I can scarcely hold my pen', wrote Hester to Robert and Louisa Noel) was about to be married to Sir George Crauford. The wedding was to be held at Ockham, with a honeymoon to follow at Ashley Combe. Lady Byron was staying and nobody would complete the party more perfectly, Ada pleaded, than their own dear Charles Babbage himself. Would he come for a week?

> or if you really cannot (tho I am sure you *can*, if you *will*) stay so long, then pray come for the night even . . . we all much desire *your* presence. For although our party for the occasion is very small & quiet, Miss King & ourselves feel that your long friendship with all of us, with myself most particularly, makes you especially to be remembered & wished for. So pray consider this & that weddings do not happen twice.
>
> Yours ever,
> *AAL*

Ada Lovelace – although her accuracy in dating correspondence can never be trusted even to be within the right year – appears to have written to Babbage on 6 February 1843. The following day, Babbage noted that he met with the young countess under what he succinctly described as 'new circumstances'. Those changed conditions, it is fair to guess, related to Ada's recent translation and to Babbage's proposal as to what she should do next.

Babbage had always been his own worst enemy, and it was a trait he demonstrated with peculiar force in 1842. Visiting England at the beginning of the year to attend the christening of Queen Victoria's first son, the King of Prussia was eager to inspect English technology. Urgently invited to the Royal Society on 30 January for an especially arranged morning meeting with this potential royal sponsor for his unbuilt machine, Babbage failed to show up. Later that year, when Ada was doing her best to bring Babbage together with journalists and editors who might drum up interest in the Analytical Engine – just as Dionysius Lardner, back in 1834, had done for the Difference Engine in the *Edinburgh Review* – the capricious inventor once again stayed away.

Babbage's excuse to Ada for not joining her on this occasion was that he needed to keep himself free for 'a possible discussion with Sir R. Peel'. Babbage's behaviour during his meetings with the overworked Tory prime minister proved disastrous. Instead of allowing Sir Robert time to consider whether he could offer financial support from the government for Babbage to start building his second machine (its estimated size was equivalent to a small steam engine), Babbage began to hector him. Back in 1822, Peel had personally recommended a government subsidy for developing the Difference Engine. In November 1842, after two encounters with a furious Babbage, Peel folded his hands and walked out. There would be no further discussions.

Meanwhile, Count Luigi Menabrea, a brilliant young military engineer who had attended the 1840 Turin conference (where he may have heard Babbage lecture and certainly examined drawings of the unbuilt Analytical Engine), had published in a Swiss journal a lucid account of its projected appearance, workings and capability. (The choice of a French publication was reasonable at a time when French was still the common language of scientific reports; Menabrea himself spoke French well enough to serve later as an ambassador to Paris.)

Menabrea's account, covering twenty-three pages, appeared in the respected *Bibliothéque universelle de Genève* in October 1842. Richard Taylor, editor of a London journal specialising in academic articles from abroad, approached not Babbage but his diminutive and fiercely ambitious friend Charles Wheatstone, when seeking a translator for the Italian's work. Charles Wheatstone took the commission straight to Ada. To Babbage, the result of that meeting came in February 1843 as a complete – and seemingly delightful – surprise.

ᘯᕉᘰ

For Ada, Charles Wheatstone's timing was excellent. Her health had been bad during 1842 (Hester King's letters to Robert Noel's wife in Dresden mentioned that Ada was suffering from a new digestive problem, following several months of undefined respiratory difficulties 'which caused us all a good deal of uneasiness'). Ada's health had not been improved by the news that Medora, out of funds and reduced to borrowing from the servants whom Ada had innocently recruited, had done a bunk from her rented chateau in Toulon and gone to seek legal redress in Paris. (The haste of her departure was underlined by the shocking information that Miss Leigh had undertaken the journey on public transport without wearing a hat.)

A distraction both from illness and her troublesome half-sister was always welcome to Ada. It's hard to imagine any diversion that could have appealed to her more vividly than the proposal which Charles Wheatstone placed before her at St James's Square.

Eight years earlier, back in the autumn of 1834, Ada had been an excited witness to Babbage's discussions with Mary Somerville of a new and entirely different form of machine to the old and uncompleted Difference Engine. Since then, as Ada's friendship with Babbage progressed, she had often declared her hopes of helping to bring this later project to completion. Talking with Wheatstone, she agreed upon the urgent need to present Menabrea's description of what was by then known as the Analytical Engine to an English audience. Taylor had issued an end of July deadline. What mattered now was that an impartial and informed report should be made accessible. Ada accepted the commission. By the end of November 1842, she had set to work.

∽

Nineteenth-century scientific translation did not have to be precise. Mary Somerville, as Laplace cordially acknowledged, had gone beyond him in her interpretation of his own major work. Ada, translating Menabrea, was more cautious. Fluent herself in French, she produced a clear English version in which one slip (too much has since been made of a misread 'cas' for the 'cos' of a cosine) was notably overlooked by both Wheatstone and even Babbage himself. Those two brilliant men saw no flaw; what they did approvingly note was the clarity of Ada's single footnoted adjustment to Menabrea's text.*

It was Babbage, according to his own entertaining (but frequently unreliable) autobiography, who now proposed that Ada should put to further use her exceptional knowledge of his cherished project. Menabrea had described the components of the machine based upon what he had been shown in Turin, engraved on

---

* Menabrea had written in his concluding paragraph that – in literal translation – 'all of the parts, and all of the wheelwork, of which the immense apparatus is composed, have been studied as has their action, but they have not yet been combined'. Ada restated him thus: 'The plans have been arranged for all the various parts, and for all the wheelwork, which compose this immense apparatus, and their action studied; but these have not yet been fully combined together in the drawings and mechanical notation.' Progress was being stressed. Ada's other and far more significant footnotes were added at a later stage (Taylor's *Scientific Memoirs*, 1843, p. 670).

wooden blocks and also in stereotyped plans, drawn by Babbage's son. The Italian mathematician and engineer explained how these components would be deployed (with particular attention to the innovative use of instruction cards carrying – as Menabrea was the first to note in print – the equivalent of algebraic formulae). He also observed the considerable simplification of time-consuming intellectual labour that would result from the Engine's operations. '[W]ho can foresee the consequences of such an invention?' Menabrea asked in his conclusion. Ada's challenge was to answer that question, above all by showing that Babbage's embryonic Engine was more than just an improved calculating machine. The bounds of 'mere *arithmetic*' had now been overstepped, Ada would write in the 'Notes' that formed her extended commentary on Menabrea's report:

> the Analytical Engine does not occupy common ground with mere 'calculating machines'. It holds a position wholly its own; and the considerations it suggests are most interesting in their nature ...
>
> A new, a vast, and a powerful language is developed for the future use of analysis, in which to wield its truths so that these may become of more speedy and accurate practical application for the purposes of mankind than the means hitherto in our possession have rendered possible.*

Reading those visionary words today, it's hard to accept that they were written a hundred years before the birth of electronic computers as we know them today.

Composing her notes to Menabrea's article over the early spring and summer of 1843, Ada Lovelace aimed to describe and demonstrate the importance of Babbage's invention in clear language. As

---

* Ada's quotes within this chapter are referenced in the text from the original article page numbers.

the best popular science writing still does, she used visual analogies to illustrate her points.

As a mathematician, Ada had reached a level high enough to describe Babbage's machine and discuss it with the inventor. But it is not as a mathematician that we respect her. What is remarkable about Ada Lovelace's published 'Notes' – the only completed scientific writing that she appears to have produced – is the evidence they provide that, through the combination of an intuitive intelligence and her awareness of the years of discussions and planning that lay behind the unbuilt Engine, a young Victorian woman glimpsed its significance for a world that was not yet ready either for it or for her.

The birth of the computer did not depend solely upon Lady Lovelace, but she unquestionably belongs to the history of that genesis. Armed with hindsight, we see how close Ada came to predicting not only the arrival of the universal computer, but the potential of technology to transform the way we function. Her perception would prove to be as suggestive and retrospectively influential as Mary Shelley's dark vision, in 1816 (after a memorable night of storytelling in the company of Ada's exiled father, out in a rainswept villa overlooking Lake Geneva), of the birth of bio-engineering.

Neither woman changed the world in which they lived. Uniquely, both Lovelace and Shelley foresaw the role that technology might have to play in transforming a world they never knew.

လၐၐ

Armed with a six-month deadline (Richard Taylor required copy by the end of the summer of 1843), Ada set to work on writing up the 'Notes' soon after Hester's February wedding. Reading through her translation of Menabrea, Ada identified seven points at which to add a series of her own notes (A to G) correcting or augmenting the Italian engineer's skilful exposition. In note A – by which Babbage was so delighted that he implored her not to change a single word – Ada used Menabrea's account of the Difference Engine's limitations as a stepping stone to her own perception of what the unbuilt Analytical Engine might potentially be enabled to achieve.

Among the longest of Ada's seven commentaries (it covers ten printed pages), Note A introduced the possibility that the Engine would act upon other things besides number. Music, a subject close to Ada's heart, offered a striking example.

> Supposing, for instance, that the fundamental relations of pitched sounds to the science of harmony and of musical composition were susceptible of such expression and adaptations, the engine might compose elaborate and scientific pieces of music of any degree of complexity or extent. [694]

How would the engine succeed in doing this? Menabrea had explained the method of using numerous punched cards that Babbage had adapted from Jacquard's celebrated loom. Ada, while thoughtfully advising readers in a later note (C), to visit one of the two London Science Halls at which a Jacquard loom could be observed in action, used the analogy of mechanised picture-weaving to create one of her own most striking images, while pointing to the technical advance upon Babbage's earlier machine. The Difference Engine used cards only to print off the results of its (purely arithmetical) calculations:

> The distinctive characteristic of the Analytical Engine, and that which has rendered it possible to endow mechanism with such extensive faculties as bid fair to make this engine the executive right-hand of abstract algebra, is the introduction into it of the principle which Jacquard devised for regulating, by means of punched cards, the most complicated patterns in the fabrication of brocaded stuffs. It is in this that the distinction between the two engines lies. Nothing of the sort exists in the Difference Engine. We may say most aptly that the Analytical Engine *weaves algebraical patterns* just as the Jacquard loom weaves flowers and leaves. [696]

The image she had selected was both just and memorable. It paved the way for a more dramatic perception. Where Babbage had set out to design a superlative producer of tables, Ada glimpsed the possibility of programming a single piece of fixed hardware (a rather substantial one, admittedly) to do any form of computation. Always conscious that the purpose of her task was to attract project support, Ada hinted at the unforeseeable uses to which the Engine might be put, had she the space and 'were it in actual existence'. [700] In Note A, she contented herself with declaring that the Analytical Engine would be both simpler to build than its predecessor and 'much more powerful'. [701]

Simpler, perhaps, but there was no getting around the fact that the machine Babbage hoped to create was enormous. In Note B, without dwelling upon this point, Ada described what was to be far the largest element: a storehouse designed to contain ('at least') two hundred columns of discs. Here, Ada transformed Menabrea's correct, but flat image of a column of circular discs into the more vivid 'pile of rather large draughtsmen ... each counter having the digits from 0 to 9 inscribed on its *edge* at regular intervals'. [701]

While Ada's imaginative gift for making the invisible apparent is one of the most successful aspects of her 'Notes', this is not primarily what has led her to be seen as a significant figure in scientific history. Throughout her seven notes, over and again, Lady Lovelace returned to the idea of the Analytical Engine's potential to meet the challenges of a future world. In Note E (requiring a detailed use of the trigonometry that she had only recently mastered), Ada again stressed this point through reference to the Engine's adaptability. It might be supposed, Ada wrote, that a machine which gave its results in numerical form could work only with numbers. But this, she announced in the old assertive voice of her mathematical correspondence with De Morgan, was an error.

The engine can arrange and combine its numerical qualities exactly as if they were *letters* or any other *general* symbols; and in fact it might bring out its results in algebraical *notation*, were provisions made accordingly. It might develope [*sic*] three sets of results simultaneously, viz. *symbolic* results (as already alluded to in Notes A. and B.); *numerical* results (its chief and primary object; and *algebraical* results in *literal* notation. [713]

Babbage, as Ada acknowledged in her next sentence, had actually made no plans for his Engine to do any such thing, but Babbage's plans were never going to hold his more boldly imaginative interpreter back. As Stephen Wolfram has stated in a fine recent analysis of Ada's 'Notes': 'Babbage did not know what he had; Ada started to see glimpses and successfully described them.'

Ada Lovelace, in her personal correspondence, often made claims about her own powers that bordered on the preposterous. Where Babbage's invention was concerned, she reined back that impulse. In Note F, she remarked that the engine could be used to determine 'that which human brains find it difficult or impossible to work out unerringly' [722]; in Note G, another ten-pager that has become the most famous of all Ada's 'Notes', she cautioned the reader against any temptation to overrate Babbage's invention.

To exaggerate the powers of the Analytical Engine, Ada wrote, would invite the reverse to take place. Certainly, Babbage had devised a means of improving the pace of scientific progress. Nevertheless, there must be no supposition that the inventor had created the 'thinking machine' that Lady Byron had loosely termed it back in 1833. 'The Analytical Engine has no pretension whatever to *originate* anything,' Ada wrote in one of her most quoted and discussed statements. Babbage agreed.

Having cut the machine (so to speak) down to size, Ada built it up again in a final and remarkable endeavour. Menabrea, indicating the Analytical Engine's sophistication as a computer of numbers, had introduced the name of Jakob Bernoulli, the deviser, back in 1713, of a series of numbers which continue to play a basic theoretical role in surprisingly many aspects of mathematics. Working with this sequence of ugly-looking and increasingly complicated fractions, Bernoulli himself claimed to have been able to compute his first ten numbers in fifteen minutes; Ada, painstakingly drawing up what today looks like the first computer program (William Lovelace proudly inked it in before carrying it off to display to neighbours and friends), offered an example by which the Analytical Engine was shown to be capable of computing fifty Bernoulli numbers in a minute. This was a task which neither the earlier Difference Engine nor its precursors could have addressed.* It was Ada's most striking demonstration – the chart showed informed readers how a string of instructions from punched cards would guide the machine through a progressive sequence of events – of the Analytical Engine's potential value to any country willing to cough up the considerable funds required to build it.†

৩৩

Ada visited her mother in Leicestershire at the beginning of 1843, while her husband travelled to Germany, seemingly to glean new architectural ideas for the ongoing transformation of East Horsley Place into Horsley Towers, his own magnificently idiosyncratic take on a Bavarian schloss.

In 1843, the cost of William Lovelace's Surrey fantasia (fifteen woodland bridges, new access roads, a lake, cloisters, a chapel, a courtyard, a tower and a gigantic hall formed only a portion of the grand project) was mounting by the minute.

Lavishing money on his building projects, William remained tight-fisted with his wife. Anna Jameson, writing to the Noels in Dresden in January 1843, chattily confided that Lady Byron wished

---

* In 2008, Stephen Wolfram's 'Mathematica' program was used to compute the ten millionth Bernoulli number (one that would have taken Babbage's Engine several thousand years to achieve). It took 'Mathematica' a little less than six days. Ada was, of course, using Bernoulli numbers only as a way of showing off the powers of the engine.

† No precise figure for what that cost would have been is currently available.

her extravagant son-in-law would augment a £300 a year allowance that scarcely enabled Ada to pay the wages for Suzette, her new French maid. (Ada would soon solve the problem by eschewing maids altogether.) But it was Annabella herself who had set the level of Ada's allowance. Why, seeing Ada in need, did her mother not intervene?

The answer may have lain in Lady Byron's growing awareness of her son-in-law's chief weakness: a fierce family pride that, with time, would encase him like a suit of armour. William Lovelace was already smarting from the news that the country would not welcome his services as secretary of state. (He had put his name forward in 1840.) A humbled Crow, it is fair to guess, would have brooked no Hennish interference. Annabella wanted no scenes, but Ada's lack of money, combined with her husband's flair for spending it, would become increasingly problematic as the decade wore on.

It was not money worries but the increasingly bizarre behaviour of Medora Leigh, out in France, that offered the severest challenge to Ada's concentration as she worked to complete her seven notes to Menabrea's *Memoir*. Passionately loyal to her mother and furious at the way that Lady Byron's generosity had been abused, Ada found it impossible to remain detached during the final stages of her mother's ill-judged attempt to offer maternal care to an increasingly aggressive young woman.

By March 1843, word had reached London that Medora was seeking legal support for her rights as Lady Byron's adopted daughter from Pierre Berryer, one of France's foremost lawyers. Delegated to act as Annabella's representatives, Selina Doyle and her sister Adelaide reported from their own Paris lodgings that Miss Leigh was living at an expensive hotel on Place Vendôme, claiming that it befitted her rank. She had taken the story of how she had been brutally cast aside by Lady Byron to the ear of a sympathetic Henry Bulwer (brother of the more famous novelist) at the British embassy.

It was at this point that Ada revealed her own pent-up feelings. Again and again, in a letter scrawled across many tightly written pages, 'Elizabeth' (Medora no longer) was invited to remember the poverty from which she had been rescued by 'my mother ... *She*, on whom of all people in the world you have the least natural claim'. Had Miss Leigh forgotten all that she owed to them? 'Remember what you were at Paris – grateful for *any* countenance from me. You had scarcely dared to hope it ...'

> You have but *one* course to pursue – submission to your benefactress; and if you have one spark of good feeling or of prudence, you will at once hasten to acknowledge your rash and ungrateful conduct and regret for it.

Ada's letter was of little help in resolving an increasingly rancorous dispute, but by April, out in Paris, a new avenue of possibility had opened. Selina Doyle had heard Victor Beaurepaire speaking in a curious way about Miss Leigh. Commenting upon one of her rare moments of tranquillity, he remarked that it made her easier to handle. (*'Elle est plus tranquille aujourd'hui et prête a faire tout ce qu'on veut.'*)

Was Medora perhaps mad? The juvenile educationalist Louisa Barwell, requested by Lady Byron to set down her recollections of a memorably uneasy stay at Moore Place in 1842, readily confirmed that Miss Leigh had appeared to her to be deranged. ('I think I then told you that I believed her reason was not sound, and whenever I have since reflected upon her conduct, I have always come to the same conclusion, that she was insane – and this has been in my own mind a melancholy excuse for all the sad & distressing conduct I then witnessed.')

On 24 April, Annabella despatched her old friend Dr King to Paris with a letter of ultimatum. Either Medora could accept Lady Byron's orders, or she could face being completely cut off. Seeing what might be coming her way – Dr King had recently opened a genteel asylum in Brighton – Medora turned upon her visitor. An offer (one that Lady Byron had not authorised Dr King to make) to increase her allowance from £150 to £300 – the same sum that was annually paid to Ada by her husband – was scornfully rejected. Reviewing the visit in her hand-scrawled memoir, Medora recorded that the meek and somewhat bewitched Dr King had been both intimidating and abusive.

Fixed at the forefront of Medora's mind was the fact that the £3,000 deed yielded up in 1842 by Mrs Leigh now belonged by rights to herself. It seemed to her that Lady Byron, who had lodged the document with her own solicitors precisely in order to prevent Medora from cashing it in, had actually stolen her property. (That the £3,000 gift could only be validated by Lady Byron's death was not the kind of detail to interest a destitute young woman who believed that the world had wronged her.)

It was the quest for the deed – and further funding – that brought Nathalie Beaurepaire, swiftly followed by Medora, little Marie and a kindly admirer called Captain Barrallier, back into Ada's life.

୧୨୯

By June 1843, when Medora arrived in England on the arm of her new chevalier (she did have a perfect genius for finding them), Ada had reached the final stages of writing up her notes to Menabrea's article. It was that month in which she decided to make use of the Bernoulli numbers to demonstrate the superiority of the Analytical Engine over all earlier designs. By the beginning of July, Ada was ready for Lovelace to ink in the pencilled numbers on her laboriously calculated chart.

Sadly, none of the correspondence between Babbage and his interpreter has survived from the earlier months of Ada's endeavours. By June, however, an agreeably collegiate relationship had been established: it was one that entitled Ada to describe herself to Robert Noel, on 9 August, as 'a completely *professional* person'. Dates, especially on Ada's side, frequently went by the board as she dashed off a flood of requests, reproaches, entreaties and teasing messages to Babbage. Written on tiny sheets of paper, they were – on at least one occasion – carried to the local railway station by Ada herself, running along as fast as she could go. At other times, they were conveyed to Dorset Street by one of the smartly liveried footmen who, as Ada had once told De Morgan when something went awry at St James's Square, must get used to her own special way of doing things, if they wished to please ...

Pleasing Ada, in the summer of 1843, meant carrying her latest missive from St James's Square to Marylebone, waiting for Babbage to write out his response and then hastening back through the dusk to a pale, reed-thin and often breathless Ada, pondering the challenging details of one of her charts or hunched over her latest tussles with that difficult trigonometrical Note E.

Determination is the quality that shines through all of Ada's endeavours. 'I will have it *well*, & *fully* done; or not at all,' she instructed Babbage on 26 June; a few days later, she was ready to boast that her husband, an admiring observer of her tables and diagrams, was 'quite enchanted with the beauty & symmetry that they displayed'. Flirtatiously, she wrote of herself as 'a fairy' and made fun of her chivalrous courtship by Frederick Knight,* the Lovelaces' closest neighbouring landowner at Ashley Combe. 'I am *anything* but *My Ladyship* to him,' she teased before scolding Babbage for altering her notes and revisions when ('poor little Fairy') she was working 'like the Devil on his behalf'. 'I *must* beg you not,' she rebuked him on 1 August, as she finalised Note B. And, in the same letter: 'I wish you were as accurate, as much to be relied on, as I am myself.' Her criticisms were not groundless: on one occasion, Babbage carelessly deleted an entire paragraph of her work. 'I suppose I must set to work to write something *better*, if I can, as a substitute,' Ada sighed. 'However, I should be decidedly inclined to *swear* at you, I will allow.'

---

* Recently returned from living in Europe, 31-year-old Frederick Knight was enchanted by Ada. It was probably Knight that Ada was thinking of on 27 June 1850, when she told Woronzow Greig that she '*had not a leg to stand on*' some seven or eight years earlier. Advice to behave with more discretion had been ignored, for 'I was then young & *plucky* & had no mind to be put down about anything at all.' (Betty Toole, *Ada, the Enchantress of Numbers* (Strawberry Press, 1992), pp. 359–60).

Babbage's mistake was not the only cause for curses in the late summer of 1843: '... the fact is I am plagued out of my life just now,' Ada admitted to him on 19 July. Lovelace was fretting about the cost of his new building projects; more to the point, the unpaid Beaurepaires were growing increasingly truculent. To send a letter to Annabella emblazoned, across its envelope, '*Lady Byron – Femme de mauvaise foi*' was bad enough, but now Nathalie had carried her tale of woe to the French embassy in London, where Ada was blamed for having originally engaged the couple in Paris under false pretences. (Medora's status as an unmarried mother, which had been concealed by Ada and Lady Byron, would have caused any high-grade servants to reject that work as prejudicial to their own reputation.) Sighing, Ada laid aside her 'Notes' to pay a visit of her own to the Comtesse St Aulaire, the ambassador's friendly wife. Lady Byron, angry and alarmed at the growing prospect of a public scandal, wanted a full report.

Nathalie had proved to be a compelling storyteller. Madame St Aulaire had apparently heard everything to do with Medora, and, alas, 'everything else too ...' Naturally, the ambassador's wife (who would become a close friend of Ada's) was filled with 'indignation and horror', but not enough to stop her from listening to an hour's worth of delightfully shocking tales. It was with some difficulty that Ada obtained her hostess's reluctant promise of total discretion.

Written on 25 July, Ada's long letter to Lady Byron allows us to see how delicately she had to juggle the different aspects of her life. First, she gave her mother a full and detailed account of the interview with the ambassador's wife. Only after sympathising with the toll that 'this horrible affair' must be taking upon Lady Byron's delicate health, did Ada admit that she herself was now suffering from acute and almost daily pain.

Sir Charles Locock, known as 'The Great Deliverer' for his services to the Queen, had been devoted to Ada ever since he attended her for the birth of her first child. Lady Lovelace's medical symptoms baffled him. As soon as he thought he had found the answer, another variant emerged. Wanly, she joked to her mother about the '*amusement* in being so curious a riddle'; heroically, she accepted that no imminent relief from suffering was in sight. Locock had even told her that her mysterious ailments might be beyond cure. That fatalistic edict, offered when Ada was only twenty-seven and at what felt like just the beginning of her professional life, was hard to accept. It was entirely typical of Ada to turn a sentence of permanent invalidism into a chance for new opportunities. Why should not pain be connected to her intellectual progress? What if she looked upon it as a condition of – rather than an impediment to – 'all that wonderful & available mental power which I see grounds to believe I am acquiring ...'?

> I will willingly bear *anything* if this be so. What would be to
> me dreadful, would be mind & activity impeded by health. Give
> me *powers* with *pain* a million times over, rather than *ease* with
> even *talents* (if not of the highest order).

It is easy to mock the extravagance of Ada's valiant declarations – she wrote in this same letter of 25 July about 'the great laboratory of my brain' and in another that she dashed off earlier in the same month to Babbage, about the 'almost *awful* energy & power [that] lie yet undeveloped [*sic*] in that *wiry* little system of mine'. She boasted, too, in that same letter to Babbage of 4 July, about how, within a decade, 'the Devil's in it if I haven't sucked out some of the life-blood from the mysteries of this universe, in a way that no purely mortal lips or brains could do'.

Ada had been advised by Locock to use prescribed measures of both laudanum and claret to assuage her sufferings, but the clarity of her scientific writing shows how little impact that remedy had upon her intellectual powers, even when she spoke of drinking three glasses of wine for supper. Few people, not even a mother who had no taste for fanciful hyperbole, mocked Ada during her lifetime for her ambitious imaginings. Perhaps, knowing Lady Lovelace at first-hand, her friends and family understood – far better than we through the exalted medium of her letters – how much a young woman who was not yet thirty needed to create the image of herself as an indestructible and almost superhuman force. Armed with that prodigious ideal, Ada could combat the recurrent periods of intense physical pain that assailed her with ever increasing ferocity.

⁗

The almost daily shunting to and fro of Ada's notes and Babbage's revisions was still in play at the beginning of August, the month in which Richard Taylor's volume was due to be printed. Reading over her notes once again, Ada reported to Babbage that she was 'quite thunderstruck at the *power* of the writing'. It pleased her especially that there was no sense of the author's gender. She was in agreement with her husband that each of the notes should carry the initials 'AAL', simply by way of an identity to connect to any future work. Ada, in 1843, had no doubt that there would be plenty of that.

Writing to her mother in an undated letter during this same summer, Ada stressed the relief that mathematical work had offered as an escape from 'the tortuous & nefarious documents & affairs which have recently so painfully engaged much of our energy & attention'. The reference was to the fact that Medora, having finally obtained the deed, was still causing trouble. John Hobhouse made astonished note in his diary for 15 August that a young woman called Miss Leigh had contacted him, claiming to be Byron's daughter and asking for money. ('Can it be *the* daughter who eloped with Trevanion who married her sister?' Hobhouse asked himself, indicating by his marked emphasis that he knew exactly what the rumour was.) Even Augusta herself was approached ('I once more remind you that I am your child'), but without success, since Mrs Leigh had nothing left to give. Possibly, Annabella or Ada did help out. Somebody other than Barrallier must have provided the funds that kept Medora and Marie fed and sheltered in London until

May 1844, when Medora finally managed to cash in the deed and returned to France.*

⋍⋍

Back in August 1843, a proud Ada finally presented Lady Byron with the literary child she called her 'firstborn'. Not aspiring to be either so eloquent or brilliant as his grandfather, he was nevertheless, so Ada believed, worthy of pride. At the very least, he bore testimony to 'a most indomitable industry ...' A bold prediction followed. 'He will make an excellent head of (I hope) a *large* family of brothers & sisters ...'

Annabella could have asked for nothing more. It was all she had wished for. 'Mother of Ada', she cooed. Had Ada not demonstrated by her work that this maternal title might be 'as good a passport to posterity (if I am to have one) as "the wife of Byron"'.

⋍⋍

It was just as the end of Ada's intellectual labours came into sight that a new problem had arisen. The primary purpose of publishing her translation and the added notes had been to revive public interest in Babbage's new invention and to secure enough of an investment for it to be built. It was completely without warning, at the beginning of August, that Babbage produced a preface of his own and declared his wish for it to be integrated with Ada's article.

---

* A granite headstone, engraved with her maiden name and a quotation from Byron, has only since 1960 marked Medora's previously obscure grave at Lapeyre, a rural hamlet in south-west France. Married to a soldier's servant, Georges Taillefer, in 1847, the year after giving birth to a son, Medora died in 1849 of smallpox, aged thirty-five. Her daughter, Marie, ejected from the convent where she had been placed, was subsequently spotted (in 1872) gambling at Baden-Baden by George Eliot. (The novelist made memorable use of this scene in the opening of *Daniel Deronda*.) Medora's son, Elie Taillefer, entered the church and worked in an area local to Lapeyre, where he remained scandal-free and was much respected.

This was appalling news. No master of diplomacy, Babbage had seized upon the excuse of writing a preface – one which both Ada and the publisher read with growing dismay – to harangue the British government for having let him down. Such a public display of aggression threatened to undo all the benefits of Ada's endeavours. Asked to reconsider, Babbage lost his temper. He would do no such thing. If Lady Lovelace didn't like his preface, then Babbage would publish it with Taylor, while she, having requested the publisher to release her, could take herself and her precious work elsewhere.

Towards Babbage, Ada remained admirably calm and rational. Writing to her mother about him from St James's Square on 8 August, she described herself as harrassed and perplexed. 'We are in fact *at issue*,' Ada admitted, adding that she had reached the conclusion that their friend was 'one of the most *impracticable*, *selfish*, & *intemperate* persons one can have to do with'. A new and 'very frightful' crisis in her health could be directly attributed to the misery of being torn in two directions by Babbage and by the editors, while striving to keep the peace.

Two days earlier, Ada had gone so far as to inform Mr Babbage that his current course of action was 'suicidal'. By the middle of the month, she had taken advice from William and her staunch supporter, Charles Wheatstone. Back at Ockham, Ada composed a fourteen-page letter (it was written on uncharacteristically large sheets, almost as if she meant to convey the impression of a legal document) to her recalcitrant colleague.

The degree of Wheatstone's involvement remains unclear, but it seems likely that he supported the intriguing proposal that Ada now presented, with her husband's approval. The letter began with flattery, reminding the touchy inventor that Ada's only wish was to see Babbage's genius given its due. On the matter of publication, however, she stood firm; there would be no withdrawal.

It was only after this that Ada proceeded to the plan that had perhaps been in the minds of herself, Lovelace and Wheatstone all along. How would Babbage feel about allowing Lovelace and herself to take over the project? Babbage could appoint his own referees, but – in return for allowing his friends to conduct the business of getting the Engine built – he must promise to place himself at Ada's disposal. Carelessness would not be tolerated: '& can you promise not to *slur* & *hurry* things over; or to mislay, & allow confusion & mistakes to enter into documents & etc.?' While he, Babbage, would naturally retain complete control of the machine's design, all else would be arranged by his patrons. What did he think?

Ada was clearly apprehensive about the inventor's reaction. A final sentence wondered whether he would now dismiss 'the lady-fairy' from his service. The following day, Ada wrote again, to backtrack. Perhaps it would be better after all if Babbage ignored the whole idea and behaved 'as if nothing had passed'.

And so he did. A note in his personal records stated, without offering an explanation, that Lady Lovelace's proposals had been rejected. Babbage did, however, back down about his preface. The memoir and 'Notes' were published (prefaceless) on 25 August 1843 in an edition of 250 copies, of which Ada received 100 and Babbage fifty. By 9 September, the inventor was almost ready to resume his old, teasing relationship with the young woman he now addressed as 'the Enchantress of Number'. Almost, but not quite. Of course, he would love to visit her down at Ashley Combe, Babbage wrote, and perhaps he ought to bring along Arbogast's *Du calcul des dérivations* so that the two of them could discuss 'that horrible problem – the three bodies'.

The allusion to the French mathematician was deliberately malicious. Ada had referred to Arbogast in her 'Notes'. By offering to bring along the book, Babbage was hinting that she hadn't read it. But her tussle with Babbage had taught Ada to give as good as she got. While informing the inventor that she (naturally) already possessed Arbogast's book and would be happy to discuss it with him, Ada passed along a glowing personal tribute to her 'Notes' from Augustus De Morgan. 'I never expected that *he* would review my crude young composition so favourably,' Ada remarked with just a hint of menace. De Morgan had powerful friends and Babbage took the point. 'You should have written an original paper,' Babbage grovelled on 12 September. 'The postponement of that will how-ever only render it more perfect ... Ever my fair interpretress, your faithful slave ...'

By the following year, all bitterness had evaporated and Babbage and Ada had safely resumed their easy, quasi-familial role. But it was Charles Wheatstone, not Babbage, who was willing to spend five hours in November 1844 advising Ada on how best to proceed in her scientific endeavours.

Writing to William later that same day, Ada sounded both flattered and excited. 'Wheatstone has given me *some* very strik-ing counsels,' she told her husband on 25 November 1844. Ada had apparently been planning to expand her observations on the Analytical Engine, but Wheatstone dissuaded her. 'Don't be vexed at this,' Ada reassured William, 'a subject is fixed on instead, so it will make no difference, & I can as easily do one as the other ...'

Here, in her immediate readiness to apply her mind to a new project, is evidence of the degree to which Ada had – as she proudly claimed to Woronzow Greig – become a truly professional person. The boost to her confidence of seeing her own clear work in print, with herself identified as the author, had been immense. All that she now lacked was the means to transform herself into a scientist. It seemed, following her conversation with Wheatstone, that help might be at hand.

PART THREE

Visions

'*I hope to bequeath to the Generations a Calculus of the Nervous System*'

ADA LOVELACE TO WORONZOW GREIG,
15 NOVEMBER 1844

CHAPTER EIGHTEEN

THE ENCHANTRESS
(1843–4)

'Science is no longer a lifeless abstraction floating above the heads of the multitude. It has descended to earth. It mingles with men. It penetrates our mines. It enters our workshops. It speeds along with the iron courser of the rail.'

MICHAEL GARVEY,
The Silent Revolution (1852)

Towards the end of 1843, having worn herself down the previous summer in her heroic endeavour to promote Charles Babbage's unbuilt machine, Ada Lovelace suffered an unusually grave lapse in her health. Writing to Sophia De Morgan – and entreating her not to tell Lady Byron – Ada confided that learning she was not pregnant had, nevertheless, offered great solace. 'I don't the least mind all I have suffered,' she wrote. 'I think *anything* better than that.'

Of all her family roles, motherhood was the one that Ada least relished. She had been admirably supportive of William's sisters, while vainly striving to improve relations between her husband and the unremittingly hostile Lady Hester King. As a daughter, she had proved affectionate and loyal throughout Lady Byron's painful tussles with Medora Leigh and her quasi-keepers, the Beaurepaires.

As a mother, however, Ada was both negligent and capricious. True, she had written in an uncertainly dated letter to her mother about how tears had 'rushed' to her eyes as she watched little Lord Ockham stepping carefully through a dance with his sister. Eager to believe that she had detected signs of genius in her small daughter, Ada had also predicted that the gifted Annabella, aged seven, would become a great artist.

Such moments of tenderness were rare. From the time of embarking upon her translation of Menabrea, Ada's mind was focussed upon her own scientific career. Writing to Charles Noel in Dresden in August 1843 about finding a teacher for the Lovelace family, Ada was far more interested in obtaining the latest scientific information from Germany (the admired heartland of scientific study) 'as to the microscopical structure and changes in the brain, nervous matter, & also in the blood', than in the academic credentials of Herr Kraemer, Charles's candidate for her children's tutor.

Nevertheless, there was no denying that a competent instructor was required to take care of three small children whose parents' Unitarian beliefs prohibited young Viscount Ockham and his siblings from attending conventional (Anglican) schools. The thing to impress upon Herr Kraemer, as Ada explained to her cousin Robert at careful length, was that he would be working for 'a completely *professional* person'. As such, she herself was unable '(were I even fitted by *nature*, which I am *not*), to associate much personally with my children, or to exercise a favourable influence over them by attempting to do so'. While there would be no regular or frequent association with the Lovelaces themselves, Kraemer would receive instructions on what principles to deliver his lessons, with special attention to the inculcation of religion based upon solid Unitarian foundations ('subject of course to our more special direction than perhaps in any other matter') and well-balanced habits of empirical observation.

It is not perhaps surprising that Dr Kraemer would prove unable to meet such a demanding standard. Hired in the autumn of 1843, his peremptory dismissal was hastened by the fact that Lady Byron had found a more suitable candidate. Summoned to join her mother in October at the genteelly unfashionable resort of Clifton (Brunel's great suspension bridge had not yet linked Clifton to the thriving port of Bristol), Ada heard Annabella's proposal. Presented in Lady Byron's quiet but always decisive tones, Dr William Carpenter sounded ideal.

It was Annabella's philanthropic work that had brought her into contact with the Carpenters. Dr Lant Carpenter, a leading Unitarian educationalist who suffered from depression, had drowned in 1840, while travelling around Europe on a prescribed health tour. At the time Annabella arrived at Clifton, his widow and eldest daughter Mary were both working at the celebrated Bristol school inaugurated by the late Dr Carpenter. Mary, then aged thirty-six, would later become one of Annabella's closest allies and a co-trustee of her papers, while her first cousin, Harriet Martineau, would become one of Lady Byron's greatest champions. In the early autumn of 1843, however, Lady Byron's interest was focussed more sharply upon Mary's younger brother.

Handsome, clever and highly ambitious, the Edinburgh-educated William Carpenter had already made his name as the author of *Principles of Human Physiology*, an account of developmental theories of life which paid prudent tribute to 'our continued dependence on the Creator'. Recently married, young Dr Carpenter was a rising academic in need of a steady income and secure accommodation. That was where the Lovelaces came in.

Anxious to see her unruly grandchildren given a sterling education while Ada concentrated on her burgeoning scientific career, Lady Byron intended Carpenter to act both as tutor and watchdog, one who would ensure that her daughter was not pushing herself beyond her strength. What Lady Byron did not factor into her plans was the effect that Ada's celebrated parentage and charismatic personality was likely to have upon a socially insecure academic who – as William Lovelace would later remark – was excessively susceptible to the charms of a pretty woman.

'I like to please people's eyes and indeed ears and all their faculties as much as I can,' Ada jauntily informed her mother in an undated letter that was probably written a year or two before meeting Dr William Carpenter. The effect of this flirtatious streak in Ada's nature was predictable. Dr Carpenter, arriving with his wife for a first interview at Ashley Combe in late November 1843, was flattered by the rapidity with which the young Lady Lovelace ('more delightful than ever,' her doting husband wrote to the Hen after Ada's return from Clifton on 1 November) took him into her confidence, both about her children and about herself. Within the first week of meeting Carpenter, Ada had told him about her teenage escapade with a tutor at Ealing. She had also spoken mysteriously of 'present troubles' from which the smitten academic impulsively decided it was his mission to release her. In early December, after agreeing to a provisional engagement as tutor for one year, Carpenter was invited to visit Ada after dinner, at her London home.

For a married woman to ask her children's married tutor to call on her alone and late at night was a clear signal of more than professional interest. Summoned to the bedroom-cum-office that Ada spoke of as her 'sanctum', Carpenter was made privy to further confidences about his young employer's private life. By mid-December, the relationship was intimate enough for Ada to entreat him to cheer her with 'a few *kind* lines – I need them'. Quoting these words back to her on 15 December, Carpenter asked permission to sign himself as 'Your affectionate friend'.

It was here that the trouble began. Already promised £400 a year, Carpenter now felt sufficiently emboldened to lay out his requests to 'the *really kind friend* which I believe you wish me to regard you'. He wanted a free house in which to entertain his friends, a horse of his own – presumably from the Ockham stud funded by Annabella – and the freedom to go to London to give lectures as and when he wished. Furthermore, he would only consider work that kept him within easy reach of the City. Remote Ashley Combe, where the King children were used to spending a blissful part of every year, was out of the question.

It may seem that Carpenter was asking for quite a lot. In his defence, he was no ordinary tutor. A published academic with the genuine promise of an appointment as the Fuller Professor of Physiology (1844–8) was justified in seeking some concessions for educating a trio of undisciplined children. (A governess, Miss Cooper, was independently recruited to act as nursery supervisor.)

Carpenter's mistake lay, not in his demands, but in misreading Ada's volatile personality. In January 1844, following one of the young countess's sudden breakdowns in health, Carpenter did something – it seems he had already kissed her – at which she took offence. Icily, Ada indicated that he had stepped beyond his role. She had wished only to be friendly. Perhaps the question of his employment should be reconsidered.

Carpenter was both furious and alarmed. Without telling Ada (on whom he inflicted a lengthy defence of the absolute purity of his intentions), he elected to write separately and at considerable length (concision was not Dr Carpenter's forte) both to her husband and her mother. Annabella was sufficiently displeased by his revelations to seek advice from Joanne Baillie about alternative teachers for her grandchildren. William Lovelace, offered Carpenter's commiseration for having to deal with such a feckless wife, grew incandescent with rage. 'I was completely *stunned*,' an injured Carpenter told Ada on 19 January after reading her husband's response. 'Though I saw that I had made a great mistake, I could not see *in what* …'

Carpenter, thanks to Ada's good-natured intervention on his behalf, was still offered the tutor's post. The request for a free house at Ockham was confirmed, together with his generous salary. Gratitude, grudgingly, was expressed. 'That you are a peculiar – *very peculiar* – specimen of the feminine race, you are yourself aware,' Carpenter informed his future employer on 24 January. Resentment seeping from his pen, he assured Lady Lovelace that 'the barriers' of social position would never again be transgressed. Nevertheless, he owed her a debt of thanks.

Would not a word from you as to liberties I had even *offered*, damn me with Lord L. Lady B. and the world? I feel that you *must* have done your best for me and for yourself to have extricated me as you have done; and to lead to the continuance of the wish that the educational engagement should continue.

᎒Ꮆ

William Carpenter's appointment as the Lovelace children's tutor – a role in which he would in fact acquit himself quite well during his trial year – proved timely. His employment coincided with the time at which Ada's brave words about her readiness to endure – and even to make a research subject of her physical suffering – were put to the test.

Ada's health suddenly deteriorated during the midwinter of 1843–4. Dr Locock was shaken when he saw for the first time what he described as a 'mad' look in his patient's eyes. 'He told me that it was really peculiar, & horrible to a spectator,' Ada confessed to her mother in an undated note. Put on a light diet and in a state of strict isolation, Ada acknowledged the need for such prudent measures when she found that she could not even cope with the stress of a short visit from a cherished family friend, the Yorkshire vicar Samuel Gamlen. 'I could not bear it for more than 10 minutes,' a wistful Ada admitted to her mother in a second undated note.

My brain then began to turn & twist, & my eyes to burn. I referred him [Gamlen] to you for everything about me … & merely said a few little facts as to the present … I cannot but *weep* over my inability to see so many who I would wish to see. It is *sad, sad, sad* to me.

Six weeks after Christmas 1843, Ada was still living in enforced solitude at St James's Square. On 10 February 1844, while eager to visit Woronzow and Agnes Greig, she felt obliged to warn these dear friends not to be startled by the strangeness of her swollen features. William was piteously thanked for the worry that he expressed ('What a *kind kind* mate *ou* is. Your sweetest letter (just received) has almost made me cry. It is so *wise,* yet so *tender.*') But William himself was contributing to Ada's fragility. 'I do not feel I am fairly dealt with in this,' Ada wrote from her London sickroom after her absent husband complained that the children were not always made immediately available to visit him either at Ashley Combe or East Horsley. 'Either thro' negligence or intention on your part, you give me *no notice* of *anything* scarcely ... I am expected to make no objection, & manifest no surprise, however *impromptu* the thing may be, & however unpleasant for what I had planned.' After scolding her husband for behaving in a way 'very pernicious to our mutual happiness', Ada smoothed her Crow's ruffled feathers. '*Pray* write to me, if only 6 words. I am quite miserable about you because I know you are unhappy, & fancy you have an unkind bird.'

Reading the tender letters that the Lovelaces exchanged during this time, it becomes clear that, despite their many spats and disagreements, Ada and her husband remained powerfully attached to each other. Lovelace had been infuriated by Dr Carpenter's suggestion that Ada was an unfeeling wife. But it was always easier for a diffident and reclusive man to demonstrate emotion through his fanciful buildings than in words. In the Great Hall of the newly transformed Horsley Towers, *Crede Byron* was proudly chiselled into one of the mighty beams that William himself had engineered (Brunel was pleasingly complimentary). Fretting about the absent Ada's health – he was alone down at Ashley Combe in the summer of 1844 – Lovelace set out to create a new sea pool and elaborate grotto for a wife who now placed her faith in swimming to cure her ailments. Visiting Brighton that summer, while the children went to Somerset and Carpenter took time off for his own career, Ada lodged herself at 38 Bedford Square, adjoining the seafront. Taking dutiful daily immersions from a bathing machine in a daring black one-piece, rounded off with a pair of stout leather boots, the novice sea nymph was soon envisaging herself as 'an *independent* & *skilful* swimmer ... *Perseverance* will do the business, I feel no doubt.'

Exercise was the solution, or so a hopeful Ada now persuaded herself. In between despatching instructions about the proper strength and length of gymnastic ropes to be installed in their various homes, she diverted William with accounts of her visit to a travelling circus (where the appearance of an elephant was an exciting novelty) and Brighton's zoo, where an adventurous monkey ripped through her sleeve and drew blood. 'This is my year of *accidents*,' poor Ada sighed, having already managed to break her nose and undergo '*some hours*' of dental surgery.

Exercise did not mean that Ada had weaned herself off the combination of claret and drugs prescribed by her favourite doctor. Ada's mother – Annabella had a horror of opiates – argued for the safer route of mental control. Harriet Martineau, a woman for whose industry and intelligence Lady Byron had considerable respect, attributed her recovery from uterine cancer entirely to the power of mesmerism. The letters about her unconventional cure were published the following year, but in 1844, they were already being shared and widely discussed among Martineau's friends. Here, surely, was the answer to Ada's predicament, one that would protect her uncommon and precious mind from being needlessly addled by stimulants?

Used to having her way, Lady Byron found herself on this occasion in the minority. Neither Dr Locock, nor his medical colleagues, nor even the opinionated William Carpenter believed that mesmerism could cure physical illness. Moreover, as Ada sharply informed her mother on 10 October 1844, the doctors believed that the experiments with mesmerism that she had voluntarily undergone back in the summer of 1841 might even have caused her current ills. It wouldn't do. In fact, Miss Martineau might herself benefit from the advice of a young lady who now wrote with brimming confidence of 'my advancing studies on the nervous system' and of ways that the world might yet benefit from her suffering.

And with that, Ada was off, overpowering her mother with a verbal extravaganza of all the thoughts and schemes that coursed unchecked through her shifting, skimming mind. She wrote of the authority with which she had learned to discipline Annabella's small namesake. ('Gentle as I am in general, yet when she *is* naughty, I am well aware that I give no quarter ... I am a changed being at once.') Ada went on to predict her personal destiny. She would become either a sun or a vagrant star. ('Solemn decree'.) The Sun, perhaps. And what planets should she permit to orbit her solar self?

> Oh! I must arrange some Comets too, by & bye. No complete planetary system without. Heavens! How shall I get any comets? I think I must myself be the chief Comet & not merely one of the Planets. Yes – that will do.
>
> At least I am an amusing Bird, if not a very wise one, with my repentances, my Suns, Planets, Comets, &c, &c, &c.
>
> I really believe that you hatched me simply for the entertainment of your old age, that you might not be ennuyée.

In part, Ada was simply playing with ideas and seeking to entertain a mother who she knew was going through sad times. To whom else, she sweetly asked, could she rattle on in such a lunatic vein, and yet be understood? 'I grow so fond of my old Hen, who understands all I can say & think so much better than *any one*.'

Annabella was in need of consolation. The summer of 1844 had been blighted by a bitter quarrel with Edward and Fanny, her favourites among all the Noels, when they jointly attacked Lady Byron for undervaluing Edward's skills as an educationalist.* (Ada had acted as the peacemaking go-between, but without success.)

---

* Local insurrections had forced Edward and Fanny back to England from Euboea. Angry altercations began when Lovelace suggested that Edward could become a land agent like his brother, with no loss of social status. Things worsened when Fanny defended her husband's right to be made a principal at his own school, rather than running one of the village schools set up by Annabella. The provision of a Warwickshire house at Leamington Spa (where Lady Byron owned property) did not lessen the touchy Edward's sense that he had been insulted. The quarrel with Annabella was never patched up, but Edward, as a widower, became her younger grandson's most respected advisor on family history.

And then, within a single month, death robbed Annabella of Harriet Siddons, of a beloved godson, Hugo de Fellenberg Montgomery, and of the Swiss school reformer for whom the late Mr Montgomery had been named. Advising Hugo's young widow, while comforting Mrs Siddons's bereaved daughter, Annabella wore herself out. Gossipy Mrs Jameson, visiting the woman she now regarded as her closest friend, was dismayed. Lady Byron had been 'more white and tremulously weak than I had ever seen her,' she confided to the American author, Miss Catherine Sedgwick, the following year. 'I was shocked ... Of all human beings she is the one most necessary to my heart & to my mental and moral well-being ... uniting in her extraordinary character and peculiar destiny all I most love with all I most reverence.'

To Annabella's grieving friends, it seemed as if the delicate, waxen-faced little widow had reached the end of her journey. They should have known better. If we look for one quality shared by Lord Byron, his wife and his daughter, it is the ability to take us by surprise. Byron could shift from love to hate within the space of a sentence. Ada and Annabella could lie at death's door on one day and be shaping destinies on the next. By mid-November, Lady Byron was well enough to visit Ockham and form a view of her grand-children's progress. Ada, while persuaded that the 'many *exciting expeditions*, and *irregular amusements*' devised by Dr Carpenter had proved the 'very *making*' of her firstborn, was less than impressed by the tutor's influence over her daughter: ('her *spirits are too much for her*; she *speaks* in a coarse vulgar voice, walks with a *heavy masculine brusque* step ... is nothing short of perfectly *odious*'.)* Lady Byron, who was extremely fond of her little namesake, disagreed. 'I think Dr Carpenter is on the right track,' Annabella announced. By way of reward for his good work, she offered to pay the tutor a thousand-pound bonus in lieu of lost lecture work, and to fund necessary renovations to his house at Ockham. (Carpenter

---

* To Carpenter himself, Ada wrote of her daughter's need of 'a profession' and suggested, presciently, that it might be that of an artist. (AAL to W. B. Carpenter, n.d. 1844, Dep. Lovelace Byron 44, fol. 16.)

had complained that it was both poky and damp.) Always shrewd, Lady Byron made it clear that the money would be paid only when Dr Carpenter had satisfactorily completed his term of trial.

And Ada? Brilliant, impetuous, magnificently ambitious Ada? It's hard to withhold admiration from a young woman who resolved to turn her personal battle against debilitating illness into a journey of discovery that would reap benefits for the world. While Charles Darwin would transform the garden of his country home into a vast outdoor laboratory, Ada – increasingly restricted to hobbling around the interior of a bedroom or study for her daily exercise – set out to make a clinical study of her own afflicted body. Writing to her mother in November 1844, Lady Lovelace bravely dwelt upon the value of possessing

> a frame so susceptible that it is an *experimental laboratory* always about me, & inseparable from me. I walk about, not in a Snail-Shell, but in a *Molecular Laboratory*. This is a new view to take of one's physical frame, & amply compensates me for all the sufferings, had they been even greater.

&

Ada had made her anonymous debut in the world of science in the late summer of 1843. By November 1844, Lord Byron's daughter was known to be the clever young woman who had written the 'Notes' expanding upon Menabrea's description of Babbage's unbuilt Engine. Mary Somerville had sent compliments upon the clearness with which she had illustrated a very difficult subject (a real homage from the translator of the fiendishly difficult writings of Laplace). Augustus De Morgan had not only written to praise Ada to herself. Answering a question from Lady Byron about his opinion of her daughter's intellect, De Morgan had boldly stated that Ada was, if the risk to her delicate health could be taken, capable of going beyond them all, of looking into realms of knowledge that were not yet apparent. It was as if De Morgan had intuited the then unimaginable fact that his former pupil would be perceived, over a century later, as the predictor of modern computer technology.

Buoyed by such an encouraging reception, but held back by recurrent ill health, Ada resolved to make a laboratory of her own frail body. But how was it to be done? To whom could she look for help?

By 1844, interest in Babbage's projected machine was already being overtaken by the growing impact of Michael Faraday's discovery, back in 1831, of electromagnetic induction, establishing the principles upon which the first electrical generator and transformer could be built. Professor Charles Wheatstone, Faraday's close friend, had meanwhile developed the first telegraphic system to be put into use in England. By November 1844, the Wheatstone telegraph was already being described as the 'nervous system' of the nation. It was an image that chimed precisely with Ada's bold new plan to use electricity and magnetism to create 'a *calculus of the nervous system*'. This was the intriguing proposal that she had submitted to Woronzow Greig on 15 November. Two weeks later, she invited Charles Wheatstone to her home for a discussion that lasted for five hours. It was the possibilities opened up by Wheatstone's electrical transmission systems – rather than the railway tracks in which her canny mother had started to invest – that had captured Ada Lovelace's enterprising imagination.

It may have been because Charles Wheatstone did not have to answer for the consequences to Lady Byron (whom he had never met) that he felt less anxiety than Augustus De Morgan about encouraging his protégée – Ada was thirteen years younger than himself – to push her enquiring intelligence to its limits. Ada looked upon her well-received 'Notes' as the foundation for a future and much larger career. It was Wheatstone – the instigator and first reader of Ada's Menabrea translation, the kindly advisor on how best to deal with Babbage's ill-conceived anonymous preface – who now appeared most eager to assist that career into life.

The connection that Wheatstone wanted Ada to explore was with German science. He had already encouraged her to translate certain papers by Georg Ohm, the German analyser of Wheatstone's ingenious device for measuring electrical usage. (It is still referred to as 'the Wheatstone bridge'.) Wheatstone next proceeded to the unexpected proposal that Lady Lovelace should use her social position to become the secret scientific advisor and mediator for the queen's German husband.

Wheatstone knew what he was talking about. His father, a maker of musical instruments, had taught music to Princess Charlotte. (Wheatstone himself invented a primitive form of the concertina and later presented one to Ada.) Acting in his role as the first professor of experimental philosophy (or applied science), at King's College London, the ingenious Wheatstone had contrived an electrically triggered cannon salute across the Thames to greet Prince Albert on his first visit to the college in 1843. The crushing failure of that dramatic salvo from the new riverside Shot Tower (the galvanic battery that should have triggered it was damp) bore unexpected fruit: it caused the sympathetic prince to ask the inventor about his technique. A friendship formed. By the time of his November discussion with Ada, Wheatstone understood how intensely frustrated Albert felt about his exclusion from the world of English science. The prince longed to contribute. 'Wheatstone says none but some *woman* can put him in the right way, & open the door to him towards all he desires,' Ada reported to her husband, before explaining the plan that their friend had unfolded to her.

... *if* I can take a certain standing in the course of the next few years, the Prince would on some occasion speak to me about science, and that in that case, if I happily seize the moment, I may do for science an *inestimable benefit*; for all the Prince wants is a sensible *advisor* & *suggester*, to indicate to him the *channels* for his exercising a scientific influence.

The idea of acting as a royal advisor was intriguing. Closer to Ada's own line of interest was the fact that Charles Wheatstone's closest friend in the world of science was the very man she was currently urging to become her collaborator. Electricity was what quickened Ada's interest now. Nobody in England knew more about electricity in 1844 than Michael Faraday.

Faraday had first seen Ada Lovelace back in 1839, the year in which Alfred Chalon's prettified portrait of the young countess was being displayed in the windows of London's most fashionable print shops. Faraday liked the look of her so much that the superstar of electrical science persuaded Charles Babbage to secure an image for him from the sitter herself.

It was Babbage who gave the relationship its first friendly nudge. Observing Faraday and Ada deep in conversation at one of his soirées on 9 September 1843, he sat down that same night to send Faraday the recently published Menabrea 'Notes', while adding a glowing tribute to 'that Enchantress who has thrown her magical spell around the most abstract of Sciences and has grasped it with a force which few masculine intellects (in our own country at least) could have exerted over it'.

Silence followed.

In October 1844, Ada took the initiative into her own hands. Presenting herself to Faraday as 'the bride of science', she asked permission, not only to work alongside him, but to become his soulmate. 'For many years,' she informed the startled scientist, 'I have desired to be admitted to intercourse & friendship with you; & to become in some respects your disciple.'

Ada was not exaggerating. She had been hearing about Michael Faraday, a man old enough to be her father, since childhood. Ada was eleven when Faraday began giving his famous Christmas lectures for the young at the Royal Institution. At the time when little Ada was first pondering the span of a rainbow's arc, Faraday was already experimenting with electromagnetism. Self-taught and with no formal knowledge of mathematics, Faraday was the principal advisor on electricity and magnetism for Mary Somerville's *On the Connexion of the Physical Sciences* (1834). Faraday's name appeared at least fifteen times in Somerville's index. (Babbage, by contrast, appeared just once.)

'I have a spell of *some sort* about me ...' Ada had boasted to Woronzow Greig in 1841. Returning to the idea in a letter sent to her mother shortly before her first appeal to Faraday, Lady Lovelace remarked again upon 'the power *I know I have over others*'. It was to this most Byronic aspect of Ada's seductive personality that a dazed Michael Faraday was about to be subjected.

The silence which had ensued after their first meeting at Babbage's home was partly due to a crisis in Faraday's personal life. A nervous breakdown had been followed by the enigmatic dismissal of himself and members of his family from the strict Sandemanian sect in which Faraday himself had long served as a respected elder. (The rupture was serious; Faraday was not reappointed for sixteen years.) The feyness apparent in Ada's first overture may have appealed to a man who, while reading the Bible, marked out the passage in Daniel that states: 'And at that time shall *Michael* stand up, the great prince which standeth for the children of thy people ...' More likely, Michael Faraday, a keen admirer of Lord Byron's poetry, was genuinely impressed by Wheatstone's praise for a young woman who combined imaginative intelligence with what seemed to him (but not John Herschel) to be a first-rate mathematical mind.*

Faraday may have been intrigued by Ada's background and her blandishments, but he was not to be so easily conquered as William Carpenter. Faraday had recently turned down a request from the elderly and eminent Maria Edgeworth to visit his home.

---

* 'I find myself in reading her notes at a loss in the same kind of way as I feel when trying to understand any other thing which the explainer himself has not clear ideas of.' John Herschel to Charles Lyell, 15 November 1844, Royal Society, *Herschel Letters*, vol. 22. ff. 210–11. Herschel nevertheless had a very friendly correspondence with Ada (Dep. Lovelace Byron 172, fols. 1–29.)

Ada was firmly informed that he was not well enough for collaborative endeavours. Neither did Faraday share her declared belief in the bond between religion and science: 'there is no philosophy [science] in my religion'. However, where many would have laughed at Ada's proclaimed desire to become 'High-Priestess of God's works as manifested on this earth', Faraday received the news of her ambition with pleasing gravity. Really, there could be no doubt that 'with your deep devotion to your subject you *will attain* it,' he wrote back in this same long letter, while adding kind hopes – clearly, he had been briefed about Ada's poor health – that her life would be sufficiently prolonged to do so. But he did not want a collaborator.

Faraday had underestimated both Ada's perseverance and her complete disregard for conventional behaviour. On 24 October (her second letter crossed Faraday's response to her first), she wrote again, begging the esteemed scientist only to write when it felt comfortable, and to regard her 'as a mere *instrument*'. Three days later, she hailed Faraday as 'one of the *few* whom it is an honour & privilege to know on this earth'. On 8 November, Ada sought permission to visit 'your philosopher's cell, just to look about me there'. More boldly, Ada announced her plan to make Faraday's own researches into 'my *hinge* & *centre* for an Electrical Article' that she planned to write in the coming year for the *Quarterly Review*. (References to other unidentified articles already in the pipeline also appear in this same letter.)

By now, Lady Lovelace had almost achieved her goal. A bewitched Faraday – in a letter that is missing from this intriguing correspondence – seemingly compared the endeavours of himself, a mere 'tortoise', to the dazzling 'elasticity of intellect' of her ladyship (a tribute that Ada swiftly shared with an impressed Lady Byron). Ada, whose physical diminishment of herself formed a regular part of her epistolary flirtations, now briskly shrank into 'a little brown bird' who would sit quietly at his side, but only if Mr Faraday would first promise to let the little bird pay a visit, and promise not to be cross at receiving such a giddy letter. 'I *mean* it to make you *laugh*. At any rate you must, I am sure, perceive that you have a very good-natured creature to deal with in yours most sincerely *AAL*.'

Ada's wish was granted. By 15 November, she was even apologising for having failed to make a return visit to his house in Albemarle Street. But she had not yet succeeded in luring him to her home. Faraday made one further feeble effort to escape ('You drive me to desperation by your invitations. I dare not and must not come and yet ...') before he yielded to the siren's call. 'We must talk *business* & *science* next time,' a gratified Ada announced on 1 December.

The subject of the meeting which took place on 28 November 1844 (one day before Ada's lengthy discussion with Wheatstone) remains unknown. Religion is a possibility. Ada's opening letter had engagingly presented herself as a regular hotch-potch of world faiths, although 'in truth I cannot be said to be anything but myself'. Perhaps they discussed the extraordinary discrepancy between Ada's physical fragility and the unfailing vigour of a mind which – as she had told him on 13 November, 1844 – '*keeps me all compos* and happy'. Certainly, the relationship had progressed. Three days after that encounter, Ada confided to Faraday her love of going about 'incog.' – that is to say, as 'Mrs William King' – and without the trappings of a rank that she professed to disdain. ('I have in fact roughed it thoroughly, as they say ...')

Relations had grown friendly enough for Lady Lovelace to admit to Faraday – as Ada very rarely did – how much care she took to mask her physical sufferings from strangers. Plans were hatched for further meetings during February 1845, but – it was often the case with Ada's grand projects – her plans for an article about electricity fizzled out. Her interest in Faraday's work remained vivid. Later that year, she eagerly followed the news that Faraday had succeeded in manipulating the course of light by magnets and thick sheets of glass. Ada's own final ambition – seemingly to replicate the effect of sunlight on raindrops – would owe much to her knowledge of Michael Faraday's work.

What was the project on which Ada hoped to collaborate with Faraday back in November 1844, at the time of her lengthy conversation with Charles Wheatstone? The answer emerges from her correspondence with another, less scientifically minded man: Woronzow Greig.

In that same November, Greig, who had been acting as Ada's researcher for a year, decided to play a little joke. An extraordinary, anonymously authored book had just been published. It was called *Vestiges of the Natural History of Creation* and it proposed that the world had emerged from a fire-mist, that men had evolved from apes and that life might yet be generated in a laboratory. Written by Robert Chambers, a member of the Scottish publishing family, the book became a literary sensation. Nobody knew who had written it. Some pointed to William Carpenter and others to George Combe.

It says much for Ada's standing in the scientific world, just one year after the publication of her 'Notes', that many believed Byron's brilliant daughter to be the modest author of *Vestiges*. Babbage, perhaps a little jealously, twitted Ada about it. Old Joanna Baillie, convinced of her authorship, gasped to Annabella at the genius of 'that wonderful creature', her daughter. William Lovelace, rather gratified by all the attention his wife was receiving, told John Hobhouse that everybody seemed to think she'd written the book. Who was he to deny it?

Ada herself was enchanted by Greig's notion of demurely presenting her with the very book that everybody was declaring she had written. Having signed herself with particular gratitude ('With Many Many Thanks'), she rewarded her old friend by sharing with him the secret of her latest project: a calculus of the nervous system. What she intended, so Greig was now informed, was to create what Ada ambitiously defined as 'a *law* or *laws*, for the mutual actions of the molecules of *brain*; (equivalent to the *law of gravitation* for the *planetary* & *sideral world*.)'. The problem that faced her, as she explained it in her lengthy letter, was purely practical. She needed to learn how to carry out practical trials on body parts: 'viz: the brain, blood, & nerves, of animals'.

To us, it may sound either as though Ada had gone mad or as though she had been burying her nose in the imaginative pages of that contemporary masterpiece, *Frankenstein, or The Modern Prometheus*.* But William Lovelace, as ambitious as the Hen for Ada's success, had heard and approved his wife's project; Greig, the legally trained, rational and sober-hearted son of Mary Somerville, neither questioned Ada's sanity nor withdrew his services as her devoted researcher.

On 5 December 1844, Ada wrote again to Greig. His friendly invitation to a play was brushed away with a reminder that she had not set foot in a theatre for over two years. All Ada wanted from him at present was a means of access to that most un-woman-friendly treasurehouse of researchers: the Royal Society. Had she not earned the right? 'I really have become as much tied to a *profession* as *you* are,' Ada pleaded to the lawyer. 'And so much the better for me, I always required this.'

A rare view for a woman to take of herself in the mid-nineteenth century, it was one in which Ada Lovelace was assisted by the quiet support, not only of Woronzow Greig, Charles Wheatstone, Lord Lovelace and her own mother, Lady Byron, but by the reassurance in 1844 that Michael Faraday, then regarded as the greatest scientist of the day, had confidence in her declared belief that she – Lord Byron's daughter – had been singled out to act as 'the *High-Priestess* of God's earthly manifestations.'

Great things were evidently in store.

---

* A book which Ada seems never to have read. It is not known whether she ever met *Frankenstein*'s creator, but these two remarkable women lived alongside each other in London's small scientific world from 1822 to 1851. Mary Shelley died in London, just one year before Ada. (See www.mirandaseymour.com for a blog about possible connections.)

CHAPTER NINETEEN

THE LADY FROM PORLOCK

(1844–9)

On 14 November 1838, the *Taunton Courier* excitedly reported that Fyne Court, the home of Somerset's most eccentric squire, had received a visit from the Earl of Lovelace and his lady, accompanied by a large party of their friends. In the absence of the owner, Mr Andrew Crosse, the callers were given a tour of the house and grounds. Apparently, they had been 'much gratified' by what they saw.

There was nothing novel about visiting country houses in the absence of their owners. Fyne Court was old, handsome and enhanced – if you liked that kind of thing – by a garden that featured crumbling follies, ponds, bridges and a serpentine lake (complete with grotto-style boathouse). Those were not the attractions, however, that had brought the Lovelace contingent of scientists, journalists and county folk out on a twenty-mile jaunt across Exmoor, in search of a lonely manor settled deep within the Quantock Hills.

Given the fact that Andrew Crosse grew up in an area that seems to have drawn the romantic poets to it like iron filings to a magnet (Wordsworth and Coleridge were living nearby when Crosse was in his early teens), and through the landscape of which they all roamed at will, it's surprising that Mr Crosse's name does not appear more frequently in literary history. Born at Fyne Court in 1784, Crosse was running the family estate by the age of twenty-one. A tall, ruddy-cheeked and deeply religious man (he bore a striking physical resemblance to his one-time Somerset neighbour, Robert Southey), Crosse was an amateur poet whose passion for science owed something to his upbringing (his father had been friendly with both Benjamin Franklin and Joseph Priestley), something to a sympathetic master at his Bristol boarding school and much to the simple fact that he was himself a clever, well-off man living in an age when science had become a fashionable home pursuit.

By the time that Andrew Crosse married Mary Anne Hamilton in 1809, he was a man obsessed. Five years later, visitors found the once elegant ballroom of Fyne Court transformed into a gigantic electrical laboratory, containing its own power storage supply within the fifty barrel-sized glass Leyden jars that had been provided by a friendly fellow scientist, G. S. Singer. Above them in the gallery (from which Crosse sometimes personally regaled his guests with an organ recital), an elaborate apparatus for measuring atmospheric electricity was connected to long lines of copper wiring that were strung between the swaying branches of an avenue of majestic beeches (trees that still flank the approach to Crosse's home).

History does not report what the inhabitants of the local hilltop village of Broomfield thought of Andrew Crosse, but the experiments that regularly took place at Fyne Court – especially when a storm was up – often provided an electrical display (one home-made flash was alleged to have towered tall as the mast of a ship) that won the squire his local reputation as 'the thunder and lightning man'. Kind to his tenants (those who wished it received free electrotherapy treatment for their ailments, courtesy of their landlord and his wife) and always hospitable to his visitors, Crosse never refused a welcome to uninvited guests. Humphry Davy, Charles Babbage and the Shelleys were among those who visited Fyne Court hoping to see wonders revealed, and departed wondering only how Crosse and his family managed to survive in a household of such untrammelled chaos.

In 1836, Crosse performed the infamous experiment that had first caught the interest of the Lovelaces. Mary Shelley, back in 1819, had published *Frankenstein*, a novel which dared to suggest that a scientifically constructed corpse could be shocked into a state of sensibility. Medical halls and lecture theatres had already offered show-stopping evidence of how electricity could cause a dead man (women's bodies were never used) to raise an arm, clench a jaw, clasp a hand. Mary Shelley's fiction raised the stakes by granting Victor Frankenstein's unfortunate creature the power to feel emotions and to react to the experience of withheld parental love.

Andrew Crosse had done nothing so remarkable, but his discovery nevertheless created a public sensation. Speaking to a local electricity society in 1836, Crosse casually reported the emergence of tiny, living mites after he had dripped a chemical mixture on to electrified red ironstone. To Crosse, a devoutly Christian believer, it seemed clear that the *Acarus crossii*, as the mites came swiftly to be named, resulted from some unidentified contamination in his process. Simultaneously hailed as a modern Prometheus and hounded by death threats for having dared to challenge the laws of divine creation, the amateur scientist found it impossible to subdue the storm of excitement he had unwittingly provoked. While evidence backed Crosse's denials (the results of the only attempt to replicate the experiment, conducted under an air-tight bell jar by a surgeon, W. H. Weekes, were never formally confirmed), the idea of spontaneous generation was too alluring to be abandoned. When Robert Chambers began to write *Vestiges of the Natural History of Creation*, and to suggest that life could be created in a laboratory, he had Crosse's experiment in mind. The story of the seemingly life-generating crystals played a small but significant role in the daring survey of modern science that Chambers set before the public in 1844. (The Crosse family were understandably annoyed by this fresh exposure to a publicity they did not welcome.)

It was curiosity about the *Acarus crossii* that had caused the Lovelaces to escort that inquisitive houseparty to Fyne Court back in 1838. (Four years later, Ada had written to interrogate Crosse about the mysterious mites, but was simply referred to the experiment carried out by Weekes.) Later still, in the autumn of 1843, when Ada was away at Clifton with her mother, the reclusive squire and his younger son, Robert, had ventured back across Exmoor to visit the Lovelaces at Ashley Combe. Crosse's conversation, according to a disappointed William Lovelace, had proved considerably less sparkling than his enthralling electric experiments had suggested.

Absorbed in embellishing his cliffside palace, Lovelace had been more eager to show off Ashley Combe's towers and terraces than to listen to Andrew Crosse's troubles in dealing with a household that could no longer be governed by his invalid wife. The visitor's slowness of speech was enough to drive a man mad, William groaned to Ada before shifting his letter's theme to a more engrossing topic: was his dear Bird keeping up her harp practice at Clifton? Never must she forget how much the Crow loved to hear her play.

A year later, Ada herself initiated a correspondence with Andrew Crosse. It was at precisely the same time that she first made contact with Michael Faraday. The countess was seeking any means she could find to further her scientific career, no easy thing in a world that strove to exclude women from any significant activity whatsoever. Ada's reason for approaching both Crosse and Faraday was that both scientists were known to carry out most of their experiments in private, far from the masculine precincts of lecture theatres and college laboratories. An added bonus in the case of Crosse was the fact that Fyne Court lay less than twenty-five miles from the Lovelaces' home-grown Somerset Alhambra.

To Andrew Crosse, as to Michael Faraday, Ada Lovelace indicated the seriousness of her own commitment by identifying herself as a 'bride of science'. A reference to her wish to practise galvanising frogs' legs may have suggested that Ada was in some ways a little behind the times; such experiments had been carried out forty years earlier. Ada's interest was nevertheless patently sincere, while the Menabrea 'Notes' – these were sent to Crosse twice over, once by Ada and again by her proud husband – offered evidence of a luminously intelligent and adventurous mind.

It was for quite another reason that Lord Lovelace encouraged both Ada's correspondence with Andrew Crosse and the plan that she hatched in November 1844 to pay a personal visit to Fyne Court.

Devoted though the couple were at that time (Ada told the Hen that her dear Crow's nature grew more beautiful every year, while Lovelace wrote to Lady Byron of his longing that everybody should recognise the nobility and even the 'grandeur' of the Bird's glorious mind), the earl was an orderly man. His wife's undisciplined habits drove him almost to distraction. Respecting Ada immensely for her courage and independence, her husband nonetheless thought it admirable that, after sacking an unsatisfactory maid, his wife briefly chose to fend for herself. He thought it splendid that Ada now packed her own travelling cases, mended and even made her own clothes, dressed and laced herself and even – when ill – prepared her own modest supper in a saucepan hung over the bedroom fire.

What irked Lord Lovelace was Ada's vagueness. Payments were forgotten. Books were borrowed from lending libraries and seldom returned. As many as three harps might be simultaneously ordered for trial, and none of them given back to the hard-up instrument-maker for years on end. And as for Ada's work habits: it was extraordinary, the meticulous Lovelace lamented to a sympathetically clucking Hen, that anyone could be so neat as their brilliant Bird in the arrangement of her wardrobe and yet so chaotic in the order and dating of her notes and papers.

Writing to Lady Byron about her daughter's proposed visit to Fyne Court, Annabella's 'affectionate son' (for so a devoted Lovelace now unfailingly signed himself) was determined to be frank. He wanted his wife to visit Crosse's unruly home as a warning of what could happen when disorder was permitted to rule. With better organisation at home, the earl was convinced that Andrew Crosse could have become a respected figure in the world of science. As it was, Crosse was perceived as a charming eccentric, an amateur experimenter whose one notorious achievement had been the product of his own ineptitude. Crosse would act as a caution to Ada.

At first, all went according to plan. Andrew Crosse paid a second visit to Ashley; Lovelace, citing illness as an excuse for not joining them, loaned his coach and coachman, John, so that Ada and Crosse could together travel back in comfort to Fyne Court.

The journey provided time for fruitful exchange. Reference was surely made to *Vestiges* and the *Acarus crossii*, but most of their time, as Ada reported to her spouse, had been occupied in outlining her great plan for a calculus of the nervous system. Mr Crosse had been impressed, especially by the quietness of her reasoning and the soundness of her premises. He did not, Ada was pleased to announce, regard her ideas as 'mere enthusiasm'.

The success of the visit can be judged by Ada's response to Fyne Court's freezing temperature. This was late November: Ada's circulation was so poor that she habitually slept, even in high summer, in a thick flannel dressing-gown worn over her nightwear. Yet, it was in a spirit of positive gaiety that she sent out her first bulletin from Andrew Crosse's home at 9.30am, while sitting alone and breakfastless, huddled in her shawl and boa stole beside an unlit fire, within a silent and shuttered house.

Lovelace had been right about one thing. Ada readily agreed that Fyne Court was chaotic. ('I never saw the like.') Meals arrived by chance and ended at whim. (The Crosses had talked to her about science until one in the morning upon that memorable first night.) One room was entirely in ruins. Others had been sacrificed to Mr Crosse's need for space in which to conduct his electrical experiments. The lantern-lit cellars looked more like a surgeon's theatre than a wood and coal store. There was only one working lavatory in the house, off at the far end of what served as a drawing room. Often as not, the door to it was locked and the key mislaid.

Ada seemed to be describing a madhouse, one which was considerably less organised than an actual London madhouse patronised by Lady Byron and Elizabeth Fry.* Unfortunately for Lord Lovelace's

---

* Visiting Rouen asylum – supposedly a model of its kind – in 1838, a shocked Annabella compared the use of permanent leg chains to kindly Hanwell, where mentally disturbed inmates were encouraged to garden and practise handicrafts, and where solitary confinement ended as soon as the patient felt willing to socialise. In 1834, she made Hanwell the subject of a laudatory poem. Orderliness, in Annabella's methodical view, was crucially connected to mental stability. She would have been appalled by Fyne Court.

plans, Ada loved Fyne Court. Here, so she joyfully informed her husband, she was treated, not as an empty-headed peeress or – at best – as Byron's daughter, but as a professional colleague. If she felt ill, she could simply withdraw to her room. (Ada had given Andrew Crosse advance warning of her ongoing and 'terrible' physical affliction and of her imperative need to be alone when battling it.) Scientific discussion was the order of the day. Never for a single moment was Lady Lovelace treated as that inferior being: a woman.

The focus of Ada's letters home, from the very start, was less upon her host than on his eldest son. Six years older than herself, John Crosse struck Ada as being both well-read and highly intelligent. A good mathematical mind was apparently combined with a strong sense of humour and a lively relish for strenuous debate. John was planning to spend six months of the following year in Berlin, studying all that was new there in the world of German science. Meanwhile, Ada coolly proposed to her husband that the young man – she emphasised John's great youth with deceptive care – should become her colleague and assistant. Perhaps John could come and live at Ockham, where he would be able to keep her mind up to the mark by stimulating discussions of her views. 'This is very useful and good for me,' Ada announced to her husband on 24 November. The Crow, delighted, reported to Lady Byron the good news that their clever Bird had at last found the support that she required for the scientific endeavours in which both her husband and mother so ardently wished her to succeed.

༄

As the daughter of one of Europe's most notorious rakes, it was inevitable that gossip would always hover close to Lady Lovelace. While the scandal often emerged from the hostile camp presided over by Lovelace's resentful mother at Woburn Park, the stories which reached John Murray's dining table in December 1844 – from whence they were reported back to Ada and her mother as 'public news' – had originated at Ockham. Ada, writing to Woronzow Greig about how she planned to combat these malicious tales, dismissed them as unfounded and absurd. Her mother, she told Greig, had 'quite chuckled' at Ada's plan to embarrass the 'Traitor' by confronting him with her 'great eyes' and delivering his own malicious words straight back to his face.

It was soon after this that a newspaper item appeared in which it was hinted that Lady Lovelace was on over-friendly terms with a Somerset neighbour. The newspaper was behind the times: the admirer named was not John Crosse, but Frederick Knight, the genial country neighbour with whom Ada often rode out both on Exmoor and in London, although never without her husband's calm assent. (Ada, reporting this particular titbit to Babbage in July 1845, thought it hilarious.)

Not all the gossip could be blamed upon spiteful in-laws, chatty servants and nosy visitors. Ada herself was hopelessly indiscreet, as her impulsive revelations to Dr Carpenter had already shown. In the opening months of 1845, she began to confide in Woronzow Greig.

Evidently, the countess's new relationship with John Crosse was causing her to question her marriage. Early in that November, Ada had been writing about William Lovelace with exceptional affection. Now, just after her first visit to Fyne Court, Ada abruptly told Greig that no husband could suit her, and that it was a 'cruel & dreadful' mockery to hear the lawyer talking about conjugal kindness. Lord Lovelace, however well-meaning, was incapable of understanding her. ('He is a good & just man. He is a *son* to me ... But it has been a hopeless case ...')

And then, with one of those lightning impulses that had so often baffled her father's friends, just as the well-meaning Greig began to offer advice, Ada changed her mind. On 12 February 1845, eight days after describing the relationship with her husband as 'hopeless', Lady Lovelace ordered Greig to forget all she had said. She did not regret her marriage. Nobody could suit her better than Lord Lovelace. 'More than this you cannot desire in reason,' she entreated, forgetting that it was she herself who had introduced the whole awkward subject. It was nonsense, she pleaded now. Her mind had been distracted by other affairs 'quite unconnected with any of my own'.

Reading that puzzling allusion to her sudden interest in affairs 'quite unconnected' with her own, it seems possible that Ada was already pondering John Crosse's glib tales of financial hardship and wondering how to help him. Money, as Crosse was quick to intimate, was what he required from a woman whose access to immense wealth offered considerable temptation to a man who possessed little of his own.

Sexual frustration may also have contributed to Ada's sudden outburst against her husband. In January 1845, the countess had only just turned twenty-nine. Her multiple ailments included gynaecological problems which would later manifest themselves, agonisingly, as a large sore in her cervix. An inability to enjoy sex might well have given rise to the despair that Ada betrayed to Greig, drawing back only when she belatedly realised the risk attached to confiding in her husband's oldest friend. Much of Ada's correspondence was later destroyed, with a view to protecting her reputation. Whether an emotionally passionate relationship with John Crosse was ever physically consummated remains an unknowable mystery.

∽

On an intellectual level, John Crosse and Ada soon found a subject upon which they could collaborate. In the summer of 1845, Roderick Murchison's old ally in geological studies, Adam Sedgwick, published an eighty-five-page denunciation of the anonymously authored *Vestiges* in the *Edinburgh Review*. It was the longest article that the magazine had ever published (and it was the last review that Sedgwick was ever asked to write).

For Ada and her proud family, it had been quite enjoyable, until this point, to see herself being identified by a number of eminent people as the author of a book that was already in its fourth edition and that would continue to be a huge seller until the end of the century. However, while it was gratifying for her to note that Sedgwick was keen to identify her as the author of *Vestiges* (he spoke only of a woman, but there was no other female contender in the field), Ada was far from pleased by Sedgwick's chauvinism. Only a woman, so he wrote, could have written in such a giddy, skipping, illogical style about a subject of such importance as the genesis of mankind. Poor research (in Sedgwick's jaundiced view) again indicated a woman's hand. No woman (this was an astonishing observation by a man who was well acquainted with the scrupulously methodical and industrious Mary Somerville) was capable of the 'enormous and continued labour' required for scientific work.

John Crosse's bone of contention was with *Vestiges*, rather than Sedgwick. As embarrassed as his father had been by the spotlight that Andrew Crosse's discovery of sentient mites had thrown upon a reclusive family, he resented the way in which Robert Chambers's controversial book revived interest in this awkward topic. (Chambers had even included letters from Weekes, the surgeon whose own experiments between 1842 and 1844 led him to believe in the notorious *Acarus crossii*.) Studying Sedgwick's extended diatribe alongside Chambers's book, Ada and Crosse decided to present their own appraisal of *Vestiges*.

It was unthinkable that Lady Lovelace (or even the coy 'AAL') should acknowledge her contribution to John Crosse's essay. Ada nevertheless betrayed her close involvement by the anger with which she wrote to Charles Babbage on 2 September about the 'infamous' way that a certain Mr John Crosse ('I have *leave* to mention his name to you') was being treated by the *Westminster Review*. Crosse's contribution was filled with printer's errors and had been ignominiously positioned at the end of the magazine.

The *Westminster* may have been careless in editing Crosse's piece, but relegating it to the final pages was a deliberate decision. By September, already sated by Sedgwick's interminable rant in the July issue of the *Edinburgh Review*, the public wanted no further attacks upon a book which was widely admired. Neither, as the owner (Sir William Molesworth, a friend of the Lovelaces) or the editor (William Hickson) must have concluded, was it useful to give prominence to a piece which criticised *Vestiges*' treatment of the 'acarus Crossii [*sic*], or *horridus*' resulting from Andrew Crosse's 1836 experiment.

There was nothing wrong with challenging the author of *Vestiges* for his suggestion that electricity was involved in 'the shrub-like crystallisation of frozen moisture on windows'. (This was 'a fatal blunder', Crosse and Ada justly scolded; 'none so bad'.) Overall, however, the tone of the collaborators was shrilly assertive. One chapter of *Vestiges* (on the mental capacity of animals) 'appears to us altogether erroneous'. Chambers' Malthusian proposal that mankind could be subjected to a mathematical diagnosis was dismissed as 'downright nonsense'. Such jaunty writing did not suit the pages of the soberly intelligent *Westminster Review*. No further reviews by John Crosse and his invisible colleague would grace its pages.*

Charting the progress of Ada Lovelace's secretive relationship with John Crosse is not easy. One fact stands out. Following that first husbandless stay at Fyne Court in November 1844, the countess began to carve out a more independent life for herself. At the end of August 1845, after spending three weeks with her mother at a village house

---

* The little that has been identified of Ada's published writings outside the Menabrea 'Notes' and contributions to her husband's occasional articles about the science of agriculture is frankly disappointing. In 1842, she reviewed a novel called *Morley Einstein*, three volumes of tosh in the silver-fork genre that was popular at the time. The author was the prolific George Payne Rainsford James. Ada's claim to have admired its stance on penal reform and the arts and sciences makes one wonder how closely she had read a book which says so little upon these topics. Frequent references in her letters to her mother about papers on which she was working suggest that she planned to write many more reviews and articles. The only other one that seems to have survived, again written in collaboration with John Crosse, was of the pioneering experiments in mesmerism being carried out in Germany by Baron von Reichenbach. The unpublished review, which contains early observations about photography, suggests that Crosse himself was no feminist. Reading Ada's own approving comment on the Baron's use of experiments that could be undertaken by amateurs of both sexes, he excised it.

in Kirkby Mallory (the main Noel home had been rented out on a long lease to a widowed Lady de Clifford), the countess retreated to Brighton where – as her husband teased her – she lived in such privacy that not even the notoriously inquisitive Mrs Jameson could find her. Lovelace's prophecy proved correct; Anna Jameson left Brighton at the end of the summer in a state of perfect ignorance about Ada's whereabouts.

Writing to Woronzow Greig from the partially completed Horsley Towers on 24 November 1845, Ada boasted of the '*positive*' and 'conclusive proofs' she had received at Brighton that her incognito was successful. Plans were being hatched for a new way of life and they were not only driven by a sick woman's need for seclusion and Brighton's bracing air. By the following summer, Ada had persuaded her unsuspicious mother to subsidise the furnishing of a permanent pied-à-terre in Brighton's Russell Square, one of the smartest areas in town. (Annabella's untypical lack of interest in her daughter's activities was due to the fact that she was preoccupied by innumerable philan-thropic and educational enterprises, both in England and America.)

Of all Ada's letters to her mother, the one that she wrote to the preoccupied Lady Byron from Brighton on 8 July 1846 was the most affectionate. She began by apologising for the expense of the Russell Square furniture, pointing out that it had been of the simplest kind, 'much of it being only such as is used in servants' rooms'. What mattered was that she now possessed a first little home of her own, a cosy nest to which she could retreat. Ada's elated tone makes it tempting to assume that John Crosse had become a regular visitor to Russell Square.

'*This* life, backwards & forwards, between home & here, suits me delightfully,' Ada informed her mother, in full underlining mode.

> I return *home con gusto* always. – Much of the comfort I am
> now enjoying I owe to you, – & I feel so grateful for it, – that
> I do not well know how to say so *adequately*! I think of it
> often ... Every night & every morning I go to sleep thinking 'I
> owe my comfort to the *Hen*!'

And how – whether in Brighton or elsewhere – did the illicit couple pass their stolen hours? If we can trust Ada's own testimony, the answer is touchingly innocuous. Back in 1844, following her first visit to Fyne Court, a relieved Lady Lovelace told Andrew Crosse that she had discovered in her own pocket the little gold pencil that she had been so very anxious not to have left behind at his home. Drawing up her will eight years later, Ada carefully specified that Mr John Crosse was to receive the instruments contained in her gold writing case, and to make use of them 'habitually, in remembrance of the many delightful & improving hours we have jointly passed in various literary pursuits'.

Hard though it is to credit, intellectual affinity may have been the prime stimulus of Ada's secret love affair.

∽

Speculations about the nature of Ada's relationship with John Crosse should not obscure the strength of the family bond that continued to unite the Hen, the Bird (as Lovelace and Annabella continued lovingly to refer to Ada) and the Crow (who relished his nickname enough to make occasional playful use of a gaunt black bird in lieu of his signature).

The difficulty of removing William Carpenter from their lives had occupied screeds of inter-familial correspondence in 1845. In truth, the Lovelaces had never entirely trusted Carpenter after the opening spat in their relationship. The move from Ockham to nearby East Horsley provided a perfect excuse to end it. The tutor's trial year was up and there was no home adequate to satisfy his (rather grand) requirements at the new estate. Carpenter's desperate eagerness to stay on beyond his appointed term – despite having secured a professor's chair and regular work as a lecturer at the London Hospital and University College – suggests that he valued his post and liked his employers better than they did him. But pride was also at stake. Back in 1844, Lady Byron had paid the tutor a £200 advance upon a promised £1,000 to do up a house for his family. Now, there was

to be no house and Lady Byron required Carpenter's written gratitude for the £300 she was still willing to offer, irrespective of the
purpose for which it was used. If thanks were not forthcoming – or
rather, an apology from the impetuous tutor for having prematurely
assumed that Lady Byron would be less charitable – the sum would
not be paid. Thanks extracted, and due obeisance made, the money
was handed over.

Annabella could be chillingly legalistic where money was concerned, but she had no reason to offer such a generous sum to a man
who, however well-meaning – he carried the children off to see the
sights of London and on various jolly outings in Surrey – had been a
troublesome employee. Carpenter's demands for improved terms had
rarely slackened, while his habit of gossiping about a fiercely private
family had caused Lovelace, on 22 August 1845, to describe him as
'a villainous incendiary'.

Overqualified as a children's teacher, Carpenter had never succeeded in winning over the 9-year-old and stubbornly wayward
Viscount Ockham. Mrs Jameson, meeting with young Annabella
towards the end of the tutor's trial term of employment, was shocked
by the little girl's neglected air. 'I never saw a child to whom a firm,
cheerful & *tender* influence was more wanting,' she wrote to Lady
Byron.

Mrs Jameson was also aiming a shaft at the child's absent mother.
Ada, until her early thirties, remained singularly detached from her
offspring. Back in 1839, she had cared enough to insist – in keeping
with her Unitarian beliefs – that little Ralph must not be formally
christened. By 1845, she was happy to yield the 6-year-old boy's
upbringing entirely to her mother, while leaving Lovelace to oversee
conscientious Miss Cooper, the governess to their older two children.

Ada's withdrawal from the conventional maternal role meant that
the earl, while always able to draw upon the Hen for calm advice,
was obliged to take an active interest in his children. A stickler for
discipline, he tried to control everything, from the hour at which
the children rode out upon their ponies to the hour at which Miss
Cooper began her schoolroom duties. A clock stood within sight of

the earl's bed and his door was always wedged open. Miss Cooper habitually commenced her duties fifteen minutes late. The impulse to provoke such a time-conscious employer must have been irresistible.

Lord Lovelace's children never learned to love their father in the way that they did the small, upright figure of whom little Ralph once sweetly observed that 'Granma' reminded him of a cow licking her newborn calf, while Lady Annabella relished the occasional treat of being allowed to unpin and brush her grandmother's waterfall of light-brown hair.* Their grandmother had a gentler manner, but the earl, in his own gruff way, did his best. Taken out of context, Lovelace's actions can sound harsh. But it was not so unkind for a father to ask a 9-year-old Victorian boy to write his granny a short letter in Latin about the tearing of his riding cape on a bramble bush. While it was thoughtless to threaten a habitually inattentive pupil (Byron Ockham again, on 19 August 1845) with putting him in the blinkers of 'a nasty, dirty horse' if he did not sit up and listen, a threat is not equivalent to a deed and Ockham was a very reluctant pupil.

It was the remembered tedium of sharing his dinner table with William Carpenter (together with the tutor's wife and their starchy visitors) that caused Lovelace to reject his mother-in-law's prompt offer to engage a replacement tutor. (Annabella ended by hiring the phrenologically impeccable Mr Herford herself, as a special tutor to young Ralph.) Meanwhile, advised by an anxious mother-in-law that Ada was far too ill to assist him, Lord Lovelace resolved to educate the children on his own.

Writing to her esteemed son-in-law from Kirkby Mallory on 21 August, Annabella bleakly described Ada's health as 'of a very unfavourable character'. She herself planned to remain in Brighton in order to assist in any way that her daughter might require. Ada also admitted that she was indeed in a bad way. 'You poor dear

---

* There was always a striking contrast between what Lady Byron preached and what she practised. Writing to Ada on 30 August 1848, while Ralph was still in his grandmother's care, she announced that moral obedience should be obtained by 'physical obedience ... obedience resulting from fear'. There is no hint in the family memoirs that such tyranny was ever employed.

patient thing – my own bird – the news you give me of the abcess tears my heart,' Lovelace wrote to Ada in Brighton on 30 August. On 12 October, he despatched one of his most tender notes, hoping that his dear Bird might soon again 'spread her brilliant wings in the sight of the admiring crow & her young'. Two days later, he confessed to Ada his terror that she might become too ill to perform the work, both in science and music, that she so loved ('one of the saddest of my many sad reflections about you').

It's impossible to doubt that William Lovelace, although often selfish and increasingly obsessed by his social position in the world, remained deeply attached to his fragile, clever wife. Meanwhile, his new paternal responsibilities turned the earl's thoughts to religion.

Lovelace never came closer to his mother-in-law than in their discussions about God. What, speaking as one convinced Unitarian to another, should he tell the grandchildren? Naturally, Lovelace wished to acquaint his eldest son and daughter with the New Testament: how could he do it without warning them that the Bible was 'mistaken' and the text 'interpolated with fables'? Should he confess that he did not believe in the Immaculate Conception? Ada had suggested bringing young Annabella to Brighton, where she could be educated by the earnestly religious wife of Dr King, their old family friend. But what should they do when Mrs King's beliefs contradicted their own Unitarian tenets? Was it right to force such young children to choose whom they should trust?

These questions, for people like the Lovelaces and Lady Byron – they believed that Jesus was a good man, but not the son of God – were difficult to address without causing gossip. John Cam Hobhouse was genuinely shocked when Ada (after seating her father's oldest friend next to herself at a London dinner party in June 1846) confessed that she did not believe in immortality.

John Hobhouse was not a warm man, but he had grown fond of Byron's unconventional daughter. In 1845, she visited his home expressly to see the curly-haired and broad-shouldered bust of her father that Hobhouse had commissioned in Rome, in 1817, from the admired Danish sculptor Bertel Thorwaldsen. A month earlier, Ada had expressed her distaste for Thorwaldsen's full-length statue of the poet, a grand memorial for which Hobhouse had vainly struggled to secure a place in Westminster Abbey.* Confronted by this smaller and more lifelike bust of the father she had never known, Ada came visibly close to tears. Her host was touched.

Discussing Ada's lack of religious faith at dinner in the summer of 1846, Hobhouse was alarmed to see how ill his young hostess looked. While noting in his diary for 3 June 1846 that the Lovelaces seemed 'much attached' to each other, he sadly predicted that their happiness, 'if happy they are, will soon be at an end'.

A few days later, Ada apologised to the grandson of Byron's publisher for having fainted while dining at his house. The Murrays had assumed for one dreadful moment that all was at an end. Their guest's capacity for miraculous recovery remained as extraordinary as the swiftness of the attacks that she described to Mr Murray as spasms of the heart. A week later, Ada was well enough to host an intriguing dinner party of her husband's contriving.

Over twenty years later, much public merriment would be expressed when Harriet Beecher Stowe, launching her passionate defence of the late Lady Byron, would describe the reclusive Lord Lovelace as 'a man of fashion'. Back in 1846, however, Stowe's description seemed to fit. Newly situated at Horsley Towers (Ockham Park had been conveniently rented to Stephen Lushington), William wanted to expand his social circle. One of his letters instructed Ada to invite the eminent geologist Sir Roderick Murchison to stay, simply because of the Murchisons' access to a large and influential group of friends. In the country, William began making week-long visits to those fellow landowners who shared his passion for Gothic architecture. In London, shortly after Ada's collapse at John Murray's house, the earl urged his wife to invite a fashionable Italian lady to dine at their home.

Light-hearted references in Ada's letters to 'Countess Italia Italia'

---

* Nevertheless, both Ada and her mother had supported Byron's right to a place in the abbey. The rejected statue was finally granted a place in the Wren Library at Trinity by its new master, William Whewell. Byron would not be granted a memorial in the abbey until 1969.

have led biographers to deduce that Lord Lovelace was planning to entertain Teresa Guiccioli at St James's Square. But Byron's ageing inamorata was still in Italy (from where Mrs Jameson maliciously reported to Lady Byron on 12 November 1846 that the fair *contessa* had lost her looks and even her pleasant smile, while still displaying a superabundance of radiant hair). In fact, and to Ada's consternation, the exotic lady whom her husband was so anxious to invite to dinner was the notorious Countess Ida von Hahn-Hahn, author of *Countess Faustine*, a book about a beautiful courtesan. The infamous authoress, so an apparently gratified Lovelace had been accurately assured, bore a striking resemblance to none other than his own wife.

The problem was not with the countess, nor with her book, but with her companion. Turning to Babbage (an unlikely master of etiquette) for advice, Ada expressed uncharacteristic concern about society's view. She herself did not mind if the countess brought along her lover, Baron Bystram. Lovelace himself was entirely open-minded on such matters. But what would others say? Would such behaviour get her into 'a scrape with the other *lady-guests*', or even with society in general? No further mention being made of the dinner invitation, it seems that the plan was abandoned. The incident stands as an intriguing example of Ada's Byronically unpredictable nature.

Where Lovelace's own difficult family were concerned, Lady Lovelace remained fiercely loyal to her husband. On 22 June 1846, Ada fired off a furious letter to William's maternal uncle, reminding Lady Hester's brother – in the haughty third person – of 'the repeated & unjust condemnations of Lady Lovelace's husband during this series of years', accusations which had caused her own feelings for Lady Hester to have passed beyond forgiveness. Secretly, however, Ada knew that her odious mother-in-law's claims to be terrified of her eldest son were not without justification. William did have a fearsome temper. Visiting Ashley Combe that autumn, Ada herself was briefly exposed to the blackness of spirit that may have helped to earn her husband his teasing nickname of the Crow.

The details are vague. The Lovelaces drove along the coast to Minehead, where they dined with old friends, the Pearces, who offered their frank opinion that Byron Ockham and his sister were turning into rude little beasts. (The Pearces' criticisms were confirmed by Ada's request to her mother on 7 October to find a governess who could teach better manners to her outspoken daughter. Young Byron's impudence was a continual source of anxiety.)

The Pearces' comments rankled. After dinner, while still seated at the table, the earl lost his temper and vented it on Ada. Backed by her shocked hosts, Ada decided not to go back to Ashley that night. Instead, she went straight from Minehead to join her mother at Moore Place, Lady Byron's Surrey home. She said nothing about her return. Lovelace, she believed – and Lady Byron agreed with her daughter – deserved a fright.

He got one. Dismayed and crestfallen, Lovelace told the Pearces that he believed his wife had gone for good. Six weeks later, accompanied by young Ralph and his new tutor, Ada was welcomed back to Ashley Combe. Lovelace was all deference and affection. The Hen's advice had been spot on, Ada cheerfully reported to her mother. A stern peck from his little brown Thrush was all that had been required to bring her moody old Crow back into line.

Further evidence of Ada's closeness to her mother at this time surfaced ten days later. Writing to Annabella from Ashley Combe on 29 November, Ada confirmed that everything was going smoothly and according to the plans that the two of them had hatched during her stay at Moore Place. Stroppy little Lord Ockham was to be packed off to Kirkby the following year for a few months of tuition in schoolwork and estate-craft training by Charles Noel. Ralph, accompanied by Mr Herford, would shortly be returning to live with his grandmother at Esher. Lovelace's proposed annual payment of £100 towards his youngest son's upkeep sounded about right, Ada added. It wasn't much, but any more would give William a feeling that he had the right to intervene: this was something that neither Ada nor her mother wished to happen. Ada, it is clear, favoured her mother's skills as an educationalist and mentor over those of her husband.

The year 1846 ended with a crash. On 10 December, her thirty-first birthday, Lady Lovelace wrote to tell her mother that she had just undergone a near brush with death. Out driving a light open phaeton with Lovelace late at night on the treacherously steep and narrow lanes around Ashley Combe, an accident had occurred. The sporty little carriage overturned, flinging Ada herself into the verge. The huge wheels came off; the night air was filled with the sounds of grinding metal and the high whinnying of the horses. For one terrifying moment, flat on her face in the muddy depth of a country ditch, Ada believed herself in hell.

Ada's account was shocking. (She spared her mother nothing when relating the daily dramas of her life.) But why had the Lovelaces risked their lives by careering through narrow combes and twisting lanes on a dark December night in that most precarious of vehicles, a rickety high-wheeled phaeton? Had they quarrelled? Had the driver been drunk? Whose hands had held the reins?

Although no explanation was forthcoming (the incident was never again mentioned), it is tempting to speculate that the thirty-year-old countess was guiding the horses herself when her thoughts drifted off, whirling her away into that hidden and feverish drama of a life that was beginning to spiral out of control.

By December 1846, Ada's beloved John Crosse was involved with another woman. Five months later, he married Susan Bowman. Their child (the first of three) was born, but not registered, in March 1848. Crosse himself, when in London, resided at Park Street, near Grosvenor Square. His secret wife was despatched to live at Reigate, a quiet little town in Surrey. Nobody, even in Reigate itself, had the faintest idea that John Crosse was Bowman's husband. The reasons for this curious act of subterfuge remain obscure.

Even in December 1846, when the carriage accident occurred, Ada must have suspected that something odd was going on from the fact that her lover had started to press her for financial assistance. Seemingly, Crosse told Ada only that he needed to buy and furnish a house in Reigate. How much more – if anything – he may have disclosed remains unclear: all incriminating correspondence on both sides was destroyed in the 1850s.

What Ada did know by December 1846, the month of the carriage accident, was that Crosse wanted money and that she had agreed to provide it. The question of precisely how a wife living on a miserly allowance of £300 a year was to lay her hands on ready cash without arousing the suspicions of her husband and a fiercely prudent mother was the problem that now began to dominate Ada Lovelace's turbulent existence.

CHAPTER TWENTY

VANITY FAIR

(1847–50)

Although William Thackeray wrote his finest novel during the
mid-1840s, he set his savagely witty lesson in the art of survival –
the survival of the toughest, not the best – thirty years earlier, in
the time of the Napoleonic Wars. Becky Sharp carved her road to
social success through an England in which a shocked young Percy
Shelley saw starving, homeless families crying by the roadside. In
1812, Ada's father spoke out for the rights of the machine-smashing
weavers of the Midlands; these were people whose existences, so the
well-travelled Byron claimed, were more wretched than those he had
observed in any part of Eastern Europe.

Ada Lovelace, who would always prefer reading facts to fictions,
may not have followed the serial parts in which Thackeray's novel
first appeared in 1847. But by 1847, she herself was a participant
in the devastating social divide that his book covertly portrayed.
The Hungry Forties were the years of revolution and famine, the
years when great fortunes were made and lost. In Ireland, potato
blight was starving a million people to death. A further million
emigrated, never to return. Out in Rome, that exceptionally resil-
ient Irish invalid Miss Mary Montgomery joined forces with Anna
Jameson's friend Ottilie von Goethe, to raise money for her destitute
compatriots by means of a grand subscription ball. (The Irish-born

Mrs Jameson, writing to tell Annabella that she herself would not attend the ball, expressed unease about such a blatant conjunction of wealth and poverty.)

In 1848, revolution swept through Europe. Its force petered out in England, where the great Chartist march ended with the people's leaders being shepherded across the Thames from Kennington, in three small, metered public carriages, on a rainy April afternoon. Universal suffrage and democratic reform would have to wait.

A generous contributor to the relief of famine in Ireland, Lady Byron viewed atrocious social conditions at home as a call to arms. As with her earlier purchase of land in Greece to honour Byron's crusade, she took inspiration from her late husband's youthful challenge to a heartless government.

Back in 1816, Byron had stood up for the weavers and their rights. In 1843, the beleaguered frame-workers rose again. When 25,000 signatories petitioned for the right to work, the government averted its eyes. Annabella took action. Throughout the Hungry Forties and on into the next decade, Lady Byron lavished money on new schools, churches and hospitals upon her huge Midlands estates. Charles Noel was once again instructed to care for the poor, rather than their patron. Greeting an embarrassed Lady Byron in 1851 by doffing their caps in gratitude for the 'many sums of money' that had come their way, the Leicestershire villagers and farm folk were rewarded with a brisk reminder of the 10 per cent bonus gift awaiting anyone prepared to entrust Lady Byron with their savings for future investment.

Annabella Byron, had she been born a century later, might have become the model director of a bank. Ruthlessly stingy to any employees whom she believed had wronged her, she was a meticulous keeper of records and fulfiller of legal commitments. Distributing funds wherever she felt they might best serve society, she never for a second lost sight of what was being done with her money.

A clear example of Annabella's combination of financial acumen with a stern social conscience surfaces in a remarkable letter written in January 1846 to Elizabeth Rathbone, a Quaker friend in

Liverpool. Lady Byron's topic was the misappropriation by a certain Mr Johns of the funds of a philanthropic trust that Annabella had set up. Those funds, as she had just discovered, were being used, without her permission, for Mr Johns's other and less noble projects. A reprimand had been followed by their swift recall for investment by Mrs Rathbone's more biddable son-in-law, John Paget, a barrister at the Middle Temple. 'I have written to Mr J. Paget,' Annabella informed Mrs Rathbone in her best regal style (tenants often commented upon Lady Byron's similarity to Queen Victoria), 'from whom I shall hope to obtain more details than it is Mr Johns' habit to give.'

The letter to Mrs Rathbone offers useful insights into the enlightened nature of Annabella's social views. Alluding to Cardinal Newman's recent denunciation of Mrs Rathbone's old friend Joseph Blanco White as insane (White had questioned both the authority of the Gospels and the divinity of Christ), Lady Byron grew indignant and then passionate. Was it not disgraceful that such a 'superior' thinker as Mr White should be treated as a lunatic, while criminals 'of the low & ferocious classes' – people who might more justifiably be considered mad than he – were sent to the gallows instead of to St Luke's Asylum, where 'humanising experiments' might reform their behaviour? Had Mrs Rathbone read the excellent new pamphlet against capital punishment? 'But this being a subject I have so much at heart, is apt to lead me on . . . A heated head bids me stop.' Calming herself, Annabella asked for news of the Rathbones' good friend Dr Beecher, a member of the American group of abolitionists and reformers among whom Lady Byron also moved.*

Given his mother-in-law's rare combination of altruism with

---

* This seems to be the earliest indication of a connection between Lady Byron and her future defender, Dr Beecher's daughter, Harriet. It was cemented by the friendship that she formed in 1849 with Dr Elizabeth Blackwell, the first woman to be listed on the UK medical register. The English-born Blackwell had become close to Lyman Beecher and his wife during the early 1840s, when she lived in Cincinnati. (In England, Annabella helpfully introduced her to the young Florence Nightingale, whose own vocation for nursing Lady Byron was discreetly supporting.)

financial acumen, it is unsurprising that William Lovelace chose, in the mid-1840s, to cede administration of the two Ockham schools to Lady Byron and the widowed Stephen Lushington's sisters-in-law, now snugly settled into the old King home. The Ockham schools had been going downhill. One of Annabella's first actions was to sack a matron who was taking older girls out for evening jollities at the local pub and entertaining young men in her rooms until 2am. Slowly, the schools began to recover their reputations.

As Annabella's philanthropic zeal waxed, William Lovelace's waned. Depressing proof of this fact emerged in 1848 when, two weeks after the doomed Chartist march, Lovelace told his 12-year-old heir that 'the poor' had thankfully become 'too poor to cause trouble'. Further evidence of how far Lovelace was removed from social reality surfaced in a request for Ada to send along his article on 'Nobility' to her new friend, Charles Dickens. Had Lovelace ever bothered to read Dickens's novels, he would have known how savagely the aristocracy were pilloried in that author's works.

At home, Lovelace continued to pour money that he could ill afford into the enlargement and enhancement of his country estates. While the handsome house in St James's Square was reluctantly exchanged in 1846 (at the close of a ten-year lease paid for by Annabella) for smaller lodgings in Belgravia, on Grosvenor Place, William continued to pursue a buying spree of his own. In 1847, he was eyeing up a former King home, the majestic Dunsborough Park, as a real bargain at £4,000. (Annabella's always-eloquent silence quelled that particular folly.) At Ashley Combe, the new boathouse, grotto and cliffside garden terraces now grandly ascended to a bal-ustraded 'Philosopher's Walk' that Lovelace and Ada had playfully named for Charles Babbage, one of their most frequent visitors. At Horsley Towers, only Ada's modest request to be provided with a cold 'plunge bath' (to improve her sluggish circulation) was rejected by her husband as an unnecessary extravagance.

Ada would always adore Ashley Combe. At Horsley Towers, sandwiched between the virtuous circle of female dependants who inhabited Stephen Lushington's new home at Ockham Park, and the army of clergymen, doctors and philanthropically minded ladies who surrounded Annabella at her nearby Esher home (the ten-year lease on Moore Place did not expire until 1851), Ada felt trapped as a caged bird. Whenever the door cracked open, she took flight.

Flitting between Somerset, London, Esher and Brighton, Ada was kept informed of the improvements by which her husband hoped to lure her back into captivity at Horsley. In August 1845, Lovelace described the turret chamber in which, perched above her own swan-studded lake, he wished his brilliant wife to renew her mathematical studies. He had, he tempted her, equipped one of the lancet windows with a telescope through which Ada might enjoy a splendid view of the queen's quarters at Windsor Castle.

Lovelace's blandishments were resisted. On 15 November 1848, Ada cautiously told her mother about the anticipated pleasure of inhabiting what sounded to be the '*most delightful*' new tower room at Horsley, so long as it was warm and dry. A year later, however, Lovelace was informed of his delicate wife's continued reluctance to shiver to death in a dank lakeside chamber.

Ada's absence could be overlooked by a man who now cared for almost nothing beyond his own grand designs. (The Lovelace children's letters from this time are filled with references to Papa's obsession with tunnels, earthworks and brickmaking.) Seated next to the Archdeacon of Westminster (Wordsworth's nephew) at a London dinner in May 1849 hosted by Lord Rosse, Lovelace paid scant attention to accounts of the scientifically minded Irish peer's remarkable new telescope, the largest ever yet designed. 'We talked architecture & monuments all through dinner,' William boasted to his mother-in-law; the next day, the earl toured the abbey's roof with the Dean, before setting out for a further round of architectural exchanges with like-minded friends at Trinity, his old Cambridge college. Back in Surrey, Lovelace swapped views about chromatic brickwork with Henry Drummond of Albury, a rich, witty and ardently religious banker for whom Augustus Pugin was embellishing an old manor house with no less than sixty-three differently decorated chimneys.

Architectural historians tend to sneer at Albury (just as they do at East Horsley). William worshipped it.

Few aspects of his own most idiosyncratic creation pleased William more than the tall tower in which he aspired to house (or imprison) his wife. By December 1849, a huge window had been opened above Horsley's new grand staircase. Its sole purpose was to shed a glare of daylight into the entrance to Ada's 'Mathematics Room'. A month later, after five years of remodelling – and with thought at last given to the degree of warmth required for such a slender and sickly inhabitant – Ada's study was complete. Four new paintings of Ashley Combe had been recessed into the panelled and mirrored walls, while a new-fangled speaking tube had been installed, through which Ada might issue commands for her daily needs. As a final touch, a portrait of Lord Lovelace himself, dashingly attired in the scarlet-and-gold dress uniform of his official position as Lord Lieutenant of Surrey, surveyed the room from above the entrance door. 'You will,' the artist's proud sitter promised a once-again absent Ada on 6 January 1850, 'be very gay.'

∽∾

Back in 1838, Annabella Byron had believed that she was doing the right thing when she persuaded Prime Minister Melbourne to upgrade an ill-treated William King to the rank of Earl of Lovelace. She rejoiced when her son-in-law became Lord Lieutenant of Surrey, while his younger brother had to content himself with the less significant role of high sheriff. What Lady Byron had not fully grasped was the damage that might be done by the persistent social rivalry between Locke King and his detested older brother, William Lovelace.

Throughout the 1840s, the mischief-making Lady Hester King continued to fuel hostility between her sons. Stories leaked out that William had unjustifiably held back items of furniture that legally belonged to Locke; that he was destroying the beautiful old woods around Ockham for timber sales; that he was selling off the family house. Every single time, the story was traced back to William's mother at Woburn Park.

Lady Hester's mind was clear upon one particular point: William Lovelace was never going to overshadow his sibling in Surrey, the county most closely associated with the King family's history. If William bought a village near Guildford, then his brother must have one near Weybridge. If William built a fine new house near Ockham, then Locke must have a bigger one near Woburn. (Designed by Sir Arthur Blomfield, the immense Brooklands Park was finally completed in 1862.) There was one crucial difference: money. Locke King, always his mother's pet, was lavishly subsidised both by the generous legacy left to his mother when Lord King died, and by the considerable personal wealth of Lady Hester's own West Country family, the Fortescues. William Lovelace, who usually raised money by selling off parcels of his land, was due to receive no more than Ada's fairly modest wedding dowry until the time of Lady Byron's death. Locke could afford to be extravagant. His elder brother had been tempted into living far, far beyond his means. As the 1840s drew to a close, William Lovelace was confronting the possibility of financial ruin.

Even before the demands made upon her by John Crosse, Ada herself was struggling to make ends meet on an allowance of merely £300 a year. It's hard to see how she managed. In London, she was still paying for John Thomas's musical tuition. At Ashley Combe and East Horsley, she was responsible for the upkeep and maintenance of several horses and six dogs, including a Dalmatian called Sirius, a spaniel called Luna and a large, beloved dog called Nelson. Harps; textbooks; day clothes and shoes; the wages of a maid whom she was once again employing; extra tuition in languages, music and art for the children: these were just a few of the costs for which Ada was responsible.

Had Ada not been involved with John Crosse, it's possible that she would have taken up a generous offer made by her mother in 1845 of a long, large and interest-free loan. Instead, fearful of discovery (Ada always had difficulty in hiding secrets from the sharp-eyed Lady Byron), she chose to struggle on.

In 1848, a year in which the intensity of Ada's relationship with the newly married Crosse was matched by his growing demands upon her purse, Lady Lovelace undertook a secret negotiation. Woronzow Greig was asked to approach Henry Currie, the former owner of Horsley Towers, and request a loan of £500. Although puzzled that the countess had not applied for help to her own family, the banker agreed. On 1 May – writing from the house on Cumberland Street into which the Lovelaces had moved after a year's sojourn at Grosvenor Place – Ada explained that she could not borrow from a husband already burdened by 'heavy expenses'. Promising that the debt would be paid off, with interest set at 5 per cent, within three years (it took four), her chief concern was that William should remain in the dark. He must not know about this loan.

Greig, like Henry Currie, was puzzled that Ada did not simply apply to her apparently wealthy and affectionate husband for aid. When Ada finally decided to do so in December 1848, William refused. He did, however, promise to cover the cost of his wife's new ballgowns. This pledge was less bizarre than it sounds. In December 1848, the elderly Duke of Wellington was being courted and entertained at Brighton, where Ada was visiting her mother. The duke had been an early supporter of the Babbage project for which the Lovelaces were still quietly seeking investment. A beguiling, persuasive and exquisitely dressed Ada might yet help to restore the Lovelace family fortunes.

Two elegant dresses, brought to Brighton by her daughter's new maid (Mary Wilson, who shared Ada's passion for dogs, had been caring for Babbage's mother until the old lady's recent death), aroused Lady Byron's suspicion that something was afoot. Struggling to avoid the steely blue stare which had once subdued her father, Ada floundered, evaded and finally stumbled into deceit. Greig was expected to visit Brighton within the month; on 5 January 1849,

Ada dashed him off a frantic note of warning. Her request for an increased allowance had been confessed to Lady Byron, as had William's refusal. All else that she had told him about her debts was secret – and must remain so. Greig kept his word. No trace of these mysterious confidences survives.

Henry Currie's loan of £500 did not go far towards meeting John Crosse's financial requirements and Ada's own debts. In March 1849, the countess made a second urgent application for financial help to her husband from Moore Place, where Ralph and Annabella were living under the care of Lady Byron. While William's response was cool, he promised to drive over to Moore Place from East Horsley, to discuss what could be done. The meeting was unsatisfactory; shortly afterwards, Ada borrowed an additional £300 from Wharton and Ford, the solicitors who had always looked after Milbanke and Noel affairs. Neither William nor her mother was informed of the loan.

It remains unclear to what degree Lady Byron was aware of the Lovelaces' financial problems. (Two years later, Annabella would bitterly reproach Ada for not having come to her with a direct appeal for help.) In 1849, however, Lady Byron sensed enough to propose lavishly underwriting the purchase for her daughter and son-in-law of a new London home in the crescent of Great Cumberland Place. Little Lady Annabella was thrilled by the fact that their new home had speaking tubes and a comfortable schoolroom (there were many complaints about the spartan one at Horsley Towers). William's delighted response (Such spacious rooms! Such elegance! Such health-giving air!) suggests that the Lovelaces' previous accommodations must have been of a very inferior quality. It's unlikely, however, that Lady Byron understood why the possession of a grand London address was considered to be of such significance.

∽᪻᪻᪻∽

A handsome home in the capital was immensely helpful to the commercial and diplomatic strategy upon which both Ada and Lovelace were already embarked. In 1843, Ada had put forward a business proposal to raise investment for Babbage's unbuilt machine. That project was one that – despite Babbage's initial refusal – the Lovelaces had never abandoned.

Simply stated, the earl and his wife wanted to loan Babbage their name and social influence in exchange for control of the finished machine and a satisfactory return from its future use. By 1846, an attentive Babbage was being promised an introduction to the banker-owner of Albury. (Ada repeatedly emphasised Henry Drummond's great wealth.) The following May, Babbage dined privately at Grosvenor Place, for the sole purpose of conducting a business talk with Lord Lovelace. A month later, Ada described a second and similar discussion as having been of 'real importance'. On 6 February 1849, as Ada prepared to array herself in her new silk ballgown for the purpose of charming the Iron Duke into supporting their scheme, Lovelace cautioned her that they owed it to Babbage 'not to promote his cause by inferior means'. Sadly, there is no sign that Ada's persuasive skills bore fruit.

Ada loved the ingenious and unexpected mind of Charles Babbage, the fatherly friend to whom she now often playfully signed her letters 'yours filially'. While the project for the unbuilt Analytical Engine's future proceeded with frustrating slowness, other and slightly less respectable plans for raising funds were being hatched. A pet one was discussed in 1847, when Babbage visited the Lovelaces at the same time that William Nightingale first brought his daughter Florence to stay.

Florence Nightingale's visit was a bit of a coup for Ada, who knew how much the younger woman idolised Lady Byron.* She had already heard about Florence's own mathematical skills from Lovelace, a regular guest of the Nicholson family at Waverley Abbey, the Surrey estate at which, in the summer of 1843, a convalescing Florence had secretly coached a young Nicholson cousin in maths.

* The Nightingales' connection to Ada's family dated back to the friendship between her own Milbanke grandparents and Florence's grandfather, William Smith, an abolitionist and early convert to Unitarianism. Florence's aunt, Julia Smith, was one of Lady Byron's chief confidantes.

(Ada herself was then hard at work at nearby Ockham on her Menabrea 'Notes'.) Florence provided the inspiration for a wistful poem that suggests the younger woman remained an enigma to Ada ('But still her spirit's history / From light and curious gaze concealing'), but it was Florence's father who interested Charles Babbage.

William Nightingale, like Babbage and Ada, was fascinated by mathematical games and puzzles. It is fair to guess that it was this member of the Nightingale clan to whom Ada frequently referred within the private correspondence that she now embarked upon with Charles Babbage.

Writing his memoirs after the deaths of both Ada and her mother, Babbage recalled a project he had developed during the 1840s for an automaton that might be able to play intellectual games of skill. (Tic-tac-toe, along with chess and draughts, were offered as examples.) If he could produce such an ingenious and entertaining machine, might it be sold to the public at large, thus raising money for the Analytical Engine to be built *without* all the burden entailed by outside investment? 'A friend, to whom I had early communicated the idea, entertained great hopes of its pecuniary success.' Just who could this hopeful friend of Babbage's have been, if not the entrepreneurial Ada Lovelace?

On 30 September 1848, Ada made her first known reference to ongoing discussions with Babbage about '*Games*, and notations for them'. The inventor had just been staying at Ashley Combe and Ada sweetly told him in this same letter that even the rain-filled skies 'are weeping unceasingly over yr. departure'. At the end of an especially affectionate letter, almost as an afterthought, she urged Babbage to get in touch with the Nightingales, who had apparently begged him to write to them. Three weeks later, Ada wrote again, this time with reference to a favourable article that had just appeared in the *Athenaeum* about Babbage's engines. ('Let the Government *answer* it, if they *can*!') This time, Lady Lovelace alluded not only to letters from 'the Birds', who threatened to be 'angry' and fail to 'sing' if he did not respond, but to the potentially lucrative system upon which Babbage and she were now at work.

> You say nothing of Tic-tac-toe – in yr last. I am alarmed
> lest it should never be *accomplished*. I want you to complete
> *something*; especially if the something is likely to produce *silver*
> *& golden* somethings ...

The hope of financial gain could hardly have been more clear.

It was towards the end of 1848, on 19 December, that Ada first mentioned sending Babbage 'a *book* which I think will interest you'. On 11 February 1849, she promised to send him 'the *book*' (always underlined) to keep during the three days that she would be spending with her mother. On 27 February, Ada wrote again, hoping that Babbage had understood something she had written out very clearly, for his particular interest. On 20 September, while urging him to come and spend an entire month on their beautiful Somersetshire estate, Ada reminded her friend of the need for 'the *new cover*' (underlined) for the book. If she came straight up to London from Surrey, would he like to travel to Somerset with her, by the new express train?

> There is a great deal I want to explain to you, which can't be by
> letter. I can't decipher satisfactorily some indications in the work
> in question.

Seven days later, Ada expressed relief that Babbage had turned up, however unexpectedly, while the Lovelaces were entertaining at their London home. He was just back from Paris, which she considered 'a most excellent step'. She had been 'particularly glad' to see him, whatever the circumstances; it was 'a very good thing as regarded the *book*'.

Many theories have been produced about that mysterious book, as well as about the role that was being played as a messenger by Mary Wilson, Babbage's former servant. But the fact that this very same book was shown at a later date to Sir David Brewster, an eminently respectable Scottish scientist who took a keen interest in the Analytical Engine, suggests that there was nothing especially sinister afoot. That said, it seems reasonable to assume that a plan for making money was being discussed, and that it involved the use of a mathematical system – to which both Ada and Babbage were contributing ideas – in a book that they shunted back and forth (with Mary Wilson as its carrier). Probably, Lovelace knew what was afoot. Lady Byron, known for her aversion to any form of gambling or speculation, was kept in the dark.

ᏯᎶ

Back in 1846, Lovelace's sister Hester Crauford had written to Lady Byron from her marital home near Pisa, to hope that Ada had recovered well enough 'to let her quicksilver loose again'. The Craufords' own worries about health had always been focused upon Sir George (it was for this reason that the couple had gone abroad), but the news that reached the Lovelaces in the spring of 1848 was of Hester. Already the mother of a little boy called Charles, Hester had died while giving birth to her second son. Characteristically, Lady Hester King wasted no time in informing the heartbroken widower that she herself had never recovered from the shock of her daughter's heartless defection. Replying with as civil a letter as he could muster, Sir George explained how greatly he had adored his wife. 'A heart like Hester's, I never did find, and never shall find again upon earth,' he wrote on 12 April, while asking his mother-in-law to believe that Hester had never hated her, as the bitter old woman now claimed. 'It was from the *house* that she was estranged,' Crauford vainly pleaded. He received no response.

Ada was desolate. She had loved Hester Crauford like a sister. Anguish of a similar nature was felt by Annabella in February 1849, when news reached Lady Byron of the death of gentle, affectionate Sophy Tamworth, the orphaned older cousin with whom she had grown up at Seaham. That first and always fondly remembered home had been haunting Lady Byron's thoughts. In 1847, while suffering a long spell of ill health, Annabella wrote a tender account of her own northern upbringing, in which she attributed the birth of her powerful impulses towards philanthropy to parents who deserved more recognition, as she now believed, for their many acts of kindness to the local poor. The death of William Melbourne in November 1848 was dutifully recorded by his cousin; the loss of Cousin Sophy went far deeper. Evidently, there had been a falling-out at some point in the past between Annabella and members of Sophy's family. It comforted Lady Byron to learn from Sophy's brother, Lord Scarsdale, that no rancour now remained: there was 'nothing to forgive'.

છગ

The older generation were falling away. The closest bond holding together that intense little triangle of the Hen, the Bird and the Crow throughout the 1840s was that of a second threesome: the children.

Mr Herford, the tutor selected by Annabella after William Carpenter's belated exit, arrived at Ashley Combe in November 1846, bringing with him a reticent and distinctly undernourished 7-year-old Ralph. Lady Byron's attitude to meals was notoriously vague (on one occasion, she entirely forgot to provide lunch for her guests); nevertheless, both Ada and Lovelace respected Annabella's grandmotherly skills and her evident enjoyment of the role.

On 28 January 1847, Lady Byron notified the childless Robert Noel that she would shortly be taking over the supervision of both Ralph and his 9-year-old sister, her namesake. She herself would be dividing her time between a new house at Southampton and her customary home at Esher. The children, living at Moore Place, would have the company of little Hugh Montgomery and the Bence-Joneses. (Lady Gosford's eldest daughter, Millicent, was occupying the second of Annabella's two Esher houses, together with her Irish husband and three small children. It suited Annabella's needs to have a doctor on call; Henry Bence-Jones was an experienced physician.)

All began well. The Irish-born Miss Lamont, Ada's own first attendant, was recruited to take care of young Annabella and to instil what Ada (remembering the Pearces' account of her daughter's insolence) described as the manners '*peculiarly* appropriate to this young lady'. Visiting her beloved friend in the early summer of 1847, Anna Jameson congratulated Lady Byron upon a marked improvement in her granddaughter's behaviour: 'excellent stuff in that child'.

Ada did not question her mother's decision to take Ralph off on his own to the seaside for a while (Ralph was the most sickly of the three children). Neither did she protest when – possibly for the same reason – Ralph and his tutor were despatched to Hofwyl in 1848. Republican Switzerland remained a safe haven amid the revolutionary storms. Although Ralph pined for the company of his sister during a lonely sojourn in the second Mr Fellenberg's house, away from the other boys, it was nevertheless this first short foreign adventure that engendered his lifelong passion for mountaineering and grandly isolated landscapes.

Annabella King began her lifelong habit of diary-keeping in 1847. It seems to have been a comfort during the long periods of Ralph's absence. Comically prosaic at times ('the morning went, the afternoon came'), the diary also reveals how close the relationship was between the two namesakes, old and young. Lady Byron was at her best in this relationship, fondly recording the child's first jokes and puns and making sure – thanks to the Bence-Jones family next door – that she was not too lonely. Besides long foraging expeditions for mushrooms and blackberries in the nearby Ockham woods, there were picnics at Claremont (accompanied by a flock of tin cows and goats), rides (the little girl was given her own small mount, a pony called Seagull) and many presents. One that especially excited a child whose future would be spent as an intrepid traveller in the Middle East was a book called *Travels in Persia*. The two Annabellas read it together at Lady Byron's Southampton house.* Nevertheless, Annabella missed her mother and beautiful Ashley Combe. It was

---

* Young Annabella was becoming a voracious reader. When aged thirteen, she read both Mrs Gaskell's *Mary Barton* and Dickens's *Christmas Stories*. While partial to travel books, she also read that year a French course in maths, Brewster's *Martyrs of Science*, a study of ozone, Lalande's *Logorhythms* and Vasari's *Lives of the Painters* (*Wentworth Papers*, British Library, BL 53817 and 54091).

beyond her understanding that Mamma could not look after her because she had no governess to provide.

One of Ada's motives for borrowing money from Henry Currie had been that she wanted to assume personal responsibility for her daughter's education. By 1848, she was in a position to do so. The governess she had found, Miss Wächter, was recommended to her by Robert and Louisa Noel at a time when many clever young German women were forced into exile by political events on the Continent.

First, however, Annabella had to be extricated from Moore Place, where she was happily assisting Miss Lamont to 'make things' intended to raise money for the suffering Irish. Ada's excuse was that Miss Lamont had been behaving in an unseemly fashion.

Like her father, Ada, who could be so progressive and even revolutionary in her ideas, could also be breathtakingly conventional. Back in 1835, she had been outraged by the portrait-painter Margaret Carpenter's habit of stretching herself out, in full view of their guests, upon the drawing-room carpet at Ockham. Poor Miss Lamont's crime was merely to have introduced her young pupil to friends of her own, met by chance while strolling through Esher.

Ada was outraged. It was not to be tolerated, she stormed to her astonished mother; Charlotte Stamp, that paragon among governesses, would have been horrified! Such behaviour was absolutely unacceptable in 'families of my circle'. Five days later, a command was delivered for the sacking of Miss Lamont and the immediate restoration of Lady Annabella to her parents.

Ada's bizarre outburst came in April 1848, when she had just received the news of Hester's death, while agreeing to the painful decision that her oldest and favourite child – Byron Ockham was not yet twelve – should go to sea the following year. But Ada was also seizing a pretext to reclaim her only daughter, a child who displayed increasing signs of possessing a sensitive spirit and a rare gift for art. (Her tutor at Moore Place was a colleague of Ruskin's, Thomas Boys.)

The appointment of Miss Wächter as Annabella's new home governess proved an unqualified success. Lovelace liked the young

woman, Annabella adored her, and Lady Byron offered no opposition. In October 1848, Ada rather tactlessly informed her mother
that Annabella had improved under the new governess's care. 'She
is not like the *same* girl,' the proud mother announced from Ashley
Combe on 10 October; five days later, while extolling her daughter's
exceptional love for natural history and animals, she declared the
delightful Miss Wächter to be all that a mother could desire. As a
result, Annabella had grown 'remarkably *well*, & wonderfully *happy*'.

Ada's growing affection was reciprocated. In an undated
December letter from the following year, a wistful young Annabella
wrote a poignant letter from Horsley, to tell her ailing mother how
much they all – herself, Papa, Miss Wächter and the dogs – were
missing her and longing for her return.

ॐ

Ada's older children, Byron and Annabella, had been deliberately – and somewhat peculiarly – named by their grandmother,
as a homage, as if to mirror a marriage of which her memory was
retrospectively creating an increasingly distorted view. By 1849, all
the blame for that marriage's failure had been placed – within Lady
Byron's own mind – upon the unconscious shoulders of Augusta
Leigh: the same woman whom Annabella had once held as dear to
her as a sister. Augusta's name had scarcely been mentioned since
Medora's wine-and-fantasy-based disclosures of 1841. Eight years
on, Medora was dead – at the pathetically youthful age of thirty-
five – and the very thought of Mrs Leigh prompted anxious questions
in Lady Byron's mind. What would future generations think of her
for having left her famous husband? How would she be judged by
her own descendants?

It was during 1849, after one of many lengthy sojourns with
Stephen Lushington's family at Ockham, that Annabella decided
to consign a large number of her private papers to his sister-in-law.
Frances (always known as 'Fanny') Carr was impressed with the
importance of protecting these precious documents – their owner

stipulated a minimum of thirty years – from the eyes of curious outsiders. Doubtless, Miss Carr was also provided with a slanted version
of the past; by 1849, Annabella's fondness for confiding secrets had
become dangerously allied to her eagerness to remember what she
wished had happened, as opposed to what had actually occurred.

It was also at the beginning of 1849 that Lady Byron acquired a
new and pleasingly responsive friend, one who seemed ideally suited
to become her future champion. Frederick Robertson, a personable
and intelligent young man, had long been – unknown to Annabella
herself – her ardent admirer. While staying at Cheltenham three
years earlier, he had defended Lady Byron's name from idle gossip
with the enigmatic phrase: 'I have reasons.' In the autumn of 1848,
while taking a holiday health break in Bohemia, Robertson met
Robert Noel who, discovering that the handsome clergyman was
working at Brighton, promptly supplied an introduction to his own
revered relation.

Ada, who was visiting with her mother in Brighton early in
1849, while preparing to charm the elderly and stone-deaf Duke of
Wellington, disliked Frederick Robertson from her first glimpse of
his curly brown hair and sapphire-blue eyes. But Lady Byron was
bewitched, charmed by the obliging Robertson's willingness to see
her as she now viewed herself: the woman who (had she only been
allowed) could have redeemed her adored husband from the hell into
which a wanton elder sister had led him. By 1849, William Lovelace
was proving to be a less biddable adoptive son than in the past. Here
was the ideal substitute: an intelligent, thoughtful and principled
young man who never questioned Lady Byron's veracity and never
doubted the accuracy of her recollections. Robertson should be her
recorder; from him, her grandchildren would learn Lady Byron's
own indisputable account of the past.

Frederick Robertson arrived in Lady Byron's life at the moment
when her oldest grandchild's fate had been temporarily settled by

booking little Lord Ockham on to a ship bound for Van Diemen's Land (Tasmania). It was, so Lovelace and Ada had unhappily agreed in February 1848, the best that could be done for their recalcitrant eldest son. But this was to be no ordinary voyage. Byron Ockham left Plymouth aboard the *Swift* in June 1849. He was just thirteen years old. It would be over three years before – as a young man of sixteen – he would return to England.

Of Lord Byron's three grandchildren, his namesake was the one he would most readily have identified as a chip off the old block. Ockham was only five when Annabella scolded his parents for allowing the Lovelace heir to grow up as a backstairs boy, 'the servants' plaything'. Nothing changed. Spending most of his early life down at remote Ashley Combe, Ockham grew fond of the roughly spoken Porlock labourers and builders who taught him jokes and practical skills. Aged ten, he was teaching his siblings how to swear. Aged twelve, while being educated in Brighton by the eminently worthy Dr William King and teaching tricks to a pet puppy, Frisk, Ockham was writing letters to Ralph – aged nine at the time – which (so Lovelace, having intercepted one such private missive, opined) were infected by a 'free and easy tone' that leaned towards 'downright impertinence'.*

A new line was taken in 1848. Sending Ockham and his new personal tutor to reside with Charles Noel's family at Peckleton House in Leicestershire was part of a plan to prepare a small and stubborn viscount for his future duties as a great landowner and peer of the realm. Charles Noel would instruct him about land management; Mr Pennington was paid £110 per annum to present Latin, Greek, German and the sciences to the boy in short and easily digestible lessons. A descent into a local mine for educational purposes was permitted (the boy was much struck by the hardship inflicted upon horses living underground). All forms of drawing – young Byron had developed a naughty gift for caricature – were banned.

Engagingly affectionate and physically attractive (Ockham

---

* Reading Ockham's immature but jolly letters to his brother, it's hard to see what the fuss was about.

had dark curly hair, an olive skin, brilliant eyes and the muscular hands of a young blacksmith), the Lovelaces' eldest child never had difficulty in winning friends. Rebellious and hard to teach though Ockham was ('he is so slow that I do not suppose you could get more out of him,' Charles Noel told Ada on 11 April 1849), Charles nevertheless doted upon his young lodger.

Here at Peckleton, although the Noels had two small daughters of their own, there was never any sense of sexual unease. Reunited with his family at Ashley Combe in the autumn of 1848, troubling ghosts of the past arose to haunt the present. A curious set of letters that passed between Ada and her mother reveal that both of them were haunted by the same fear: what if Ockham had inherited his grandfather's troubling attraction to a female sibling? Byron was '*never alone*' with Annabella, Ada reassured her mother, while stressing in the same letter of 6 November that there were indeed 'many reasons to keep them apart'.

Unlike her husband, Ada became anxious even about allowing their oldest son to visit Ashley when little Annabella was also there. Lady Byron, while approving of her daughter's concern, went further still, suggesting that Ralph should also be separated from his sister. Reluctantly, Ada agreed. She would see to it that Ralph was '*never alone* with Miss W[ächter] and Annabella at Horsley,' she wrote back, 'supposing that is your wish'.

Miss Wächter, who personally found Byron Ockham to be an irresistible little charmer, was baffled by this strange insistence upon separation between the siblings. The first effect of her elder brother's charismatic personality upon Lady Annabella's manners and ideas might prove disquieting, the governess conceded; nevertheless, 'the real and more lasting effects' of sisterly friendship with such a beguiling youth were surely 'very valuable'.

Ada was torn. Evidently, she shared her mother's uneasiness. And yet, she adored her firstborn son. (A letter written in July 1848 fondly described young Byron, just home from Brighton, as 'brown as a nut, & looking more *manly* in face, and strikingly handsome'.) He, of Ada's three children, had always been the most eager to canter out with his mother across Exmoor, to show an interest in her beloved pack of dogs (Sirius the swift Dalmation was his favourite, while his sister preferred Nelson, the big family dog) and to tease her, proposing that Papa's grand tower room at Horsley would be 'a capital place to have tea'. Ockham was always the first to sense his mother's mood, the one who knew just how to make her laugh.

A solution to the concern about the children's intimate relationships was already in place. Plans for Byron to go to sea had been made and advice was now taken from the Lushingtons and Greigs, both families being possessed of excellent naval connections. Ada dreaded his going. In the autumn of 1848, she began pleading with her mother to send Ralph home for a while, because of the long separation between the brothers – she sadly wrote that it might be one of 'very many years' – which lay ahead. Lady Byron remained nervous and obstinate. Ralph was only permitted to rejoin his own family in October 1849, when young Lord Ockham was safely away on the other side of the world. And still, Lady Byron dreaded repetitions of the past. Ralph must be tutored separately from his sister, she wrote. The children should at all times be *watched*.

Ada agreed.

කිවෙ

The decision to book Ockham as a midshipman on to the *Swift* for this particular voyage across the world was equally strange, and strangely fortuitous. Both at Harrow and later, at university, William Lovelace and William Greig had studied alongside an exceptional man. Today, his statue occupies a position of honour on O'Connell Street in Dublin; back in July 1848, William Smith O'Brien was a charismatic leader of the Young Ireland movement, a man who had been arrested when he called for armed rebellion in the cause of Irish independence. O'Brien was the first Irish rebel who had been born into the landed gentry; with Queen Victoria embarrassingly due to pay a visit to Ireland within a few months of his conviction, the Irish rebel's sentence was hastily commuted from hanging to being transported to Van Diemen's Land, along with his three principal collaborators.

The *Swift*, then, was a convict ship with a difference. Here, in place of dark holds filled with sick children, pregnant women and desperate men, were four well-educated and elegantly dressed prisoners who strove to hold tedium at bay during a three-month voyage by playing backgammon and chess. And by chat.

Chat must surely have encompassed talking to a young man who bore the intriguing name of Byron Ockham and who turned out to be the son of O'Brien's Trinity colleague, now married to Lord Byron's daughter. The *Swift*'s crew consisted of only sixty-six men, and a midshipman's duties would certainly have taken him to the deck where the four Irish prisoners passed much of their time. To Byron (who would later preach the virtues of the French Revolution to his younger brother), Smith O'Brien must have seemed a true hero, a man who had placed his convictions first and who – Byron Ockham was there to see him set ashore at Van Diemen's Land on 27 October – honourably refused to accept the 'ticket-of-leave' which would have allowed the gallant prisoner parole and considerable freedom.

Byron's experiences on board the *Swift* confirmed a road upon which – even at the tender age of thirteen – he was already firmly set. For the rest of his short, strange life, Lord Ockham would always take the side of the underclass against the privileged group into which he had been born. Arriving at Valparaíso on the *Daphne* in the summer of 1850, the 14-year-old Byron promptly led an unofficial project to divert water from the verdant hilltop garden of Admiralty House into that of a far less privileged – and doubtless very grateful – Chilean neighbour. Invited because of his rank to attend an elegant ball, the mutinous viscount accepted – and sent a midshipman chum along to masquerade as Lord Ockham in his place. It was a pity, Ockham's kindly new Captain mused, that such 'a very clever but wild young fellow' had been given 'no chance of starting well in life'. Captain Fanshawe was not ready to write the boy off. He only doubted that Ockham would ever fit the aristocrat's role for which he had been bred.

Back in England, Ada pined in vain for letters from her habitually uncommunicative son. In September 1849, she had been informed that the *Swift* was on course and that her boy was in good spirits. Then, nothing. Fears grew. In December, Lady Byron lowered Ada's spirits by mentioning a dreadful incident in which a young boy had been kidnapped by a Portugese slaveship and drowned. Not until February 1850 did a navy-stamped package arrive to relieve the anxious mother. Lovelace, for his part, was delighted by the improvement he perceived in Ockham's attitude towards his parents. By May that year, the complacent earl was calling at Moore Place to boast to its new inhabitant, the exiled Duchesse d'Orléans, a lady with whom he was eager to curry a friendship, that there was nothing to beat the British Navy for teaching a boy discipline.*

On 7 June 1850, the proud father received a brisk comeuppance. Ockham's long-awaited first letter from Chile had arrived. It was addressed, not to his father – but to his 10-year-old brother, Ralph. Sharing his displeasure with a sympathetic Hen, Lovelace complained that his seafaring heir's epistle (as ever, the inquisitive father had been unable to resist opening it) was filled with low and vulgar jokes. Was it for this that they had expended so much careful planning?

Lovelace grumbled; Ada, longing for the safe return of her favourite child, continued to believe that Ockham would astonish them all. Writing to Charles Babbage, back in November 1848, Ada had claimed that her oldest boy would prove to be the tortoise who beat the hares, only 'by & bye'.

Byron Ockham would do so still. Ada was sure of it.

---

* Following the arrival of the deposed French king Louis Philippe and his family at Claremont House in 1849, William Lovelace had persuaded his reluctant mother-in-law (Annabella had rejoiced at the royal family's fall) to loan the second of her two houses at Esher to Victoria's elderly cousin, the duchesse. Possibly, the earl expected this to lead to some sort of royal favour. It didn't.

CHAPTER TWENTY-ONE

THE HAND OF THE PAST
(1850–1)

In 1850, Ada found herself enjoying an unusually protracted spell of robust good health. Making the most of this unfamiliar sense of well-being during an autumn visit to the Lake District, the 34-year-old Lady Lovelace managed both to climb up to the 900-metre-high plateau that crowns Helvellyn and to attempt the marginally lower ridge of Skiddaw, where only bad weather forced her to halt. 'The mountain air & mountain life does wonders,' Ada exulted to her mother, before adding her intention of returning for further and bolder ascents.

The trip to Cumbria formed the climax to a tour that (ironically, as it turned out) was planned as a diversion from the Lovelaces' ongoing worries about money. No investors had shown an interest in supporting the building of Charles Babbage's pioneering but expensive machine. The plans for marketing a games-playing automaton that were discussed in Ada and Babbage's shared 'book' had come to nothing. Providing Annabella with a home education was a continuing expense for which Ada had undertaken personal responsibility. A more problematic expenditure, since she could discuss it with nobody (Ada herself knew only a carefully edited version of the truth), was John Crosse's ongoing need to provide for his secret family.

Early in December 1849, Lady Byron had made her son-in-law

a welcome loan of £4,500 to assist with the purchase of 6 Great Cumberland Place. A further £1,500 was offered later that month. The loan was generous, but it was insufficient for the requirements and aspirations of a very ambitious earl. (Having been thwarted in his desire to become secretary of state, Lovelace now had his eye fixed on obtaining a post at the Admiralty.) At the beginning of 1850, however, the Lovelaces secured a secret benefactor.

In 1846, Anna Jameson and her niece Gerardine [*sic*] had formed part of the elopement party that accompanied the newly-wed and fled Elizabeth Barrett and Robert Browning from Paris to Pisa. Living abroad, Mrs Jameson relied upon Lady Byron to invest the substantial income she was accruing back in England, the fruits of her successful career both as art historian and travel writer. Annabella's financial acumen was becoming legendary. Anna Jameson's investments grew. Her letters of gratitude were heartfelt.

Seeking financial aid at a time when she did not dare ask her mother to produce more than a meagre £50 travel fund for her autumn tour, Ada bethought herself of the indebted and always friendly Mrs Jameson. On 9 February 1850, Anna was summoned for a visit to Horsley Towers. Ada's note was imperious. She herself was just off to see little Ralph at Southampton, where Lady Byron was supervising her younger grandson's schooling at Drew's Academy. Mrs Jameson was instructed to send her response to William, who 'is anxious to know as soon as possible. He hopes you will not say us Nay ...'

Sitting in Horsley Towers' newly furnished Great Hall beneath Phillips's celebrated portrait of Lord Byron in Albanian dress (the poet stood between Mrs Carpenter's painting of Ada as a bride and Hoppner's painting of his wife as a child), Mrs Jameson might have wondered why the owners of such a splendid home and such fine possessions were short of money. Nevertheless, perhaps at this initial point – and certainly later on – Anna agreed to help out with a loan, while promising to say nothing to her appointed soulmate, Lady Byron. That recklessly given assurance of secrecy was to have devastating consequences for a treasured friendship.

Money continued to leak away. In May 1850, Ada evinced her first flicker of real interest in a sport that offered the possibility of raising a fortune by the use of her mathematical skills. Lady Byron, meanwhile, had just paid a visit to Horsley with the objective of meeting one particular fellow guest. Lord Clare, now stoutly middle-aged, had been Lord Byron's first great love. Sadly, no record survives of what thoughts were shared, perhaps because of an anxious grandmother's greater concern about young Annabella, who had just had her first period. It was at precisely this stage and at the same age (thirteen) that Ada had been struck down by the paralysis that crippled her for almost three years. Writing to reassure a worried Lady Byron on 30 May, Ada promised that every care would be taken of her granddaughter's health. Only the quietest forms of exertion would be permitted; nothing reckless. These comforting words were an afterthought, tacked on to the end of a letter that was largely devoted to Ada's latest interest.

Voltigeur was a three-year-old Yorkshire-bred colt belonging to Thomas Dundas, 2nd Earl of Zetland. The Zetlands had been friends of the Milbanke family since Annabella's childhood at Seaham. Paying a March visit to Aske Hall, the Zetlands' Yorkshire home, Lovelace heard little beyond his host's high expectations for their exceptional horse.

Lord Zetland's hopes had been confirmed on 29 May, when his colt won the Derby, the world's greatest flat horse race, historically held on the downs at Epsom. Merrily, Ada's letter of the following day warned her mother to look out for reports of Lord Lovelace's imminent destitution, due to the reckless gambling of his wife. To write in this way to a mother who loathed all forms of speculation – Lady Byron had even distributed anti-gaming posters in the casino-rich town of Wiesbaden, back in 1838 – was typical provocation by a saucy daughter who loved to tease her mother. Lady Byron was not amused to hear that her giddy darling was 'in danger of becoming a sporting character'. Her silence had its usual effect. The subject was dropped.

The year 1850 was one of vigorous social activity for the

Lovelaces. In March, the earl had visited both Aske and Floors Castle, the Duke of Roxburghe's enormous Scottish residence. Early in May, plans were hatched to welcome an eminent American historian to their own new London home. (Ada was a keen admirer of William Prescott's 1843 masterpiece, *The History of the Conquest of Mexico*.) Robert Noel, paying a rare visit to England from Dresden, was invited to join a gathering of scientific luminaries at Great Cumberland Place at the end of that month. At the opera, William and Ada weighed the merits of 'the Swedish nightingale' Jenny Lind against her rival, Henriette Sontag, and found in favour of the sweet-toned German soprano. Dutifully attending two royal balls, Lady Lovelace was still angling for the post of unofficial scientific advisor to the queen's husband. Instead, to her annoyance, she learned from Woronzow Greig that her name had once again become the subject of scandalous gossip. A certain gentleman had been identified – but Greig refused to divulge his name.

The haughty tone of Ada's response contrasted oddly with the fervency of her denials. Such stories were pitifully out of date, she wrote. Did Greig (Ada wrote to him, as she did to Babbage and Wheatstone, man to man, using his surname alone) not know that the mere fact that she was Byron's daughter meant that she was saddled with a new lover every three years – and would be until she was too old for such silly tales to carry conviction? No need for Greig to mention the gossip to her mother, who was well used to hearing such foolish gossip. Lovelace, however, must be informed. The name of this mystery lover had better be supplied to her at once.

Ada's tone was both defensive and aggressive. Was she afraid that John Crosse had been identified by a sharp-eyed friend? It's hard to tell. Sophia De Morgan was mentioned as a prime culprit in the spreading of injurious tales. But Ada expressed no guilt. She acknowledged nothing. As before, Greig was reminded of a line beyond which it was unwise for him to step. Lady Lovelace might choose to confide in him; she would never accept interrogation or criticism.

It was, nevertheless, important for Ada not to offend the Greigs in the summer of 1850. Woronzow had played a large part in arranging for Byron Ockham's transfer to the *Daphne*, captained by his own friend Edward Fanshawe, and now safely anchored at Valparaíso. Meanwhile, Agnes, Greig's gentle Scottish wife, had just volunteered to chaperone young Annabella around Europe, an expedition of the same kind that Ada herself had enjoyed as a young girl. The project suited Mrs Greig, who had been seriously ill during the previous year. It also freed the Lovelaces to pursue their plan for a round of northern visits.

Money worries were still preying on Ada's mind as she prepared for the autumn tour. Writing to her daughter out in Germany on 25 August, she confessed to her horse-loving child that economy had compelled the sale of several of their favourites from the stud. As a further saving, only the Wilson siblings, Stephen and Mary (the Babbage family's former servants), would accompany the Lovelaces down to Ashley at the end of the year: 'rents are half paid, we are in some difficulty . . .'

One of the greatest treasures to which Ada possessed unfettered access was the Lovelace diamonds. This magnificent set of jewels, given to his wife at her marriage, formed a regular feature of William's letters to Lady Byron as he questioned – always a little anxiously – how they were being cared for. The idea of raising money on the jewels first lodged itself in Ada's mind in July 1850, when she asked Charles Babbage to arrange for a private inspection of 'the *diamonds*' at the 'Exhibition d'Industrie', adding that this 'would help me'. Since Ada cared nothing for diamonds, it's hard to see why she would have thought such an experience useful, if not to assess the sale value of Lord Lovelace's most prized heirloom.*

---

* Tempting though it is to correct the date here to the opening of the Great Exhibition (1851), Ada needed no special permission to view the gems when all was open to the public. More likely, she was hoping for an advance private inspection of the celebrated Koh-i-Noor diamond, which the 13-year-old Duleep Singh brought over from India in July 1850 as part of the Treaty of Lahore negotiated by Lord Dalhousie after the conquest of the Punjab. Babbage was preparing a guide for the 1851 Exhibition, which probably gave him special access rights.

Ada's worries were not alleviated by the insistence of Lady Byron that her daughter should be constantly available to provide companionship to herself as and when a widowed mother might require it. On the brink of the Lovelaces' northern tour, Annabella stepped up the pressure. Their departure date was set for the last week in August; on 19 August, two piteous requests for a last little glimpse of Lady Byron's only child reached Great Cumberland Place. Accusations followed. How could Ada have neglected to visit Moore Place the previous week, when she was staying at Horsley Towers, a mere half-hour's drive away?

Annabella knew how to tweak her daughter's conscience. Truly, they had believed the Hen still to be at Brighton, responded Ada within an hour. Of course, she would try to rectify such an oversight. Indeed, she would take the London train down to Esher that afternoon and then return to the city on that same night. But the Hen must promise not to become '*frightened* or *astonished* or otherwise affected' if she failed in the attempt. The Bird was going to do her best.

Ada was always vulnerable to Lady Byron's reproaches, but she had become wearily familiar with her mother's methods. Further complaints from Moore Place were forestalled by posting a precise itinerary. Referring to their money difficulties with artful indirectness, Ada experimented with using a bit of emotional blackmail. A lack of funds, she hinted, might well oblige the Lovelaces to linger on at Ashley Combe after the trip 'by way of *economy*'. Ashley was the one place from which Lady Byron could not reasonably demand daily companionship. It was too remote, and Ada knew it. The implication was clear; if Annabella wanted her daughter to nurse and humour her, very well. But she must pay for the privilege.

The response was predictable. Perhaps from meanness, but more probably from habitual obstinacy, Lady Byron refused to be drawn. If extravagance forced her profligate children into seclusion, so be it. They and she must endure the consequences.

The autumn tour began with a long-promised visit to Knebworth, a Hertfordshire mansion which Edward Bulwer-Lytton had richly Gothicised in the style most admired by William Lovelace.* From there, the travellers proceeded to William and Fanny Nightingale's Derbyshire home, Lea Hurst, and on to Thrumpton Hall, a recently 'improved' Jacobean mansion in Nottinghamshire inhabited by Captain George Byron and his young wife, Lucy Wescomb, who owned the house.

George had been Ada's childhood friend, but no record survives of whether the cousins discussed Newstead Abbey, the nearby house at which the Lovelaces planned to pass a few days. George Byron's father had spent many happy months roaming through the Newstead woods in search of rabbits and pheasants to shoot, while his more brilliant cousin was off being lionised in London. Probably, Ada admired the young garden oak being grown at Thrumpton, an offshoot from one that Byron, as a boy, had planted at Newstead. The sturdy sapling was a gift from Newstead's new owners, the Wildmans, of whom both George and Lucy Byron spoke with great affection. (Wildman had apparently just turned down an offer from Barnum to purchase the celebrated scrap of bark on which Byron and Augusta had carved their initials.) Ada's own feelings about Newstead remained ambivalent. She was half-dreading the visit.

On 7 September, the Lovelaces arrived at the house which was now Thomas Wildman's home. Ada's mother, who had paid just one covert, inquisitive visit to Newstead shortly after her separation from Byron in 1816, had seen the old house at its lowest ebb, grown almost as derelict as the gaping, glassless window (a relic of the ancient abbey) that soared above it. Since then, under Colonel

---

* The Knebworth archive contains three letters from Edward Bulwer-Lytton to his young daughter Emily written in June 1847, when EBL hoped the Lovelaces might soon visit his home. Emily, living alone at Knebworth in unhappy circumstances, feared Ada's 'disastrous influences', but her father thought the young countess might prove 'a good friend' to his nervous and intelligent daughter. Three days earlier, he had described Ada to Emily as 'a very remarkable person, extremely original – but too prononcée for my taste, womanly in mienne [sic] but masculine in mind' (Letters of 16 and 19 June 1847, Knebworth Archive, Box 88).

Wildman's energetic ownership, a transformation had taken place. A fortune had been lavished upon the rescue mission which, at the time of Ada's visit, was virtually complete. Showing off his achievement with forgivable pride, the kind-hearted colonel – he had spent days swotting up on scientific subjects in advance – was baffled by Ada's reticence. Surely, it must give dear Lady Lovelace pleasure to see how faithfully he had followed the old designs? Why did she look so sad? He could not understand it. It was not until the third day of Ada's visit that Colonel Wildman dared directly to ask her for the reason. Talking to her sympathetic host about her growing regrets that the abbey was no longer a Byron house, Ada seemed transformed, a different woman.*

Her correspondence reflected the change that had taken place. Arriving at Newstead, Ada had confided to her mother on 8 September a feeling of overpowering sadness. ('All is like death around one; & I seem to be in the Mausoleum of my race.') William, meanwhile, sent the Hen dismissive accounts of a dreary village filled with poachers and stocking-makers. Newstead itself was nothing compared to Horsley Towers. Wildman's interiors were overdone. As for the miserable little church at nearby Hucknall Torkard, where Byron was buried: 'The tablet I need not describe.'

It's evident that William Lovelace had not yet registered the shift in his wife's feelings. (Before she left Newstead, Ada told Wildman that she wished to be buried there, and to lie at her father's side.) On 15 September, while snugly lodged at Radbourne Hall, the elegant Derbyshire family home of Captain Byron's mother, Ada informed her own mother about her change of heart. If visiting Newstead had begun as a descent into the grave, a resurrection had taken place. 'I do love the venerable old place & all my wicked forefathers,' Ada

---

* Visiting the abbey in 1857 as part of a tourist jaunt, Nathaniel and Sophia Hawthorne heard the tale of Ada's visit and her change in manner from their voluble landlady at a nearby inn. Sophia, a great admirer of Lord Byron (Nathaniel was said to resemble the poet), recorded the story in her journal. Washington Irving popularised the anecdote in *Bracebridge Hall*, a book which included his own visit to the iconic Newstead.

declared. An ancient prophecy was mentioned, predicting that the Byrons would leave the house at the very time that her father sold it, and 'that it is to *come back* [two heavy underlinings] in the present generation'.

Ada gave no thought to what the impact of such a bold declaration on her mother was likely to be. For herself, thoughts of Newstead – and indeed, her mother – were swept aside a couple of weeks later when her hosts at Aske Hall, the Zetlands, invited Lady Lovelace to accompany them to Doncaster, to see how their Derby-winning colt would fare in two of the last big events of the flat-racing season. William, off to investigate new agricultural methods in Lincolnshire, agreed to rejoin the party on the third day.

Doncaster Races took place, as they still do, on a pear-shaped track. Unlike today, there were then no stands and no barriers. No rules of etiquette kept separate classes of racegoers apart. The sense of communion on a mud-spattered field was close to that of an old-fashioned point-to-point: informal, boisterous and electrically intimate. As at Epsom, crowds of the Zetlands' employees and tenants had come along to bet and cheer their 'Volti' on to triumph in the St Leger, before collecting the prize money (no horse appeared to compete against him) in the Scarborough Handicap.

Lord Lovelace arrived at Doncaster in time to see their friends' athletic colt beat his greatest rival of the age, Lord Eglinton's The Flying Dutchman, in a hair-raising tie-breaker for the Doncaster Gold Cup. (The two horses were the only runners and Eglinton's jockey had been drinking hard before the race.) Writing to his mother-in-law, Lovelace observed that his clever wife was being admired by all for her skill in picking out the best points of a horse, while he – poor chap – had succeeded only in having a few pounds picked from his pockets. Ada's maid had apparently turned a little profit on her bets, but their silly coachman had lost 18 shillings – not enough to stop him from trying his luck again. As for Ada:

> I am threatened with proofs by an eager ardent avis, that *this* business is profitable – much more so than the *training* them . . .

Nobody knows what conversations and encounters had taken place at Doncaster prior to William's arrival, but it was here that Ada took the fateful decision to retrieve the Lovelace fortunes by making a new kind of book.

Arriving back at Aske in time to share the celebrations, Ada collapsed and had to take to her bed, where (so she assured an alarmed mother on 26 September) she was miraculously restored to health by the Zetlands' wonderful physician. His name was Dr Malcolm and – as Ada prudently failed to add – he took a keen interest in his captivating patient's explanations of how she could use her mathematical skills to outwit experienced bookmakers on the turf. Ada's problem was that she – as Byron's somewhat notorious daughter – could never allow her own name to be used for placing bets. But if Lady Lovelace could find a few obliging friends to help, friends who might like to make a little money themselves by the use of her computations . . .

Dr Malcolm encouraged her. Working for the Zetlands, the doctor had plenty of contacts in the bookmaking world. Why should Lady Lovelace not rally up a circle of discreet enthusiasts like himself and form her own private ring? He had the names. She had the brains. How could she – how could *they* – lose?

Writing to her mother at this momentous time, Ada demurely reported how much she liked the Zetland's prizewinning colt. Voltigeur was both quiet and amiable: 'a most *earnest, conscientious* sort of horse'. She could as well have been talking of Tam o'Shanter and Zigzag, the horses on which she loved to ride out across Exmoor. About her thoughts for a racing future, there was not a word.

Evidence that Ada's enterprising mind had alighted upon a new interest continued to surface through the rest of the autumn. A puzzled but dutiful daughter, back from her educational tour of Germany, and visiting her grandmother, was asked to hurry over to Horsley and despatch to Ada the doubling dice that she would find there, lodged within a backgammon board. Meanwhile, Charles Babbage received a message on 1 November about the usefulness of 'Erasmus Wilson' in helping her mistress to a new cure and of Ada's urgent need to meet Babbage's *'medical friend'* as soon as she her-self returned to London from her hill-climbing exploits in the Lake District. ('Some very thorough remedial measures must be pursued,' Ada warned him, '– or all power of getting any livelihood in *any* way whatever, will be at an end.')

It sounded almost like a threat. Since Ada was simultaneously boasting to her mother and Agnes Greig that her northern physician (Dr Malcolm) was responsible for an astonishing improvement in her health, 'Erasmus Wilson' was surely a code for Mary, the servant who had once worked for Babbage and who was now placing dis-creet bets on her mistress's behalf. It's reasonable to surmise that the curiously underlined *'medical friend'* was in fact a potential recruit for Ada's ring of investors.*

By Christmas 1850, while paying a visit to her mother at Esher, Ada was studying the new season's printed programme for steeplechases. All the best bets had been clearly marked up for her by one of Dr Malcolm's tipsters. In a word, Lady Lovelace was hooked.

৩৩

At any other moment in her cautious life, the prudent Lady Byron might have been thoroughly alarmed by Lovelace's allusion to Ada's fancy for becoming a breeder of horses. (William himself seems to have been largely unconscious of Ada's enthusiasm for placing bets until the following spring.) But Annabella had been sidetracked by her daughter's altered view of Newstead, and the bold admiration with which she now extolled her father and his gambling forebears. Of what use was the careful version of past events that she herself had recently revised and polished and submitted to an admiring Frederick Robertson for his approbation, if Ada were to embrace

---

* It would be easier to interpret Ada's puzzling letter to Babbage as being con-cerned (as it purports to be) with the writer's health, had it had not been written while Lady Lovelace was shinning up mountains in the Lake District and boast-ing of her wonderfully restored health.

her unredeemed papa? What could Lady Byron herself do to regain ascendancy over her wilful daughter?

Initially, Annabella resorted to threats. If this was how Lord Byron was to be viewed, then she would play no further part in the upbringing of her grandchildren. They would never see her again! Somewhat, but not entirely, soothed by pleading letters of reassurance that her version – and only her version – of the past would prevail, Lady Byron came up with a new proposal. If Ada loved Newstead so much, then she should have it. William could appraise its value. The money could be raised by selling some of the Wentworth estates around Birmingham. The idea, once Annabella began to consider it (the feelings of the poor Wildmans were entirely disregarded), proved curiously appealing. The house would be her gift to Ada, but the person who owned Newstead – just as she still owned everything to do with the Wentworth estates – would be herself. Annabella, not Ada, would become the presiding angel of Byron's ancient home.

The Lovelaces were not averse to the Hen's proposal. 'Will you sometime write me a letter about a possible *exchange* of *Newstead*,' Ada wrote to her mother on 24 December. She added that Lovelace thought that a deal might indeed be done without too much impact on the Wentworth property. The possibility of acquiring the abbey intrigued them both.

And then, with no explanation, the whole fantastic plan was dropped. By January 1851, Ada (while up to the neck in her plans to set up a racing ring) was making pleasant arrangements for the Wildmans to come and stay at Horsley with Captain Byron and his wife.* Annabella, meanwhile, her mind aswirl with the turbulent emotions that talk of Newstead had brought rushing to the surface, was diverted by another connection to the past.

---

* Declining on 29 March 1851, on account of 'poor George's health' (although the invitation to Horsley was planned for the following winter), Lucy Byron asked Ada to tell her the truth about something. It's unclear whether Lucy had heard rumours about buying Newstead, but it is noteworthy that the Wildmans also turned down the Lovelaces' invitation. (Lovelace Byron Papers.)

Augusta Leigh's raffish old husband had died at the age of seventy-nine in May 1850, the month of Voltigeur's first triumph at Epsom. By the end of the year, largely on account of her late husband's outstanding debts, Augusta was destitute. She still had her rooms at St James's Palace. What she lacked, as ever, was ready cash. She knew that Lady Byron had recently reconciled herself with Mrs Villiers. Was this not the ideal moment to remind Byron's wealthy little widow that there still existed a sister for whom she had, at one time, felt the most tender sentiments of affection?

The moment was indeed timely. Annabella's lengthy conversations with the attentive Frederick Robertson had recently included a pious wish that she might meet with Augusta Leigh for one last occasion. On New Year's Day 1851, she told the impressionable clergyman that – as for herself – she 'loved her still. I cannot help it.' On 8 January, Lady Byron dropped a hint about the tales she might tell Mr Robertson – if she wished – about the true nature of Byron's relationship with his older half-sister.

This was awkward. Anybody living in Lady Byron's circle would have had to be exceptionally ill-informed not to have heard, by 1850, at least a whisper about Byron's scandalous relationship with Augusta Leigh. Nervous of causing offence, Robertson expressed careful surprise – and even horror. Could it be that Byron and Mrs Leigh ...? Was his 'dreadful fancy' based upon fact? It was. Expanding graciously, Lady Byron offered the receptive cleric that version of the past to which she herself was now entirely wedded.

Byron had always loved her. Even after his wife left him, he had written those very words. 'I was his best friend,' Annabella had recently reminded her daughter (17 September 1850), before quoting Byron's passionate declaration ('I did – do – and ever shall – love you.') But he was not allowed to love her. Another, more wicked influence had prevailed. Augusta Leigh, jealous of a young wife's spiritual power over the husband she had left, had twisted the evidence. Acting (admittedly under Annabella's own instructions) as the marital go-between during the last eight years of Byron's life abroad, Mrs Leigh had fuelled her brother's hatred of his wife. She had manipulated the truth. This gospel testimony of Lady Byron – ever since Medora had produced in the winter of 1840–1 her own imaginative version of past events – had become plain fact. All that was lacking, as Annabella explained to her fascinated listener, was the oral proof, the confession that only Augusta Leigh herself could provide.

A wiser clergyman might have smiled. Robertson, while widely admired in Brighton as a magnificent speaker – and a very handsome man – was both naive and an unconscionable prig. The actress Fanny Kemble, visiting Brighton in the late autumn of 1850, had been appalled to discover that Lady Byron, urged on by Robertson, was planning to write a cautionary preface to the readers of a new cheap edition of Byron's works. Fanny, who had always opposed the public view of Byron's widow as a cold-hearted prude, believed the enterprise would do great harm to her old friend. 'I had always admired the reticent dignity of her silence,' Kemble wrote in her entertaining *Records of Girlhood*. And besides, 'what *could* Byron do to the young men of 1850?' But Annabella was not to be dissuaded.

> 'Nobody' she [Lady Byron] said, 'knew him as I did … nobody knew as well as I the causes that had made him what he was; nobody, I think, is so capable of doing justice to him, and therefore of counteracting the injustice he does to himself, and the injury he might do to others, in some of his writings.'

The clinching argument for this ludicrous project (it never saw the light) had come from Frederick Robertson. It was he, so Mrs Kemble learned, who had solemnly advised Lady Byron of the dangers of her husband's poetry 'to a class peculiarly interesting to him … and of course his [Robertson's] opinion was more than an overweight for mine'.

With such an ally at her side, Lady Byron was ready for action. Her opportunity came in February 1851, when word reached her from Admiral Lord Byron (Captain George's father) that Miss Emily Leigh had been in touch regarding her mother. A response was promptly issued. A week later, Augusta herself wrote to accept Lady Byron's proposal for a meeting. It might, Augusta hopefully wrote, do both of them good to have a free and frank discussion after so long a silence. She welcomed this opportunity to clear the air.

Annabella does not appear to advantage during the elaborate negotiations over which, counselled by Robertson at every step, she presided during the next few weeks. Augusta, who had never been on a train in her life, was instructed to make her way alone to Reigate station. There, at a convenient but obscure destination midway between Brighton and London, an inconspicuously dressed servant (meaning, he would wear no livery buttons on his coat) would meet and conduct Mrs Leigh to a nearby – and flawlessly sedate – coaching inn called The White Hart. Following her brief introduction to a neutral witness, the two women would be left alone. Augusta's feeble protests about this sudden inclusion of a stranger at such an intimate occasion were crushed by Annabella's representation of Robertson as 'the Genius of the Soul's World'. One might as well (so Lady Byron haughtily implied) deny a birthplace to the Christchild as exclude the Reverend Frederick Robertson of Brighton from the Reigate inn.

The interview took place in a back room at The White Hart on 8 April. No records were made. Later, however, Annabella recalled her dismay at realising that Mrs Leigh, an inveterate chatterbox, meant to produce nothing more confessional than a babble of pleasantries. 'Is that all?' Lady Byron had burst out. 'I felt utterly hopeless, and asked to be left alone to compose myself.' Rejoining Robertson and their bewildered guest after this moment of solitude, Annabella moved into attack mode. Armed with assertions of which a list had been prepared ('*you* kept up hatred; *you* put things in a false light'), she tried to coerce a response. Eager to please, and thus to get some financial recompense for her journey, Augusta agreed that her brother had often uttered 'dreadful things'. She refused to say that she had encouraged him. Pressed harder, Mrs Leigh grew annoyed. Lady Byron had been allowed to bring Mr Robertson along as her supporter. Well, she had one, too: Sir John Hobhouse. Augusta was ready to state that Hobhouse had once actually warned her not to be so unflinchingly loyal to Annabella – unless she herself actually wished to lose her brother's affection.

This declaration was the modest boast that tipped the balance of Annabella's fiercely governed mind. 'At *such* a testimony I started up,' Lady Byron admitted afterwards. 'I was afraid of myself . . . the strongest desire to be out of her presence took possession of me, lest I should be tempted beyond my strength'. Some answer was tearfully jerked out, some phrase about a kind blessing that she now felt herself unable to confer – and the meeting was over.

Annabella had once described Byron's sister as having been born in a state of moral idiocy. The validity of that brusque observation was never more pathetically apparent than in Augusta's readiness to view the Reigate meeting as a success. Writing to thank Annabella for her 'exertions', she 'could not resist' signing herself as 'Yours affectionately'. A furious Annabella responded that the required confession had been entirely inadequate. Adding not one word of reciprocal affection, Lady Byron signed her answer: 'Farewell'. Growing apprehensive, Augusta wrote again, this time to offer Frederick Robertson proofs of her innocence. Impossible, the clergyman bleakly responded on 21 May. Such proofs could only be produced in the presence of Lady Byron and the word 'farewell' was surely clear enough? There would be no further meetings. Mrs Leigh could console herself with the thought of clearing her conscience at another encounter, one 'which must be heard very, very soon, when you meet God face to face'.

And that was that.

While the Reigate meeting and its aftermath do not reflect well upon either Lady Byron or her advisor, it is worth noting that Augusta's half-sister, the widowed Countess of Chichester, wrote some years later expressing a friendly desire to meet with Annabella at Brighton. Apparently, Lady Chichester wanted to express the deep gratitude 'I have ever entertained of yr kindness to my Sister & several members of her unfortunate family'.

There's no doubting the sincerity of Lady Chichester's words. Clearly, she was recalling the unpleasant drama of Medora. It's likely that she was also remembering how promptly Annabella had paid the bills and offered to cover the cost of all that was required for comfort when Augusta, just six months after the Reigate meeting, lay at death's door. Possibly, Lady Chichester had also learned from Emily Leigh of Lady Byron's final moment of humanity, a written wish that Emily might whisper to her mother '*from me* the words Dearest Augusta – I can't think they could hurt her'.

On 5 October 1851, Emily reported that she had done as requested. Her mother seemed much pleased and affected. She had made a lengthy response. Only – alas for a hungry Annabella, still yearning for that unreceived confession – Mrs Leigh had lost her voice. 'I could not hear distinctly,' Emily wrote. '– I dare say she will mention the subject again.'

She never did. On 12 October 1851, Augusta Leigh died in faded dignity, attended by her daughter and a physician, in the rooms at St James's Palace that she had inhabited for thirty-three years. On 16 October, Annabella, who had been lingering at a London hotel in the vain hope of a last-minute summons, wrote on black-edged paper to ask if she might be allowed to visit her god-daughter, to hear a private confidence that would never be shared. That Emily had none to offer was, perhaps, as well. Augusta's secrets, if indeed she had any to disclose, would assuredly not have gone untold.

None of Byron's family attended Mrs Leigh's interment at Kensal Green. On 2 July 1852, however, Annabella wrote to inform Emily that, despite appearances, she had always been her mother's truest friend. 'Mine is not a nature in which affection can pass away,' Lady Byron announced: 'nearly forty years have shown this in regard to her'.

There is no doubt that Annabella herself believed this remarkable statement to be no less than the truth.

The Lovelace children once again spent the Christmas of 1850 in sep-arate places. Lord Ockham remained in Chile under the supervision of the Greigs' friend, Captain Fanshawe. Annabella had been shifted from Lady Byron's home, to the Greigs, and on to Ockham, where old Stephen Lushington treated her as a cherished grandchild of his own. (A glimpse of their affectionate relationship peeps through accounts of afternoon games of billiards and the lawyer's teasing comments about Annabella's salamander-like love of a blazing fire.) Meanwhile, Ada's younger son, Ralph, remained in fog-drenched London with his mother, where Ada herself – between paying snugly wrapped visits with Babbage to the semi-completed and ice-cold 'Glass House' in Hyde Park – scolded the boy for his sulks about the absence of Ockham's promised tales of his nautical adventures. (If any such letters did arrive, we might suspect that Lord Lovelace saw fit to confiscate them.)

Aged eleven, Ralph was beginning to make his own complex personality felt. Ada, writing to her mother in December 1850, following a happy reunion with the Greigs and her daughter at their London home, reported that Ralph's new tutor, Mr Kensett, was taking a firm line with his stroppy little pupil, and that she approved.

While Lord Lovelace pondered his chances of getting into the Admiralty (Ada agreed with Lushington that her husband was too touchy and impractical for such a post), his wife's private thoughts dwelt continuously upon how to lay hands on the money of which both she and the earl increasingly stood in dire need. Going abroad was a popular move back then, both to escape debts and to improve poor health. Mrs Somerville had done it. So had the Brownings. Perhaps the Lovelaces should follow suit? Lady Byron (despite the inevitable sacrifice of Ada's company) favoured this course. By 23 December 1850, Ada was ready to pursue it.

I think we shall let our house in May, & go to the *Pyrenees*,
I am not joking. I reflected on yr suggestion, & soon got
accustomed to it. It frightened me at first ... It would *set me up*
for years (& set our *purses* up too).

The idea was not abandoned; Ada mentioned it again on 21 April
1851 as a project for the following month – 'but nothing is yet settled'. By May, however, Ada's health was too seriously impaired for
a journey abroad to be considered. She had, besides, embarked at
full tilt upon an entirely different enterprise, the nature of which her
mother was to learn in full only after its catastrophic failure.

By January 1851, Ada had set up her ring of fellow gamblers and
was ready to beat the bookies at their own game. John Crosse was
involved, while Babbage was evidently aware of what was going on.
A certain William Nightingale, identified as the father of two sons,
may have been connected to Florence's family. Almost nothing is
known about Mr Fleming, but it is likely that he was a friend of the
Zetlands' physician, Doctor Malcolm, since the two names are often
mentioned in conjunction. Malcolm himself was a man of modest
means who, like Ada, was struggling to live on £300 a year. Richard
Ford was another matter.

Sir Richard Ford was a gentleman of means. The author of
Murray's celebrated *Handbook to Spain* was a brilliant art
historian (he introduced Velázquez's paintings to their English
audience), and a close friend of George Borrow. An ardent traveller in post-Napoleonic Europe, Ford had returned to England
in the 1830s to create Heavitree House, a Spanish-style recon-
struction of an Elizabethan cob cottage, perched on a hilltop
just outside the city of Exeter. Ford had been at Trinity College,
Cambridge, ten years before William Lovelace. Like William, he
was a self-taught architect. The two men knew each other well.
In 1835, Ford was one of the first to hear about his friend's young

bride and to share with a mutual acquaintance William's enthusiastic account of her.

> From the Baron's account she [Miss Ada Byron] must be
> perfection ... highly simple, hateth the city and gay world,
> and will not be likely to turn up her nose at you and me, the
> respectable aged friends of her lord.

In 1849, Sir Richard Ford had lost both his mother and his wife. (His second marriage to Mary Molesworth, sister to the owner of the *Westminster Review*, would not take place until the summer of 1851.) In the winter of 1850–1, then, Sir Richard Ford was a lonely widower. It is clear that his main contact in the racing ring was Ada herself, it is also incontrovertibly apparent from Ford's involvement that William Lovelace must have known something about what was going on. While it remains impossible to establish just how much William was personally involved in the booking and laying of bets, the presence of his friend in Ada's ring makes it clear that Lord Lovelace was never an innocent bystander.

It was Ada, however, who led the way and her elderly ring were awed by the (initially) elaborate nature of her strategies. On 13 January, a respectful Richard Ford told Ada that he and Nightingale (Ford referred to him as 'the sportive Nightingale') were planning to meet in London 'to talk over the wonderful combinations in your letter'. A financial innocent himself, Ford frankly stated that he would never want to bet more than £5 and that he imagined 'making a book' to be like 'living at the brink of a precipice' (27 January). Nevertheless, Ada's confidence was infectious. '£3,000 this year!' Ford exclaimed in another undated letter. 'How my mouth waters at such draughts. But by what magic is such a sum to be obtained & how is Chiles [Samuel Chiles was a Vauxhall-based bookmaker, seemingly recommended by Dr Malcolm] become so suddenly consumed into the depositing of thousands from not having a halfpenny?'

Ford's willingness to be drawn into Ada's net of speculators reminds us of just how dangerously alluring Byron's daughter could be. By March 1851, Sir Richard himself was paying regular visits to bookmakers to negotiate terms and deals about which he patently had not the faintest degree of understanding. Between times, he advised Ada about her plans for the Pyrenees, paid visits to Horsley Towers, arranged jolly dinner parties for the ring (but only when his daughters were out of the way) and even blithely reported that he was off to dine in 'The Enemy's Camp' with Lord Eglinton, the owner of Voltigeur's greatest challenger, The Flying Dutchman.

How good was Ada at bookmaking (or more accurately, at gambling on horses)? The fact that her ring stuck with her through at least one full racing season suggests that she must have had some degree of success. Nevertheless, the few scraps of notes and papers that survive from the bookmakers themselves suggest that the excited countess was doing little more than following tips – for which she paid quite handsomely – and making judgements based on the odds that were being laid. Occasionally, a kindly tipster warned 'Her Ladyship' away from an impulsive choice. Ada, blithe as a lark despite her increasing ill health and the fact that she was now seldom able to walk for more than a few yards without pain, ignored them all.

Disaster sprang upon her like a beast from the jungle. On 1 May 1851, in what has ever since been known as The Great Match, Lord Eglinton's Flying Dutchman challenged Voltigeur ('The Flyer' and 'Volti' by now, to their adoring fans) to an eagerly anticipated rematch at York, running on the old Knavesmire course. (It was where Dick Turpin, one of the most infamous horsemen of all time, had been hanged in 1739.) The crowds were immense, since both the champions were Yorkshire bred. Many of the 130,000 people present had walked fifty miles to watch the event. Ada's ring, led by herself, had backed the Zetlands' colt.

Ada was not present in person (she was too ill to leave her bedroom at this time) to learn the catastrophic news that Lord Eglinton's horse had beaten the prodigious Voltigeur by a length. Ten days later, Teddington won at Epsom. The odds on the Derby's confidently predicted winner were 3/1. Ada, who had persuaded Lovelace to loan the impecunious Dr Malcolm £1,800 to bet against Teddington, had now in total suffered losses of £3,200, while also bearing full financial responsibility for the losses of her disappointed ring.

It remains unknowable to what extent either John Crosse or Charles Babbage were directly involved at this point in Ada's ring. It is known that Ada was personally responsible during this time for obtaining the living at Ockham for Andrew Crosse's eldest son, Robert, and that Robert's father expressed his gratitude for her assistance at a time when his son (who had a young family to support) had been seriously ill. Equally apparent from the friendly letters that Robert and Andrew Crosse wrote to Ada in 1851 is the fact that they knew nothing about either a racing or a romantic connection between Lady Lovelace and Robert's older brother, John.

Charles Babbage falls under more suspicion than Crosse because of the incontrovertible fact that his former servant, Mary Wilson, ran bet-placing errands and allowed her name to be regularly invoked in the covert dealings of the ring. But did this mean that Babbage himself was involved? The long and mysterious correspondence with Ada about a shared 'book', while it clearly predates her activity in the racing world, has helped to muddy the waters. Thus, when Babbage suddenly again mentions 'a book' to Ada on 13 January 1851, it sounds intriguing. Babbage's letter recommends that when 'the book' arrives, Ada herself should read out Sir James South's instructions to her maid, 'in order for your influence in causing them to be followed'. While it is tempting to construe South as the '*medical friend*' Ada had previously mentioned with such curious emphasis, Sir James was no doctor, but an eminent astronomer. The likelihood is that Mary Wilson was simply being instructed about the sighting of stars on certain nights, an activity that had always enthralled Ada. Nevertheless, her earlier reference to Babbage's unnamed '*medical friend*' remains a puzzle.

What is certain is that Babbage wrote to Ada on 13 May 1851, the day of the Epsom Derby, in a way that shows he knew this was a special day for her. Had she passed a good night? What were her commands for the day? She must not exert herself with writing: 'a visit from your own Lady-Bird will be sufficient'. The degree of attentiveness being shown here, on this particular date, is highly suggestive, although (once again), nothing can be confirmed.

ගෙ

Even today, our understanding of the connection between mind and body remains frustratingly theoretical. However, it's hard to dismiss the sudden decline in Ada's health following her major losses at Epsom and York. Enough concern was felt for Charles Locock to summon Sir James Clark, Prince Albert's personal physician, to diagnose one of Locock's own favourite patients. Clark's interest in the case was doubtless heightened by the fact that the patient in question was Lord Byron's daughter.

Examinations were made of the painful and intimate kind to which Ada Lovelace was now obliged to subject herself on a regular basis. A sheet masked Ada's genitalia from view as the middle-aged gentleman probed cold instruments – or even inquisitive fingers – towards her womb, searching for an explanation of the irregular bleeding and continuous pain that the 35-year-old patient endured with a courage and good humour that commanded their awed respect.

On 15 June, Charles Locock submitted their findings to the earl. For himself, while acknowledging the presence of extensive ulceration in the cervix, he was ready to describe the young countess's large internal 'sore' as 'healthy' and to pronounce that it was curable – with prudent care. Sir James Clark, long since recovered from the stain to his reputation of a misdiagnosed court pregnancy in 1839 (poor Lady Flora Hastings was in fact dying of a cancerous tumour that distended her belly), offered a grimmer diagnosis. Cancer was clearly present, he stated. Nothing could now be done to restrain it. Lady Lovelace's days were numbered.

Clark's verdict was bleak and it could not be ignored. Understandably, at the time of terrible racing losses of which he was at the very least partially aware, Lord Lovelace shrank from breaking such black news to his fragile and suffering wife. Four days later, however, the earl could restrain himself no longer. Who better to confide in than the compassionate, maternal and understanding Hen?

A few hours after despatching a long and anguished letter to his mother-in-law (he had mentioned money problems and debts, as well as the gravity of Ada's condition), Lovelace regretted the impulse. It was now that he took one of the worst decisions of his life. Instead of waiting for a response, he bolted off across the country to Leamington Spa, where Annabella was spending a few restorative days after paying a business-related visit to the nearby Kirkby Mallory estates. There, in a darkened town of immense gentility, an astonished Lady Byron opened her front door an hour before midnight, and found herself overwhelmed by a distraught, frightened and – in his present emotional state – alarmingly vehement son-in-law.

The location for Lovelace's impromptu confessional visit was as ill chosen as his timing. Leamington was a town that was filled with Wentworth properties and connections. Edward Noel was living nearby. (His wife Fanny had died here in 1847.) Charles and Mary Anne Noel frequently stayed with Annabella at Leamington during visits of the official kind that she had just been paying to her estate. Miss Montgomery, too, was a regular visitor. For Lord Lovelace to show up in the middle of the sleeping spa, emerging from his private coach at dead of night, was to set tongues wagging – and there was nothing that Lady Byron feared more in this particular part of the world than gossip.

It has never been clear just what was said during what Annabella later described as 'that hour of agony'. We know from a bitter letter that Lovelace wrote eighteen months later (17 December 1852) that the earl felt that his mother-in-law had been 'slightingly' dismissive about the severity of Ada's illness. We know from the document Annabella drew up with the assistance of Stephen Lushington at Ockham on 1 July, two weeks after the Leamington meeting, that she believed William Lovelace had betrayed his clearly understood duty to protect a wife who knew no more about money (let alone professional horse-racing) than an untutored child. Lovelace had not stood up to Ada. Instead, fearing the turbulence of his wife's powerful impulses and emotions, he had allowed her to do as she wished. He had, above all, been unforgivably irresponsible in allowing Lady Lovelace to go without him to Doncaster racecourse and thereafter, to mix with 'low & unprincipled associates'.

Writing to Lovelace a full nineteen months later (9 January 1853) about their fateful interview, in one of a series of savagely recriminatory letters, Lady Byron accused her son-in-law of having 'unconsciously' disclosed to her that dreadful night at Leamington a prospect so appalling that 'disease itself was to be looked upon as a blessing to my daughter'. That prospect was not Ada's death. It was that Lord Lovelace had allowed his headstrong and (in the view of a stern mother) financially irresponsible young wife to gamble.

Grudgingly, Annabella would eventually concede that her son-in-law appeared not to share her personal horror of speculation. 'You did not, you do not, view these things as I do,' she granted in the same chilling letter of reproach that she wrote to Lovelace on 9 January 1853. Acknowledgement of that crucial difference of view was made. Forgiveness was implacably withheld.

A month earlier, on 11 December 1852, during another of these bitter exchanges (they dragged on over a period of almost two years), Annabella reminded Lovelace once again of his behaviour at Leamington. It was his fault and his alone, she wrote then, that a devoted mother had subsequently become estranged from her only child: 'your conduct with regard to me since June 19 1851, affected my daughter most lamentably, & so long deprive[d] me of intercourse with her.'

It had not been so simple as that. On 3 July 1851, while obstinately refusing to disclose precisely what had so disturbed her during the Leamington interview, Annabella told her daughter how gladly she would have solved any financial problems, had she only been asked. The following day (tactfully omitting to point out that Lady Byron had recently begrudged loaning her daughter a few hundred pounds), poor Ada did her best to clear the air. She promised to visit her mother's Brighton home, both to see her 12-year-old son, and to discuss what she carefully referred to as 'recent occurrences'. Anxious not to have a quarrel, she mentioned the potential danger to her own delicate health of 'agitating influences'.

No settled plan was made, possibly because Ada was too ill to travel. Ten days later, Lady Byron noted that she herself had resorted to her sad practice, in times of extreme despair, of going out alone in an open boat in order to vomit up her anguish, safely out of reach of public view.

Four weeks went by.

On 8 August, a frail Ada took a train to Brighton. What was said there remains unknown, but Lady Byron did not relent. Having bidden her mother farewell two days later, Ada wrote one of her most wistfully elusive notes: 'I never remember to have quitted you with so much *regret*. *Why*, I cannot say: althou' I have some vague idea about the *whys* of the case.'

If Ada believed that peace could be restored, she deceived herself. Enduring war had been declared by the Hen upon the Crow. William Lovelace, until the end of his days, would never comprehend what he had done to merit such unyielding wrath.

On 10 April 1852, eight months on, Ada wrote to her mother to express regret that '*that* interview' (William's visit to Leamington) had ever taken place. She now wished she had taken a sterner line during her August visit to Brighton. 'I never felt so tempted to step out of all the usual bounds of filial propriety,' she wrote. But what would have been the use of pleading William's cause?

Pray do not be angry at my having the *idea* (never likely to be practically attempted) of ever *persuading* you to anything! It is only an *idea*, a wish!

'I am,' Ada added with a sudden burst of candour, 'rather unhappy about it all.'

❧

Illness was nothing new to Ada. She had spent most of her short life battling invalidism, proving over and again that the 'wiry little system' in which she took such pride would enable her to battle her way back to health. The battle continued through the months that followed William's dash to Leamington. By the late summer of 1851, it was only the frail, tormented body that could no longer keep up with Ada's passion for achievement and her absolute refusal to give up hope. 'Life *is so difficult*,' she wrote to her mother on 15 October, underlining every word; a sentence or two later, she was willing to believe that she might yet have another thirty years to enjoy before – so she hoped – a quick and gentle death.

It seems clear that Ada – however valiant her attitude – was at least partly conscious that the end was near. Her health was already failing when she split her energies into the pursuit of her two consuming passions. By the summer of 1851, she had become fatally addicted to the gambling mania which – as she was perfectly aware since the Newstead encounter with her father's ancestry – was an obsession that ran in her blood. Since then, Ada's attachment to her Byron lineage had grown steadily more pronounced.* But Lady Lovelace was also and always her mother's child and, above all, Ada longed to please Lady Byron by making her individual mark in science.

---

* On 22 August 1851, Ada asked Charles Babbage to purchase Byron's rifle and pistols from one of Augusta Leigh's sons as 'a favour to us'. Nine days later, following a day's visit from Ralph to Horsley Towers, she told her mother that the boy needed her own care. ('Set a Byron to rule a Byron! – For Ralph is a Byron – three-quarters at least.') Commenting on Augusta Leigh's death to Annabella six weeks later (15 October), Ada ominously alluded to her own dread of 'that horrible struggle, which I fear is in the Byron blood'.

CHAPTER TWENTY-TWO

RAINBOW'S END

(1851–2)

'I am spellbound until my offspring is complete, however imperfect.'

ADA LOVELACE TO LADY BYRON,
10 AUGUST 1851

'I have also an awful amount of writing to do at present.'

ADA LOVELACE TO LADY BYRON,
21 APRIL 1852

To have created, aged only twenty-seven, a boldly persuasive and articulate account of the possibilities that Charles Babbage's unbuilt machine could offer was a splendid achievement, but it is important to remember that the celebrated Menabrea 'Notes' seem visionary only to us, enlightened retrospectively by Alan Turing's generous appreciation of a brilliant predecessor. Within her own lifetime, Ada's ascendant star was quick to fade. By 1851, confronting her own mortality at the age of thirty-five, the need to prove herself as a serious player in a world dominated by men had become over-whelming. Scientific recognition of Ada was what the Hen and her own loyal Crow had always desired. It was this mark of excellence that she herself most craved.

Again and again, in the stream of letters that Lady Lovelace wrote to Lady Byron during the last full year of her life, she referred to the excitement she felt about her continuing work on 'light-filled drops'. It was in connection to this work that Ada, during the summer of 1851, pursued a new collegiate friendship with an eminent Scottish scientist. Sir David Brewster's discovery of the kaleidoscope, back in 1816, was an offshoot from a lifetime dedicated to studying the properties of light.* Both Ada and her mother had known the elderly Scotsman for years (he was close both to Babbage and Mary Somerville), but it was only in 1851 that Ada began to take a par-ticular interest in his work.

The idea may have come from her husband, always an eager sup-porter of his wife's scientific work. On 17 May, Lord Lovelace, Dr Locock, Charles Wheatstone, Adolphe Quetelet (a highly regarded French astronomer) and David Brewster had all attended a dinner in the Royal Society's splendid rooms at Burlington House.

Ten days later, the countess asked Charles Babbage to bring Brewster to see her at home, in order that she might converse with him and Adolphe Quetelet. Ada was therefore already in contact with Brewster when she suddenly decided to resume her old con-nection with Michael Faraday: 'you see what I do – ever as you like with me,' Faraday wrote affectionately on 10 June in a letter that also expressed concern about news of Lady Lovelace's weakened health. On 21 June, Ada told Lady Byron that she was working hard on 'the drops' and hoping that the great scientist would visit 'to give me his ideas on the subject'. The fact that she entreated 13-year-old Annabella on the following day to write and thank Mr Faraday for

---

* Brewster invented the kaleidoscope in 1816 and the stereoscope, a hugely popular early form of 3D photographic viewing, in 1851. He enjoyed the com-pany of clever women; in 1851, he escorted Charlotte Brontë around the Great Exhibition – and doubtless showed off his stereoscope during the tour.

his kind gift to her of a book (it was a new primer on electricity) suggests that Lady Lovelace was unusually anxious to please him. A few weeks later, on 2 August, she told her mother that Faraday's reliance upon experiments meant that he, more than Sir David Brewster, would be able to assist her researches on 'the drops'.

So, what was it that Ada was working on in her race for time against the painful cancer that was insidiously spreading up through her cervix and into her womb? What were the 'prismatic drops full of bright & various hues' to which she was still referring on 29 October 1851, when she entreated her mother to believe that she might yet achieve something, that she *had not lived in vain*'?

Surprisingly little attention has been given to this last phase of Ada's involvement with the world of science. And yet, to judge by the letters that she and her mother exchanged, that research was intended to crown the summit of Ada's brief career. The most likely explanation of her 'drops' is that Ada had turned back to the phenomenon that had captivated her as a light-obsessed child, when she wrote to William Frend to ask if he could explain how a rainbow's arc was formed. Aged thirty-five, Ada knew that a rainbow is made by the angle from the viewer at which 'white' multicoloured sunlight is refracted into its separate components at the back of a drop of rain. She knew that rainbows brighten as they approach the ground because of the lengthening of the raindrops; she knew, too, that the visible arc is part of a circle.

All of this, by the year 1851, was current knowledge. Ada's particular interest in the work of David Brewster (whose speciality was optics and the polarisation of light) and of Michael Faraday (who had demonstrated in 1845 that electromagnetism can twist a polarised ray of light shone through thick glass) suggests that her own study was related to the significance of the way raindrops refract the sun's light. It's impossible to be certain, but Ada Lovelace may well have been intuitively feeling her way towards the future invention of the spectroscope, an instrument that can replicate a prism by splitting light into its component colours. If so, she was again far ahead of her time; it is through spectroscopy that the properties of distant stars and galaxies can be measured, something that would have delighted Ada with her lifelong passion for astronomy.

Everything appeared to connect. On 2 August, Ada told her mother that she thought it better to involve Faraday than Brewster because their friend William Rutter's experiments were closer to his field. William Rutter was one of the ten men of science who in 1850 had founded the British Meteorological Society at Hartwell House in Buckinghamshire. David Brewster and Adolphe Quetelet were among the earliest members; Lady Byron and her daughter were also swiftly nominated by John Drew, a 41-year-old astronomer and geologist from Southampton. (Drew knew Lady Byron through her educational work; he had become England's youngest ever headmaster, aged seventeen, in 1826, at the Southampton school to which Annabella would send her grandson, Ralph King.)

The letters which Ada wrote to her mother during July 1851 constantly referred to the fact that she herself was working alongside William Rutter. On 5 August, she finalised plans with her mother for Rutter to conduct a privately held experiment during her own August visit to Brighton. It was agreed that a dinnertime discussion of the experiment would take place afterwards at Lady Byron's home on Marine Parade.

And then comes Ada's curveball. Firstly, she brought not Michael Faraday but David Brewster as her companion on this scientific mission. Secondly, while experiments were indeed carried out, they were not of the kind that Ada's letters about light-filled drops might reasonably lead us to expect.

Brewster and his wife were paying an October visit to Hartwell House, the family home of astronomer John Lee, when he finally recorded what he had witnessed three months earlier at Brighton. On 6 August, Lady Byron and her daughter had taken him to observe the movements of a pear-shaped ball of wax when suspended from William Rutter's fingers by a silk thread. Under Rutter's grasp, the ball rotated from left to right; dangled from the hand of a woman, the movement was reversed. And what, the shrewd old Scotsman wondered, would occur if a blindfold were in place? But Brewster himself was far from sceptical. The experiment had greatly intrigued him, and he described it with scientific care, while drawing a parallel to the prevalent rage for spirit rapping and levitation.

William Rutter's experiment was less fey than Brewster's description suggests. Its purpose was not to indicate the presence of mysterious spirits, but to demonstrate the power of electromagnetic forces within the human body. It's possible that Ada – whose interest in creating what she had grandly named 'a calculus of the nervous system' dated back to the mid-1840s – may have believed that she could draw upon this inner source of energy to overcome the physical challenges to her weakening frame.

While the link between magnetism and Ada's research into light-filled drops remains unclear, it is evident that she considered Rutter's demonstration a success. On 1 September, she reassured her mother that the 'drops' were still flowing well and that she would soon be able to offer 'a certain solid reality, upon which to *judge*, rather than to *hope*'. Lady Byron had already hoped for far too long, as her daughter acknowledged with a wistful plea: 'Have patience ... yet a *little* longer.'

Two months passed. On 29 October 1851, a poignant letter from Ada followed a brief bedside discussion with her mother. Apparently, Lady Byron's words had given 'great encouragement' and a promise was made that she might yet, 'by and bye', see 'certain productions'. But Ada's mind was clouded by pain-killing drugs. Her brave assurances shifted into a strange vision of herself presiding over regiments of numbers, 'marching in irresistible power to the sound of *Music*. Is not this very mysterious?'

လၐၐ

As Ada felt her grasp upon life slipping away, her attachment to her children grew stronger. Ralph, still living under his grandmother's supervision at Brighton and Southampton, aroused grave concern in November 1851 when he caught scarlet fever, one of the major killers in Victorian times. Lady Byron's attachment to her youngest grandchild was never more clearly demonstrated than by the fact that she herself arranged to watch over and nurse him, in her own bedroom, until the highly contagious fever had abated. Ada, helplessly fretting at a distance, urged his sister to write Ralph cheering letters, while wondering at the capricious fate that allowed the lives of both her sons to be threatened when she herself was so ill.

Byron Ockham's letters from abroad sometimes took as long as three months to arrive. When they came, poor Ada shuddered at the dangers to which his parents had exposed their oldest boy. She was not to know that Viscount Ockham, who was still only fifteen, was relating his exploits with considerably more verve than accuracy. Promises to bring home a collection of scalps ('What a very odd mind Byron's is!' Ada commented to her mother on 13 November 1851) were based on his having seen such trophies being brandished at officers by a group of marauding 'natives' during his stay at Vancouver Island. A dramatic account of his near shipwreck at Mazatlán failed to mention that the *Daphne*, when a hurricane ripped away her sails and snapped her masts in half, had been safely anchored in harbour.

Byron's adventures were, nevertheless, remarkable. In September 1851, a month before the Mexican storm, the *Daphne* had sailed along North America's western coastline from Vancouver to San Francisco. The California Gold Rush was then at its zenith. The wooden city of some 30,000 citizens was still being rebuilt after a summer fire had razed a quarter of its flimsy structures to the ground, but brothels and drinking saloons were still flourishing in the town for which the term gold-digger was coined, and where dashing, gun-toting ladies were frequently available for a fistful of glinting coins.

Had the Lovelaces made a terrible mistake in sending their eldest son to sea? Writing back to Ockham on 15 November, Ada pleaded with her jaunty sailor-son to remember that there was no real need for him to remain on the other side of the world, 'unless by yr own wish'. By the time her letter arrived, Lord Ockham was off in Mexico, helping Captain Fanshawe to take charge of the crates of silver bullion required by the British government from the owners of some of South America's most brutal and dangerous mines. Granted, this was an extraordinary way of life for a young Unitarian aristocrat who otherwise would have been swotting over his classics with a tutor, but young Byron's letters betrayed no trace of homesickness, and no evidence that he wanted to renounce his swashbuckling life at sea.

Byron Ockham's reaction might well have been different had he known how gravely ill his mother had become by the autumn of 1851. It was harder to protect his sister from the truth. By the end of October, Ada's daughter had returned home from a second journey to Europe with Agnes Greig and Miss Wächter. Writing to Mrs Greig just ahead of the September trip, Ada had asked that the young girl should be bought a pretty dress from Paris ('whatever she likes best'), and that Annabella should be shielded from the news that her beloved governess was suffering from incurable cancer.

How much did Ada know about her own state when she wrote to Mrs Greig of Miss Wächter's 'horrible doom'? Three months later, her favourite physician, the habitually optimistic Charles Locock, reluctantly acknowledged the gravity of his patient's case. On 25 November, a miserable William Lovelace broke a long silence to tell Lady Byron the ominous news. To the patient herself, Dr Locock spoke only of a slight improvement. On 28 November, Ada urged Annabella to pass the good news along to Papa. Whether Ada herself believed it is doubtful.

Nothing indicates Ada Lovelace's acceptance of her fate more touchingly than her new concern for the welfare of the 14-year-old girl who was now home from her travels and living alone at Horsley Towers with her father. Lady Byron, exhausted by nursing Ralph through scarlet fever and worried about the declining health of Frederick Robertson, was in no state, at the close of 1851, to take in a second grandchild. While Ralph was despatched for a second stay at the Fellenbergs' family home in Switzerland, Ada turned to the trusted friends who had always been quietly present in the background of the Lovelaces' lives.

Margaretta Burr was a talented watercolour painter who had taken her sketch pad along when she and her husband travelled around the Middle East with Lord Lovelace's Egyptologist friend, Sir John Gardner Wilkinson. At Aldermaston Court, a splendid faux-Elizabethan house standing above its own lake in Berkshire countryside (Daniel Burr had rebuilt it from scratch after a massive fire in the 1840s), the Burrs and Wilkinsons lived almost as a single family. On 21 November, Margaretta visited a wan and bedbound Ada in London to glean ideas for a great fancy-dress ball she was planning to welcome in the coming year. It was agreed that Aldermaston should become a second home to Ada's children during this sad and difficult time. Meanwhile, discussions with Mrs Burr about young Annabella's future encouraged Ada to adopt a new policy towards the daughter whom she now began to treat as her confidante and – as she fondly threatened '(unless you *escape* by marrying) . . . my Vice-Queen in everything'.

A vice-queen's duties were not onerous. At Horsley, where Ada's daughter gaily reported that dear, earnest Miss Wächter was urging her to be 'neat as a new *pig*' (with five underlinings), Annabella was instructed (on 29 November) to act as a grown-up hostess. She was to be sure to conduct guests around the earl's beloved tower ('You know that the *Tower* is decidedly Papa's first born, & dearer to him than kith or kin or life itself'), and prepare herself to preside at the Boxing Day Hunt breakfast, when Lovelace's new Great Hall became a sounding sea of horns, hounds and red coats. In early January (following a cosy Christmas with the Lushingtons at Ockham), Annabella was to make her grown-up debut at Mrs Burr's great masquerade, to which Papa would accompany his daughter, wearing the 'Albanian' uniform in which – so a fond wife fancied – William always looked his most Byronic.

Meanwhile, behind her daughter's back, Ada was urging her reluctant husband to play his part. Mrs Burr was counting upon him to attend the ball; Annabella could not possibly attend without an escort; William's Egyptologist friend, Gardner Wilkinson, had already picked out a pretty Spanish costume for the dear girl. And besides, Ada weakly pleaded, surely the Crow would wish to see 'how handsome and admired *yr daughter* will be!' Pressed by all, Lovelace gave in. An excited and gravely beautiful Cinderella went to the Burrs' great ball with her father at her side, a magnificent figure in his glittering uniform.

∽

Relations with Ada's mother were less easily managed. A year later (15 December 1852), Lady Byron would remind her son-in-law (while laying the blame squarely upon him) that Ada had forbidden her mother to visit their London house during the entirety of the previous February. This seems to be correct. In the correspondence, a matching gap appears between 25 January and 28 February, at which point Ada pointedly ascribed a modest sign of better health to the fact she had been allowed to rest in undisturbed solitude. Perhaps from a wish not to cause alarm to Lady Byron, she neglected to mention that her condition was nevertheless serious enough for kindly Agnes Greig and Mrs Burr to have organised a month's rota of night care, during which one of them spent each night upon a sofa close to Ada's bed.

On 4 March, the septuagenarian Stephen Lushington paid the invalid a visit at Great Cumberland Place. He was horrified by what he saw. 'The marks of reduction & suffering were very strong,' he reported to Lady Byron, while adding that Charles Locock (whom he knew well) seemed, nevertheless, to entertain hopes of a recovery.

Discreet, kind and deeply attached both to Lady Byron and her daughter, Lushington's delicate commission from Annabella was to obtain a list of Ada's debts. Expecting the worst, he was pleasantly surprised. All the same, it struck Lushington that the £450 identified by the invalid could hardly be comprehensive of Lady Lovelace's obligations. Perhaps, further debts would be recollected at some later date?

'I have an interest in Ada which neither time nor circumstance

can ever shake off,' the old lawyer confessed to Lady Byron on
30 April. Clearly, even in her weakened state, Ada Lovelace had
been able to exert her unique charm and substantially hoodwink
one of the country's shrewdest legal minds. Not only did her debts
vastly exceed the sum that she had named, but she was still using
Mary Wilson to place secret bets on horses. On 4 April 1852
(eight days before Ada first admitted to her mother that she was
still enmeshed in 'pecuniary affairs'), one of the countess's regular team of unsavoury tipsters congratulated her on a win. Lady
Byron, fobbed off with pleasant assurances that Byron Ockham
was reported to be becoming an ornament to his naval profession,
and that Ada herself was now hard at work upon 'an awful amount
of writing', was even informed that plans were still afoot for the
Lovelaces to rent out their London house and go to Spain. Ada, by
the way, had been most amused by Miss Julia Smith's analysis of
her handwriting (a sample had been sent to this decidedly amateur
graphologist by an admiring Annabella). But was dear Miss Smith
really prepared to discern that she, the enterprising and gleefully
fanciful Ada Lovelace, lacked imagination?

'Oh I am such a *sick* wretch!' Ada suddenly burst out at the end of
this long, chatty and exceptionally misleading letter to her mother.
That impetuous cry, apart from a glancing mention of the worry of
'particular circumstances' at present, was the only hint of agitation
in a letter written on the very same day that Ada was threatened
with a personal visit on 21 April 'unless I hear there is increment'
from one of the rough-mannered tipsters of whom she was becoming
increasingly afraid. The hint was heard. When Stephen Lushington
passed along the news that he suspected some form of blackmail
was afoot, Lady Byron consulted her bank book. On 19 and 21
May, she presented Lord Lovelace with the generous sum of £2,800.
Unfortunately for Ada, however, its use carried her mother's habitually firm restrictions. The money was to cover house repairs and
Ada's medical care: nothing more. Epsom and Ascot were coming
up and Lady Lovelace was desperate for cash.

It was at this point that Ada turned for help to John Padwick, a man who made his name in the racing world by fleecing young aristocrats through his moneylending arrangements. It may well have been at Padwick's request that William Lovelace (having sworn to Lady Byron that he would oppose any further gambling on horses) now provided his wife with a confidential document that authorised her to bet without a limit. Any idea that Lovelace stood outside the gambling ring was buried by this transaction. He was in it, up to the hilt.*

On 25 May 1852, the day before a rain-sodden Derby, Mary Wilson received a tip to back Hobbie Noble 'for a great stake'. Hobbie Noble (4/1) came in fourth. Little Harry – the favourite whom Ada had elected to back against strong advice – came nowhere.† 'Pray let her Ladyship understand in as certain a manner as can be supposed ...' was the menacing opening of her tipster's next note to Mary Wilson.

The game was up. Noting nervously that her mother was now determined to 'extract all furies', the countess agreed to a pre-lunch meeting at which to seek a favour that she had hitherto hesitated to request. A deal was being negotiated. Ada was ready to confess, but only if her mother produced more funds.

Tracking the sequence and guessing the content of Ada Lovelace's multiple undated confessions is like peeling the layers away from an invisible onion. What we do know about this particular revelation is that Ada, writing about it the following morning, expressed relief. She had unburdened herself of what she called 'the Dragon'. Having done so, Ada was impatient to see her mother again as soon as possible, in order 'that I may be finally satisfied *you* won't devour me'.

---

* Previously, biographers have assumed that Lovelace's letter related to Ada's betting at Doncaster. The later 1852 date adds more weight to Lady Byron's bitter sense that her son-in-law had betrayed her trust in him. At Leamington, Lovelace had promised to oppose any future attempts at gambling by his wife.
† John Padwick's notorious talent as a moneylender was not matched by his skill on the course. A month before the Derby, he sold his own horse, Little Joe. It won the race.

More information emerges from the meticulously detailed letters which Lady Byron now began despatching to Emily Fitzhugh, a trusted old friend from the Siddons family circle. (As requested, Miss Fitzhugh restored the entire cache to the sender after Ada's death.) To Emily, Annabella wrote on 9 June that firmness had been used and a confession forced, although 'tenderness in a measure neutralised my own influence & suffered a worse one to prevail'. By 'a worse one', Lady Byron could have been alluding to John Crosse, for whose continued visits to his ailing patient Charles Locock innocently petitioned to Lovelace in August, on the grounds that they were 'such a source of comfort and happiness'. Probably, Ada's confession to Lady Byron concerned her racing losses. More certainly, it included a truly shocking and unlooked-for admission.

Frantic for money, both to support the needs of a greedy lover and to cover losses suffered by herself and the ring, Ada had descended to fraud. She had arranged with Crosse to pawn her husband's most treasured heirloom: the Lovelace diamonds. In their place, doubtless with Crosse's assistance, she had substituted paste replicas. Lord Lovelace, she assured her mother, knew nothing about it. But if he did discover her crime . . . Ada made it clear that she was terrified of the consequences.

Whatever Lady Byron may have thought about this revelation, she could not bear the thought of exposing frail, unhappy Ada to her husband's wrath. Having extracted the broker's details, she arranged for the jewels to be discreetly retrieved (the sum involved was £900, inclusive of interest) and restored to a woman who would clearly never be in a position to wear them again. Lord Lovelace was not informed.

On 23 July, John Crosse paid one of a series of covert visits to Ada's London home. On that same day at Horsley, Woronzow Greig told Lord Lovelace that a little private detective work had led him to the startling conclusion that Mr Crosse was no bachelor, but a married man, one with children and with a secret home in Reigate. Lovelace, still unaware of any special significance in the friendship between Crosse and his own wife, promised to further the investigations with an interview of his own.

Secret marriages and hidden mistresses were far from rare in mid-Victorian England. Ludicrous though Crosse's improbable alibi of housing the secret family of a naughty uncle had sounded to Greig, the earl himself was in no mood to challenge the tale that Crosse set before him. Worried about money, miserable about his unreconciled feud with his mother-in-law and heartbroken at the prospect of his wife's approaching death (let alone the ongoing spectacle of her appalling sufferings), Lord Lovelace had almost reached the end of his tether. The elaborate fabrications of John Crosse were beyond his interest. Having briskly interviewed the young man and drawn up a statement of his considered opinion (that Crosse's alibi was indeed untruthful), Lovelace dismissed what he considered to be a subject of minor significance from his mind.

The intensity of Lovelace's sadness is apparent from the record of Ada's deterioration which he began on 29 July 1852, intending to monitor his wife's last moments as a memorial gift to his mother-in-law. The previous day, William had been advised of a new hard swelling in Ada's uterus; Lady Byron was simultaneously informed by Dr Locock that her daughter would be dead within two months.

Lovelace's medical journal – written in a book small enough to sit within the palm of his hand – opened at the time when his daughter was paying a week's visit from the Lushingtons' home at Ockham to her parents' London house. Anxious not to frighten the girl too much, Ada forced herself to assume the semblance of a normal routine. Each day, Lady Lovelace emerged fully dressed from the large bow-windowed room at the back of the first floor. Slowly, she dragged herself down the curving staircase to the hall. Seated at the dining-room table, she picked at morsels of a midday meal that neither she nor William had the appetite to eat. Henry Phillips, whose father had represented Lord Byron in all the glory of his Albanian attire, came in to paint a profile of Lady Lovelace, wan as a starved sparrow, her emaciated hands resting like claws upon the piano keys. On 3 August, Annabella wrote to her brother Ralph out in Switzerland that Mamma was still just able to play duets with her. Their mother seemed quite different nowadays: 'so gentle and kind ... like what I should imagine an angel to be.'

If not quite yet reformed, Ada had persuaded her mother that she did now genuinely repent for all her sins. Writing to thank the intensely religious Agnes Greig for all her acts of kindness, Lady Byron entreated the sympathetic Scotswoman to console Ada and to tell her – her words offer an appalling insight into Lady Byron's mind – that these sufferings were God's way of ministering to his erring child: 'a Father's love to bring her to Christ'. Florence Nightingale was simultaneously asked for advice about setting up a cottage hospital in Kirkby, seemingly at Lady Lovelace's request.* Lady Byron's own gift to her daughter of a book of sermons was accompanied by a much admired new life of Margaret Fuller, whose sole manuscript of her masterpiece (a study of the new Italy that was coming into being under Garibaldi's fiery leadership) vanished forever in 1850 when Fuller, her child and her young husband drowned in a shipwreck that took place just off the coast of New York. (Fuller was returning to her homeland from Italy, in order to preside over the American birth of her book.) It's true that Ada was passionately interested in America; nevertheless, it's difficult to suppose that the story of Fuller's lost masterpiece offered much solace to a young woman whose own ambitions remained so unfulfilled.

Neither young Annabella's wishes nor Lady Byron's pious endeavours would ever make an angel out of Ada. On 3 August, Lord Lovelace recorded that his wife and he held 'sad talks' about Greig's revelations concerning John Crosse. Three days later, Ada secretly received her lover. Once again handing over the diamonds her mother had retrieved, the dying countess sent Crosse straight back

---

* Florence suggested that Lady Lovelace's village hospital might follow the layout and system of Kaiserswerth-am-Rhein, a German training school for nurses where she had studied in 1851 (FN to AINB, n.d. 1852, Dep. Lovelace Byron 94, fols. 88–92).

to the same pawnbroker's on the Strand. She also – seemingly of her own free will – handed Crosse an invaluable document for possible future use to blackmail her husband. This was the 'limitless' letter of credit that Lovelace had rashly provided to his wife in order to cover her final season of racing bets.

John Crosse's visit excited old passions in Ada. During that same week, writing with a savagery that takes one's breath away, the countess told her mother that she longed for Lovelace to go away and let her alone. Contemptuously, she compared her unfortunate husband to a needy dog, one who could not leave his master. The spectacle of his grief disgusted her.

So it was one day; with the next, Ada's mercurial mind shifted into an altered set of opinions. She was consistent only in the dauntless courage with which she bore the pain, the sickness, the sleeplessness and the fear of grey oblivion that had become her daily attendants.

Only the children remained a source of real happiness. Young Annabella provided continual pleasure with a series of lively letters adorned with her own graceful pen and ink images. (An entire aviary of birds arrived, followed by comic sketches from everyday life, landscapes – it seemed there was nothing that this talented fifteen-year-old could not represent.) And then, five days after Crosse's visit, a strapping youth with bronzed cheeks and a seaman's rolling gait sauntered into his mother's room. Ada had warned her son in advance of what he would see. For herself, she was overjoyed by the tenderness of Ockham's manner and the handsomeness of his face. There was no want of feeling in him now, she rejoiced to her mother that day. 'Quite the contrary.' Down at Aldermaston, the muscular young viscount took the Burr boys out to sail on the lake in a washtub that he had rigged up with a sail. His sister meanwhile wrote to tell Ada (with seeming innocence) about a toy racing game that she had found in a box. 'It is very amusing for some people are so indescribably unlucky with their horses,' Annabella remarked to her mother on 18 August. Was the comment innocuous, or had an unusually observant girl learned more than was intended during her week-long stay at Great Cumberland Place?

Slowly, hidden truths were beginning to emerge into the light. One day earlier, a horrified Lady Byron told Lushington that she had learned from Greig of a previous and hitherto unmentioned pawning of the family diamonds, one of which Lovelace himself had been aware. What hurt her most, so she wrote, was the realisation that Ada had lied to her. 'I cannot forget that the motive made use of to move me, was the dread of his ever *knowing* of such a circumstance ...' Advised by Lushington, Annabella suppressed the urge to challenge her son-in-law. Instead, gritting her teeth, she wrote to offer peace. With it, came her wish that the two of them might learn to stop putting 'the worst construction on each other's motives'. Quoting these sentiments back to Greig on 20 August, Lovelace presciently remarked that he doubted her ability to stick to such a resolution. 'Yet my heart yearns towards Lady Byron.'

ॐ

Ada, meanwhile, was still struggling to conceal her tracks from the gaze of an increasingly suspicious and tenacious mother. On 12 August, Charles Babbage was summoned and given a draft of Ada's will. Instructions included the obtaining (somehow) of £600 from Lady Byron, to be distributed just as Babbage had been 'privately' directed in another (lost) note. Babbage was also asked to look through certain papers that Ada gave him, and to destroy what he judged unfit to preserve.

Given that Ada would surely not have wished any of her scientific work to be destroyed, it's fair to assume that the papers in question related to her secret racing life. Any surviving connection between Babbage himself and the racecourse appears only in the inventor's continuing loyalty to Mary Wilson, the woman whose name was most frequently employed in the tipsters' notes.

The fear of impending death was growing strong. 'I want *Ralph* back,' Ada pleaded to her mother on 15 August. On the same day, William was asked to remind Colonel Wildman of his promise that Lady Lovelace should be buried beside her father. Ada was to lie within the Byron vault 'at her own desire', Lady Byron informed Mrs Villiers on 7 September. Privately, Annabella resolved to erect her own monument to Ada, discreetly tucked away in the old family churchyard of Kirkby Mallory.

On 19 August, the least savoury of Ada's racing colleagues paid a visit to Great Cumberland Place. Mr Fleming had come to discuss a life insurance policy that the countess had been persuaded to take out prior to the diagnosis of a fatal disease. Its value was £600. When he left, Fleming had pocketed a signed note assigning him the entire £600, in exchange for the ten shillings he had just placed in Lady Lovelace's hand.

Did Ada know what she was doing? Or had she been frightened into doing as Fleming asked? Increasingly, as the cancer took its hold, Lady Lovelace spoke of sinister men who were trying to gain access to her room. It's likely that Mr Fleming's possible return with further demands was preying on her fearful mind.

❧

The pains were becoming unbearable. On one occasion, Lady Byron was summoned from her nearby residence at two in the morning. Together with Lovelace, she tried to soothe his writhing, screaming wife as Ada arched and scrabbled and crouched upon all fours, fighting against a pain that neither mesmerism (Annabella's contribution) nor drugs could now alleviate. Still, there were moments of respite. Ada herself could no longer even attempt to pick out the old airs and waltzes which Lovelace remembered having once charmed him so much. But she could still listen with pleasure when Fanny Kemble's graceful sister, Adelaide Sartoris, came in to sing to her. Towards the end of August, Ada asked if Charles Dickens would come and read to her about little Paul Dombey, gliding into death with the peace that poor Ada craved and could not find. Three years earlier, invited to visit her home in Brighton, Dickens had teased Byron's charmingly imperious daughter that he felt like Aladdin being summoned into the Princess Badroulbadour's bathhouse. Seeing her at Great

Cumberland Place on this final occasion, Dickens was (so Lovelace recorded in his diary) 'wonderfully struck with her courage and calmness'.

On 22 August, Annabella and Byron Ockham were allowed to pay another brief visit to their mother. Tenderly, they helped their father to bathe Ada's hands – the only action that could still bring a little relief from pain – while she talked dreamily about returning to the Lake District and how happy they might all be. That evening, Dr West, the quietly efficient doctor who was now also living in the house, reported an alarming deterioration in his patient's condition. Mattresses were hastily laid across the floorboards and propped against the walls, in order to prevent Ada from harming herself as she lashed out. 'Her energy was something very awful,' Lovelace noted in his tiny journal the next day, and yet, as Ada swept about the room, throwing aside the restraining arms of her mother and her husband, her expression had been 'wonderful'.

Lovelace himself was beginning to crack under the strain. A water bed (a thick rubber sheet laid over a tub of water) had been installed to ease her suffering as Ada became unable even to empty her bladder without cries of agony. He spent a day arranging pots of flowers at points where she could see the bright colours from her bed, while, with her mother as scribe, Ada whispered her recollection of a happy visit she had once paid alone to Charles Dickens at Gad's Hill. And at last, on 26 August, ten days after Dr West had urged Lady Byron to speed her grandson's return from Switzerland, Ralph arrived. Fearing the impact of Ada's haggard appearance upon a susceptible 13-year-old, his grandmother had delayed his return; now, Lady Byron hurried him away to join his siblings in the country, at the welcoming home of the Burrs.

There were occasional moments when Annabella found it impossible to maintain a glacial manner towards the son-in-law whom she held responsible for Ada's misfortunes. She noted them. Once, when the dying woman's torments became almost unbearable to witness, Lady Byron touched Lord Lovelace upon the arm in a sign of silent sympathy. When he remarked that his pale, waterborne wife looked like the drowned Ophelia, Annabella agreed. On 31 August, Lady Byron was sitting by Ada's bed when Lovelace tiptoed in. As he bent to kiss the dying woman's hands, Ada pulled his head down until his mouth touched her cheek (but it was only with 'a sort of instinct', Lovelace wanly wrote). Joining his hands to her mother's across the bed, she entreated them both to have mercy on her. A moment later, Ada's flickering thoughts had swerved back into the realm of nightmare. Perhaps – it was still her greatest terror – she would be buried alive? And then, when once she was dead, what sufferings still lay in store for such a wicked woman? Could they last for a million years?

Lord Lovelace had maintained his daily record of Ada's agonisingly slow decline for an entire month. The endeavour was breaking his heart. On 31 August, he made his final entry and closed the tiny pages up.

Perhaps the diary ended for a bleaker reason. On 1 September, following a private discussion with her mother, Ada asked to see her husband alone. She disclosed much – but far from all – about her secret relationship with John Crosse. Describing this interview at second hand to Stephen Lushington, Annabella said that the earl had called upon God to forgive his wife for her sins in a way that she personally considered downright Pharisaical. What shocked Lady Byron far more was the evidence that her son-in-law had lost his temper with his dying wife. Annabella had experienced one of Lovelace's fearsome rages at Leamington. She saw that same fury in his face as he emerged from the sickroom. Ada acknowledged that her husband had been very bitter towards her. However indignantly protective Lady Byron may have felt, it is hard to see how Lovelace could have been anything else.

On 21 September, Lady Byron formally took up residence in the graceful crescent house on Great Cumberland Place that she had chosen for her beloved children as their London home. She noted that she had moved in only because it was her daughter's wish.

Writing to Miss Fitzhugh six days later, Annabella ironically remarked that she believed she had the qualities necessary to govern a colony of convicts, if so required. While hardly flattering to the servants of the Lovelaces' household, the implication was clear. Lady Byron was now in charge. Anyone who displeased her was dismissed. Outside servants were brought in to follow her directions. Lovelace did not object. Neither did the two lawyers, Greig and Lushington, whose repeated visits bore witness to the fact that the last shreds of Ada's secret life were now being exposed to pitiless view, while urgent thought was applied to how much of the evidence should be destroyed.

'I dread beyond anything the idea of you living far away. If I could not see you often, I should feel so lonely now.' The words are Ada's in a note to Lady Byron which evidently predates but poignantly represents the final harrowing phase of their relationship. Writing to Emily Fitzhugh, Annabella suggested (once again) that Ada had grown truly penitent. A mass of pencilled scrawls, executed in a faint and trembling hand, appeared to bear her out. In one, a reference to verse 8 of Psalm 17, Ada asked her mother, despite everything ('*malgré tout*'), to 'keep me as the apple of thy eye, hide me under the shadow of thy wings from the wicked that oppress me . . .'

Even now, Ada's submission was not absolute. There was nothing penitent in the fierce allusion to herself as Christ to which one note now drew attention: '*You have condemned, you have killed the righteous man . . .*'

Lady Byron had become the chatelaine, but her son-in-law seldom left the house. On 7 October, however, the earl prepared an official note to state that he would be away for a few days (probably at Aldermaston with the children) and that, during his absence, 'Lady Byron should be considered in every respect as the mistress of my house'.

The timing is significant. Four days later, while the earl was still away, Annabella recorded for the eyes of Lushington – but not for those of the absent Lovelace – her dismaying discovery that Ada had allowed John Crosse to pawn her jewels a second time over at the beginning of August. This had only just emerged. Once again, Lady Byron covered the cost of the diamonds' discreet redemption. On this occasion, however, she did not restore the jewels to Ada's care.

Ada's long concealment of this second pawning was gallantly ascribed by a loyal parent to a prolonged loss of memory that could have been caused by a stroke or seizure. In fact, this was the dreadful moment at which Lady Byron was forced to accept that she could no longer trust her daughter in any respect. What she could and would still do, with passion, was to defend and exalt her. Nobody, not even well-meaning Anna Jameson, who imprudently criticised Ada for denying her a final deathbed visit, was permitted to say a single word against Lady Lovelace. (It was that unrecorded but evidently harsh comment about Ada – together with the discovery that Mrs Jameson had been a secret provider of funds to her daughter – that severed this closest of all Lady Byron's female friendships.)

∽∽

On the evening of 21 October, Byron Ockham arrived to see his mother for a last time before he returned to sea, newly commissioned as an officer. Watching him as he peeped in at Ada through a half-open door – the doctors had advised against any emotional farewells – his grandmother caught a glimpse of the wretchedness in the young man's eyes before he turned and tiptoed back down the stairs. Ockham's adoring sister came into Lady Byron's room in tears that night.

It should already have been clear from Ockham's rough manner (if not the tattoos he bore upon his hands) that such a youth would never accept the elevated rank that had been imposed upon him. (Lovelace, using every connection he knew of to secure his son an officer's rank, had even procured a glowing reference from Lord Zetland's brother, Admiral Dundas.)

Directly after leaving his mother's home, Byron stuffed the hated new uniform into a carpet bag, posted it back to Horsley Towers – and vanished. Charles Noel, who had always been more attached to this wild, affectionate boy than his own hardworking son and namesake, volunteered to track the runaway down. A discreet advertisement (no identifying name was given, but reference was made to lightly tattooed hands, a deep slow voice and a seaman's gait) enabled a detective to run the fugitive to earth at a Liverpool inn for sailors. Here, after initially denying his identity, Lord Ockham gave himself up on 9 November.

A month later, Ada's eldest son was sulkily aboard again, serving on Lord Nelson's own old flagship, the *Victory*. The posting was no sinecure (the battered old ship had been converted into a depot store that was permanently lodged at Portsmouth), but it meant that a watchful eye could be kept on the rebellious young man while decisions were taken about his future role. Helped by Greig's and Lushington's excellent naval connections, Byron Ockham was despatched in 1853 to the Malta station in the Mediterranean, soon to become a naval hub point for the Crimean War. It must have pleased Annabella to think that the boy was following in his grandfather's hallowed wake. (Byron, during his youthful travels, had spent three weeks at Malta.)

⸉⸊

Ada knew nothing about Ockham's defection. Little active consciousness remained in the twilight world that now offered Lady Lovelace only intermittent release from pain. She spoke in riddles, calling her illness a good bargain and claiming that treacherous conspirators wanted to separate her from the mother to whom she now clung. She imagined shadows into looming figures who blotted out the light from the doorway. Terrified of what lay in store for her, she nevertheless longed for death.

The end, so cruelly slow to arrive, came suddenly on the evening of 27 November. The two lawyers were paying one of their visits to sort through Ada's papers. Annabella, worn out by a long day of watching by Ada's side, had nodded off in her room when Lovelace and Greig rapped on her door. It was half-past nine. The two men gave her the news she had both dreaded and longed for. Her beautiful, eccentric, brilliant child, aged only thirty-six – the age at which her husband, too, had gone – was dead.

Accompanying the soberly dressed men to Ada's room, Annabella found herself unable to register what she had been told. How could her daughter have slipped away during one of the rare moments when she herself was not keeping watch beside her child? Could she in truth be dead? Bending over the bed, Lady Byron held her candle close to Ada's parted lips and waited, watching for a breath that would cause the flame to waver. She raised the candle higher. Ada's eyes did not open. Once again, she brought the flickering candle back to catch a breath from the pale mouth.

About to repeat the process, Annabella found herself being gently ushered out. Back in her room, Lady Byron sat at her desk, thinking. Had they only given her time, she could have shown those blundering intruders that Ada had in fact waited to die until a beloved mother was stood at her side. Picking up her pen, Lady Byron recorded in a firm hand that Ada had died at ten o'clock, while in her parent's presence. That was how it should have been. Her record would make it so.

Later, when the house was silent, Annabella went to sit beside her daughter's body. Alone, she watched the slow hardening of the haggard features that she herself had carefully sketched almost three months earlier. Too late, she regretted having agreed with Lovelace that the children – her granddaughter was actually present, fast asleep in a different part of the house – should see their mother once more, before the burial box enclosed her for the last long journey to Newstead. To remember the extraordinary, passionate Ada in all the radiant glow of her vitality: surely that was the kinder way?

Down in his study, Lord Lovelace was also awake, writing letters in a strong, steady hand that belied his own exhaustion. The burden of each was the same. Addressing Lady Hester (she had written just once, and briefly, to enquire how long Ada had left to live), he pointedly dwelt upon the exceptional humanity of his mother-in-law. 'It is fortunate that Lady Byron has been domiciled with us during this time,' Lovelace told his mother: '... her gentleness & presence of mind have been the main support of her suffering daughter as well as me'.

There is no doubt that Lord Lovelace meant what he said, and yet there was an almost obsessive note in his endless repetition, in every letter he wrote that night, of that particular mantra. Paying tribute over and again to the Hen's gentle practicality, he seemed to hope that he might yet earn her forgiveness.

CHAPTER TWENTY-THREE

LIFE AFTER ADA
(1852–3)

'The Rainbow'
Bow down in hope, in thanks, all ye who mourn
Where e'en that peerless arch of radiant hues
Surpassing earthly tints, the storm subdued.
Of nature's strife and tears. 'Tis heaven-born
To soothe the sad, the sinning and the forlorn.
A lovely loving token; to infuse
The hope, the faith that Pow'r divine endures
With latent good the woes by which we're torn
'Tis like sweet repentance of the skies,
To beckon all by the sense of sin opprest,
Revealing harmony from tears and sighs;
A pledge, that deep implanted in the breast
A hidden light may burn that never dies,
But burst thro' storms in purest hues exprest.

AAL

On 28 November 1852, the morning after her daughter's death, Lady
Byron moved into Brown's, the Dover Street hotel that had been

set up in 1837 (with her own financial support) by James Brown, one of Lord Byron's former valets, and his wife, Sarah Willis, who had briefly served as Annabella's maid at Piccadilly Terrace.* The Browns respected their guest's need for discretion. When a neatly bonneted Florence Nightingale called at the hotel the following day to offer her condolences to the woman she revered and admired above almost any other, she was informed that Lady Byron was unable to receive callers.

Thwarted in her original plan, Florence set off instead to inspect what she soulfully referred to as 'the poor house itself'. Young Annabella was still in residence, but did not appear. Lord Lovelace had accompanied the coffin (placed inside a private carriage) on the Midland railway line to Worksop, near Newstead.

And why on earth, an inquisitive Miss Nightingale pondered, would the family seek to draw attention to their link with Lord Byron, of whose incestuous relationship with Augusta Leigh all the Nightingale family had long since been informed by his widow? It did not occur to her that the hapless Lady Lovelace had chosen her own burial place.

> I thought of the words 'conceived in sin' and what an account
> that man, her father, has to render, from whose excesses her
> dreadful sufferings must date, and wondered they should like to
> bring her near him in her death.

Florence's long letter has never before been looked at in connection with Ada's death. Revealing both of Florence's own attitude to emotion ('She never lost her self command,' Miss Nightingale remarked admiringly of Lady Byron's care for her dying daughter) and of her nosiness (Lady Byron's personal maid had been coaxed

---

* Annabella's kindness to James Brown was part of an ongoing commitment to act upon what she imagined to have been her late husband's wishes. 'I know she secretly fulfils her husband's claims and honours his drafts upon posterity,' an admiring Florence Nightingale wrote in an undated letter to Parthenope, her sister.

into volunteering that it was 'a very good thing that poor Lady Lovelace was dead'), the real interest lies in the collateral detail that Florence's letter provides.

The woman who welcomed Miss Nightingale into 6 Great Cumberland Place on 29 November was none other than her own Mrs Clark, the no-nonsense housekeeper who would later travel out with her to Scutari in the Crimea. It was during discussions about Ada's apparent desire for a village hospital to be established at Kirkby Mallory that Florence had offered to loan Mrs Clark to Lady Byron as a capable (and above all, discreet) assistant. Mrs Clark's role at Cumberland Place had probably taken the form of turning and lifting the dying patient, emptying bedpans and carrying trays. It was only during the last days that Mrs Clark had been given a more delicate commission, one of which Florence now became aware. 'I am sure,' Miss Nightingale wrote to her sister:

> they may be most thankful they have Mrs Clark there to depend
> on. She has burnt everything, all the dreadful letters which
> would have broken their hearts to know of. Mrs Clark is not
> going to stay, she says she cannot bear it – but has consented to
> remain as long as they want her so much.*

∽৩৫∼

Miss Nightingale's letter helps to explain why both Dr Lushington and Woronzow Greig were visiting Great Cumberland Place on the evening that Ada Lovelace died. Evidently, this pair of trusted lawyers were still assessing what to suppress and what to preserve in order to protect the family from scandal. They did their best. The preserved family papers do not reveal Mrs Clark's presence or what the 'dreadful letters' were that she had been instructed to destroy.

---

* Mrs Clark spent the end of that bleak year at Horsley Towers. Annabella, writing to her grandmother, reported that she was a 'wonderful person' who made the schoolroom cheerful, while cooking them 'very good *dinners*' and 'nice *biscuits*' (Wentworth Papers, 54090).

When Parthenope Nightingale, many years later, obligingly searched the Nightingale family's archives for any letters that might interest Ada's son, Ralph, she reported that none had been found. Of the copious and seemingly confidential correspondence between Lady Byron and her close friend, Julia Smith (Julia was Florence and Parthenope's unmarried aunt), not one trace survives.

ༀ

On 3 December 1852, Ada's coffin – her husband had made sure that it was a handsome one (silver-handled, mounted with the Lovelace coat of arms and mantled in violet-coloured velvet) – was conveyed from Newstead to nearby Hucknall Torkard, to be laid in the crowded Byron vault alongside her father and beneath the plaque on which Augusta Leigh, naming herself as the donor, had created a last enduring link to the brother she adored. Ada's own plaque, by her specific request, carried only the dates of her birth and death, together with the information that she was Byron's daughter and Lord Lovelace's wife.

The crowds at the church gate were large. The funeral itself was an intentionally private ceremony. The widowed Sir George Crauford and Peter Locke King represented the widower's family, with the 7th Lord Byron and Charles Noel appearing for the Byron side. The only outsiders, with the exception of the Wildmans of Newstead, were the two lawyers who now faced the tricky task of reconciling Lady Byron with her unhappy son-in-law.

Woronzow Greig had wasted no time. While still at Newstead, he read aloud to Lushington the ardent appeal that he himself had prepared. Gratitude was now Lord Lovelace's chief thought, Greig wished Lady Byron to understand. Every shadow of (unjust) reproach would be withdrawn. A full admission would be made of how her son-in-law had wronged her, when visiting Leamington in June 1851, by undervaluing the real concern Lady Byron felt for her only child. The earl was willing to become as wax in her hands, to remodel as she pleased, if only Lady Byron would not abandon him in this time of affliction.

Stephen Lushington suggested a different approach. He advised that the appeal should come directly from Lovelace himself – and that it should be sent out before Lady Byron issued her own commands. The thinking was surely right, but neither Greig nor Lushington had appreciated the high degree of Lovelace's pride or of Lady Byron's stubbornness. Lovelace might well be feeling remorseful, but he was not willing to forgive the fact that the double pawning (bluntly referred to by the earl as 'the robbery') of his jewels had been concealed from him until after his wife's death. Annabella's tart response, delivered via Lushington – Lady Byron now declined to address her son-in-law directly – was that, since she herself had uncomplainingly borne the total cost of their double recovery, the earl had nothing to grumble about. He had his diamonds; what, then, was his complaint? And how dared Lovelace compare her prudent discretion to his own deceit about – and complicity in – her daughter's gambling! Annabella did not resist the opportunity to remind her son-in-law of the 'unlimited confidence' he had formerly expressed in the very man responsible for the 'robbery': John Crosse.

There is no doubt that Lady Byron was being extremely harsh. (Ralph would later hold the mean-spirited and blame-filled letters despatched to his father after the trauma of Ada's death as responsible for an ineradicable hardening in Lord Lovelace's personality.) But other elements were also at work. It was during the week that the earl received this ferocious letter (it was written on 16 December 1852) that the bereft Lovelace finally began to comprehend how deeply his beloved wife had betrayed him with John Crosse. Writing back the following day to beg the Hen for an interview – it was never granted – Lovelace described the desolation that he felt, now that 'every cherished conviction of my married life has been unsettled'. Did Lady Byron seek to augment his sorrows? If only she would tell him what, precisely, it was that he had done to displease her! All he begged for now was the chance to understand, and to be understood.

The more that Lovelace grovelled, the more merciless his adversary became. Any hint of criticism of Ada from her husband was seized upon as evidence of the wretched earl's vindictive and unforgiving spirit. And how dared he breathe a word (he hadn't) against 'the Mother whose child you depreciate & condemn *beyond measure*'!

On 11 January 1853, Woronzow Greig advised his bewildered friend to recognise that Lady Byron's views were indeed 'very peculiar' and stop arguing. Better if he had. Instead, within a day, the distraught Lovelace had ignited another row. Rashly, he accused his mother-in-law of using 'casuistry' to score cheap points. The earl had forgotten that Lady Byron always liked to have the last word in a dispute. Retreating behind a wall of silence, she simply closed the door.

Where the law was concerned, however, Lady Byron was meticulous. She promised and paid £5,000 towards Ada's debts (after deducting the cost of recovering Lord Lovelace's pawned jewels). She was scrupulous in following Ada's wishes concerning the future of the children. Annabella would spend six weeks of each year with her grandmother. Ralph would remain entirely under Lady Byron's supervision. Since Lord Ockham wanted no part of his heritage, arrangements would be made for her younger grandson to become her legal heir. Young Annabella, too, would receive a generous bequest. All this, Lady Byron was prepared to do – and nothing more.

∽✸∾

Excluded from his mother-in-law's life, Lovelace finally found a way to express his feelings when, in 1862, he decide to honour the memory of his late wife, deep within the heart of Horsley Towers.

Vaulted, spangled, pillared and painted, the earl's secret shrine to Ada Lovelace is a gilded treasure box of fantasy run wild. High above the unconsecrated altar of his private chapel, William Lovelace installed two large grey tablets. The one on the left, named for Ada, has been pointedly emblazoned with the ten commandments that Ada so often chose to ignore. Facing it across the altar is an identical slab of slate.

Not one word of eulogy or indictment appears upon the tablet that bears only Lady Byron's name. Lord Lovelace's tribute to the woman he had venerated, trusted and finally lost speaks for the depth of his bitterness by the absolute blankness of its face.

છ્ઝ

The joyous old days when the Hen and the Crow fondly conspired about how best to protect and cherish their elusive and enchanting charge, the Bird, were gone, never to return. On 9 February 1853, Annabella icily reminded her son-in-law that she held his own imprudent behaviour responsible for what she now vaguely referred to as her daughter's 'aberrations'. Greig meanwhile advised his sympathetic colleague, Stephen Lushington, that the hapless Lord Lovelace had just discovered 'an additional act of treachery' on the part of his late wife.

Prior to the final stages of her illness, Lady Lovelace had been persuaded by some of her racing acquaintances to insure her life for £600. In January 1853, Mr Fleming, Dr Malcolm and John Crosse lined up to submit their rival claims to that sum. Fleming had already persuaded the dying countess to assign him sole rights for a paltry ten shillings. Dr Malcolm, to whom Ada had earlier persuaded her husband to loan £1,800 (only £200 had been repaid at the time of her death), stated that he also deserved the insurance money, in lieu of his personal discharge of Ada's liabilities. (The fact that the Zetlands' physician had actually won £2,000 from Ada's tips went unmentioned.) John Crosse's claim took the nastier form of black-mail. He already held a cache of Ada's letters. By 9 February 1853, Lovelace knew that his wife had also given her lover the letter in which the earl had incriminated himself by personally authorising her betting activities. Crosse now threatened to publish it.

By 26 February, an exhausted Woronzow Greig was able to report to Lovelace that, while he himself had 'fairly broken down under the part which I have taken in these matters', control of this night-marish situation had been regained. Scurrilous though they were, Dr Malcolm and Mr Fleming were men who cared intensely about their social status. Artfully, Greig indicated that the only hope for each of retaining his modest perch in society was instantly to drop their spurious claims against a dead woman whose name was catnip to a hungry press. He capped this by producing a document that proved Ada had always paid – perhaps with Padwick's loans – her own racing losses. As to Ada's alleged 'gift' of the insurance policy to Mr Fleming, her signature had not been witnessed. Fleming took fright when Greig threatened him with the possibility that the insurance company might well come after him for felonious behaviour.

Greig was tough, but John Crosse was wily. By early February, Greig knew that Crosse had no interest in behaving like a gentleman. He owned 108 letters from the late countess. Many of these could further damage her already spotty reputation. By April, however, Crosse had agreed to take £600 in exchange for the eighteen incriminating letters in which Ada spoke of her love for him, together with the betting authorisation from Lord Lovelace that she had voluntarily placed in John Crosse's hands.

All seemed to be proceeding smoothly. Crosse's attorney consented to the burning of the returned nineteen documents in the presence of Henry Karslake, Lord Lovelace's Surrey solicitor. Crosse's attorney had approved the final arrangement. It was at this delicate moment of imminent exchange that Lady Byron, whom Greig and Lushington had taken care to exclude from their negotiations, discovered what was being planned.

Annabella, with some sense, opposed buying off Crosse. If he could get such a generous sum for a few letters, what more might such a man be encouraged to demand for his silence? 'Can she desire to force us into Court? What else can be her object?' a despairing Greig asked Dr Lushington on 2 April. On this crucial occasion, Lady Byron's wishes were overruled. The letters were handed over to Karslake. John Crosse's further demand (he wanted a written exoneration of his part in the betting clique) was rejected. Mr Crosse, so a disgusted Woronzow Greig informed William Lovelace on 14 April, was no better than a felon: a man entirely 'destitute of honour and principle'.

So John Crosse appeared to them all in the way that he sought to exploit, even in death, the woman whose trust he had abused during her life. Nevertheless, the fact that Ada had written Crosse ninety letters which contained nothing compromising attests that there had been another, unsexual side to this relationship, as does the further and intriguing fact that Greig was in no hurry to destroy the four packets of Crosse's letters which were still in Ada's possession when she died. (They were spoken of as being in existence months after Mrs Clark's bonfire at Great Cumberland Place.) Even the innocuous gifts which the countess strove to bequeath to Crosse (by using Charles Babbage as her unofficial executor) could argue that an intense friendship, rather than a romantic passion, had prevailed.

This was not how Ada's bequest to Crosse was perceived by Lushington and Greig. To their legal minds, it seemed pure madness to place the late countess's 'unreformed' writing box, just as Ada had left it, in the possession of such an unscrupulous man. Neither did they trust Crosse to make an appropriate selection when it came to carrying away twelve 'WORKS (not vols)' of his own choice from Ada's personal library. They did not even care to allow him the coroneted and monogrammed gold pencil case she bestowed as a souvenir of the literary interests they had shared.

The concerted attempt to make John Crosse vanish from Ada Lovelace's history proved remarkably effective. Publicly, Ada featured in the memoir later written by Andrew Crosse's second wife only as a frequent visitor and occasional witness to scientific experiments carried out at Fyne Court. Privately, John Crosse's family disapproved of his murky relationship with the countess. Bitter altercations would take place between father and son before Andrew Crosse died in 1855, pointedly bequeathing his eldest son only the suggestive gift of an organ. (John Crosse had inherited none of his father's musical skill.) Fyne Court was left to Andrew Crosse's second wife, Cornelia. In 1859, John Crosse would change his name to Hamilton in order to receive a substantial legacy from that very uncle whose name he had cheerfully impugned to William Lovelace, ascribing spurious misdemeanours to a respectable relative in order to conceal his own secret family at Reigate. Almost the first use Crosse made of that bequest was to reclaim Fyne Court for his own family seat.

Evidence survives that the enigmatic Mr Crosse did retain affectionate feelings for Ada Lovelace. He never parted with the precious relics which offer the ultimate proof of Ada's attachment to him. In 1880, John's son and namesake would inherit from his father a gold ring that Lord Byron had bestowed upon his infant daughter, together with a miniature copy of the romantic poem 'Maid of Athens', and a precious lock of Byron's hair. The fact that John Crosse chose to preserve those items as family heirlooms, suggests – at the least – that he shared Ada Lovelace's reverence for her father.*

⪼⪻

At Brown's Hotel, the owners went out of their way to comfort an honoured guest during a period in which Lady Byron came, for the first time since the separation from Byron in 1816, close to breaking point. When the lawyers, early in 1853, discreetly spoke to the distraught Lord Lovelace about Lady Byron's 'very peculiar' views, while urging him to comply with whatever his mother-in-law might request him to say, the subtext was that Lushington and Greig were dealing with an unknown quantity.

For Annabella, even more than for her son-in-law, the discovery of the near-criminal world in which her daughter had become mired was devastating. By 5 February 1853, Lady Byron felt wretched enough to tell a new confidante, the American poet and abolitionist Eliza Cabot Follen, that Ada's death had been 'necessary', and that she herself had become towards the end 'unequal to the task' of supporting her poor daughter. By the following month, the search for a

---

* John (Crosse) Hamilton's widow outlived her husband and remained at Fyne Court until a major fire in 1894 rendered the house uninhabitable. The music room and romantically arcadian gardens survive under the management of the National Trust. Brian Wright, in *Andrew Crosse and the Mite that Shocked the World* (Matador, 2015), gives the most detailed account of the younger Crosses.

culprit on whom to lay the blame for Ada's destruction had switched away from her broken son-in-law to Charles Babbage.

The extent of Babbage's role in Ada's clandestine life among tipsters and semi-criminals remains extremely unclear. The mass of Lady Lovelace's letters to Babbage that are lodged at the British Library contains (as one would expect) no hint of a link between the inventor and the horse-racing world. Yet the perseverance of his loyalty to, and defence of, Mary Wilson is hard to ignore. If Babbage had been entirely innocent, would he not have come to share Lady Byron's view of Miss Wilson, rather than vigorously opposing it?

On 12 August 1852, Ada had secretly attempted to appoint Babbage as her executor. Through this most indiscreet of men, Lady Lovelace hoped to settle all the financial problems that beset her, to make provision for Mary Wilson, and to arrange for John Crosse to receive her private legacy. She also invited Babbage to make himself a present of any twelve 'works' (possibly meaning sets, rather than single books of the kind she had tried to bestow upon John Crosse) that he might wish to take from her library after her death. Babbage carried a substantial selection of the countess's papers away with him that day. Ada had authorised him to destroy or to preserve what he thought fit. Here, once again, the evidence points towards Babbage's intimate knowledge of her private affairs. While he may never have participated in Ada's gambling activities, he most certainly knew what was going on.

Ada had not inherited her mother's legal skills. Without a witness to a will, its executor's delegated powers are redundant. This is something that Babbage was slow to realise. On 13 December, just over two weeks after Ada's death, Lady Byron issued a formal request for the return of her daughter's papers, claiming that this had been her daughter's final wish. Babbage refused. Defending himself to Stephen Lushington later that month, the inventor volunteered to provide – should Lady Byron so wish it – an account of the invaluable support that Mary Wilson had offered to Ada. It was, he believed, appropriate that both Mary and her brother, Stephen, should be rewarded. Mary herself was willing to confirm that, back on 18 August 1852,

Lady Lovelace had promised to repay her handsomely for unspecified good services.

On 5 January 1853, while considering Babbage's request, Lady Byron learned from Mrs Jameson that the inventor was holding discussions with John Murray about his wish to publish a 'memoir' of Ada. The following day, Annabella offered to pay Mary Wilson £100. Anxious to avoid any suggestion of a bribe to a woman whose chief services had been to Ada's racing ring, Lady Byron demanded written confirmation that this sum was given in lieu of any financial loss Miss Wilson had personally suffered by taking up service with Lady Lovelace. Ill-advised by the choleric Charles Babbage, Mary refused. On 25 February, Annabella decided to cut her losses and withdraw the offer, salting the wound with the observation that 'I think it well she [Mary] has not received the £100.'*

The impulse towards self-justification had always been strong in Lady Byron. On 9 March, Annabella wrote to Woronzow Greig and, at much greater length, to his mother. The subject of these two documents of record (Mary Somerville was instructed not to burn her letter) was Charles Babbage, and what incensed Lady Byron most now was that he had dared to speak ill of the dead. To Greig, she reported upon a letter from Babbage, just received, 'full of much bitter vituperation, and containing a reflection upon *her* so malignant that I cannot describe it'. Somewhat alarmingly, given Babbage's reported wish to publish a memoir, his letter amounted almost to a formal document. A solicitor had clearly overseen and revised the letter before its despatch. Babbage stated that he had himself retained a copy.

Writing to Mrs Somerville, out in Florence, Annabella attempted to reconstruct the past. Rumours (she wrote) might have reached the Somervilles out in Italy that Lady Byron had excluded Charles Babbage from her daughter's home. Such gossip was ill-founded. Ada

---

* When Charles Babbage died, he left a bequest of £3 per month to Mary Wilson, to be paid to her for the rest of her life. Since no bequest was made by him to any other employee, it may have been his way of compensating for Lady Byron's stinginess.

had 'never hinted at any wish to see him'. This was untrue. Ada had specifically requested her mother to copy out a letter from Charles Locock in which the sympathetic doctor confirmed his patient's eagerness to see Babbage. The wish had been there, but Annabella chose to draw a very fine line of distinction between the doctor's letter and Ada's own expressed desire. Mrs Somerville, while dutifully preserving Lady Byron's letter, was prudent enough not to respond.

The fault lay on both sides. Annabella blamed Babbage for helping to lead Ada down from the sunny heights of science on which Lady Byron had yearned for her brilliant child to secure an enduring and eminent position. Babbage, for his part, felt that both he and the Wilsons had been badly treated. Like Lady Byron, Babbage was a man who did not easily forgive.

Talking to an admiring American visitor a full two years after Ada's death, Charles Babbage became unexpectedly garrulous on the unexpected topic of Lady Lovelace's hatred of her mother and her husband. Of Ada herself, Babbage apparently spoke with sad affection: 'there was so much feeling in both his words and manner that I did not feel at liberty to question him as to the nature of the unhappiness of the life he was speaking of . . .' So sombre and altered was Babbage's manner at this point that the visitor, one Henry Hope Reed, was led to assume that the unknown lady at issue must have killed herself.

The interview (it appeared in an American journal several years after Mr Hope Reed's death) is fascinating in what it reveals about Babbage himself. The problem with Ada Lovelace, Babbage informed his attentive visitor, was that she was 'utterly unimaginative'. You could say anything you liked ('all sorts of extraordinary stories') and that 'matter-of-fact mind' of hers would accept them all as plain fact. Really, it was quite hilarious to see how solemnly the countess swallowed them down.

Henry Hope Reed took Babbage at his word. Yet it was Babbage himself who, while cumbersomely playful, entirely lacked the imaginative power which had enabled a visionary Ada Lovelace to foresee the possibilities inherent in his machine. Laughingly, Ada had complained to her mother of being plagued by far too vivid a mind. And yet, here stood poor Babbage in 1854, assuring a respectful visitor that the fancies and the games and the wit had all been on his side. Perhaps it was as well that Charles Babbage had never appreciated the gift of joy his own laborious jokes had proven to the dancing, quicksilver mind of his attentive Lady Bird, his glittering Fairy.

෨෧෨

The third of Lady Byron's relationships to be enduringly affected by her daughter's death was her friendship with Anna Jameson, the loquacious Irish art historian to whom – over a period of ten years – Annabella had become as close as a sister. The reasons for their estrangement were several. It was a painful shock for Annabella to learn that her gambling-obsessed daughter had turned to Mrs Jameson for financial support and that Anna had provided it, all without a word to Annabella herself. Equal pain was inflicted when Mrs Jameson, while desperately endeavouring to restore herself to Lady Byron's good graces, attacked the character of her dying daughter. Mrs Jameson loved Ada. It's unlikely that she said anything intentionally cruel. To Annabella, however, during the testing final weeks of her daughter's excruciatingly extended life, any word of criticism dropped acid upon an open wound.

A meeting between the newly estranged ladies took place during December 1852. According to a loudly distraught Mrs Jameson, the word 'friendship' was flung back in her face. To Elizabeth Barrett Browning (a woman who said her flesh crawled at the mere thought of touching Lady Byron's hand), Jameson later confided (on 18 May 1856) that the shock of being exposed to Annabella's 'inexorable' temper had almost destroyed her. Throughout 1853, nevertheless, Mrs Jameson struggled to mend bridges, while Annabella continued smilingly to deny – it was a technique that Lady Byron had honed to perfection – that her own feelings had ever altered.

On 23 January 1854, having expressed courteous regret at the reported death of Anna's mother, Mrs Murphy, Annabella rejected the peace offering of a contribution to her own private Kirkby monument to Ada (for which, as she took care to point out, no donations had been solicited or desired). On 13 February, following a further cool exchange, Lady Byron remarked that, while chilled by Mrs Jameson's 'persistent attacks', her own affection remained unchanged. Had she herself not confirmed, towards the end of 1852 (we can be sure that the meticulous Annabella had placed the copied original before her as she wrote), that she was 'as ever your Friend'?

Anna Jameson's last and fatal error was to express forgiveness, both towards Ada and to her mother. It was the offer of 'forgiveness' to herself that had made Lady Byron want to strike Augusta Leigh during their ill-fated final encounter. Extended by Mrs Jameson, whose assistance to Ada Lady Byron regarded as inexcusably disloyal to herself, forgiveness was an insult. Responding to it in that same icily courteous letter of 13 February, Lady Byron commanded 'My dearest Mrs Jameson', please, to leave the issue of who should forgive whom aside – and to allow Ada's reputation to take care of itself.

> You tell me you have 'shielded the memory of Lady Lovelace from the cruel world.' If the world is cruel, let it alone – if the 'Repentance' which is now by her own direction inscribed on the monument to her at Kirkby Mallory, cannot disarm the Pharisees they must be left to convict themselves.
>
> Your reiterated expression of forgiveness, in fact to many accusations, might *need* Forgiveness, if I were not, in so many respects, and in spite of yourself, always so truly, Your friend,
>
> *AINB*

Faced by such steely and conditional friendship, there was no more to be done. In October 1854, Mrs Jameson wrote to sever her long connection with Robert Noel, the man who had first introduced her to Annabella and to Ada. While urging him to remain 'all you can and ought to be' in his own profound friendship with his respected older cousin, Anna identified Lady Byron's coldness towards her as the reason that she herself could no longer bear to see 'any friend who reminds me of her'. Interestingly, Robert Noel made no attempt to argue with Mrs Jameson's decision. He remained devoted to Lady Byron, fondly described in one letter to her as his oldest and dearest friend. Most likely, he had already heard his cousin's version of the quarrel and of its origins.*

So far as is known, the friendship with Anna Jameson was never renewed. Requested to thank Lady Byron in 1859 for her suggestion that a fund should be organised to pay John Gibson (a well-known neo-classical sculptor) to model Mrs Jameson's head in marble, Annabella's granddaughter responded (to Mrs Jameson's niece, Gerardine) that Lady Byron denied all knowledge of the project. Nevertheless, the letter-writer was permitted to state that her grandmother would contribute £50 (a handsome sum in 1859) towards the fund.

Lady Byron had added just one condition: the name of the donor must never be revealed.

---

* On 8 April 1856, Lady Byron sent to Robert Noel's German-born wife, Louisa, of whom she was extremely fond, a list of Ada's closest friends. Henry Drummond of Albury, the Zetlands, the Molesworths and Agnes Greig were identified. Also mentioned, without comment, was Anna Jameson.

PART FOUR

The Making and Breaking of a Reputation

'She [Lady Byron] was the one person involved in that tragic story who was innocent of wrong, true in word and deed, generous, resourceful, courageous amidst crushing difficulties, and so she consistently remained for the rest of her life.'

RALPH GORDON MILBANKE,
2ND EARL OF LOVELACE, *Astarte*, 1905

CHAPTER TWENTY-FOUR

ENSHRINEMENT
(1853–60)

*'[W]hat might have been, had there been one person
less among the living when she married … Then her life
would not have been the concealment of a Truth, while
her conduct was in harmony with it (no wonder if she was
misunderstood).'*

FRAGMENT OF A THIRD-PERSON MEMOIR,
BEGUN BY LADY BYRON,
BRIGHTON, 1851

Having done all she could to protect her dead daughter's name from
being mired in a public scandal, Lady Byron's thoughts turned again
to the question of her own future reputation.

Two years earlier, she had sketched out the beginnings of a
memoir, in the hope of encouraging Frederick Robertson to publish
her history. A mass of private papers had been placed in his safe-
keeping for just that purpose. By the beginning of 1853, however,
the ill and overworked Brighton cleric (now married and responsible for two young children) was unable to contemplate such a
taxing commission. Instead, he read Annabella's fragment and

offered an honest opinion. What was needed, Robertson advised, was for Lady Byron to write the book herself, but in language that was more comprehensible and far less veiled. Why not just state Augusta's name when she wrote of her wish that there had been 'one person less living' when she married Lord Byron? And why not give her husband's dreadful sin a name instead of hinting at some unspeakably mysterious 'Truth'? Annabella could and did speak about these sensitive issues in private, among her chosen friends. Why then, once she picked up her pen, must Lady Byron become so wilfully obscure?

Lady Byron had no answer to that cogent query, except to say that the one occasion when she had come before the public to defend her parents (in the 'Remarks' printed as an inserted appendix to Moore's *Life and Letters of Lord Byron*), her words had proved of little service either to them or to herself.*

The trouble was that Annabella wanted the truth to be told and yet not to break her promise to Byron that she would protect his sister and her family. Lady Byron had never doubted that Medora was her husband's child. She believed that Byron's fear of scandal about Augusta had driven him – with her wicked Aunt Melbourne's active encouragement – into marrying herself, Annabella Milbanke, a woman he no longer loved. He might even (although this was a point upon which Annabella often contradicted herself, perhaps from genuine uncertainty) have continued sleeping with his sister during intervals of their marriage, and most especially following Ada's birth. How could Lady Byron, knowing herself to be regarded as one of England's most admired philanthropists – a woman whose generous help to the young mothers of illegitimate children was as highly praised as the progressive schools she endowed and the daringly enlightened penal system that she vigorously advocated – how could the illustrious, 62-year-old Lady

---

* John Wilson, writing in the voice of 'The Shepherd' in *Blackwood*'s popular *Noctes Ambrosianae*, in May 1830, had attacked Lady Byron, declaring that a spouse's first loyalty always lay to her husband, not her parents, however brutal the facts might be.

Byron set down such a shameless history and yet hope to escape everlasting notoriety?*

Annabella's grandchildren were very dear to her and she took great pride in them. She had always stood up for Ockham, arguing to Ada back on 30 November 1844 that while the boy had suffered 'great disadvantages' from his Somerset upbringing, there was 'much good *in* him'. Ralph, then aged seven, was praised in that same letter for being both grown up and 'full of fun', while Annabella's gift for phrase-making was fondly quoted. ('I am so happy this evening that I wish it could be pulled out like a telescope,' the child had just announced.) Now, they were growing up and their future perception of her (a topic frequently mentioned to her circle of confidantes) offered cause for legitimate concern. She was clear about how they should regard their famous grandfather: her birthday gift to 15-year-old Ralph of *Childe Harold* was inscribed with an injunction to admire Lord Byron's poems, but to distrust the great poet's personality. How could she make them understand why she had left such a remarkable man, without revealing the scandal about Byron's sexual involvement with a carelessly amoral sister, that shadowy figure about whom Annabella's own feelings remained tormentingly conflicted?

Meanwhile, Lady Byron followed Ada's last wishes where her children were concerned. Annabella King – to the considerable regret of a clever, artistic girl who adored her high-minded but gently humorous grandmother – was largely confined to the ever more fancifully embellished Surrey home that she mischievously renamed Glum Castle. Lovelace, to do him justice, oversaw an educational

---

* Listing Lady Byron's philanthropic activities would take up an interminable chapter. Here are just two examples. In 1853, possibly moved by her grandson's accounts, she strongly advocated the need to improve conditions in far-flung penal colonies such as Van Diemen's Land, while setting up two new schools at home. In 1854, she was the sole funder both of the new Five Points Mission in New York, and of Red Lodge, a refuge and school for young girls set up by Harriet Martineau's cousin, Mary Carpenter, in Bristol. Numerous other missions, schools, asylums and hospitals received both financial support and the benefit of Lady Byron's formidable administrative mind.

programme that included languages, music (Charles Hallé himself gave Annabella nine piano lessons), and even – when Ruskin came for a solitary Christmas in 1854 – drawing advice from the great man himself. But life at Horsley, enlivened only by an annual visit to Europe with Mrs Greig, was dominated by the earl's obsession with his arches and tunnels. The visits paid by Annabella to her grandmother's airy Brighton home each spring appeared to a lonely girl like scenes from a beautiful dream, one in which the happiest moments were connected to the annual reunion with her younger brother. The brevity of these cherished interludes served to increase their charm.

The plan to separate the children was maintained. Ralph – the grandson upon whom Lady Byron's hopes for the preservation of the enormous Wentworth estates were now fixed* – was compelled to remain, by Ada's wish and with Lord Lovelace's formal agreement, under his grandmother's roof for all but a short period of every year. From 1852, until 1859, when the 20-year-old youth was despatched to lodge under his tutor's roof at University College, Oxford, Ralph was educated at home in Brighton and Southampton. His resentment about this cloistered life among elderly, controlling figures emerged in a plaintive letter which his grandmother passed along to Harriet Siddons's son-in-law in 1857. Ralph's strong objections to 'the restraint of a tutor' created persistent problems, Lady Byron confided to Arthur Mair. Earlier, while seeking to lodge the travel-hungry boy (then eighteen) at the Mairs' northern home en route to his proposed lone footslog around Scotland, Annabella admitted her fears. She never minded Ralph going out to Hofwyl, where he was under supervision. She could not trust a naive and troublingly irresponsible youth to travel unaccompanied. 'To this I cannot consent.'

Lady Byron was not inflexible. It was arranged that Ralph should

---

* The estates included Kirkby Mallory, Knowle in Warwickshire (now a ward of the thriving Birmingham extension town of Solihull), part of Leamington and substantial tracts of land near Darlington in Co. Durham (where her estate was still referred to in the local press in 1834 as belonging to 'the unfortunate Lady Byron').

hike around the Highlands together with one of the Mairs' sons. He returned home radiant. Such adventures (when carefully controlled) always did the poor boy good, his relieved grandmother observed.

While Ralph's growing passion for travel became powerful enough for his grandmother eventually to stipulate in her will that he must reside in England for at least a part of every future year, she wanted her granddaughter to see more of the Continent. In 1855, Annabella visited Mary Somerville in Florence and travelled on to Germany with her Noel cousins. In 1856, while Lovelace consented to host a debutante daughter's ball at Horsley, the trouble of arranging Annabella's presentation at court fell to her grandmother.

The search for an appropriate chaperone enabled Lady Byron to make cautious overtures of friendship to those members of William Lovelace's family with whom the earl's own relationship remained glacial. In 1855, Lady Hester King had expressed an interest in Ralph's academic progress; now, Lady Byron enquired whether Lady Hester's niece, Viscountess Ebrington, might wish to undertake the task.

A hand of friendship had been offered, and was accepted. By the late 1850s, both Annabella and the younger grandchildren were paying regular visits to their King relatives at Woburn Park and Dover Street. The ground was laid at this time for Ralph (whose relationship with his own father would never become cordial) to find a future substitute in Peter Locke King, Lord Lovelace's detested younger brother. Lady Hester must have been delighted.

The question of what was to become of Byron Ockham was one which independently troubled both Lord Lovelace and his mother-in-law. Neither knew what best to do for this handsome and increasingly wayward youth. Established by the early summer of 1853 at the Malta station on the *Albion*,* a ship under the command of one of Stephen Lushington's naval relations, Viscount Ockham (or J. Aker, as Byron often now signed himself to a sister he urged to

---

* The *Albion* is also puzzlingly referred to in letters as the *Allum*. These would appear to be one and the same ship.

stand up for her rights) was well-placed to earn the promotion that his father craved. Malta stood at the centre of Britain's strategy to intervene in Russia's escalating war against Turkey. By the summer of 1853, well-informed Londoners were already siding with Turkey ('the sick man of Europe' was Tsar Nicholas's notoriously derogatory term for his targeted foe) in what was about to become Britain's largest wartime engagement since Waterloo.

Lord Lovelace, himself confined to wearing a uniform that had never seen a battlefield (he donned it for official appearances as Surrey's long-serving lord lieutenant), was keen for his oldest son to see live combat. By the late summer of 1853, however, Byron Ockham's commander had resolved to send the intractable young aristocrat home, following his persistent defiance of various orders from his superiors. Byron's infractions had included going AWOL, sneaking liquor into his berth and – worst of all – falsely accusing Captain Lushington's personal protégé, a young Mr Dundas, of stealing his own (illegally acquired) gin. Asked to apologise to the youth – a member of the Zetland family – Lord Ockham had flatly refused.

What was to be done? A plea from Charles Noel to allow the youth to join his own family's new home at Leamington Spa was brusquely rejected by Lady Byron. Annabella had formed a more romantic plan. She herself still owned large tracts of Euboea in Greece, although much of this extensive estate had been transferred to the widowed Edward Noel. What could be more appropriate than that a second Byron should take up residence in Greece? This was the proposal that Annabella asked Charles Noel to put to Lord Lovelace (all direct communication between herself and her son-in-law having been severed) on 28 August 1853.

It was not to be. Ockham, having abruptly left Lushington's ship without leave – after failing to secure his father's permission for an official release – vanished from public view. Back in England, during the autumn of 1853, a court martial was discussed. Out in the Dardanelles, the young sailor found a job on the *Inflexible*, a coal ship carrying fuel to the fleet. In 1854, he made an ill-fated attempt to start a new life in America. By the spring of 1855, after working his way back to England from New York, Byron was reluctant to undertake any more foreign adventures. For the time being, appalled by her grandson's wretched appearance and evident ill health, Lady Byron arranged for him to live under her roof at Brighton, while taking tuition from Lieutenant Arnold, a son of Rugby's celebrated schoolmaster.

Byron Ockham was not yet nineteen. Ever hopeful, a doting grandmother had faith that Ada's favourite son might yet make a success of his life.

∞

The brusqueness of Annabella's response to Charles Noel's kindly offer to care for her rebellious grandson at Leamington owed much to the fact that it was penned on 15 August 1853, the day that Frederick Robertson died. Robertson was only thirty-seven. Overworked and depressed, he died of 'inflammation of the brain', a form of stroke. Local newspapers reported that Lady Byron had joined the mourners who followed the young clergyman's coffin on foot in one of the largest funeral processions ever seen in Brighton. (In fact, Annabella – always averse to any form of self-publicity – had watched the shuffling crowds from a discreet distance.)

The loss was devastating. Robertson had been her advisor, her confidant and friend. Rumours of a love affair between the pair were groundless, but an athletic build and exceptional good looks had added to the charismatic charm for the susceptible Lady Byron of a young preacher whose vivid and erudite weekly sermons at Holy Trinity, Brighton, were regularly attended by congregations larger than the church could hold.* (It was not uncommon for London

---

* Robertson's parishioners had been outraged in 1853 by the Vicar of Brighton's refusal to enable the hard-pressed cleric to take on an assistant, one whose name had been put forward by Lady Byron in an effort to help her friend. The candidate (Ernest Tower) was the grandson of Isabella Baker, in whose house Annabella herself had been born. Later, Tower took up a post at one of Lady Byron's parishes in the Midlands.

worshippers to travel down simply for the benefit of listening to a man widely regarded as the finest preacher in the country.)

Privately, Annabella later admitted to her younger grandson that her chief regret about philanthropy was the obligation to deal with so many plain-faced men. None of them – certainly not kind, loyal, worthy Dr King, still living in Brighton and supporting Annabella in the world of good works – ever came near to replacing Robertson in her affections. The subsequent discovery that the admired cleric, married, and with two young children, had been dallying with one of Lady Byron's own social circle, the respectably married Lady Augusta Fitzpatrick, was brushed off by his fondest admirer as a mere irrelevance.

Initially, Lady Byron had wanted Robertson to present her record of an ill-fated marriage to the public. The roles were now reversed. In September 1853, after providing funds to educate Robertson's fatherless children, Lady Byron started to interview various people who might contribute to a biography of her brilliant friend. It would be modelled, so she told one of Robertson's greatest admirers, Henry Crabb Robinson, upon the hugely successful recent life and letters of Margaret Fuller that she had (somewhat insensitively) presented to her daughter shortly before Ada's death. Annabella's failure to carry this ambitious project through owed more to her increasingly poor health than to any lack of commitment. Instead, Lady Byron became an assiduous circulator of the first published version of Robertson's celebrated sermons. It's highly probable that she also commissioned the death mask of Robertson which was taken by Robert Noel (now owned by University College, London).

Crabb Robinson, who had first met Annabella in that summer of 1853 at a party for the literary phenomenon of the year, Harriet Beecher Stowe, left their discussion filled with respect for this quietly dressed and unassuming woman. 'I was much pleased with Lady Byron', the savvy old gentleman noted that night. 'I consider her one of the best women of the day.' Such words were high praise from a man who had met almost every great figure of the age, including Wordsworth and Goethe. Annabella might lack the wit that had charmed Henry Crabb Robinson when he met Madame de Staël, but he was impressed by her rare combination of intelligence and integrity. Later, he would describe Lady Byron as the noblest woman he had ever known.

∽∾

Thomas Noel – the illegitimately born relative who had presided over Annabella's wedding to Byron at her parents' home – died in the summer of 1853, aged seventy-seven. It came as a shock to Mr Noel's family to learn that the cantankerous old man had excluded the third of his four sons from his will, seemingly out of pique at Charles's readiness to manage the Kirkby Mallory estate as Lady Byron's agent. (Thomas Noel Senior regarded all Wentworth property as rightfully belonging to himself.) Charles's older brothers, Robert and Thomas Junior (author of one much admired poem, 'The Pauper's Drive'), promptly made over to Charles a generous share of their own bequests. Edward Noel proved less forthcoming.

Although it is not certain that Annabella came to Charles Noel's assistance, the likelihood is that she did, especially since the news of Charles's disinheritance came shortly after an unfortunate incident for which Lady Byron was partly to blame.

Richard Realf had just turned eighteen in 1852, when Annabella first heard about the handsome son of a Sussex blacksmith, an admirer of Lord Byron who was hoping to publish his own poems. *Guesses at the Beautiful* reads today as dreadfully as its dismal title might suggest. Perhaps Annabella, who was financially responsible for shepherding Realf's slim volume into print before proudly circulating it among her Brighton friends, was recalling her youthful patronage of Joseph Blacket, the penniless bard of Seaham. Early in 1853, mindful of the fact that poetry alone is no way for any young man without means to support himself, she packed her protégé off to the Midlands, to study agriculture with Charles Noel. Perhaps, too, she sensed an absence in the life of Charles, whose son and namesake had recently left home to work for a firm of silk merchants in London.

By the end of the year, unwelcome news reached Lady Byron's Brighton home. Richard Realf had fallen in love with the Noels' 15-year-old daughter. Alice, a quiet girl blessed with large eyes and long, strikingly beautiful blonde hair, was infatuated. Her parents were horrified, not least by the violence of Alice's passion. (A letter from Charles Noel's wife, Mary Anne, informed Lady Byron – who promptly passed the news along to Mrs Cabot Follen, her favourite American confidante – that at last the poor child's eyes had stopped glaring like the headlights of a train.)

Reprehensible though Lady Byron's indiscretion might seem in spreading family gossip, she was seeking advice. Advised by Mrs Follen, Annabella arranged for Alice's sweetheart to be despatched to America and given a teaching post at the new Five Points Mission in New York. Realf was accepted without question; Lady Byron had, after all, contributed £6,500 (in excess of £3 million in today's currency) towards setting up Five Points. By 1858, the young man was out in Kansas, fighting alongside John Brown and writing to bless Lady Byron, herself an ardent abolitionist, as his generous benefactor.

This ill-starred love story had no happy ending. Alice, adopted by her uncle after her parents' death of smallpox in 1857, became Edward Noel's eerily intimate companion. Seduced at one point by Wilfrid Scawen Blunt – seduction was a rite of passage for female guests at the future marital home of Ada's daughter – Alice never married. Richard Realf, despite a rackety existence abroad that included a bigamous marriage, never forgot his first love. When he took his own life, aged forty-six, in Oakland, California, one imaginative biographer has claimed that Realf was still wearing a locket that contained a strand of Alice Noel's bright yellow hair.*

---

* *A Passport to Hell: The Mystery of Richard Realf* by George Rathmell (iUniverse, 2002).

Annabella had struggled against ill health ever since the traumatic marital separation that marked her transformation from an active young woman into a semi-invalid whose condition – a hardening of the arteries – worsened progressively with age. On 2 February 1854, Dr King explained to her new Brighton friend, Henry Crabb Robinson, that, although often confined to working from her sick-room, Lady Byron's mental state was never impaired. She had been at her most impressive, Dr King considered (and Stephen Lushington agreed), when forced to undergo the daily agony of witnessing her daughter's slow and painful death.

King was a devotee. William Howitt, a Quaker reformer and author, offered a harsher portrait of his wealthy patron. Howitt would deliver his recollections to the popular *Daily News* in September 1869, nearly a decade after Lady Byron's death. Rankling in Howitt's mind after all those years was the memory of Ephraim Brown, a Nottingham man whose services he had once recommended to Lady Byron as a teacher in one of her Leicestershire schools. Trained up by her at Ealing, Brown had been given a post for which, according to Howitt, Brown sacrificed other opportunities. Lady Byron had then sacked him, casting both the teacher and his penniless family adrift. While it remains unclear in what way Brown had offended his employer, his banishment did not discourage Howitt from submitting further educational projects to the same hard-hearted patron.

It was during one such discussion that Howitt (as he later reported) witnessed the shocking change that ill health could wreak upon Lady Byron. Speaking with him over the dinner table at her home, and in the best of spirits, she had agreed to support and help fund Howitt's latest school proposal. Coming down to breakfast the following morning, he entered the presence of an altered woman. White as paper and cold to the touch as the North Pole (in Howitt's striking account), Lady Byron spoke only to whisper a withdrawal of her promise. No explanation was given, no apology made. The subject was closed.*

Untypical though Howitt's account sounds – Lady Byron was known and widely praised for the exceptional generosity of her philanthropy – it fits with the adamantine side of Annabella's nature that had been experienced with such pain by William Lovelace and by Anna Jameson. Undeniably, Annabella could be both harsh and unforgiving. Even her devoted granddaughter, finally listening to her father's side of the story of their terrible quarrel (this conversation took place many years after Lady Byron's death), began to wonder about the way Lord Lovelace had been treated. Annabella's own godchild, Emily Leigh, seeking help to purchase herself a home in 1855, was dismayed to receive only a bleakly pragmatic recommendation to economise by going into lodgings. Such acts of coldness were not forgotten.

৩৩

The deaths of Ada Lovelace and Frederick Robertson, together with her estrangement from Anna Jameson and William Lovelace, left Annabella in a position of emotional isolation. Philanthropy, assuredly, brought many acquaintances and admirers into her life. Her relationship with Parthenope and Florence Nightingale had deepened to the point where Lady Byron would become a recipient and proud transmitter of what amounted to Nightingale's news bulletins from the frontline, at the height of the Crimean War. But professional colleagues – women like Arabella Lawrence in Liverpool, Mary Carpenter in Bristol, Dr Elizabeth Blackwell, Harriet Martineau, Elizabeth Jesser Reid (founder, in 1849, of Bedford, London's first women's college) – were themselves energetic reformers with lives of

---

* The analogy to the North Pole suggests that Howitt's experience may have occurred at Uplands, the house near Mortlake at which Annabella laughingly described an unheated chamber in which less-favoured visitors were housed as 'the Polar Room'. Louisa Noel was among the luckier ones who was promised the cosy downstairs bedroom with its own snug German-style stove.

their own. These collaborations were of a warm but practical nature, focussed upon ways to rectify injustice and improve social conditions.

It was, then, a rare treat for Annabella to find that her plans with Henry Crabb Robinson to found a new magazine, *The National Review*, were assisting the development of a friendship that allowed her to speak freely about the one subject of which she never grew tired. Discussing Lord Byron with his widow, an intrigued Robinson enquired about the poet's own dark brand of religion. If only she could have turned her husband away from his Calvinistic beliefs and towards her own faith in a forgiving God, Annabella sighed. Did Robinson wonder that she still, after all these years, shrank from reading Byron's 1822 play (it was partly based on Goethe's *Faust*), *The Deform'd Transformed*? The play distressed her, she explained, because she read into it her superstitious husband's belief that lameness marked him out – from the first moment of his birth – as cursed by God.*

⁑

Byron Ockham's period of tuition by Lieutenant Arnold proved to be short-lived. In the summer of 1855, the young man headed north from Brighton to take a job screening coal in Sunderland. (As a child, Ockham had been greatly excited by the descent into a Midlands mine arranged by Charles Noel and his tutor.) By December, he had returned to London and signed up to a five-year contract riveting metal plates on to the iron flanks of the *Great Eastern*, the massive steamship being built at Millwall under the direction of Isambard Brunel and his engineering partner, John Scott Russell.

To an anxious grandmother, the last hope for establishing Ockham in a respectable life lay in ensuring that he had proper lodgings. Conscious that Louisa and Robert Noel were returning from Dresden, Annabella offered them her grandson as a paying lodger for three months. The case was becoming a desperate one,

---

* Mary Shelley, who copied the play for Byron and much admired it, told its author that she had greatly preferred the task to working on his *Don Juan*.

she confessed to Louisa on 26 June: 'now or never will he form desirable connections. The ball is thrown into the air – who is to catch it?'

The Noels did not step forward to catch it, and it is unlikely that Byron would have accepted such a restricting proposal. By 6 September 1856, only the viscount's sister and faithful confidante knew that he was living on the Isle of Dogs, where J. Aker's favourite pastime was to run up different flags in front of his lodgings – Russian one day, American the next – in order to cause a bit of a stir. He was saving hard with a friend, in order to buy a small schooner. He also had plans – shades of his grandfather! – to buy a bear cub. Nothing, however, was said to Byron's sister about the fact that her brother was hoping to marry Mrs Low, the divorced daughter of his East End landlord. (Conscious of his title and responsibilities, Mrs Low turned him down.)*

Unsurprisingly, Lord Ockham's twenty-first birthday was not marked at Horsley by the traditional family celebrations for an eldest son.

෴

Lady Byron's generosity was legendary among those whom she loved. Always on the move, Annabella looked upon her various homes chiefly as useful places in which to provide a refuge for any friends who were poor, unhappy or simply undergoing a time of crisis. In the autumn of 1855, the hard-up De Morgans were offered the loan for as long as they wished of a country house. Making a similar proposal in 1856 to another, much younger couple, Annabella offered George and Louisa MacDonald part of Aford House, her new residence at Ham Common, out beyond Richmond. They should have their own entrance and come and go as they pleased, she promised, but they must never feel excluded from her personal domain. 'When socially

---

* 'I would not object to a working woman as his wife,' Lady Byron told Robert Noel on 11 April 1857 (Dep. Lovelace Byron 104).

disposed, you will invite yourself,' their new friend instructed them. 'My house has often been called Liberty Hall.'*

Annabella was writing primarily to George, the 31-year-old author of 'Within and Without', a poem that Lady Byron admired for its intimations of an afterlife. MacDonald went on to write a book – if a personal intrusion can be excused – that held me spell-bound when I was a child. 'I have been asked to tell you about the back of the North Wind,' the book began.† I doubt if I was the only reader who wept when I reached the moment when Diamond, the boy-hero, is found, stretched out upon his little bed in the hayloft from which the capriciously beautiful North Wind used to carry him away on extraordinary adventures. 'I saw at once how it was. They thought he was dead,' MacDonald wrote (as the tale's narrator). 'I knew that he had gone to the back of the north wind.' And that, as MacDonald's admirers learn to accept, was the best place that any moderately unhappy and imaginative child could hope to be.

The friendship began in 1855, when Annabella wrote an admiring letter to the author of 'Within and Without'. Soon after this, Lady Byron confessed her personal longing for a spiritual reunion with a reformed and Augusta-free husband. MacDonald, as he came to know Annabella better, never doubted that – until the end of her life – she always had and forever would love Lord Byron.

Poor, lively, warmhearted and high-principled, George and Louisa MacDonald brought as much to their new friend in pleasure as Lady Byron returned to them in munificence. At the time Annabella met him, George MacDonald had exchanged his life as a country parson for badly paid teaching work in Manchester. An active frame belied MacDonald's lifelong ill health; the following year, Annabella funded

---

* It's hard to keep count of the number of houses at which Annabella lived after Ada's death. Besides various homes in Brighton, they included Aford House at Ham Common, Uplands House at East Sheen, 1 Cambridge Terrace on Regent's Park, a house in Gloucester Terrace, another which Ralph reported that she was buying from a bankrupt and, finally, two adjacent houses in the then unfashionable location of Primrose Hill.

† George MacDonald, *At the Back of the North Wind* (1871).

the couple's three-month visit to Algeria, where a dry climate helped the invalid to regain his energy. In 1858, she commissioned Augustus De Morgan's exceptionally artistic son, William, to do up the MacDonalds' home, instructing him to combine elegance with every possible comfort. It's likely that she also engineered MacDonald's 1859 appointment to lecture at Bedford, the pioneering London women's college with which Lady Byron had been closely involved for a decade.

This late-flowering friendship was one of which Lady Byron's closest friends warmly approved. Mary Montgomery, meeting them at Lady Byron's last London home in 1858, thought the MacDonalds were delightful. Crabb Robinson, encountering the couple there during the following spring, was impressed both by the boldness of MacDonald's religious views, and by (Lady Byron always favoured a handsome man) the former clergyman's arresting good looks.

George MacDonald would later become famous, prosperous and a towering influence upon other writers, notably Lewis Carroll. (Tolkien and C. S. Lewis freely acknowledged the Victorian author as their first teacher in the world of fantasy fiction.) He never forgot Lady Byron's kindness to him in more straitened times. To their children, the MacDonalds always spoke of Lady Byron as the woman who had given George hope and practical help when he most needed it. (Help included an unexpected £300 legacy in her will.) A decade later, at the absolute height of the posthumous public attack upon Lady Byron's reputation, George MacDonald made a point of dedicating his latest novel to her memory.

∽✿∾

Another and more significant friendship was formed around this time. In this case, it was generated by one of the most burning topics of the day. Abolitionism was the common cause that united Lady Byron's friends and colleagues on both sides of the Atlantic. Britain had abolished slavery in 1834; nevertheless, by 1850, over three million African slaves in America, and in other parts of the world, remained in bondage. In 1850, Ellen and William Craft were among the tiny group who escaped from the slave-owning Southern states in America and avoided recapture in the North under the draconian terms of the new Fugitive Slave Act. The Crafts began their new, free lives in England as teachers at Lady Byron's Ockham school. In that same year, Harriet Beecher Stowe started writing *Uncle Tom's Cabin*, the story through which its young author would help to change the course of American history.

By April 1853, when Mrs Beecher Stowe and her family arrived in London for the beginning of a four-month lecture tour, Stowe had overtaken even Dickens, to become the world's best-known living writer. *Uncle Tom's Cabin* had sold 300,000 copies in America during its first year of publication, despite being a banned book throughout most of the Southern states. In London, one year later, ten different dramatic adaptations of Stowe's novel were being staged. Everybody wanted to meet and pay tribute to its celebrated author.

It was, therefore, a singularly privileged group of some twenty men and women who gathered to meet Mrs Stowe on 24 May at the London home of Elizabeth Jesser Reid. It was at this occasion that Anna Jameson (still struggling to regain Annabella's friendship) introduced Henry Crabb Robinson to her former soulmate. Robinson's interest in both Lady Byron and the honoured American guest did not preclude him from observing that the most impressive person in the room was William Craft, the new Ockham school teacher. Mr Craft was, Robinson respectfully noted in his diary (while employing the problematic language of that time), 'the most intelligent-looking negro I ever saw'.

Recording at a later date the history of her friendship with Lady Byron, Harriet Beecher Stowe described that first encounter at Mrs Reid's home. She had been struck by Lady Byron's fetching appearance (slight, pale and silver-haired in a lacy widow's cap and lavender-coloured gown) and appealing manner (poised, quick and graceful). The topic of slavery was instantly raised; Mrs Stowe was astonished to find how well-informed and astute Lady Byron appeared to be, and how original in her ideas. ('Many of her words surprised me greatly, and gave me new material for thought. I found I was in company with a commanding mind.')

In 1856, the Beecher Stowes made a second visit to Europe, both to publicise *Dred* (Mrs Stowe's new novel was about the runaway slave leader of a plotted rebellion), and to attend the London stage debut of Mary Webb, the African-American actress for whom Harriet had adapted parts of *Uncle Tom's Cabin* into dramatised readings, entitled *The Christian Slave*. Arriving in the dog-day heat of August, the Stowes found London disappointingly empty of smart society. It was during this quiet period that Stowe's friendship with Lady Byron first bloomed. Annabella, who had already offered loyal support to Mary Webb and her family, invited the Stowes to visit her at home on at least two occasions. On the second, their schoolboy son Henry was introduced to Byron Ockham, a young man whose brilliant eyes and muscular physique (comparable to the Farnese Hercules, gasped well-travelled Mrs Stowe) provided welcome distraction from the subject of the viscount's unconventional lifestyle. A poised Lady Byron expressed her hope that Lord Ockham was proving to be a good moral influence upon his fellow mechanics at Scott Russell's shipyard. There was talk of his setting up a new school in the East End. Really, it was quite wonderful to observe how Lady Byron looked for the best in everybody who surrounded her, an admiring Mrs Stowe would later remark.

Following a headily aristocratic September in Scotland (where the Stowes were the guests of the Duchess of Sutherland), Harriet's husband escorted young Henry back to his American schooling. Meanwhile, Harriet, together with her married sister, Mary Foote Perkins, arranged to visit a personal hero, Charles Kingsley, at his Berkshire rectory, before embarking on her second tour of Europe. It was by happy chance that Annabella's new abode was at Ham Common, conveniently placed along the westward route from London out to Eversley, Kingsley's secluded home.

Following a satisfying expedition to Eversley Rectory, Mrs Stowe and her sister spent a night at Aford House. It was now that a key

conversation took place between Lady Byron and Mrs Beecher
Stowe. Disclosures were ventured on both sides. Harriet's confession
of her youthful adoration of Lord Byron led easily on to an unfolding
of the private history of Lady Byron's marriage. Only the slightest of
pauses occurred when Mrs Stowe confessed that she already knew
about the incest. (Her source was their mutual American friend,
Eliza Cabot Follen.) Nodding swift assent, Annabella passed on to
a thrillingly intimate account of her married life.

And what, a pale-faced and emotional Lady Byron asked at the
end of her enthralling monologue, should she do now? Plans were
once again afoot for a popular edition of her late husband's poems,
prefaced by what threatened to be a wickedly misleading account of
Lord Byron's domestic life. Was it her duty to reveal what she alone
now knew to be the Truth? Should she volunteer it herself, or . . .?

Lady Byron's hesitation was pregnant with implication. Was
Annabella hoping that Mrs Stowe would step forward with an offer
of her own services, or was she simply seeking practical advice? Mrs
Stowe herself was uncertain what was expected from her. Playing
for time, she requested a written account of past events to which she
could devote herself with scrupulous consideration. To this, Lady
Byron readily agreed.

The discussion at Ham took place at the end of October. On
5 November, Mrs Stowe returned the detailed notes (from which
Lady Byron had prudently omitted any mention of incest). Twelve
days later, on the verge of departing for Paris, Mrs Stowe announced
that she had changed her mind 'somewhat'. Better, perhaps, to publish nothing at this time. Such delicate matters should be placed in
the hands of 'some discreet friends' who could decide, after Lady
Byron's own demise, what should be done?

Perhaps Harriet sensed that she had disappointed her new
friend. Shortly before returning to America in the summer of 1857,
Mrs Stowe sent Lady Byron a gift of some little majolica vases from
Italy, together with a reassuring message of affection. 'I often think
how strange it is that I should know you,' she wrote on 5 June, 'you
who were a sort of legend of my early days – that I should love you

is only a natural result.' Omitted from this pleasing tribute was any hint of just what sort of a legend the youthful Lady Byron might have been. It was the poet, not his widow, whom an impressionable young girl had worshipped.

Henry Beecher Stowe drowned shortly after his mother's return to America. Lady Byron's silence about the tragedy hurt. 'I did long to hear from you,' Harriet confessed on 30 June 1858, 'because I know that you did know everything sorrow can teach.'

A considerable deterioration in Lady Byron's already failing health may have contributed to her neglect of a friend in need. She had moved into her final home, a tall, pleasant house in St George's Terrace, looking out at the steep green ascent of Primrose Hill. All physical endeavours had become a struggle. The next-door and smaller house was being purchased in order to create a practical ground-floor suite for her own use. Ralph, about to go to Oxford (following a meeting with a kind-hearted academic, Professor Donkin), was to be given an upstairs study all his own. A physician was in permanent residence, but the kindest of Lady Byron's nurses was her own granddaughter.

The two Annabellas enjoyed a delightful friendship, so Mrs Stowe now learned. It was one in which a 'spirit union' left plenty of room for lively mutual dissent. Together, they had been reading serialised instalments of Harriet's new novel, *The Minister's Wooing*. Tactfully (for this was not one of Mrs Stowe's finest works), Lady Byron compared it to *Adam Bede* ('the book of the season') and ingenuously wondered which would prove the more enduring.

Curiously, Annabella made no mention to Mrs Stowe of the fact that she herself was once again planning to write the story of her doomed marriage. On 18 April 1859, she heard from Anna Jones, the vicar's daughter who had kept up a friendship with both Mary Montgomery and herself ever since those miserable early weeks of 1816 when Annabella had taken refuge at Kirkby. The chief topic of Miss Jones's letter was the autobiographical book which Lady Byron had declared that she was going to write. While Anna approved ('The sooner you commence the better'), she qualified her encouragement by adding a curious rider: namely, that '*many* should give opinions and be allowed to revise & find fault'.

The project went no further. The thought of being revised and found fault with was enough to deter an author who detested criticism. But it's more likely that Annabella, growing weaker month by month, simply ran out of energy.

Harriet Beecher Stowe returned to England in the summer of 1859. Calling upon her old friend and finding an ashen-faced and greatly aged Lady Byron almost unable to speak, Mrs Stowe departed in haste. A second visit took place on a warm summer afternoon. The invalid had recovered enough strength to undertake a pleasant saunter around the garden of her London home. 'She was enjoying one of those bright intervals of freedom from pain and languor, in which her spirits always rose so buoyant and youthful,' Harriet would fondly recall. Accompanying her guest to the railway station and noting Mrs Stowe's sudden dismay at discovering she had left behind her gloves (an essential part of every proper Victorian lady's attire), Lady Byron impulsively drew off her own. That spontaneous gift, Harriet later observed, was entirely in keeping with her admired friend's noble character.

Lady Byron died quietly in her bed at St George's Terrace on 16 May 1860, on the eve of what would have been her sixty-eighth birthday. (Anna Jameson, still unforgiven, had gone to her grave just two months earlier.) Sending the news to Stephen Lushington at 5am, Annabella sadly wrote that 'my darling' had died an hour earlier, after undergoing great suffering with patient resignation. The cause of death was identified as cancer of the breast.

Lord Lovelace had never given up hope of a reconciliation. All through these final weeks, he had hovered close by, waiting for any summons from the dying woman which he might receive. It never came. On 18 May, an embarrassed and disapproving Stephen Lushington was forced to tell the unhappy earl (who was, after all, his landlord at Ockham Park) that all three of his children opposed his plan to attend the funeral. If he came, they would not. Given no option, Lovelace stayed away.

Dr Lushington himself was of course present on 20 May 1860, to see his old friend's coffin lowered into place at Kensal Green. The grave was discreet: the plain granite slab carried only Annabella's (misspelt) name, a pair of dates and her county of birth. The burial plot lay close to those of several Lushingtons. The lawyer's family had become almost an extension of Lady Byron's own.*

Travelling back from the funeral within a closed carriage together with Lady Byron's lawyer, Gerard Ford, the 7th Lord Byron made a startling disclosure. It had been made known to him – and apparently to nobody else – by the late Lady Byron that her son-in-law had visited her house and robbed her of a box of the precious letters that she had always protected from public view. Challenged by his younger son in later years, Lovelace flatly denied any such theft. It seems clear now, however, that those abstracted papers – they included letters that had passed between Annabella and Augusta Leigh in 1816–17 – were later loaned or copied for use by hostile critics at the height of the posthumous onslaught on Lady Byron's reputation. Ralph King, while convinced of his father's transgression, identified the culprit in *Astarte* (1905) only as 'a deceased relative'.†

∽∾

Lady Byron's will was – as we might expect – meticulously planned. Ralph, the principal heir of all that it was within his grandmother's power to bestow (that is to say, the enormous Wentworth estates), was instructed to add Noel and Milbanke to his surname. (Lady Byron had also taken care – while never using it herself – to claim and retain the Wentworth barony for her descendants.) Annabella (who now changed her name to Lady Anne King Noel) received, in

* Lushington himself chose to be buried, with equal lack of ostentation, in the churchyard at Ockham.

† William Lovelace's second wife, Jane Jenkins, expressed strong indignation at even this veiled allegation. It was inconceivable that her late husband would have behaved in such an underhand manner, she asserted to her stepson. Posterity has sided with Ralph.

addition to investments that provided an annual income of £3,000, all of her grandmother's jewels, trinkets and ornaments. Mary Carpenter, a trustee, was given Red Lodge, the Bristol property that Lady Byron had purchased to house and rehabilitate young women in difficulties. Edward Noel received £1,000, while £100 went to Charles Noel's son and namesake. Louisa Noel was given £500. The same sum was bestowed upon the mysterious but memorably named Thomas Horlock Bastard, a Dorset phrenologist.*

Most significant, however, was a clause in the will that concerned Lady Byron's personal papers. In 1853, the late Thomas Davison, a close friend from Annabella's early years, had been replaced as one of her three trustees by Henry Bathurst, a lawyer living at Doctor's Commons. (Henry's mother, Lady Caroline, was a close friend to Lady Byron.) Instructions were given to Mr Bathurst, together with Mary Carpenter and Frances Carr (Lushington's unmarried sister-in-law) that all of Lady Byron's papers should be immediately sealed and deposited at a bank. Lady Byron's final instruction rang crystal clear. 'I direct that no one else however closely connected with me shall on any plea whatsoever be allowed to have access.'

Near to death, Annabella believed that she was asking the trustees to act in the best interests of her family when she specified that they were to act with special thought to the welfare of her grandchildren. The intention was good. The result was to prove disastrous, both for the future defence of Lady Byron's reputation and for the peace of mind of those same beloved grandchildren whom she was so anxious to protect.

---

* The will was extensive. The list given here represents only a modest selection of Lady Byron's bequests.

CHAPTER TWENTY-FIVE

OUTCAST

Less than a month after Lady Byron's death, Harriet Martineau decided to write Annabella's life. In order to do so, she approached for their views – and anticipated approval from – those reformers and friends who were most likely to assist her by providing recollections of an esteemed colleague.

Initially, the response was warm. The approval of Mary Carpenter, a junior trustee, could be relied upon since she was Harriet's close relation. Elizabeth Jesser Reid was very much in favour, as was Mrs Reid's present houseguest, Anna Jones, a woman who had known Lady Byron for over forty years. Mary Montgomery, while herself sending along supportive messages, asked Miss Reid to convey that her own houseguest, Julia Smith (Parthe and Florence Nightingale's formidable aunt), was 'well pleased' by Miss Martineau's proposal.

That initial trail of enthusiasm went cold only when word reached Frances Carr, the senior trustee of Lady Byron's papers. Fanny – dutifully aware of Annabella's repetition in her will of her 1849 injunction (stipulating that her papers were to be withheld from family and public view, without exception, for a period of thirty years) – vetoed the project. She was not, however, able to prevent Harriet Martineau from publishing an expansive personal tribute to a woman for whom Martineau entertained both sincere affection and a high esteem.

Martineau's essay appeared in the first weeks of 1861 in *The Atlantic*

Monthly and the *Daily News*, the popular British newspaper for which she wrote on a regular basis. Martineau's tone was laudatory. Lady Byron had loved her husband until the last. 'She gloried in his fame.' Her wealth 'such as her husband left of it', had been altruistically lavished upon philanthropic causes and educational reform. An unhappy marriage was blamed both for the 'wretched health' that made Lady Byron's survival from year to year 'a wonder' even to her doctors, and for 'the few and small peculiarities' (the delicate topic of 'strained affections' was touched upon) that bespoke 'irremediable loneliness in life'. As to posterity, Martineau felt confident in stating that Lady Byron's death would not only create a sense of bereavement 'wherever our language is spoken', but that Lady Byron herself would be referred to with tenderness:

> in all future time, when popular education, and the power of women to bless society with all gentle and quiet blessings, engage the attention of lovers of their kind.

In 1861, this extravagant paean of adulation attracted not a single word of criticism.

∞

Had hostile detractors been loitering in the shadows, they might have been expected to reveal themselves in 1861, when Britain's covert support of the slave-owning, cotton-producing Southern states in the American Civil War was matched by a waning of enthusiasm for abolitionists, alive or dead. In 1862, Annabella's eldest grandson died of a ruptured blood vessel.

Lord Wentworth (a title which Byron Ockham reluctantly accepted, following the death of his grandmother,* but himself never

---

* It was Lord Lovelace who had urged his son to take on the barony, in order to keep the Wentworth title in the family. It would pass from Ralph (d.1906) to Ralph's daughter (d.1917) and then, via Ralph's sister, Anne (d.1917) to her daughter, Judith.

used) had succeeded in his modest plan to save enough from his earn-ings at the shipyard to purchase (together with an unnamed friend) a small yacht. Ockham was sailing this little craft in the Solent during the summer of 1862 when he collapsed and was taken to convalesce at Wimbledon, a village on the outskirts of south London. A puzzling location – the first cottage hospital was built there in 1869 – suggests that the descendant of Byron's publisher, John Murray, had stepped in to offer help. (John Murray III had built himself a splendid home at Wimbledon. In honour of his most lucrative client, he named it Newstead.*)

Ralph, to whom the Wentworth barony now passed, was moun-taineering on the Continent in the summer of 1862. Anne, the only one of the family who maintained regular contact with her older brother after Lady Byron's death, became a regular visitor to Wimbledon. She was holding her brother in her arms, when, aged only twenty-six, Byron King-Noel, 12th Baron Wentworth, died on 1 September 1862. In America, the *New York Times* published a colourfully anecdotal account of the young man's life at sea and in the shipyard. English newspapers were more tactfully brief, men-tioning little beyond the fact of Lord Wentworth's untimely death. Of Byron's possessions, nothing survives except for the (privately owned) logbooks of his first years at sea. Reports that a tablet was erected to his memory at the Byron church of Hucknall prove to be false. The place of burial is unrecorded for a young man who had always preferred to disappear.

Six years later, in 1868, a persevering Harriet Martineau returned to her idea of writing a life of Lady Byron. On this second occa-sion, it was Ralph who turned the project down. 'I told her kindly that Miss Carr still wishes to prevent publication,' Ralph told his sister on 2 February 1868. Disappointed but probably unsurprised, Martineau simply republished her earlier article as part of her newest

---

* Sold by John Murray IV and since demolished, 'Newstead' now lies under Centre Court, Wimbledon. A local street, Newstead Way, still marks its past presence – and offers fine views of Centre Court.

production: *Biographical Sketches (1852–1868)*. No objections were made. In 1868, it was still permissible for Lady Byron to be extravagantly admired.

Aged respectively thirty-one and twenty-nine at the beginning of 1868, neither of Ada Lovelace's surviving children had yet married. Ralph remained locked in fierce dispute with his father over his right to the Wentworth estates. (Cash-rich but land-poor since his grandmother's death, Ralph eventually bought out Lord Lovelace's lifetime interest in the inheritance, acting on the advice of his now friendly uncle, Locke King.) Anne, returning to England in the summer of 1867 after an extended stay in Italy, yielded to the pleadings of Jane Crawford Jenkins, the kind-hearted and well-meaning widow who had been married to Lord Lovelace since 1865. Reluctantly, Anne agreed to visit Horsley Towers, both to meet a baby half-brother, Lionel Fortescue King, and to hear her father's own account of his terrible falling-out, back in 1851, with Lady Byron.

Writing on 19 June 1867 to Agnes Greig (Mary Somerville's delightful Scottish daughter-in-law had become close as a second mother to Anne since Ada's death), Anne confessed that the encounter with her father had unsettled her. She had disliked hearing how harshly the earl spoke about her grandmother – '& yet it would seem she [Lady Byron] must have been much mistaken towards my Father, then as to my Mother, I must believe all that my father tells me.' Things were not, perhaps, quite so clear-cut as Anne and Ralph had been led to suppose.

On one issue, however, the siblings were united in unbreakable agreement. They both wanted access to the papers that would reveal to them the hidden mysteries of the short-lived Byron marriage. Fate was to play into their hands in the autumn of 1868, when an embarrassed Frances Carr admitted that her fellow trustees had not been able to prevent her from destroying various incriminating letters within the archive. She was anxious to compensate. By 17 October 1868 (eleven years before the official release of his grandmother's papers), a triumphant Ralph was busily sending batches of newly acquired letters and relevant documents across London to his more organised sister, for sorting and proper arrangement. Ralph described this process as a preliminary to 'the completion of the whole work'.

In the autumn of 1868, then, armed with some – but far from all – of the key papers, Ralph was planning to produce an authoritative account of his grandparents' marriage.

Unforeseen events were about to capsize this sensitive project.

ᛉᛒᚷ

Comfortably settled in Paris since 1846 with her devoted second husband, the Marquis de Boissy (a man who liked – to his wife's annoyance – to introduce her as '*l'ancienne mâitresse de Byron*'), Teresa Guiccioli never forgot that Byron himself had spoken of her as his last passion. An admired French poet and former politician had placed Teresa alongside Dante's Beatrice and Petrarch's Laura as a woman 'immortalised by love'. But Alphonse Lamartine's tribute, published in *Le Constitutionnel* in 1865, had attracted fewer readers than a mocking attack upon the lovely marquise's fidelity that Alexandre Dumas had launched with far more spirit in his own loquacious memoirs. 'O madame! madame! why have you been so faithless to the memory of the poet?' Dumas had ungallantly enquired. 'Wasn't it good enough for you, to have been Byron's mistress?'

When Monsieur de Boissy died in 1866, Teresa was still feeling incensed that Dumas, a writer of mere historical potboilers (however successful), should have dared to question her profound love for the chivalrous poet who had recently taken to sending her personal reassurances (over the spirit waves) of his yearning for that moment when his sweet Teresa (but not Augusta Leigh, and most certainly, not his wife) would rejoin him in celestial bliss.

Announced in 1867, *Lord Byron jugé par les témoins de sa vie* was published anonymously by a Parisian publisher (Amyot) in 1868. The English translation, made by Hubert Jernyngham, a courtly admirer whom Teresa bullied mercilessly, was published the following year in both Britain and the United States.*

Few of Lord Byron's former drinking cronies would have recognised their old friend in Madame de Boissy's 900-page homage to a literary angel. (The nearest equivalent to Teresa's desexed Byron was the newly sanctified Shelley with whom – as Madame's talkative spirit guide was always keen to convey – Lord Byron was now enjoying an eternity of ennobling exchanges.)

Madame de Boissy's Byron was – to be frank – a bit of a bore. He had led a life of inviolate purity (except when impertinent hussies like Lady Caroline Lamb threw themselves into his arms). He drank only water. His years of devotion to that sweet child-bride, the Contessa Guiccioli (Teresa was just ten years younger than Byron), had been supervised at all times by her sternly proper family, the Gambas. The lovers had never slept together. Byron's desire to marry the beautiful *contessa* had been blocked by the mere, inconvenient fact that she already had a husband, one under whose hospitable roof her cavalier often resided, it was true, but always under conditions of flawless respectability.

Back in 1821, Byron had laughingly described the Contessa Guiccioli to Augusta Leigh as his wife's most ardent defender. Nearly fifty years later, Teresa reserved fifty-six pages of her book (forming Chapter Twenty-two, in its entirety) for the subject of Lord Byron's marriage to a most unsuitable woman. Suddenly, here, nine years after her death, Annabella was characterised by her rival and survivor as critical, cold and, above all, spoiled. (It is Teresa we have to thank for attaching to Lady Byron those epithets that have ever since stuck to Annabella like viscous slime, when she used this chapter to condemn her as 'a spoilt child, a slave to rule, to habits and ideas as unchanging and inflexible as the figures she loved to study'.) Lord Byron's own married fidelity had been impeccable, the marquise

---

* A further work, a life of the Marquis de Boissy, (*'mon bon mari'*) remained unfinished. A third, *The Life of Lord Byron in Italy*, was published (with more praise rightly being granted to its translator, Michael Rees, and heroic editor, Peter Cochran, than to its long-winded author) in 2005.

wished her exhausted readers to understand. But the poet's tender relationship with his sister had aroused the jealousy of the chilly-hearted wife who had deserted him, refusing his heartfelt entreaties for a public explanation. Byron was forced into exile and the fault was his wife's, for

> the most atrocious part of this affair, and doubtless the most wounding to him, was precisely Lady Byron's conduct; and in this conduct the worst was her *cruel silence*! This silence it is which will ever be her crime, for by it she poisoned the life of her husband.

That '*cruel silence*', Teresa continued, had also been employed by Lady Byron to slander the immaculate name of Augusta Leigh. Silence, when so cunningly deployed, had in fact proved to be a weapon 'crueller than Clytemnestra's poniard'. So much for Lady Byron's love! (And so much as well for the reputation of a woman whom Teresa Guiccioli herself had never once met.)

It's unclear whether Ralph Wentworth ever noticed the modest *Recollections* of 1868 in which his grandmother's loyal friend at court, Amelia Murray, had paid tribute to Lady Byron as a woman who had been 'traduced and misunderstood', but who was 'worshipped' by those few who had known her well. On 6 February 1869, however, Ralph sent to his sister the first – and quite reassuring – English response to Madame de Boissy's tome. Writing under *The Times*'s habitual cloak of anonymity, Caroline Norton had expressed astonished indignation at Madame de Boissy's tone of 'persistent rancour' towards the late Lady Byron. On that same day, Richard Monckton Milnes, Florence Nightingale's former suitor, commended Mrs Norton's defence of Byron's widow to the House of Lords. The House, a little ominously, had offered no response.

Early in 1869, Ralph had other matters on his mind than the poison-tipped darts being hurled at his dead grandmother by a faded Italian beauty with time on her hands (and an obliging spirit guide to advise her on how best to fill it). On 17 March, he informed his

sister that the son of the late Mrs Villiers had given him a batch
of letters from 1852–3 in which his mother and Lady Byron had
exhanged thoughts on the indelicate subject of incest and the late
Augusta Leigh. The letters, so Ralph reported with subdued excitement, contained 'precise and complete information as to everything'.

The following day, 18 March 1869, Ralph took lunch with
Alexander Ross, the Byron-loving vicar of St Philip's in Stepney. The
two men chatted about the possibility of their co-editing a series of
letters which would reveal in Lady Byron's own words – not theirs –
her reasons for leaving her husband. Also present at the lunch, and
acting as consultants on the project, were Edward Noel and the
Reverend Augustus Byron (the 7th Lord's affable younger brother,
recently installed by Ralph as the incumbent at Kirkby Mallory).
De Boissy's book was discussed by the four diners, but only in the
context of a contemplated response to it by Sophia De Morgan, one
which Ralph – an increasingly protective guardian of his grandmother's reputation – intended to dissuade her from writing.*

On 1 June 1869, however, a thoughtfully judicious response to
Teresa's book appeared. It was the first of five anonymously authored
articles that John Fox wrote upon aspects of Lord Byron's private life
for the widely read *Temple Bar* magazine. (In 1871, Fox's articles
were collected and expanded for a book that carried what had by
then become the significant title: *Vindication of Lady Byron*.)

Fox's first essay reminded his 30,000 readers of the fact that
Lord Byron, despite Madame de Boissy's harsh characterisation of
his wife, had frequently blamed himself for the couple's separation,
while pronouncing his wife to have been irreproachable. Fox also
made the first direct allusion to Byron's incest yet to have appeared

---

* In 1875, at a chastened Ralph's request, Mrs De Morgan summarised her views
for him in a lengthy document. Like Edward Noel (who passed the startling
information on to Ralph during the lunch on 18 March 1869), Mrs De Morgan
had heard from Lady Byron that she herself had inadvertently discovered the
poet and Mrs Leigh in an undeniably compromising situation very late on in
the marriage. That disquieting incident had increased Lady Byron's eagerness to
remove her baby daughter from Piccadilly Terrace.

in print. (Madame de Boissy had ventured only a coy reference to Lord Byron's 'deep fraternal feeling' and an 'almost too passionate expression' of brotherly love.)

An otherwise cautiously expressed critique of the *Témoins*, a book that Fox plainly despised, was swept away in the furore that commenced the following month when John Paget, writing for the July 1869 issue of *Blackwood's Magazine*, offered his resounding approval for Madame de Boissy's publication.

John Paget was the son-in-law of Elizabeth Rathbone, one of Lady Byron's warmest admirers back in the mid-century world that had revolved around abolitionism and social reform. Lady Byron had at one point placed certain financial trusts into the care of Mr Paget, a barrister at the Middle Temple. Evidently, there had been a disagreement. By 1869, John Paget was fiercely hostile to the late Lady Byron. He did not need to plough through the 900 pages of the *Témoins* to dig up a story against her that would sell. All that was required was to convey the gist of Teresa's own view, while adding the thunder-and-flash effect of his own more exuberant style.

The result was electrifying. Gleefully, Paget presented the gentle Contessa Guiccioli to *Blackwood's* readers as he imagined her in the first flush of her radiant youth, married off to an evil lecher ('A fouler prostitution never profaned the name of marriage'), while arguing that Lord Byron's role as live-in cavalier to a married woman was in perfect compliance with Italian tradition. And how touching it was (John Paget remarked), to observe this sweet old lady still keeping faith with the one man she had truly loved. How right Madame de Boissy was to reproach Lady Byron for maintaining the silence by which that vile woman had knowingly, wickedly, damned her husband's noble name.

Lord Byron, following the separation from Annabella, had memorably referred to his wife – among a great many other epithets – as 'the moral Clytemnestra of her lord'. John Paget (inspired by Teresa's description of her dead rival's poisonous ways) went one better. In *Blackwood's*, that July, the august Lady Byron was compared to Madame de Brinvilliers, a seventeenth-century murderess who was beheaded and then burned at the stake for poisoning her father and two brothers. Silence (John Paget announced) had been Lady Byron's preferred form of venom: 'a poisonous miasma in which she [Lady Byron] enveloped the character of her husband – raised by her breath, and which only her breath could have dispersed'.

And now she had taken her silence to the grave! Bringing his long tirade to a finely frothing climax, Paget invited a pious – if misquoted – nod of approval from Shakespeare (*Henry VI, Part Two*) for his views: 'She dies and makes no sign – O God, forgive her.'

Annabella's family were understandably distressed by the article in *Blackwood's* (Lord Lovelace privately wrote of it to Robert Noel as 'villainous'), but they chose not to respond to it in print. Ralph had other matters on his mind. In June 1869 he lost his sister and cherished confidante to Wilfrid Scawen Blunt, a Byronically attractive, fortune-hunting and blushlessly amoral man whom an adoring Anne frequently addressed as 'My Tyrant'. (Blunt responded by calling his wealthy wife 'Stumpie', 'Little Ugly' – Anne was rather beautiful – or 'Dick'.) Just two months later, having long since recovered from an ill-fated romance with a young Icelandic girl, Ralph himself married Fannie Heriot, the giddily pretty daughter of a Newcastle clergyman. Fanny, fiercely chaperoned by a voluble Irish aunt throughout their engagement, was not yet seventeen.

On 27 August, a dapper Lord Wentworth set off (unchaperoned) with his bride to enjoy a fashionable seaside honeymoon in Boulogne. The couple had only reached Dover when an extremely worried lawyer caught up with his client and presented Ralph with a slim package containing the equivalent of a ticking bomb.

Within Gerard Ford's folder was an advance copy of Harriet Beecher Stowe's opening – and entirely unsolicited – salvo in defence of the injured Lady Byron. Due for publication in America on 1 September in *The Atlantic Monthly*, 'The True Story of Lady Byron's Life' comprised a twenty-nine-page essay which was due to appear simultaneously in England (in a paraphrased and annotated version) in *MacMillan's Magazine*.

Mrs Stowe's publicly declared motive for rushing into print was the outrage she had felt both at reading John Paget's article for *Blackwood's* (the British magazine was immensely popular with American readers) and at the silence with which its vicious allegations had been greeted. To Ralph Wentworth and Gerard Ford, the American novelist's indignation felt manufactured. Officially, Paget's anonymously authored article had been published in July, but nineteenth-century magazines were notoriously late in issuing their final copy. Gerard Ford believed – and Ralph shared the lawyer's scepticism – that Mrs Stowe had already been preparing an animated response to de Boissy's book when John Paget wrote his piece. *Blackwood's* simply offered a conveniently topical peg upon which to hang her own sensational tale. It was one that could be relied upon to raise the profile of an author whose sales were not what they had been back in the 1850s, before the outcome of a hideous civil war robbed abolitionism of its market value. Ford was especially angry that the advance copy of Mrs Stowe's article had reached his legal office only – and, he believed, quite deliberately – when it was too late for steps to be taken to prevent its publication.

ᙚᙓᙚ

John Paget's assault upon Lady Byron's reputation had caused little more than an unpleasant flutter of gossip. It was Stowe's 'True Story' that raised the storm from which Lady Byron's name has suffered enduring damage.

Much of the fault was due to Mrs Stowe's own careless haste. By the late summer of 1869, she had heard much – but far from all – of the complicated history of the Byron marriage and separation. Assistance had come from her friend Eliza Follen, one of Lady Byron's chief confidantes.* (It was from Mrs Follen that Mrs Stowe had first heard about Byron's incest.) But Mrs Stowe had

---

* Mrs Follen had also helped Harriet Martineau with her article about Lady Byron, back in 1860, negotiating a payment by Mr Fields at *The Atlantic Monthly* of $2 a page. (Martineau Letters, CRL, University of Birmingham.)

personally seen no documents, other than Harriet Martineau's laudatory essay and a handful of prudently reticent letters from Lady Byron herself.

Such a lack of precise information would prove singularly unfortunate, both for Lady Byron and her daughter. Unburdened by the facts, Mrs Stowe believed that the Byrons – at the time Annabella left her husband – had been married for two years, not one. The error was grave. It placed Lady Byron in the position of a complicit, knowing witness to the incest which had resulted in Medora's birth in the summer of 1814. Of Ada Lovelace, Harriet Beecher Stowe evidently knew almost nothing. William was dismissively set aside in the article as a mere 'man of fashion'. The absence of reference to Ada encouraged Victorian readers to assume that Lord Byron's daughter, his rare, extraordinary child, had been cut from the same cloth as her patently trivial spouse.

The response to Mrs Stowe's initial publication was dramatic. In America, 15,000 readers of *The Atlantic Monthly* promptly cancelled their subscriptions, nearly causing James T. Fields's revered magazine to go out of business. Privately, Oliver Wendell Holmes enquired whether dear Harriet was quite certain of the dreadful fact (the incest) that she had so boldly asserted in print. Writing from England on 10 December 1869, George Eliot rebuked Stowe for her thoughtlessness in unveiling what was a private family scandal.

In January 1870, an undaunted Mrs Stowe returned to the fray. *Lady Byron Vindicated* disclosed by its title alone that this book was to be no mere hagiography. John Stuart Mill had pointed the way forward. His *The Subjection of Women*, published in 1869, was admired by Stowe for its emphasis upon the slavery of women, a topic which fitted well with the subject upon which she had justly established her reputation. But the use of the word 'vindicated' in her title connected Stowe's new book more directly to Mary Wollstonecraft's feminist polemic of 1792 (*A Vindication of the Rights of Woman*). Eight decades later, women's rights were back on the agenda in America. *Lady Byron Vindicated* was written with that large audience of disenfranchised voters well to the fore in the mind of Mrs Stowe.

Paget's article for *Blackwood's* had followed Madame de Boissy's lead in criticising Lady Byron for a silence (about the reason for leaving her husband) which, when writing her earlier article, Mrs Stowe had been at pains to defend. It was, she had stated with admiration in 'True Story', a 'perfect silence'. *Lady Byron Vindicated* marked a change of stance. Ill-treated by a brutal husband, Lady Byron had not said enough. She had neglected a public duty by failing to broadcast the ghastly details (the incest) of a disgraceful tale. Wealthy, philanthropic, strong-willed and formidably intelligent, who could have been better placed than Lady Byron to light the way forward, to offer enslaved wives a more lofty position from which to seek equality and escape humiliation?

Warming to her theme, Mrs Stowe berated one old-fashioned *Blackwood's* reviewer who had praised a certain widow (not Lady Byron) for concealing the brutal way in which her husband had treated her. Reverting to her finest declamatory style, Mrs Stowe set up a caricature of what she conceived such men as this widow's admirer to want:

> helpless, cowering, broken-hearted, abject women given over to the animal love which they share alike with the dog – the dog, who, beaten, kicked, starved, and cuffed, still lies by his drunken master with great anxious eyes of love and sorrow ...

While such passages as this made for sumptuous reading at the breakfast table, they bore no relation – as even Lady Byron's worst enemies conceded – to the behaviour of Byron's wife. (Nobody had ever accused Lady Byron of acting like a whipped dog.) But it was not Mrs Stowe's impassioned defence of the right of abused wives to speak out that caused the real, persisting disquiet. It was the fact that a respected author, first in an article and then in the book that followed it, had set down in flaunting, naked print the fact of an incestuous relationship which she believed to have continued, with his wife's knowledge, throughout the entire period of Lord Byron's marriage.

∽◎∾

Lady Byron Vindicated fanned the flames, but it was 'The True Story' that had ignited the fire in which Annabella's hard-won reputation as a good-hearted and progressive social reformer was to be incinerated. *The Tablet*, slyly remarking that Mrs Stowe's article was a godsend to the British press in a September that was short of news, noted that, in Newcastle alone, three versions of 'The True Story' had been published by the end of the month. Tickets for Mr Charles Larkin's Newcastle lecture upon 'The Byron Scandal' were said to be selling out fast. William Howitt had meanwhile rushed his own unkind recollections of a generous patron into print on 4 September, in the *Daily News*. Three days later, the *Pall Mall Gazette* published a dignified letter in which Ralph truthfully stated that his grandmother's written account of the marriage and separation (in a letter which she had despatched to Mrs Stowe at her request, and which Harriet had duly returned) contained no mention of incest. On 11 September, *The Athenaeum*, rising to the defence of the 'retired, gentle, pure and modest life' of Augusta Leigh, slyly enquired whether Mrs Stowe had sullied her soul by taking payment for her hideous diatribe. (She had, and of course they knew it.) Elsewhere, the *Edinburgh Review* found it impossible to review even such a harmless work as the late Henry Crabb Robinson's diaries in October 1869 without alluding to the scandalous talk about Lady Byron.

Privately, Ralph said of the onslaught by the press upon his late grandmother's reputation that both he and his sister felt as though they had been driven out into a storm, stark naked. Publicly, ordered by their father to hold their tongues, the siblings maintained an unhappy silence. It can't have been easy. In October 1869, and again in January 1870, helpfully supplied with papers by the Leigh family, by John Murray, by Hobhouse's daughter, Lady Dorchester* – and even by Lord Lovelace himself – the lawyer Abraham Hayward started a new and long-running hare in the *Quarterly Review*. Lord Byron, so Hayward now declared, would never have slept with Mrs Leigh, she having been a mother figure, 'being so much older', and 'not at all an attractive person'. William Lovelace, meanwhile, was advised by a helpful relative on 8 November 1869 that busy Mrs Stowe had sent over to London a batch of various proofs. One, edited by a certain Charles Mackay, appeared to contain a memoir by the late Medora Leigh. With luck, Mackay's book would prove too bad to appear in print. Still, perhaps Lord Lovelace might wish to intervene? Lovelace, writing back to his informant (Lord Chichester was Augusta Leigh's nephew), explained that his hands were tied both by a personal horror of publicity and by the unfortunate fact that Lady Byron and he had not even been on speaking terms when she died. Publicly, at least, Lord Lovelace declined to intervene.

Nothing by now was too bad to be served up to a gossip-hungry public, whipped into a raging fever by journalists who wrote about Lady Byron as if they were prosecuting an indicted criminal (with a shrewd eye on the gallery of enthralled spectators). Charles Mackay, the editor of Medora's alcohol-fuelled ravings, appealed for a redeemed Lord Byron to be acquitted in 'that Great Court of Conscience'. Lady Byron's employment of the two escaped slaves at Ockham School was touched upon only so that Mackay might shockingly denounce their patron as a 'n****r-worshipper' (although he himself did *not* use asterisks). John Fox, while praising Annabella's work as a progressive reformer in *Temple Bar* (October, 1870), added fuel to the flames by suggesting that it was not incest, but sodomy – a crime that under English law was punishable by

---

* On 15 February 1886, one Henry Carlisle begged Lady Dorchester to return the letters that she had loaned to Abraham Hayward, of which Hayward 'would gladly be rid', as the letters were now causing 'trouble' from Lord Wentworth. The mystery of why Lady Dorchester's father, Lord Broughton (formerly Sir John Cam Hobhouse), ever came into possession of the Byron–Melbourne correspondence remains unsolved. (Lovelace Byron Papers).

death – that had caused Lady Byron to leave her husband. Buggery (Fox strongly implied) would justify Lady Byron's public silence: how could any wife speak out upon such a subject?

Appeals were frequently – and vainly – made for the elderly Stephen Lushington to speak out about the past. Privately, however, in January 1870, Lushington confided to Lady Byron's only male trustee, Henry Bathurst, that his client had been spurred into leaving her husband by Byron's disgraceful boast of having recently lain between two naked prostitutes, fondling both, while pondering which of them he should bring home to dwell alongside his wife. Incest was not – it had never been – the reason for Lady Byron's departure. So a still shocked Stephen Lushington recalled, and Bathurst took the esteemed lawyer at his word. In public, Lushington continued to maintain silence regarding the private life of a client whom he continued to revere until his death, at Ockham, in 1873.

January 1870 was the month in which the attacks reached their climax. John Paget had already compared the late Lady Byron to a murderess. Now, *Blackwood's* rhetoric-intoxicated maestro urged all self-respecting women to save their own souls by abhorring and condemning her, every woman, that is, 'who had not sunk into a state of degradation lower than that of the lowest prostitute that ever haunted the night-houses of the Haymarket'. There, within those depths into which no respectable female would ever venture to peep, Miss Martineau's model of virtue glared shamelessly up from her own iniquitous pit. As for the household over which this deplorable hypocrite had presided at 13 Piccadilly Terrace, such an establishment would excite disgust even in 'the wretched and vicious neighbourhoods' in which (Mr Paget could only coyly imagine) such dreadful places might actually exist.

So much for Lady Byron. Mr Paget was nevertheless eager to grant her noble husband a clean bill of health. He quoted (in this same January article) the indignant words of a Mr Delmé-Radcliffe, who had recently informed readers of the *Telegraph* that the rumour of Byron's incest was 'a lie – an odious damned lie, upon my soul, a lie – a wicked lie'. The late Sir John Cam Hobhouse (long since transformed from one of Byron's rowdiest drinking cronies into Lord Broughton, a portly pillar of Victorian society) was also invoked for for his stirring defence during the 1840s of Lord Byron's entitlement to a monument in Westminster Abbey.* *And why not?* demanded Paget. Byron had been an eminent poet. More than that, as Lord Broughton himself had been proud to declare, 'he was, in the best sense of the word, a gentleman!'

Perhaps the most discomforting aspect of the savage attack upon Lady Byron that a reckless Mrs Stowe had inadvertently unleashed is the evidence that only John Fox and Eliza Lynn Linton (anonymously publishing a series of calm, fair-minded pieces in the *Saturday Review*) gave any thought at all to Lady Byron's descendants. Mrs Stowe herself had expressed unconvincing amazement that any living members of the family might yet survive with whom she could have consulted. (Had she really never heard of Ralph, who was living at his grandmother's house during Mrs Stowe's three visits to England, or of Anne, the intelligent, artistic granddaughter in whom Lady Byron took such pride?) The truth would seem to be that Mrs Stowe launched her grand defence without ever attempting to make contact with a family who were certain (as Mrs Follen had surely advised her) to obstruct such an indiscreetly assertive attempt at an apologia.

Equally hypocritical, however, were the widespread professions of shocked disbelief at the tale of Byron's incest. That story (as the journalists admitted in their colourful comparisons to loathsome reptiles and ancient denizens of the sewers) had been slithering around private dinner tables and publishers' backrooms ever since the year of the Byrons' separation. Shock suited the framing of a new heroine, one who was ripe for their sugar-stuffed Victorian audience. Alongside their pleasing image of the virginal Teresa Guiccioli, the journalists now placed an even more ludicrous caricature of Augusta Leigh: a quiet angel of the hearth at whose knee, each night, her innocent children knelt to lisp their prayers.†

---

* Byron had to wait until 1969 to be granted his place in the abbey.
† John Paget created this celestial image for *Blackwood's* (January 1870).

Presented with the uplifting portrait of such a saintlike sister (it was one which the gentlemen of the press continued to embellish for their readers' delectation until well past the end of the century), the public's consciousness of Lord Byron's incest dwindled to the status of a hideous mirage, the deluded fantasy of his jealous and consummately deceitful wife.

In England, Mrs Stowe herself was pardoned for what was perceived as a blunderingly inaccurate, but well-intended enterprise. In France, where Harriet's defence of Lady Byron had incurred the unyielding hostility of Madame de Boissy, Teresa was still consoling herself in 1870 with the thought that readers of Mrs Stowe's hateful book seemed now to believe that Lady Byron had, at best, been mad enough to merit permanent confinement in an asylum.*

In 1871, Ralph Wentworth's young wife gave birth to a girl, Ada Mary (always known as Molly), at their London home. Lord Wentworth's happiness was short-lived. On 7 July of the following year, a crestfallen Ralph wrote to tell his sister that it was 'physically impossible' he could have been responsible for Fannie's second pregnancy. The father-to-be was a certain James Blyth, a military man who owned a home near Reading. This second child of Fannie's died in infancy. Ralph had already left the country, after bestowing Molly (whose paternity he now also had cause to doubt) upon the Blunts, a well-intended solace for their recent loss of newborn twins. Judith, the Blunts' only surviving child, was born in February 1873.

Humiliated and considerably impoverished by his fickle wife's fondness for jewels and gambling, Ralph remained abroad through the mid-1870s. Following Fannie's death in 1878 (and an ill-considered, swiftly terminated engagement to an American author,

---

* Madame de Boissy's uninhibitedly malevolent letters about both Lady Byron and Mrs Stowe were to Madame Emma Fagnani (whose husband, Giuseppe, she had commissioned to paint twinned portraits of the late Lord Byron and herself). They are great fun to read and are in the Byron papers held at *HRC*, Box 7.15.

Julia Fletcher), he returned home. In 1880, Lord Wentworth embarked upon a happy second marriage, one that had been actively encouraged – in an unconscious echo of the role played by Annabella in matchmaking Ada to William Lovelace – by the bride's mother. Mary Stuart-Wortley proved to be both a loving wife to Ralph and a talented successor to his architect father. Working in collaboration with Charles Voysey, Mary continued William Lovelace's exuberantly imaginative redevelopment of the villages of Ockham and East Horsley. Ralph and Mary never had – and seemingly did not regret the absence of – children of their own.

By 1880, having returned from years of travelling in the Middle East, the Blunts had settled at Wilfrid's family home, Crabbet Park in Sussex. Here, a handsome house newly designed by the multi-talented Lady Anne Blunt was surrounded by the park in which the couple managed their celebrated stud of Arabian horses. Ralph and his second wife had meanwhile moved into an immense new home on Swan Walk, Chelsea, a corner house which had been built to Ralph's specific requirements during his years abroad.* (Fannie's gambling debts and jewel purchases were evidently not on quite the prodigious scale that her distraught husband's letters had once suggested.)

It was Wentworth House that became, from 1880, the headquarters for discussions about the family papers with which Ralph had grown understandably obsessed. Just along the road in Cheyne Row, and always ready to sympathise with his difficulties, Sophia De Morgan shared a house with her agreeable and very social daughter, Mary. Nearby, slowly gathering together various anecdotes and fragments of literary history for fictional use in *The Aspern Papers* (1888), lived that most anglicised of American writers, Henry James.

The acknowledged and most direct source for his story about

---

* The house overlooks the Chelsea Physic Garden. Building work had been supervised in Ralph's absence by the avuncular Augustus Byron, one of Lord Wentworth's staunchest allies.

the ethics of literary collection was the tale related to James about a hopeful Bostonian's courtship of the ageing Claire Clairmont. (Edward Silsbee, from 1872–5, was an attentive lodger in the Florentine house where Miss Clairmont and her niece then presided over a treasure trove of letters from the time when she had given birth to a daughter, Allegra, accepted by Lord Byron as his own.) By 1887, when the London-based writer began work on his wonderful novella, Henry James was also intrigued by Lord Wentworth's tireless pursuit of any papers that could throw light upon the historic scandal of the Byron marriage. It is fair to assume that the trials of an obsessive collector stirred the imagination of a writer whose attentiveness to 'données' (inspiring ideas) was second to none.

Ralph's lifelong endeavour to restore honour to his grandmother's besmirched name resulted in numerous battles. He made no public response in 1883, when *The Athenaeum* published a series of fifty-year old Byron and Leigh letters intended to demonstrate that the talk of incest had been a malicious fabrication. In 1886, however, the eminent Leslie Stephen added a lengthy essay on Lord Byron to his heroic and home-produced *Dictionary of National Biography*. In these august pages, the father of Virginia Woolf (a man whose own daughter not long after this would be molested by an older half-brother) loftily dismissed the allegations against Augusta Leigh as 'absolutely incredible', the jealous ramblings of a scorned wife whose reasons for leaving her husband had never been established. Stephen also (much to the delight of the Leigh family) suggested that Mary Chaworth, rather than Augusta, had been the enduring object of Byron's secret love. Another step had been laid on the stairs ascending to a purified Mrs Leigh – and leading down to the already grubby realm inhabited by a desanctified Lady Byron.

Challenged by an infuriated Ralph about his allegations, an unphased Leslie Stephen requested evidence to the contrary. In 1887, while conceding that the letters produced by Lord Wentworth had indeed entirely undermined his own assertions, the ageing author-editor proved too enfeebled to undertake his promised revisions, or even a modest errata note. The *DNB* entry on Lord Byron, somewhat shockingly, remained unaltered. Instead, Sir Leslie volunteered his services as a consultant as to which letters should be included in Ralph's own first discreet submission to the historic controversy.*

The redemptive intentions of Ralph's book, *Lady Noel Byron and the Leighs*, were apparent from the fact that he completed it on his grandmother's birthday (17 May) and dedicated it to his parents. Quoting a line from Carlyle's *French Revolution* as his inspiration ('Where thou findest a lie that is oppressing thee, extinguish it'), Ralph focused his attack upon the reviewers of 1869–71 who had first set out to make a monster of Lady Byron and a martyr of Mrs Leigh. Augusta, so Ralph now stated, had been neither pure nor upright, nor even conveniently plain. She had never been slandered by Lady Byron. In fact, Augusta's own family had thanked Ralph's grandmother for her generosity. (As evidence, Ralph cited the 1856 letter in which Augusta's widowed half-sister, Mary Chichester, had requested a meeting with Lady Byron, in order to convey her own heartfelt gratitude on behalf of the 'unfortunate' family of Mrs Leigh.)

Diligently though the arguments were set out and substantiated by the letters of which Ralph by then owned the largest collection in the country, the tiny print run of a mere three dozen copies for *Lady Noel Byron and the Leighs* (1887) ensured that its influence was negligible. Recipients of the hand-delivered copies (primarily friends and relatives) already shared Ralph's view: these sympathisers included his sister, his brother-in-law, various Noels, the De Morgans, and Ralph's sympathetic young half-brother, Lionel, born in 1865 from Lord Lovelace's second marriage.

Lord Lovelace, perhaps because (in characteristic fashion) he was

---

* As later with *Astarte* (privately published for Ralph Lovelace in 1905), Leslie Stephen's advice to Ralph leaned always towards the vindication of Augusta Leigh. It was Stephen, in both cases, who persuaded Ralph to omit the most self-incriminating and confessional of Mrs Leigh's letters to Lady Byron and Mrs Villiers.

off busily building himself a vast new home – his fourth – near Lake
Torridon in north-west Scotland, was unavailable for comment.

In 1893, the old earl died. Lionel, who had been left Horsley
Towers and the Scottish estate, while Ashley Combe and Ockham
Park went to his older brother, touched Ralph's heart by instantly
offering to send him the family portraits that still adorned Horsley's
Great Hall: the Margaret Carpenter painting of Ada, in the year
of her marriage; the Albanian portrait of Lord Byron; Hoppner's
representation of little Annabella Milbanke in a high-waisted white
dress. Brought back to Wentworth House,* these striking images
were on show by 5 February 1895, when Henry James, accompanied
by his London neighbour, Mary De Morgan, was invited over to
view the most incriminatingly incestuous letters that were by now in
Ralph's possession. (Loaned the Byron–Melbourne correspondence
by Hobhouse's daughter, Lady Dorchester, Ralph prudently made
copies.)

Returning to his own home later that night, Henry James recorded
in his notebook that he had already been considering a brother–sister
drama when he was shown the letters. James went a little further,
stating for his own peace of mind that nothing so 'nefarious' as the
Lovelace letters had even crossed his mind.

So Henry James said and doubtless he believed what he wrote
down. But when he went on to write *The Turn of the Screw* (1897),
was the novelist's perception of the strange, hidden relationship
between the two children of Bly – Miles and Flora – and their
ghostly alter egos, Peter Quint and Miss Jessel, affected by what he
had read and heard two years earlier at Wentworth House? Might

---

* Relations between Ralph and his father had not been improved by William
Lovelace's demand in 1867 for £80,000 to renounce his technical ownership of
Lady Byron's Wentworth estates. They had worsened when he refused to allow
his son to inhabit either Ashley Combe or Ockham during his own lifetime.
By 1893, Ockham, rented out to Lady Norbury for almost two decades after
Dr Lushington's death, had fallen into terrible disrepair. Ralph and his wife
would spend a fortune, and many years, restoring Ralph's beloved childhood
home to habitable use. (Ashley proved to have been only a little less neglected.)
Meanwhile, the couple remained at their comfortably modern home in Chelsea.

Byron's letters to Lady Melbourne, and to Augusta, have contributed to the sense of something lubricious and elusive, never quite
visible, that makes James's self-styled 'potboiler' feel so troubling
to its readers? Had Ralph talked about his grandmother's strange
insistence that young Byron Ockham should be kept away from his
sister at all times? Impossible to prove, the disturbing influence of
the letters that Henry James was shown by Ralph Lovelace, upon
his own story of two intensely close siblings and their ambiguous
interpreter, merits, perhaps, a consideration that it has not, as yet,
received.

∽♋

The final stage in Ralph's long battle to reclaim the high ground for
his grandmother was triggered by a disagreement arising from John
Murray's end-of-the-century edition of Byron's letters. Handsomely
bound in gold and sea-blue cloth, the volumes were annotated
and edited by Rowland Prothero. Ralph withdrew from his role
in the project as editor-in-chief after reading *The Times* review of
Volume 3, in which the anonymous reviewer asserted (once again),
that it was now clear that Lady Byron had no reason to leave her husband. To Ralph, it seemed that Prothero and Murray had combined
to strengthen the case against his grandmother, and to vindicate
Mrs Leigh. Determined to proclaim the truth, once and for all,
the 2nd Lord Lovelace now embarked upon the immense project
that would absorb him almost until his death in 1906. (Mary, his
widow, recalled that her often sad and distrait husband had never
appeared so calm and at ease as when he was at work upon this final
endeavour.)

Huge, unwieldy and cumbersomely written, *Astarte, or A
Fragment of the Truth* (Ralph's title alluded to the female figure in
Byron's *Manfred*) remains a cobwebbed treasure trove for Byron
scholars. But it is not the hagiography one might expect. Ralph spoke
candidly about what he now recalled as a miserable upbringing and
an unsatisfactory education. He deplored some of his grandmother's

'despotic' ways.* *Astarte* nevertheless offered the clearest account that had yet been provided of the Byron marriage, together with the clearest justification for Annabella's departure from it. Privately, however, Ralph blamed his grandmother's parents for their excessive influence upon a conscientiously dutiful daughter. Leaving Byron, so Ralph Lovelace had come to believe, was the source of all his grandmother's sorrows. Like Henry Crabb Robinson, Ralph never forgot the wistfulness with which Lady Byron talked about her husband during her own last years, as if entombed within a prison of her own regrets.

Ralph died peacefully while standing on the terrace at Ockham one warm early evening in August 1906. Eight months earlier, he had received a courteous tribute to *Astarte* from Henry James (who gently expressed the wish that its author had been just a little less reticent).† It may have been as well that Lord Lovelace died just before the publication of a book (*Lord Byron and his Detractors* deliberately echoed 'Lord Byron and his Calumniators', the title of John Paget's scurrilous essay for *Blackwood's* in January, 1870) in which John Murray IV and Rowland Prothero stubbornly asserted that no substantial proof had yet been provided of Mrs Leigh's guilt. Without the admission that Lady Byron had failed to obtain from an evasive Augusta Leigh at their ill-fated Reigate encounter, so Lord Byron's staunchest defenders asserted, Ralph Lovelace's charge of incest remained unproven.

---

* 'Despotic' was a word much used of Lady Byron by her later detractors, including Mrs Langley Moore. It had first appeared in an 1888 letter, in which the elderly Anna Jones remarked to Ralph that Lady Byron was 'despotic' about the accuracy with which her own words should be reported to future generations. That description was one that resonated with the 49-year-old recipient, as he began to reflect upon his grandmother's firm supervision during his early life.
† Henry James had become a firm friend of both Ralph and Mary Lovelace. In 1909, he and John Buchan (whose wife was Mary Lovelace's niece) would be asked around to Wentworth House by Ralph's widow, in order to attest the value of certain letters due to be deposited at the British Museum. Buchan, shocked by what he read, wrote in his later memoir of the 'ancient indecency' at which his cooler colleague (who had of course seen most of the 'incest' letters already) had apparently turned not a hair.

In 1907 (in a book commissioned by John Murray IV), Richard Edgcumbe entered the lists with *Byron: The Last Phase*. The truth, so Edgcumbe laboriously explained to credulous readers, was that the bearer of Byron's secret child had been his first love, Mary Chaworth. Augusta had gallantly faked a pregnancy in order to save from social disgrace a married woman to whom Mrs Leigh, like her brother, remained deeply attached. Every incriminating verse that Byron had addressed to his beloved sister had in fact been written to Mary Chaworth. Entertaining to read, Edgcumbe's book is best treated as an extravagant fiction.

How much did Rowland Prothero and John Murray IV know of the true story? The awkward answer peeps through Marie Belloc Lowndes's record of a conversation which took place on 4 December 1911. Dining at the Murrays' Wimbledon home, Hilaire Belloc's clever older sister learned that her host privately accepted the story of incest, but believed that he, as the indebted descendant of Byron's own publisher, had a duty to suppress that fact.

In 1920, the widowed Mary Lovelace made her own contribution to the reclamation of Lady Byron. To a second and expanded edition of *Astarte,* Mary now added the letters which Ralph himself had been criticised for excluding. (The fault was not altogether his: Lady Dorchester had refused to permit the inclusion of Byron's most revealing letters to Lady Melbourne, while the discreetly manipulative Leslie Stephen had dissuaded Ralph from publishing several self-incriminating letters written by Mrs Leigh.) Writing an affectionate memoir of her husband during that same post-war period, Ralph's widow quietly emphasised the burden that the issue of his grandmother's reputation had become for him, and how hard an honourable man had always striven to do what he believed to be right.

Forty years of experience of dealing both with Lady Byron's papers and a sensation-loving press had taught the second Lady Lovelace the value of discretion. Writing about Ralph's sister in 1920, three years after Anne's death, Mary glided placidly over the details of the Blunts' bizarre and frequently wretched marriage. (It had ended in 1906, the year of Ralph's death.) Instead, she dwelt upon Anne's exceptional courage, resilience, vigour (she could still vault on to a horse at the age of seventy-seven) and high intelligence. Blessed (in her sister-in-law's admiring words) with the mind of a scholar, the heart of a child and the soul of a saint, Anne had spent her last ten years living in Egypt. She died as Baroness Wentworth in 1917, having outlived her niece, Molly King-Noel (the title's previous bearer since Ralph Lovelace's death), by just six months.

Judith, Anne's only child, was divorced from her artistic husband, Neville Lytton, in 1923. The couple had been married for twenty-four years. Like her mother, and like Ada, Lady Lytton (also known as Baroness Wentworth) had an uncommon affinity with animals, and above all, with horses. When she died in 1957, the Crabbet Stud still comprised seventy-five of the world's most beautiful horses, colourful murals of which adorned the ceilings of Crabbet Park, the graceful house designed by Judith's mother. The stud was later sold – and subsequently dismantled – by one of Judith's two daughters, Lady Winifrid Tryon. The house, happily, survives.

∞

Houses, as much as their owners, have stories to be told. Seaham is now a spa. Halnaby has gone. Newstead Abbey's future is currently far from secure.

Horsley Towers was sold by Ralph's widow, Mary Lovelace, in 1920 to the great aircraft designer Sir Thomas Sopwith. Now a hotel, it retains the exterior and many of the internal features of William Lovelace's extravagant creation, including the chapel, Ada's tower and the mausoleum in which William and his second wife were buried. In 2018, a magnificent self-portrait of Sir Hubert Herkomer still hangs in Horsley's entrance hall, signalling its architectural influence upon Lululaund, the Bavarian polymath's own spectacular fantasy home (long since destroyed) at Bushey, in Hertfordshire.

Woburn Park has gone. At nearby Brooklands, Hugh Locke King

created England's first motor-racing track in 1907. (The house, built by Lady Hester King for her favourite son, is now a college.) The Lovelaces' house at Ashley Combe has been demolished. So has Kirkby Mallory, better known today as Mallory Park, a motorbike track. The church and graveyard survive, as does Ada's unkempt shrine.

Fire destroyed the main house at Ockham Park in 1948, seven years after Mary Lovelace's death. The family papers escaped the blaze, having been stored in the separate stable block (which survives). In 1957, they were moved to Crabbet, to be divided between Judith Lytton's two daughters and her son, grandfather of the present Lord Lytton.

POSTSCRIPT

Lady Byron's fate, following her mauling at the hands of the gentlemen of the Victorian press, was to continue to be perceived as they had described her. Ralph's two books, reaching a tiny, well-informed audience, caused no shift in the public's perception of her as a coldly vindictive woman. Neither, in 1929, did Ethel Colburn Mayne's redemptive account of a maligned philanthropist. Visitors to Kensal Green need sharp eyes to discover Lady Byron's name on the 1885 Reformers' Memorial. (She is listed alongside Barbara Bodichon, John Stuart Mill, Elizabeth Fry, Josephine Butler and Robert Dale Owen.)

Thirty years after the publication of Mrs Mayne's book, access to the Lovelace Papers was independently granted to Malcolm Elwin (working on the papers held at New Buildings, a house on the Crabbet Estate, by the Earl of Lytton) and to that ardent Byronophile, Doris Langley Moore (working on the papers held at Crabbet by Lord Lytton's sisters).* It was unfortunate for Lady

---

* In 1972, the collections were separately placed on loan to the Bodleian Library (as the Lovelace Byron Papers) and to the British Library (as the Wentworth Papers).

Byron, already in the doghouse, that neither Elwin nor Moore liked her. Malcolm Elwin's books (the second of which was completed by another hand and published after his death in 1973) confirmed the grim portrait of Lady Byron given in works by Mrs Moore, books which reached a far wider audience.

A respected authority upon Lord Byron, Langley Moore's enduring prejudice against his wife has exerted an unfortunately baleful influence. The origin of her somewhat excessive devotion to the poet and his works, as her unpublished memoir makes clear, was touchingly romantic. Growing up in Johannesburg, where her father was the editor of the *Sunday Times*, Doris Langley-Levy became addicted to Byron's works at an early age. Her father gave her a copy of *Childe Harold* in 1917, when she was just fifteen years old; when she arrived in England six years later, Langley-Levy was carrying the book and had set her heart on entering the world of Byronic studies. Warmly supported by John Murray VI ('Jock'), she went on to write several magnificent books about the poet. The strength of her attachment to him is apparent in the fact that she was married while standing upon the – rather fragile – slab that covers the Byron family vault at Hucknall Torkard. (The slab has since then been placed under a protective raised box with a see-through lid.) While Robin Moore became the biographer's official husband, it is hardly an exaggeration to state that his wife's heart, until the day she died, belonged to Lord Byron.

Immense though Mrs Moore's contribution to the world of Byron scholarship has been, her espousal of the poet resulted in a uniquely skewed take upon his life. Viewing herself almost in the role of a consort, it proved impossible for Moore to take an impartial view of the actual wife who had, after a single year, abandoned Lord Byron and left his house. She herself, she must have felt, would never have shown such disloyalty.

Drawing upon the wealth of family letters which was placed in her hands at Crabbet and working in close correspondence at all times with Leslie Marchand, the magnificent second editor of Byron's letters (Rowland Prothero was the first), Mrs Moore used that rich resource to create an unforgettable portrait of Lady Byron as a neurotic hypochondriac, a mutton-stuffing glutton, a grudging giver and a humourless despot.

The truth about Annabella, as Julia Markus set out to demonstrate in *Lady Byron and Her Daughters* (2015) – following the trail explored by Ethel Coburn Mayne (1929) and Joan Pierson (1992) – is both more complex and more nuanced. Annabella was undeniably a controlling, over-legalistic and often difficult woman, one whose enlightened attitude to reform and whose generous use of a great fortune to improve social conditions went hand in hand with an attitude that can, at best, be described as interventionist. She did bear grudges, as William Lovelace discovered to his cost. Loyal to her friends and kind to the less fortunate of her family, Annabella never ceased to love the captivating and capricious genius with whom she lived as his wife for just one year. As the mother of his child, she did what she sincerely believed was best for a young woman whose personality resisted moulding. She took great pride in Ada, never ceasing to encourage her in her studies, while worrying about her always fragile health and changeable spirit. She turned against William Lovelace only when she felt that he had betrayed his position as a fellow guardian of this precious, but erratic, young woman. At the time of her death, Lady Byron commanded almost universal respect, admiration and – from those who had known her as a loyal friend – love.

Annabella's daughter has suffered a different fate. After a century of obscurity, Ada Lovelace stands in danger of becoming lost behind the growing radiance of a reputation that perceives her largely as an icon: an exceptional female pioneer of computer technology.

In 1869, Ada Lovelace signified nothing more to Harriet Beecher Stowe than the fact that she was married to an aristocrat. Not until the 1950s and the dawn of the computer age did it begin to be realised just how exceptional a contribution Byron's daughter made to a technological future that she would have embraced with delight. It is a future that has retrospectively embraced her. In 2018, we have an Ada Lovelace Day, a NASA language named in her honour, two documentaries about her and a burgeoning Ada Institute for Digital Technology. There are blogs about Ada, courses upon Ada, conferences about Ada, exhibitions about Ada, biographies of Ada, a (magnificent) graphic novel about Ada and children's books about Ada. In Britain and America, the name of Ada Lovelace now carries as much, if not more, weight than that of her celebrated father.

Ada revered her father. In celebrating Lovelace's powerful intelligence and her predictive gifts, however, it is crucial that we recognise the twin sources of Ada's extraordinary personality: that combination of her mother's enquiring, scholarly intelligence with her father's imagination and volatile temperament; a dangerous blend of fierce self-discipline and unbridled euphoria.

Ada Lovelace spent most of her short life trying to live up to her mother's high expectations, while striving to compete against a father who increasingly haunted her imagination. Poetically, he soared above her; in personality, with all its attendant risks, Ada was – and gloried in being – the daughter of Lord Byron, through and through.

Annabella's role in controlling and encouraging the Byronic side of her daughter's vivid personality cannot be overestimated. We can never hope to understand Lady Byron if we fail to accept how torn she was between a romantic desire to see her beloved husband recreated – Annabella's tender pride in Ada's own late-flowering (and not terribly good) poetry speaks for itself – and a prudent terror of seeing reborn in her child the violent demons that she had personally confronted in her husband.

One thing is certain. Lady Byron followed her husband's wishes concerning his daughter to the letter. Ada was brought up – and brought up with far greater consideration, sympathy and love than has been granted in the past – by her mother. But the setter of the ground rules – the watchful advisor from afar during the first eight years of his daughter's life – was that astonishing, legendary father whom Ada never knew.

TIMELINE OF EVENTS

10 December 1815	Birth of Augusta Ada Byron
15 January 1816	Lady Byron leaves her husband
25 April 1816	Byron leaves England (for permanent exile)
3 July 1822	Babbage announces his designs for calculating engines to Sir Humphry Davy
19 April 1824	Byron dies at Missolonghi
1826–8	Lady Byron takes Ada on a Continental tour
May 1829	Following an (unrelated) attack of measles, Ada enters a three-year period of semi-paralysis
1831	Michael Faraday demonstrates electromagnetic induction
1833	Ada endangers her reputation with an attempted elopement
5 June 1833	Ada first visits Babbage's house with her mother and sees a portion of the Difference Engine
1834	Ada begins mathematics lessons with Mary Somerville and attends a lecture about Difference Engine 2 and the need for funding
February 1835	Ada suffers a medical breakdown
April 1835	Lord Melbourne becomes prime minister under King William IV

8 July 1835	Ada marries Lord King at Fordhook, Ealing
12 May 1836	Birth of Byron Noel, later Viscount Ockham
22 September 1837	Birth of Anne Isabella King
30 June 1838	William King is created 1st Earl of Lovelace
2 July 1839	Birth of Ralph Gordon Noel King
June 1840	Ada starts to study mathematics with Augustus De Morgan
11 August 1840	Lord Lovelace is appointed Lord Lieutenant of Surrey
August 1840	Charles Babbage goes to Turin and presents plans for the unbuilt Analytical Engine at a scientific symposium
Autumn 1841	Ada suffers a further medical breakdown
October 1842	Luigi F. Menabrea publishes his account of the Analytical Engine in French (based upon diagrams shown by Babbage in Turin in 1840)
August 1843	Ada's translation of Menabrea's paper is published, with additional 'Notes' by herself as AAL
January 1844	Ada has another breakdown

November 1844	Ada meets John Crosse at Fyne Court in Somerset.
	In London, she corresponds with Michael Faraday, meets with Charles Wheatstone and discusses the possibility of becoming Prince Albert's scientific advisor
28 August 1849	Death of Elizabeth Medora Leigh in Aveyron, France
late August 1849	Byron Ockham goes to sea for three years
Autumn 1850	The Lovelaces visit Newstead Abbey and Ada's interest in betting finds an outlet at Doncaster racecourse
January 1851 – May 1852	Ada leads a private gambling ring and suffers serious losses
June 1851	Following severe haemorrhages, Ada's doctors diagnose cervical cancer
12 October 1851	Death in London of Augusta Leigh
27 November 1852	Ada dies at 6 Great Cumberland Place
16 May 1860	Lady Byron dies at St George's Terrace, Primrose Hill
1 September 1862	Death in Wimbledon of Viscount Ockham
February 1869	The first – and cool – response in print in the UK to Teresa Guiccioli's long book about Byron, in which Lady Byron is denigrated

July 1869	John Paget, in *Blackwood*'s, supports the Guiccioli account and follows her lead in attacking Lady Byron
Summer 1869	Ralph Wentworth marries Fanny Heriot; Anne King-Noel marries Wilfrid Scawen Blunt
September 1869	Publication in the UK and the US of Harriet Beecher Stowe's magazine article, 'True Story', in which she defends Lady Byron against the previous attacks
January 1870	Publication of Harriet Beecher Stowe's expanded, rethought defence of Lady Byron, as *Lady Byron Vindicated*
18 October 1871	Death of Charles Babbage
1888	Leslie Stephen publishes a *DNB* essay on Byron, in which Lady Byron is again denigrated
1889	Ralph Wentworth privately publishes *Lady Noel Byron and the Leighs*
29 December 1893	Death of William Lovelace; Ralph Wentworth becomes 2nd Earl of Lovelace
1905	Publication of *Astarte*, Ralph Lovelace's assessment of the Byron separation and defence of his grandmother against previous attacks upon her reputation
1906	Death of Ralph Lovelace at Ockham Park

1917   Death of Ralph's sister, Lady Anne Blunt, Viscountess Wentworth, following the death of his daughter, Ada Mary (Molly) in the same year

1920   Publication of *Astarte*, edited by Mary, Countess of Lovelace, with additional material

NOTE ON ADA'S HEALTH

Nobody has yet succeeded in identifying just what it was that Ada Lovelace suffered from. Although her early and severe attack of semi-paralysis followed upon measles, it is very rare indeed for measles to cause such a drastic collapse of health. (The last reported case was in 1964.) The cause of Ada's death is not in doubt, but what are we to make of the continual breakdowns in health, the violent mood swings, the desire for solitude (expressed to Andrew Crosse before her first visit to his Somerset home) when one of these attacks afflicted her and – most perplexingly of all, perhaps – the 'mad eyes' referred to by Charles Locock and the swollen facial features which remained in evidence, as Ada wrote in one apologetic letter, to Agnes and Woronzow Greig, for several days?

A thyroid condition is not applicable, since this would have been accompanied by an increase in weight and Ada – as her images clearly show – became increasingly emaciated. (Anorexia cannot be ruled out; Ada's father dieted ferociously to keep himself trim and Ada's husband made it clear that he detested overweight people.)

A condition called cyclothymia holds out a possible answer. A cyclothymic personality will undergo rapid changes of mood, periods of depression and weight loss. Professor Edgar Jones also suggests that Ada's way of dealing with early traumas might have led to what is clinically described as the 'somatising' (or suppressing) of a source of emotional distress, which would emerge in the form of a rash or bodily pains.

It has been suggested that her father suffered from epilepsy and that this, together with a bipolar condition, might help to explain his violent rages and swift recoveries, often – this was notably the case in a remarkable incident that took place in a Cephalonian monastery during the last months of Byron's life – with a state of complete amnesia about what had taken place. But epilepsy does not, Professor Jones explains, usually pass from a father to a daughter. Ada's own temperament, although highly erratic, was uncommonly sweet. The temper she showed as a little girl did not emerge in her adult life.

Possibly, she shared her father's allergy to alcohol. Byron could drink wine with impunity, but not spirits. (The Cephalonian incident, during which Ada's father barricaded himself into a room and hurled furniture at all who tried to enter it, was preceded by a great bout of gin-drinking.) The prescription given to her by the eminent Charles Locock for laudanum and claret as a cure for her ailments was probably not ideal. It is unclear whether, or how much, it exacerbated her condition. Ada herself blamed mesmerism at one point, which only shows how little she knew about the source of her affliction.

I am very grateful for the thoughts given to me on this perplexing topic by Professor Edgar Jones, by Dr Penny Sexton, by Dr Geoffrey Wong and by Dr Anthony Rockwell.

ACKNOWLEDGEMENTS

All through the research and writing of this book, I've been supported and encouraged by goodwill the like of which I've never before experienced. It also helped that the Society of Authors very generously provided me with a grant and that the always generous Harry Ransom Center at Austin, Texas, provided a fellowship that enabled me to visit their collection. David McClay, formerly at the National Library of Scotland, and Mary Clapinson, who originally catalogued the Lovelace Byron Papers on loan to the Bodleian, gave more of their time than any mere biographer should expect. Thank you both, so much.

I am above all indebted to Lord Lytton and to Katy Loffman at Paper Lion, for gracious permission to read and quote freely from the Lovelace Byron Papers. Without this act of kindness, my whole project would have been in ruins.

In no particular order, a tremendous debt of thanks is due to:

Giuseppe Albano, Geoffrey Bond, Mark Bostridge, Robin Byron (13th Lord), Colin Harris, Henry Cobbold, John and Celia Child-Villiers, the Right Hon. Kenneth Clarke, the late Peter Cochran, Nora Crook, John Fuegi and Jo Francis, David Oldrey, Lord Zetland, Lady Howard de Walden, Gillian O'Keefe, Professor Ursula Martin, Dr Christopher Hollings, Professor Betty Toole, Professor Richard Holmes, Sammy Jay, Stephen Wolfram, Doron Swade, Dana Kovarik, Dr Nick Booth, Jenny Childs at the Cadbury Research Collection, Lady Selina Hastings, Professor Samuel Baker,

Professor Roger Louis, John and Virginia Murray, Fiona MacCarthy, Elizabeth Garver, Helen Symington at the NLS, Professor Graeme Segal and Dame Marina Warner, John Pulford and the Brooklands Museum team, Oliver Davies, Georgina Ferry, Sir Drummond Bone, Lord and Lady Ralph Kerr, Jill Weston, Dr Nicholas Woodhouse, Surrey History Centre, Benjamin Ringer, David Sneath, Sally and Henry Machin, Professor William St Clair, Sydney Padua, Professor David Brailsford (whose YouTube exposition of Babbage's work is exquisitely lucid) and Dr Adrian Johnstone (who is engaged with a team that includes Doron Swade on Plan 28, a Royal Holloway project to build Babbage's Analytical Engine by the 2030s).

Thanks are due always to that prince among agents and wisest of counsellors, Anthony Goff. At Simon & Schuster, I am blessed in the enthusiasm and support of my dear chief editor, the wonderful Suzanne Baboneau. I owe much to the patience and input of Karl French (structural editor), Jo Whitford (senior project editor) and Liane Payne (for her beautiful maps and family trees). Sue Stephens is the sort of publicist that writers dream about (in a very good way). Douglas Matthews remains – always – the most thoughtful and satisfying of indexers.

Despite such generous help, work in such a controversial field is bound to result in errors and questionable assertions (I'm thinking of the tricky question about which of Babbage's private discussions in 1834 relate to Difference Engine 2 and which to the Analytical Engine). All such faults and misconceptions are of my own making.

At home, thanks to my son Merlin Sinclair for mathematical input, and Talia and Shira Sinclair, two of Ada Lovelace's most ardent admirers. A significant part of Lovelace's fanbase comprises young girls who admire her spirit and achievement. May you all grow up to have Ada's intelligence, imagination and perseverance, with none of her problems.

Last, my greatest debt is to Ted Lynch, the morale-booster, unflagging enthusiast and patient co-editor who helped to shape and clarify my first draft. Without you at my side and on my side, my dearest Ted, this long-planned book would not be here.

SELECT BIBLIOGRAPHY

While the list given here by no means represents everything I have read, it offers guidance to anybody keen to pursue any of the multiple strands in the story.

I would especially recommend anybody interested in Ada to seek out on YouTube *The Ada Project* by Conrad Shawcross, RA, which uses a hacked assembly line industrial robot to evoke the questing spirit of a remarkable young woman.

Books and articles relating to Annabella Milbanke, Lady Noel Byron

Beecher Stowe, Harriet, 'The True Story of Lady Byron's Life' in *Macmillan's Magazine* (UK) and *Atlantic Monthly* (US), September, 1869.

——*Lady Byron Vindicated* (London, Sampson Low & Son, 1870).

Blessington, Marguerite, Countess of, *Conversations of Lord Byron* (London, H. Colburn, 1834).

Crane, David, *The Kindness of Sisters: Annabella Milbanke and the Destruction of the Byrons* (London, HarperCollins, 2012).

Elwin, Malcolm, *Lord Byron's Wife* (London, Macdonald, 1962).

——*The Noels and the Milbankes* (London, Macdonald, 1962).

——*Lord Byron's Family* (London, John Murray, 1975). Completed by a second hand.

Fox, John, *The Vindication of Lady Byron* (London, R. Bentley, 1871). Largely comprising a series of essays published in *Temple Bar*, with added text.

Fox, Sir John, *Byron, A Mystery* (London, Grant Richards, 1924). Written by the approving son of the above author, with assistance from Mary, Countess of Lovelace.

Graham, T. Austin, 'The Slaveries of Sex, Race and Mind: Harriet Beecher Stowe's "Lady Byron Vindicated"', *New Literary History*, vol. 41, no. 1 (Winter 2010), pp. 173–90.

Gross, J. D., *Byron's 'Corbeau Blanc': The Life and Letters of Lady Melbourne* (Texas, Rice University Press, 1997).

Guiccioli, Teresa, Marquis de Boissy, *Témoins*, translated as *My Recollections of Lord Byron* (London, R. Bentley, 1869). Worth seeking out for the influential and damaging chapter devoted to Byron's marriage.

Lovelace, Ralph, *Lady Noel Byron and the Leighs* (private circulation, 1887).

——*Astarte: A fragment of truth concerning George Gordon Byron, Sixth Lord Byron, recorded by his grandson* (London, Christophers, 1905, 1921).

Markus, Julia, *Lady Byron and Her Daughters* (New York, W. W. Norton, 2015).

Mayne, Ethel Colburn, *The Life and Letters of Anne Isabella, Lady Noel Byron* (London, Charles Scribner, 1929).

Murray, John and Rowland Prothero, *Lord Byron and His Detractors* (London, private circulation, 1906).

Pierson, Joan, *The Real Lady Byron* (London, Robert Hale, 1992). Includes a useful section about the Noel family.

Taylor, Brian W., 'Annabella, Lady Noel-Byron: A Study of Lady Byron on Education', *History of Education Quarterly* vol. 38, no. 4 (1998), pp. 430–55.

Books, music, articles and online material relating to Ada Byron, Countess of Lovelace

Babbage, Charles and Ada Lovelace, *Sketch of the Analytical Machine Invented by Charles Babbage with notes by the translator*, extracted from *Scientific Memoirs* (London, R. and J. E. Taylor, 1843).

Brailsford, David, *Babbage's Analytical Engine*, YouTube, https://youtu.be/5rtKoKFGFSM. All of Professor Brailsford's online lectures about Babbage are invaluably lucid and lively.

Essinger, James, *A Female Genius: How Ada Lovelace Lord Byron's Daughter Started the Computer Age* (London, Gibson Square, 2014).

Ferry, Georgina, 'Ada Lovelace: In search of a "calculus of the nervous system"', *The Lancet*, vol. 386 (2015).

Hammerman, Robin and Andrew L. Russell, *Ada's Legacy* (Vermont, Morgan & Claypool, 2015).

Howard, Emily, *The Lovelace Trilogy*, opera (2011).

Lethbridge, Lucy, *Ada Lovelace: Computer Wizard Of Victorian England* (London, Short Books, 2001). For younger readers, not wholly accurate but a great place to start, together with Sydney Padua.

MacFarlane, Alistair, 'Alistair MacFarlane on the first-ever programmer: Ada Lovelace', *Philosophy Now*, issue 96 (2013).

Martin, Ursula has headed and written some of the most insightful recent explorations of Ada Lovelace's work as a mathematician. Some can be found online at: http://www.tandfonline.com/doi/full/10.1080/17498430.2017.1325297

Moore, Doris Langley, *Ada, Countess of Lovelace, Byron's Legitimate Daughter* (London, John Murray, 1977).

Padua, Sydney, *The Thrilling Adventures of Lovelace and Babbage* (London, Particular Books, 2015).

Spufford, Francis and Jenny Uglow (eds), *Cultural Babbage: Technology, Time and Invention* (London, Faber & Faber, 1996).

Stein, Dorothy, *Ada: A Life and Legacy* (New York, MIT Press, 1985).

Swade, Doron, *The Cogwheel Brain: Charles Babbage and the Quest to Build the First Computer* (London, Little, Brown, 2000). Doron Swade masterminded the Science Museum model of Babbage's calculating engine, comprising 8,000 parts, completed in 2002.

Toole, Betty A., *Ada, the Enchantress of Numbers: A Selection from the Letters of Lord Byron's Daughter and Her Description of the First Computer* (California, Strawberry Press, 1992).

Whitbourn, James, 'Ada', for soprano, alto, tenor, bass choir and piano (Chester, Chester Music, 2015). Commissioned to mark the 200th anniversary of the birth of Ada Lovelace; words by Lord Byron.

Wolfram, Stephen, *Idea Makers: Personal Perspectives on the Lives & Ideas of Some Notable People* (Illinois, Wolfram Media, 2016).

Woolley, Benjamin, *The Bride of Science: Romance, Reason and Byron's Daughter* (London, Pan Macmillan, 2015).

Lord Byron

Austin, Alfred, *A Vindication of Lord Byron* (London, Chapman & Hall, 1869).

Edgcumbe, Richard, *Byron: The Last Phase* (London, John Murray, 1909; Hamburg, Severus, 2012).

Eisler, Benita, *Byron* (London, Hamish Hamilton, 1999).

Grosskurth, Phyllis, *Byron: The Flawed Angel* (Massachusetts, Houghton Mifflin, 1997).

Jeaffreson, John Cordy, *The Real Lord Byron* (London, Hurst & Blackett, 1883).

MacCarthy, Fiona, *Byron, Life and Legend* (London, John Murray, 2002).

Marchand, Leslie, *Byron: A Portrait* 3 vols (London, John Murray, 1957).

——*Byron's Letters & Journals*, 13 vols (John Murray, 1973–94).

Moore, Thomas, *Life and Letters of Lord Byron*, 2 vols (London,

John Murray, 1830; 1831; 1873). The 1831 edition contains Lady Byron's 'Remarks'.

Prothero, Rowland (ed.), *The Works of Byron: Letters and Journals*, 6 vols (London, John Murray, 1898–1902). This contains a great deal of useful additional information not published by Marchand.

Walker, Violet, *The House of Byron* (Shrewsbury, Quiller Press, 1988). Only for those who are interested in Byron's antecedents (the family tree is the most extensive I have seen) and would like to know more about Ada's paternal lineage.

Other useful books to consult

Bakewell, Michael and Melissa, *Augusta Leigh: Byron's Half-sister, A Biography* (London, Chatto & Windus, 2000).

David, Deirdre, *Intellectual Women and Victorian Patriarchy* (New York, Cornell University Press, 1987).

Fox, Celina (ed.) *London: World City 1800–1840* (London, Yale University Press, 1992).

Gunn, Peter, *My Dearest Augusta* (London, Bodley Head, 1968).

Hobhouse, John Cam, Baron Broughton, *Recollections of a Long Life* (London, John Murray, 1910).

Holmes, Richard, *The Age of Wonder: How the Romantic Generation Discovered the Beauty and Terror of Science* (London, HarperPress, 2009).

Origo, Iris, *The Last Attachment* (London, John Murray, 1949).

Secord, James A., *Victorian Sensation: The Extraordinary Publication, Reception, and Secret Authorship of Vestiges of the Natural History of Creation* (London, Chicago University Press, 2000).

Trevanion, Henry *The Influence of Apathy* (unknown publisher, London, 1827).

Winstone, H. V., *Lady Anne Blunt: A Biography* (Gloucester, Barzan, 2003).

NOTES

ABBREVIATIONS

BL – British Library

BL&J – *Byron's Letters & Journals* (ed. by Leslie Marchand)

CRL – Cadbury Research Library (University of Birmingham)

DLM – Doris Langley Moore (Archive of transcriptions and notes in private collection)

HRC – Humanities Research Center, Austin, Texas

LKC – Locke King Collection (Brooklands Museum). The papers identified in these notes are from boxes 9 and 10

MSBY – Somerville Papers (Bodleian Library)

NLS – National Library of Scotland (Murray Papers, still being catalogued for reference)

NYPL – New York Public Library (Berg Collection)

WP – Wentworth Papers (British Library)

Where no source is provided in these notes, the originals are in the catalogued and extensive Lovelace Byron Papers (Dep. Lovelace Byron) held by the Bodleian Library by permission of the present Lord Lytton and initially placed on loan by Lord Lytton's father.

Quotations from Hobhouse's *Diary* are always connected to the late Peter Cochran's excellent online edition (https://petercochran.wordpress.com/hobhouses-diary/). The original diaries can be found at BL, Add MS 56532–5 and Berg Collection volumes 1 and 2 (New York Public Library).

The letters from Lady Anne Blunt to her mother, grandmother and brothers are in WP, Add MS 54090–540097.

AAB;   mark the change of status from Augusta Ada Byron (1815–), to
AAK;   Augusta Ada King (1835–), to Augusta Ada Lovelace (1838–52)
AAL –

AIK;   mark the change from Lady Annabella King (Ada's daughter), to
AINK;   Annabella Noel King (1860–), to Lady Anne Blunt (1869–1917)
AB –

AL –   Augusta Leigh

BO –   Byron, Viscount Ockham (Ada's eldest son)

RGK; RW;   mark the change from Lord Ralph Gordon King (1839–) to Baron
RL –   Wentworth (1862–), to 2nd Earl of Lovelace (1893–1906)

EML –   Elizabeth Medora Leigh

AIM; AIB;   mark the change of status from Anne Isabella Milbanke (1792–),
AINB –   to Anne Isabella Byron (1815–), to Anne Isabella Noel Byron
(1822–60)

JM and   mark the shift in Annabella's parents, in 1816, from Judith and
JN; RM   Ralph Milbanke to Judith and Ralph Noel
and RN –

MN –   Mary Noel (Annabella's great-aunt)

SL –   Stephen Lushington

WK; WL –   mark the change from Lord (William) King (Ada's husband) in 1838
to William, 1st Earl of Lovelace

Dates in square brackets indicate conjectured dates

Chapter One: Anticipation (1761–92)

p. 3   She likes to make up stories: from AINB's 'Auto Description', written
at age thirty-nine, *c.* 1831, Dep. Lovelace Byron 131, fols. 184–90.

Chapter Two: A Very Fine Child (1792–1810)

p. 6   the county folk flocked in to see their Annabella 'as if she had been
something miraculous': JM to MN, 12 and 27 October 1793, Dep.
Lovelace Byron 17, fols. 166, 167–8.

p. 7   'one of the finest girls of her age I ever beheld,' Mrs Baker of Elemore
gushed: Isabella Baker's addition to a letter from JM to MN, 10 March
1797, Dep. Lovelace Byron 18, fols. 42–3.

p. 7   'she was a *very fine Child*': JM to MN, 22 June 1794; 3 September 1797
and 30 May 1795, Dep. Lovelace Byron 18, fols. 21–2; fols. 60–2.

p. 7 'Annabella's Mama is determined to do it': Sophy Curzon (later Lady Tamworth) to JM, 26 May 1794, Dep. Lovelace Byron 11, fols. 141–2.

p. 8 'but she will judge for *herself* & cannot be *made* to *like* any body': JM to MN, 26 June 1798, Dep. Lovelace Byron 18, fols. 58–9.

p. 9 'the *Angel* ... regrets the Sea and the Sands': Sophy Curzon to JM, 26 May 1794, Dep. Lovelace Byron 11, fols. 141–2.

p. 9 '... I believe it is the bathing makes the sun & air catch her skin so much': JM to MN, 25 August 1797, Dep. Lovelace Byron 18, fols. 58–9.

p. 9 Bessy hankered after the privileged world into which she had briefly stepped: R. Anderson Aird, *Notes on the Parish of Seaham* (booklet, 1912), p. 12.

p. 10 she had expressed outrage in 1797 at the English government's persecution of 'the poor oppressed Irish': JM to MN, 24 September 1791 and 24 May 1797, Dep. Lovelace Byron 17, fols. 155–6; Dep. Lovelace Byron 18, fols. 51–3.

p. 10 'She saw that the execution was as good as the Intention': AINB, 'Recollections of Seaham', 1847, Dep. Lovelace Byron 14.

p. 11 'very gentle and good': *The Athenaeum*, November 1869, p. 669.

p. 11 'You never forgot one word of your speech nor was any fear discernable in your speech': AIM, 7 November 1803. Playfully inscribed on the back of the paper: 'Compliments – No.1. – praises – to be sold only to those on whom the compliments are made. Price a good deal, viz. 2s.'. Dep. Lovelace Byron 117, fol. 1.

p. 12 'A peace would set all afloat again': JM to MN, 31 May 1794 and 24 May 1795, Dep. Lovelace Byron 18, fols. 17–18, 51–3.

p. 15 'nearly resembling the heavenly, in the divine illumination of that countenance of hers': Sarah Siddons to JM, both quotations from the same letter of 11 July 1810, Dep. Lovelace Byron 14, fols. 102–4.

p. 15 whose 'natural simplicity and modest retirement' was accompanied by 'a ... charming manner': Joanne Common, *Seaham Hall Historical Project*, 1998, p. 10, extracted from University of Durham SEQ 40.

Chapter Three: The Siege of Annabella (1810–12)

p. 17 'she is to be shunned by all who do not honour iniquity': Ethel Mayne, *The Life and Letters of Anne Isabella, Lady Noel Byron* (Charles Scribner, 1929), p. 29.

p. 20 for 'a character so far beyond what any of your years possess': Lady Auckland to AIM, 26 July 1811, Dep. Lovelace Byron 62, fols. 8–12.

p. 21 Annabella's readily bestowed friendship did nothing to speed her progress to the altar: George Eden (later Lord Auckland) to AIM, 26 July 1811, DLM transcript.

p. 22   'an unfounded pursuit of other objects?': Vere Foster (ed.), *The Two Duchesses* (Blackie & Son, 1898), pp. 348–9.

p. 22   'I would give the world to go back for six months ...': Augustus Foster to Elizabeth, Duchess of Devonshire, 26 May, 1812, *ibid.*, p. 365.

p. 22   'I shall live in hope for you,' the duchess wrote: Elizabeth, Duchess of Devonshire to Sir Augustus Foster, 28 May and 4 July 1812, *ibid.*, pp. 368, 372.

p. 23   'she was much embarrassed', Mrs Lamb wrote; worse, she 'has never mentioned you since': Mrs George Lamb ('Caro George') to Sir Augustus Foster, 31 August 1812, *ibid.*, pp. 373–4.

p. 24   'I do not believe that Mac[kenzie] has any thoughts of me though I am sure Lady Seaforth has': AIM to RM, 14 and 13 April 1812, Dep. Lovelace Byron 29, fols. 90–1.

p. 25   'I am much the fashion this year. Mankind bow before me, and womankind think me somebody': AIM to RM, 9 April 1812, Dep. Lovelace Byron 29, fols. 33–4.

p. 26   'Farewell old Woman – make yourself merry with thinking how merry I am': AIM to JM, 11 July 1811, Dep. Lovelace Byron 29, fols. 23–4.

p. 27   'If she sometimes is mistaken as to the best method of securing your comfort': Dr Fenwick to AIM, 2 February 1812, Dep. Lovelace Byron 69, fols. 43–5.

p. 28   'I therefore propose not to be in London till this day fortnight ...': AIM to JM, n.d. but probably 9 or 10 February 1812, two weeks before her departure for London, Dep. Lovelace Byron 18, fols. 47–9.

p. 28   'for a time [it] gave her the appearance of blooming health': AIM to JM, 24 February 1812, Dep. Lovelace Byron 18, fols. 51–3.

Chapter Four: Entering the Lists (1812–13)

p. 29   '*Childe Harold ... is on every table, and himself courted, visited, flattered and praised*': Vere Foster (ed.), *The Two Duchesses* (Blackie & Son, 1898), pp. 375–6.

p. 29   Miss Milbanke's reserved manner and air of 'quiet contempt': Byron to AIM, 26 September 1814, *BL&J*, vol. 4.

p. 30   'I was astonished – overpowered – I could not believe it': Byron to AIM, enclosing a cutting about Annabella from Caroline's letter to himself, 9 October 1814, *BL&J*, vol. 4.

p. 32   Lord Byron was 'without exception': AIM to JM, 16 April 1812, Dep. Lovelace Byron 29, fols. 33–4.

p. 33   'But these are all, has she no others?': Byron to Lady Caroline Lamb, 1 May 1812, *BL&J*, vol. 2.

p. 34   'the cleverest most agreeable, absurd, amiable, perplexing dangerous fascinating little being that lives': Byron to Lady CL, [April] 1812, *ibid*.

p. 37   'As to Love, that is done in a week': Byron to Lady Melbourne, 18 September 1812, *ibid*.

p. 38   'the result of all this seems to me': Lady Melbourne to Byron, 29 September 1812, in Jonathan David Gross (ed.), *Byron's 'Corbeau Blanc': The Life and Letters of Lady Melbourne* (Rice University Press, 1997), pp. 118–121.

p. 41   'I am never sulky': AIM to Lady Melbourne, 21–25 October 1812, *ibid*., pp. 124–6.

p. 41   'till you can attain this power over Yourself never boast of your command over yr passions': Lady Melbourne to AIM, 25 October 1812, *ibid*., pp. 126–7.

p. 42   'After so full an explanation you will perhaps take off my *stilts*, and allow that I am only *on tiptoe*': AIM to Lady Melbourne, October 1812, n.d. but after the 25th. *ibid*., pp. 133–4.

p. 42   'if she does not misunderstand me nor my views': Byron to Lady Melbourne, 12 February 1813, *BL&J*, vol. 4.

p. 43   'Perhaps, unconscious as I was, the engagement was then formed on my part ... but every time I felt more pain, & at last I shunned the occasions': AIM, Journal, 6 May to 26 June 1813, quoted in Ethel Mayne, *The Life and Letters of Anne Isabella, Lady Noel Byron* (Charles Scribner, 1929), p. 55.

p. 44   Caroline Lamb was merely signalling a frenzied wish to recapture her lost lover's interest: Lady Melbourne to Byron, 7 July 1813, in Gross, *op. cit*., pp. 142–3.

p. 45   'I have not the skill – ': Byron to Lady Melbourne, 18 July 1813, *BL&J*, vol. 4.

p. 45   'In particular I would not have it known to Ly Melbourne ...': AIM to Byron, 22 August 1813, NLS.

Chapter Five: An Epistolary Courtship (1813–14)

p. 48   humbly sought permission to address her as 'My dear friend': Byron to AIM, extracted from letters written on 6 and 26 September, and 10 November 1813, *BL&J*, vol. 3.

p. 49   Annabella was to be his mentor, not his confidante: Byron to AIM, 26 September 1813, *ibid*.

p. 49   the kind of young woman who 'enters into a clandestine correspondence': Byron to Lady Melbourne, 28 September 1813, *ibid*.

p. 50   'What I want is a companion – a friend rather than a sentimentalist': Byron to Lady Melbourne, 19–21 February 1814, *ibid*.

p. 51 'He has never yet suspected me,' she sighed: AIM to Lady Gosford, 1 and 3 December 1813, Dep. Lovelace Byron 72, fols. 81–4.

p. 52 'the moment I sunk into your friend ... you never did – never for an instant – trifle with me': Byron to AIM, 12 February 1814, *BL&J*, vol. 4.

p. 52 'six hundred in heart and in head & pursuits about six': Byron to AIM, 19 February 1814, *ibid*.

p. 56 'My doubt then is – and I ask a solution – whether you are in any danger of that attachment to me': AIM to Lord Byron, 6 August 1814, NLS.

p. 57 'Not, believe me, that I depreciate your capacity for the domestic virtues ...': AIM to Lord Byron, 13 August 1814, NLS.

p. 58 'It never rains but it pours': Narrative Q, 1816, one of the many documents in which Annabella revisited the circumstances of the engagement and the marriage (Dep. Lovelace Byron 130, item 4). The lettered labelling ('Q' etc.) was later added by Annabella's grandson, the 2nd Earl of Lovelace. (See notes to Ch. 6).

p. 61 'I stood on the opposite side of the fireplace': Malcolm Elwin, quoting one of Annabella's several later re-statings of the courtship and her marriage, in *Lord Byron's Wife* (Macdonald, 1962), pp. 227–8.

p. 63 'if there is a break – it shall be *her* doing not mine': Byron to Lady Melbourne, 13 November 1814, *BL&J*, vol. 4.

p. 63 'everything is in your power': Lady Melbourne to Lord Byron, 18 November 1814, in Jonathan David Gross (ed.), *Byron's 'Corbeau Blanc': The Life and Letters of Lady Melbourne* (Rice University Press, 1997), pp. 187–8.

p. 63 'Ma Mignonne': Byron to AIM, 16, 20 and 28 November 1814, *BL&J*, vol. 4.

p. 63 that a visitor 'has found out a likeness to your picture in Mignonne': AL to Byron, 15 December 1814, NLS. Annabella, when finally in possession of all Augusta's correspondence relating to her own situation, sent the letter on to Mrs Leigh's intimate friend, Theresa Villiers, as evidence of what double-dealing had been in play. Copies of the Augusta–Annabella letters are in WP, Add MS 31037.

p. 65 'I do not see any good purpose to which questions of this kind are to lead': Byron to AIM, 22 December 1814, *BL&J*, vol. 4.

Chapter Six: A Sojourn in Hell (January to March 1815)

p. 68 'gazing with delight on his bold and animated face': Hobhouse's *Diary*, transcript by Ralph, 2nd Earl of Lovelace, from the original in NYPL. But see also p. 487 for the much more accessible Cochran online edition of Hobhouse's *Diary*.

p. 69 'is very engaging in his manners ... Papa says he could never be tired of

listening to him': Mary Noel (daughter of the Revd Thomas), writing
from Kirkby Mallory, to Henrietta Jervis, in Bath, 10 January 1815,
Dep. Lovelace Byron 21, fol. 126.

p. 70   advice that Noel decided to ignore: AIB to her lawyer, Stephen
Lushington, 19 February 1816, quoting a letter from the Revd Thomas
Noel, Dep. Lovelace Byron 88, fols. 14–16 and 25–6. Eight days
earlier, she told Stephen Lushington that it was John Hobhouse who,
following his return to London in the summer of 1815, 'had instigated,
more than anyone else, the behaviour that has disunited us'.

p. 70   and a request to wear it in remembrance of the donor: see note to p. 69,
'is very engaging in his manners ...'.

p. 72   Jane Minns ... was herself looking back over a gap of fifty-four years:
Interview with Jane Minns, AIB's former maid, *Newcastle Daily
Chronicle*, (1869).

p. 72   'You would think ... that we had been married these fifty years': Byron
to Lady Melbourne, 3 January 1815, *BL&J*, vol. 5.

p. 73   the personality which Walter Scott privately described as 'irritable to
the point of mental disease': Sir Walter Scott to Lady Anne Barnard
(1824–5, n.d.), Charles Mackay (ed.), *Medora Leigh, A History and
Autobiography* (R. Bentley, 1869), p. 84; Byron to AIB, 17 November
1821, *BL&J*, vol. 9.

p. 74   'It is so like him *to try and persuade* people that *he is disagreeable*':
Augusta Leigh's letters, except where otherwise indicated, exist in
original and transcript form in the Lovelace Byron Papers. A set
of copies is also at HRC (Byron Papers, Misc III) and at the British
Library Manuscripts, Add MS 31037. Annabella's account comes
from Narrative Q, July 1816 (see Ch. 5, note to p. 58, 'It never rains
but it pours'). The letter identification of AIB's statements and narratives follows that chosen by the 2nd Earl of Lovelace, the first person
to read his grandmother's copious records in full. I have relied upon
the meticulous (although often in shorthand) copies made from the
originals, when held at Crabbet, by DLM.

p. 74   '*bereaved of reason* during his paroxysms with his wife': Hobhouse's
Diary, 12 March 1816, from a part of Lord Lovelace's transcript (see
note to p. 68, above, 'gazing with delight').

p. 75   'well, and as happy as youth and love can make them ...': JM to
Sir James Bland Burges, 27 January 1815, Burges Papers (Bodleian
Library, Oxford).

p. 75   Annabella had left Seaham for Halnaby looking like 'a flower': Mrs
Clermont to Lady Gosford's new son-in-law, Dr Henry Bence-Jones,
11 October 1846. Bence-Jones had been recruited by Annabella to care
for her family's old and mentally enfeebled friend. It was at this time
that Bence-Jones himself began to research some of the story around

the separation and first interviewed Jane Minns (see, note to p. 72 above, 'Jane Minns ...').

p. 76   Lady Melbourne, busily urging her protégé to put himself under his wife's affectionate direction: Lady Melbourne to Byron, 31 January 1815, in Jonathan David Gross (ed.), *Byron's 'Corbeau Blanc': The Life and Letters of Lady Melbourne* (Rice University Press, 1997), pp. 279–81; Byron to Lady Melbourne, 2 February 1815, *BL&J*, vol. 4.

p. 77   Lady Byron resolved to omit such scenes: AL to AIB, n.d., Tuesday, 1815, has evidently taken the phrase 'ramble-scramble' from Annabella's previous letter to her. Dep. Lovelace Byron 79, fol. 67.

p. 78   Byron ... had 'vastly' enjoyed his stay at Seaham Hall: Byron to Tom Moore, 8 March 1815, *BL&J*, vol. 4. Annabella's expectations of pregnancy were confirmed by the end of that month.

p. 79   It made up for the coldness and the 'sort of unrelenting pity': Annabella set her memories of the visit down in Statements R, Q (R being an expansion of Q, written in late 1816 or early 1817) and G (1816), to which she added extensive passages late in 1816 and again in the following spring. This process of revision and addition was still being carried out in the 1850s, for the purpose of providing a factual record and as part of the foundation for a book. Fact, by 1850, was becoming hard to distinguish from wishful interpretation. (See note to p. 74 above, 'It is so like him'.)

p. 79   'My heart is withered away, so that I forget to eat my bread': The level of the 'deep horrors' can be gauged by the fact that Annabella felt it necessary to write in shorthand (Statement G, 1816) that Byron claimed to know his sister wore drawers, 'with an emphasis perfectly unequivocal'. (See note to p. 74 above, 'It is so like him'.)

p. 79   Mrs Leigh 'submitted to his [Byron's] affection, but never appeared gratified by it': AIB, Narrative S, confirmed in Narrative R (late 1816 to 1817). The narratives were reports, rather than legal statements. (See note to p. 74 above, 'It is so like him'.)

p. 80   she 'did not wish to detain us': *ibid.*

Chapter Seven: Unlucky for Some: 13 Piccadilly Terrace (1815–16)

p. 84   'Hey diddle! diddle': I am indebted to Sammy Jay at Peter Harrington for a viewing of the violin and the poem (23 July 1815). The poem has never been published. The violin's provenance and authenticity remains alluringly unproven, but the signature is in Byron's hand. It is privately owned.

p. 85   'It was an instant of revenge ... and her voice of kindness extinguished it': Statement K, late 1816 (see Ch. 6, note to p. 74, 'It is so like him').

p. 86   'I believe he burnt it afterwards': Narrative S, written as part of a sequel to Narrative Q, July 1816 (see Ch. 6, note to p. 74, 'It is so like him').

p. 86   'My Night Mare is my own personalty [*sic*]': Byron to Douglas Kinnaird, 20 January 1817, *BL&J*, vol. 5.

p. 86   'I meant to marry a woman who would be *my friend*': Statement F, March 1817 (see Ch. 6, note to p. 74, 'It is so like him').

p. 87   'unless there is a woman (and not any or every woman) in the way': Byron's journal, 26 November 1813, *BL&J*, vol. 3.

p. 88   'B has just found out an Etymology for Blücher's name which is quite in your way': AIB to RN, 15 August 1815, Dep. Lovelace Byron 29, fol. 109.

p. 88   'B said it was a memento left us by our honoured parent': AIB to JN, 17 August 1815, Dep. Lovelace Byron 29, fols. 111–12.

p. 88   'gratefully acknowledged by B's voracious stomach': Ethel Mayne, *The Life and Letters of Anne Isabella, Lady Noel Byron* (Charles Scribner, 1929), p. 184.

p. 89   'She is diffident – she is very young, not more, I think, than nineteen': Anna Eliot Ticknor (ed.), *Life, Letters & Journals of George Ticknor*, 2 vols. (Houghton Mifflin, 1900), vol. 1, p. 53.

p. 89   'as if he were not to see her for a month': Ticknor, *op. cit.*, p. 50.

p. 90   'a good kind thing ... the best little wife in the world': Both tributes were cited by AIB in Narrative F, March 1817 (see Ch. 6, note to p. 74, 'It is so like him').

p. 90   whether 'there ever was a better or even brighter, a kinder or a more amiable & agreeable being: Byron to Thomas Moore, 8 March 1816, *BL&J*, vol. 5.

p. 90   'Annabella I am sure requires country air': JN to Byron, 11 August 1815, NLS.

p. 91   'I always feel ... as if I had more *reasons* to love you': AIB to AL, n.d., Tuesday evening, early August 1815, in Rowland Prothero (ed.), *The Works of Lord Byron*, 6 vols. (John Murray, 1898–1902), vol. 3, pp. 210–12.

p. 91   A coded 'Not *frac.*' signified 'not fractious': Byron to AIB, 31 August 1815, *BL&J*, vol. 4.

p. 92   'I was very ill,' she later recalled: Statement G, 1816 (see Ch. 6, note to p. 74, 'It is so like him').

p. 92   Byron's own was signed, as Annabella's had been, with the mysterious '-A—da': Byron to AIB, 1 September 1815, *BL&J*, vol. 4.

p. 93   amidst 'the very distressing circumstance to which we must look forward': AIB to JN, 7 October 1815, Dep. Lovelace Byron 29, fols. 134–5.

p. 95   'In short,' wrote Annabella, 'they *yelped* and he *snapped*': AIB to RN, 4 November 1815, Dep. Lovelace Byron 29.

p. 97　'God knows what he may do': Statement by Mrs Clermont, 22 January 1816 (see Ch. 6, note to p. 74, 'It is so like him').

p. 97　Annabella credited Augusta's reassuring company with having prevented her from doing so: AIB to Lady Melbourne, 4 January 1816, Jonathan David Gross (ed.), *Byron's 'Corbeau Blanc': The Life and Letters of Lady Melbourne* (Rice University Press, 1997), pp. 331–3.

p. 97　'for a considerable time before my confinement he [Byron] would not see me': Statement B, added shortly afterwards to AIB's first statement of 18 January 1816, to her mother. Underlinings probably indicate where Annabella's mother felt that the record would carry most weight. (See Ch. 6, note to p. 74, 'It is so like him')

p. 98　'The impression ... made upon my mind': Mrs Clermont, see note to p. 97 above, 'God knows what he may do'.

p. 98　Byron had spoken out to him against marriage: 'talking of going abroad': Hobhouse's *Diary*, 25 November 1815, see note on p. 487.

p. 102　'would probably say that she has seen Lord B appear personally fond of me': AIB, Statement to JN at Kirkby, January 1816, and additional statement relating to the nurse, March 1816 (see Ch. 6, note to p. 74, 'It is so like him').

p. 102　'Amongst other unkind things said to me': Additions to Statement made by AIB to her mother at Kirkby Mallory, 18 January 1816 (see Ch. 6, note to p. 74, 'It is so like him').

p. 103　'She [Annabella] cryed': Mrs Clermont's Statement, see note to p. 97 above, 'God knows what he may do'.

p. 104　According to her later statements, this was the only occasion upon which Lady Byron feared for her life: Statement U, 'Desultory', partly dictated by AIB to Mrs Clermont, March 1816 (see Ch. 6, note to p. 74, 'It is so like him').

Chapter Eight: The Separation (1816)

p. 108　the expectation of Byron's imminent arrival remained firmly in place: The 1816 separation correspondence between AIB and AL is given in Rowland Prothero (ed.), *The Works of Lord Byron*, 6 vols. (John Murray, 1898–1902), vol. 3, pp. 210–12. It is also in WP, Add MS 31037.

p. 109　'Lady Byron into the country – Byron won't go!': Hobhouse's *Diary*, 17 January 1816 (see note on p. 487).

p. 110　'a fine affair in their imagination your absence – & my story!': AL to AIB, 19 January 1816, Coleridge and Prothero, *op. cit.*, vol. 3, p. 320.

p. 110　had a 'too confiding disposition': Sir Francis Doyle to AIB, 18 July 1816, Dep. Lovelace Byron 68, fols. 18–19.

p. 112　she broke down, on certain occasions, in hysterical fits of sobbing: Statement by Mrs Fletcher to John Hanson, n.d., NLS.

p. 113   'She will break my heart if she takes up the thing in bitterness against
          him': AIB to Mrs Clermont, 22 January 1816, Dep. Lovelace Byron
          66, fol. 5.

p. 113   'I would not but have seen Lushington for the World': JN to AIB, 25
          January 1816, Dep. Lovelace Byron 36, fols. 12–14.

p. 114   the lawyer had privately 'deemed a reconciliation with Lord Byron
          practicable': SL to AIB, 31 January 1830. Lushington's letter was pub-
          lished by AIB with his consent in her privately circulated 'Remarks'
          in Moore's 1830 biography of Byron.

p. 114   'It is worth the sadness if it brings anything good to him': AIB
          Memorandum, 27 January 1816, in Malcolm Elwin, *Lord Byron's
          Wife* (Macdonald, 1962), p. 379.

p. 115   'Kate! I will buckler thee against a million!': Byron to AIB, 3 February
          1816, *BL&J*, vol. 5.

p. 115   In an afterthought addressed to Mrs Clermont, the carrier of her
          letter to Lushington's home: Byron to AIB, 8 February 1816, *BL&J*,
          vol. 5; AIB's 'Remarks' on this letter were sent to Mrs Clermont on
          13 February 1816, for transmission to Lushington.

p. 115   Lady Melbourne asked her brother Ralph why he had instructed
          friends 'to give the event every possible publicity': Lady Melbourne
          to RN, 12 February 1816, in Jonathan David Gross (ed.), *Byron's
          'Corbeau Blanc': The Life and Letters of Lady Melbourne* (Rice
          University Press, 1997), p. 314.

p. 116   marvelling at 'the unexampled gentleness, goodness, and wise for-
          bearances': Ethel Mayne, *The Life and Letters of Anne Isabella, Lady
          Noel Byron* (Charles Scribner, 1929), p. 259.

p. 116   'he had been guilty of the offence which, of all offences, is punished most
          severely': Thomas Macaulay, '*Letters and Journals of Lord Byron; with
          Notices of his Life*, by Thomas Moore', *Edinburgh Review*, June 1831.

p. 117   Byron's boasts to Annabella 'of his adulteries and indecencies': S. M.
          Waddams, *Law, Politics and the Church of England: The Career of
          Stephen Lushington 1782–1873* (CUP, 1992), p. 114.

p. 118   Lushington confirmed that 'when I was informed by you of facts
          utterly unknown ... my opinion was entirely changed': SL to AIB, 31
          January 1830, *ibid.*, see note to p. 114 above, 'the lawyer had privately
          "deemed ...".'.

p. 118   'I am in boundless respect of her,' Lushington would write years
          later: SL to Frances Carr, his sister-in-law, n.d. 1852, quoted in Joan
          Pierson, *The Real Lady Byron* (Robert Hale, 1992), p. 32.

p. 119   'Oh– Bell– to see you thus stifling and destroying all feeling, all affec-
          tions – all duties': Byron to AIB, 4 March 1816, *BL&J*, vol. 5; AIB,
          'Reasons for my return urged by Mrs Leigh', 5 March 1816, DLM
          transcript.

p. 120   Reshaped by the super-cautious Stephen Lushington, it became a
          nebulous web of conditionals: Lushington's Statement is given in full
          in Ralph Milbanke, Earl of Lovelace, *Astarte: A Fragment of Truth
          Concerning George Gordon Byron, Sixth Lord Byron* (Christophers,
          1905 and 1921), pp. 46–8; see also Elwin, Malcolm, *Lord Byron's
          Wife* (Macdonald, 1962), p. 441.

p. 121   her brother, while deranged, could once have committed 'some act
          which he would not avow': AL to Francis Hodgson, 14 March 1816,
          Dep. Lovelace Byron 84, fols. 220–6.

p. 122   Byron's royal admirer, young Princess Charlotte, declared that she
          had wept 'like a fool': HRH Princess Charlotte to Miss Mercer
          Elphinstone, April 1816, Lady Charlotte Bury, *The Diary of A Lady-
          in-Waiting*, edited by Francis Steuart, 2 vols. (J. Lane, 1908), vol. 1,
          p. 399.

p. 123   she described her own 'most tender affection for — . What is the
          reason?': AIB, journal fragment, 16 September 1820, Dep. Lovelace
          Byron 117, fol. 4. Punctuation has been altered here to make the orig-
          inal author's meaning clearer. Annabella's original gives the blank for
          the omitted name followed without a break by '—what is the reason?'

p. 124   From Augusta – with whom he had just parted for the last time – he
          had asked only that she should keep him informed: Byron to AL, in a
          brief postscript, 15 April 1816, *BL&J*, vol. 5.

Chapter Nine: In the Public Eye (1816–24)

p. 125   if Harriet Beecher Stowe's memory of her impressions as a 5-year-old
          were to be trusted: Harriet Beecher Stowe, 'The True Story of Lady
          Byron's Life', *Atlantic Monthly*, September 1869.

p. 125   'I think my noble friend is something like my old peacock': Walter
          Scott to J. B. S. Morritt, 16 May 1816, in John Gibson Lockhart,
          Memoirs of the Life of Sir Walter Scott (Robert Cadell, 1845), p. 332.

p. 126   'True Jedwood justice was dealt out to him': Thomas Babington
          Macaulay, '*Letters and Journals of Lord Byron; with Notices of his
          Life*, by Thomas Moore', *Edinburgh Review*, June 1831.

p. 127   the privately printed and widely distributed 'Remarks' of 1830 in
          which Annabella defended her dead parents: AINB, 'Remarks' (on
          Moore's *Life of Lord Byron*) were privately printed and widely dis-
          tributed in March 1830, following the publication in January 1830
          of Moore's first of two volumes. In 1831, the 'Remarks' were bound
          into a new edition of Moore's book, at Annabella's request.

p. 129   'people at Ely and Peterborough Stared at us very much, and Mama said
          we were Lionesses – pray what does that mean?': AIB (writing, as she
          frequently did, as Ada) to JN, 11 June 1816, Dep. Lovelace Byron 30.

NOTES497

p. 130 Initially, Byron refused to believe it: Byron to John Murray, 21 December 1822, *BL&J*, vol. 10.

p. 131 Lady Melbourne remarked that Lady Byron's face was 'sad and strained': Lady Melbourne to Hobhouse, 18 October 1816, in Jonathan David Gross (ed.), *Byron's 'Corbeau Blanc': The Life and Letters of Lady Melbourne* (Rice University Press, 1997), pp. 331–3. (This long letter offers a perfect example of how Lady Melbourne operated behind the scenes in her protégé's life.)

p. 132 'the only important calumny that ever was advanced against you': P. B. Shelley to Byron, 29 September 1816, in Frederick L. Jones (ed.), *Letters of Percy Bysse Shelley* 2 vols. (OUP, 1964), vol. 2, pp. 363–4.

p. 133 'in fact I am the one *much* the more to blame ... *quite* inexcusable': AL to AIB, 17 September 1816, while enclosing a letter from Byron, Dep. Lovelace Byron 79, fols. 139–40.

p. 134 Annabella remarked that Byron's satire was 'so good as to make me smile at myself': Ethel Mayne, *The Life and Letters of Anne Isabella, Lady Noel Byron* (Charles Scribner, 1929), p. 283.

p. 134 The journal, as its publisher proudly pointed out, carried 'an article on a great Poet': John Murray to AIB, Friday, 7 February 1817, Dep. Lovelace Byron 94, fols. 70–1.

p. 135 as even Annabella had to admit – Scott had 'not expressed, but I think directly implied': AIB to Theresa Villiers (about the *Quarterly Review* article), 6 March 1816, Dep. Lovelace Byron 114.

p. 136 'but to injure, and then to desert, and then to turn back and wound her widow'd privacy': *Blackwood's Magazine*, August 1819. Byron never discovered whether the author was either Scott's son-in-law, John Gibson Lockhart, or John Wilson, a regular writer for *Blackwood's*. Wilson wrote the piece.

p. 137 'I was thought a devil, because Lady Byron was allowed to be an angel': Marguerite Blessington, *Conversations of Lord Byron with the Countess of Blessington* (H. Colburn, 1834), pp. 160–1.

Chapter Ten: In Search of a Father

p. 141 'The little boy [Hugo, an orphaned nephew of Mary Montgomery] is a very nice child': AAB to AINB, 7 December 1824, Dep. Lovelace Byron 41, fols. 15–16.

p. 142 He asked for his daughter to be taught music (in which neither parent had any skill) and Italian: Sending an Italian book to her friend Harriet Siddons's daughter, Elizabeth, Annabella wrote: 'The language is beautiful, so do not get the translation. I wish your Mother could enjoy the original.' AINB to Elizabeth Siddons, 13 June 18[34], HRC, bound vol. 1 of the Byron Collection.

p. 143   'Is the Girl imaginative? ... Is she social or solitary': Byron to AL, 12
          October 1823. AINB to AL, 1 December 1823, both in Ethel Mayne,
          The Life and Letters of Anne Isabella, Lady Noel Byron (Charles
          Scribner, 1929), pp. 196–7.

p. 143   'Her prevailing characteristic is cheerfulness and good-temper': AINB
          to AL, 1 December 1823, *ibid.*, pp. 196–7.

p. 143   Byron's 'pertickeler wish' had been that his valet should carry a mes-
          sage to his wife and child: William Fletcher to John Murray, 21 April
          1824, 43531 NLS.

p. 144   she begged him – vainly – to recall what her husband's final message
          to her had been: Mayne, *op. cit.*, p. 297.

p. 144   'the fiercest Animals have the rarest number in their litters': Byron, 6
          November 1821, *BL&J*, vol. 9.

p. 145   'I had a strange prepossession that she would never be fond of me':
          AIB to Theresa Villiers, 11 November 1818, Dep. Lovelace Byron 114,
          fols. 190–1.

p. 145   'She looked round the Bed and on the Bed, and then into the Closet':
          JN to AIB, 5 September 1817, Dep. Lovelace Byron 37, fols. 37–8.

p. 146   her 'dearest wish to prove a better child than she [Lady Noel] has yet
          found me': AIB to Harriet Siddons, 20 September 1817, HRC, bound
          vol. 1 of the Byron Collection.

p. 147   'Hastings will be good for me': AIB to Harriet Siddons, 27 March
          1820, *ibid.*

p. 147   Contemplating the dreary years ahead of enacting 'a calm perfor-
          mance of duty': AIB to Harriet Siddons, 11 May 1821, *ibid.*

p. 150   'No person can be more rational, companiable [*sic*] and endearing
          than this rare child': Lamont Journal, 20–22 June and 7 July 1821,
          Dep. Lovelace Byron 118, item 5.

p. 153   A letter addressed to Cousin George's mother, now also known as
          Lady Byron, proudly announced her near perfect command of Spanish
          and Italian: AAB to 7th Lady Byron, 7 December 1824, Dep. Lovelace
          Byron 168. Ada, although she scarcely knew her Aunt Augusta, was
          a resolute user of her own full name. Others addressed her as 'Ada'.
          Ada always signed herself as Augusta Ada, or 'A. A.'

p. 153   She could understand her mother's enduring affection for gentle Sophy
          Tamworth: AAB to AINB, 9 September 1824, Dep. Lovelace Byron
          41, fols. 13–14.

p. 155   'tho from the accidental delay of a letter, my consent may have been
          inferred by the party in question': AINB to John Murray, 31 March
          1826, NLS.

p. 156   After glumly admitting that it had been 'quite shocking' of her to
          announce she did not believe in prayers: AAB to AINB, 1 and 3 June
          1826, Dep. Lovelace Byron 41, fols. 27–8, 30–1.

p. 158   her mother could now manage to scrawl in her own hand the simple words 'much better': AAB to AINB, 3 February 1828, Dep. Lovelace Byron 41, fols. 54–5.

p. 158   Ada admitted that there had been times when 'I really thought ... you could not live': AAB to AINB, 8 April 1828, Dep. Lovelace Byron 41, fols. 67–9.

p. 159   'I have got a scheme about a ... steamengine': AAB to AINB, 4 April 1828, Dep. Lovelace Byron 41, fols. 63–6.

p. 160   'very gentle ... just a little pottering thing ...': AAB to AINB, 12 October 1828, in a letter playfully addressed 'To the Right Honourable *Immortal* Grand *Crockery* Panjandrum Lady Noel Byron from the little Panjandrum of *Clay* – Oh Alas!', Dep. Lovelace Byron 41, fols. 70–3.

p. 160   Flying had been abandoned for the creation of 'my Planetarium': AAB to Sophia Frend (later De Morgan), 4 February 1829, Dep. Lovelace Byron 171, fols. 16–17.

Chapter Eleven: A Rainbow's Arc (1829–35)

p. 165   Augusta, whose only concern was to please the beguiling Henry, announced in April 1829 that she felt personally 'very hurt': AL to AINB, 20 April 1829, Dep. Lovelace Byron 84, fols. 68–70.

p. 165   Perhaps, the answer is best summed up by Annabella: AINB to Theresa Villiers, 11 May 1852, Dep. Lovelace Byron 114.

p. 167   By 1 December, Annabella was feeling angry enough to identify Lushington to young Lizzie Siddons: ANB to Elizabeth Siddons (later Mair), 1 December 1829, HRC, bound vol. 1 of the Byron Collection.

p. 167   'From your representations and the conclusions you draw': AINB to AL, 17 January 1830, 43411, NLS.

p. 170   To Henry, she despatched a plaintive squawk of command: The letters between Medora, Trevanion and Augusta, dating from February 1831, were published in Ethel Mayne, *The Life and Letters of Anne Isabella, Lady Noel Byron* (Charles Scribner, 1929), pp. 343–4. At the Bodleian, the main holding of Medora's letters is in Dep. Lovelace Byron 85–6 (to AINB) and 68 (to Selina Doyle). Miscellaneous letters to her are in 87, fols. 1–60.

p. 171   'poor Mrs Leigh and all connected with her are mad': Michael and Melissa Bakewell, *Augusta Leigh: Byron's Half-Sister* (Chatto, 2000), p. 336.

p. 172   Selina Doyle and she were struggling to read German together, she told Robert Noel: AAB to Robert Noel, 27 August 1830, Betty Toole, *The Enchantress of Numbers* (Strawberry Press, 1992), p. 42.

p. 172   Laughing at her own 'disputation habits': AAB to Arabella Lawrence, n.d., summer 1830, Dep. Lovelace Byron 172, fols. 180–2.

p. 173   'it will be so nice ... and I shall have no trouble in making up my mind
         about anything': AAB to Arabella Lawrence, n.d., Sunday, August
         1830, Dep. Lovelace Byron 172, fols. 184–5.

p. 175   'No creed. No scripture books': AINB to Elizabeth Blackwell, 27 May
         1851, in Julia Boyd, *The Excellent Doctor Blackwell: The Life of the
         First Woman Physician* (Sutton, 2006), pp. 126–7.

p. 176   'God knows I have enough of it, and a great plague it often is': AAL
         to AINB, 21 April 1840, Dep. Lovelace Byron 41.

p. 176   by August, in Brighton, Ada was able to boast to Selina Doyle's ille-
         gitimate niece, Fanny Smith: AAB to Fanny Smith, 5 August 1832,
         Dep. Lovelace Byron 112, fols. 94–100.

p. 178   'as far as they could without actual penetration': Woronzow Greig,
         Memoir, MSBY Dep. b. 206, folder MSIF 2–4.

p. 178   Miss Byron's public disgrace had just been avoided: Sophia De
         Morgan, *Threescore Years and Ten: Reminiscences of the late Sophia
         Elizabeth De Morgan* (London, 1895), p. 89.

p. 178   a consequent debt of gratitude 'of which I am so sure I shall never need to
         be reminded by you': AAB to WK, 28 June 1835, Toole, *op. cit.*, pp. 76–7.

p. 178   'I cannot consider that the parent has any right to direct the child':
         AAB to AINB, 19 May 1833, Dep. Lovelace Byron 41, fols. 85–8.

p. 180   'my illustrious parent' had looked 'very pretty indeed': AAB to Fanny
         Smith, 9 November 1833, Dep. Lovelace Byron 112, fols. 94–100.

p. 180   Over a decade later, she would offer a heartfelt apology for the way
         she had behaved as a wilful teenager: AAL to AINB, n.d. November
         1844, Dep. Lovelace Byron 42, fols. 152–8.

p. 182   '[For] nothing but *very close & intense* application': AAB to Dr
         William King, 9 March 1834, Toole, *op. cit.*, pp. 53–4

Chapter Twelve: Mathematical Friendships (1834–5)

p. 183   the Irish novelist Lady Morgan decided she resembled 'one of the
         respectable twaddling chaperones one meets': H. V. Morton, *A
         Traveller in Italy* (Methuen, 1964), pp. 482–4. Morton's delightful
         account of Mrs Somerville brings her to life with remarkable skill.

p. 184   'while her head is among the stars her feet are firm upon the ground':
         Maria Edgeworth to an unnamed friend, 17 January 1832, quoted in
         Mrs Somerville's posthumously published and heavily edited *Personal
         Recollections* (John Murray, 1873), p. 156. (Edgeworth was fascinated
         by the scientific world, although not herself a contributor to it.)

p. 184   Mary and her husband were fond of telling the story: Mrs Somerville's
         posthumously published *Personal Recollections* (1873) cite Laplace's
         tribute to her from a personal encounter in Paris. Maria Edgeworth
         confirmed his high opinion in an 1822 letter to her mother. Laplace,

she said, had observed that Mrs Somerville could not only understand, but correct him. (C. Colvin (ed.), *Maria Edgeworth: Letters from England 1813–44* (OUP, 1971), pp. 371–2.)

p. 185   'the most extraordinary woman in Europe, a mathematician of the very first rank': David Brewster to J. D. Forbes, 11 September 1829, *Forbes Papers*, University of St Andrews Library.

p. 186   'Ada was much attached to me,' Mrs Somerville would later recall: Mary Somerville, *Personal Recollections*, *op. cit.*, Ch. 10.

p. 186   By 24 March, Ada was boasting to Dr King: AAB to Dr William King, 24 March 1834, Dep. Lovelace Byron 172, fols. 131–4.

p. 186   'You must *trammel* your mind …' he warned: Dr King to AAB, 24 April 1834, Dep. Lovelace Byron 172, fols. 132–9.

p. 189   'The logarithmetical Frankenstein': *London Literary Gazette and Journal of Belles Lettres, Arts, Sciences, Etc* (1832) commenting on Babbage's appearance at a meeting of the newly formed British Association for the Advancement of Science.

p. 190   subsidising an invention which – unlike James Watt's steam engine – had been developed without any prototype: The reference is made in Dionysius Lardner's defence of Babbage in the *Edinburgh Review* (July 1834, pp. 266–7).

p. 191   Sophia Frend later described how, 'young as she was', Ada had immediately grasped the concept: Sophia De Morgan, *Memoir of Augustus de Morgan* (1882; republished by Elibron Classics, 2005), p. 89.

p. 191   'We both went to see the *thinking* machine': Lady Byron to Dr William King, 21 June 1833, Dep. Lovelace Byron 77, fol. 217.

p. 192   'I am afraid that when a machine, or a lecture, or anything of the kind, come[s] in my way': AAB to Mary Somerville, 8 July 1834, MSBY, Dep. c. 367, folder MSBY-2.

p. 192   'Ada does not think anything the world offers worth trouble, except Music': AINB to Elizabeth Siddons, n.d. 1834, HRC, bound vol. 1 of the Byron Collection.

p. 193   'The risk to man and beast – the desperate gambling among the spectators – the futility of the object': AINB to Harriet Siddons, n.d., HRC, bound vol. 1 of the Byron Collection.

p. 193   'I feel my intellect reviving …': AINB to Harriet Siddons, 8 August 1834, HRC, Bound vol. 1 of the Byron Collection.

p. 194   'My dear Annabella. You must pardon my scolding!': AAB to Lady Annabella Acheson, 5 December 1834, Dep. Lovelace Byron 168, fols. 28–9. Ada's early mathematical writings were freshly transcribed and put online in 2016 by Dr Christopher Hollings and Professor Adrian Rice (see Ch. 15, note to p. 224, '*Festina lente*').

p. 194   'indeed I think I *am* making great progress': AAB to Annabella Acheson, 26 November 1834, Dep. Lovelace Byron 168, fols. 25–7.

p. 195　It was 'in the highest department of mathematics – I understand it to include the means of solving equations that hitherto had been considered insoluble': AINB, unpublished diary, 15 December 1834, Dep. Lovelace Byron 117, fol. 1.

p. 195　During her autumn at Wimpole Street, she wrote a poem in which God the Father was boldly replaced by a maternal deity: AINB to Elizabeth Siddons, 3 October 1834, HRC, bound vol. 1 of the Byron Collection.

p. 196　His new idea, so she firmly noted, was 'unsound': AINB, unpublished diary, 15 December 1834, 17 November 1834, Dep. Lovelace Byron 117, fol. 1.

p. 196　'In a few weeks I dare say I shall be quite strong': AAB to Mary Somerville, 20 February 1835, MSBY, Dep. c. 367, fols. 2–3.

p. 197　a newly ebullient Ada declared, 'even better than waltzing': AAB to Mary Somerville, n.d. April 1835, MSBY, Dep c. 367, fol. 3.

Chapter Thirteen: Ada's Marriage (1835–40)

p. 200　'nothing shall be wanting on my part to you and for you ... to meet all your wishes will always be my first duty's pleasure': The private history of the Lovelaces and Lady Hester has recently been identified within an archive held at Brooklands Museum. Long before William King (Lovelace)'s nephew, Hugh Locke King, built the Brooklands race track, William's younger brother, Peter Locke King, built a large (and surviving) house close by. This house was where the Locke King archive was stored and – due to a breakdown of relations between the two halves of the family – where it remained, unseen. It was returned to Brooklands from a King family house in South Africa during the 1990s. The papers identified in these notes are from boxes 9 and 10 in the Locke King Papers, Brooklands Museum.

p. 202　'I thought to myself how few young men whom one meets at balls would talk with so much feeling about their country church': AAB to William King from Fordhook, 8 June 1835, Dep. Lovelace Byron 165, fols. 1–39.

p. 203　'How I envy your chaperon his ride with you': William King to AAB, n.d. June 1835, *ibid*.

p. 203　'Now do not be angry with me, because I have only just spoken the truth – neither more nor less': AAB to William King, 28 June 1835, *ibid*.

p. 203　Annabella praised Lord King, not merely as 'a man of rare worth and superior abilities': AINB to Harriet Siddons, 9 June 1835, HRC, bound vol. 1 of the Byron Collection.

p.205　'Dear little Canary Bird, may the new "cage" be gladdened by your notes': AINB to AAK, 9 July, 1835, Dep. Lovelace Byron 47.

Chapter Fourteen: An Unconventional Wife (1836–40)

p. 206   A disappointingly pompous George Ticknor, calling in at Fordhook
to inspect Lady Byron's Ealing school: Anna Eliot Ticknor (ed.), *Life,
Letters & Journals of George Ticknor*, 2 vols. (Houghton Mifflin,
1900), vol. 1, p. 53.

p. 206   'for the first time in my life – I may say that I feel without a care on
earth...': AINB to Harriet Siddons, 22 July 1835, HRC, bound vol. 1
of the Byron Collection.

p. 207   'These catastrophes are very frequent in my house, I think I will act
being in a rage next time...': AINB to Elizabeth Siddons, [July] 1835,
HRC, bound vol. 1 of the Byron Collection.

p. 208   'I want my Cock at night to keep me warm': AAK to William King, 8
and 9 October 1835, Dep. 165, fols. 1–39.

p. 208   '*Ou* won't hurt her I think, will *ou*?': AAK to William King, 11 March
1838, Dep. 165, fols. 80–119.

p. 208   Chatting to Mary Somerville's attentive son during the 1840s about
her sexual life: All of Ada's extravagant confidences to Woronzow
Greig were recorded in his brief private memoir (MSBY, Dep. b.
206, folder MSIF 2–40). Greig had also heard some of the stories
from Lady Byron in or before 1835, when he was delegated to
transmit the outline of Ada's escapade to William King. Ada spiced
up the details. Sophia De Morgan, writing to Lord Wentworth in
1875, stressed Ada's delight in shocking her listeners. Greig was a
susceptible man.

p. 209   The result, in the view of a displeased Ada, was that she looked like 'a
crop-eared dog': AAK to Mary Somerville, 1 November 1835, MSBY
Dep. c. 367, folder MSBY-3.

p. 209   The likeness to Lord Byron was declared by her to be 'most striking': AAK to AINB, 29 October 1835, Dep. Lovelace Byron 41, fols.
111–15.

p. 210   Writing to their mother, Ada teased that warnings would be sent if
either Martha or Mary decided to elope: AAK to Mary Somerville,
10 February 1836, MSBY, Dep. c. 367, folder MSBY-3.

p. 210   Writing a character portrait of her daughter during the early years
of Ada's marriage: AINB, 'Portrait' of Ada, dated 1840 by William
Lovelace, but it may have been written much earlier, Dep. Lovelace
Byron 118, fols. 86–7.

p. 211   'Hester and I are very happy together,' Ada told William: AAK to
William King, 1 August 1836, Dep. Lovelace Byron 165, fols. 40–79.

p. 212   'You will however I trust remember that *if either at present or at any
future time*': AAK to Lady Hester King Sr, 11 June 1837, LKC.

p. 213   'No matter ... The occurrence of last week will of course now be blotted out from the record of events': AAK to Lady Hester King Sr, 12 February 1838, LKC.

p. 213 The fault was theirs, she wrote fiercely back to Lady Hester's brother on 23 June 1846: AAL to Lord Fortescue (Lady Hester King Sr's brother, formerly Viscount Ebrington), 23 June 1846, LKC.

p. 214 'Our school is doing so well, that I am very anxious it should do better': AAL to AINB, Wednesday [1838], in Betty Toole, *Ada, the Enchantress of Numbers* [sic] (Strawberry Press, 1992), pp. 104–5. Doubtless altered for readability, Toole's quotation from Babbage should read 'The Enchantress of Number'.

p. 214 'Ada teaches so that one cannot help learning,' an admiring friend had exclaimed: AINB, 'Portrait' of Ada, Dep. Lovelace Byron 118, fols. 86–7.

p. 215 Fond personal recollections played a larger part than phrenological diagnosis when Robert described Miss King: R. R. Noel, *Notes biographical and phrenological illustrating a collection of casts (of skulls)* (published for private circulation, 1883; Senate House Library, UCL).

p. 215 Her letter, although spiky, stopped just short of a sneer: Hester King Jr to Louisa Noel, 4 August 1839, regarding the Alfred Chalon 1838 portrait. This correspondence is in WP, Add MS 54089.

p. 216 Little Byron, described by Hester to Robert Noel's wife as 'an exceedingly odd boy': Hester King Jr to Louisa Noel, 14 September 1839, WP, Add MS 54089.

p. 216 'Now Ma may go ... Ma can go downstairs': AAL to AINB, n.d. 1838–9, see Toole, *op. cit.*, pp. 113–14.

p. 216 Ada wondered how her mother found the patience to suffer so much tiresome 'chatteration': AAL to AINB, n.d. March 1840, Dep. Lovelace Byron 41.

p. 216 Hester King described Lady Byron to the Noels as a besotted granny: WP, Add MS 54089.

p. 216 Lady Lovelace finally admitted to her mother that she would never have chosen to bear a child: AAL to AINB, 12 December 1840, Dep. Lovelace Byron 41, fols. 194–5.

p. 217 'to say the truth I do not think Mr H. Fellows knows much about the Trinity or the Unity either': AAK to AINB, n.d. September 1837, Dep. Lovelace Byron 41.

p. 217 It was in the same playful tone as in her letters to Fanny that Annabella wrote to Ada from Germany: Ethel Mayne, *The Life and Letters of Anne Isabella, Lady Noel Byron* (Charles Scribner, 1929), p. 374.

p. 218 In June 1837, Ada fired off an opinionated letter to Mrs Somerville: AAL to Mary Somerville, 22 June 1837, MSBY, Dep c. 367, folder MSBY-3.

p. 219 'a very bright light a good way farther on': AAL to Charles Babbage, 16 February 1840, BL, Add MS B37192.

p. 220   'I hope you are bearing me in mind': AAL to Charles Babbage, 16
          February 1840, BL, Add MS B37192.

p. 220   Writing to her absent mother that month: AAL to AINB, 20 October
          1840, Dep. Lovelace Byron 41, fols. 170–4.

Chapter Fifteen: Ambitions and Delusions (1840–1)

p. 223   'The discovery of the Analytical Engine is so much in advance of my
          own country': Charles Babbage to Angelo Sismondo, in Anthony
          Hyman, *Charles Babbage: Pioneer of the Computer* (Princeton
          University Press, 1982), p.185.

p. 224   '*Festina lente*,' De Morgan reproved her on 15 September 1840: All
          Augustus De Morgan's correspondence with Ada is in box 170 in the
          Lovelace Byron Papers. I am indebted to Christopher Hollings and
          Adrian Rice for early use of their transcriptions, now available online,
          and to Ursula Martin for introducing me to the first papers that have
          seriously examined Ada's mathematics. These are now online. The
          most relevant to De Morgan's influence is: http://www.tandfonline.
          com/doi/full/10.1080/17498430.2017.1325297

p. 224   'I work on very slowly,' Ada sighed to her mother: AAL to AINB, 21
          November 1840, Dep. Lovelace Byron 41.

p. 225   'I have materially altered my mind on this subject,' she confessed to
          her tutor: AAL to Augustus De Morgan, 22 December 1840, see note
          to p. 224 above, '*Festina lente*'.

p. 227   'the importance of *not* being in a hurry': AAL to Augustus De
          Morgan, 10 November 1840, see note to p. 224 above, '*Festina lente*'.

p. 227   'The moving force of mathematical invention is not reasoning but
          imagination': Robert Perceval Graves, *Life of Sir William Rowan
          Hamilton* (3 vols., Hodges, Figgis, 1889), vol. 3, p. 219.

p. 227   'Imagination is the *Discovering* faculty': AAL, 'Essay on Imagination',
          5 January 1841, Dep. Lovelace Byron 175, fol. 231.

p. 228   'I feel bound to tell you that the power that Lady L[ovelace]'s thinking
          has always shewn': Augustus De Morgan to AINB, 21 January 1844,
          Dep. Lovelace Byron 67, fol. 9.

p. 229   '... the less I have *habitually* to do with children the better': AAL to
          AINB, 12 December 1840, Dep. Lovelace Byron 41, fols. 194–5.

p. 229   'His affable, communicative, manly & I may say elegant manners,
          charm people much': AAL to Louisa Barwell, 5 January 1841, Dep.
          Lovelace Byron 63.

p. 230   'You have always been a kind & real & most invaluable friend to *me*':
          AAL to Charles Babbage, 12 January 1841, BL, Add MS B37192.

p. 230   'one of the most logical, sober-minded, cool, pieces of composition (I
          believe) that I ever penned; the result of much accurate, matter-of-fact,

reflection & study': AAL to AINB, 6 February 1841, Dep. Lovelace
Byron 42, fols. 12–16.

p. 231   'The services which I am so willing to render are not asked ... A Right
Honourable wall surrounds me': AINB to Ralph King, 7 September
1855, Dep. Lovelace Byron 61.

p. 232   And thus, as she argued in a long and earnest letter to Harriet Siddons:
AINB to Harriet Siddons, 11 February 1836, HRC, Bound vol. 1 of
the Byron Collection.

p. 233   'The great thing is not to delay as the people are starving': The quotations are from David Herbert, *Lady Byron and Earl Shilton* (Hinckley
& District Museum, 1997), pp. 40–1. More detail appears in Harriet
Martineau's unpublished correspondence and notes. These were collected from various fellow reformers in 1860, following Lady Byron's
death (CRL, XHM121–31).

p. 233   'So many mothers came that it seemed each child had two Mothers!':
AINB to Harriet Siddons, June–July 1840, HRC, bound vol. 1 of the
Byron Collection.

p. 235   Mary Montgomery was willing to view Mrs Leigh as 'one of the wickedest woman ever born': Mary Montgomery was quoted in Sophia De
Morgan's long letter of record to Lord Wentworth about his mother
and grandmother, 9 April 1875, Dep. Lovelace Byron 187, fols. 62–76.

p. 236   'I can believe – alas! that I should confess it – even to you': Anna
Jameson to AINB, 13 December 1840, Dep. Lovelace Byron 75. Mrs
Jameson seems to have burnt, as requested, Lady Byron's description
of Augusta Leigh's misdoings.

p. 237   'She [Medora] knows that the throat of my conscience is small': AINB
to Lady Olivia Acheson, in Ethel Mayne, *The Life and Letters of Anne
Isabella, Lady Noel Byron* (Charles Scribner, 1929), pp. 353–4.

p. 237   'I would save you, if it be not too late, from adding the guilt of her
death to that of her birth. *Leave her in peace*!': AINB to AL, 20
January 1841, WP, Add MS 31037.

p. 238   'It *well* paints your whole principle & character; – at least it does so
to *me*': AAL to AINB, 11 January 1841, Dep. Lovelace Byron 42, fols.
8–11.

Chapter Sixteen: A Cuckoo in the Nest (1841–3)

p. 239   '*But if you knew one half the harum-scarum extraordinary things I
do*': AAL to Woronzow Greig, 31 December 1841, MSBY, Dep. c. 367,
MSBY-9.

p. 241   Ada described the following year as 'a frightful crisis in my existence':
AAL to WL, n.d. April 1842, Dep. Lovelace Byron 166, fols. 1–49.
Much of the letter was devoted to explaining Ada's newly discovered

vocation ('poetry, in conjunction with musical composition, must be my destiny'), while warning her husband not to impede it.

p. 241   'I should tell you that I did not suspect the daughter as being the result of it [the incest]': AAL to AINB, 3 March 1841, Dep. Lovelace Byron 42, fols. 28–30. The eight-day gap between this letter and Annabella's revelation of incest on 23 February suggests that Ada was answering a second revelation, concerning Medora's parentage. This would explain the more challenging and sceptical tone of Ada's second letter.

p. 242   'Indeed the last fortnight is rather a convincing proof that nothing can': AAL to Sophia De Morgan n.d. spring 1841, Dep. Lovelace Byron 171, fols. 16–17.

p. 243   'A *new language* is requisite to furnish terms strong enough to express my horror': AAL to William Lovelace, 8 April 1841, Dep. Lovelace Byron 165, fols. 160–89.

p. 244   'it is impossible to know her without loving her – or to look into her mind without respecting all she has done': Anna Jameson to AINB, 28 August 1841, Dep. Lovelace Byron 75.

p. 244   Annabella confessed that the presentation of her protégée was nevertheless causing friction: AINB to Harriet Siddons, 7 August 1841, HRC, bound vol. 1 of the Byron Collection.

p. 245   'I think he has bequeathed this task to me! . . . I *have a duty* to perform towards him': AAL to ANIB, n.d. 1841, Dep. Lovelace Byron 42.

p. 245   'You know I am a d—d odd animal!': AAL to Woronzow Greig, 31 December 1841, MSBY Dep. c. 367, MSBY-9.

p. 246   'I am quite in a fuss about my mathematics, for I am much in want of a lift at the moment': AAL to Augustus De Morgan, June 1841, Dep. Lovelace Byron, box 170.

p. 247   'My intended journey to Town is only on particular business': AAL to Augustus De Morgan, 27 October 1841, Dep. Lovelace Byron, box 170.

p. 248   Seemingly bewitched by the 'waywardness, beauty & intangibility': Doris Langley Moore, *Ada, Countess of Lovelace: Byron's Legitimate Daughter* (John Murray, 1977), p. 161.

p. 248   'a naughty sick Bird': AAL to William Lovelace, n.d. June 1841, Dep. Lovelace Byron 166, fols. 50–100.

p. 249   The results, judging by Dr Kay's unpublished journal: the unpublished journal is held in the Kay-Shuttleworth Papers at the John Rylands Library, Manchester, ref. 219, 1/25.

p. 249   'tho really what use an old Crow would be to me I know not': AAL to William Lovelace, n.d. July 1842, Dep. Lovelace Byron 166, fols. 50–100.

p. 250   In the spring of 1842, Ada's letters sound as though she has suddenly vaulted into our times: AAL to William Lovelace, n.d. but recording her activity, Thursday, half past four, *ibid.*

p. 250   '... and the more scope I have in prospect for it, the more settled, calm & happy, does my mind become': AAL to William Lovelace in two letters written during the spring and summer of 1842, *ibid*. 'And if so, it will be poetry of an unique kind': n.d. *ibid*.

p. 253   she described him to Lovelace as allegedly '*very handsome* and attractive': AAL to William Lovelace, n.d. July 1842, *ibid*.

p. 253   Her affectionate message of congratulation, so he told a gratified Ada: Sir George Crauford to AAL, 3 November 1842, Dep. Lovelace Byron 168, fols. 199–200.

p. 255   'I could not read of that meeting without great pain': Both letters are in Ethel Mayne, *The Life and Letters of Anne Isabella, Lady Noel Byron* (Charles Scribner, 1929), p. 362.

p. 255   'And then came all sorts of vituperations': AAL to AINB, [23] July 1842, Dep. Lovelace Byron 42, fols. 56–8.

p. 256   'I cannot bear to think of the folly': AAL to WL, n.d. July 1842, Dep. Lovelace Byron 166.

p. 256   It was sad that 'a nice stingy Old Hen, (especially about *horses* ...)' should be feeling bereft: AAL to AINB, 25 July 1842, written two days after Medora's departure to France, Dep. Lovelace Byron 42, fols. 58–60.

p. 256   'I know you would prefer such a state of things ... dear Mate': AAL to William Lovelace, n.d. July 1842, Dep. Lovelace Byron 166, fols. 50–100.

p. 257   'Time must show. To say the truth, I have less ambition than I had': AAL to Woronzow Greig, 16 December 1842, MSBY Dep. c. 367, MSBY-9.

p. 258   'Wheatstone has been with me a long while today': AAL to William Lovelace, n.d. December 1842, Dep. Lovelace Byron 166, fols. 50–100.

Chapter Seventeen: My Fair Interpretress (7)

p. 259   'so happy that I can scarcely hold my pen,' wrote Hester to Robert and Louisa Noel: Hester King Jr to Robert Noel, 8 February 1843 (WP, Add MS 54089).

p. 259   'or if you really cannot (tho I am sure you *can*, if you *will*) stay so long': AAL to Charles Babbage, 8 February 1843, BL, Add MS B37192.

p. 263   'the Analytical Engine does not occupy common ground with mere "calculating machines"': From Note A, in Ada's Translator's Notes to M. Menabrea's Memoirs, *Scientific Memoirs, Selected from the Transactions of Foreign Academies of Science and Learned Societies and from Foreign Journals*, ed. by Richard Taylor (1843), vol. 3, p. 697. Further quotations from the article and translation in Chapter 17 will provide only the relevant page number.

p. 267 'Babbage did not know what he had; Ada started to see glimpses and successfully described them': Stephen Wolfram, *Idea Makers: Personal Perspectives on the Lives & Ideas of Some Notable People* (Wolfram Media, 2016), p. 96.

p. 269 She had taken the story of how she had been brutally cast aside by Lady Byron: Selina Doyle to AINB, 21 March 1843, Dep. Lovelace Byron 68, fols. 123–4.

p. 270 'You have but *one* course to pursue': AAL to EML, 24 March 1843, Dep. Lovelace Byron 172, fol. 204.

p. 270 '*Elle est plus tranquille aujourd'hui et prête a faire tout ce qu'on veut*': Selina Doyle to AINB, 25 March 1843, Dep. Lovelace Byron 68, fol. 124.

p. 270 'I think I then told you that I believed her reason was not sound': Louisa Barwell to AINB, 9 April 1843, Dep Lovelace Byron 63.

p. 271 Medora recorded that the meek and somewhat bewitched Dr King had been both intimidating and abusive: Charles Mackay (ed.), *Elizabeth Medora Leigh: A History and an Autobiography* (R. Bentley, 1869), pp. 149–50. Mackay was the father of the novelist Marie Corelli.

p. 272 'I will have it *well*, & *fully* done; or not at all': All of the quotations in this paragraph and its predecessor are taken from the 1843 June–August letters published (but with rationalised dates that often conflict with Ada's own) in Betty Toole's *Ada: The Enchantress of Numbers* (Strawberry Press, 1992), Ch. 10.

p. 275 'quite thunderstruck at the power of the writing': AAL to Babbage [n.d. August] 1843, BL, Add MS B37192.

p. 275 'Can it be *the* daughter who eloped with Trevanion who married her sister?': Hobhouse's *Diary*, 26 July 1843. See note on p. 487.

p. 275 'I once more remind you that I am your child': See note to p. 271 above, 'Medora recorded ...' The letter from Elizabeth Medora Leigh to Augusta Leigh, 15 August 1843, is in the Pierpont Morgan Library, New York, and is reprinted in full by Doris Langley Moore, in *Ada, Countess of Lovelace: Byron's Legitimate Daughter* (John Murray, 1977), pp. 184–5.

p. 276 At the very least, he bore testimony to 'a most indomitable industry ...': AAL to AINB, n.d., but probably the first week of August 1843, DLM transcript.

p. 276 'as good a passport to posterity (if I am to have one) as "the wife of Byron"': AINB to AAL, n.d. 1843, *ibid.*

p. 277 A new and 'very frightful' crisis in her health: *ibid.*

p. 277 Back at Ockham, Ada composed a fourteen-page letter: AAL to Charles Babbage, n.d. August 1843, BL, Add MS B37192.

p. 278 'that horrible problem – the three bodies': Charles Babbage to AAL, Dep. Lovelace Byron 168, fols. 49–50 (all Babbage's letters to AAL are in this section).

Chapter Eighteen: The Enchantress (1843–4)

p.283 *'Science is no longer a lifeless abstraction'*: Michael Garvey, *The Silent Revolution: or The Future effects of Steam and Electricity upon the Condition of Mankind* (W. and F. G. Cash, 1852), p. 3.

p. 283 'I don't the least mind all I have suffered': AAL to Sophia De Morgan, 21 December 184[3], Dep. Lovelace Byron 171, fols. 16–17. Betty Toole, in *Ada: The Enchantress of Numbers* (Strawberry Press, 1992), suggests 1844, but 1843 sits better with a reference to the bad effects of intensive mathematical work (the Menabrea 'Notes') undertaken six months earlier.

p. 284 'as to the microscopical structure and changes in the brain, nervous matter, & also in the blood': AAL to Robert Noel, 9 August 1843, Dep. Lovelace Byron 173, fols. 155–8.

p. 286 She had also spoken mysteriously of 'present troubles': W. B. Carpenter to AAL, 27 November 1843, Dep. Lovelace Byron 169, fols. 119–24.

p. 287 Annabella was sufficiently displeased by his revelations: Joanna Baillie to AINB, 19 December 1843, Dep. Lovelace Byron 62.

p. 287 'I was completely *stunned*': W. B. Carpenter to AAL, 24 January 1844, Dep. Lovelace Byron 169, fols. 119–24.

p. 288 'Would not a word from you as to liberties I had even *offered*': W. B. Carpenter to AAL, *ibid*.

p. 288 'My brain then began to turn & twist': AAL to AINB, 5 p.m. Monday, n.d. [early 1844], DLM transcript.

p. 289 'What a *kind kind* mate *ou* is': AAL to William Lovelace, n.d. [early 1844], Dep. Lovelace Byron 166, fols. 101–25. Toole, *op.cit.*, suggests 1845 or 1846.

p. 289 'I do not feel I am fairly dealt with in this': AAL to William Lovelace, 10 April 1844, *ibid*.

p. 290 'an *independent* & *skilful* swimmer …': AAL to William Lovelace, 14 August 1844, Dep. Lovelace Byron 166.

p. 290 'This is my year of *accidents*': AAL to William Lovelace, 15 August 1844, Dep. Lovelace Byron 166.

p. 290 In fact, Miss Martineau might herself benefit from the advice of a young lady who now wrote with brimming confidence of 'my advancing studies on the nervous system': AAL to AINB, 10 October 1844, Dep. Lovelace Byron 42, fol. 150.

p. 292 Lady Byron had been 'more white and tremulously weak than I had ever seen her': Anna Jameson to Catherine Sedgwick, July 1845, Catharine Maria Sedgwick Papers, Coll. 2, Massachusetts Historical Society.

p. 292 Ada, while persuaded that the 'many *exciting expeditions*, and *irregular amusements*': AAL to AINB, 10 October 1844, Dep. Lovelace Byron 42, fol. 150.

p. 292   'I think Dr Carpenter is on the right track': AINB to AAL, 20 November 1844, Dep. Lovelace Byron 55, fols. 126–85.

p. 293   a frame so susceptible that it is an *experimental laboratory*: AAL to AINB, 11 November 1844, Dep. Lovelace Byron 42, fol. 150.

p. 295   '... *if* I can take a certain standing in the course of the next few years': AAL to William Lovelace, 29 November 1844, Dep. Lovelace Byron 166.

p. 296   'that Enchantress who has thrown her magical spell around the most abstract of Sciences': Charles Babbage to Michael Faraday, 9 September 1843, Frank L. James (ed.), *Correspondence of Michael Faraday* 6 vols. (Institution of Electrical Engineers, 1996), vol. 3.

p. 296   Presenting herself to Faraday as 'the bride of science': Michael Faraday's letters to Ada can be found in Dep. Lovelace Byron 171, fols. 44–53 and in Henry Bence Jones, *Life & Letters of Michael Faraday* (Longmans, Green and Co, 1870). Ada's letters to Faraday are published in Frank L. James (ed.), *Correspondence of Michael Faraday*, 6 vols. (Institution of Electrical Engineers, 1996), vol. 3.

p. 300   'With Many Many Thanks': AAL to Woronzow Greig, 15 November 1844, MSBY, Dep. c. 367 MSBY-9.

p. 301   'I really have become as much tied to a profession': AAL to Woronzow Greig, 5 December 1844, *ibid.*

Chapter Nineteen: The Lady from Porlock (1844–9)

p. 302   Born at Fyne Court, Crosse was running the family estate: The best account of Crosse and his family is given by Brian Wright, *Andrew Crosse and the Mite that Shook the World: The Life and Work of an Electrical Pioneer* (Matador, 2015).

p. 306   His wife's undisciplined habits: WL's letters to ANIB in the autumn of 1844 are in Dep. Lovelace Byron 46.

p. 307   He did not, Ada was pleased to announce, regard her ideas as 'mere enthusiasm': AAL's letters to her husband about the Fyne Court visit are in Dep. Lovelace Byron 166.

p. 309   Her mother, she told Grieg, had 'quite chuckled': AAL to Woronzow Greig, 5 December 1844, Betty Toole, *Ada: The Enchantress of Numbers* (Strawberry Press, 1992), pp. 305–6. AAL's letters to Greig in 1844–5 are in MSBY, Dep. c. 367, MSBY-9.

p. 309   'He is a good & just man. He is a *son* to me ... But it has been a hopeless case ...': AAL to Woronzow Greig, 4 February 1845, in Toole, *op. cit.*, pp. 313–14.

p. 310   'quite unconnected with any of my own': AAL to Woronzow Greig, 12 February 1845 MSBY, Dep. c. 367, MSBY-9.

p. 311   capable of the 'enormous and continued labour' required for scientific work: James A. Secord, *Victorian Sensation: The Extraordinary Publication, Reception, and Secret Authorship of Vestiges of the Natural History of Creation* (University of Chicago, 2000), p. 242.

p. 314 'habitually, in remembrance of the many delightful & improving hours we have jointly passed in various literary pursuits': Ada's bequest to John Crosse, Dep. Lovelace Byron 175, fol. 161.

p. 315 'I never saw a child to whom a firm, cheerful & *tender* influence was more wanting': Anna Jameson to AINB, 3 January 1845, Dep. Lovelace Byron 75.

pp. 316 'You poor dear patient thing': WL to AAL, 30 August 1845, DLM
–17 transcript.

p. 317 'one of the saddest': WL to AAL, 2 September 1845, *ibid.*

p. 317 how could he do it without warning them that the Bible was 'mistaken' and the text 'interpolated with fables': William Lovelace to AINB, n.d. but seemingly July/August 1845, DLM transcript.

p. 318 their happiness, 'if happy they are, will soon be at an end': Hobhouse's *Diary*, 3 June 1846 (see note on p. 487).

p. 318 'a man of fashion': Harriet Beecher Stowe supplied this description of Lovelace, a man whom she had never met, in *Lady Byron Vindicated* (Sampson Low, Son & Marston, 1870), p. 443.

p. 319 Would such behaviour get her into 'a scrape with the other *lady-guests*': AAL to Charles Babbage, 18 November 1846, BL, Add MS B37192.

p. 319 'the repeated & unjust condemnations of Lady Lovelace's husband during this series of years': AAL to Lord Fortescue, 22 June 1846, LKC.

p. 319 Secretly, however, Ada knew that her odious mother-in-law's claims to be terrified of her eldest son: Lady Hester King Sr's self-justifying explanation of her mistreatment of William Lovelace seems never to have got beyond the drafted memorandum that is in the Locke King archive at Brooklands.

Chapter Twenty: Vanity Fair (1847–50)

p. 320 Promising that the debt would be paid off: AAL to Henry Currie, 1 May 1848, Dep. Lovelace Byron 168.

p. 324 Lady Byron viewed atrocious social conditions at home as a call to arms: AINB to AAL, 25 February 1848, *LP*. Her contribution to funds in the Irish famine, together with her philanthropic work in Leicestershire, is clearly identified in the 1860–1 correspondence of Harriet Martineau, at a time when Martineau was gathering material to write a biography of Lady Byron (Martineau Papers, 125–30, CRL).

p. 324 Greeting an embarrassed Lady Byron in 1851 by doffing their caps in gratitude for the 'many sums of money': *Leicester Journal*, 16 June 1851.

p. 325 Calming herself, Annabella asked for news of the Rathbones's good friend Dr Beecher: AINB to Elizabeth Rathbone, 17 January 1846, HRC, Byron, box 5.6.

p. 326 Lovelace told his 12-year-old heir that 'the poor' had thankfully become 'too poor to cause trouble': WL to BO, 26 April 1848, Dep. Lovelace Byron 167, fols. 3–4.

p. 326 Further evidence of how far Lovelace was removed from social reality surfaced: WL to AAL (n.d., but probably *c*.1848), DLM transcript.

p. 328 'You will,' the artist's proud sitter promised a once-again absent Ada on 6 January 1850, 'be very gay': WL to AAL, 29 December 1849 and 6 January 1850, Dep. Lovelace Byron 164, fols. 1–40.

p. 333 'A friend, to whom I had early communicated the idea, entertained great hopes of its pecuniary success': Charles Babbage, *Passages from the Life of a Philosopher* (Longman, 1864), p. 353.

p. 333 her first known reference to ongoing discussions with Babbage about '*Games*, and notations for them': AAL to Charles Babbage, 30 September 1848, BL, Add MS B37192. All quotations from Ada's letters to Babbage in this chapter are from this collection.

p. 334 'You say nothing of Tic-tac-toe': AAL to Charles Babbage, 18 October 1849, *ibid*.

p. 335 'A heart like Hester's, I never did find, and never shall find again upon earth': Sir George Crauford to Lady Hester King Sr, 12 April 1848, LKC.

p. 336 there was 'nothing to forgive': Sophy Tamworth's brother had succeeded their father as Baron Scarsdale in 1837. AINB to William Lovelace, 28 February 1849, Dep. Lovelace Byron 67, fols. 125–7.

p. 337 '*peculiarly* appropriate to this young lady': AAL to AINB, 20–22 April 1847, Dep. Lovelace Byron 43, fols. 3–8.

p. 337 'excellent stuff in that child': Anna Jameson to AINB, 28 June 1847, Dep. Lovelace Byron 75.

p. 338 Such behaviour was absolutely unacceptable in 'families of my circle': AAL to AINB, 28 April 1848, Dep. Lovelace Byron 43, fols. 25–8.

p. 339 'remarkably *well*, & wonderfully *happy*': AAL to AINB, 15 October 1848, Dep. Lovelace Byron 43, fols. 60–6.

p. 339 In an undated December letter from the following year: AIK to AAL, December 1850, WP, Add MS 54091.

p. 340 'I have reasons': Marilyn Thomas, *The Cleric and the Lady: The Affair of Lady Byron and F. W. Robertson*, Forum on Public Policy: A Journal of the Oxford Round Table, vol. 2008, no. 2, p. 404.

p. 341 a 'free and easy tone' that leaned towards 'downright impertinence': William Lovelace to AINB, 27 November 1846, DLM transcript.

p. 342 Byron was '*never alone*' with Annabella': AAL to AINB, 6 November 1848. All the quotations given here about the children are from DLM's transcripts. Nothing – other than Lady Byron's controlling habits – was deduced from them in her Life of Ada. The originals are in Dep. Lovelace Byron 43.

p. 342 'the real and more lasting effects' of sisterly friendship: AAL to AINB, 15 October 1848, Dep. Lovelace Byron 43, fols. 60–6.

p. 344 'a very clever but wild young fellow' had been given 'no chance of starting well in life': Alice E. J. Fanshawe (ed.), *Admiral Sir Edward Gennys Fanshawe, GCB: A Record. Notes. Journals. Letters* (Spottiswoode, 1904), p. 264.

Chapter Twenty-one: The Hand of the Past (1850–1)

p. 346 'The mountain air & mountain life does wonders': AAL to AINB, 23 September 1850, Dep. Lovelace Byron 43, fols. 126–8.

p. 347 William, who 'is anxious to know as soon as possible. He hopes you will not say us Nay ...': AAL to Anna Jameson, 9 February 1850, Bonn University Library, Germany.

p. 349 The name of this mystery lover had better be supplied to her at once: AAL to Woronzow Grieg, 27 June 1850, MSBY Dep c. 367, folder MSBY-9.

p. 350 'rents are half paid, and we are in some difficulty ...': AAL to AIK, 25 August 1850, Dep. Lovelace Byron 67.

p. 350 she asked Charles Babbage to arrange for a private inspection of 'the *diamonds*' at the 'Exhibition d'industrie', adding that this 'would help me': AAL to Charles Babbage, 23 July 1850, BL, Add MS B37192.

p. 351 Truly, they had believed the Hen still to be at Brighton: AAL to AINB, 19 August 1850, Dep. Lovelace Byron 43.

p. 352 The autumn tour began: The account of the autumn tour and the discussions of Newstead are taken from the Lovelaces' copious letters to Lady Byron, in Dep. Lovelace Byron 43 and 46, transcribed by DLM and partly published in Betty Toole, *Ada: The Enchantress of Numbers* (Strawberry Press, 1992), pp. 366–71.

p. 354 'I am threatened with proofs by an eager ardent avis': WL to AINB, 23 September 1850, DLM transcript.

p. 356 'Some very thorough remedial measures must be pursued': AAL to Charles Babbage, 1 November 1850, BL, Add MS B37192.

p. 359 'Nobody' she [Lady Byron] said, 'knew him as I did': Frances Kemble, *Records of a Girlhood* (Henry Holt, 1880), pp. 167–8.

p. 360 'to a class peculiarly interesting to him': *ibid*.

p. 361 'At *such* a testimony I started up,' Lady Byron admitted: The quotations here are from Ethel Coburn Mayne, *The Life and Letters of*

Anne Isabella, Lady Noel Byron (Constable, 1929), in the account of the meeting which she gives on pp. 408–10. Her description of the encounter remains the most balanced of the many in existence.

p. 362   'I have ever entertained of yr kindness to my Sister & several members of her unfortunate family': Lady Chichester to AINB, 25 May 1856, Dep. Lovelace Byron 65, fols. 251–3. Ralph Lovelace alluded to this letter in *Astarte*, in order to demonstrate the high regard in which his grandmother had been held by Augusta's family. Mary Chichester was Augusta's widowed half-sister.

p. 362   'I could not hear distinctly,' Emily wrote: Emily Leigh to AINB, n.d. May 1852, Dep. Lovelace Byron 85.

p. 364   'I think we shall let our house in May': AAL to AINB, 10 December 1850, Betty Toole, *Ada: The Enchantress of Numbers* (Strawberry Press, 1992), p. 377.

p. 365   'From the Baron's account she [Miss Ada Byron] must be perfection': Sir Richard Ford to [name unknown] Addington, n.d. June 1835, Rowland Prothero (ed.), *Letters of Richard Ford* (John Murray, 1905), p. 185.

p. 365   'to talk over the wonderful combinations in your letter' ... he imagined 'making a book' to be like 'living at the brink of a precipice': Sir Richard Ford to AAL, 13 and 27 January 1851, Dep Lovelace Byron 171, fols. 129–130.

p. 367   'in order for your influence in causing them to be followed': Charles Babbage to AAL, 13 January 1851, Dep. Lovelace Byron 168.

p. 368   'a visit from your own Lady-Bird will be sufficient': Charles Babbage to AAL, 13 May 1851, Dep. Lovelace Byron 168.

p. 369   'that hour of agony': AINB to William Lovelace, 9 January 1853, Dep. Lovelace Byron 46, fols. 257–9.

p. 370   'disease itself was to be looked upon as a blessing to my daughter': AINB to WL, *ibid.*

p. 370   'your conduct with regard to me since June 19 1851': AAL to WL, 11 December 1852, Dep. Lovelace Byron 46, fols. 236–9.

p. 371   'I never remember to have quitted you with so much regret': AAL to AINB, 3 August and 10 August 1851, Dep. Lovelace Byron 43.

p. 371   'Pray do not be angry': AAL to AINB, 10 April 1852, Dep. Lovelace Byron 44.

p. 372   'Life is so difficult': AAL to AINB, 16 October 1851, Dep. Lovelace Byron 43.

Chapter Twenty-two: Rainbow's End (1851–2)

p. 377   The experiment had greatly intrigued him, and he described it with scientific care: Sir David Brewster, diary entry for 21 October 1851, in

Margaret Gordon, *The Home Life of Sir David Brewster* (D. Douglas, 1869), p. 254.

p. 377 'Have patience ... yet a little longer': AAL to AINB, 1 September 1851, Dep. Lovelace Byron 43.

p. 377 'marching in irresistible power to the sound of Music': AAL to AINB, 29 October 1851, Dep. Lovelace Byron 43.

p. 378 'What a very odd mind Byron's is!' AAL to AINB, 13 November 1851, Dep. Lovelace Byron 43.

p. 378 'unless by yr own wish.' AAL to Byron Ockham, 15 November 1851, Dep. Lovelace Byron 167, fol. 10.

p. 379 'whatever she likes best': AAL to Agnes Greig, 29 August 1851, MSBY, Dep. c 367, folder MSBY-10.

p. 380 wearing the 'Albanian' uniform in which – so a fond wife fancied – William always looked his most Byronic: AAL to AIK, 22 and 28 November 1851, Dep. Lovelace Byron 167, fols. 238–43.

p. 381 'how handsome and admired *yr daughter* will be!': AAL to WL, n.d. December 1851, Dep. Lovelace Byron 166, fols. 126–85.

p. 381 'The marks of reduction & suffering were very strong': SL to AINB, 4 March 1852, Dep. Lovelace Byron 89.

p 382 'I have an interest in Ada': SL to AINB, 30 April 1852, Dep. Lovelace Byron 89.

p. 382 'Oh I am such a *sick* wretch!': AAL to AINB, from letters written on 4, 12 and 21 April 1852, Dep. Lovelace Byron 44.

p. 382 Ada was threatened with a personal visit on 21 April 'unless I hear there is increment': A surprising number of the tipsters' scrawls survived Lady Byron's fierce pruning of the archive. I have also drawn on DLM's detailed notes on tipping and racing notes in the original, pre-Bodleian collection of Lovelace Papers, since I could not identify every item to which she referred in Dep. Lovelace Byron 172, fols. 30–60.

p. 383 'Pray let her Ladyship understand in as certain a manner as can be supposed ...': *ibid*.

p. 384 'tenderness in a measure': AINB to Emily Fitzhugh, 9 June 1852, Dep. Lovelace Byron 69, fols. 118–269, in the form of a journal.

p. 384 'such a source of comfort and happiness': Charles Locock to William Lovelace, 20 August 1852, Dep. Lovelace Byron 173, fols. 1–25. The letter was later copied out by Annabella for the benefit of her lawyers.

p. 386 'so gentle and kind': AIK to RGK, 3 August 1852, WP, Add MS 54093.

p. 386 'a Father's love to bring her to Christ': AINB to Agnes Greig, n.d. 1852, MSBY Dep c. 367, folder MSBY-7.

p. 387 'It is very amusing for some people are so indescribably unlucky with their horses': Anne Isabella King to AAL, 18 August 1852, WP, Add MS 54091.

p. 388 'Yet my heart yearns towards Lady Byron': WL to Woronzow Greig, 20 August, 1852, MSBY Dep c. 368, folder MSBY-1.

p. 395 'It is fortunate that Lady Byron has been domiciled with us during this time': William Lovelace, from 6 Great Cumberland Place, to Lady Hester King Sr, 27 November 1852, LKC.

Chapter Twenty-three: Life after Ada (1852–3)

p. 397 'The Rainbow': Ada's sonnet was inscribed on the 1854 monument that her mother ordered to be erected in a remote corner of the churchyard at Kirkby Mallory. A few (silently corrected here) errors in punctuation, together with the misdating of Ada's birth to 27 December 1816 and the alteration of her name from 'Augusta Ada' to 'Ada Augusta', indicate that Lady Byron herself never saw the completed monument. It was engraved with a biblical quotation that either Ada or her mother (or both) picked out before her death. The most relevant phrase was the final one: 'And if he have committed sins, they shall be forgiven him.' (James 5:15). The shrine takes the shape of a niched altar and is now rather neglected. Several Byron graves are close by.

p. 398 'I thought of the words "conceived in sin"': Florence Nightingale to her sister, Parthenope, Monday, dated by editor as 'after 29 November, 1852'. Lynn McDonald (ed.), *Florence Nightingale on Society and Politics, Philosophy, Science, Education and Literature* (2003), vol. 5, pp. 759–62, in *Collected Works of Florence Nightingale*, 16 vols. (Wilfrid Laurier University Press, 2000–2012). Florence appears to have believed that Ada had inherited syphilis.

p. 399 'they may be most thankful they have Mrs Clark there to depend on': *ibid.*

p. 400 The earl was willing to become as wax in her hands: Woronzow Grieg, draft letter to AINB, 2 December 1852, MSBY Dep c. 367, folder MSBY-6.

p. 401 Annabella did not resist the opportunity to remind her son-in-law of the 'unlimited confidence' he had formerly expressed: AINB to WL, 16 December 1852, Dep. Lovelace Byron 59, fols. 338–40.

p. 401 'every cherished conviction of my married life has been unsettled': WL to AINB, 17 December 1852, DLM transcript.

p. 403 'an additional act of treachery': Woronzow Grieg to SL, 9 February 1853, Dep. Lovelace Byron 90, fols. 36–7.

p. 403 while he himself had 'fairly broken down under the part which I have taken': Woronzow Greig to WL, 26 February, 1853, Dep. Lovelace Byron 171.

p. 404 'Can she desire to force us into Court?': Woronzow Greig to SL, 2 April 1853, Dep. Lovelace Byron 90, fols. 38–9.

p. 404   a man entirely 'destitute of honour and principle': Woronzow Greig to WL, 14 April 1853, Dep. Lovelace Byron 171.

p. 405   They did not even care to allow him the coroneted and monogrammed gold pencil case: Ada's bequest to John Crosse, Dep. Lovelace Byron 175, fol. 161.

p. 406   In 1880, John's son and namesake would inherit from his father a gold ring: Information about John Crosse's later life is gratefully taken from Brian Wright, *Andrew Crosse and the Mite that Shocked the World* (Matador, 2015).

p. 408   'full of much bitter vituperation, and containing a reflection upon *her* so malignant that I cannot describe it': AINB to Woronzow Greig, 9 March 1853, MSBY Dep c. 367 folder MSBY-4.

p. 408   Rumours (she wrote) might have reached the Somervilles: AINB to Mary Somerville, 9 March 1853, MSBY Dep c. 367, folder MSBY-1.

p. 409   'there was so much feeling in both his words and manner': Henry Hope Reed to Alexander Bache (n.d. 1854). The letter appeared in *The Southern Review*, 1867. Extracts are published in Appendix 1 of Sydney Padua, *The Thrilling Adventures of Lovelace and Babbage* (Particular Books, 2015). Professor Reed drowned on the steamship *Arctic* while returning to America from Europe in September 1854.

p. 411   Lady Byron remarked that, while chilled by Mrs Jameson's 'persistent attacks': AINB to Anna Jameson, 13 February 1854, HRC, Byron O/S box 14.

p. 411   she herself could no longer bear to see 'any friend who reminds me of her': Gerardine Macpherson, *Memoir of the Life of Anna Jameson* (Roberts Bros, 1878), pp. 281–3.

p. 412   Nevertheless, the letter-writer was permitted to state that her grandmother would contribute £50: AINK to Susan Zilari, 3 May, 1859–60, HRC, Byron box 6.3.

Chapter Twenty-four: Enshrinement (1853–60)

p. 417   'I am so happy this evening': AINB to AAL, 30 November 1844, Dep. Lovelace Byron 55.

p. 418   The visits paid by Annabella to her grandmother's airy Brighton home each spring: AINK to AINB, n.d., WP, Add MS 54093.

p. 418   'To this I cannot consent': AINB to Arthur Mair, 15 August 1857, HRC, bound vol. 1 of the Byron Collection.

p. 420   By the spring of 1855, after working his way back to England: Byron Ockham's obscure movements can be partially tracked by reading the letters about him to AINB from his always concerned and affectionate sister (WP, Add MS 54093).

p. 422 'I was much pleased with Lady Byron,' the savvy old gentleman noted that night: Henry Crabb Robinson, 17 September 1853, in T. Sadler (ed.) *Diary, Reminiscences, and Correspondence of H. C. Robinson* 2 vols. (Macmillan, 1869); *London Review*, xxxiii, October 1869 – January 1870, p. 326 (in a review of the above mentioned book).

p. 428 'now or never will he form desirable connections': AINB to Louisa (Mrs Robert) Noel, 26 June 1855, Dep. Lovelace Byron 103, fols. 99–211.

p. 429 'When socially disposed, you will invite yourself': AINB to George and Louisa MacDonald, 1856, Joan Pierson, *The Real Lady Byron* (Robert Hale, 1992), p. 297. It was another friend, Thomas Carlyle, who provided the name 'Liberty Hall' for Annabella's Irish style of hospitality.

p. 430 Crabb Robinson, encountering the couple there during the following spring, was impressed: H. C. Robinson, 16 April 1859, in Sadler, *op. cit.*, vol. 2, p. 396.

p. 431 'the most intelligent-looking negro I ever saw': H. C. Robinson, 24 May 1853, *ibid.*, p.340.

p. 431 'Many of her words surprised me greatly, and gave me new material for thought': Harriet Beecher Stowe, *Lady Byron Vindicated, or a History of the Byron Controversy* (Sampson Low, Son & Marston, 1870) Pt. 2, Ch. 1.

p. 432 On the second, their schoolboy son Henry was introduced to Byron Ockham: Harriet Beecher Stowe's views are paraphrased from the account she provided in *Lady Byron Vindicated*, pp. 145–6.

p. 433 And what, a pale-faced and emotional Lady Byron asked at the end of her enthralling monologue, should she do now?: *ibid.*, in paraphrase.

p. 433 'I often think how strange it is that I should know you': Harriet Beecher Stowe to AINB, 5 June 1857, in Charles Beecher Stowe, *The Life of Harriet Beecher Stowe* (Sampson Low, Son & Marston, 1889).

p. 434 Lady Byron compared it to *Adam Bede* ('the book of the season'): AINB to Harriet Beecher Stowe, 31 May 1859, Beecher Stowe, *op. cit.*, p. 50.

p. 434 'The sooner you commence the better': Anna Jones to AINB, 18 April 1859, Dep. Lovelace Byron 76, fols. 30–61.

p. 435 'She was enjoying one of those bright intervals of freedom from pain and languor': Beecher Stowe, *op. cit.*, p. 152.

p. 435 That spontaneous gift, Harriet later observed, was entirely in keeping: *ibid.*

p. 436 Travelling back from the funeral: Gerard Ford to RL, 12 January 1887, Dep. Lovelace Byron 184, fol. 53.

p. 437 The will was extensive [fn]: Dep. Lovelace Byron 152, fol. 19.

Chapter Twenty-five: Outcast

p. 439   'She gloried in his fame.': Harriet Martineau, *Biographical Sketches* (Arlington, 1868), pp. 316–25, in which the 1860 *Daily News* article was reprinted as part of a collection taken from Martineau's essays and reviews for that paper. The Martineau correspondence about the project is in HM 131–8, CRL.

p. 441   '& yet it would seem she [Lady Byron] must have been much mistaken': AINK to Agnes Greig, 19 June 1867, MSBY Dep c. 367, folder MSBY-7.

p. 442   'O madame! madame!': *Memoirs of Alexandre Dumas, Père* (Michel Lévy Frères, 1852–6). Dumas included a short, spontaneous life of Byron, during which he recalled – with merry disrespect – his own encounter with a flirtatious and golden-haired Contessa Guiccioli in Rome.

p. 442   When Monsieur de Boissy died in 1866, Teresa was still feeling incensed: Mary R. Darby Smith: *La Marquise de Boissy and the Count de Waldeck, Memories of Two Distinguished Persons* (J. B. Lippincott & Co., 1878), p. 27. Smith describes a spirit encounter with Byron at Madame de Boissy's Paris home in March 1868. His messages, faithfully transcribed by their recipient, the marquise, are notably lacking in wit or originality. They speak only of his devotion to Teresa Guiccioli and his interest in her visitor (as a Byron-lover).

p. 445   'precise and complete information as to everything': Ralph Wentworth to AINK, 17 March 1869, WP, Add MS 54093–7.

p. 449   Writing from England on 10 December 1869, George Eliot rebuked Stowe: Joan D. Hedrick, *Harriet Beecher Stowe: A Life* (OUP, 1994), p. 467.

p. 450   Reverting to her finest declamatory style, Mrs Stowe set up a caricature: Harriet Beecher Stowe, *Lady Byron Vindicated, or a History of the Byron Controversy* (Sampson Low, Son & Marston, 1870), pp. 78–9.

p. 455   a crestfallen Ralph wrote to tell his sister that it was 'physically impossible': Ralph Wentworth to Lady Anne Blunt (formerly AINK), 7 July 1872 (and all correspondence between these two), WP, Add MS 54093–7.

p. 465   The strength of her attachment to him is apparent: I am indebted to Virginia Murray for the detailed reader's notes to Doris Langley Moore's unpublished memoir, and to Sir Roy Strong (25 and 26 March 2015) for background details, based upon his friendship with Langley Moore. Lady Selina Hastings (2 February 2015) supplied the account of the Hucknall wedding. Her mother, Margaret Lane, was a close friend of Mrs Langley Moore. Her account of the Hucknall wedding is confirmed both in the memoir and in a letter written by Mrs Langley

Moore to Robert Innes-Smith (18 February 1988), in which she play-fully suggested that they might yet repeat the exhumation of Byron's corpse that had been carried out in 1938. Mr Innes-Smith had sent her the account by James Betteridge (the young caretaker who was present at the 1938 disinterment) of Byron's appearance. The features, so Betteridge affirmed, had been 'easily recognisable from the many pictures we had seen'. Byron's skin had turned the colour of dark stone (Robert Innes-Smith, *Sunday Telegraph*, 7 February 1988). It would appear that this was accurate, and that Hobhouse's inability (in 1824: see Cochran online diary) to recognise the lifeless features of his old friend may have been due to his emotions.

PICTURE CREDITS

PAGE 5: Portrait of William King in dress uniform, signed, inscribed and dated 'Sevilla 1831' (oil on canvas), José Gutiérrez de la Vega (1791–1865), private collection, courtesy Kalfayan Galleries, Athens/Thessaloniki (top left); portrait of Lady Hester King, Sr, 1832 (oil on canvas), John Linnell (1792–1882) © Brooklands Museum archives, reproduction of the image courtesy of Penelope Daly (top right); Lady Hester King, Jr, Brooklands Museum archives (middle left) and Reverend Sir George Crauford (middle right) c.1844 (oil on canvas), Eden Upton Eddis (1812–1901) © Brooklands Museum archives; East Horsley Towers sale of notice © Brooklands Museum archives (bottom).

PAGE 6: Obituary portrait of Charles Babbage (1791–1871) published in *The Illustrated London News*, 4 November 1871. Portrait derived from a photograph of Babbage taken at the Fourth International Statistical Congress, London, July 1860 / Wikimedia Commons (top left); Mary Somerville (1780–1872), self-portrait (oil on panel) © Somerville College, University of Oxford (top right); Analytical Engine © Science Museum / Science & Society Picture Library, all rights reserved (bottom).

PAGE 7: Portrait of Ada Lovelace (daguerreotype), Antoine Claudet (1843–1849), private collection (top); portrait of Ada Lovelace, September 1852, Lady Byron, Bodleian, Lovelace Byron Papers (bottom).

PAGE 8: Portrait of Byron Ockham (1836–1862) (top left) and portrait of Ralph Wentworth (1839–1906) (top right) (daguerreotypes), Antoine Claudet (1843–1849), private collection; Lady Anne Blunt (1837–1917), c.1900, held at the Fitzwilliam, Cambridge, in the Scawen Blunt Collection (bottom).

INDEX